Taming Texas

Captain William T. Sadler's Lone Star Service

Stephen L. Moore

State House Press
Austin, Texas
2000

Copyright © 2000 Stephen L. Moore
All Rights Reserved

Library of Congress Cataloging-in-Publication Data

Moore, Stephen L.
Taming Texas : Captain William T. Sadler's Lone Star service / by Stephen L. Moore.
p. cm.
Includes bibliographical references and index.
ISBN 1-880510-68-5 (alk. paper)
ISBN 1-880510-70-7 (deluxe ed. : alk. paper).
ISBN 1-880510-69-3 (pbk. : alk. paper)
1. Sadler, William Turner, 1797-1884.
2. Soldiers—Texas—Biography.
3. Pioneers—Texas—Biography.
4. Legislators—Texas—Biography.
5. Texas—History—Revolution, 1835-1836.
6. Texas—History—Republic, 1836-1846.
7. Texas—History—1846-1950. 8. California—Gold discoveries.
9. Anderson County (Tex.)—History—19th century. 10. Houston County (Tex.)—History—19th century. I. Title

F390.S15 M66 2000
976.4'04'092—dc21   00-036519
[B]

Printed in the United States of America

First Printing

cover design by David Timmons

cover painting: Sherman's First Skirmish *by Charles Shaw.*
Courtesy of the San Jacinto Museum of History Association

STATE HOUSE PRESS
P.O. Box 15247
Austin, Texas 78761

CONTENTS

Prologue 1

One. **Texas Bound: Lamar And The "Unassuming Gentleman"** 5
- SADLER'S EARLY YEARS 7
- ALABAMA RIVER TO NEW ORLEANS 15
- RIVER PASSAGE TO NATCHITOCHES 20

Two. **Pioneers of the Fort Houston Settlement** 25
- WAGONS WEST FROM NACOGDOCHES 29
- THE ORIGINAL TOWN OF HOUSTON 35
- THE TEXAS REVOLUTION 36
- FORMATION OF THE EARLY TEXAS RANGERS 38

Three. **Sadler's Rangers and the Nacogdoches Volunteers** ... 39
- THE NACOGDOCHES VOLUNTEERS MARCH OUT 45
- THE FALL OF THE ALAMO AND THE GOLIAD MASSACRE ... 47

Four. **A Time To Fight: The Fork In The Road** 51

Five. **Rendezvous With Santa Anna: The Battle of San Jacinto** 59
- SHERMAN'S FIRST SKIRMISH 60
- DAWNING OF A NEW FREEDOM 63
- THE CAPTURE OF SANTA ANNA 72

Six. **Post-San Jacinto: A New Threat in East Texas** 77
- DRIVING THE MEXICAN ARMY FROM TEXAS 78
- THE PARKER'S FORT ATTACK 80
- COMPLETION OF FORT HOUSTON 86
- THE NEW LIFE, THE NEW WIFE AND THE NEW COUNTY 91

Seven. **Cordova's Rebellion and General Rusk's Texas Militia** 97
- THE RISE OF CORDOVA'S REBELLION 100
- GENERAL RUSK'S MILITIA TAKES TO THE FIELD 103
- DEFENSE OF FORT HOUSTON 105
- THE VIOLENCE ESCALATES AGAIN 110

Eight. **Mabbitt's Skirmish and The Battle of Kickapoo** 115
- BATTLE AT KICKAPOO VILLAGE 124

Nine. **The Edens-Madden Massacre** 131
- AFTERMATH AT SAN PEDRO CREEK 139

Contents

Ten.	**The Republic's New First Regiment of Infantry** 141	
	SADLER'S TEXAS LAND GRANTS 145	
	PRESIDENT LAMAR REVAMPS THE TEXAS MILITARY 149	
Eleven.	**Sadler's Appeal To President Lamar** 159	
	NEW DEPREDATION BRINGS CALL TO ACTION 163	
Twelve.	**Frontier Freedom: The Cherokee War** 167	
	THE ASSEMBLY OF TEXAN TROOPS 172	
	"BETWEEN TWO FIRES": FINAL NEGOTIATIONS FAIL 178	
	JULY 15: THE EVENING ENGAGEMENT 181	
	JULY 16: FINALE AT THE DELAWARE VILLAGE 186	
Thirteen.	**Transition Years Of A Young Nation** 195	
	EXPULSION OF THE CHEROKEES 197	
	PROTECTING AUSTIN'S FRONTIER SETTLEMENTS 200	
	THE EARLY 1840S IN HOUSTON COUNTY 203	
	HOME FRONT POLITICS 207	
Fourteen.	**The End of a Republic: Ninth Congress** 209	
	THE TEXAS CAPITAL IN WASHINGTON 209	
Fifteen.	**The First Legislature Shapes the New State** 219	
	CREATING A NEW COUNTY 228	
Sixteen.	**Early Anderson County And The Second Legislature** . 239	
Seventeen.	**California Gold, Texas Railroads And The Civil War** . 251	
	THE CALIFORNIA GOLD RUSH 252	
	LIFE IN 1850S ANDERSON COUNTY 256	
	EARLY RAILROADS IN TEXAS 258	
	FINAL CALL TO DUTY: THE CIVIL WAR 263	
	TERRELL'S 34TH TEXAS CAVALRY REGIMENT 266	
Eighteen.	**Final Years of a Texas Veteran** 271	
	DEADLY TWISTER ON SADLER PLANTATION 273	
	PROVIDING FOR THE CHILDREN 275	
	PENSION PAPERS AND A NEW LAND GRANT 277	
	A FINAL WISH OBSERVED 280	

Appendices
A: RANGER/FRONTIER UNITS OF TEXAS, 1835-1839 287
B: COMPLETE MUSTER ROLL OF THE NACOGDOCHES VOLUNTEERS . 297
C: ROSTER OF PARTICIPANTS IN THE CHEROKEE WAR 298

CONTENTS

D: CAPTAIN SADLER'S TEXAS LAND GRANTS 307
E: SADLER FAMILY IN LINCOLN COUNTY, NORTH CAROLINA . 308
F: FAMILY TREE OF WILLIAM TURNER SADLER 313

Chapter Notes 331
Bibliography 355
Index 363

Other Rosters/Lists:
THE PILGRIM PREDESTINARIAN REGULAR BAPTIST CHURCH . . 27
THE NACOGDOCHES VOLUNTEERS OF SAN JACINTO 46
BATTLE OF SAN JACINTO: ORGANIZATION OF TEXAS TROOPS 64
BATTLE OF SAN JACINTO CASUALTIES 71
PARKER'S FORT MASSACRE: MAY 19, 1836 84
FORCES OPERATING FROM FORT HOUSTON, OCTOBER 1838 . 112
BATTLE OF KICKAPOO: SUMMARY OF FORCES 116
BATTLE OF KICKAPOO: KNOWN CASUALTIES 128
THE EDENS-MADDEN MASSACRE OF HOUSTON COUNTY, TEXAS 135
ORIGINAL OFFICERS OF THE FIRST REGIMENT OF INFANTRY, 1839 . . 154
POSTMASTERS OF EAST TEXAS IN 1839 162
THE CHEROKEE WAR: COMPOSITION OF TEXAN FORCES 177
JULY 15TH CHEROKEE ENGAGEMENT: TEXAN CASUALTIES . . 184
NECHES BATTLE CASUALTIES: JULY 16, 1839 190
SENATE OF THE NINTH CONGRESS OF THE REPUBLIC OF TEXAS . . . 212
HOUSE OF REPRESENTATIVES OF THE NINTH CONGRESS . . . 213
TEXAS HOUSE OF REPRESENTATIVES: THE FIRST LEGISLATURE 221
TEXAS HOUSE OF REPRESENTATIVES: THE SECOND LEGISLATURE . . . 245
SADLER'S ASSISTANCE TO EMANCIPATED BLACKS 272

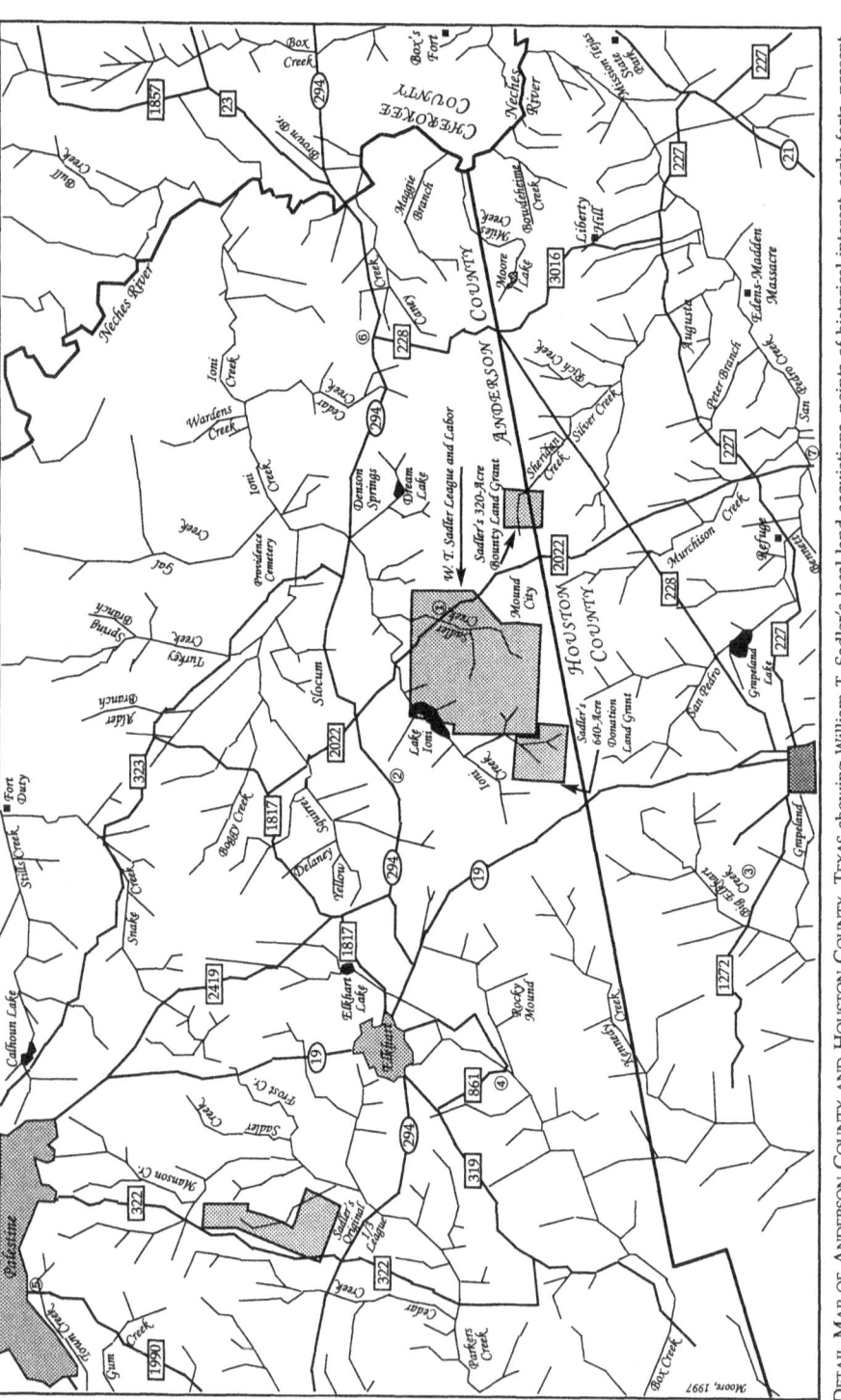

DETAIL MAP OF ANDERSON COUNTY AND HOUSTON COUNTY, TEXAS showing William T. Sadler's local land acquisitions, points of historical interest, early forts, present communities and paved highways and farm roads. Key to numbered items: ① Captain Sadler Centennial Marker and cemetery; ② McLean-Sheridan Massacre Marker; ③ Parker Cemetery (including markers of Rev. Daniel Parker, Dickerson Parker and Miles Bennett); ④ Pilgrim Predestinarian Regular Baptist Church Marker and Pilgrim Cemetery; ⑤ Fort Houston markers; ⑥ early Muse community (later known as Hickory Grove) and cemetery; and ⑦ site of the old Fort Brown.

The Republic of Texas
March 2, 1836 - February 19, 1846
Map of Major Towns, Settlements and Forts of 1839
(Showing only heavily populated areas of Texas)

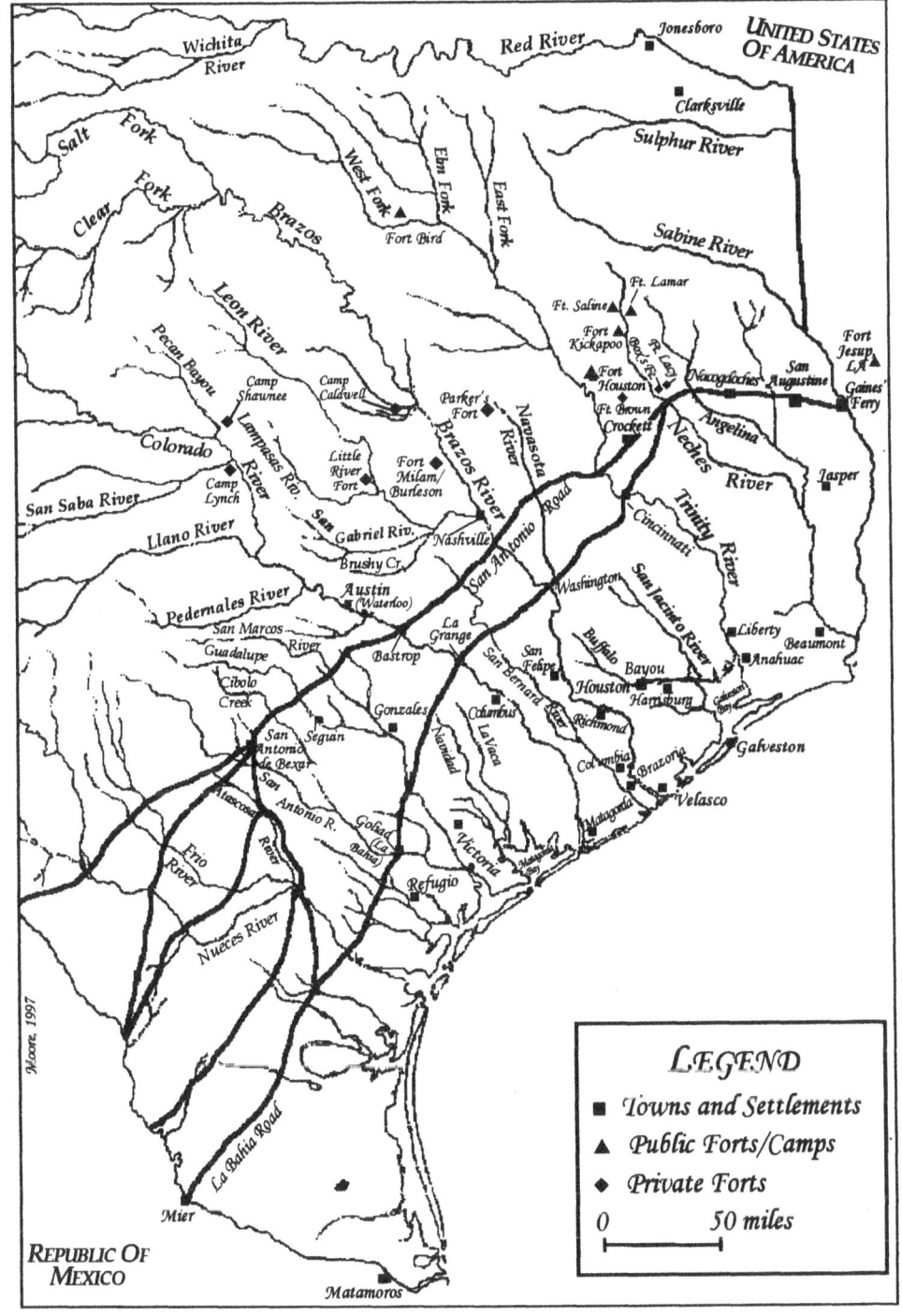

PROLOGUE

In accordance with his final wishes, the death of William Turner Sadler in 1884 was observed quietly and without fanfare. More than two weeks passed, in fact, before even his closest friends became aware of his demise. According to an obituary printed in the local newspaper, Sadler was "of singularly modest and retiring disposition, being desirous of avoiding all glorification for the past."

In contrast to this peaceful final chapter, his life's story had been colorful and bold as it was played out during the early years of Texas history. He had first roamed the vast lands of this state while it was still a province of Mexico and had permanently settled there before the Republic of Texas was created in 1836. During the republic's early years, Sadler had fought in a number of the battles which helped the country secure its independence from Mexico and the safety of its frontier settlements from violent Indian uprisings. He went on to serve in the House of Representatives during the late days of the Republic of Texas and the first years of the new state.

From the Texas Revolution to the Civil War, W. T. Sadler was involved in the conflicts which shaped the future of the Lone Star State. He fought in battles and passed legislation with some of the more prominent names associated with Texas, including Sam Houston, Mirabeau B. Lamar, Thomas J. Rusk, Edward Burleson, Sidney Sherman, Albert Sidney Johnston, Anson Jones, John S. "Rip" Ford, John H. Reagan and James Pinckney Henderson.

This manuscript is more a tracing of Sadler's steps through key events of Texas history than it is a true biography. The events leading to the early Indian depredations and militia battles of East Texas in which he participated are explored with new detail, with the inclusion of muster rolls for such battles as Kickapoo and the Cherokee War. The early history of Houston County, Texas, and Sadler's hand in shaping Anderson County, are also examined with respect to the other men who served as these counties' first leaders. The *Palestine Herald-Press* in a 1969 article on Sadler wrote, "Anderson County owes its existence in part and perhaps its name to a hero of the Battle of San Jacinto who served in the Congress of the Republic of Texas and in the First State Legislature during the period when Anderson County was created out of Houston County."

Born over two-hundred years ago in Lincoln County, North Carolina, Sadler and his family settled in Putnam County, Georgia, in 1817. Despite owning his own farm, he was taken by the opportunities of Texas and made his first pilgrimage in 1822 to scout out land during the time Stephen F. Austin was developing his first colonies of settlers. Another decade would pass before Sadler became serious about carving out his own future in the new lands of Texas. After selling his Georgia farm, he departed in

1835 and traveled much of the way in company with Mirabeau B. Lamar, a future hero of San Jacinto and President of the Republic of Texas.

During his early years in this new territory, three races were waging war with each other over the possession of Texas: the Anglo-American "Texans," the native Indians and the Hispanic mestizos of Mexico. From the emigrant town of Nacogdoches, Sadler and other pioneers struck out into the untamed lands of East Texas near Cherokee Indian land. The settlement they developed later became Fort Houston, an early stockade against attacks by hostile Indian bands which roamed this area of the country. After the Texas Revolution broke out in 1835, Sadler became captain of a frontier ranger company that served between the Brazos and Trinity rivers. His company, formed on January 1, 1836, did the initial construction on the frontier post known as Fort Houston in present Anderson County. Charged with protecting the new settlements from attacks by Mexican troops and Indians, these revolutionary companies were among the very first to be considered "Texas Rangers."

As news spread of the final stand of Lieutenant Colonel William Barret Travis and his gallant defenders of the Alamo in San Antonio, Sadler's rangers were disbanded at Fort Houston. Finding the Texas Army at the Colorado River, most of them joined a company known as the "Nacogdoches Volunteers." These men joined Colonel Sidney Sherman's Second Regiment and fought bravely under General Sam Houston at the crucial Battle of San Jacinto, in which Texas won her independence from Mexico in 1836.

The following ten years of the Republic of Texas were difficult for pioneers living in the frontier settlements. Spurred on by Mexican rebels, the Indians of Texas began engaging in savage depredations upon the helpless citizens, looting and burning their homes, murdering, scalping, and even taking hostages.

The absence of a unified army in the post-San Jacinto years gave rise to the Texas Militia structure. The militia's mounted volunteer companies were called upon in times of crisis to uphold the law and restore peace. W. T. Sadler was captain of such a volunteer company and his men helped quell the Cordova Rebellion of 1838, culminating in the Battle of Kickapoo on October 16, 1838, in present Anderson County.

Before Captain Sadler and his men could return to the community where their loved ones had been left behind, a band of Indians committed a violent assault on the home of John Edens. In what became known as the Edens-Madden Massacre, a raiding party attacked these families, slaughtering and scalping most, burning down the home and then retreating into the night. Nine were left dead and two women were severely wounded. Sadler returned from battle to find his young wife and child mutilated and burned.

After this, he donated his livestock and crops to the Texas Militia, taking a promissory note which would not be paid until almost a decade later. After several more bloody depredations against frontier families, Sadler wrote a bitter letter to his old friend, President Lamar, urging him to allow the militia to visit the marauding Indians "with the same kind of warfare that they give us." Under Lamar's direction, the First Regiment of Infantry of the Texas Army was created in 1839 to serve as the new means of frontier defense.

Sadler was commissioned as captain of one of the companies of the First Infantry in January 1839, and he commanded a post called Fort Brown in Houston County. He and his men served with Thomas Rusk and Edward Burleson in the Cherokee War, fighting in the key battles along the Neches River in which Chief Bowles and his Cherokees were ultimately defeated. Sadler is said to have fired a shot that downed the Indian leader. He also commanded another infantry company into early 1840 on the remote frontiers near present Austin, Texas.

While names such as John Coffee Hays and William "Bigfoot" Wallace stand out as leaders of the Texas Rangers in the 1840s, the earliest ranger and militia companies have received far less acclaim. Most of those earlier outfits, such as Sadler's, were hastily formed to defend against some frontier menace, but few achieved any degree of recognition. This text attempts to look not just at Captain Sadler but some of the other lesser known frontier freedom fighters of his time. Focusing mainly on the battles and periods of unrest in which he was involved, the goal is also to bring out new details of some of these actions.

Tragically, many of the names, military records, company muster rolls and other important documents regarding some of the early Indian battles in Texas have been largely erased through time and a fire in 1855 in the General Land Office which destroyed a good portion of the Republic of Texas records. For example, a precise muster roll of all those fighting the Cherokees at the important Neches battle cannot be completed because there are no extant rolls for some of the companies participating.

In 1844, Sadler was elected as the Houston County Representative to the House of the Ninth Congress of the Republic of Texas. Eight years after winning their independence, Texas' congressmen found themselves meeting to legislate in the upstairs gambling hall of a saloon in a dingy riverside town! After annexation in 1845, Sadler served in the First and Second Legislatures of the State of Texas.

In his later years, Sadler participated in the California Gold Rush of 1849, was involved in the early railroads of Texas, served as an early postmaster in both Houston and Anderson counties, and fought for the Confederacy in the Civil War. After the War Between the States, he was one of the few to offer a new start to his county's free blacks by providing fertile farm land from his vast land holdings. Although a member of the Texas Veterans Association, he did not actively participate in its proceedings. The county he helped establish, Anderson County, had an agricultural base but has continued to grow. Thanks to transportation, retail and wholesale trade, oil and gas production, finance and service industries, the population in 1990's census was 48,024.

As with many Republic of Texas records, time has swallowed much of the keepsakes he acquired in these early days. What became of some of Captain Sadler's relics, such as a pouch of gold dust from California, a dagger he wrestled from one of Santa Anna's soldiers at San Jacinto, the musket he used, and a whiskey flask he carried in battle, remains a mystery.

Having spent much time in Houston and Anderson counties during my youth, I have seen the sites of most of the historic events described in this text. My grandmother, Evaline Kolb Moore, once took me to the site of the Edens-Madden Massacre where her great grandfather lost his first wife to the Indians. Through her stories of Captain Sadler, I became interested enough in my ancestor to write a short biographical sketch on him for a school project back in 1980. Her cousin Jerry Sadler, a former legislator, Texas Land Commissioner, and Railroad Commissioner, also spent time with me at Moore Lake in Houston County to tell me about early Sadler history.

Sixteen years later, I became interested enough in Texas history to want to find out more about Sadler and what kind of experiences he endured. Over the course of my research, many members of the Sadler family were helpful in turning up old documents and family history, including Howard C. Sadler, Patrick D. Sadler, Laverne Sadler Marsh, Joan Coker Smola, Jo Ann Day Freeman, Jane Taylor Linkswiler, and my father, Marshall L. Moore Jr.

My family has owned land in present Anderson and Houston counties since 1835. Descendants of Captain Sadler still live in small towns and rural areas of these counties. My grandparents retired in extreme northeast Houston County and built Moore Lake on Miles Creek. My father's grandparents lived for years in an old dogtrot log home on eighty-five acres between the present communities of Liberty Hill and Augusta. They had acquired this land from the descendants of early county pioneer John Sheridan.

My initial goal in compiling this text was to learn more about my great-great-great grandfather's involvement in the history of Texas. During this process, I found that his was a heritage not unlike that of many other immigrants whose contributions have gone largely unsung. In the evolution of the Lone Star State, Sadler was actively involved in the bitter fights for independence, the frontier hardships endured by thousands of pioneer settlers, and in the early legislation which helped Texas recover from its tremendous debts and rise to the proud state that it is today.

The fact that his children honored his final request to be buried quietly and without demonstration was noble. For his life's accomplishments to have continued unrecognized would be a shame.

Chapter One

TEXAS BOUND: LAMAR AND THE "UNASSUMING GENTLEMAN"

June - July 1835

The hot afternoon summer sun beat down on the banks of the Alabama River, baking the shoreline into a gently cracking crust in June of 1835. The river was in good navigable condition, although the water level was down slightly for this time of year.

From its Indian derivations, the word "Alabama" translates to "great water" or "great river"; the native Indians had long understood the value that bodies of water played in the basic human game of survival. For the early U.S. explorers and immigrants, the river systems of North America were also a basic means of travel.

The Alabama River was one of the key means of transport throughout the state of Alabama in the mid-1830s. From the thriving city of Montgomery, just south of center in the state, this river twisted and snaked more than two-hundred crooked miles to the port city of Mobile, located on the banks of Mobile Bay and at the mouth of several converging rivers.

Passage down such waterways in 1835 was aboard the latest travel innovation, the steamboat. Since Robert Fulton's first steamboat of 1807, the first such boat to appear in western waters in 1812 had been the Fulton-built *New Orleans*, which ran two-thousand miles down the Ohio and Mississippi rivers to reach the home port whose name she bore.[1] Steamboats on America's great waterways flourished in the early 1820s and 1830s as rivers became a major means of transporting crops and immigrants. This transportation was aided greatly in 1832 when the United States government began appropriating money for the improvement of the "Western Rivers."[2]

These wooden workhorses made for a more exciting means of travel, although generally more dangerous. Even if river snags did not tear the boats apart, many were lost to boiler explosions or overheated fireboxes' setting fire to the fuel wood stacked near them. The average life of early steamboats on many rivers was only five years, although on the busy rivers the owner could expect a boat to pay for itself in five months.[3]

The blast of a whistle was heard before the little steamboat *Little Rock* slowly chugged around a bend between the Alabama's high bluffs. One of the side paddle wheels came to a stop while the other backpaddled rapidly to ease the boat's wooden hull to the bank of the small community of Washington, the first stop below Montgomery. Few aboard had any interest in this little river settlement of about two-hundred souls, but the boat did take aboard one traveler who was bound for Mobile. Thus far this man had journeyed by land from his home in Georgia, taking the road from the eastern border of Georgia and Alabama through Opelika and Tallassee into Montgomery. To a promising new frontier located west of the Sabine River he carried most of his worldly possessions, including enough money to purchase land and cattle.

This passenger made his way aboard on June 19, 1835, and paid his fare of a few dollars as the steamboat crew secured additional wood for fuel. Shortly thereafter, the sidewheel paddles bit into the Alabama as the steam whistle announced the departure of the *Little Rock*, small compared with some of the mighty riverboats which would journey along the major rivers. These early steamboats were called side-wheelers, powered by a single mighty steam engine that turned the big wooden paddles like plows through the water. At slightly more than one-hundred feet in length and twenty feet wide, the *Little Rock* had a very shallow draft for clearing sand bars and a flat keel to prevent her from digging into underwater obstructions.

Aboard the *Little Rock*, thirty-six-year-old Mirabeau Buonaparte Lamar was a little disappointed with the lack of company for the river trip. Most of the passengers were illiterate farmers. The only other passenger with whom he had held much conversation since boarding the steamboat just upriver at Montgomery, Alabama, was a U. S. Army lieutenant named McKenzie.[4]

Lamar was bound from his home in Putnam County, Georgia, for the expanding pioneer territory called Texas. His father, John Lamar, had moved the family in 1808 from its old property in Jefferson County (near Louisville, Georgia) to its new home in Putnam County, near the growing community of Milledgeville (Georgia's early capitol). John Lamar named his sons after areas of history that were of interest to him: Lucius Quintus Cincinnatus,

Jefferson Jackson, Thomas Randolph and Mirabeau Buonaparte. Mirabeau had been born on August 16, 1798, on the old Jefferson County homestead. His new home near Georgia's Little River became known as "Fairfield."[5]

After picking up the latest passenger in Washington, Alabama, the *Little Rock* proceeded on her way toward Mobile. Soon thereafter, Lamar discovered that this new passenger came from his own home county and knew his family. In a 193-page journal of his travels, Lamar wrote:

> Sitting one evening on the bow of the boat, an unassuming and intelligent gentleman approached me and inquired how far south I intended to prosecute my journey. I answered that I was on my way to Texas. "I am pleased to hear it," he replied, "for I am thither bound myself and shall be pleased with company." On inquiring, I found that he was from Putnam County, [and] that he knew me well; was first cousin to William Moreland, my brother-in-law. His name was Sadler.[6]

* * * *

SADLER'S EARLY YEARS

The fellow Georgian Lamar met on the *Little Rock* was thirty-seven-year-old William Turner Sadler. His father, Nathaniel Milton Sadler of English ancestry, was born in 1770 in Virginia and eventually become a wealthy plantation owner in Georgia. Prior to moving to Georgia, Nathaniel Sadler's family resided in what was originally Tryon County, North Carolina. This county was later broken up into Rutherford County and Lincoln County, the latter named after American Revolution hero Benjamin Lincoln.

Sadler's grandparents were Thomas and Martha Rose Sadler Jr., who were married in 1764 in Brunswick County, Virginia, and the parents of seven children. Thomas and Martha Sadler were dismissed from the Quaker Church when Thomas refused to free his slaves on the account of his wife, who had brought them into their marriage. After Thomas Sadler passed away in late 1794, Martha followed her children to North Carolina. Following her death in 1803, all but one of the Sadler children eventually moved on to points south and west of Lincoln County. Nathaniel Milton Sadler, the third child of Thomas and Martha, inherited a slave named Lewis from his mother's will.[7]

Shortly after moving to North Carolina, Nathaniel married Phebe Tucker Moreland on March 24, 1796, in Lincoln County. Just over a year later, their first child, William Turner Sadler, was born on July 26, 1797. The family lived a short distance from Lincolnton, the county seat which had been provided for by the 1784 General Assembly. The first court house and jail were made from logs in 1785; a new frame court house was erected in 1788. The first United States census was taken in 1790 and listed 1,405 heads of white families in Lincoln County. Located about thirty miles northwest of present Charlotte, North Carolina, this county's present size measures only ten miles wide by thirty miles long.[8] At least two prominent figures of early Texas history would immigrate from Lincoln County: attorney James Pinckney Henderson, who became the first Governor of the State of Texas in 1846; and Kenneth Lewis Anderson, who became the last Vice President of the Republic of Texas in 1844.

The 1800 census of Lincoln County lists four related Sadler families. The first was Nathaniel Milton Sadler, his wife Phebe and their two sons under the age of ten, one being William Turner and the other possibly Peterson G. Sadler, whose birthdate has never been clearly established. Nathaniel is also shown as owning seven slaves at this time. The second listed family was that of William Rose Sadler Sr. (Nathaniel's brother), his wife Nancy Turner Moreland, and their four children. The third was that of Henry Sadler (an uncle to Nathaniel and William Rose), his wife and seven of their ten children. An eighth child of theirs, Jeremiah Sadler, is on the 1800 census as a head of household with a wife and three children.

The 1810 census of Lincoln County shows Nathaniel and Phebe Sadler to have five children and eleven slaves. They had one daughter under two years (Emaline Sophia), two sons over ten years (William Turner and his brother), and two sons under ten years (infant Theophilus Sadler and another son whose name is unknown). (See Appendix E for information on the Sadlers in Lincoln County.)

Nathaniel and Phebe Sadler sold their land in North Carolina in late 1817 and bought land in early 1818 in Putnam County, Georgia, which had been created in 1807 from Baldwin County. In Georgia, the Sadlers had three more known children: Charles Wesley Sadler in 1818, Martha Matilda Sadler in 1820, and Nathaniel Milton Sadler II in 1823. The oldest daughter of the family, Emaline Sadler Walker, later gave birth to Nathaniel Sadler Walker who would serve as a personal physician to General Robert E. Lee during the Civil War.[9] The 1820 Georgia census shows Nathaniel

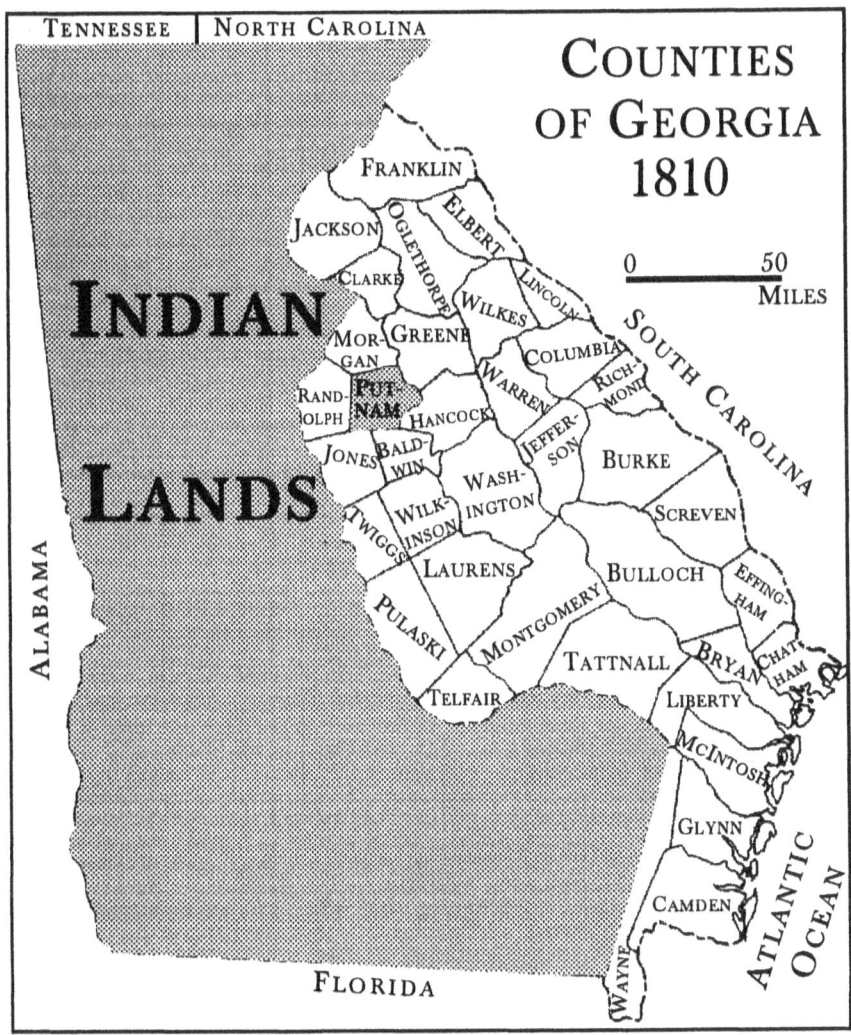

The State of Georgia as it appeared in 1810, shortly before William Turner Sadler's father moved their family from North Carolina to Putnam County, Georgia, in 1818. Modified from "Hall's Original County Map of Georgia Showing Present and Original Counties and Land Districts, 1895."

Sadler, his son William T. Sadler and James Sadler Sr. (Nathaniel's nephew) all to have residences in Putnam County.

The lure of cheaper land prices had no doubt brought Nathaniel Milton Sadler and his family to Georgia, where he accumulated vast holdings of land, cattle and slaves. His plantation home and properties became known as "Sadler's Hill Plantation." The family's old two-story log home has been restored and still stands in Georgia on Sadler Hill.

Relatively little is known of William Turner Sadler's early years in Georgia. Following his younger days in school, he is said by family sources to have studied civil engineering and to have been a surveyor. His great-grandfather, Thomas Sadler Sr., was known to have been a skilled land surveyor in Brunswick County, Virginia, as early as 1741.[10] William Sadler is also said to have fought in the Seminole and Creek Indian Wars in Florida. Two of his brothers, Theophilus and Peterson G. Sadler, are known to have served in Meriwether's Company of Cooper's First Batallion, Theophilus as a private and Peterson a first corporal.[11]

Despite owning a farm in Putnam County, W. T. Sadler was not intent upon living out his life in the expanding state of Georgia. The well-heralded territory of Texas offered undeveloped lands made fertile by fourteen rivers, many of which flowed toward the Gulf of Mexico. He became serious about exploring this area and had made his first pilgrimage to Texas in 1822 to scout out land just after Mexico

The two-story Nathaniel Milton Sadler plantation home in which William Turner Sadler and his siblings were raised has been restored and still stands in present Putnam County, Georgia. Photo courtesy of Laverne Sadler Marsh.

had become independent from Spain in 1821. After arriving in Nacogdoches, Sadler set out on a northwesterly course that brought him to the rich lands lying between the Neches and Angelina rivers.

At that time, the lands lying between where these rivers came together were considered to be "Indian Territory." While Texas was still under Spanish rule, the Cherokee Indians under their Chief Bowles had petitioned the King of Spain for a grant of this land. Because Mexico was fighting Spain for its independence, Spain approved this grant to the Cherokees on the condition that the Indians help them defeat the Mexicans. Spain, and the Cherokees, eventually lost. The Cherokees thereafter claimed this land and began a petitioning act with Mexico to claim it rightfully. Ironically, their request for this land would eventually become contingent upon their aiding the Mexicans in driving out the new Texan settlers.[12]

Sadler passed through this Indian territory and crossed the Neches River into an area east of the present Anderson County town of Elkhart. That night he camped on the upper reaches of Ioni Creek near the village of the Ioni Indians. The next few days he spent in scouting this area until finding the land he wanted for his own future homestead. Soon after this expedition, he returned to Georgia to make preparations for settling permanently in Texas.[13]

This promising land of Texas soon became Sadler's quest. The opportunity for settlers to acquire new land in Texas was possible due to the ground-laying negotiations with Spain and Mexico by a man named Moses Austin, but it was his dedicated son Stephen Fuller Austin who actually recruited and organized the first white settlers into the new territory. Stephen Austin first scouted out the new land in 1821, just as Mexico was gaining its independence from Spain. Known as the "Citizen Empresario" or just the "Empresario" of Texas, Austin obtained approval for his colonization contract in Mexico City in 1823 and returned to Texas for the deliverance of land titles to "The Old Three Hundred," original settlers who were waiting for him.[14]

Austin's first colony town, San Felipe de Austin, was formed in September 1824 by the issuance of titles to the settlers by his land commissioner, the Baron de Bastrop. According to an official census taken in the fall of 1825, this colony had eighteen-hundred citizens, including 443 slaves.[15] Through the word of those who had visited and through newspaper stories back east and up north, Texas continued to grow during the late 1820s and early 1830s. The official census of 1831 showed that Austin's settlements had a total population of 5,665.[16]

Stephen F. Austin maintained a register and required all migrating men or families to apply for permission to settle. The contract application process was not overly complicated. Immediately upon arrival, each new settler presented himself to Austin and registered his name, marital status, his family information, specifying the number and sex of his children, the place of his nativity, his age, where last from, and occupation. After depositing recommendations attesting to his Christian morality and good habits, the settler then took an oath to support the federal and state constitutions. After this, the settler then became an official "applicant" and was given a permit by Austin or his representative, Samuel M. Williams.[17]

The applicant then had thirty days in which to notify Austin of his choice of land. The petition for land was submitted on stamped paper in both English and Spanish. Instructions were then given to the surveyor to survey the applicant's land and plat the property. After this was completed, certain fees were due before the commissioner issued the land title. The stamped paper itself cost two dollars, the commissioner's fee was fifteen dollars, secretary Williams required ten dollars for all of his clerical arrangements, and Austin himself required fifty dollars during the early 1830s. Austin's fee was justified by law as he was the one who had secured by his own expenses and labors the privilege for settlers to obtain complete titles of land without excessive complications.[18]

Austin was due ten dollars upon receipt of title and another forty dollars a year later. He accepted payment in cash, cattle, mules, hogs, and even corn. For unmarried men such as Sadler, only half this fee was due to the Empresario of Texas because unmarried men were generally granted only one-quarter league of land. By the end of 1833, a total of 750 land titles had been issued in Austin's various grants from the state, plus 310 in the original grant from the national government.[19]

New settlers of Austin's land were normally entitled to one labor (177.1 acres) of land for farming and twenty-four labors for cattle raising. These twenty-five total labors equalled one league of 4,428.4 acres. The unusual measurements of land were derived from the Spanish measurement of a *vara*, a linear measure of varying value which Texas finally settled as being 33.33 inches.[20] While most unmarried men only received a quarter of a league (about 1,107 acres), some were granted a third of a league (about 1,476 acres). This grant of land could be augmented to a full league once the settler became married. These lands were required to be cultivated or occupied within six years.[21]

This receipt from Putnam County, Georgia land records was the source of capital William Turner Sadler needed to acquire his new land in Texas. Signed on February 4, 1834, this document deeded his fifty-acre farm to his father for the sum of $300.

The future state of Texas derived its name from the local Tejas Indians. The area near the Neches River where Sadler scouted out land is in present Houston and Anderson counties. In addition to the presence of the native Indians, this land was bountiful with deer, buffaloes, wild turkeys, pigeons and panthers. There were also two Spanish missions located in this area from earlier times. Mission San Francisco de Los Tejas, named after Saint Francis (founder of the Franciscan brotherhood), was constructed in 1690 by Spanish soldiers under explorer Captain Alonso de León. Mission Tejas was located along the Old San Antonio Road in what is now Houston County. A second mission was built during the same time, Mission Santísimo Nombre de María located further north near the Neches River.[22]

As Sadler was preparing to stake his claim in this new territory, population in Texas was swelling. In 1820 there were only about two-thousand settlers, but by 1834 the population had climbed to twenty-four thousand. Of these, twenty-thousand people were Anglo-Americans or, more properly, "Texans."[23] Texas was split into three territorial departments: Bexar, the southernmost territory which bordered Mexico and included the settlements of Bexar, Goliad, San Antonio and Victoria; Brazos, farther east along the coast and including the towns of San Felipe, Gonzales, Columbia and Matagorda; and Nacogdoches, which stretched to the Red and Sabine rivers which separated Texas from the United States territories. The Nacogdoches Department included the towns of Nacogdoches, San Augustine, Liberty and Jonesboro, and its population in 1834 as estimated by Juan N. Almonte of Mexico was nine thousand.[24]

In the Nacogdoches Department, Sadler had located the land which closely resembled the fertile farmland of his father's plantation. To raise the capital necessary to purchase land, cattle and the necessities to start his own plantation, he decided to part with his Georgia property. On February 4, 1834, he sold his fifty-acre farm to Nathaniel Sadler for three-hundred dollars. Although this could have been his brother, Nathaniel Milton II, this sale more probably was made to his father. According to the sales slip, William T. Sadler's land was located "in the fourteenth district of Baldwin, now Putnam County adjoining." This receipt, as signed and sealed by Sadler, marked the beginning of this man's future. Three-hundred dollars, although not an enormous amount of money, would buy a small fortune of land in Texas in 1834.

Having converted his personal holdings to cash, Sadler prepared to set forth for the land of Stephen F. Austin. Ahead of him lay a

Fellow Georgian Mirabeau B. Lamar was Sadler's traveling companion through Alabama, Mississippi and Louisiana.

Lamar fell ill near the Texas border and Sadler continued on to Nacogdoches. Their lives would continue to cross at the Battle of San Jacinto, while Lamar was President of the Republic of Texas, and when both men served together in the Texas House of Representatives.

Courtesy of the San Jacinto Museum of History.

trying journey through both new settlements and areas that had never been settled. When William Turner Sadler bade goodbye to Georgia and his family, he would see neither again for many years.

* * * *

ALABAMA RIVER TO NEW ORLEANS

As previously described, Sadler made the acquaintance of Mirabeau B. Lamar shortly after boarding the steamboat on the Alabama River on the evening of June 19, 1835. From Washington, Alabama, the energetic *Little Rock* chugged between the Alabama's high bluffs, beyond which lay fertile grounds well adapted to cotton and corn crops. After passing another small community, the little steamer passed the larger settlement of Selma before arriving at the former state capital of Cahawba in Dallas County. Flooding along the Alabama had moved the capital away from the

The early river steamboats in use in 1835 were side-wheelers whose paddles were usually driven by a single engine. William T. Sadler and Mirabeau B. Lamar used three such steamboats during the course of their travels through Alabama and Louisiana en route to Texas. According to Lamar, the Little Rock *was one of only thirteen boats on the Alabama at this time.*

river and would eventually force the abandonment of some of the early riverside communities, including that of Washington.

Cahawba (now spelled Cahaba), by land only about sixty miles from Montgomery, was viewed by Lamar as a city "in a state of improvement." The *Little Rock*, in fact, stopped long enough here for Lamar and his companion William Sadler to journey together into town where Lamar was able to renew associations with some of the people with whom he had done newspaper business some fifteen years before.[25]

As the Texas-bound pair became acquainted, Sadler found that Lamar had quite a varied past from his early Georgia days. Lamar had developed a love for history as a youth while growing up in Putnam County and attending nearby Powelton Academy for one term. This school boasted a strong curriculum, but after his first term he was sent to Eatonton Academy, which was closer to home and strengthened by a new headmaster. His cultural education resulted in a love of oil painting and in poetry, the latter a trademark for which he would become known. In 1819 Mirabeau Lamar had begun a general mercantile business with a friend, but he sold out to his friend by year's end as business dwindled.[26]

Turning next to journalism, Lamar became co-publisher and part-time editor of the *Cahawba Press* in Cahawba, Alabama. While experimenting in writing, he also used this vehicle to publish some of his early poetry. He had then left behind the *Cahawba Press* in 1822, returning to Georgia and joining the staff of Governor George MacIntosh Troup as secretary. Among the topics concerning the

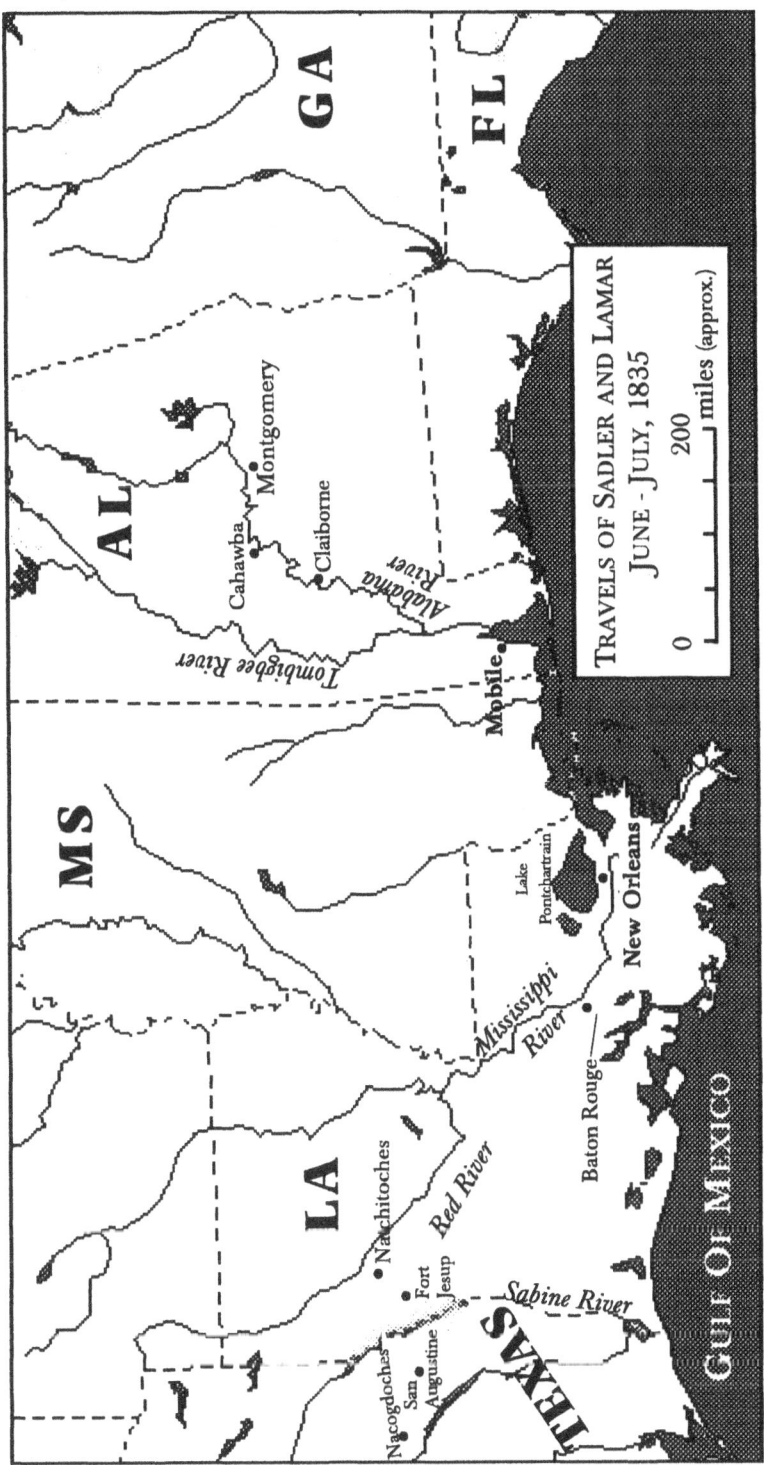

En route to Texas in 1835, W. T. Sadler met another man from Putnam County, Georgia – Mirabeau B. Lamar. Together, the pair continued the one thousand-mile journey to the new territory via steamboat, stagecoach and even one of the first trains.

Georgians at the time was the spread of white settlers into Creek Indian territory. Lamar commanded a corp of military volunteers, and the unit's first muster was that of welcoming elderly French explorer Marquis de Lafayette, who was visiting the area.[27]

After Governor Troup's term ran out in December of 1825, Lamar married Tabitha B. Jordan on January 1, 1826. His young wife's health was poor, but she did deliver them a daughter, Rebecca, late in 1827. He soon began his own paper, entitled *Columbus Enquirer*, which began appearing regularly in 1828. The following year he was elected as State Senator for Muscogee County and completed a year in office. While he was a candidate for a return to office the next summer, his wife Tabitha succumbed to tuberculosis on August 20, 1830. Mirabeau Lamar was deeply troubled; he withdrew from the senatorial race and sold his newspaper to take up traveling about the area for almost two years. Regrouping, he finally returned to politics in 1832, running unsuccessfully for Congress. He ran again in 1833 for Congress but was again unsuccessful even though he bought back half of the *Enquirer* to give himself a voice. Following these two losses, Lamar was hit hard again with three more: his sister died in the spring of 1833; his father died that summer, and his beloved older brother Lucius committed suicide on July 4, 1834.[28] Whereas Sadler was traveling to Texas to secure his future, Lamar was more or less trying to leave his past behind him.

Adding these failures and tragedies to the recent death of his wife, Lamar was not in good mental health by late 1834. His physical health was also suffering. He decided that his remedy should be a drastic change of his environment: moving to the free territory beyond the Sabine River to a land where a man could carve out a future for himself. It was the pioneering frontier called Texas.

* * * *

From Cahawba, the *Little Rock* made good time downriver, where the communities were less frequent for much of this stretch. About 150 miles above Mobile it passed the town of Claiborne. Below this city were many large plantations, beautiful to view but all subject to flooding when the Alabama escaped her banks. The junction of the Tombigbee and Alabama rivers was about fifty miles above Mobile. Below this flatland junction the rivers became known as the Tensaw and Mobile rivers, the latter used by the *Little*

Rock on Sunday, June 21, for her final run to the city of Mobile. This area was also low and flat, with live oaks and blue cranes becoming more prevalent as the steamboat moved toward the bay.

Mirabeau Lamar noted an eagle's nest in a tree by the water's edge, and the boat's pilot told him that it had been a familiar sight on the Alabama for many years. Of their arrival in Mobile, Lamar wrote:

> Long before we reach Mobile we wind our way through a flat marshy country that can never be subjected to the plough and hoe. The city rose to view about 7 miles off. We approach it by twilight. A storm has cooled the atmosphere and it is delightful and refreshing. Our journey closed with the close of day. It was Sabbath evening. No noise, no bustle of business greeted our entrance. All was tranquil and placid, and as far as I can judge of the feelings of the passengers, they partook of the serenity of the weather and peacefulness of the scenery around them.[29]

The passengers sought lodgings for the night, but Lamar found that there was not a room available for him at the luxurious Mansion House. He noted that the use of his military rank, however, allowed their fellow traveler Lieutenant McKenzie to receive a "handsome apartment." Lamar and his fellow travelers took their bags to the nearby Alabama Hotel, where "room was more abundant and titles less necessary."[30]

Located at the base of the Mobile River, the city of Mobile in 1835 had a population of about ten thousand. Lamar found it to be in "a most rapidly progressive state" and that it had risen from a dirty river town into a growing city "with beauty unrivaled and wealth unbounded."[31]

After a short stay in Mobile, Sadler and Lamar caught a stage coach bound for New Orleans on Wednesday, June 24. They departed in a heavy rain storm, with Lamar's riding atop the box with the driver for a better view of the countryside. From his perch he noted the Nunnery in the town of Summerville and then the Catholic College in the next town of Springhill. Following this, "we were whirled over 30 miles of pine country as level as a die and as barren as a molehill, which brought us to Portersville on Lake Ponchartrain."[32] The passengers also learned from the driver that he was making his last mail run to New Orleans on this trip because mail was being readied for water transportation between the two big cities.

The stage delivered the travelers to the steamboat *Otto*, which carried them overnight to a railroad depot. One of the country's first railroads ran five miles from Lake Ponchartrain into New Orleans, and this locomotive trip was certainly a memorable event for Sadler and his traveling companion. On the morning of Thursday, June 25, the men left the *Otto* and boarded the new train, which transported them rapidly into New Orleans in twenty minutes. Lamar, for one, was not moved by the sanitary conditions found in this populous city, "The first thing that arrested my attention was the extreme filthiness of the place. I had often heard of the sickliness of New Orleans, but now, instead of being surprised at its mortality, I wonder how any human being can exist there."[33]

Indeed, the state of affairs in New Orleans was quite disturbing. Robberies and street quarrels were daily events, with many quarrels turning into deadly duels in which one of the combatants was forever silenced. Sadler and Lamar tried to look past the lawlessness and take time to take in some of the cultural sights of the big town. Although most theatres were closed during the summer, Lamar attended two plays in the French Quarter, which he enjoyed little due to his "ignorance of the language." He estimated that this city of "fruitful adventure" would expand from its population of 50,000 to more than 500,000 in a short period of time.[34]

RIVER PASSAGE TO NATCHITOCHES

Lamar had plans to sail from New Orleans to Matagorda, while Sadler would be proceeding directly toward the East Texas town of Nacogdoches. Upon advice from an acquaintance on June 27, Lamar instead opted to try the Red River passage on the next available steamboat to Natchitoches. Sadler and Lamar continued their journey together toward Texas on June 30, securing passage on the steamboat *Romeo*.[35]

The Mississippi River was quickly becoming crowded with riverboats. By Lamar's count, there were seventy-two boats in operation on the Mississippi River as of 1835.[36] Despite ever-improving steamboat designs, the dangers of river travel would persist for decades. The high sediment content of the muddy waters could form an island in an eddy within just a few years. On the Mississippi alone, more than four-thousand travelers were killed or injured in steamboat accidents between 1811 and 1850.[37]

The single-engined *Romeo*, a side-wheeler of perhaps 160 tons and 120 feet in length, departed about 2:00 p.m. for its journey to the junction with the Red River. In his journal, Lamar noted the elegant mansions shaded by wide-spread oak trees near New Orleans. As the steamboat moved away from the city, however, the living conditions quickly deteriorated.

> The whole country up the river exhibits but one unvaried aspect: the private residences are small and inelegant; very few highly improved places. About 100 miles above New Orleans a church stands on the banks of the river. It looks solitary and useless. I was much disappointed in the appearance of the crops. They were not so luxurious as I expected. Cane was small and corn was inferior to that of the Alabama River. Cotton was good, but [there was] little of it. The settlements looked not like plantations, but like military encampments.[38]

Lamar was impressed with the *Romeo*'s captain, a "noble, honest" man who possessed gentlemanly qualities that he found to be "uncommon" in riverboat captains. The *Romeo* stopped long enough before breakfast on July 1 to pick up a female passenger just south of the settlement of Plaquemine to the left of the river. Two more big bends and two more miles of the river brought the little steamer to the thriving city of Baton Rouge, which stood on a bluff to the river's right. Its name meaning "red stick," Baton Rouge was a station for U.S. soldiers in the 1830s and was located on the Mississippi 130 miles above New Orleans.[39]

About thirty miles upriver from Baton Rouge, the *Romeo* passed the town of Bayou Sara on the right hand bank. This rich cotton-growing area was a major source of river shipping of cotton bales down to New Orleans. The Mississippi River was joined by the Atchafalaya River at a point about fifty-seven miles above Bayou Sara and about three miles below the mouth of the Red River. The Atchafalaya, believed to have split at one time from the Red River, continues a southerly course and empties into the Gulf of Mexico.

The *Romeo* reached the Atchafalaya at about 9:00 p.m. on Thursday, July 2, 1835. Work still continued on clearing these rivers for safer passage. A great water-logged jam of flotsam and debris, piled high with floating trees and known as a raft, had been cleared in 1833 by snagboats under command of Captain Henry Miller Shreve to enable steamboats to open trade between New Orleans and Natchitoches (pronounced "Nak-a-tosh"), Louisiana. Several years later, Shreve and his partners organized the Shreve Town

Company on a bluff above this river's northern Louisiana area, and the town was incorporated in 1839 as Shreveport.[40]

After leaving behind the mighty Mississippi, the *Romeo* headed due north for about eight miles to a junction of the Atchafalaya and Red rivers, at which point the Red River splits and turns toward Bayou Natchitoches. Lamar described the differences in these bodies of water.

> In ascending the Mississippi, and after entering into the Red River, the water becomes clearer. I was gratified at this, as I was weary of washing in the turbid waters of the Mississippi. But in a few hours' run, I was disappointed: for I found that the appearance of limpidness that belongs to the Red River was owing to the clear, transparent waters of the Black River emptying into it. After leaving the mouth of the Black River, the Red River assumed the deep complexion which gives it its appropriate name. This River Red divides into a great number of branches, which leave the main channels at one point and enter it again at another. Each branch has its appropriate name.[41]

After entering the wide mouth of the Red River, the steamboat chugged along several miles before river banks could once again be clearly made out. This area of Louisiana was prone to flooding due to the low banks. Such floods kept the river branches fluctuating in their courses, and one bad flood in 1832 had moved the Red River miles eastward from the town of Natchitoches. This settlement was still accessible, however, by steamboats traveling up the Little River, which itself was becoming less navigable each year.

Bountiful cotton crops were evident in this area of the Red River, although the planters did not have enough field space allotted for hay for their horses. On board the *Romeo* were a number of large bales of hay for sale to these planters. Moving westward and up the Little River from the Red, the steamboat finally delivered its passengers to Natchitoches early on Sunday, July 4.

Here, Sadler and Lamar found much of the town's younger inhabitants "drunk as deacons and funny as fiddlers, throwing the whole town into a state of wild uproar."[42] Although the Texas-bound travelers were a little taken aback that the people's behavior continued into Sunday, Lamar soon found that "the people were only keeping the Fourth of July, which at once unraveled these extravagant gambols."[43]

Located about four-hundred miles by water from New Orleans, French-established Natchitoches was the oldest and most remote city in Louisiana. The Texas-bound travelers found it also to be a dirty town full of inhabitants who were improving their settlement largely by preying on the funds of the Texas immigrants passing through their area. Mirabeau Lamar arrived here sick with a "burning fever" which would plague him for several days as he lay recovering in a boarding house, alternately shaking with the chills and burning up with fever. In the process of recovery, he was "swindled by a Scottish physician" and was left with a less-than-high regard for Natchitoches, "never met I with a community more selfish, unfeeling, and ready to prey upon the necessities of fellow-creatures."[44]

Sadler parted company with Lamar in Natchitoches for the final leg of his thousand-mile journey back to Texas. Although he had established a friendship with his Georgian companion, Sadler was not prepared to tarry any longer in returning to his land claim. Lamar wrote that he found Sadler to be a truly congenial traveling partner in "all matters clever and pleasant, and together we journeyed until we reached Natchitoches on the Red River, where we separated, he for Nacogdoches and I brought to anchor by a burning fever."[45]

Acquiring a horse was little problem in this town, and from Natchitoches it was roughly a forty-mile trip to the Sabine River, which marked the Texas border. The road passed through the U.S. post of Fort Jesup. Named for Brigadier General Thomas Sidney Jesup, Quartermaster General of the U. S. Army, this post had been established in 1822 on a ridge between the Red and Sabine rivers, twenty-two miles southwest of Natchitoches, and served to protect the Louisiana and Texas borders. Past Fort Jesup, most of the route was barren countryside. Lodging and feed for horses were obtainable by the numerous immigrants who traveled this road from a number of area residents.

From Natchitoches, the road to Texas via the Sabine was known as the Old San Antonio Road or by its Spanish name, El Camino Real (the "King's Highway"). Established in 1691 as a direct route from Moncolva, Coahuila, to the Spanish Indian mission settlements of East Texas, El Camino Real ran for 540 miles through Texas from the Gaines Ferry to Paso de Francia on the Rio Grande River.[46]

Texas was entered from Louisiana by taking a ferry across the Sabine River into San Augustine County. The ferry was operated by James Gaines, one of the earliest Texas settlers and also the county's earliest *alcalde* or justice of the peace. Once across the narrow, muddy stream that separated the province of Texas from the United States, it was approximately thirty miles into San Augustine, a flourishing young town of about four-hundred settlers. Again, Sadler did not stay long before continuing down the King's Highway into Nacogdoches. He arrived around July 10 after covering about one hundred and twenty miles from Natchitoches and having spent more than a month since departing home in Georgia.

Left by his fellow Putnam County traveler, Mirabeau Lamar soon recovered from his ailment and departed Natchitoches on July 15, arriving in Nacogdoches on July 22. The former Georgia politician would become an important player in the early history of Texas, and his path would continue to cross that of William T. Sadler over those years.

Chapter Two

PIONEERS OF THE FORT HOUSTON SETTLEMENT

July 1835 - December 1836

William Sadler found Nacogdoches to be bustling with Texas immigrants upon his arrival in July of 1835. Named for the Nacogdoche Indians who had originally inhabited the area, this city had originally been visited by the La Salle Expedition in 1687. A mission named Nuestra Señora de Guadalupe de los Nacogdoches had been established with a settlement as early as June of 1716, thus giving the town bragging rights to being the "oldest town in Texas."[1]

This settlement was later abandoned due to negotiations between France and Spain, but in April of 1779 Gil Antonio Ibarvo and his followers resettled Nacogdoches. The Spanish had recognized this area to be an important gateway from the East to the Spanish possessions of North America. Ibarvo built the Old Stone Fort as a warehouse for merchandise his people smuggled between Natchitoches in Louisiana and the Indians of Texas. The first Texas newspapers were established here in the early 1800s, and although the settlement was almost completely destroyed by Spanish forces, Dr. James Long and three-hundred followers entered Texas in 1819 and occupied the Old Stone Fort. From here they helped organize early Texas with a provisional government that eventually became known as the Republic of Texas. Unrest with the Spanish continued, culminating with the Battle of Nacogdoches on August 2, 1832.[2]

This battle was a result of orders to the locals by the commandant of Nacogdoches to surrender their arms and declare in favor of Antonio López de Santa Anna, a former army commander who later became President of Mexico. Rebel forces under James W. Bullock and Vicente Cordova attacked a Mexican force near the

The Old Stone Fort, *as it looked it pioneer days. This house, sixty feet in length, twenty feet wide and twenty feet in height, was built in 1779 and was a prominent structure in Nacogdoches when Sadler arrived in July 1835. The Old Stone Fort has since been refurbished and is now a museum on the campus of Stephen F. Austin State University.* Early illustration drawn for the *Houston Press.*

Angelina River and captured the commandant, José de las Piedras. By the battle report of rebel settler James Bowie, thirty-three Mexicans were killed and about eighteen wounded in exchange for three Texans killed and seven wounded. This rebellion has been credited with making possible the organization of the impending Texas Revolution.[3]

Tensions continued between the more aggressive Texans and the Mexican troops in Texas, who had been sent by Santa Anna to control the rising flow of Texan immigrants. By 1835 the new settlers far outnumbered the native Mexicans who lived in Texas territory, and their number was increasing.

Thomas Jefferson Rusk, a lawyer from South Carolina who had arrived in Nacogdoches just months before Sadler, was destined to reach great fame in Texas. In a letter to his wife on February 15, 1835, he found the climate to be "mild and pleasant." Rusk wrote that Nacogdoches had "about 300 Americans and about 200 Spaniards and the country all around is settled up with Americans and the land is fine and the country affords all the conveniences and most of the luxuries of life and those who will be prudent and industrious here must become wealthy very soon."[4]

An industrious person, W. T. Sadler was quick to purchase the rights to the land he desired. First Class Headright Certificate No. 492 shows that he bought one-third of a league (1,476 acres) in

THE PILGRIM PREDESTINARIAN REGULAR BAPTIST CHURCH OF EAST TEXAS Original Members *(As of March 5, 1836)*		
ELDER AND WIFE	Annie Parker Crist [1]	John Grigsby Jr. [6]
Daniel Parker [+]	Stephen Crist [1]	Louisa T. Grigsby [6]
Martha "Patsey" Parker [+]	Rebecca Davidson [1]	James Jordan [4]
MEMBERS	Robert Davidson [1]	Joseph Jordan [2]
Armstead Bennett [7]	Polly Denson [5]	Prudence Jordan [4]
Faith Bennett [7]	Thomas C. Denson [5]	Robert A. Love [4]
Harriet Bennett [6]	Elizabeth Eaton [2]	Oliver Morris [4]
Mary Bennett [6]	Polly Eaton [2]	Isaac Parker [3]
Permelia Bennett [6]	Rachel Eaton [2]	James W. Parker
Stephen Bennett [6]	Richard Eaton [2]	John Parker [+]
Sally Brown [+]	Nancy Faulkenberry [2]	Lucinda Parker [3]
Julious Christy [+]	Garrison Greenwood [2]	Lucy W. Parker [3]
Rachel Christy [+]	John Gregg [6]	Pheby Parker [+]

[+] Listed as charter members of origination of church on July 26, 1833 in Crawford County, Illinois. Julious and Rachel Christy were given letters of Dismission on August 11, 1833.
[1] Received into church by letter on August 11, 1833.
[2] Received into church by letter on October 20, 1833 in Clayburn Parish, LA.
[3] Received into church by letter Saturday, April 5, 1834, in Austin's Colony, Texas.
[4] Received May 31, 1834. Morris dismissed Nov. 15, 1834.
[5] Received into church by letter on September 5, 1835.
[6] Received into church by letter on February 6, 1836.
[7] Received into church by letter on March 5, 1836.
   Source: "Records of an Early Texas Baptist Church." *The Quarterly of the Texas State Historical Association,* volume XI, no. 2 (October 1907): 85-156.

Nacogdoches from an agent named Severio Arocha. Arocha had been originally assigned this land on May 2, 1835.[5] Many early documents incorrectly show this man's name as "Rocha," including county maps later filed with the General Land Office. Original Sadler deed transactions record the name as Arocha. The 1830 Census shows a large group of Arochas in San Antonio and one Arocha family settled in Nacogdoches by that time. This one-third league was located approximately sixty miles due west of Nacogdoches, in an area that is now south of the present city of Palestine.

From Nacogdoches, Sadler prepared to settle in the area he had scouted out near the Neches River in 1822. His newly acquired land fell into what was currently Nacogdoches County but what would later become Anderson County. Very few white settlers had yet ventured out that way, as a number of Indian tribes still resided in the lands. The earliest known white settlers to venture into this vicinity had been a large group of immigrants from Illinois who established the first non-Catholic church in Texas.

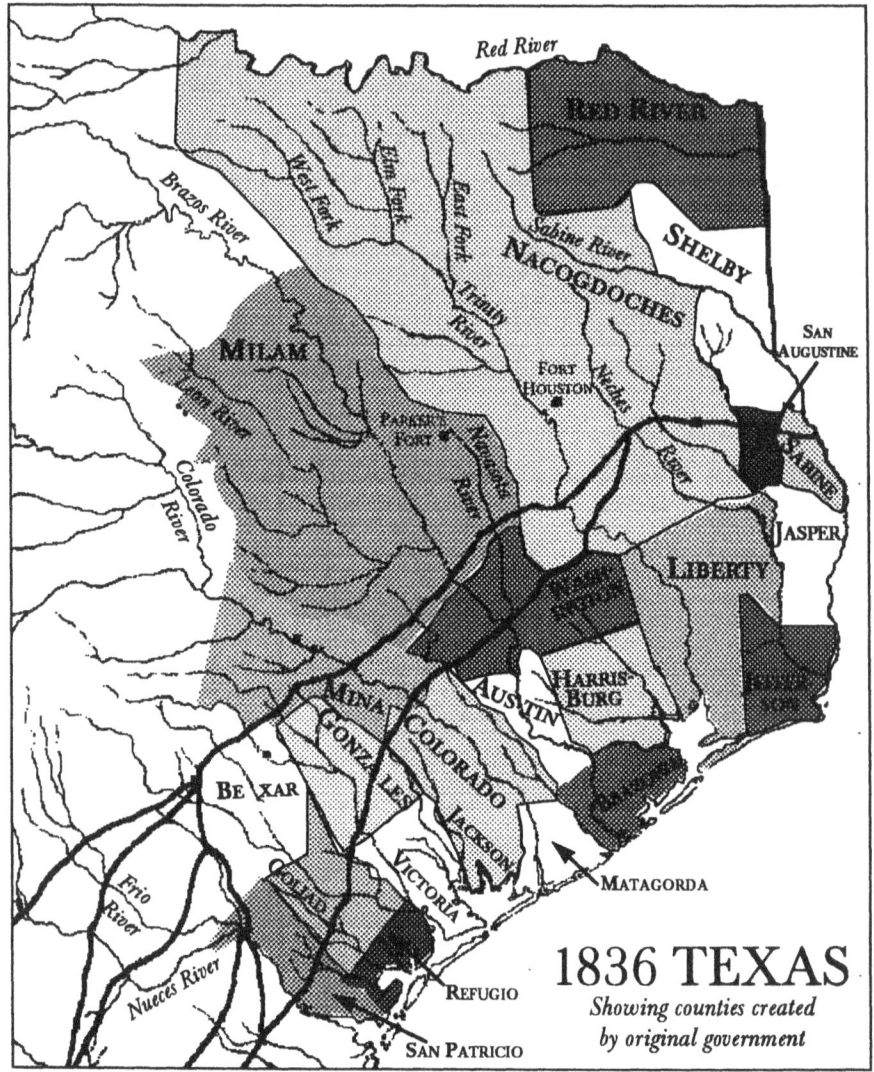

The territory of eastern Texas in 1835 included vast expanses of unsettled areas. In early 1836, the provisional government of Texas created a number of counties from the previous land "departments." Also shown are the major roads of this time. West of Nacogdoches, Sadler and his fellow pioneers established a settlement that later became Fort Houston.

These settlers were led by Daniel Parker Sr., who had been born in Culpepper County, Virginia, in 1781 and moved later to Franklin County, Georgia, where he was a licensed Baptist preacher by 1803. He married Patsey Dickerson and continued to preach in Georgia and Tennessee until the couple moved to Illinois in 1817, settling near the town of Palestine in Crawford County. Daniel Parker visited Texas in 1832 and found that Mexican law forbade his organizing a Protestant church in Texas territories but did not forbid the immigration of an *already organized* Protestant church. With this little problem solved, Parker returned to Illinois and gathered a following for a church that was named the Pilgrim Predestinarian Regular Baptist Church.[6]

Parker's Baptist church was organized near Palestine on July 26, 1833. His church members, friends and kinsmen then loaded their belongings into wagons and began their journey. Among the families to follow the church from Illinois to Texas were the Bennetts, Browns, Kennedys, Jordans, Greenwoods, and Lagows. Daniel and Patsey Parker brought their five sons, Dickerson, Daniel Jr., Benjamin, Isaac Duke and Kalbe, and two sons-in-law, Joseph Kennedy and Reuben Brown. Daniel's elderly father, John Parker, also made the journey with his five other sons: James W., Isaac, Silas, Joe A., and Benjamin F. Parker.[7] The Pilgrim Church settlers passed through Logansport, Louisiana, en route to Texas, and were joined by members of the Eaton and Faulkenberry families.

These settlers stopped long enough on San Pedro Creek in present Houston County to build their first fort near the present town of Grapeland. Known as Brown's Fort, this was where Elder Daniel Parker and his sons built their homes. His father, Elder John Parker, and sons James W., Silas M. and Benjamin F. Parker all continued on farther west to near the Navasota River, where they built Parker's Fort in present Limestone County near the town of Groesbeck.[8]

The settlers of the Pilgrim Predestinarian Regular Baptist Church would be the closest colonies to the one that would be established by Sadler and his companions and would become closely intertwined in Sadler's later life.

* * * *

WAGONS WEST FROM NACOGDOCHES

A small group of Texas settlers departed Nacogdoches in July 1835 with horses and cattle to pull their wagonloads of food, tools, provisions, and the personal effects they would need to forge out a new existence in the untamed territories where each had acquired his grant of land. This group, who would be the first white settlers of present Anderson County, Texas, consisted of William T. Sadler and the families of John Crist, William M. Frost, Garrison Greenwood and Joseph Jordan.[9]

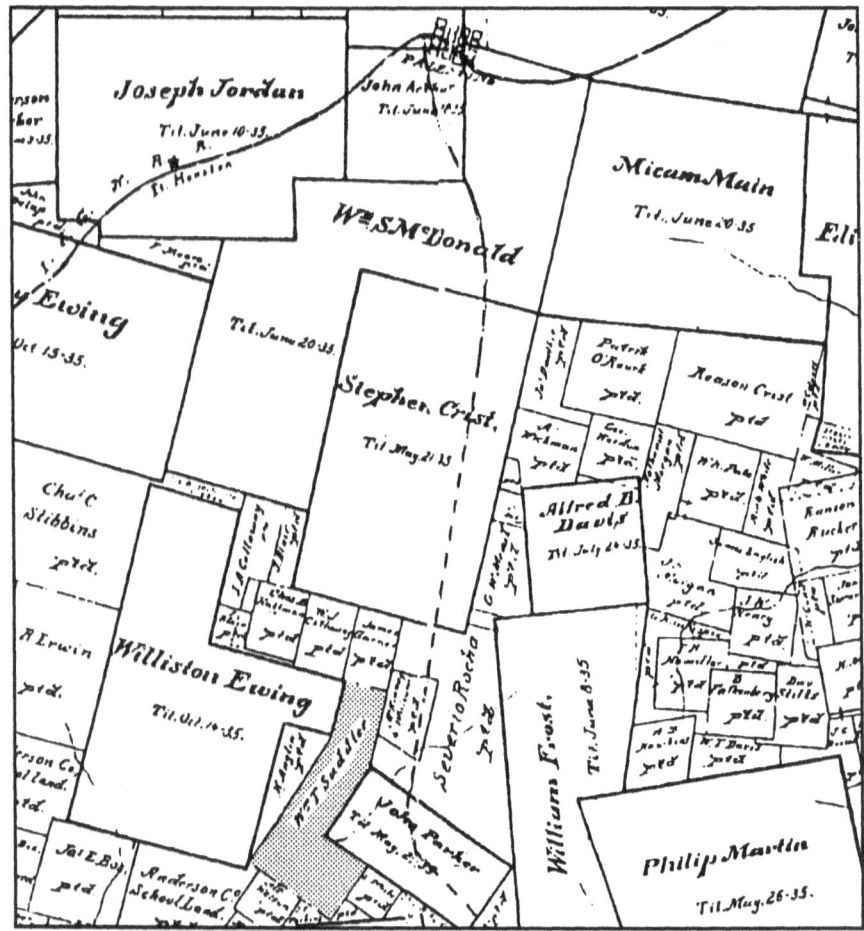

This cross-section of an early map from the General Land Office of Texas shows the original headright owners of land in the vicinity of Fort Houston. William T. Sadler's original 1/3 league (the shaded area) was purchased from Severio Arocha (both men's names are misspelled on this map) in 1835. Also shown is the future town of Palestine in what became Anderson County.

Greenwood, thirty-six, Crist, twenty-nine, and Jordan (Greenwood's father-in-law) were all originally with the Parker family wagon train from Illinois. Their families, along with that of William and Nancy Frost, farmed and harvested crops in 1834 in present Grimes County before moving in 1835 to the present Anderson County area. Garrison and Elizabeth Jordan Greenwood by that time had eight children. Joseph and Elizabeth Estes Jordan brought sons Levi and James, and the latter's wife Prudence. Frost had gained title to a league and labor of land in this area west of

Nacogdoches on June 8, 1835. Two days later, on June 10, Jordan had title to his own league and labor, on which the Greenwoods lived for a time.

Sadler and his companion settlers moved forward into a territory of the Nacogdoches Department approximately fifty miles beyond the extremes of the current frontier settlements. These bold travelers were armed with rifles yet very vulnerable to Indians as they crossed the Angelina River and later the Neches River. They continued on approximately twenty miles west to a location that was about eight miles east of the Trinity River.

This spot chosen, about two miles southwest of the present town of Palestine in Anderson County, had a "magnificent spring" where "tradition has it that the water gushed forth from the earth."[10] On these fertile lands Sadler and the families of Crist, Frost, Greenwood and Jordan began a small community that would become known as the "Fort Houston Settlement." The tract of land where the main settlement developed belonged to Joseph Jordan.

Soon after the Fort Houston Settlement had been established, the initial small group of settlers was increased by the arrival of other families. Early maps of this part of Texas show the names of the men owning the land surrounding this developing community to be John Arthur, John Crist, Stephen Crist, John Delap, Williston Edley Ewing, William Kimbro, James Madden, Micham Main, William S. McDonald, Daniel M. McKenzie, Elias G. Myers, Dickerson Parker, William H. Smith, and Jacob Snively.

The small settlement of Crists, Frosts, Jordans and W. T. Sadler was quickly joined by the families of Abram and Valentine Anglin, Roland William Box, James Edward Box, George Washington Browning, Daniel LaMora Crist, Stephen Crist, George T. Lamoin, Pleiades Orion Lumpkin (twenty-seven-year-old son of former Georgia Governor Wilson Lumpkin), and William S. McDonald.[11] McDonald would become the first justice of the peace for the area and Browning became the first commissary of the post of Fort Houston.

Of these other early settlers, Stephen and wife Annie Parker Crist were members of the Parker's Pilgrim Predestinarian Church. At this time, the couple had five children: Daniel Murry, twelve, George W., ten, Cicero, eight, Benjamin, seven, Martha "Patsy", five, and Elizabeth, three. After settling here, the couple had four more children. Stephen's brother Reason and half-brother Daniel LaMora Crist (from his father's second wife), twenty-one, also settled on land in the area at this time.[12]

The Fort Houston Settlement was near enough to the Trinity River that the settlers would use this river in future years for passage down to the new town of Magnolia. The site chosen in 1835 was near the junction of the early Nacogdoches and Pecan Point (near Red River) roads, close enough for families to benefit from the river without having to be concerned about flooding problems.[13] The farmland here lay between the Trinity and Neches rivers among the red hills, which were thickly covered with pine trees, large oaks and colorful sweetgums. A fine saline (salt spring) was only about four miles away, and many springs and creeks made excellent water sources for livestock. These benefits were in addition to the financial considerations for the early East Texas settlers; even five years later in 1840, those who purchased their land could still acquire a league for the price of five hundred dollars.[14]

The need for permanent housing was the first concern for the pioneer Fort Houston settlers. The approach of winter in a few months necessitated a sense of urgency to the task of establishing comfortable quarters. Building these early structures was a true community effort. John Crist made the boards for the first homes in present Anderson County from logs that were cut by William Sadler.[15]

The 1,476 acres Sadler acquired from Severio Arocha was located just southeast of the main Fort Houston settlement and was almost L-shaped. His original one-third league bordered with a number of pieces of land, including that of Arocha, John Parker, Williston E. Ewing, James Gardner, Stephen White, J. P. Perkins, Abram Anglin and Allen T. Nelson. A small creek that ran near his land was named "Saddler Creek," the improper spelling taken from the title later filed with the General Land Office of Texas.

A distinctive early landmark of this area was a line of cedar trees planted by the Indians long before the arrival of white settlers from Nacogdoches. This tree line, serving as a trail for early Indians, began at a point where three creeks, Saddler's, Crist and Frost's Creek, came together about a mile off the old Magnolia Road at a spot known as Rocky Point or Rocky Knob.[16] This trail of cedar trees, planted approximately a half mile apart, ran through the land of the Fort Houston settlement and continued north to the top of the Texas territory.

Aside from this original land acquisition, Sadler was entitled to receive a separate one-third league for being an early Texas settler. Once married, this grant could be increased to a full league and labor. For this second land tract he chose a location several miles

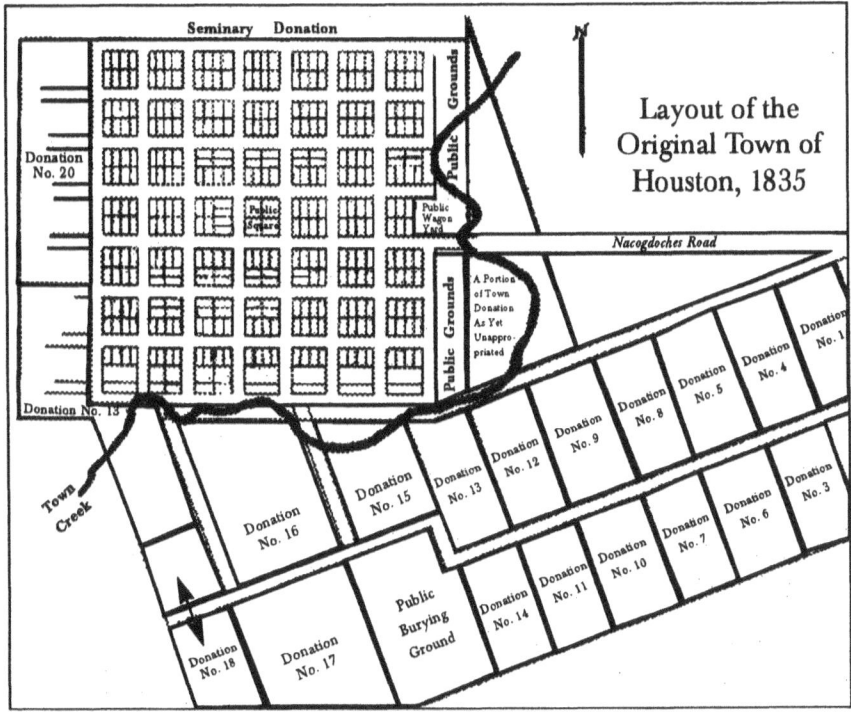

Rendition of the original map of the town of Houston drawn by William S. McDonald. He and Joseph Jordan encouraged immigrants to move to the settlement where Sadler and other pioneers had first settled the previous summer. The town was surrounded by Town Creek, and land was set aside for public grounds, a wagon yard and a public square.

east and slightly south of the first piece of land. Sadler's surveying skills came in handy as he accomplished the original surveys of this property. Although he would not receive clear title to his own grant of a league and labor until 1838 after being married, he eventually decided to build his home upon this land rather than the original one-third Arocha league.

This property would include *another* creek that is also spelled improperly as "Saddler Creek" on modern Texas maps. This Sadler Creek branches from a larger creek known as Ioni Creek. Rising by present U.S. Highway 287 southeast of what is now Elkhart in Anderson County, Ioni Creek runs northeast for 17.5 miles to its mouth on the Neches River, five miles east of Denson Springs. This stream was named for the Indians who had previously established a village along its heavily wooded banks.[17]

The land he settled upon had long been considered that of the Ionet Indians, whose name was later changed to "Ioni" Indians by the white settlers. The peaceful Ionies had their main village in a little valley cove on Ioni Creek. The Ionies maintained a prosperous business, trading with the newly arriving white settlers in the future years. Near the creek, they had grown large peach and plum trees, many of which still stand near the old village.[18]

One of Sadler's daughters, Martha Tucker Sadler Kennedy, later gave a statement to Miss Kate Hunter, an Anderson County school teacher who collected a good deal of this county's history, on July 17, 1927.

> My father, W. T. Sadler, came to Texas in 1835 from Putnam County, Georgia. He came unmarried and settled near the old Ioni Village. At that time there were Indian wigwams there and an Indian graveyard, but no Indians; they had been driven out.
>
> Wild plum thickets grew along Sadler Creek and Ioni Creek on Sadler land. My father related that every summer when the plums were ripe, the Indians would return to gather the fruits but never bothered any one nor were they bothered. These Indians never farmed; they were hunters and gatherers.

Camping at distances eighteen to thirty-five miles from the Fort Houston settlement were an abundance of Indian tribes, from the Ionies to the less peaceful Kickapoos, Caddos, Kichais and Tehuacanas. Sadler's property was located near the main road from Mexico City which passed through San Antonio, where it branched north to St. Louis and east to the Natchez Trace and the Atlantic seaboard. This road, later dubbed the "beef trail," would be a source of great sights in the future as herds of market-bound cattle and countless settlers traveled past.[19]

On this property he acquired cattle and hogs to raise as he slowly built a plantation in the likeness of his father's back in Putnam County, Georgia. The fertile soil was immediately accessible to plows in this area, and good food crops such as corn could be had the same year. So far, the opportunities of Texas were proving to be everything that Sadler had hoped for.

* * * *

The Original Town of Houston

The Fort Houston Settlement pioneers wasted little time in establishing a town to attract more settlers. Joseph Jordan and William McDonald, who owned adjoining properties north of Sadler's land, laid out the town which they called Houston. It was named for Sam Houston, who was at this time a prominent citizen of Nacogdoches from which the settlers had recently arrived.[20]

The *Telegraph and Texas Register*, the only newspaper for Texans at this time and published since October 10, 1835, at San Felipe de Austin, carried an article in its December 2, 1835, issue which announced the establishment of the new East Texas town of Houston. It described the town as being laid out on the east side of the Trinity, about forty miles north of the San Antonio Road.

> It contains between three and four hundred building lots and a large quantity of outland. The situation is said to be handsome, salubrious, and well-watered: surrounded by fertile, well-timbered land, and is about 6 miles from a good steamboat landing on the Trinity. The town is intended to be on the roads leading from Nacogdoches and Pecan Point to the falls of the Brazos. Within a few miles of it there are two large and good salines.

The town of Houston was divided into forty-nine blocks which were in turn divided into six or eight lots, each numbered. The rest of the town was plotted to include a public burial ground, a church block, seven acres designated for "seminary" purposes, two public watering places, and a town square with provisions made for a large public wagonyard. The road to Nacogdoches ran east and west through the town, and a small branch now called Town Creek formed a semi-circle about the town's southern and western extremes.[21]

The conditions established by Jordan and McDonald, the latter owning a mill south of town on the branch known as Town Creek, were basic. A five-hundred-acre donation of land was set aside for assignment to the first twenty settlers to build and occupy these donations for a one-year term that would commence on January 1, 1836. After one year of occupying this land, the said tenants would have clear title to their land. Among the first to settle in Houston were James E. Box, Daniel Crist, Randolph W. Davis, H. A. Delespine, Benjamin W. Douthit, George E. Dwight, Eli Faulkenberry, James W. Gardner, G. Glenn, Alexander Joost,

Washington Lewis, Oliver Lund, Alexander E. McClure, John McLinn, Shadrack H. Moore, Benjamin Parker, Silas M. Parker, William Perry, Edmund H. Persons, Richard Sparks, James Wilson, and William R. Wilson.[22]

During the early months of this community, the structure known as "Fort Houston" was also established. Early records of Garrison Greenwood indicate that the settlers began the blockhouse of native pine in the fall of 1835; the stockade was added later by soldiers in 1836. The earliest farmers to use this fort at night for protection were the families of Joseph Jordan, William Frost, Garrison Greenwood, Abram Anglin, John Crist and W. T. Sadler.[23]

THE TEXAS REVOLUTION

While Fort Houston's settlement was growing, Texas went to war. Efforts to inaugurate a war for independence had begun as early as 1826 in East Texas with the Fredonian Rebellion and had continued with the Battle of Nacogdoches in 1832. While in Mexico to present petitions of the Convention of 1833, Stephen F. Austin was arrested and held prisoner until July 1835. Antonio López de Santa Anna began a hostile campaign to seize power of Mexico, which he accomplished by late 1834. Santa Anna then sent a large contingent of soldiers to Texas, stationing them in the coastal settlement of Anahuac by January 1835.[24]

William Barret Travis led a group of volunteers in a march against Anahuac in June and forced the Mexican commander to surrender his post. Austin returned from his imprisonment in Mexico in October and encouraged the settlers to join him in rising up against Santa Anna. As Austin organized his men, an act of defiance occurred at Gonzales on October 2, 1835, when approximately 160 Gonzales Texans reclaimed a cannon that had been given the city by Mexico in 1831 for protection against Indian attacks. The Texans under Colonel John Moore stood defiantly, with their cannon and a banner that read "Come and Take It", before about one-hundred Mexican soldiers. Several long range volleys were exchanged, a Mexican private was killed, and the Mexican troops fled as the Texans advanced.[25] This revolt at Gonzales was a boost for the settlers' morale and is credited as the opening battle of the Texas Revolution.

Stephen F. Austin personally led a volunteer army against San Antonio, where General Martín Perfecto de Cos had increased Mexican forces in the town to about eleven-hundred soldiers in response to the Texan uprisings. In East Texas, officials in

Nacogdoches labored at soothing relations between settlers and the more than six-thousand Cherokee Indians who lived between the west side of that town and the Neches River. Mexican agents were suspected of trying to influence the two Cherokee leaders, Chiefs Bowles and Big Mush, to fight the Texans.[26]

A company of Texans on October 9 overwhelmed meager Mexican forces in the town of Goliad, killing one Mexican, wounding three and capturing twenty-four others. The Texans also seized the enemy's munitions supply, which included three-hundred muskets, powder, lead, and several cannons.[27] In other October actions, Colonel Jim Bowie, Captain James W. Fannin and a force of ninety Texans fought four-hundred Mexican soldiers near Mission Concepción on October 28. Some sixty Mexicans were reported killed at the cost of the first Texan killed in the revolution.

Small skirmishes continued into November. The General Convention of Texas adjourned on November 14 at San Felipe after electing provisional leaders. Stephen Austin (previously General of the Army of Texas) with William Harris Wharton and Branch T. Archer were appointed as commissioners to the United States to solicit aid for Texas in the revolution. Henry Smith, a former delegate of the Convention of 1833, was elected the Governor of Texas and Sam Houston the commander of the army. Houston, a former Tennessee governor and close ally of U. S. President Andrew Jackson, was a veteran of the U.S. Army, having fought bravely in the Seminole and Creek Indian Wars. Houston would command a regular army of men recruited for two-year enlistments but would not have authority over the six-hundred-man volunteer army at San Antonio, which was soon placed under the command of Colonel Edward Burleson.[28]

Burleson's officers decided in early December to give up their seige against Mexican forces in San Antonio. Colonel Ben Milam, however, spoke out sharply against this decision, uttering the inspirational call of "Who will follow old Ben Milam into San Antonio?"[29] The volunteer forces rallied with Milam and Burleson, and his officers agreed to organize an attack on the provisional capital city. Despite icy weather, the Texas volunteer forces began their assault on December 5 against the fortified stone buildings of San Antonio, whose key defensive structure was the heavily gunned Alamo.

After four days of heavy fighting throughout the "Alamo City," two-hundred Mexicans were killed and Mexican General Cos' remaining eleven-hundred troops finally surrendered at the Alamo on December 9. Some twenty-five Texans were wounded and four were killed, including Ben Milam. The capture of the Alamo provided the Texas Army with large amounts of muskets, powder, cannon and ammunition. News of their loss at Bexar, the Mexican municipality of San Antonio, was quickly received by Santa Anna.[30]

Victorious leaders in Goliad announced that the former province of Texas was now a free and sovereign state independent from Mexican rule. The first flag of Texas independence, a white cotton cloth whose red inked center sported a severed arm and hand clutching a drawn sword, was unfurled on December 22 in Goliad.[31]

* * * *

FORMATION OF THE EARLY TEXAS RANGERS

With the meager forces of the Texas Army concentrated in central Texas, a new means for protecting the frontier settlements was soon created. Stephen F. Austin had called a "Permanent Council" in October 1835. Representatives from each of the Texas municipalities went forth to help organize the affairs of the revolution. Representing the Nacogdoches municipality was Daniel Parker Sr., who on October 17 offered a resolution to create a corps of Texas Rangers.

Three "superintendents" of the rangers were instated: Silas Mercer Parker would direct twenty-five men to protect the frontiers between the Brazos and Trinity rivers; Garrison Greenwood would maintain ten rangers on the east side of the Trinity to the Neches; and Daniel Boone Friar with twenty-five rangers would patrol the areas between the Brazos and Colorado. Parker and Friar would rendezvous their men at the Waco Indian village on the Brazos River as a central point, while Greenwood's rangers would headquarter at the new Fort Houston settlement.[32]

The first known use of the term "rangers" in Texas had been for ten men employed by Stephen F. Austin in 1823. Other small bands of men were employed by Austin at various times over the following years to ward off bands of Indians who threatened his colonists.[33] It was not until the outbreak of the Texas Revolution, however, that the ranger corps was formally organized.

With this fabled corps of frontier defenders, W. T. Sadler would soon begin to make a name for himself in Texas.

Chapter Three

SADLER'S RANGERS AND THE NACOGDOCHES VOLUNTEERS

January 1 - March 25, 1836

In the Fort Houston settlement, superintendent of rangers Garrison Greenwood selected William Sadler, a single man who was a veteran of the Seminole and Creek Indian Wars, to be captain of his frontier unit. As such, Sadler then became responsible for raising his own company of volunteers for the territory between the Trinity and Neches rivers.[1]

When the Permanent Council of Texas met again in November, it resolved on November 9 to add another Texas Ranger unit of twenty men under the superintendence of George W. Davis to cover the frontier from the Colorado River to the Guadalupe.[2] Also on November 9, Daniel Parker recommended that his brother Silas Parker's request for ten additional rangers be authorized for the Brazos/Trinity area.[3] This assembly then addressed the future needs of the regular army, a militia structure, and also a corps of 150 rangers which was authorized on November 24, 1835. This resolution provided for three companies of fifty-six men each. The first captains (Isaac Watts Burton, William W. Arrington and John James Tumlinson) were elected on November 28, and Robert McAlpin Williamson, a lawyer and newspaper editor with a wooden leg who was known as "Three Legged Willie", was appointed major in charge of the ranger service.[4]

Captain Sadler spread the word that he was forming a volunteer mounted ranger unit. Those interested gathered to enlist in the East Texas town of Houston in present Anderson County on January 1, 1836. One of these new enlistees was twenty-one-year-old Daniel LaMora Crist, who later stated that he "was a private in Captain William T. Sadler's Company No. 10 of Mounted Rangers of independent volunteers under order of the Government."[5] Area

> **OATH OF IDENTITY.**
>
> *Samuel G. Wells* of the town of *Butler* county of *Freestone* in the State of *Texas* on this *8th* day of *August* One Thousand Eight Hundred and *Seventy Three* personally appeared before me, the undersigned, a Justice of the Peace for the county and *State* above mentioned, and *Samuel G. Wells* who being duly sworn according to law, declares that he is the identical *Samuel G. Wells* who was a *Private* in Captain *Wm. J. Sadlers* Company *No. 10* of the — Company of *Mounted Rangers* that he enlisted on the *1st* day of *January 1836* for the term of *Three Months* and was discharged at *Fort Houston (Anderson Co)* on the *1st* day of *March 1836* by reason of *the Fall of the Alamo.* —
>
> *Saml. G. Wells*

Captain Sadler's Texas Ranger Company *was formed at Fort Houston on January 1, 1836, during the Texas Revolution. Evidence of the unit's existence can be found in such archival documents as this oath of identity from the Pension Papers of Samuel G. Wells.* Texas State Library and Archives Commission, Republic of Texas microfilm series OCLC#37449683, reel 244, frame 650.

resident Daniel Parker Jr. also joined Sadler's company on New Year's Day and later served as a witness for the service of fellow ranger Samuel G. Wells.[6]

Each of Sadler's new privates enlisted for the three-month period spanning January 1 - April 1.[7] Although no muster roll of this unit has survived, the other members of Sadler's ten-man unit are believed to be Daniel Doubt, John Crawford Grigsby, William Calvert Hallmark, James Madden, Philip C. Martin, and Dickerson Parker.[8] These men and Captain Sadler all later joined a company known as the Nacogdoches Volunteers near the Colorado River, prior to San Jacinto but *after* that company had originally formed.

Sadler is known to have kept company with twenty-three-year-old Dickerson Parker, older brother of Private Daniel Parker Jr. Both were sons of the Elder Parker who had brought the first non-Catholic church to Texas.[9] Of the other rangers, Crawford Grigsby and his family migrated with the Parker family in 1834 to present Houston County. His parents, John and Louisa Thompson Grigsby Jr., had settled in the area of the present community of Augusta. William Hallmark, thirty-one, was one of fourteen known children of George William Hallmark, who had settled in present Houston County in 1834.[10] Philip Martin, a North Carolina native, had immigrated to Texas in 1824 and was granted a league of land on May 26, 1835, just east of Sadler's one-third league. James Madden, thirty-one, had also been granted land in 1835 near the Fort Houston settlement.[11]

Sadler's ranger unit is listed on several documents as "Company No. 10," a name that would have been indicative of size rather than the total number of ranger units in existence. Captain Sadler referred to his men as the "Houston Company" in a document he signed in March 1836.[12]

Those men joining were required to furnish their own horse, arms and clothing and were to be supplied with one-hundred rounds of powder and ball. Ammo for the regional ranger companies was drawn by the superintendents from John Lott in Washington-on-the-Brazos, where a vast quantity of ammunition was deposited. In return for being properly equipped, they were paid $1.25 per day as privates. In the event of no horse, the captain would "cause a horse to be purchased for said private and charge him with the same, in the settlement of his quarterly accounts."[13] Officers received the same per diem rate as privates, but they were paid the same as officers of equal rank and grade in the U.S. Army.

Each new ranger unit was assigned specific duties. On the western frontier, Captain John Tumlinson's company, also formed on the first of January, was assigned to build a blockhouse at Hornsby's Station on the headwaters of Brushy Creek, about thirty miles northwest of present Austin.[14] Captain Sadler's company was similarly assigned to construct a blockhouse, the main fortification for what would become known in East Texas as Fort Houston.[15] The rangers under Silas Parker were fortunate enough to have Parker's Fort, near the Navasota River, from which to operate. Parker's initial twenty-five-man ranger company, under command of Captain Eli Hillhouse, was in service "for the purpose of frontier defense" by late October 1835.[16]

Even as the new ranger corps was taking shape, the Texas Army's volunteer forces had been dwindling during the Texas Revolution. President Santa Anna had used his time well, regrouping his forces and pushing forward into Texas in early 1836 with a harsh plan to drive all Texas settlers from the countryside. While another force under General José Urrea advanced along the Gulf Coast, Santa Anna and approximately fifteen-hundred troops surprised the Alamo defenders in San Antonio in February 1836. The commander of the Texas forces in San Antonio, Lieutenant Colonel Travis, and his co-commander Jim Bowie, sent urgent dispatches on February 23 to other Texas commanders at Goliad and Gonzales. Travis' men were gathered in the old Alamo fortress for protection but needed immediate reinforcements. "We are determined never to retreat," read one message received by Colonel Fannin in Goliad.[17]

The Texan garrison at the Alamo held but a little more than 150 gallant defenders who, under Travis, pledged to "never surrender or retreat." The one-thousand-plus Mexican troops who first arrived in San Antonio were continually augmented over the next few days until their number surpassed three thousand. Fighting between the forces occurred in the streets around the Alamo as Mexican troops tried to move in artillery and to cut off the Texans' water supply.

Lieutenant Colonel Travis continued to send almost daily dispatches of the fighting. He estimated on February 24 that his little forces could not last more than two more weeks and sent a message to Gonzales with another call to "the people of Texas and all Americans in the world" for help. Stating that he had not yet lost a man after twenty-four hours of Mexican bombardment and cannonade, Travis made a desperate appeal.

> I call upon you in the name of liberty, of patriotism and everything dear to the American character, to come to our aid with all dispatch . . . If this call is neglected, I am determined to sustain myself as long as possible and die like a soldier who never forgets what is due his own honor and that of his country.
> Victory or death.[18]

This strong statement motivated hundreds of new Texas settlers to fight. New volunteers for the Texas Revolution immediately turned out as the word spread, but they were to be too late to reinforce the besieged Alamo defenders.

* * * *

Travis' message drew an immediate reply in Gonzales from Major Williamson, who had not yet managed to raise all three companies of his ranger corps. He sent word on February 25 to his rangers that the Mexican Army had arrived in San Antonio and that the Texan forces had retreated to the Alamo.[19] Williamson ordered Captain Tumlinson's company into Gonzales to help with the current crisis. Private Noah Smithwick recalled that "the invasion of Santa Anna necessitated our recall" and that all advanced positions "were ordered abandoned, and the forces to concentrate at Gonzales, whither every available man was urged to repair forthwith."[20]

Word took a few days longer to reach the remote frontiers of East Texas. Captain Sadler was stationed in the town of Houston when he first heard of the plight of the Alamo defenders. He and his rangers were busily working on the main blockhouse of what had become known as Fort Houston. His grandson, Robert Roach Sadler, related in 1921 to Anderson County's historian that

> I've heard my grandfather say they were working on the house (which house I don't know), when they got news that San Antonio had fallen, and that Fannin's men would be massacred if they didn't get some relief, and he and a party of men (I don't know who) started to their relief.[21]

The Texas Rangers were revamped again during early March. Two new senior officers, Colonel Jesse Benton and Lieutenant Colonel Griffin Bayne, were appointed. By mid-March, orders had gone out to ranger companies such as Captain Sadler's to disband and join the army. In pension papers filed more than thirty-five years later, several of his men stated the date to be "about the first day of March" 1836. Private Daniel Crist's papers state that Sadler's men were "discharged at Fort Houston on the first day of March AD 1836 by reason of the fall of the Alamo, when they were called to the Army of San Jacinto."[22] This company was more likely broken up in mid-March. Crawford Grigsby is known to have attended Daniel Parker's Pilgrim Church on Saturday, March 5, and Sadler's men did not leave the present Houston County area until March 19. Another ranger captain, Stephen Townsend, is known to have received his orders to join the army on March 16.[23]

The work on Fort Houston remained incomplete and would not be resumed until other rangers took up station there in the summer of 1836. Within a short period of time, William Sadler and seven men from his Houston Company struck out for Gonzales to join the Texas Army. Two of his former privates, Sam Wells and Daniel

Crist, stayed behind to help protect the women and children of the Fort Houston settlement. Wells joined Captain Thomas S. McFarland's Texas Volunteers. This unit, which did not see action at San Jacinto, included other Fort Houston area residents Williston Ewing, Miles Bennett, Stephen Bennett, John Parker and Reuben Brown.[24] Daniel Crist later served in Captain Mike Costley's rangers as a private through September 1836.[25]

Many of the senior officers of the rangers joined the Texas Army during the next month. Major Williamson and Captain Isaac Burton ultimately joined the cavalry as privates; Captain John Tumlinson joined Captain William Heard's Company F as a private; superintendent George Davis joined as a private in Captain Moseley Baker's Company D; and Captain Sadler was soon to take the rank of private in another volunteer company.

In San Antonio the situation was tense. From the Alamo, the top-ranking Mexican-Texan, Captain Juan Seguín, and an aide rode to Gonzales on February 29 for reinforcements. Led by veteran scout John W. Smith, thirty-two Gonzales rangers under Lieutenant George C. Kimbell, joined by Captain Albert Martin, slipped into the Alamo on Tuesday, March 1, bringing the total number of defenders inside to about 187.[26] They also brought with them the defiant "Come and Take It" flag from the October 2 Gonzales battle.

Scout John Smith was sent over the walls on the night of March 3 with a final message for help to the delegates of the General Convention of Texas being held at the small town of Washington-on-the-Brazos. The Convention's delegates had declared the independence of Texas on March 1 and had worked non-stop into March 2 writing and signing their formal Declaration of Independence for Texas.[27] The Convention would then spend the next seventeen days and nights forming the draft for the Republic of Texas's Constitution.

Also important was the fact that Governor Henry Smith's provisional Texas government ceased to be when the fifty-eight delegates formally elected the men who would now run the free and sovereign Republic of Texas. The key elected officials were David G. Burnet as President, Dr. Lorenzo de Zavala as Vice President, Secretary of Treasury Bailey Hardemann, Secretary of Navy Robert Potter, Attorney General David Thomas, Secretary of State Samuel P. Carson, and as Secretary of War, Thomas Jefferson Rusk.[28]

The fighting at the Alamo grew to such a desperate point on March 5 that Lieutenant Colonel Travis paraded his 185 remaining defenders on the grounds of the old mission for an emotional speech. "Our fate is sealed," Travis told his men, since the promised reinforcements could not possibly arrive soon enough to save them from the increasing pounding they were taking.[29] Several wounded and sick men, including the brave Colonel Jim Bowie, lay on cots. Travis is said to have drawn a line in the dirt with his sword and asked those who would stay to fight to their deaths to step across. David Crockett and his band of Tennessee followers quickly stepped across, while Bowie and some of the wounded had to be carried across. Only one fifty-year-old private refused, and he slipped over the walls that night to make his escape.[30]

* * * *

THE NACOGDOCHES VOLUNTEERS MARCH OUT

Far from the Alamo, a volunteer company that Sadler's rangers would soon join was formed in Nacogdoches on March 6, 1836. The word had spread that help was needed in San Antonio. Many of these men were residents of the area which later became Houston County, and most were new to Texas. One of the earliest enlistees of this Nacogdoches company was nineteen-year-old Alfred M. Hallmark, whose brother William Hallmark was one of Sadler's rangers.[31] John Swanson Yarbrough Jr., seventeen, came from Ouachita Parish in Louisiana in 1835 to join his father, Swanson Sr., who had come to Nacogdoches in 1832 to apply for land.[32] Both father, son and other son Joseph Randolph Yarbrough headed for Nacogdoches to enlist.

Other future Houston County residents of this company included five young men of the Box family. Four were brothers, John Andrew, thirty-two, Nelson A., twenty-eight, Stillwell, and Thomas Griffin Box, nineteen, all sons of Stephen F. Box who had brought his wife and five sons to Texas as one of the first settlers of the present Crockett, Texas, area. James Edward Box, twenty-two-year-old cousin of the Box brothers, was a son of John M. Box, who came to Texas from Tennessee in 1833 on covered wagon and horseback and settled in what is now north Houston County.[33]

The large bunch of Nacogdoches County residents formed their company with about forty men on March 6, calling themselves the "Nacogdoches Volunteers." In the process of organizing, the men elected thirty-one-year-old Hayden S. Arnold as captain. A Tennessee native who had migrated to Texas in 1835, Arnold had previously enlisted in the volunteer auxiliary corps on January 14, 1836.[34] Robert W. Smith from North Carolina was named first lieutenant and Isiah Edwards became the second lieutenant.[35]

> ## THE NACOGDOCHES VOLUNTEERS OF SAN JACINTO
> Second Regiment Texas Volunteers, First Company Infantry Roster *
>
> **OFFICERS:**
> Hayden S. Arnold ...... Captain
> Robert W. Smith ...... 1st Lt.
> Isiah Edwards .... 2nd Lt.
> Thomas D. Brooks..... 1st Sgt.
> Samuel Leeper .... 2nd Sgt.
> William P. Kincannon .. 1st Corp.
> Samuel Phillips .... 2nd Corp.
> **PRIVATES:**
> Howard W. Bailey
> John T. Ballard
> James Edward Box
> John Andrew Box
> Nelson A. Box
> Thomas Griffin Box
> Henry Mitchell Brewer
> John W. Carpenter
> Henry Larkin Chapman
> Daniel Doubt
> John Crawford Grigsby
> William Calvert Hallmark
> Elias Edley Hamilton
> John W. Harvey +
> Peter W. Holmes
>
> James Madden
> Philip C. Martin
> John McCoy
> John W. McHorse
> Stephen McLinn
> George R. Mercer
> James Mitchell
> Jose Molino
> John Moss
> William Nabors
> Dickerson Parker
> Leroy Pruett
> Martin J. Pruett
> David Rusk
> William Turner Sadler
> William Bennett Scates
> Stephen Franklin Sparks
> John B. Trenary
> Jesse Walling
> Madison Guess Whittaker
> William F. Williams
> John Yancy
> John Swanson Yarbrough Sr. ++
> John Swanson Yarbrough Jr. ++
>
> * This roster only indicates those who fought at San Jacinto. For a complete roster of the Nacogdoches Volunteers, see Appendix B. Six other company members were sick and stayed with the baggage at Harrisburg: Stillwell Box, Keeton McLemore Jones, Alfred M. Hallmark, William Henry Vardeman, John C. Walling and Joseph Randolph Yarbrough.
>
> + Some early rolls show a "John Marvey" to have fought at San Jacinto, but this was later decided to have been John Harvey listed twice on Capt. Arnold's roll by mistake.
>
> ++ Nacogdoches Volunteer rolls show only "Swanson Yarborough". Family records indicate that father *and* son fought at San Jacinto, with the son being killed in the battle.

All of Arnold's original company had been in Texas for less than two years, except John McCoy who had brought his family to Texas in 1828. At forty-one years of age, McCoy was the oldest man of the company. The youngest member at this point was nineteen-year-old William F. Williams, born in Tennessee on June 14, 1816. The men under Arnold's command had come from Alabama, Georgia, Louisiana, Mississippi, Missouri, North Carolina, Tennessee and Virginia, and all were willing to fight for their republic. Also among the group was a native of Nacogdoches of Mexican descent named José Molino, whose name incorrectly appears on some rosters as "Hosea Maloney, Mexican".

Two more men, Leroy and Martin Pruett from Georgia, joined on March 7, shortly before the unit marched out. Other men would continue to be added to Captain Arnold's company over the next month. Another company of Nacogdoches County volunteers under Captain Leonard H. Mabbitt was later formed, but it arrived too late to join the historic San Jacinto battle.

Arnold's revolutionary company was but one example of the four different categories of Texas military in 1836: the Volunteer Army of the People, the Regular Army, the militia, and the frontier ranging companies. The Volunteer Army, organized in October 1835 by Stephen F. Austin, kept its recruits in service with the promise of land and money. The second military group was the newly created Regular Army of Texas, established by the provisional government on November 13, 1835, and patterned after the U.S. Army. At full strength, the Texas Army would consist of one brigade of 1,120 men, divided into a regiment of artillery and one of infantry, each led by a colonel and containing two battalions of five fifty-six-man companies.[36]

The militia of Texas, while not as regimented as the Regular Army, would play an important role in the defense of the Republic in the coming years. The fourth group was the early Texas Ranger corps recently created. During the republic years, these mounted frontier lawmen were given a variety of titles: mounted riflemen, minutemen, spies, mounted gunmen and rangers.[37]

* * * *

THE FALL OF THE ALAMO AND THE GOLIAD MASSACRE

Just as the Nacogdoches Volunteers were formed on March 6, William Barret Travis and his 188 brave Alamo defenders were being overrun. As many as 1,544 Mexicans died in the assault in San Antonio, but the Texans, fighting hand-to-hand once the Mexicans finally entered the fortress, soon were overcome. Cannon fire kept Santa Anna from personally joining the frey until organized resistance had been crushed. In a boastful report to his government in Mexico City, he claimed that more than six-hundred Texans had been killed.[38]

The slaughter was horrific. Santa Anna ordered no prisoners, and at least six Texans in the hospital barracks were executed with bayonets.[39] Even after the last of the 183 Alamo defenders was dead, Mexican soldiers fired point blank into their bodies and jabbed them with knives and bayonets. That night, Santa Anna ordered the mutilated bodies burned. He spared only three Americans: Susanna Dickinson, wife of slain Captain Almeron Dickinson, her fifteen-month-old daughter, and Travis' slave Joe. They were sent to Gonzales to spread word about what would happen to rebels who resisted the Mexican Army.[40]

The Washington-on-the-Brazos Convention was hurriedly broken up as news of the Alamo's troubles began arriving. The convention had appointed Sam Houston to be Commander-in-Chief of the Texas Army. General Houston departed for Burnham Crossing on the Colorado River on March 6, where he planned to take command of his Texas forces against the threat of Santa Anna's advancing troops. Some delegates returned to their families, while others headed at once to join the army.[41]

Mexican patrols had had other skirmishes with small bands of Texans near Agua Dulce and San Patricio, and these had proved fatal for about one-hundred Texans. Houston ordered troops under James Fannin in Goliad to rendezvous with the troops of James Neill and Edward Burleson in Gonzales. When Sam Houston arrived on March 11 at this Guadalupe River community of about five-hundred people, he secretly felt that rumors of the fall of the Alamo must be true.[42] He took steps to organize his military forces by officially appointing Edward Burleson as colonel, Sidney Sherman as lieutenant colonel and Alexander Somervell as major of the Texas Army. By March 13, word was out officially that the entire garrison at San Antonio had been slaughtered. This bitter news was brought to Gonzales by Texas scouts under Erastus "Deaf" Smith and Henry Wax Karnes, who had found Susanna Dickinson, her small daughter and two black ex-slaves.[43]

Fierce battles continued between some of the smaller Texan forces and the Mexican troops. About fifteen Texans and more than eighty Mexicans were killed or wounded in a day-long action on March 14 at an old mission known as La Bahía in Refugio. Texan forces slipped out of the mission after dark and tried to escape. The company known as the "Kentucky Mustangs" under Captain Amon King was spotted by Indians who were in cooperation with the Mexicans. Following a twelve-hour battle with the Mexican forces, at least five of King's men had been killed or wounded, as were twenty enemy soldiers. King surrendered to General José Urrea under the condition that his men be treated as prisoners of war. Soon after surrendering, however, the thirty brave Refugio defenders, under previous orders from Santa Anna, were marched two by two in front of the mission and shot at point-blank range.[44]

Following the Alamo's fall, Captain Sadler and seven of his rangers departed for the Colorado River to join the Texas Army, where their services were more desperately required. Those leaving Fort Houston with Sadler are believed to be Daniel Doubt, Crawford Grigsby, William Hallmark, James Madden, Philip Martin, Daniel Parker Jr. and Dickerson Parker. These men all joined up with Captain Arnold's company after its departure from Nacogdoches.[45] Dickerson Parker and his brother Daniel Jr. would both miss a significant event of their family's history while fighting for Texas.

Traveling down the San Antonio Road to where it met the Trinity River, Sadler and company on March 19 crossed aboard the ferry operated by Nathaniel Robbins. Since they were en route to join the army to fight, the rangers did not pay the customary one dollar fare for transporting them. Robbins was instead provided with a payment-due voucher which Sadler endorsed as "Paymaster for the Houston Company."

By March 17 General Houston's troops, having received word of the Alamo's fall, had retreated back to the Colorado River near the present town of La Grange. Here, they waited for all straggling civilians to cross the river safely. News that the army was falling back spread a wave of fear across the Texas frontier. Settlers grabbed whatever possessions they could carry or put on a wagon and fled from their homes. The dramatic number of civilians fleeing eastward grew so fast that the retreat became known as the Runaway Scrape.

San Jacinto bound. Sadler and seven of his rangers crossed the Trinity River aboard Nathaniel Robbins' ferry on March 19. Sadler signed this claim at the little Houston County community of Randolph as "Paymaster for the Houston Company." Audited Republic Claims, Texas State Library and Archives Commission, microfilm reel 88, frame 269.

The Texan Army camped out on the east bank of the Colorado River, while a Mexican force of about eight-hundred men under General Joaquín Ramírez Sesma camped on the west bank of the river about two miles upstream. Houston's troops remained near the Colorado for six days as the general gathered intelligence on the various advancing Mexican forces.[46]

As Mexican troops advanced eastward from San Antonio, a fierce battle was fought on March 19 near Coleto Creek by about three-hundred soldiers under Colonel Fannin. His men had fallen back about ten miles from Goliad when they were engaged by Mexican infantry and cavalry units under General Urrea. Fighting from mid-afternoon through the night, Fannin's men killed or wounded an estimated 250 Mexicans before being finally overwhelmed. About sixty of the Texans were killed or wounded, and the remaining men were taken prisoners of war. Another force of about eighty men under Captain William Ward, the second surviving bunch from the La Bahía fight at Goliad, was also captured on March 23.[47]

From San Antonio, General Santa Anna sent word that all the Texans captured from these smaller battles since the fall of the Alamo "should be treated as pirates."[48] In Goliad, approximately 350 Texans were marched outside of the fortress of La Bahía under the premise that they would be moved elsewhere. About a mile from the fort, they were halted and the Mexican troops opened fire on the helpless men from point-blank range. Swords and bayonets were used to finish off the wounded, although about thirty men managed to escape the massacre. After the Mexican troops returned to La Bahía, some fifty wounded men left behind at the fortress were also executed. Texan leader Colonel Fannin was taken outside the church separately, blindfolded, and shot in the head.[49]

The effect of the slaughters at the Alamo, Refugio and Goliad would have a profound effect upon the fighting psyche of the Texan forces. Captain Hayden Arnold's company of Nacogdoches Volunteers was well along its two-week travel down the King's Highway. From Nacogdoches to Washington-on-the Brazos was a distance of about 160 miles. En route, they met an express which was carrying intelligence of the fall of the Alamo and the massacre of Fannin and his men. John Harvey, a twenty-six-year-old of Tennessee origin, later wrote that "this news augmented our courage and hurried us on."[50] There would be no mercy for Santa Anna's troops whenever Sam Houston chose to engage.

Chapter Four

A TIME TO FIGHT:
THE FORK IN THE ROAD

March 26 - April 19, 1836

When Captain Arnold's company joined forces with the Texas Army on March 26, they found tall, bearded, thirty-year-old Colonel Sidney Sherman on the Colorado River. When the Texas Revolution broke out, Sherman had sold his cotton-bagging factory in Newport, Kentucky, and used the proceeds to finance an unruly fifty-two-man company of Kentucky volunteers.[1]

Sherman was now in charge of approximately 350 men who were camped several miles farther upriver from Sam Houston's main forces. This fiery leader had asked permission of Houston to cross the river and engage a large force of Mexican troops, but he was ordered not to provoke the enemy this day.[2] General Houston had received word by this time of the massacre of Fannin's men, and he passed the word for the army to retreat. On the day that the Nacogdoches Volunteers joined up, Colonel Sherman read the retreat orders from Houston, a command which was immediately met with strong criticism.

Sherman's forces reluctantly fell back from the Colorado and marched. They were joined the next morning by the companies of captains Amasa Turner, William S. Fisher and Richard Roman.[3] The Texas Army reached the Brazos River and stayed the night of March 28 in the town of San Felipe, where Sherman caught up.

According to William Sadler's pension papers, he and his rangers joined the army at Dewees Crossing, named for William D. Dewees' ferry, about twenty-five miles southeast of La Grange and seven miles from the present city of Columbus, on the Colorado. They were assigned to the Nacogdoches Volunteers, where at age thirty-eight Sadler became the second oldest man of the unit.

Colonel Sidney Sherman in an 1835 oil painting by an unknown artist. As one of the senior officers under General Sam Houston in the Texas Army, Sherman was given command of the Second Regiment, which included the First Infantry Company to which William Sadler was attached. Colonel Sherman would prove to be a valiant leader in the impending Battle of San Jacinto.
Courtesy of the San Jacinto Museum of History Association.

The next morning, March 29, brought much unrest among the troops as Houston ordered the men to fall back once again. This time, he called for the soldiers to follow him north up the Brazos River to the plantation headquarters of the region's richest man, Jared Groce. Known as "Groce's Retreat," this plantation was about twenty miles from San Felipe and would prove to be a good source of food supplies. The 160-foot steamship *Yellowstone* was at Groce's loading cotton for transport down the river.[4]

The rain came down in torrents as the Texans slogged through mud and water toward Groce's. Many grumbled bitterly about Sam Houston, and two company commanders, Wylie Martin and Moseley Baker, refused to follow. They asked for and received permission to station their men near the San Felipe crossing of the Brazos and the crossing near Fort Bend (now Richmond).[5]

While these companies remained behind to fight the Mexicans, Houston's men spent two days covering the eighteen miles back through flooding creeks to Groce's, where camp was set up. Secretary of War Thomas Rusk soon joined Sam Houston on April 4, on the west side of the Brazos River where the Texans were camped. President David Burnet and the rest of his new government's cabinet had retreated from Washington-on-the-Brazos on March 17 after the Convention had completed writing the Constitution of the Republic of Texas. Burnet sent word with Rusk to stop the retreat of the Texas Army. "The enemy are laughing you to scorn," Burnet wrote General Houston. "You must fight them. You must retreat no farther. The country expects you to fight."[6]

When the Mexican forces approached the Brazos on April 7, only Captain Baker's defiant company remained behind to prevent the enemy from crossing. As this small group bravely fought Santa Anna, the cannon fire could be heard plainly in the Texan camp. Secure in this location, Sam Houston chose to send out his scouts for intelligence, all the while facing increasing pressure from his commanders to attack.[7]

Houston now had under his command about nine-hundred men, having lost several hundred thus far to basic belligerence and to the Runaway Scrape. Those who remained at Groce's were organized into an army and put through daily drills to prepare them as a regimented unit. Colonel Sherman was given command of the Second Regiment of Texas Volunteers, which would soon include nine companies.[8] Among these was Captain Arnold's Nacogdoches Volunteers, which now became known as the First Infantry Company of the Second Regiment. The army's First Regiment, under Colonel Edward Burleson, was largely composed of regular army men.

Five new volunteers joined Captain Arnold's company on April 12, 1836: Howard W. Bailey, Henry M. Brewer, Thomas D. Brooks, Henry Chapman and Stephen F. Sparks. All five had entered service in Nacogdoches on March 8 and had been engaged by the government in various services.[9] They were ordered on April 6 to report to General Houston, whereupon they were enlisted into the Nacogdoches Volunteers. Thomas Brooks, a school teacher from William Settlement near Nacogdoches, became the company's first sergeant. Stephen Sparks, later a president of the Texas Veterans Association, who turned seventeen just five days before joining Arnold's company, was now the baby of the outfit.

During two weeks of camping out at Groce's, and also when it was on the move, the Texas Army was supplied with intelligence by an effective spy unit. Some of the most well known from this group were "Deaf" Smith, Henry Wax Karnes, Colonel Robert Eden Handy and a free black from San Antonio named Hendrick Arnold. Arnold, playing the part of a fugitive slave, and dark-complexioned Smith playing a simple-minded old man with poor hearing, reportedly even entered Mexican camps to collect intelligence.[10]

The Texans were soon on the move toward Harrisburg, crossing the Brazos in the rain on April 12 and 13, using the steamer *Yellowstone* and a small sailboat. Bolstering the Texans' defenses on

"El Presidente." *Antonio López de Santa Anna Pérez de Lebron, the Mexican president and leader of the Mexican army which slaughtered the Texan defenders at the Alamo. Santa Anna and his army then began a push to drive out all white settlers from the lands of Texas.*
Oil portrait, courtesy of the San Jacinto Museum of History Association.

April 15 was the arrival of the first cannon, a twin six-pounder nicknamed the *Twin Sisters*. This artillery piece was donated by the citizens of Cincinnati, Ohio, and was hauled from Harrisburg out to the army by Leander Smith (brother-in-law of Thomas Rusk), who was under command of John A. Wharton.[11] The *Twin Sisters* were then presided over by a brand-new artillery corps, placed under command of Lieutenant Colonel James C. Neill.

East of the Brazos River, the men were growing more discontented. Private John Harvey from Sadler's company noted

Sam Houston *was criticized by many in the army for not fighting Santa Anna sooner. On the evening of April 19, however, he delivered a motivational speech from horseback that his troops needed. This 1892 "Equestrian" oil painting by Stephen Seymour Thomas depicts General Houston leading his forces into battle at San Jacinto.* Courtesy of the San Jacinto Museum of History Association.

that "men began leaving the Army to take their families out of danger."[12] As the army moved to Donohue's farm on April 14, located six miles southeast from the previous camp at Groce's, some grumbled that Houston intended to retreat all the way to Nacogdoches. Passing through present Hempstead in Waller County, the Texas Army was rejoined by the survivors from the companies of captains Baker and Martin, who *had* attacked the

Mexicans. Captain Baker openly criticized Houston for not joining the fight.[13]

On the morning of April 16, the Texans were on the move again. At a point about fifteen miles east of Donohue's, they reached a crucial fork in the road. One route would lead them toward Nacogdoches and eventually the United States, while the other road curved southeasterly for Harrisburg and the Gulf Coast. Colonel Sidney Sherman later explained that Colonel Tom Rusk, the new Secretary of War, was responsible for the order that came to turn for Harrisburg.[14] This turn at the fork in the roads caused word to swiftly spread through the men that Sam Houston had finally decided to fight!

* * * *

After passing this critical juncture, the army left the fleeing civilians to make it on their own for Nacogdoches. Only Captain Wylie Martin's company was ordered to stay with the thousands of civilians on their trek. Many soldiers chose to follow this crowd, but the majority were ready for battle with Santa Anna. From the Second Regiment's First Company, young Stephen Sparks recalled, "The road (to Harrisburg) was new and boggy, and the prairies covered with water." The few wagons available "were insufficient to travel very fast, so we soon began to bog down."[15] The rainy, exhausting conditions took their toll on Houston's men and many became seriously ill with flu conditions.

In the meantime, three main forces of Mexican troops were sweeping eastward across southern Texas. On the northern end, one force under General Antonio Gaona moved through Bastrop before turning on a more southerly route for Harrisburg. To the extreme south, the bloodthirsty troops under General Urrea, who had recently effected the Goliad Massacre, moved from La Bahía to Victoria and then on toward Matagorda on the coast. Santa Anna's own forces had passed through the charred remains of San Felipe on April 9 and arrived in present Richmond on April 12.

Having become fixated upon a scheme to capture the Texas government's cabinet, Santa Anna learned that President Burnet, Vice President Lorenzo de Zavala and the other senior members were only thirty miles beyond the Fort Bend crossing on the Brazos River. The Mexican dictator led his six-hundred men into Harrisburg on April 15 to find that Burnet and his cabinet had only narrowly escaped to New Washington, a small settlement on the northern banks of Galveston Bay. In his rage at missing his prey, Santa Anna ordered Harrisburg burned, and the printing presses, which had produced the *Telegraph* and most recently the Texas Declaration of Independence, were destroyed.[16] Colonel Juan Almonte was sent on a futile chase after Burnet, but the Texas leaders had moved from New Washington to Galveston Island. Santa Anna torched the new settlement of New Washington before deciding to move his troops toward the presumed location of Sam Houston's forces at Lynch's Ferry on the banks of the San Jacinto River.

The Texas Army reached Buffalo Bayou on April 18, opposite from the smoldering ruins of Harrisburg, and there set up camp after 4:00 p.m. Sadler and his fellow First Company infantrymen arrived "tired and hungry, so we all scattered to look for something to eat," wrote Stephen Sparks.[17] Texas spies Henry Karnes and Deaf Smith had a productive day, capturing a Mexican captain and two couriers. The Mexicans sported Alamo spoils, including deerskin wallets inscribed with the name William Barret Travis. Even more important was the discovery of a number of letters intended for Santa Anna. These were translated for General Houston by Major Lorenzo De Zavala Jr., the Vice President's son, and revealed the strength and positions of Santa Anna's forces.[18]

General Houston left Harrisburg on April 19, but he had less than one-thousand men at this point. Some 258 men, most of them sick from exposure and from diseases they had taken from the dirty civilians previously tagging along with the army, were left behind at this camp opposite Harrisburg.[19] From the Nacogdoches Volunteers, at least six sick men were left behind at Harrisburg who would miss the impending battle: privates Stillwell Box, Keeton Jones, Alfred Hallmark, William Vardeman, John Walling and Randolph Yarbrough.

The majority of the troops hiked along the flooding Buffalo Bayou, more than three-hundred yards wide in places, to find the easiest crossing point. Before the crossing was made, General Houston delivered his first formal speech of the campaign. The men formed a square formation so that he and Colonel Rusk could sit on their horses in the center. In the Nacogdoches Volunteer company to which Sadler was attached, fellow infantryman John Harvey noted that Houston "formed us in solid column, rode into our midst and delivered to us one of the best speeches."[20]

Houston told his men to remember the Alamo when they entered into the battle. At the conclusion of this speech, the second-in-command of the First Regiment, Lieutenant Colonel Alexander Somervell, remarked, "That speech made me damned sure of one thing: no man in this army will be taken prisoner."[21]

The Secretary of War, Colonel Rusk, next spoke to the assembled army in an equally inspiring speech. He cried out at one point, "May I not survive if we don't win this battle!"[22] The speech session soon broke up with cheers of "Remember Goliad!" "Remember La Bahía!" and "Remember the Alamo!"

Chapter Five

RENDEZVOUS WITH SANTA ANNA: THE BATTLE OF SAN JACINTO

April 20-22, 1836

Following these speeches, most of the army crossed Buffalo Bayou on an old leaking ferryboat. "It was so small that only 12 could cross at a time," noted one of Sadler's fellow soldiers.[1] The *Twin Sisters* and an ammunition wagon were sent across on a hastily assembled raft. Once across, the Texas troops marched silently down the right bank until an hour before daylight, at which time they were ordered to rest. Exposed to a cold north wind, the soldiers slept on the damp ground.[2] After resting for a few hours, the Texas Army marched on to Lynch's Ferry, near the junction of Buffalo Bayou and the San Jacinto River, during the early morning hours of April 20. General Houston then had his men take up positions along five-hundred yards near the ferry, hiding largely in a grove of live oaks.

Under the command of Sidney Sherman were both the Second Regiment and a sixty-one-man cavalry troop unit. W. T. Sadler's old traveling companion, Mirabeau Lamar, had recently returned from a trip back to Georgia and had now managed to join this cavalry unit during the march to Buffalo Bayou. A new group of men arrived from Galveston in the early morning hours to report to Sam Houston. One of these men who would fight with the cavalry on the following day observed the wide variety of cultural backgrounds displayed by the men gathered around their campfires in the pre-dawn hours.

[They were] all unwashed, unshaven for months, their long hair, beard and mustachoes, ragged and matted, their clothes in tatters, and plastered with mud. In a word, a more savage band could scarcely be assembled; and yet many – most indeed, were gentlemen, owners of large estates, distinguished some for oratory, some for science, and some for medical talent.... But here, oppressed and trampled on, their homes made desolate, their wives and children driven out from the fair habitations which were rising in the wilderness, all had turned out, determined, even desperate, to defend their country and avenge the Alamo and other horrible atrocities.[3]

* * * *

Sherman's First Skirmish

While some of the soldiers found and slaughtered several cows for breakfast, Texas spies soon reported the Mexicans to be moving toward Lynch's Ferry, near which General Houston had halted. Wednesday, April 20, was partly cloudy with a slight chill in the air as Sidney Sherman led forty cavalrymen out to scout near the charred remnants of New Washington. They met an advance Mexican patrol and killed four of the enemy soldiers. Sherman rode back to the Texas camp to alert Sam Houston of the enemy's presence at about 1:00 p.m.

While Sherman's men held watch, Houston ordered his troops to lie down to conceal their numbers. Even as Houston and Sherman spoke, Mexican troops had advanced within sight of the Texas forces.[4] The cavalry troops quickly towed to the scene the *Twin Sisters*, which had not even been test-fired due to a shortage of cannonballs! The thirty cannoneers under Lieutenant Colonel James Neill moved their weapon about ten paces onto the open prairie. Behind them at the edge of the timber were the two infantry companies of Lieutenant Colonel Henry Millard. Behind these companies were the sixty-eight cavalrymen, and riflemen from Colonel Edward Burleson's First Regiment were on the right wing.[5]

Santa Anna saw the meager Texan force on the prairie and sent a company of Mexicans to a cluster of trees halfway between the two armies. As both challenge and insult, Santa Anna had his musicians play the evil "Deguello" (the "no quarter" song he had also played at the Alamo) as his soldiers opened fire on the Texans.

Under cavalry protection, the Mexicans advanced their cannon *Golden Standard* fifty yards and fired the first shot, which sailed through the trees over the Texas camp and splashed into the bayou. The *Twin Sisters* fired its first shot ever for Texas, and its load of

Sherman's First Skirmish. *Colonel Sherman defiantly led a sixty-eight-man cavalry unit into a skirmish with Santa Anna's advance forces on April 20, 1836. This painting by Charles Shaw depicts Private Mirabeau B. Lamar, Sadler's former traveling companion, in a dramatic rescue of a downed soldier which earned him a battlefield promotion to Colonel of the Texas Cavalry.* Courtesy of the San Jacinto Museum of History Association.

broken horseshoes landed to the right of the Mexican force. One of the *Golden Standard*'s first shots fell into the Texas position and wounded Lieutenant Colonel Neill. In return, the Texans quickly wounded a Mexican captain. General Santa Anna was on horseback in view of the Texans at times, but he fell back with his main army as the two cannons slowly fired away at each other over some three-hundred yards' distance.[6]

The *Twin Sisters* scored one direct hit that damaged the Mexican cannon and killed two of its pack mules. As firing ceased for a while, Sidney Sherman rode to General Houston around 4:00 p.m. and appealed for approval to seize the *Golden Standard.* Houston ordered Sherman not to provoke a general action, but Sherman instead chose to advance with his sixty-eight-man cavalry and Colonel Tom Rusk, who was also on horseback. The Mexican artillery commander, Colonel Pedro Francisco Delgado, had his cannon quickly withdrawn at this time. Fifty dragoons (Mexican infantrymen) advanced onto the battlefield from the woods under Captain Miguel Aguirre. From his saddle, Aguirre taunted,

"Soldados God Dammes, venga aquí," meaning, "God damn soldiers, come here."[7]

The Texans took this verbal challenge and tore into the Mexican soldiers, wounding two.[8] Santa Anna ordered two companies of riflemen into the fight as many of the Texas cavalrymen dismounted their horses and took to their rifles. The Texans drove back the Mexicans, but many came into serious danger.

Colonel Rusk was penned in during the second Texan advance and might have been captured had not Mirabeau Lamar charged in on his large stallion and knocked down a Mexican horseman, opening an escape route for himself and the Secretary of War. Lamar then saved the life of nineteen-year-old Walter P. Lane, who had been knocked from his horse. Lamar shot a Mexican lancer who was preparing to kill the boy while Lane, later a brigadier general for the Confederacy, escaped on the back of the horse of another cavalryman.[9]

At one point in the action, a detachment of Mexican troops advanced through the edge of the timber on one side close enough to allow some of the Second Regiment to fire at them. One of these participants noted that "a warm discharge of small arms took place, without, however, any very serious effect."[10] Sadler's First Company fellow infantryman John Harvey later wrote that "we had a good deal of fun mixed with danger that day."[11]

Both sides pulled back after this battle on the afternoon of April 20, with the Texans suffering three wounded, including Lieutenant Colonel Neill and an artillery private named Devereaux Jerome Woodlief. The third man, a regular army officer named Olwyn J. Trask, later died from his wounds. Following this battle, Colonel Sherman had heated words with General Houston for not allowing the rest of the army to join the fight.

Evening chow for the Texans included captured bread and coffee to go with the soldiers' usual boiled beef. The light from numerous campfires illuminated the night around the San Jacinto battleground as the Texas and Mexican armies camped within one mile of each other. Santa Anna's camp was on an eminence with a marsh and a lake behind him, a thicket of woods to his right which followed the edge of the marsh, and an open plain ahead and to the left. The Mexican leader had his tents pitched under a cluster of hardwoods, while his men worked into the night building a defensive breastworks fortification of saddles and supplies.

Around the Texas campfires, men were certain that the coming morning would bring the long-awaited major clash with Santa Anna.

Dawning of a New Freedom

Reveille was sounded at 4:00 a.m. on April 21 in the Texas camp by the drum beat from a freed former slave named Dick who was part of the four-man Texas Army band. A brisk thirty-eight degrees greeted the soldiers, who began preparing for the day's actions. In the Mexican camp, Santa Anna was up long before sunrise, watching the Texans through his spyglass. In the Texas camp, many noted with disgust that General Houston slept right through the pounding of Dick's drum.[12]

As the sun rose, the weather faired and the temperature began to rise. Texas scouts observed a force of five-hundred reinforcements approaching the Mexican camp around 8:00 a.m., these men being led by General Martín Perfecto de Cos, the brother-in-law of Santa Anna. One of Karnes' scouts gave the news to Sam Houston, which he had expected due to the earlier mail intelligence.

General Houston promoted Mirabeau Lamar to full colonel in charge of the cavalry for his bravery the previous day. The man whom Lamar had saved, Walter Lane, was promoted from private to second lieutenant of the artillery corps. Houston then called a war council of his senior field officers, which included Rusk, Sherman and now Lamar, to debate whether or not to attack in the afternoon. Only two junior officers voted to attack this day.

It was decided to destroy Vince's Bridge to prevent General Cos and his men from entering the San Jacinto battleground. Texas scout Deaf Smith and six volunteers were selected, but before departing on this duty, Smith and newly promoted Second Lieutenant Walter Lane rode out from the Texas camp and used a spyglass to count tents in the enemy's camp some six-hundred yards away. Smith came back and reported to Sam Houston that he estimated there to be more than fifteen-hundred men, a fairly accurate estimate. Smith then gathered his volunteers and two axes before setting out to destroy the crossing at Vince's Bridge.

Despite reluctance to attack this day from some of his junior officers, General Houston ordered his troops to be paraded at 3:30 that afternoon to prepare for an attack on Santa Anna's army. Some estimates placed the Texas army's strength at around 780, although more than nine-hundred men later claimed to have been present. The fate of Texas now rested upon the shoulders of these men. Houston began his final inspection of the troops, moving from the extreme right wing toward the left.

Battle of San Jacinto
Organization of Texas Troops As of April 21, 1836

COMMANDER-IN-CHIEF'S STAFF
Sam Houston	Major General
John Austin Wharton	Adjutant General
George W. Hockley	Inspector General
William G. Cooke	Ast. Insp. General
John Forbes	Commissary Gen.
James Collinsworth	Aide-de-Camp
William H. Patton	Aide-de-Camp
Alexander Horton	Aide-de-Camp
Lorenzo de Zavala Jr.	Aide-de-Camp
Robert M. Coleman	Volunteer Aide
Robert Eden Handy	Volunteer Aide
James H. Perry	Volunteer Aide
Thomas J. Rusk	Secretary of War

MEDICAL STAFF
Alexander W. Ewing	Surgeon General & Artillery Surgeon
Lemuel Gustine	Cavalry Physician
Junius Wm. Motley	Houston's Physician
William M. Carper	Surgeon for Regulars
William F. Davidson	Surgeon for 1st Reg.
John P. T. Fitzhugh	Ast. Surgeon 1st Reg.
Anson Jones	Surgeon 2nd Reg.
Shields Booker	Ast. Surgeon 2nd Reg.
Nicholas D. Labadie	Ast. Surgeon 2nd Reg.

ARTILLERY CORPS
James Clinton Neill	Lt. Colonel
Isaac N. Moreland	Captain
William S. Stilwell	1st Lieutenant

CAVALRY CORPS
Mirabeau Buonaparte Lamar	Commanding
Henry Wax Karnes	Captain
William H. Smith	Captain
James R. Cook	1st Lieutenant
Walter Paye Lane	2nd Lieutenant

REGULAR ARMY
Lt. Col. Henry Millard	Commanding
Capt. John M. Allen	Acting Major

COMPANY A
Andrew Briscoe	Captain
Martin Kingsley Snell	1st Lieutenant
Robert D. McCaskey	2nd Lieutenant

COMPANY B
Richard Roman	Captain
Nicholas Mosby Dawson	2nd Lieutenant

FIRST REGIMENT TEXAS VOLUNTEERS
Edward Burleson	Colonel
Alexander Somervell	Lt. Colonel
James W. Tinsley	Adjutant
Horatio N. Cleveland	Sgt. Major

COMPANY A
William Wood	Captain
Joseph Rhodes	1st Lieutenant
Samuel Raymond	2nd Lieutenant

COMPANY B
Amasa Turner	Captain
William J. Miller	1st Lieutenant
William M. Summers	2nd Lieutenant

COMPANY C
Jesse Billingsley	Captain
Micah Andrews	1st Lieutenant
James A. Craft	2nd Lieutenant

COMPANY D
Moseley Baker	Captain
John Pettit Borden	1st Lieutenant
John Freeman Pettus	2nd Lieutenant

COMPANY F
William Jones E. Heard	Captain
William Mosby Eastland	1st Lieutenant

COMPANY H
William Warner Hill (sick)	Captain
Robert Stevenson	Acting Captain
Harvey H. Swisher	1st Lieutenant
Adolphus Hope	2nd Lieutenant

COMPANY I
William S. Fisher	Captain
William H. Steele	1st Lieutenant
Robert W. Carter	2nd Lieutenant

COMPANY K
Robert James Calder	Captain
John Sharp	1st Lieutenant
M. H. Denham	Acting 2nd Lt.

SECOND REGIMENT TEXAS VOLUNTEERS
Sidney Sherman	Colonel
Joseph L. Bennett	Lt. Colonel
Lysander Wells	Major
Edward B. Wood	Adjutant
Bennett McNelly	Sgt. Major

FIRST COMPANY
Hayden S. Arnold	Captain
Robert W. Smith	1st Lieutenant
Isiah Edwards	2nd Lieutenant

SECOND COMPANY
William Ware	Captain
Job S. Collard	1st Lieutenant
George A. Lamb	2nd Lieutenant

THIRD COMPANY
William M. Logan	Captain
Franklin Hardin	1st Lieutenant
Benjamin J. Harper	2nd Lieutenant

FOURTH COMPANY
David Murphree	Captain
Phineas Ripley	1st Lieutenant
Peter Harper	2nd Lieutenant

FIFTH COMPANY
Thomas H. McIntire	Captain
John Porter Gill	1st Lieutenant
Basil G. Ijams	2nd Lieutenant

SIXTH COMPANY
James Gillaspie	Captain
Matthew Finch	1st Lieutenant
A. L. Harrison	2nd Lieutenant

SEVENTH COMPANY
Benjamin Franklin Bryant	Captain
John C. Hale	1st Lieutenant
Archibald Lewis	2nd Lieutenant

EIGHTH COMPANY
William Kimbro	Captain
James Rowe	1st Lieutenant

NINTH COMPANY
Juan Nepomuceno Seguin	Captain
Manuel Flores	1st Sergeant
Antonio Menchaca	2nd Sergeant

To the extreme right was Colonel Lamar's sixty-man cavalry, followed by two regular infantry divisions under Lieutenant Colonel Henry Millard. To the left and slightly ahead of these divisions were the thirty men of the artillery corps with the *Twin Sisters*. Next to them was Colonel Ned Burleson's First Regiment, where Houston stopped to listen to company commanders giving motivational speeches. To the extreme left of the battlefield was Colonel Sidney Sherman's Second Regiment, which included William Sadler's First Company under Captain Arnold.

Houston wrote in his official report of the action that the "troops paraded with alacrity and spirit, and were anxious for the contest. Their conscious disparity in numbers seemed only to increase their enthusiasm and confidence, and heightened their anxiety for the conflict."

General Houston stopped in front of Sadler's company and had a conference with Tom Rusk, deciding that the Secretary of War should stay with Sherman's regiment at the start of the attack. After the battle was joined, Rusk would then ride across the field to report to Houston how the Second Regiment was doing. At about 4:00 p.m., Houston trotted his horse Saracen in front of the troops and ordered loudly, "Trail arms! Forward!"

Spyglasses had shown no movement whatsoever in the Mexican camp as the Texan troops pushed forward across the San Jacinto battleground on April 21, 1836. The artillery company hauled the *Twin Sisters* up the rising slope toward Santa Anna's camp as the nine-hundred-yard-wide wall of Texans advanced on the Mexicans. Forward across the battleground marched the regulars under Colonel Burleson and Lieutenant Colonel Millard, while on the extreme right of the Texans rode Lamar's cavalry. On the extreme left of the advancing Texas forces was Colonel Sherman's infantry regiment.

Sherman's men moved quickly and silently through the mossy oaks and tall grasses of the little thicket which ran along the edge of the marsh. They advanced with good cover toward the Mexican camp, with almost no chance of being spotted until they were within the last one-hundred yards. The tree cover and a slight rise in the ground toward Santa Anna's forces disguised their movements well. All sources, including General Houston's official report, agree that Sherman's Second Regiment on the left wing reached the enemy first.

Taking aim, the first volley of musket fire arose from Captain Arnold's First Company and was joined by the fire of hundreds of other men. The last one-hundred yards to the Mexican breastworks were covered at a fast pace as the conflict opened with a fury at 4:30 p.m. At the moment of the Texans' attack, at least two high-ranking Mexican officers were drinking champagne in their tent while General Santa Anna had retired to his own tent with a mulatto girl who had been captured three days before. As chaos befell the Mexican Army, its leader was being distracted by Emily D. West, who some claim to be the inspiration for the song "The Yellow Rose of Texas."[13]

For many of Sherman's men, their first shot was the only volley they had time to fire, for the fighting quickly became hand-to-hand as the Second Regiment swarmed over the right end of the Mexican breastworks. This end of the Mexican camp was occupied by the regiments of General Cos and Colonel Juan Almonte. William Sadler and his fellow men of Captain Arnold's First Company are believed to have been the first to attack, as recorded by infantryman Stephen Sparks.

> My captain's company was the front of the regiment, and we marched in double file. We were ordered not to fire until we could see the whites of the enemies' eyes. When we got within 300 yards of the ditch we were ordered to charge, and we charged in double file. There was only one man in front of me who fired before I did, and so I got the credit for firing the second gun on our side. We had out-traveled the first regiment, and had driven Almonte about 200 yards before the first regiment got near Santa Anna's breastworks. We charged with such fury that the Mexicans fled in a very short time.[14]

From Burleson's First Regiment in the clearing, Captain William Heard later witnessed "a sharp fire" taking place at the edge of the woods as Sherman's regiment advanced. As recorded in the 1860 *Texas Almanac*, Heard wrote:

> In a few moments I looked in that direction and saw the Mexicans running along the edge of the woods, and Sherman and his men after them. This greatly encouraged me and those near where I was. We shouted at the top of our voices: "Yonder they go, boys, and Sherman after them!" This happened when our regiment was some distance from the enemy, and before we had fired a single shot. Sherman and

his men pursued them in hot haste, and they crossed the breast-work where it joined the timber.[15]

The Mexicans began firing back on the Texans, but they had clearly been caught off guard. Colonel Sherman was given credit for being the first to shout "Remember the Alamo! Remember Goliad!" The Texas field musicians opened up with a popular tune called, "Will You Come to the Bower" once the shooting erupted. The other Texan forces rushed into battle, many men firing their first shots at as close as fifty yards distance. General Houston rode down the lines shouting, "Fire away! God damn you, fire!"[16]

Secretary of War Tom Rusk and his young aide, Dr. Junius William Motley, took off across the battlefield to report to General Houston on the Second Regiment's gallant fighting. As they neared Houston, Motley was knocked from his horse by a copper ball shot through the stomach, which would later prove fatal. While Rusk was close to Houston, the general's horse Saracen was suddenly struck by a volley of five shots. As the stallion sank slowly to the ground, Houston dropped off to the ground and quickly was provided a shorter, riderless horse below which his long legs dangled because he could not use the stirrups. Houston was shot in the ankle and his second horse was killed at the same time. Moving to his third horse, Houston continued on in the charge against the Mexican Army.

In the midst of the Mexican camp, Sherman's regiment was in fierce combat. Few men had bayonets on their rifles, so their firearms became warclubs once the opportunity to reload was lost. The Texans used their muskets and rifles to bash the enemy and many of their guns were broken off at the breech.

During the close-quarters duel, Private Sadler was attacked by a Mexican soldier wielding a straight-bladed dagger. In the ensuing wrestle, Sadler won possession of the dirk, which would remain a prized possession of his for many years. Captain Hayden Arnold's expensive London Younger gun, which he valued at $35, was shot nearly off at the breech. During the continued action, his gun was entirely broken and discarded on the battlefield.[17] The rest of Arnold's First Company fought in equally valiant fashion.

After-action reports would show no men killed or wounded from the Nacogdoches Volunteers, but a discrepancy exists concerning Swanson Yarbrough Jr. and his father, Swanson Sr. The family's Bible, a common place for early families to record their genealogical information, indicates that both father and son fought on April 21 in Captain Arnold's company and that Swanson Jr. was killed at San

Jacinto. Texas land grants were later issued for service of both John Swanson Sr. and John Swanson Jr. in the Texas Army.[18]

The Second Regiment routed the newly arrived troops under General Cos, most of whom had been lying down asleep before the shooting began. Many of these men rushed into battle without even their guns. From the center of the battlefield the *Twin Sisters* fired away, steadily pounding the Mexican forces. Santa Anna's own cannon, the *Golden Standard*, only fired three rounds before a shot from the *Twin Sisters* hit the Mexican cannon's water bucket, wounding or scaring off most of the gunners. General Manuel Castrillon stood stoically beside the cannon, even as the advancing Texas companies captured the cannon and peppered him with rifle balls.[19]

Santa Anna himself emerged from his tent to find his army being overrun by the Texans. His soldiers were being mown down before him and all attempts to organize a strong stand were lost in the madness. A servant finally offered a horse to Santa Anna, who took it and rode from the battle unharmed. The Mexicans were literally routed, and a massive slaughter took place about four-hundred yards from the Mexican forces' breastworks. "Where our two regiments got together, and the Mexicans rallied," wrote Stephen Sparks, "about 10 acres of ground was literally covered with their dead bodies."[20]

At this point, a Mexican cavalryman jumped his horse into a boggy slough and the rider and horse promptly sunk under the muck, all except the rider's head and the horn of his saddle. Captain Arnold's company found they could jump from one bank of the marsh pit to the saddle and then from the saddle to the other side of the slough. About fifty men of the Second Regiment used this irregular method of pursuing the fleeing Mexican troops. Young Private Sparks slipped and struck his knee on the dead cavalryman's bayonet, leaving a painful wound in his knee that slowed his pursuit for some moments.[21]

Having advanced through the enemy camp, William Sadler and Dickerson Parker continued their pursuit of the routed Mexican soldiers. Sadler later related to Parker's grandson how Parker shot one Mexican out of the tree from which he had apparently taken cover.[22]

Colonel Rusk checked on his younger brother David Rusk, who was part of Arnold's volunteers. Arnold told Rusk that his younger brother had acquitted himself well in the fighting after the Secretary of War had departed to report to Houston. David Rusk had stopped long enough to call for help when he found his friend, nineteen-year-old Alphonzo Steele, lying wounded on the field; he then continued on with Arnold's company into the fight. Colonel Rusk and David both helped the wounded Sam Houston from his saddle at the end of the day, and blood was dripping from the general's boot. W. T. Sadler's granddaughter, Diamond Sadler Kolb, later related that her grandfather had also assisted the wounded general from his saddle.[23]

Controversy raged for years after the battle that Sam Houston was not the leader published reports later made him out to be. Several witnesses declared that Houston ordered his forces to halt midway in the battle but that Tom Rusk countermanded the order. In support of this claim is an account by Dr. Nicholas D. Labadie, who observed Colonel Rusk and Dr. Motley riding in full gallop toward the left rear of the forces when Houston ordered the halt. Labadie reported that Rusk immediately countermanded this direct order, shouting at the top of his voice, "If we stop we are cut to pieces. Don't stop – go ahead – give them hell!"[24]

Sidney Sherman wrote a letter to *The Galveston Weekly News* of June 23, 1855, which stated that even the influence of General John Wharton "did not avail at the time Houston called a halt, for Rusk did, in violation of Houston's positive orders, take the responsibility of ordering the troops to advance." Sherman felt that this halt "would have sacrificed my regiment, as it was then engaged in the timber on the enemy's right." Although Wharton urged the continued advance just as strenuously as Rusk, Sherman felt that the Secretary of War was the only person that could

> with any propriety assume the command. On his doing so, Houston called upon men to bear witness that the responsibility would not fall upon him, and then he left the field. The battle was won, and the Commander-in-Chief has had no use for the witnesses he called upon.[25]

Sam Houston would deny to his death that he had ever given such an order. Rusk later wrote that he only recalled Houston ordered some men that had became entangled in a bog to halt and reform. Whatever events actually transpired in the heat of battle would not seriously affect the rising popularity of Sam Houston in Texas.

In Santa Anna's campground, the main battle lasted less than twenty minutes, but the slaughter would continue until sundown. Many enemy soldiers fled through the woods toward Peggy's Lake

Slaughter at Peggy's Lake. *This painting by Charles Shaw depicts the vengeance taken by Texans upon the fleeing Mexican soldiers beyond Santa Anna's campground.* Courtesy of the San Jacinto Museum of History Association.

behind their camp, where they tried to swim across to a little island. A number of Texans followed and cut them down as they ran, swam or popped their heads up from the water. Other soldiers used their personal knives, hatchets and firearms to pummel the perpetrators of the massacres at the Alamo, Goliad and La Bahía. The Texas commanders faced a very difficult time stopping the slaughter. Most men remembered the stories of the brave Texans executed in the past months, and many had no intention of showing any mercy themselves. Some of the more renegade Texans even removed scalps.

Colonel Sherman and his men began taking prisoners of those Mexicans who chose to surrender. Hundreds were quickly rounded up about the camp, including Colonel Juan Almonte, an English-speaking aide of Santa Anna's. Almonte's men surrendered three miles from where the fight first began in their own camp. Sherman, Rusk and others retired back to the Texas camp after sunset, where they found that Dr. Alexander Wray Ewing had diagnosed General Houston's wound as a compound fracture of the right tibia and fibula, just above the ankle.

Despite his wound, Houston was concerned with interrogating Almonte during the evening of April 21. Almonte told him that Santa Anna had fled the battleground, and Houston knew that San Jacinto would not be a real victory without the Mexican leader.

Battle of San Jacinto Casualties
April 20-21, 1836

KILLED OR MORTALLY WOUNDED (12)
Benjamin Rice Bingham
Lemuel Stockton Blakey
James Cooper *
Mathias Cooper
Thomas Patton Fowle
Giles Albert Giddings *
John C. Hale
George A. Lamb
Dr. William Junius Motley*
Ashley R. Stephens *
Olwyn J. Trask * [1]
John Swanson Yarbrough Jr.[2]

WOUNDED (32)
C. D. Anderson
Washington Anderson
Moseley Baker
Jesse Billingsley
James Cumba
Joseph Smith Edgar
Calvin Gage
Albert Edward Gallatin
Sam Houston +
Allen Ingram +
W. F. James +
George Washington Lewis +
Thomas H. Mays
James Clinton Neill [1]
James Nelson
William A. Park
Michael Putnam
Elbridge Gerry Rector
George Washington Robinson +
William H. Smith
Alphonzo Steele +
John Files Tom +
Thomas C. Utley +
Logan Vandever +
Elijah Votaw
Martin Walker +
William S. Walker +
George Waters
Leroy Wilkinson
William Carvin Winters +
Devereaux Jerome Woodlief +[1]
William Foster Young +

* Mortally wounded; died soon after Battle of San Jacinto.

+ Considered to be seriously wounded, but recovered.

[1] Casualty of April 20 skirmish.

[2] According to Yarbrough family records; not on official San Jacinto casualty rosters.

Still, it had been a monumental battle in which the Texans had surprised and virtually wiped out their Mexican resistance. Estimates were that 630 Mexicans were killed, 208 wounded and about 730 captured. Texas losses during the battle were seven men killed outright, five so badly wounded that they would shortly die, and thirty-two others wounded. General Houston's official report shows that about six-hundred muskets, three-hundred sabers, two-hundred pistols, several hundred mules and horses, and about $12,000 were rounded up from the Mexicans.

Following the battle, Henry Karnes and Deaf Smith set out in pursuit of the fleeing Mexican leaders. Karnes called for all those with loaded guns to follow, and about eighteen did including Elisha Clapp of Nacogdoches. Clapp took off after four fleeing Mexicans and killed one, although return fire from the others forced him to retreat. Karnes soon found evidence of someone's having bogged their horse down in Vince's Bayou and then taken off on foot into a nearby thicket. He sent Smith back to the Texas camp to ask for volunteers, as he was certain Santa Anna would be found in the thicket after dawn. About one-hundred mounted guards, mostly men who had muskets, were chosen from the volunteers. They were positioned in a patrol line across the prairie during the night to prevent Santa Anna from escaping from his thicket.[26]

In the Texas camp, more than seven-hundred Mexican prisoners were held in a crude stockade made from debris from the battle, with the *Twin Sisters* loaded and pointing into their midst should someone try to flee. During the night, the Texan guards held wax candles that had been found in the Mexican camp. Among President Santa Anna's other loot were baskets of champagne, which was soon being passed among the victorious Texans for toasts this night.

THE CAPTURE OF SANTA ANNA

Before dawn on April 22, Colonel Ned Burleson led out a search party of thirty horsemen for Santa Anna. Sam Houston correctly predicted that the Mexican general would have disguised himself as a common soldier. Having departed the battleground on horseback in company with his secretary, Ramon Caro, Santa Anna and Caro both dismounted their horses once they entered the boggy marshes near Vince's Bridge. When his afternoon siesta with Emily West had been interrupted, Santa Anna had fled in what he had readily available: white silk drawers, a linen shirt with diamond studs, red morocco slippers and a fine gray cloth vest with gold buttons.

The Mexican general spent the night in tall grass near the bayou and after dawn crossed a waist-deep creek before finding a deserted slave quarters on the Vince ranch. There he donned some old slave clothes, including a blue cotton round jacket, cotton pantaloons, an old hide cap, and he used a blanket from the horse as a serape. He still, however, wore the diamond-studded linen shirt and morocco slippers. With that, Santa Anna set off again down the bayou.

That afternoon, Sergeant James Austin Slyvester and five other men (privates Sion Record Bostick, Alfred Miles, Charles P. Thompson, Joel Walter Robison and Joseph D. Vermillion) were on horseback near the destroyed Vince's Bridge at about three when Sylvester sighted five deer and rode off after them. As he was preparing to shoot, the herd suddenly took fright and dashed away. Looking around to see what had spooked them, Sylvester saw a man moving toward the destroyed bridge and then hide in some tall grass. He was captured and brought back to camp as just another Mexican private.

Only when the Texan patrol brought Santa Anna near the prisoner area did the truth slip out. A number of the Mexican soldiers exclaimed, "El Presidente! El Presidente! General Santa Anna!" at the sight of their leader. Mexican officers yelled for the men to

"Shut your mouths!" but it was too late. Two of Sadler's company, Howard Bailey and Stephen Sparks, were standing near the prisoners when the captured general was led in. Sparks wrote that the prisoners began "jumping to their feet, and clapping their hands, and saying, 'Santa Anna.'"[27] According to the story he related to his own children, William Sadler approached the prisoner and pulled back his ragged cotton jacket to reveal the fine linen and jeweled studs underneath.[28]

The great "Napoleon of the West", as he had once boasted himself to be, was led to where the wounded General Houston was lying on a mattress from Lorenzo de Zavala's house. One witness from the cavalry wrote that he stood beside Lamar and Karnes who were in conversation near Houston when this ragged prisoner, "bespattered with mud, was ushered before us."[29] Santa Anna then

Standing in memory of the Texans who fought with great courage, the San Jacinto Monument rises 575' 4", making it the tallest stone monument in the world. This museum stands just east of Houston, Texas, in the middle of the historic 1836 battleground where Texas independence was won from Mexico.
Author's collection, courtesy of the San Jacinto Museum of History Association.

Santa Anna Surrenders to Houston. *This painting by Charles Shaw interprets the meeting between the opposing generals, considered to be one of the most famous events in Texas history. Dirty and still wearing his disguise, captured General Santa Anna is brought before the wounded General Houston on April 22. Private Sadler acted as an early interpreter for Houston before Colonel Almonte was summoned. General Houston's broken leg is being tended to by Dr. Alexander Ewing beneath a mighty oak tree. Among the others in this depiction are Colonel Sidney Sherman, behind Houston, and "Deaf" Smith, seated beside Houston.* Courtesy of the San Jacinto Museum of History Association.

broke into Spanish and announced to the Texans who their *prisonerno de guerra* truly was.

According to witness Sergeant Moses Austin Bryan, the general's confession in English translated to "I am Antonio López de Santa Anna, President of Mexico, Commander-in-Chief of the Army of Operations and I put myself at the disposition of the brave General Houston. I wish to be treated as a general should when a prisoner of war."[30]

Present near Houston for this first exchange with Santa Anna was Private W. T. Sadler, who as a student of civil engineering in Georgia had studied some Spanish. According to one of his grandsons, Sadler was instrumental in translating Santa Anna's historic first statements to General Sam Houston, statements which amounted to the surrender of Mexico![31]

Tom Rusk and Lorenzo de Zavala Jr. soon joined the gathering crowd, and Santa Anna immediately acknowledged de Zavala, whom he had known before the revolution with Texas. Most of the Texans present were in favor of shooting or hanging the murderous Mexican leader, but Houston would not have anything of the sort.

General Houston's Spanish was not adequate for the necessary negotiations. One biographer of Tom Rusk noted that during the early exchange "several translators were used."[32] In addition to Sadler, others known to have been used during the early questionings were Moses Austin Bryan, young de Zavala and finally, Colonel Almonte, who spoke good English and who had been captured the previous evening.

Almonte then acted as interpreter for most of the two-hour parley, with Secretary of War Rusk now doing most of the talking for the Texas side. Houston called for Santa Anna to surrender all the troops under his command, although the actual agreement reached called for the withdrawal of Mexican troops rather than an absolute surrender. Houston wisely chose to keep Santa Anna alive as his prisoner to guarantee the safety of his own forces.[33]

Texas independence had been won!

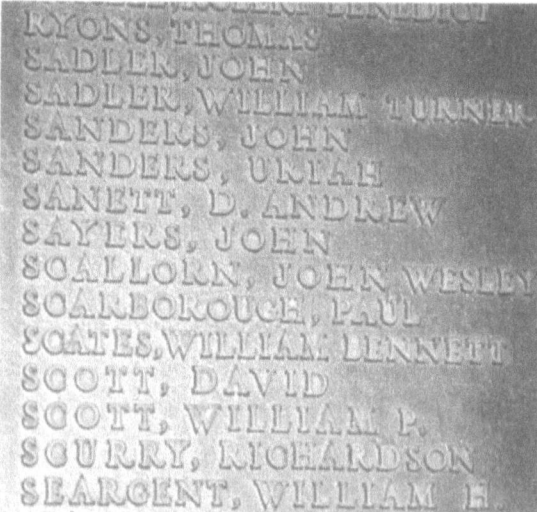

This honor role (above) within the San Jacinto Museum of History displays the names of the men who fought in the skirmish on April 20 or in the main battle on April 21. Sadler's name can be seen on the closeup to left. Although some sources have listed the two as brothers, the John Sadler listed above William Sadler is not known to be closely related.
Author's collection, courtesy of the San Jacinto Museum of History Association.

Chapter Six

POST-SAN JACINTO:
A NEW THREAT IN EAST TEXAS

May 1836 - Early 1838

Following the great victory at San Jacinto, Santa Anna signed a surrender dispatch that ordered his three senior subordinates, generals Vicente Filisola, José Urrea and Antonio Gaona, to countermarch back to Victoria and San Antonio to await further orders. Texas scout Deaf Smith was given copies of this dispatch to deliver to the commanders of the remaining troops. During the process of so doing, Smith and his men captured Santa Anna's brother-in-law, General Cos, and returned him to the Texas camp also.[1]

Sadler and his fellow soldiers of Captain Arnold's company were among those who shared the responsibility of guarding the Mexican prisoners in the days following San Jacinto. The miserable weather of the preceding weeks, with cool night air and hours of marching in the rain, continued to take its toll on the company, however. One of Sadler's company mates wrote that "we were all taken with chills and fever" and that some of the men had to be discharged.[2]

From the spoils of the battle, a chest of Santa Anna's containing more than $12,000 was used to pay the Texas soldiers a fee for their service. Each soldier was also given eleven dollars credit to purchase Mexican artifacts at an auction of the spoils of war held by Colonel Sherman on April 26. Sherman himself purchased $341.25 worth of the auction goods.[3]

Sherman, Captain Arnold and almost all of the senior officers of the Texas Army signed a letter which was presented to General Houston on May 3. They asked Houston "to present to Col. William Christy of New Orleans a saddle and bridle said to have belonged to Gen. Cos, taken in the Battle of San Jacinto on the 21st of April; and to assure him of our heartfelt gratitude towards him for the zeal used by him in our favor in our darkest days."[4]

DRIVING THE MEXICAN ARMY FROM TEXAS

The wounded General Houston was reluctant to engage the remaining Mexican forces, although he was so urged by many of his subordinates. He instead sent companies under Henry Karnes and Juan Seguín to observe the retreat of the main forces. Interim Texas President David Burnet reached the army headquarters camp near San Jacinto on May 1, where he found Secretary of War Tom Rusk determined to pursue the Mexican army. Rusk was held back, however, until the basic outlines of peace treaties were signed by Santa Anna at Velasco (present Surfside, Texas) on May 14.[5]

During this period of inactivity, a number of reinforcement volunteers were arriving to join the Texas Army. Many volunteer units arrived to enlist in the days following the historic conflict. At the same time, some men began to depart their companies over the weeks following San Jacinto as the immediate crisis subsided. Muster roll notes show that James Madden was discharged from Captain Arnold's First Company on April 22, the day after the battle. (Madden, however, is not listed on the official honor roll as having fought at San Jacinto.) Several others who had been sick and left to guard the baggage near Harrisburg rejoined Arnold's company.

Also during this period, Tom Rusk was offered both a commission as brigadier general and command of the army to replace Sam Houston, who was suffering from his ankle wound. Houston resigned from the army on May 5 and General Rusk officially took command. Newly appointed Secretary of War Mirabeau Lamar then instructed Rusk to organize his troops and follow the retreating Mexican forces at a distance safe enough to prevent clashes.[6]

W. T. Sadler had the chance to renew his acquaintances with his old traveling companion, Colonel Lamar, during the period shortly after the Battle of San Jacinto. Both men apparently shared the common desire to drive the remaining Mexican forces from their young Republic, for documents show that Sadler's service with Captain Arnold's company ended on May 13 and, on this same date, he and a number of other men transferred their enlistments into the service of a company formed under Captain Leander Smith that was to be among those to track the Mexican forces. Smith, a brother-in-law to General Rusk, had arrived in Texas during the revolution and had been instrumental in bringing the *Twin Sisters* to the aid of the Texas Army.

Smith's company fell under Colonel Sherman's Second Regiment. Sherman himself led an advance cavalry unit which moved out after General Filisola's retreating troops. This group reached Victoria on May 22, where they were joined by Captain William Strickland's independent cavalry company, recently arrived from Mississippi. Together, Strickland and Sherman's cavalry groups soon pushed on for Goliad, where the scouts under Karnes and Seguín had been monitoring Filisola.[7]

The infantry companies under General Rusk followed slowly west on foot, arriving in Victoria in late May. After a brief rest, Rusk's troops marched twenty-five miles farther to Goliad. There, on June 3, a proper military funeral, including a general parade of the troops, was held at 9:00 a.m. The bones of the Goliad defenders had been collected and placed into a single grave, and several of Fannin's command who had miraculously escaped the massacre were in attendance as mourners. In a moving address to the army, Rusk praised the brave men who had fought at La Bahía and condemned the murderous Mexican forces. "While the names whom he murdered shall soar to the highest pinnacle of fame," he stated of Santa Anna, "his shall sink down to the deepest depths of infamy and disgrace."[8]

After about a week in Goliad, Rusk brought most of his soldiers back to the Guadalupe River near Victoria. Still fully expecting the Mexican army to return to fight, he considered this area more secure than Goliad for gathering the newly arriving reinforcements. By this time, the volunteers whose enlistments were up were leaving, and Rusk's forces had dwindled to a mere three-hundred men. Camp Victoria was established during the second week of June at a point about three miles above the town on Spring Creek.[9]

Private Sadler received his last payment from Captain Arnold's company on May 30, shortly before the former Nacogdoches Volunteers unit was disbanded on June 6. Sadler and his new company under Captain Smith, however, remained on duty with the Second Regiment in Victoria.

A warning, from Henry Teal and from Henry Karnes of the cavalry scouts at Matamoros, that a Mexican army was about to return to Texas brought a flurry of commotion as Camp Victoria was being established. The scouts sent this information via messenger in the handle of his riding whip, and the letter delivered to Rusk thus became known as the "whip-handle dispatch."[10] Actually, the Mexican troops had truly retreated and by early June had reached Matamoros. By the time Santa Anna's once proud soldiers crossed back into their own country, they were half starved and wearing only tatters. The threat they still posed, however, compelled the Texas government to issue an urgent appeal for volunteers to join the army. Recruiting to fight in Texas had also been done in the United States, from which the largest portion of the new recruits arrived.

From its lowest point of about three-hundred effectives in Goliad, General Rusk's army rapidly gained strength once again as U.S. and Texan volunteers arrived. During the first days of July, a large group of mounted men from Mississippi under Brigadier General Felix Huston of Natchez and about two-hundred volunteers under General Thomas Jefferson Green of North Carolina arrived at Camp Victoria. Volunteers under these men had arrived by steamboat at Velasco as the Texas government struggled with how to return Santa Anna to his country.[11]

The Texas Army grew in size, until General Rusk reported by July 8 that he had twelve-hundred men in camp.[12] These were not the men, however, who had fought and conquered Santa Anna's troops. Most of those men had long since departed, and those who stayed through June soon left as the new enlistees arrived. Order was returning in Texas, and the settlers who had fled during the Runaway Scrape slowly returned to their homes.

Those who had been with the army for longer periods of time now chose to leave the military affairs to others. Captain Smith's company was broken up, and he returned immediately to Nacogdoches. He found many members of his family sick with fever and sent a letter to his brother-in-law, General Rusk, on July 12. Smith wrote that "I can't leave them sick" and would therefore give up his commission unless "I can have a command in the army."[13]

Private William T. Sadler, having fulfilled his three-month enlistment with a month to spare, also chose to leave the army's affairs to the new soldiers. His pension papers indicate he "was honorably discharged at Victoria, Texas by Gen. T. J. Rusk on or about the 1st day of July, AD 1836." Sadler then struck out for East Texas to find what had become of his property in the four months of his absence.

* * * *

THE PARKER'S FORT ATTACK

As the Mexican troops withdrew and the Texas Army tried to regroup, the frontier settlements had been left largely to fend for themselves in the days following the Texas Revolution. A new and deadly threat was beginning to be felt in the eastern territory. The Indians of Texas shared a rising discontent with the white men who were being allowed to take over lands that they had lived upon for decades. For the new settlers, there were enough of the various Indian tribes present to raise great concern. A report made to the government in 1836 made the following estimate of Indian strength in Texas at the time.

Wacos	400
Tehuacanas	200
Tonkawas	800
Coushattas	350
Alabamas	250
Comanches	2,000
Caddos	500
Lipans	900
Smaller Bands [1]	800
Cherokees and their associate bands [2]	8,000
Total:	14,200

[1] Includes: Kichais, Ionis, etc.
[2] Includes Biloxis, Choctaws, Delawares, Iowanes, Kickapoos, Quapaws, Shawnees, and others.[14]

Of course, not all of these Indian tribes were warlike. The Ionis who visited William Sadler's land were very peaceful individuals who were interested only in farming and hunting the lands. On the other hand, the Cherokees, Caddos and Kickapoos would come to be regarded as being much more violent.

The Cherokees Indians had their own alphabet and educational standards above that of many other Texas-based tribes. Some of them even owned negro slaves. The Cherokees had come into Texas around the time of Stephen F. Austin from the Carolinas, Georgia and western Virginia. Although promised land by the Mexican government early on, they had never been given clear title by Mexico, leading them to distrust the Mexican agents who continued to visit them.

The Indians instead began to place more trust in Sam Houston, who was known to them as "the Raven." Houston and Colonel John Forbes had reached a treaty with Texas Cherokee leader Chief Bowles (whose name "Bowl" was a rough translation of his native

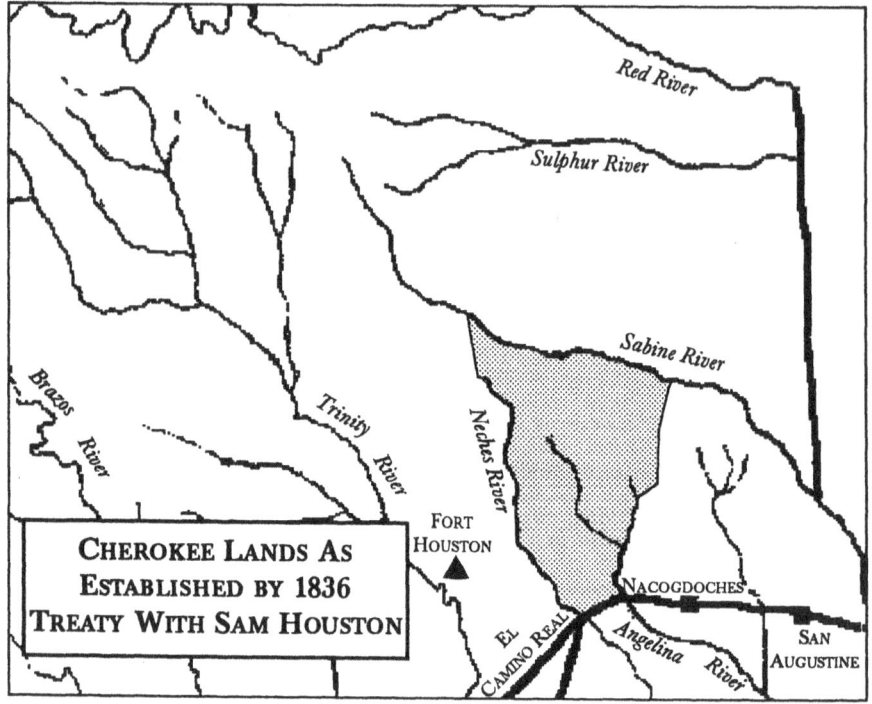

name "Duwali") on February 23, 1836. Houston is said to have presented to Chief Bowles a black military hat, a silk vest, a handsome sash and a sword, which the leader would carry until his death. Bowles' Cherokee village at this time was located in present Rusk County about nine miles north of present Henderson, Texas.[15]

This treaty gave the Cherokees land west of El Camino Real. This grant began on the west at the point where the road crossed the Angelina River. It ran up the Angelina until it reached a large creek below the great Shawnee village. Then the boundary ran with this creek to its main source and from there it followed a course due northeast to the Sabine River. It then followed the Sabine northwest to the extreme northern border of the new Cherokee lands. The boundary moved south to where it intersected the Neches River. It then followed the Neches to El Camino Real and then up the road to the point of origin on the Angelina. This area, approximately fifty miles long by thirty miles wide, covered all of present Smith and Cherokee counties plus western portions of Rusk and Gregg counties and the northeast portion of Van Zandt County.[16]

In the months following San Jacinto, Sam Houston was elected the President of the Republic of Texas. The First Congress of the

Old Fort Parker was completed in March 1834, by Elder Daniel Parker and families of his early Predestinarian Baptist Church. The fort consisted of two-story blockhouses built on opposite corners, and within were two rows of log cabins. The surrounding stockade fence was built of split cedars which were buried three feet in the ground and left extending about twelve feet high. This reconstructed structure stands in the Old Fort Parker State Historical Park, located between Groesbeck and Mexia, Texas, off Highway 14. It is also the site of the bloody Parker's Fort Attack of May 19, 1836. Photo by Marshall L. Moore Jr.

Republic, however, had refused to recognize the treaty lands Houston had granted to the Cherokees. Mexican agents were thus successful in stirring up the Indians against the white settlers who were "stealing" their land. The result was the beginning of a bloody series of Indian raids against frontier Texas settlers.

One of the earliest such raids, and one that is perhaps the most well known in Texas Indian War history, involves the Parker family which had brought the first non-Catholic church to Texas. This raid, occurring May 19, 1836, involved a combined force of hundreds of Comanches and Kiowas and took place just after the Mexicans had been defeated at San Jacinto. This attack was made on the Parker settlement, which was also home to a ten-man Texas Ranger company under Captain James W. Parker.

Parker's Fort was located near the headwaters of the Navasota River in present Limestone County, most of which was still consid-

PARKER'S FORT MASSACRE: MAY 19, 1836	
RESIDENTS:	Sarah Parker Nixon
Elisha Anglin	Benjamin Parker [1]
Abram Anglin	Capt. James W. Parker
Seth Bates	Martha Duty Parker
Silas H. Bates	James W. Parker Jr.
George E. Dwight	Francis Marion Parker
Mrs. G. E. Dwight	Martha Patsy Parker
Dwight children	Elder John Parker [1]
Mrs. Duty [2]	Sallie White Parker [2]
David Faulkenberry	Silas Mercer Parker Sr. [1]
Evan Faulkenberry	Lucy Duty Parker
Samuel Frost [1]	Cynthia Ann Parker [3]
Mrs. Samuel Frost	John Parker [3]
Robert Frost [1]	Silas Parker Jr.
S. Frost children	Orlena Parker
Elizabeth Kellogg [3]	Luther M. Plummer
Oliver Lund	Rachel Parker Plummer [3]
Mrs. Loreno D. Nixon Sr.	James Pratt Plummer [3]
Loreno D. Nixon Jr.	

[1] Killed by the Indians May 19, 1836.
[2] Wounded May 19, 1836.
[3] Taken hostage May 19, 1836.
Note: Names that are indented indicate names of young children of the parents listed immediately above them. The names and exact number of children of Samuel Frost and George Dwight are unknown.

ered wilderness country as of 1836. The next nearest white settlement from Parker's Fort was that of the Fort Houston Settlement near Sadler's home. Parker's stockade-like fort was a series of cabins surrounded by a bulletproof wall to keep out the Indians. This settlement's patriarch was seventy-nine-year-old Elder John Parker and his slightly older wife, Sallie White "Granny" Parker.

Under his supervision, the fort had been started in 1834, and as of May 19 there were about thirty-eight residents (see chart). Among these were three of John Parker's sons: Benjamin Parker, a single man; ranger captain James W. Parker and family; and ranger superintendent Silas Mercer Parker Sr. and family. Many of the other inhabitants of Parker's Fort were relatives of the family.[17]

The church had an official meeting on April 2, 1836, and certain provisions were made to keep up the church's Constitution and Church Book in the event of the congregation's not meeting again at its regular meeting place. It was recorded that "it appears that the members of this church are like to scatter by reason of the apparent danger and unsettled state of the country."[18]

The feared danger became reality about 9:00 a.m. on May 19 when several hundred Indians appeared in the prairie near Parker's Fort. Benjamin Parker, one of the rangers, went out alone to dissuade them from fighting, but he was surrounded and killed. The whole force of Indians then erupted into horrible war yells and descended upon the little pioneer fort. Ranger superintendent Silas Parker was killed while bravely fighting outside the fort. Mrs. Rachel Plummer and her infant child, James Pratt Plummer, were taken captives.[19]

Young Comanches especially were taught to prove themselves as being brave in combat; physically striking an opponent in battle was far more courageous than merely shooting the same person from a distance. Scalping an enemy while still alive was considered a great feat. This grisly act involved using a sharp knife to remove the entire scalp with ears if possible, although the raiding process often left insufficient time to take the entire scalp.

Elder John Parker tried to escape with his wife and Mrs. Elizabeth Kellogg but made it less than a mile before they were overtaken. Parker was stripped, murdered and scalped, while his wife was stripped, speared and left for dead. Mrs. Kellogg was taken captive. During the assault on the interior of the fort, rangers Samuel M. Frost and his son Robert were killed while heroically defending the women and children inside.

When the Indians first appeared, Sarah Nixon hurried away to the fields to alert some of the rangers including her husband Loreno Nixon Jr., Captain James Parker and Luther Plummer, who were working away from the fort. Plummer hurried to inform the others in the field: Silas Bates, Abram Anglin and David and Evan Faulkenberry. The rangers rushed back toward Fort Parker to fight. En route, James Parker met his fleeing family and took them to shelter in the Navasota River bottom. Nixon arrived back at the fort unarmed in time to see Lucy Parker, wife of the murdered Silas Parker, and her children being overtaken by the Indians.

Two of Lucy Parker's children, Cynthia Ann and John Parker, were taken captive by the Indians. Nixon's life was saved by David Faulkenberry, who appeared with his rifle and also saved Lucy Parker and her two other children. Nixon, his wife, Dwight's family and the survivors of the Frost family all escaped toward the hiding place in the river bottom. Bates, Anglin and Faulkenberry arrived too late to fight the main group of Indians, who were beginning to depart. They carried away with them five captives: Mrs. Elizabeth Kellogg, Cynthia Ann and John Parker, Mrs. Rachel Plummer, and her infant son James Pratt Plummer. Five men of the Parker and Frost families had been killed. Although found stripped and bloody, the elderly "Granny" Parker survived, as did the also severely wounded Mrs. Duty.

Bates, Anglin and Evan Faulkenberry returned the following morning, May 20, and secured horses and supplies for the ride to Fort Houston. A party from Fort Houston then returned to bury the dead and look for survivors. Captain James Parker, two other men and nineteen surviving women and children spent six days in the wilderness without food before being found by a party near the old San Antonio and Nacogdoches road crossing near the Navasota River.

As for the Indian captives, Mrs. Kellogg was eventually ransomed and delivered to Nacogdoches six months later, where Sam Houston paid $150 to a band of Delawares for her return. Rachel Plummer was eventually ransomed and returned to her father, James Parker, on February 19, 1838, twenty-two months after her capture. Six months after being seized at Parker's Fort she gave birth to a child, but it was brutally murdered in her presence. Rachel Plummer dictated an account of her ordeal with the Indians and died one year after being returned to her father. Mrs. Plummer's son, James Pratt, was also ransomed, taken to Fort Gibson in 1842 and delivered to his surviving grandfather in February of 1843. He lived out a full life and became a respected citizen of present Anderson County.

The other two Parker's Fort hostages, Cynthia Ann and John Parker, became the most well-known Indian captives of Texas. John Parker became a famous Indian warrior, marrying a Mexican girl and leading his own tribe for a time before quitting them and eventually fighting for the Confederacy with a Mexican company. His nine-year-old sister, Cynthia Ann Parker, lived for twenty-five years with the Indians and gave birth to two sons, one of whom became the famous Comanche chief Quanah Parker. Upon her return to civilization near Waco, her uncle, Colonel Isaac Parker, son of Elder John Parker, helped Cynthia Ann remember her name and brought her back to Anderson County where she finally passed away in 1870.

COMPLETION OF FORT HOUSTON

The horrible story of the Parker's Fort attack is but one of many raids staged by the Indians during their uprisings following the Texas Revolution. The fort was abandoned for some time, and

The original Fort Houston was located in present Anderson County and served as a frontier ranger station during the Indian conflicts of Texas between 1835-1839. The early structures of this post were started by the first settlers, including Sadler. During early 1836, Sadler's ranger company continued work on the blockhouse. Another ranger company completed the work that summer. Several years after the Cherokee War, Fort Houston was abandoned and the main structure eventually became part of the Judge John H. Reagan home in Palestine, Texas. Near its original site now stand two State of Texas historical markers.
Photo by Marshall L. Moore Jr.

many of the survivors came to settle in or near Fort Houston, including David and Evan Faulkenberry, Abram Anglin, and James Parker. By the time William Sadler returned to this area in the fall of 1836, work was well underway to fortify the little settlement near his land.

Prior to his appointment as commander of the Texas Army, Sam Houston at Nacogdoches had been informed that a true fort was needed in the area, and thus Fort Houston was properly established. Following San Jacinto, Houston sent a company of fifty emigrant volunteers under Captain George Washington Jewel, newly arrived in Texas from Nashville, to the Houston settlement in the summer of 1836.

A second company was added to the project, a volunteer ranging company under Captain Michael Costley. Born in 1809, Costley had served in the Texas Army from June 22 to September 22, 1836, after which he returned to his Nacogdoches home to lead his First Company of Texas Rangers. This mounted group was under Hugh McLeod and patrolled the Bexar Road between the Angelina and Neches rivers during the fall of 1836.[20] Among Captain Costley's company were Daniel L. Crist, Dr. Elisha DeBard, Martin Lacy, John Sheridan, Benjamin Vansickle, John C. Walling and Dr. James Jefferson Ware.

Costley and Jewel's companies set to work building the fortress at Fort Houston, adding to what had previously been established in late 1835 and early 1836 by the settlers and Sadler's rangers. The Secretary of War also required these troops to construct two additional blockhouses and a ferryboat at the upper crossing of the Trinity River. The men refused to complete the additional labor on the west bank of the Trinity, although they did complete Fort Houston. These belligerent men raised Jewel to the rank of major, informing Sam Houston that they had come out to fight and "would be damned if they were going to work for anybody."[21]

Houston refused to acknowledge Jewel's promotion, sending word that these men would not be paid if they did not behave. Captain Costley's company refused to be disciplined and opted to accept discharges on December 11, 1836. "Major" Jewel's men, under Squire Haggard since Jewel's promotion, spent their time patrolling the area about Fort Houston.

The fort these rebellious volunteers had built was a solid fortification which was described as measuring 150 by 80 feet. There were two rows of cabins inside Fort Houston's walls, with at least one two-story blockhouse from which its defenders could direct fire down upon attackers.

In her notebooks on Anderson County, Mary Kate Hunter, who had many occasions to see this fort, describes Fort Houston.

> [It was] a building made of heavy hewn logs, about 25 feet square, 10 feet high, with but one entrance, strongly barred from within. On top of this structure was placed a second story, about eight feet high, jutting over the first about two feet all round, with portholes (for rifles) for directing fire laterally, also sufficient openings between the lower and upper story through which to shoot perpendicularly, any daring savage who might approach the wall, either for the purpose of entrance or firing the building.

Named for the leader at San Jacinto, Fort Houston served as a safehaven for the settlers who were gathering in larger numbers about the area. In Nacogdoches County, Captain Elisha Clapp's ranging company was disbanded about the same time that Sam Houston discharged Costley's rebellious company. This left only Jewel's forty-four rangers in service for the first few months of 1837. These men had moved on from Fort Houston by March 1837, thus leaving the little Fort Houston Settlement on its own.

There is no evidence of a formally organized force operating from Fort Houston during the next year and a half. This area fell under what was later known as Captain Sadler's militia district. Without the Texas government's financial support, such units were strictly voluntary, were raised only at times of crisis and were filled out by local residents armed with their own weapons. During most of 1837 and early 1838, it appears that Sadler and his men were the only source of protection in this area for the residents.

* * * *

In the months following the victory over Mexico, the Republic of Texas had voted during the first Monday of September 1836 on three candidates for President: Sam Houston, Stephen F. Austin and Henry Smith. Houston won with little effort thanks to his great fame from the San Jacinto victory. The First Congress of the Republic of Texas took office on October 3, 1836. Austin was made Secretary of State, although he passed away on December 27 during his term. The third candidate, Henry Smith, became Secretary of the Treasury. Mirabeau Lamar was Houston's vice president. Houston relieved Rusk of command of the unruly Texas army and returned him to being secretary of war. General Felix Huston, one of the U.S. volunteers arriving in Texas after San Jacinto, was made commander of the army. Other positions included Samuel Rhodes Fisher as secretary of the navy, James Pinckney Henderson as attorney general, and Robert Barr as postmaster general.

During this same time, the dissident Indians tribes of East Texas were uniting and growing stronger. In Nacogdoches Sam Houston tried to use his influence to calm the Cherokees and continued to work into 1837 on placating Chief Bowles, the leader of the more warlike Cherokees.

Bowles was the son of a Scotch-Irish father and a Cherokee mother. Born in 1756, he was said to have had red hair, was slightly freckled, and not as darkly tanned as some of his fellow braves. With sixty warriors and their families, he had moved into Spanish-owned Texas and settled along the Trinity River near present Dallas. Attacks on Bowles' own colony by hostile Indians forced his Cherokee band to migrate to a wooded section of East Texas north of the present town of Henderson.[22]

During the summer of 1836, Indian representatives had held conferences with Mexican officials in Matamoros in Mexico just across the Rio Grande River. General José Urrea, a Texas

Revolution veteran who now commanded Mexican troops in Matamoros, reassured a group of visiting Cherokees that they owned their lands, not Texas. Urrea and the Indians decided that the Cherokees would postpone a planned raid on the Texans until they could be supported by the Mexican Army.[23]

The diplomatic challenge of 1837 was thus to establish control over the Indians as they grew increasingly hostile against Texas settlers, spurned by the Mexican rebels to take action. The Republic provided defense to the frontiers during 1837 with a few companies of rangers and mounted gunmen.

It was not long before the Caddo Indians and other more hostile tribes again began making depredations against East Texas settlers. Details of some of the first acts of aggression by the Indians in this area are documented in a letter dated January 27, 1837, written by Daniel McLean, the first settler of what soon became Houston County. McLean had first come to Texas in 1812 with the Gutierrez-Magee Expedition, had been one of only ninety-three survivors of a deadly Indian battle on the Medina River on August 18, 1813, and had in 1821 become one of the "Old Three Hundred" original settlers of the Austin Colony.[24]

McLean wrote to his son James, who was in school at the time in Natchitoches, that he had recently lost some of his horses. "The Indians have been in the neighborhood a few days back and have stolen every horse that Mr. Greenwood had," he related. "Since they have stolen two from the rangers at Houston, we may suppose that at the rise of the grass they will be on all sides."

McLean also related that a family near the Brazos River had recently been killed and that a party of fourteen men three weeks previously had attacked a force of approximately one-hundred Indians. This was a unit under ranger officer George Erath, who fought on January 7 on Elm Creek in present Milam County. With superior numbers and by using the cover of dense brush, the Indians (believed to be Caddoes and Cherokees) managed to kill two of Erath's men before the whites were forced to retreat to a safer area. McLean also felt that the Mexicans were "generally believed to be making every preparation to invade us in the spring. It is supposed that there [are] from four to six thousand troops at Matamoros and several thousand more coming on. We get no news authentic."

Ironically, the next major encounter with hostile Indians occurred against the white settlers of the newly established Fort Houston on the day after McLean's letter was penned. On January

28, 1837, six rangers, eighteen-year-old Abram Anglin, David Faulkenberry, Evan Faulkenberry, Benjamin W. Douthit, James Hunter, and Columbus Anderson, had left the fort to search for strayed hogs in the Trinity River bottom. Finding some of them, Hunter and Douthit were sent back to Fort Houston to fetch a canoe.[25]

In their absence, the other four were attacked by a band of Indians on the Trinity River at a point known as Bonner's Ferry. Anderson was mortally wounded, although he managed to swim the river and crawl two miles before dying. David Faulkenberry, severely wounded, also swam the river and crawled about two-hundred yards away before succumbing to his wounds. The Indians later claimed that David's son, Evan Faulkenberry, fought like a wild man, killing two Indians and wounding a third. Severely wounded and already scalped, he was said to have jerked from his captives' grasp and swum halfway across the Trinity before dying.[26] The fourth man, Abram Anglin, although hit by a bullet in the thigh, managed to swim the river and escape on horseback with James Hunter, one of the two men who had returned from Fort Houston in time to witness the Indian attack.[27]

This was the closest incident to the citizens of the Fort Houston settlement since the attack on Parker's Fort the previous May. With the recent departure of Major Jewel's troops from Fort Houston, the local citizens inhabiting the fortress were terrified. These men then appealed to Sam Houston in 1837 by petition for better defense, as the Indian raids were now occurring at their own back door. Houston, then in Nacogdoches, was unable to provide troops but did give them help in acquiring a large gun from Fort Jesup, the U.S. Army post near the Louisiana border.

Houston sent the Fort Houston settlers a note to present to Fort Jesup's commandant. They were given a 12-pounder cannon weighing 963 pounds that they transported back to Fort Houston and properly mounted for use against the Indians. The story of this gun's presence spread quickly, and many felt that it would prevent the Indians from ever making a direct attack on this fort.[28]

* * * *

THE NEW LIFE, THE NEW WIFE AND THE NEW COUNTY

In the midst of these rising Indian tensions, Captain Sadler resumed farming on his property. Corn was one of his principal crops and he soon purchased a number of hogs and cattle and began working on his home. He also finally made preparations to begin a family.

Sadler was married in March 1837 in Nacogdoches County to Mary Murchison, a daughter of Martin Murchison who had been born in South Carolina and later spent some years in Alabama. Martin Murchison brought his wife, oldest son John and daughter Mary to Texas in 1835. John Murchison, born about 1807, had then enlisted in the volunteer army from April 24 to July 24, 1836, before settling back to farming in East Texas.[29] The Murchison family lived several miles south of Sadler's home in an area of present northern Houston County that had become known as Murchison's Prairie.

William and Mary Sadler's new home was located just north of the current county line of Anderson County. Although he owned one-third of a league of land near Fort Houston, Sadler chose to establish his permanent homestead closer to the Neches River. Now married, he was able to take possession of a full league and labor of land from Texas for meeting the requirements of an early settler. It was on this large piece of land that he settled, although he would not receive clear

W. T. Sadler and his new wife established their home in present Anderson County after their marriage in early 1837. It was located just south of where **Saddler Creek** (right) crosses Farm Road 2022. Although incorrectly spelled, this creek is one of two in the county named after Sadler. Author's collection.

title to it until early in 1838 after present Houston County was firmly established. Settlers moving into Texas prior to March 2, 1836, were generally issued First Class Headrights for a league of land. The couple's home was located across a cornfield from a cluster of trees that stands beside present FM 2022 near the community of Percilla, Texas.

Should the Indians of the area become a threat again, Sadler and his Fort Houston area volunteers could expect little help from the Texas Army. Since its peak enlistment in July 1836, the army's numbers had steadily decreased. Albert Sidney Johnston was appointed commander of the Texas Army with the rank of brigadier general, but his second-in-command, General Felix Huston, challenged him to a duel for the post. Johnston was seriously wounded and had to depart Texas for some time to recover. In his absence, command of the army went to Colonel Samuel Rogers on May 7. On May 18, President Houston furloughed all the two-thousand-man army except for about six-hundred men. This number dwindled as men began quitting the service and once again the benefit of the few Texas Rangers companies in existence became apparent.[30]

The lack of proper protection on the early Texas frontiers left the doors open for the more hostile Indians to pillage the generally helpless settlers. Another assault occurred just a few miles from Sadler's new home on May 10, 1837. Two of the area's earliest residents, Dan McLean and his brother-in-law John Sheridan, were considered expert Indian fighters and were employed at times by the area's settlers as guides and protectors. While assisting the locals to recover stolen horses, both men were ambushed and killed by Indians. Near the present community of Slocum on FM 2022 now stands a Texas State historical marker which identifies the site of the McLean-Sheridan Massacre near Sadler's home. Sheridan's wife Lucinda traveled to the scene of the massacre with an oxcart shortly thereafter and brought back the bodies to be buried on their respective properties several miles south.[31]

Despite the dangers of this area, Sadler and his wife chose to remain in their new homestead. Shortly after this latest massacre, the First Congress of Texas took steps to shape Nacogdoches County into a more manageable size. Sadler's San Jacinto infantry captain, Hayden Arnold, was at this time the Nacogdoches County electee in the House of Representatives, which had gone into session on October 3, 1836. As Chairman of the Committee on Counties and Country Boundaries, Arnold introduced a bill on Tuesday, June 6, 1837, to establish the County of Houston.

The leaders of Nacogdoches had already petitioned for the creation of said county some six weeks previous. Among the numerous signers of this petition included many men Sadler knew well: Colin Aldrich, Elisha Anglin, William Anglin, Miles Bennett, Stephen Bennett, Nelson Box, Stephen Box, Thomas G. Box, Reuben Brown, Elisha Clapp, Stephen Crist, Reason Crist, Andrew E. Gossett, Elijah Gossett, Joseph Jordan, Martin Murchison, Benjamin Parker, Daniel Parker Jr., Dickerson Parker, J. D. Parker, Isaac Parker, John Wortham, Joseph Randolph Yarbrough, and Swanson Yarbrough Sr.

The act establishing Houston County was approved and signed by Sam Houston on June 12, 1837. The new county had the following boundaries:

> Beginning on the East bank of the Trinity River at a point two leagues above the mouth of Kickapoo Creek, from Thence in a northwesterly direction to the Neches, at the mouth of Big Pine Creek; Thence up the Neches to the 32nd degree of North latitude; Thence due West to the Trinity River; Thence down said river to the place of beginning, form[ing] a county to be called and known by the name of HOUSTON COUNTY.

William Sadler's land thus fell into Houston County and would remain as such until he later helped establish present-day Anderson County. The first officials of Houston County elected to serve in September 1837 included Colin Aldrich as chief justice, James Madden as sheriff, Stephen White as district clerk, Jacob Allbright as county clerk, and John Box, John Gregg, John Grigsby and Elijah Gossett as justices of the peace. John H. Kerchoffer was named president of the Board of Land Commissioners, with Elijah Gossett and John Wortham his associates. Samuel G. Wells, who had served under Captain Sadler in 1836, was Kerchoffer's clerk and George Aldrich became the first county surveyor.

Despite the development of Houston County, it would not have its own congressional representatives until the Third Congress of 1838. Sadler and sixty-one of his new county's citizens sent a petition to the Congress on September 4, 1837, criticizing the new ad valorem tax law. In other actions, the petitioning settlers set to work creating a town for their county seat. The land was provided from the headright of Andrew Edwards Gossett, and Gossett and his father, Elijah Gossett, were thus permitted to name the new town. They chose the name "Crockett" after the family friend from Kentucky who had been slain at the Alamo.

President Sam Houston called a special session of the Second Congress on September 26, 1837. Representing Nacogdoches County for this session was the former secretary of war, Thomas Rusk, who made the rebellious Indians a major issue for the Republic of Texas. President Houston was committed to pursuing a peaceful course with the Indians and to preventing encroachments upon their rights, although their land was not officially titled by either Texas or Mexico.

As Chairman of the Military Committee in the House, Rusk was largely responsible for a bill that would formally organize the Republic's militia.[32] This bill would finally recognize and provide payment for some of the volunteer outfits, such as Captain Sadler's, which had been protecting their respective colonies during the early days of the Republic. Houston vetoed this bill, although Rusk was able to rally the vote of the Congress to override the President's veto. This accomplished, a joint session of the two houses then elected Rusk as major general of the militia.[33]

Indian depredations against Texas settlers during 1837 declined from the previous year. The white settlers near Bastrop suffered a few killed in Indian encounters. In Nacogdoches County, the McLean/Sheridan and Faulkenberry/Anderson slayings had been the most serious incidents. Following George Erath's fight in January, the most serious Indian battle of the year occurred in November 1837 when a party of seventeen rangers under Lieutenant A. B. Vanbenthuysen and Lieutenant Alfred H. Miles encountered seven Kichais near the forks of the Brazos River. One of the Kichais was killed, and the Texan force continued on until reaching the upper Trinity River on November 10. This force was then attacked by approximately 150 Wichitas, Kichais and Caddos, many armed with rifles. Many of the Indians were killed, but the rangers lost ten men, including Lieutenant Miles. The survivors under Lieutenant Vanbenthuysen reached the northeast frontier and rejoined another force.[34]

Other than these incidents, an uneasy peace with the Indians of Texas was largely maintained throughout the year following the revolution against Mexico. The growth and colonization of Texas continued to flourish in 1837 as immigrants continued to pour in from all parts of the United States. New towns and new counties began springing up throughout the year. The farming season of 1837 was excellent, and cotton and food crops were bountiful. The sale of land on Galveston Island during the year led to the establishment of a rapidly growing port town called Galveston. The Second Congress in Columbia, Texas, on November 4, 1837, even appropriated $280,000 for the establishment of a new Texas Navy consisting of six armed ships: an 18-gun brig, two 12-gun barques, and three 7-gun schooners.[35]

Despite these advances in establishing necessary defenses for its future protection, the Republic of Texas unwittingly opened the door for further deadly assaults against its settlers via a resolution adopted by the Congress on December 16, 1837. The Congress' Indian Committee, headed by Chairman Isaac Watts Burton, declared President Houston's previous land treaty with Chief Bowles to be null and void. In his committee's report of two months prior, Burton wrote:

> Resolved by the Senate of the Republic of Texas that they disapprove of and utterly refuse to ratify the Treaty or any articles thereof concluded by Sam Houston and John Forbes on the 23rd day of February, 1836, between the Provisional Government of Texas of the one part, and the "Head Chiefs," "Head Men," and Warriors of the Cherokees on the other part. Inasmuch as that said treaty was based on premises that did not exist and that the operation of it would only be detrimental to the interests of the Republic, but would also be a violation of the vested rights of many citizens.[36]

The passage of this resolution was another insult to the Indians and instigated further uprisings against the post-San Jacinto settlers of Texas.

Chapter Seven

CORDOVA'S REBELLION AND GENERAL RUSK'S TEXAS MILITIA

January - October 1838

The General Land Office of the Republic of Texas was opened on January 4, 1838. Now married and eligible for his league and labor of land, Captain Sadler was quick to carry out the necessary paperwork. He rode into Crockett and presented his Headright Certificate No. 26 to Houston County's Land Commission Office. As signed by Marcus P. Mead, Elias Moore and Charles H. Nelson, the county's deputy surveyor, Sadler was granted the 24th Land Certificate of the young county.

George Aldrich, County Surveyor of Houston County, completed the required survey of the William T. Sadler Headright on February 8 and 9, 1838, after which his notes were examined and the land was approved on March 20, 1838. By Aldrich's field notes, the original 20,469,970 square varas he surveyed included seven labors of arable land for plowing and cultivation and nineteen "labors of pasture land." Black jack markers were used by the early surveyors to designate boundary lines, which were generally formed by a body of water, a distinctive landmark, or the edge of another's property. With distances indicated in varas (vs.), Aldrich's field notes of the Sadler Headright give an indication of early surveying techniques.

Beginning at Parker's south boundary stake, whence a black jack bears S 81° E dis. 12 4/10 a black jack N 1°W dis. 8 vs. Thence S 20° W 130 vs. William Frost's N boundary of league stake, whence a Hickory S 35° W dis 6 6/10 vs. a black jack S 48 ° E 6 4/10 vs. Thence with Frost line N 70 ° W 1510 vs Parker's Creek 6 ft W C S 1920 vs. stake at Ewing's line a

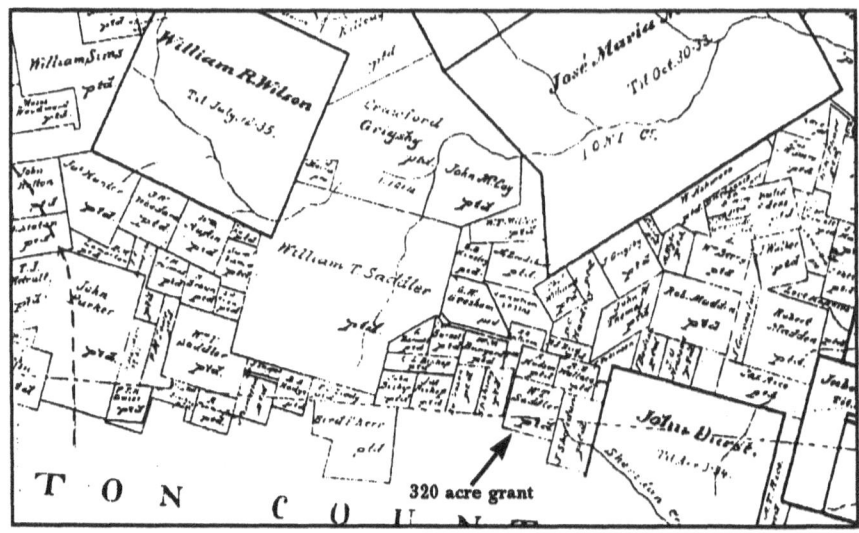

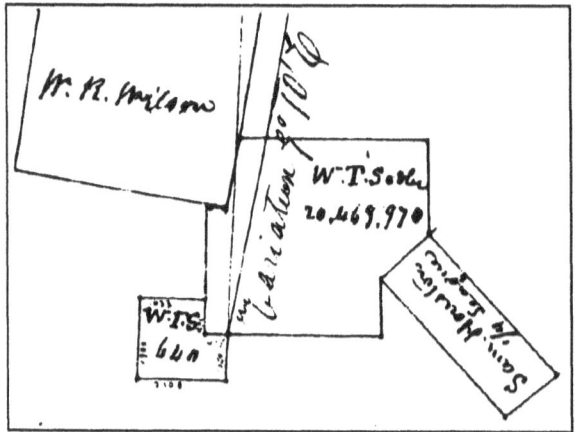

Captain Sadler was granted his headright on Ioni Creek for a league and labor (4,605.5 acres) in Houston County in 1838. This early map (above) shows the adjoining properties to his headright. To right is the original survey sketch of Sadler's headright as it appeared in 1847. Note that his 640-acre grant for San Jacinto service adjoins the southwestern corner and that Sam Houston once owned the 1/4 league to the southeast.

Hickory N 38 °W dis. 4 vs. a Red Oak S 45 W 4 4/10 vs. Thence with Ewing line . . .

In its rectangular shape, the headright of Wm. T. Sadler bordered the lands owned by William Frost, John Parker, Edley Ewing, Samuel Phillips, a one-quarter league awarded to President Sam Houston, William R. Wilson, and then back to its point of origination at Choctaw Bayou. Aldrich's original survey showed this headright to be "part on the waters of the Trinity River SE of Fort Houston," with the balance "on the western waters of the Neches." A new survey of this property in 1877 would show it to be in present Anderson County about 15.5 miles south and east of

Palestine. This league and labor included a portion of Ioni Creek and a tributary to the Ioni which was named "Saddler Creek." This was the second creek named after Sadler, the first being on his one-third league.

As for Sadler's other piece of land, the Board of Land Commissioners for Nacogdoches County was provided "satisfactory evidence" by him on March 30, 1838, that he was indeed the assignee of Severo Arocha's Headright Certificate No. 492 for a one-third league of land. By the records of the General Land Office in both cases, Sadler had to present duplicate certificates issued by the Republic of Texas. It is likely that his originals were lost during his service in the Texas Army in 1836.

The opening of the Land Office created a flood of land claimants and surveying parties who invaded what was previously Indian-held territory. As could be imagined, numerous small battles with the Indians occurred, and attacks against the white settlers increased.

President Houston went to Nacogdoches in February for peace talks with the Indians, who were becoming restless with the Congress of the Republic of Texas' refusal to recognize their 1836 treaty. In early 1838 Chief Bowles had moved his village from the spot north of present Henderson, Texas, to a location that was west of present Alto, Texas, in southwestern Smith County. Bowles began a prosperous business of selling salt from the Neches Saline farther north, and President Houston had appointed Martin Lacy as a trader to the Cherokees to supervise their saline business.[1]

Lacy established a home at an elevated spot near present Alto along the King's Highway that would later be known as Lacy's Fort or Fort Lacy. Despite the fact that the Neches Saline was within the boundaries of territory that had been accorded to the Cherokees by Houston's 1836 treaty, this commodity would not be left exclusively to the Indians' use.

The Senate of the Republic of Texas had appointed a three-man committee in May 1837 to study the Indian situation, and their report was presented in October of the same year. Much attention was paid to the large band of Cherokees, whom they found were led by their war chief, Bowles, and their civil or diplomatic chief, Big Mush (called "Gatunwali" in his native tongue). In a cruel twist for the Cherokees, the committee found that this tribe had no rights given to them by either the Mexican government or Sam Houston's treaty, and they were deemed "the most savage and ruthless" of frontier enemies.[2]

The Senate then took moves to ratify a treaty with the Anadarkos and Ionis, moving to isolate two tribes which had long been considered "associates" of the Cherokees. As related, the Senate in December 1837 had officially nullified the Houston Treaty with the Cherokees. Once the land offices reopened, hundreds of new titles were issued to settlers for land that was once considered to be Cherokee territory. The land of William T. Sadler and his fellow Fort Houston settlers was part of the Cherokees' 1833 claim against Mexico.

Secretary of War Barnard E. Bee and Colonel George W. Hockley managed to sign a treaty of peace with the Tonkawas at Houston on April 11, but it soon became clear that the Cherokee issues were far from over. Chief Bowles became increasingly displeased with the futile efforts of Houston, to whom he had given a daughter in marriage and whom he had made an honorary chief in the Cherokee nation. After a visit by Bowles to see him in Houston, a disgruntled President Houston reported to the Texas Senate in May 1838 that ignorant Texas settlers were invading the Cherokees' properties and "goading the Indians to desperation."

After this meeting, Bowles complained that Houston was no longer a chief of the Cherokees but rather the "Great Father" of the white people. His tribe hosted a council of Indian chiefs on June 14, with chiefs from the Delawares, Kickapoos and Coushattas present. All were disappointed that Sam Houston's promises to them were going unfulfilled. The groundwork had thus been laid for the Indian resistance that would soon be felt by the white settlers.

* * * *

THE RISE OF CORDOVA'S REBELLION

Under Sam Houston's leadership, Congress had first passed legislation on December 6, 1836, which established the essential militia structure for frontier defense, but thereafter Congress refused to appropriate any money to this effort. The Second Congress of Texas in late 1837 reduced the militia to one division, under the command of a major general, containing four brigades each commanded by a brigadier general. The initial general officers selected by Congress were Thomas J. Rusk as major general, with Edward Burleson, Moseley Baker, Kelsey H. Douglass and John Dyer commanding the first to fourth brigades, respectively.

The original districts for the brigades in 1837 were as follows: the First Brigade under Burleson included all areas west of the

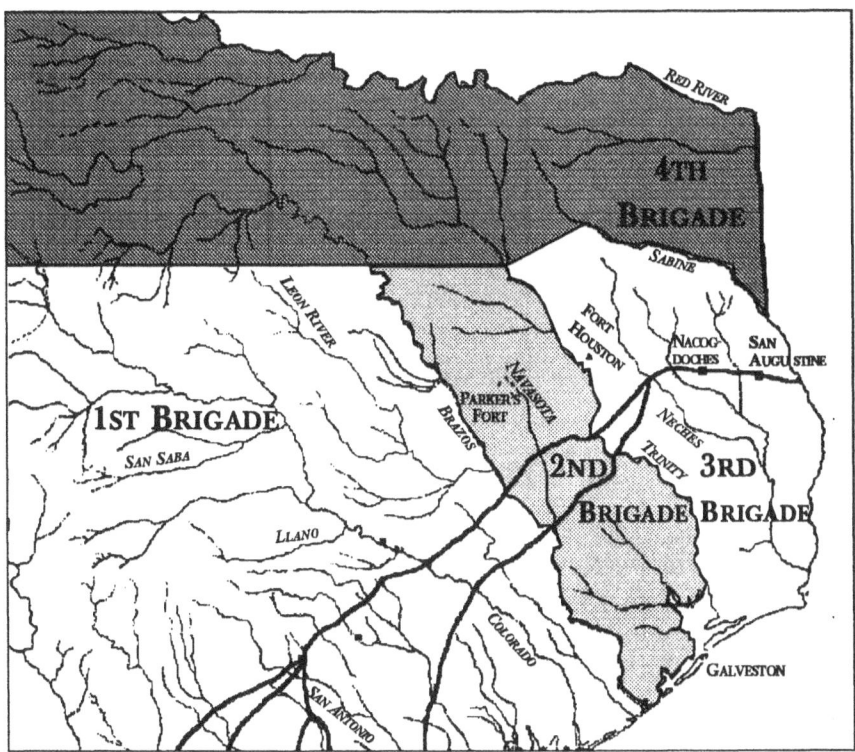

Militia Brigade Districts of the Republic of Texas in 1838. An act of Congress in December 1837 established these four brigade districts, with the following brigadier generals as their respective commanders: First Brigade, Edward Burleson; Second Brigade, Moseley Baker; Third Brigade, Kelsey Douglass; and Fourth Brigade, John Dyer. Captain Sadler's volunteer rangers of Houston County fell under Douglass' Third Brigade.

Brazos; the Second Brigade under Baker included the territory between the Brazos and Trinity; the Third under Douglass included the country between the Trinity and the Sabine; and the Fourth under Dyer the area north of the Sabine. During 1838 the militia's organization was still somewhat shaky, and its strength was strong only during crisis situations. In 1838, before organized military companies could be pulled together in 1839, volunteer militia companies such as Sadler's did the fighting against the Indians.[3]

By standards established in 1835, militia members were between sixteen and fifty years of age and were generally in companies of fifty-six men. The early militia companies used their home towns as an organizational hub and elected a captain to lead the unit. If the population was great enough to form three full companies, a major was elected to command all three companies. Towns capable of composing four militia companies could elect a lieutenant colonel, and a five-company town elected a brigadier general.[4]

Against Sam Houston's wishes, the Congress of Texas had passed a bill that took command of the militia away from the chief executive. Although Tom Rusk became the effective commander of the militia, an adjutant general with the rank of colonel actually presided over the actions of the Texas Militia. The first such chief militia officer had been Warren D. C. Hall, who was appointed on October 11, 1835. Five others followed Hall until Rusk's friend Hugh McLeod was appointed on October 24, 1837. McLeod would be Adjutant General of the Texas Militia until October 1, 1841.[5]

The first true test of the militia's effectiveness was put in motion during the summer of 1838 when an uprising later dubbed the "Cordova Rebellion" forced Major General Rusk to call up the troops. During the early months of 1838, a Mexican agent named Pedro Julián Miracle was sent from Matamoros with a force of Mexicans, soldiers and Indians to unite the various Indian groups and Mexican Texans against the white Texas settlers. On July 5, Miracle's rebels met on the Trinity River with Vicente Cordova, a former Mexican judge and *alcalde* (mayor) of Nacogdoches who had been forced out of office when the Republic of Texas was established.[6]

Cordova, aided by Juan Flores, Juan Cruz and John Norris, had gathered a band of rebel Indians thought to include some Cherokees, Caddoes and Coushattas and about two-hundred revolutionary Mexicans who resided in Texas in and around Nacogdoches. This force moved to Chief Bowles' Cherokee village on July 9, and soon thereafter a conference was held between several Indian chiefs, Miracle's forces and Cordova's rebels. Cordova then moved on to meet with other Indian tribes in the area to enlist them in the Mexican rebellion.[7] This force then pitched camp on the Angelina River about twenty miles southwest of Nacogdoches.

The first outbreak of violence from Cordova's rebellion occurred on August 4, 1838, when a party of Texans out recovering stolen horses from a Mexican settlement in Nacogdoches County was fired upon on its return trip. One man was killed, and the incident led to a search party's discovering over one-hundred Mexicans, headed by Cordova and Norris, encamped on the Angelina.[8] Another early August attack by Cordova's forces resulted in the murder of two brothers, Matthew and Charles Roberts, and their relative, William Finley.[9]

****

GENERAL RUSK'S MILITIA TAKES TO THE FIELD

The rise of Cordova's Rebellion gave Major General Rusk the ammunition he needed to raise more than twenty companies of the Third Militia Brigade. On August 10 Sam Houston, deciding that the Cherokees were in league with the Mexican rebels, allowed Rusk to raise the militia and station some of them at the lower crossing of the Angelina River. While Rusk's companies served as field reinforcements, President Houston worked in Nacogdoches to keep the Cherokees from joining the rebels.[10]

Operating in the field with Rusk were Adjutant General McLeod and aides de camp Davis S. Kaufman and Charles S. Taylor. Militia companies in service with Rusk's Third Brigade under Brigadier General Kelsey Douglass and Colonel Willis H. Landrum included the rifle companies of captains Wesley W. Hanks, William M. Keeling and David Laird, and the mounted companies of captains Hugh W. Augustine, Samuel C. Box, Andrew Caddell, Joseph Durst, George English, Robert K. Goodloe, George W. Hooper, Alexander Horton, James D. Long, David Muckleroy, James Reily, David Renfro, David Rusk, Lewis Sanchez, Robert W. Smith, Hiram B. Stephens, James F. Timmins and Charles M. Walters.

General Rusk was impatient to go after the rebels while Houston negotiated. When he received information that the Mexicans had crossed the Angelina River into what was Cherokee country and were headed for the village of Chief Bowles north of Nacogdoches, Rusk decided that it was time to move. Cordova had thus far been successful in enlisting a small number of Cherokees and Coushattas into this rebellion. In defiance of Sam Houston's orders, he took his militia from Nacogdoches directly toward the Cherokee village. The Nacogdoches troops stopped at Lacy's Fort for two days while scouts monitored the Indians. Texas scouts under Major Henry Augustine soon found that the Mexican rebels had fled camp, but they were quickly located some two miles from the Cherokee village. Rusk debated for two days whether or not to attack the Cherokees.

Convinced that the Cherokees were not involved with the Cordova Rebellion, Rusk in a letter to Houston warned that he still did not propose to talk much with "a set of infernal scoundrels" who had caused the deaths of innocent women and children.[11] All appearances were that the Cordova rebels had moved on toward the Kickapoo village to the northwest. Having arrived at Fort Houston on August 14, Rusk and Douglass marched their forces into Bowles' town. Sam Houston wrote to Bowles the same day, trying to convince him to give up the idea of fighting.

A peace talk in Rusk's camp on August 15 with ten Indian chiefs helped to postpone the Mexican rebels' operation for a short time.[12] Near the Cherokee village, Rusk learned that forty of the Cordova rebels had fled toward the headwaters of the Trinity River, while the rest were planning to filter back into their settlements. Some of Douglass' force pursued Cordova's rebels for a short distance before Rusk decided that the threat was no more and returned his men to Nacogdoches. One of these volunteers, William Y. Lacy, later wrote,

> We pursued them about 40 miles, found his men had scattered, and supposing that they had left the country and gone to Mexico, we returned home, disbanded our forces with the exception of two companies of cavalry, commanded by L. H. Mabbitt, and sent [them] to Fort Houston for the protection of that frontier.[13]

While the rebels were deserting the Indians, Rusk's force turned and marched back to Nacogdoches. Most of the militia companies were disbanded in Nacogdoches as of August 18, under the orders of President Houston. In a letter to Rusk, Houston wrote, "The brave men who have so promptly rallied to their country's defense, it is hoped, will soon be discharged, and return to their homes." Houston admitted that the enemy, although dispersed, "may again unite at some point, so as to annoy a portion of our population."[14]

Rusk wrote Vice President Lamar that this "timely demonstration of force" through Indian country stirred up fear in the Indians. Colonel Hugh McLeod endorsed Rusk's action and criticized President Houston for hindering Rusk's work "in every way with his orders."[15] The buildup to war stalled for a time as Houston pacified the Cherokees by having General Rusk take steps to have the Cherokee's boundary surveyed, despite having rejected the treaty a year earlier. The Cherokees came under intense study by Texas over the next month.[16]

Two days after Rusk had disbanded his militia, documentary evidence was obtained that proved the Mexican agents had been making proposals to the Indian leaders. On August 20, the chief

Mexican agent Captain Pedro Julián Miracle was killed on the Red River. Instructions from General Vicente Filisola were found on his body which instructed him to visit with the leaders of the Indians of Texas. The letter also revealed that Miracle had paid recent visits to the Cherokee and Kickapoo villages. It also detailed a meeting between Chief Bowles, Cordova, and rebels from Nacogdoches. Miracle had also visited the Chickasaws, Caddos, Kichais and Shawnees while attempting to arrange meetings with the Wacos and Tonkawas.[17]

The emergence of these papers caused a wave of outrage that could not be ignored by President Houston. The Texas Militia under Thomas Rusk was not directly supervised by the President of the Republic, and the two leaders had significantly different views toward the treatment of the Cordova Rebellion insurgents.

The 1838 general election for President of the Republic of Texas would have a profound effect upon how the Indians were dealt with in the future. Running for office were Mirabeau B. Lamar, James Collinsworth, Peter W. Grayson and Robert Wilson. After a bitter campaign of mudslinging, Grayson shot and killed himself. Collinsworth leaped from a steamer into Galveston Bay the day before election and drowned himself. Lamar easily defeated Wilson in the general voting on September 3, 1838.[18] Before he and Vice President David G. Burnet could be inaugurated on December 9, however, their republic would see considerable bloodshed.

* * * *

DEFENSE OF FORT HOUSTON

Despite the big 12-pounder cannon acquired by the residents of Fort Houston, the Indians in their area had been thoroughly incited by the Mexican rebels and were drawing blood. The local citizens of the town of Houston were frightened by the presence of numerous Indians, and they reported their property's being stolen at an alarming rate. A letter was drafted by the leading men of the fort on August 25, 1838, and sent to President Houston. In part, it informed the President that

> our property has been stolen, our houses and farms infested and surrounded, our families alarmed and ourselves compelled to desert our homes on account of depredations committed by our Indian neighbors. We would further beg leave to suggest as our settled conviction that from our

isolated situation and sparseness of our population, this settlement will be compelled to desert our property and protect our women and children from the tomahawk and scalping, or more cruel horror of Indian captivity. This subject is most respectfully submitted to the consideration of the Executive and some protection earnestly but strongly solicited in our truly unpleasant and distressing situation. The Indians who are doing mischief in this neighborhood are supposed to be principally the Kickapoos ....[19]

The Fort Houston letter of appeal was signed by twenty-five men: P. O. Lumpkin, William S. McDonald, Alexander McKenzie, Carter T. McKenzie, John S. Delap, W. B. Shearer, Lacy McKenzie, Richard C. Dixon, Albert G. Persons, Spencer Hobbs, George H. Duncan, Larkin Robertson, John Crist, William T. Smith, John Smith, William Craigheay, Stephen Crist, Jacob C. Morrow, M. Theo Carter, John T. Brown, John W. Carpenter, William M. Frost, Humphries Ussery, Benjamin Persons and George W. Browning. These citizens requested an early answer because they did "not feel safe to remain with our families in our present situation unless prompt measures are taken for our relief."

In October 1838, prior to the Battle of Kickapoo, the original **Fort Houston** *was the gathering point for the volunteer companies of Captain Sadler and three others under Major Leonard Mabbitt. This sketch of Fort Houston was made by Robert Howarton.* Courtesy of the Anderson County Historical Commission.

Even after Rusk had sent most of his forces back home after President Houston's orders, nearly a dozen volunteer companies organized by Rusk remained in service to defend the most exposed positions of the East Texas frontiers.[20] In response to the appeal of Fort Houston's citizens, President Houston sent Major Leonard Mabbitt with three companies of his cavalry on assignment to Fort Houston. Mabbitt's force, the First Battalion of the Third Brigade of Volunteer Rangers, was on duty at Fort Houston by September 27, 1838. The companies under Mabbitt's command were those of Captains James Bradshaw, Squire Brown and Jacob Snively, the latter having commanded a company in the area since the Texas Revolution. The largest of these three was that of Captain Brown, who was promoted into this command on September 22 after having joined this company's formation on August 30, 1838.[21]

After arriving at Fort Houston, a number of the local citizens not already part of Captain W. T. Sadler's ranging company now joined Squire Brown's company. On September 28, Brown's mounted gunmen roll increased with the enlistment of James E. Box, Daniel Crist, William Frost, Alexander McKenzie, Lacy McKenzie, Jacob Morrow and John Wilson from Fort Houston's settlement. John W. Carpenter, another signer of the Sam Houston petition and a former Nacogdoches Volunteer at San Jacinto, joined Brown's company on October 4.

Operating south of Fort Houston's settlement was the volunteer ranger company of Captain Sadler, which continued to grow in size as the Indian hostilities increased. Although independence had been obtained, the very deadly presence of the Indians still had to be dealt with before peace on the prairies could be obtained.

Just south of Sadler's property line near what is the present Anderson-Houston County line rises a high, rounded hill known as Houston Mound. As one of the highest eminences in the area, this hill was said to have been used when the militia and local citizens needed to gather in emergencies. Signal torches were lighted on Houston Mound (west of present Mound City) and on another high point north of present Grapeland, Texas.

Sadler's informal company operated loosely in the area from Box's Fort, a private structure built by Roland Box and his family in 1835 about one and a half miles east of the Neches River, to Brown's Fort near the present town of Grapeland. Many of Sadler's volunteers were residents of the little community surrounding Brown's Fort on San Pedro Creek. Among those of the early Pilgrim Church who had settled here were the children and families of Reuben and Sarah Parker Brown, Armstead and Faith Bennett, Levin and Abigail Dixon, Stephen and Annie Parker Crist, Joseph and Abigail Parker Kennedy, and Samuel G. and Pheby Parker Wells. Brown's Fort would be vacated around 1840 when the Pilgrim Church finally settled into its permanent residence near the present community of Elkhart in Anderson County.

Although no muster roll has survived time, Crockett resident John Wortham, thirty-four, appears to have been Sadler's first lieutenant and John Edward Nite, thirty-three, his third-in-command. Wortham's closest neighbors, Phillip and Martin Walker, are also known to have been attached to the county's early ranger service.[22] Some of Sadler's rangers would continue to serve in Houston County for another year, with command of his company passing first to Wortham in November and later to Solomon Adams.

When the word for volunteers was spread in early October, many joined Sadler's unit from the little settlement of Augusta just northeast of Brown's Fort. This community's earliest settlers included the families of Dan McLean, John Sheridan, John Edens, George W. Wilson, and James and Robert Madden. McLean and Sheridan, of course, had been slain by Indians the previous year.[23]

Among others comprising Sadler's company were Robert Madden, who had come to Texas with his siblings and their father John in 1832, brothers thirty-three-year-old Balis Edens, twenty-four-year-old Darius H. Edens and eighteen-year-old John Silas Edens (D. H. and John Silas had served in the Texas Army after San Jacinto for three-month terms), and John Murchison, Sadler's brother-in-law who had served in the Texas Army from April 24-July 24, 1836, in Leonard Mabbitt's company. Several members were signers of the recent Fort Houston petition including John Crist, Stephen Crist, Spencer Hobbs, P. O. Lumpkin and William T. Smith.

It became evident to the men on duty near Fort Houston that the Cordova Rebellion was far from over. Cordova's rebels had successfully enlisted the Kickapoos, whose village was located north of Fort Houston in what is now the northeastern corner of Anderson County, to their cause, and the rebellion's forces were thus at their peak shortly after Rusk had been ordered to disband his companies in Nacogdoches.

Mabbitt's men patrolled the frontier of Houston County from the Trinity eastward toward the Neches. His patrols and foraging parties were frequently harassed by Indians who were acting in cooperation with Cordova's forces.[24] Mabbitt's reports to General

Rusk helped encourage the general to recall his forces in early October.

General Rusk correctly felt that the Indians were stockpiling whiskey, lead and powder during this lull, and Texas scouts soon discovered that Indian camps were on the move. The stage had been set for what was to be a bloody war with the Indians and a tragic period for W. T. Sadler.

* * * *

With the approach of cooler weather, Major General Rusk decided it was time to take to the field again to quell Cordova's Rebellion. From Nacogdoches he sent a letter to the citizens of Houston County on October 1, 1838, to authorize the raising of two to three-hundred volunteers "to defend the country and chastise the Indians."[25]

Rusk also wrote to Major Elisha Clapp, who had been the third senior officer on his staff during the previous summer campaign, in San Augustine on October 1, authorizing him to raise 150 volunteers for protection of the frontier and to go out against the Indians. After rounding up volunteers, Clapp was instructed to join General Kelsey Douglass and his volunteers at Fort Houston on Monday, October 15.

Clapp found no shortages of volunteers to engage the Indians and wrote to Rusk from San Augustine on the evening of October 5.

> On this day we had a meeting of the neighborhood & out of forty men, thirty six turned out as volunteers.
>
> I have not heard from Fort Houston since you received express from Maj. Mabbitt. I have no doubt but that the Indians and Mexicans are embodied near Kickapoo village and in all probability we can get a fight near home. We are in the need of ammunition & cannot effect a campaign without it. I would like to hear of Maj. Douglass' success in raising volunteers. It may be that we need all that we can get. I would go against them myself but I do not think it would be a prudent measure unless I have a larger force. Your order to raise men for our protection I must inform you met with universal hallelujahs & hurrahs, it being the first legal order of the kind ever sent forth officially to our country . . . .
>
> Elisha Clapp

The Killough Massacre. This marker, made of native stone, stands as a memorial to the eighteen members of the Killough family who were killed or captured by the Indians on October 5, 1838. The marker is located in what is now northern Anderson County, near the little community of Mount Selman. Author's Collection.

* * * *

THE VIOLENCE ESCALATES AGAIN

As Major Clapp, Captain Sadler and other Texan leaders were assembling their volunteer outfits, the Indians continued on their warpath through October. On October 5, an attack was made on the Killough family which lived on a creek just inside the Cherokee claim just south of the Neches Saline. Aware of the presence of Cordova's forces in the area, Isaac Killough Sr., his four sons and their families went to their fields to harvest their crops before winter. An unarmed group of the family was ambushed and killed en route to the fields. The rest of the Killoughs and their neighboring families fled for their lives as the Indians descended and began slaughtering the families.[26]

Isaac Killough Sr. died in his yard with eighteen bullet wounds, and the entire George Wood family had been killed when the massacre ended. Between the Wood, Barakias Williams and Killough families, eighteen family members were murdered or captured on October 5. More than half the family members managed to escape and find horses for the long ride to safety with their wives and children.

The Killough family's surviving members implicated the Cherokees, but the slaughter might actually have been conducted by a combined force of Shawnees and Biloxis.[27] The Killough massacre occurred about six miles east from the Kickapoo Village in the extreme north of what is now Anderson County. Many of the survivors made their way to Lacy's Fort about forty miles away. This was the largest and bloodiest depredation in early East Texas history, surpassing even the Parker's Fort attack. One early Texas historian attributed these slayings to Cordova's Mexicans and Indians.[28] The resulting excitement caused General Rusk to call for volunteers to gather at Lacy's Fort. Two of the surviving Killough brothers, Allen and Nathaniel, would quickly become involved in the East Texas Indian campaign.

Fort Lacy was located along the Old San Antonio Road on the southern boundary of Cherokee land on the outskirts of present Alto on Highway 21. The structure itself was the former home of Martin Lacy who, as a private in Captain Costley's company, had helped to build Fort Houston during late 1836. The local Kickapoo and Biloxi Indians became increasingly hostile in 1838 as he was operating a trading house, so Lacy built the fortifications around his farmhouse. During the course of the Cordova Rebellion, Fort Lacy would become a key operations and supply house for many companies of the Third Militia Brigade under Major General Rusk.[29]

While he was busy recruiting for General Rusk's next expedition, Major Elisha Clapp received notice of the Killough attack and ordered Captain Sadler's company to march to Fort Houston to join Major

Lacy's Fort, located near the present town of Alto, was a refuge for the survivors of the Killough Massacre of October 5.
Author's Collection.

COMPOSITION OF FORCES OPERATING FROM FORT HOUSTON: OCTOBER 1838
FIRST BATTALION, THIRD BRIGADE, VOLUNTEER RANGERS
MAJOR LEONARD H. MABBITT, COMMANDING

CAPTAIN BRADSHAW'S MOUNTED RIFLEMEN

James Bradshaw... Capt.	George Isaacs	Benjamin A. Vansickle
James Allison... 1st Sgt.	Nathaniel Killough	Dr. James Jefferson Ware
PRIVATES	B. Lacey	Elijah Wheeler
William Allison Jr.	John Marshall	Alexander White
Andrew Jackson Click	Jacob Pruett	John "Young" Williams
Dr. Elisha J. DeBard	Len Pruett	Leonard Williams
Beverly Greenwood	Martin J. Pruett	Thomas Williams
James Hall	William Robinson	

CAPTAIN BROWN'S MOUNTED GUNMEN

Squire Brown..... Capt.	William M. Frost	J. P. Mosley
C. T. Crawford... 1st Lt.	Calvin J. Fuller	James O'Neal
George F. Martin 2nd Lt.	Ponton Fuller	M. L. Phillips
Samuel Brooks .. 1st Sgt.	Amos H. Gates	T. J. Quesenberry
H. Gilliland .... 2nd Sgt.	James Gilliland	Isaac Raines
Eler D. Hanks .. 3rd Sgt.	William P. Gilliland	Joel D. Raines
Charles Shanks .. 4th Sgt.	Charles Gilmore	Jon D. Raines
David F. Webb 1st Corp.	Alfred M. Hallmark	Wiley Rogers
C. C. White .. 2nd Corp.	Isiah Hamilton	Thomas M. Scott
Thomas Hanks 3rd Corp.	T. J. Hanks	William Scott
Wm Thompson 4th Corp.	Augustin Blackburn Hardin	Joseph Shanks
PRIVATES:	E. R. Harris	Daniel Smiley
L. L. Artage	Charles Johnson	John Smith
William Bates	A. T. Jones	J. H. Smith
Thomas Berry	Jesse H. Looney	Robert Waggoner
James E. Box	Mathew Mabin	J. Walker
Newton Brownfield	Daniel Marteth	W. G. Walker
Daniel Buez	Alexander McKenzie	B. W. Watson
Julius Bullock	Lacy McKenzie	James Weeks
John W. Carpenter	John D. Miller	John White
James Cartwright	John Mitchell	John Wilson
Daniel L. Crist	Jacob C. Morrow	

Mabbitt. Before departing, Sadler and the other men old enough to have families left their loved ones in the care of older men and women. Several of the families of his men were gathered in the home of John Edens, located a few miles south of the present southern boundary of Anderson County near the present community of Augusta on San Pedro Creek. Edens was a Tennessee native who had emigrated to Texas in 1831 and father of three of Sadler's privates.

CAPTAIN SADLER'S MOUNTED RANGERS

William T. Sadler . Capt.	Jacob Crist	Robert Madden
John Wortham ... 1st Lt.	John Crist	Thomas Mitchell
John Edward Nite 2nd Lt.	Stephen Crist	John Murchison
Thomas Hays Orderly Sgt.	Balis Edens	Benjamin Parker
PRIVATES:	Darius H. Edens	Daniel Parker Jr.
Britton H. Adams	John Silas Edens	Dickerson Parker
Sephus Adams	John C. Gallion	William H. Pate
Solomon Adams	John Crawford Grigsby	Dr. William Perry
William H. Adams	Mathew Dewey T. Hallmark	Elijah B. Reneau
John Bascus	William Calvert Hallmark	P. T. Robinson
Armstead Bennett	Green Benjamin Hardwick	William T. Smith
Stephen Bennett	John A. Harris	Hiram C. Vansickle
Samuel C. Box	James Head	John Walker
Thomas Griffin Box	Spencer Hobbs	Martin A. Walker
Reuben Brown	Dr. William G. W. Jowers	Phillip Walker
George W. Browning	Joseph Kennedy	Samuel G. Wells
Daniel M. Crist	Pleiades Orion Lumpkin	

CAPTAIN SNIVELY'S MOUNTED RANGERS

Jacob Snively ..... Capt.	Delores Cartenas	John Rovan
John H. Davis ....1st Lt.	Charles Chevallier	John Rowan
James W. Cleveland 1st Lt.	Josiah Taylor Childers	M. McRoy
William W. Umsted 2nd Lt.	William Cobb	Justus Shearwood
M. D. Boyd .... 1st Sgt.	James Dickerson	Augustus W. Slawson
Jackson Ward .. 2nd Sgt.	James G. Dixon	James Triplett
John Jacobs .... 3rd Sgt.	Joseph Durst	Samuel Turner
J. D. O'Kelly ... 4th Sgt.	Henry Gough	William Henry Vardeman
John W. Fowler 1st Corp.	John Hunter	Moses Wells
B. Steward.... 2nd Corp.	James G. Hyde	George Washington Welsh
William W. Wade .Bugler	Michael P. Kelley	Samuel W. Wilds
PRIVATES:	Joel Langham	John Wright
James Alexander	William McKaughn	
A. J. Blythe *	Joseph Meradith	*Transferred into this company
A. W. Blythe*	Stewart Meradith	on Sept. 21 from Captain
Champain Blythe *	Benjamin Moore	Brown's company. Roster does
George A. Box	John C. Morrison	not include five men who joined
Sebastian Box	Asa Rolling	Capt. Snively's company shortly
Joseph Buffington	Louis Rose	after Kickapoo.

As Sadler's company headed for Fort Houston, another significant attack on East Texas settlers occurred on October 8. William F. Henderson's twenty-five-man surveying party was working on land claims far beyond the white settlements on Richland Creek in present Navarro County when they were attacked by an estimated three-hundred Indians. Early estimates claimed these to be Kickapoos. In a long and bloody afternoon gunfight about sixteen Texans were killed, plus some of the Indians. One of the five Texan survivors of this action was Walter P. Lane, a San Jacinto veteran, who was shot in the leg.

* * * *

In Nacogdoches, General Rusk was under pressure to round up another group of volunteers to resist this latest Indian uprising. Almost all of the men who had followed him on the July-August 1838 expedition had been discharged into civilian life. When word arrived of the Killough massacre and the other such attacks in the Houston County area, Rusk hastily reassembled his men on October 10 and prepared to set out for Fort Houston to join Major Mabbitt's forces there.

At 10:00 a.m. on October 11, Rusk received news from a courier of Cherokee agent Charles H. Sims that the villages of Chief Bowles and Big Mush were deserted.[30] Rusk prepared to move at once for the Kickapoo Village, where earlier intelligence on Cordova's forces indicated them to be gathering. Chief Bowles had written to Rusk telling him that he was leaving because of threats against him by both Indians and Mexicans. Big Mush, one of his former Indian conspirators, wrote to Rusk informing him that Bowles' mixed Cherokee Indian and Mexican forces were camped at the Kickapoo's village.[31] This information indicated a divisive split in the Indian leadership in which the Cherokees had been governed jointly by the two chiefs. Bowles had been the War Chief, while Big Mush had been the Political Chief. Rusk departed before lunch on October 11 with more than fifty men.[32]

Although meager in size, Rusk's force was joined by more men en route, and he hoped to meet with the companies under Major Mabbitt before confronting the Indians. From Fort Houston, Major Mabbitt had more than 175 men formed in four companies that would greatly benefit General Rusk's cause.[33] They marched from Fort Houston to join Rusk in the field, but Mabbitt's men would have more than a little difficulty in effecting this rendezvous.

Chapter Eight

MABBITT'S SKIRMISH AND THE BATTLE OF KICKAPOO

October 12-16, 1838

While General Rusk's troops marched toward Fort Houston, the four companies at Fort Houston under Major Mabbitt were well aware that Cordova's rebel forces were preparing to make a stand at Kickapoo Springs in the Neches area. Rusk had directed Mabbitt to meet him at Fort Duty, four miles west of the Neches River and about ten miles from Fort Houston.

Fort Duty was on the league and labor of Richard Duty, who had built a two-story log cabin in 1837 which measured twenty-four feet square. Earlier settlers had built homes here near the Snake and Stills Creeks but had been driven back to Nacogdoches in 1836 by the Indian harassment. Duty lived on the second floor of the home, while on the first floor as many as forty local settlers would sleep during Indian danger. Richard Duty himself was later shot by Indians during an attack and died in his fort.[1]

Mabbitt started on his way to Fort Duty, leading the formation with his two companies commanded by captains Bradshaw and Snively. Following him was the volunteer company of Captain Sadler, and bringing up the rear of the procession was the large ranging company of Captain Squire Brown. The trail leading toward the Neches and Fort Duty did not allow widespread groups of horses, so the companies generally filed along behind each other. Unbeknownst to these Texans, there were watchful eyes in the thickets around them who intended to use the forest's cover to their best advantage.

At a point about six miles east from Fort Houston on October 12, the trailing forces of Texans in Major Mabbitt's force were ambushed by a group of Indians and by Mexicans of Cordova's

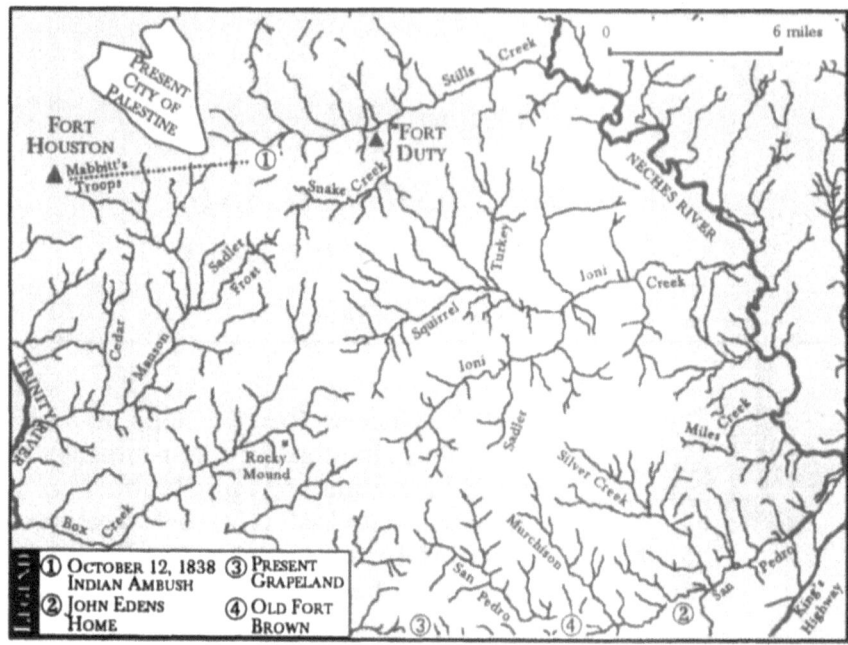

Map showing relationship of the location of the ambush against Major Mabbitt's Fort Houston troops to the John Edens Home near present Augusta where some of Captain Sadler's men left their loved ones.

forces led by Juan Flores and Juan Cruz.² The last Texans were marching a mile or more behind Mabbitt's leading forces when they were attacked. Caught completely off guard by a flurry of gunfire, these men were said to have "displayed great gallantry" in this ambush, but they did suffer casualties.

The brunt of the assault fell upon Captain Brown's rearmost company. Four of his men were killed during the fighting: Julius Bullock, John W. Carpenter, Thomas M. Scott and John Wilson. Carpenter had fought with Captain Sadler at San Jacinto and had only recently been among the signers of Fort Houston's appeal for help to Sam Houston. A survey of the battlefield later showed that Carpenter and a Caddo chief likely exchanged lethal shots with each other simultaneously from about thirty yards. Carpenter may have pursued the chief for some distance, because their bodies were found approximately half a mile from the area of the main skirmish.

The main fighting occurred on the path where Mabbitt's forces were ambushed, but firing continued on into the woods nearby as the Texans rallied to drive off their attackers. There is no record of anyone from Sadler's company being wounded, but Captain

Battle of Kickapoo: October 16, 1838
Summary of Forces: Third Brigade Texas Militia

COMMAND STAFF:

Thomas Jefferson Rusk	Major General
Hugh McLeod	Adjutant General
Major David Spangler Kaufman	Volunteer Aide-de-Camp
Major James Reily	Volunteer Aide-de-Camp
Major Isaac Watts Burton	Volunteer Aide-de-Camp
Major Baley C. Walters	Brigade Commander
Major Leonard H. Mabbitt	Brigade Commander

COMPANY ROSTERS:

CAPTAIN BOX'S MOUNTED RIFLEMEN

James Edward Box Capt.	Darius H. Edens	James Head
William Young Lacy 1st Sgt.	William M. Frost	Spencer Hobbs
PRIVATES:	John C. Gallion	Pleiades O. Lumpkin
John Bascus	Amos H. Gates	Alexander McKenzie
Samuel C. Box	Alfred M. Hallmark	Thomas Mitchell
Thomas Griffin Box	Mathew D. T. Hallmark	Jacob S. Morrow
George W. Browning	William Calvert Hallmark	Elijah B. Reneau
Daniel M. Crist	Green Benjamin Hardwick	Hiram C. Vansickle
Balis Edens	John A. Harris	William W. Wilkinson

Note: Captain Box's company was created on October 14, 1838 at Fort Houston. William M. Frost, William Lacy, Alexander McKenzie, Jacob Morrow and A. H. Gates received from Captain Brown's company and W. W. Wilkinson from Captain Brookfield. All others transferred from Captain Sadler's company.

CAPTAIN BRADSHAW'S MOUNTED RIFLEMEN

James Bradshaw .. Capt.	George Isaacs	Benjamin Anderson Vansickle
James Allison ... 1st Sgt.	Nathaniel Killough	Dr. James Jefferson Ware
PRIVATES	B. Lacey	Elijah Wheeler
William Allison Jr.	John Marshall	Alexander White
Andrew Jackson Click	Jacob Pruett	John "Young" Williams
Dr. Elisha J. DeBard	Len Pruett	Leonard Williams
Beverly Greenwood	Martin J. Pruett	Thomas Williams
James Hall	William Robinson	

CAPTAIN BROOKFIELD'S MOUNTED RANGERS

Wm. C. Brookfield . Capt.	John P. Barnett	G. W. Henchett
Presley Gossett .. 1st Sgt.	John E. Clapp	Joseph Lopez
William Gossett . 2nd Sgt.	Mills I. Eason	Alfred M. Liles
John Allbright Orderly Sgt.	Ira P. Ellis	Zachariah Maddan
PRIVATES	Richard B. Finch	John A. Muncriff
Refugio Ballensweller	James L. Gossett	Ira C. Shute

Captain Brown's Mounted Gunmen

Squire Brown .... Capt.	Ponton Fuller	Isaac Raines
Corley T. Crawford 1st Lt.	James Gilliland	Joel D. Raines
George F. Martin 2nd Lt.	William P. Gilliland	Jon D. Raines
Samuel Brooks .. 1st Sgt.	Charles Gilmore	Wiley Rogers
H. Gilliland .... 2nd Sgt.	Isiah Hamilton	Thomas M. Scott
Eler D. Hanks .. 3rd Sgt.	Thomas J. Hanks	William Scott
Charles Shanks . 4th Sgt.	Augustin Blackburn Hardin	Joseph Shanks
C. C. White .. 2nd Corp.	E. R. Harris	Daniel Smiley
Thomas Hanks 3rd Corp.	Charles Johnson	J. Smith
Wm Thompson 4th Corp.	A. T. Jones	J. H. Smith
Privates:	Jesse H. Looney	Robert Waggoner
L. L. Artage	Mathew Mabin	J. Walker
William Bates	Daniel Marteth	W. G. Walker
Thomas Berry	John D. Miller	B. W. Watson
Newton Brownfield	John Mitchell	James Weeks
Daniel Buez	J. P. Mosley	John White
James Cartwright	James O'Neal	
Daniel L. Crist	M. L. Phillips	
Calvin J. Fuller	T. J. Quesenberry	

Captain Durst's Mounted Volunteers

John Durst .... Capt.	Robert Bean	Jackson Little
James D. Long .. 1st Sgt.	Wily Burrow	Hugh Rennerd
Theodore B. Starks Ord. Sgt.	Levi B. Dikes	John Roark
Solomon Harkil .. Corp.	Asa Dorsett	Antonio Sanchez
Russell Roark .... Corp.	Peter Harper	Elbridge G. Sevier
Privates	___ Herby	
Isaac Bean	Adam Johnson	

Captain Sadler's Mounted Rangers

William T. Sadler . Capt.	Reuben Brown	Daniel Parker Jr.
John Wortham ... 1st Lt.	Jacob Crist	Dickerson Parker
John Edward Nite 2nd Lt.	John Crist	William H. Pate
Thomas Hays Orderly Sgt.	Stephen Crist	Dr. William Perry
Privates:	John Silas Edens	P. T. Robinson
Britton H. Adams	John Crawford Grigsby	William T. Smith
Sephus Adams	Dr. William G. W. Jowers	John Walker
Solomon Adams	Joseph Kennedy	Martin A. Walker
William H. Adams	Robert Madden	Phillip Walker
Armstead Bennett	John Murchison	Samuel G. Wells
Stephen Bennett	Benjamin Parker	

Captain Smith's Nacogdoches Company

Robert W. Smith .. Capt.	Jeremiah Bailey	Henry M. Rogers
Stephen F. Sparks 1st Lt.	William Bromley	Samuel Rogers
Wm. W. Taylor.. 2nd Lt.	Ambrose Hulon Crain	Luis Sanchez
Eli G. Sparks ..... 1st Sgt.	Theodore Dorset	Hiram B. Stephens
Privates	Delores Martinez	Heartwell Twaisime
Elijah Anderson	James McAnulty	Robert H. Watkins
Howard Bailey	Edward Price	Daniel Weeks

Captain Snively's Mounted Rangers

Jacob Snively .... Capt.	Sebastian Box	Benjamin Moore
John H. Davis ... 1st Lt.	Joseph Buffington	John C. Morrison
James W. Cleveland 1st Lt.	Delores Cartenas	Asa Rolling
William W. Umsted 2nd Lt.	Charles Chevallier	Louis Rose
M. D. Boyd .... 1st Sgt.	Josiah Taylor Childers	John Rovan
Jackson Ward .. 2nd Sgt.	William Cobb	John Rowin
John Jacobs .... 3rd Sgt.	James Dickerson	Mack McRoy
J. D. O'Kelly ... 4th Sgt.	James G. Dixon	Justus Shearwood
John W. Fowler 1st Corp.	Joseph Durst	Augustus W. Slawson
B. Steward .. 2nd Corp.	Henry Gough	James Triplett
William W. Wade . Bugler	John Hunter	Samuel Turner
Privates:	James G. Hyde	William Henry Vardeman
James Alexander	Michael P. Kelley	Moses Wells
A. J. Blythe	Joel Langham	George Washington Welsh
A. W. Blythe	William McKaughn	Samuel W. Wilds
Champain Blythe	Joseph Meradith	John Wright
George A. Box	Stewart Meradith	

Captain Williams' Volunteer Company

Joseph Williams .. Capt.	Levi P. Cadenhead	Lyman H. Matthews
James Fisher ..... 1st Lt.	Davis Cook	John A. Medford
John Deen ..... 2nd Lt.	Thomas Cook	Daniel Meredith
Wm. Laucer Orderly Sgt.	Thomas Cox	Isaac Stokely
Privates	William Curl	George T. Walters
John Able	Levi Ford	Robert Walters
Durham Avant	James Foster	Tillman Walters
R. P. Banks	Asbury Griggs	Wayne Walters
Zachariah W. Bottoms	Thomas Grison	William Wasnell
Henry Mitchell Brewer	Isaac Hicks	Joseph E. White
James Brewer	Jesse C. Kincannon	James Windsor
John Brewer	George W. Knox	Martin Windsor
William Brewer Jr.	John Lively	
James Brown	Joseph Looce	

Brown's company suffered two more wounded, First Corporal David F. Webb and Private Lacy McKenzie.

Captains Snively and Bradshaw returned quickly with Major Mabbitt to engage the enemy, but the Mexicans and Indians took flight through the forest. An accurate determination of the size of the rebel forces could not be made, but it was clear that they did not want an organized fight. Mabbitt's forces were credited with killing five Indians, including the chief.[3] Some of the Indian bodies were dragged from the battlefield for ceremonial burials.

Major General Thomas Jefferson Rusk, commander of the Texas Militia during the Indian battles of 1838 and 1839. He had previously served as the first Secretary of War for the Republic of Texas. Rusk led the companies of Captain Sadler and eight others in the Battle of Kickapoo Village on October 16, 1838. Courtesy of the San Jacinto Museum of History.

Mabbitt and his men hastened onward to their rendezvous with General Rusk's Nacogdoches forces. They reached the campground at the Jack Still place (east of present Palestine) well after nightfall and told the story of their ambush. One of Rusk's men, William Y. Lacy, the son of Indian agent Martin Lacy, recalled, "That night we were reinforced by Col. Mabbitt's command from Fort Houston. On his march to join us, his rear guard was attacked by (Cordova's) forces."[4]

The next morning, October 13, Rusk and Mabbitt's forces began their march back westward to Fort Houston to organize. En route, they passed back over the scene of the previous day's skirmish. "In looking over the battleground, we found a Caddo chief evidently killed by Carpenter, as they were lying within 30 feet of each other," wrote Lacy.[5] The casualties of the Cordova skirmish were carried back to Fort Houston, and the combined forces under Mabbitt and Rusk were known to have spent the night of October 13-14 at the fort. All four casualties of this fight were buried in unmarked graves in the Fort Houston cemetery.[6]

During the following day, October 14, Major Mabbitt and General Rusk took the time to better organize their troops. Another mounted "spy" company was organized and placed under command of Captain James E. Box. A veteran of the Nacogdoches Volunteers at San Jacinto, Box was promoted from Brown's unit for his actions in the fight two days previous. William Lacy from Rusk's forces became his first sergeant, or second-in-command. The majority of the other men now under Box's command came from Captain Sadler's company.

The overall group at Fort Houston was under command of Major General Rusk and his friend Colonel Hugh McLeod, the Adjutant General of Texas. In addition to several aides-de-camp, the Texan forces were directly under the command of majors Mabbitt and Baley C. Walters of Nacogdoches. Among the other company commanders from Nacogdoches was Captain Robert W. Smith, who had been first lieutenant of Sadler's San Jacinto company two years before.

Some accounts say that Rusk had up to seven-hundred men with him, but Rusk's own count of his men on October 14 was that "my force amounted to about 200 men."[7] By best count, it would appear that Rusk and McLeod actually had just over 260 men at their discretion as of this date. Records from Captain Box's company show that the volunteer privates on this Indian expedition were paid $25 per month, the first sergeant $40 per month and the militia captain $60 per month.

General Rusk did not disguise the fact that he expected a confrontation with the Indians and Mexican rebels. He used some of his last hours at Fort Houston on October 14 to write to his brother in Nacogdoches of the action he would soon be faced with. Postmarked from Fort Houston, Rusk's letter stated:

> I am just about taking up the line of march from this place to the place where the Indians are said to be encamped, which is about 25 miles from here. Their numbers are variously estimated at from 150 to 600 warriors. My effective forces will be under 200 men – I know well that should I succeed no one will find fault, but should I fail I shall be abused for imprudence.
>
> If Gen. Houston and some others had been guided by feelings of patriotism and not by low and selfish purposes, I should have had in the field at least 500 men; but let success or misfortune attend my efforts. I have the consolation of knowing that all my efforts have been directed to my country's good. If the Indians are not routed, the frontier will be laid in ruins and if that is done the people of Texas will have to fight two-thirds of the Indians on the U.S. frontier ....[8]

That Rusk expected a hellacious fight was evident by his closing line, "If cut off, I shall leave my wife and children much less than many men have sold lots for in the City of Houston, who never paid anything for them except a sacrifice of Principle." The leader of the Texas Militia promised to send his brother David more news in four days, but he closed his letter as the troops started to move. He reminded his brother, in the event he did not return, that he was owed four-hundred acres of land by James Smith, for which he had already paid.

In perhaps the first after-action account of the impending engagement, Colonel Hugh McLeod wrote to President-Elect Mirabeau B. Lamar on October 22 of Rusk's strategy.

> The General resolved to move on at once after the enemy, seeing that a victory was necessary to give the people breathing time and confidence. He did not march direct to the Saline, as he feared they would perceive his approach and retire before him. He marched first to Fort Houston, laid in what supplies he could procure, and marched then across towards the Saline.[9]

The Kickapoo village was located approximately thirty miles to the northeast of Fort Houston and about 2.5 miles south-southeast of the present town of Frankston. En route on the afternoon of October 15, Mabbitt's men spotted a few Indian braves passing the abandoned Kickapoo village. They were believed to be carrying meat to Cordova's forces.[10] Rusk's troops marched northeast until shortly before sundown, at which time it was decided to set up camp for the night for mutual protection.

The men pitched camp for the night of October 15-16 at the old Kickapoo Village in the extreme northern corner of Anderson County. The village was perhaps a half mile northwest of the Neches River on a horseshoe bend of Kickapoo Creek, a small tributary of the Neches. The camp's spot was chosen in a defensive area that they believed could prevent a surprise attack.

Cordova's rebels had been tracking the movements of Rusk's troops, and they soon announced their presence. Rusk recorded that at 10:00 p.m., the "enemy attempted to fire the woods around us, but failed."[11] Probably using gunpowder, the Indians tried unsuccessfully to trap the crowded Texans in a deadly forest fire.

The fires fizzled out but the woods around the Texas camp were obviously filled with Indians. The camp itself was arranged in a

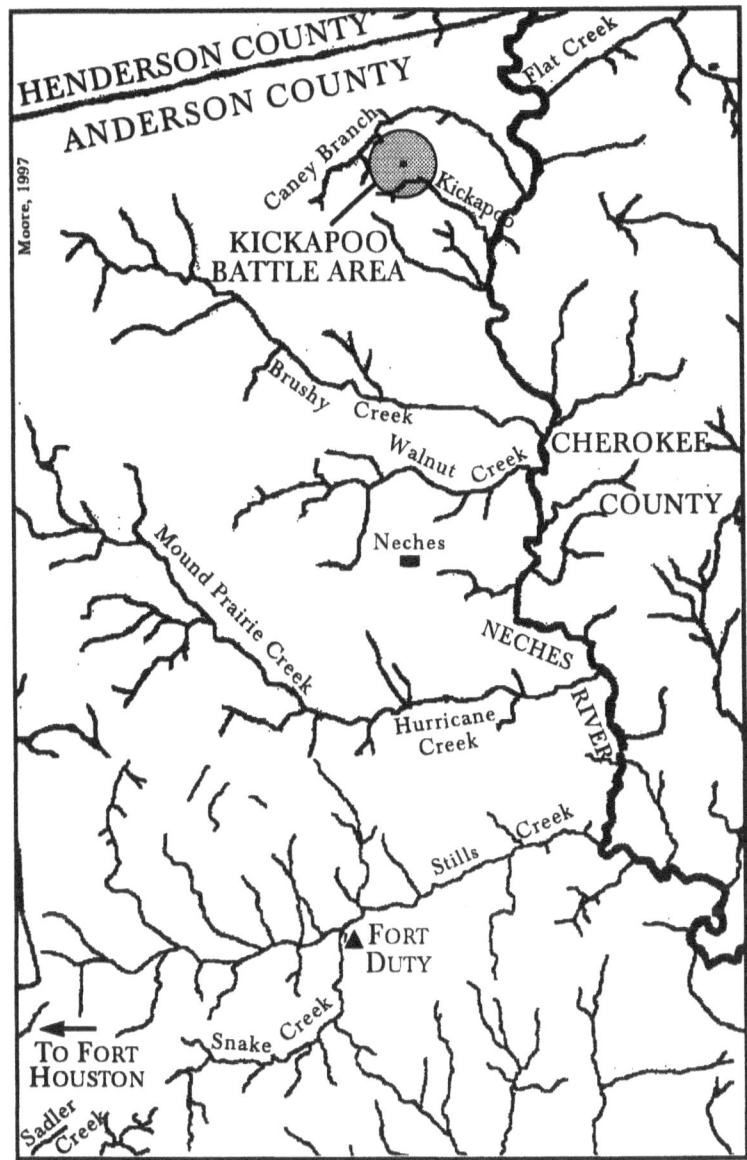

Battle of Kickapoo: October 16, 1838

This map shows the area of present Anderson County in which the Battle of Kickapoo occurred. From Fort Houston, General Thomas J. Rusk, commander of the Texas Militia in 1838, led nine volunteer companies, including that of Captain Sadler, of mounted gunmen to Kickapoo Village. On the morning of October 16, their camp was assailed by an estimated force of 250 Indians and Mexican rebels.

After suffering one man killed, at least a dozen more wounded and some thirty-five horses killed, Rusk's Texas forces managed to kill or wound an estimated seventy of the rebels. This campaign is also referred to as the "Kickapoo War."

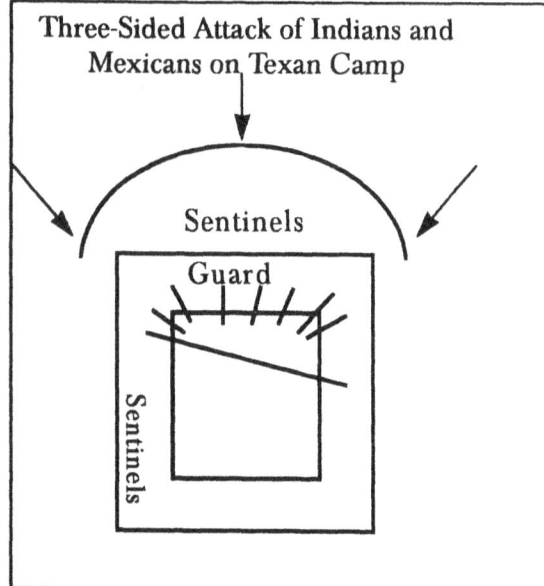

The Battle of Kickapoo, also called "The Kickapoo War," was fought on October 16, 1838. Captain Sadler's militia company was in the thick of the action and one of his volunteers was seriously wounded. This illustration of the square-shaped Texan camp is based on the sketch of Col. Hugh McLeod in an October 22 letter to President Mirabeau Lamar.
(See Gulick's Papers of Mirabeau Buonaparte Lamar, *Volume II, 266.)*

square with the horses effectively tied off in the center. Posted on two ends of the square was a sentinel, plus a guard who was stationed with the horses to prevent them from being stolen. Those who could sleep during this tense night were awakened on at least one occasion by gunfire from the uneasy Texas sentinels. During the night, two of Cordova's spies were fired upon by the Texas guards and one horse was seized from them.

* * * *

BATTLE AT KICKAPOO VILLAGE

Long before the sun peeked through the hardwoods and pines of the East Texas forest near Kickapoo Creek on October 16, hundreds of Indians and Mexican rebels were sneaking in toward the Texan camp. Just after daybreak, the forest around the militia camp suddenly erupted with gunfire and war whoops in yet another surprise attack. The attacking force was later estimated to be at least several hundred and was known to have included the Kickapoos plus Delawares, Caddos, Coushattas, a few Cherokees, some Kichais and Cordova with his rebel Mexicans.[12]

The first light of dawn and the very misty conditions of a lightly falling rain made it very difficult for the Texans to see their attackers.[13] The main attack on the Texas camp was made against the

At the site of the battle on Kickapoo Creek in Anderson County now stands a Centennial Marker which reads "Site of the Kickapoo Battlefield. Here Thomas J. Rusk with 200 Texans on October 16, 1838, attacked a band of hostile Indians and allied Mexicans, molesters of frontier settlements, and routed them."
Author's collection.

northern head of the square, and the first shots were fired within forty yards of the guard. Mexican and Indian attackers also fired from the upper eastern and upper western corners of the square-shaped campground, catching the unsuspecting Texans with fire from three sides. Due to the three-pronged attack, the Texans were "compelled to maintain the square," as Colonel McLeod wrote.

The companies which had slept in the extreme northern end of the camp ended up bearing the brunt of the assault. These were the companies of Captains Sadler, Snively, Box and Bradshaw under command of Major Mabbitt.[14] Ironically, these were the same men who had already been involved in the skirmish with Cordova's men on October 12.

The Indians had the advantage of being able to use large trees from which to fire behind. The woods were very open, giving them fairly clear shots at their enemies. This afforded them "an admirable opportunity for their favorite tactics of fighting behind a cover."[15]

Captain Sadler escaped the fight without injury, although nearly every man at the head of the camp's square had his clothes cut by flying steel balls. One of his fellow Texans, Colonel McLeod, later wrote that, "it was the closest shooting I ever saw to do so little execution."[16]

No one from Sadler's company was killed although his brother-in-law was seriously wounded in the head. John Murchison, fighting alongside Sadler, was knocked down by a direct hit. Anderson County historian A. J. Fowler later described young Murchison's wound at Kickapoo.

> He there received a ball in the forehead between the eyes, which knocked him down, but did not penetrate the skull. The thick, bony structure in the region of the eye arrested the force of the ball, which was partially spent. The ball lodged in the socket of the left eye against the eyebrow. Whence it was extracted, the wound resulted in no permanent injury to health or vision. Those who know the determined will of the man, jocularly remarked that his head was too hard to be penetrated by a bullet.[17]

General Rusk noted that the enemy attackers maintained a cavalry stationed on a hill just out of gun range, and he believed they were waiting to ride down upon any Texans who attempted to escape the ambush. Rusk at one point attempted to draw out some of his attackers by personally advancing twenty paces out from the camp and shouting, "You damned cowardly bastards! Come out and show yourselves like men!"[18] Their only response was wild yells and the continued firing of their rifles.

After about fifteen minutes of heavy fire's being exchanged, the shots began to die down around the camp. At this point, Rusk ordered a portion of his force to remain and protect the camp while he led the remainder of the companies in a charge against their attackers. The Texan offense sent the rebels fleeing on foot and horseback through the woods, and they were pursued for three quarters of a mile before Rusk ordered the men back to camp.

This motley force of attackers was estimated by Hugh McLeod to be about 250 men of various nationalities, including "Mexican negros, Coushattas, Caddoes, and some thought Keechies (Kichais)."[19] As for the number of attackers, Rusk wrote that "The force of the enemy I had no means of ascertaining, but it must have been very considerable, as the ground occupied by them was near half a mile in length."[20]

Once the chase against the Indians was given up, Rusk's forces made their way back to camp to assist the wounded. Eleven Indians were found dead on the ground, and the grass was full of trails of blood of others who may have been dragged away. Several blankets and other Indian belongings were found that had been dropped in flight.

Rusk wrote that Caddos, Coushattas, Biloxies, one Cherokee and two Mexicans were found among the dead.[21] The Texans later heard that the Indian force lost about thirty killed. Rusk felt that the blood trails his men found indicated that at least seventy Indians besides the eleven found had been wounded or killed. Most of the Indians fell within forty or fifty feet of the Texas lines. Afterwards, the enemy had fled in all directions in the dense forest.

McLeod also wrote that "Among the dead and the nearest to our camp was a Cherokee named Tail. Bowles says he was a bad Indian -- that he never could manage him and that he was well killed."[22]

Records of the Texan forces show that they suffered twelve men wounded and about thirty-five horses killed. Among the wounded was Daniel Crist of Fort Houston who was wounded in the hip and hand on October 16. The rifle balls were cut out by Dr. William Perry.[23] Private James Hall from Captain Bradshaw's company was badly wounded, but the camp surgeon felt that he would pull through. W. B. Killough, a survivor of the Killough Massacre, later wrote that his uncle Nathaniel was shot through the shoulder during the Kickapoo battle.[24]

This battle was later commonly referred to among Texans as the "Kickapoo War." Today, a Centennial Marker located along Highway 19 south of the town of Frankston in northeastern Anderson County stands in testament of the 1838 battle. The actual battlefield along Kickapoo Creek is believed to be located on the farm behind this sign. Once the Texans had Cordova's rebels on the move, the battle actually carried on over some distance in the vicinity of the old Indian village, Kickapoo Creek and the Neches River. Residents along a rural farmroad that follows the creek for some distance claim to still find arrowheads and other evidence of the early battle.

The Texans had held their own against the Mexican and Indian forces. It was a telling defeat for Vicente Cordova, and his rebellion had been effectively quelled for the time being by the strong showing of Texas forces. Cordova himself returned to Mexico, where he would remain until he and Flores could organize a new rebel force the following year.

The Battle of Kickapoo
Known Casualties Of October 16, 1838

Name	Rank/Rate	Company	Remarks
Thomas Berry	Private	Capt. Brown	Wounded
M. D. Boyd	First Sergeant	Capt. Snively	Wounded
Daniel L. Crist	Private	Capt. Brown	Wounded
Dr. Elisha J. DeBard	Private	Capt. Bradshaw	Wounded
James Hall	Private	Capt. Bradshaw	Wounded *
George Isaacs	Private	Capt. Bradshaw	Wounded
Michael P. Kelly	Private	Capt. Snively	Wounded
Nathaniel Killough	Private	Capt. Bradshaw	Wounded
John Murchison	Private	Capt. Sadler	Wounded
Mack McRoy	Private	Capt. Snively	Wounded
James Triplett	Private	Capt. Snively	Wounded
Dr. J. Jefferson Ware	Private	Capt. Bradshaw	Wounded
Thomas Williams	Private	Capt. Bradshaw	Wounded

* Died from his wounds on December 17, 1838.

Following this battle, Rusk wrote to Chief Bowles of the Cherokees, telling him that he had punished the Mexicans and Indians and that his men had killed one Cherokee. He also warned Bowles to keep his braves away from the Mexicans and advised the Cherokee chief to come to Nacogdoches soon with Chief Big Mush to hold a talk on the matters.[25] The Cherokees explained that they had been absent from their village during the Kickapoo battle because they had heard of the first fight on October 12. Chief Bowles feared that the whites would blame his people and come to destroy them and their villages.[26]

After the Kickapoo fight on October 16, General Rusk regrouped his men and immediately withdrew from the area. He and most of the men would head back toward Nacogdoches to reorganize and to call out more men for the war with the Indians. The wounded Texans were carried on litters to Fort Houston to recover. Among these was Sadler's brother-in-law, John Murchison. Murchison eventually recovered from his head wound and moved to La Grange the following year, from where he represented Fayette County in 1840-41 during the Fifth Congress of the Republic of Texas.[27]

Another wounded local was Dr. Elisha DeBard, whose wife learned of his painful wounds, packed provisions, and traveled on horseback with a faithful negro slave from Nacogdoches to Fort Houston to nurse her husband back to health. The DeBards later moved to Fort Houston, where Dr. DeBard became close friends with General Nat Smith, who had moved his family to the fort in late 1838.[28] The critically wounded Private James Hall survived until December 17 before dying from his wounds and being buried in the Fort Houston cemetery.

While at Fort Houston, Rusk's troops took the time to document their losses. At least three horses from Sadler's company had been killed, as evidenced by claims filed against the Republic of Texas for compensation. Robert Madden lost a gray mare that company mates P. T. Robinson and Crawford Grigsby, called upon to place a value on this personal property, estimated to be worth one-hundred dollars. John Walker's "hay horse was lost in the battle on the 16th," and its value was declared to be fifty dollars by fellow soldiers William H. Adams and Thomas Hays.

The claims were penned on October 19 at "Headquarters, Fort Houston" and were endorsed by Thomas Rusk. Sadler also authenticated each with "I certify that the above-named was a member of my company and lost the horse stated above. William T. Sadler, Capt."[29]

John Murchison was issued a certificate by Captain Sadler for the loss of a mare that was estimated at $275. He was paid $200 by a joint resolution approved by President Lamar on February 1, 1840 for a "horse killed in the battle that was fought by General Thomas J. Rusk against the hostile Indians and Mexicans on the 16th of October 1838 near the Kickapoo Village."[30]

Major General Rusk wrote a letter to the *Telegraph and Texas Register* in Houston which was published in the newspaper on November 3, 1838. He summed up the Battle of Kickapoo and then gave credit to his fellow officers.

> It would be difficult to find language to do justice to the officers and men: all fought with a spirit and determination seldom equalled. The officers in the action were Adj. Gen. McLeod, Maj. Kaufman, Maj. Reiley, and Maj. Burton, Volunteer Aids-de-Camp, Majors Walters and Mabbitt, Captains Box, Bradshaw, Snively, Smith, Williams, Durst, Sadler, Brookfield and Brown.

Shortly after arriving at Fort Houston, Captain Sadler and a group of his men struck out for the San Pedro Creek community in Houston County to check on their families. Victorious in battle, these men would soon find that they had lost greatly at home.

Chapter Nine

THE EDENS-MADDEN MASSACRE

October 18, 1838

Having been warned that the Kickapoos and Cherokees were on the warpath, the citizens of the area near San Pedro Creek, located slightly southwest of the present community of Augusta, gathered in the local households for mutual protection. The Indians, stirred up by Cordova's Rebellion, were believed to be rampaging with the intention of killing white people who had encroached on their lands. Captain Sadler and some of the men from his ranger company had left their siblings, wives and children at San Pedro Creek while they fought with Major Mabbitt in the two battles of Kickapoo.

Their families were gathered in the home of fifty-five-year-old John Edens, who had brought his family to Houston County from Illinois around 1831. By best count, there were nineteen men, women and children under the care of Edens and three other men: his thirty-three-year-old son-in-law James S. Madden (who had obtained a title to a league and labor of land in this area as of October 15, 1835); Martin Murchison (Sadler's father-in-law); and Elisha Moore, an older prospector who was temporarily visiting Texas from Alabama.

John Edens' San Pedro Creek home was a large wooden building of two main rooms with a dogtrot through the center. It was typical of the early East Texas farm homes, which used the dogtrot style to create natural air conditioning from the prevailing breezes. A number of recently constructed log homes in this area of Houston County had created a neighborhood of sorts.

Knowing that most of the able-bodied white men had gone off to fight, the blood-thirsty Indians descended upon the little Edens home on the cold, frosty night of Thursday, October 18, 1838.

Various early sources that discuss this attack give credit (or blame) for this event to the Cherokees, the Anadarkos or the Caddos. This little settlement was fairly surrounded by Indian tribes, ranging from the nearby peaceful Ionis on Sadler's land to more warlike bands of Anadarkos, Coushattas and Alabamas, who lived nearby on the Trinity River.[1]

The tribe most likely to have committed this attack was the Kickapoos, known to have been stirred up by the recent rebellion. In support of this are the statements of Elias Vansickle before the county court of Nacogdoches on January 25, 1839. He had been captured by Cordova's rebels on October 1, 1838, at the Neches Saline and was held hostage by these Mexicans and Indians for nearly three months. Vansickle stated, that while a prisoner in their camp,

> Some Kickapoos, a large number, came in and stated that they had killed the families of Eden and others, near Mustang Prairie, Houston County.[2]

The Edens family has presented two other possible motivations for the attack. One unlikely account is that the massacre was perpetrated by about a dozen Indians who were captured following the Kickapoo battle on October 16 and taken to Fort Houston, from where they escaped. No known account, however, mentions the capture of any Indians following the battle. Another theory that was later presented was that John Edens' land was situated on what was once an Indian campground on the banks of the San Pedro and that the Indians considered it to be sacred land.[3]

Regardless of which tribe was responsible and their precise motivation, the Indians waited until well after darkness on October 18 to make their move. Eleven well-armed Indians rode in on horseback that evening and were spotted heading toward San Pedro Creek. The braves passed by the home of William P. Davis, located a mile and a half from the Edens home, and were counted by some females at the Davis home around 9:00 p.m.[4]

The Edens home was quite crowded with all of the women and children under the care of the four older men. Aside from the dogtrot log home, there were several other buildings on the property including an outhouse and a little cabin for the family's slaves. Among the women present were Mrs. John Edens, Mrs. Sarah Hall Murchison (stepmother of Captain Sadler's wife), Mrs. Mary Murchison Sadler, Mrs. Lucinda Elizabeth Edens Madden (wife of James Madden), and Mrs. Nancy Halhouser Madden (wife

The Edens-Madden Massacre *of October 18, 1838, occurred in a dogtrot style log cabin in northern Houston County. The women and children were slaughtered in one room while the men were apparently trapped in the other room. Shown is Stephen F. Austin's 1838 cabin, which was reconstructed with original materials in San Felipe, Texas.* Author's collection.

of Robert Madden). The other inhabitants of the Edens home this night were at least eight young children of these women and a negro slave named Patsy.

The Indians waited until everyone had gone to bed for the night, watching as the men took to their own room. Apparently, some of the men had just checked on their children for a goodnight "chat" and were retiring back to their own room at the moment of attack.[5] The women, children and Patsy, the Edens family servant, were across the dogtrot in the other room with many of the guns. By the light of a bright moon, the Indians slipped up beside the house quietly before erupting with horrible "war whoops and yells fiendish...."[6]

Several Indians guarded the door to the room occupied by the men while several others burst into the other room with the women and children. With tomahawks and scalping knives in hand, the Indians proceeded to butcher their helpless inmates. The women cried out for help, but they were prevented from escaping and the men were prevented from coming to their rescue. According to one Texas historian, escape was prevented by "one powerful and hideous demon, guarding the doorway by spreading his arms and legs from side to side and grasping the lintels with his hands, all the while yelling and gloating rapturously over the bloody, sickening scene of death wrought within."[7]

All accounts seem to agree that the Indians attacked the grown women before moving on to the children. Lucinda Edens Madden, wife of James Madden, was savagely attacked. One chop of the tomahawk severed her collarbone while a second cut through two ribs near her spine. After a third blow opened a horrible gash in her back, Mrs. Madden "fell senseless upon the floor and was abandoned as dead."[8] With great physical force, the barbaric savages spared no mercy on the other women.

Captain Sadler's wife Mary was among the first to die. She and her stepmother, Sarah Murchison, and Mrs. John Edens quickly fell to the tomahawks and scalping knives while the raging Indians slashed into the other women and their defenseless children. One of the first published accounts of the Edens-Madden Massacre relates the horrible fate of one of the women slaughtered after Lucinda Madden had passed out. "Another lady was tomahawked and fell dead into the fireplace, her life's blood flowing so profusely as to extinguish the flames, and leave the fiends to complete the slaughter in semi-darkness."[9]

In one of the neighboring houses on the other side of San Pedro Creek, another group of women and children had gathered in the John Grigsby Jr. house this night. Young Ruth Ann Grigsby, sister of one of Sadler's rangers, and her family plainly heard the war whoops of the Indians and the terrified screams of women and children. Many of those in the Grigsby home fled barefooted into the cover of the woods in the creek bottom where they hid all night.[10]

In the crowded women's room of the Edens home, the wooden floors became saturated with blood as the occupants were brutally massacred. Three women, including Mary Sadler, were already dead. The Indians went after the children and remaining women with their tomahawks, and Nancy Madden, wife of Robert Madden of Captain Sadler's company, suffered a shot through her ear and a tomahawk wound in the back of her shoulder.

In the wild melee of attacking Indians and screaming children, Nancy Madden somehow managed to crawl from the room and burst into the men's room where she "fell exhausted by fright and loss of blood."[11] Assuming her to be mortally wounded, Martin Murchison and Elisha Moore quickly took this opportunity to slip out the door. They were immediately confronted by several savages on the threshold. Without time to shoot, the two older men took flight and were pursued for a mile or more through the woods by

THE EDENS-MADDEN MASSACRE OF HOUSTON COUNTY, TEXAS OCTOBER 18, 1838		
Names of those present:	Age: (where known)	Fate:
JOHN EDENS FAMILY		
John Edens	55	Escaped from the house.
Mrs. John Edens	-	Killed by the Indians.
Emily Edens	16	Killed by the Indians.
Caledonia Edens	3	Killed by the Indians.
Melissa Edens	1	Carried to safety by Patsy.
ROBERT MADDEN FAMILY		
Nancy Halhouser Madden	-	Seriously wounded; survived.
Mary Madden	3	Killed by the Indians.
JAMES S. MADDEN FAMILY		
James S. Madden	33	Escaped from the house.
Lucinda Elizabeth Edens Madden	31	Seriously wounded; survived.
Balis Erls Madden	9	Escaped from house and hid.
Robert Madden	7	Killed by the Indians.
Seldon Madden	5	Killed by the Indians.
MARTIN MURCHISON FAMILY		
Martin Murchison	48	Escaped from the house.
Mrs. Sarah Hall Murchison	-	Killed by the Indians.
Lycurgus Murchison	1	Killed or taken by Indians.
WILLIAM T. SADLER FAMILY		
Mrs. Mary Murchison Sadler	-	Killed by the Indians.
Sophia Sadler	infant	Killed by the Indians.
OTHERS PRESENT		
Elisha Moore	-	Escaped from the house.
Patsy	56	Edens servant; saved three people.

several of the braves. Murchison and Moore eventually outmaneuvered their pursuers, who probably went back for easier sport at the homesite.[12]

Once the Indians were distracted by the escape of the first two men, the other two, John Edens and James Madden, took advantage of the confusion to escape unhurt in another direction. John Edens was said to have fired one shot with an old horse pistol into the other room during the fight, but he was pulled away by one of the other men.[13] As would be expected, many later criticized the four older men for not fighting to their own deaths to save more of the women and children.

There were a large number of children in the women's room, and only two survived. Two of John Edens' daughters, Emily and

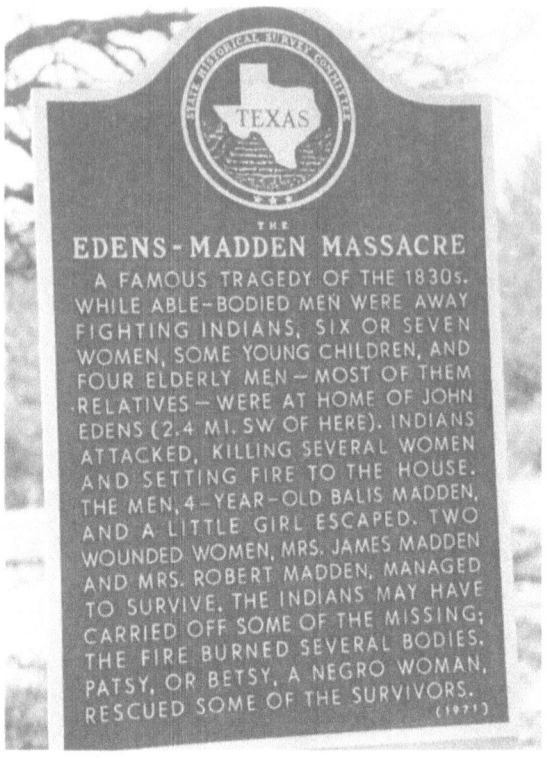

This marker is one of two erected by the State of Texas to commemorate the Edens-Madden Massacre of Houston County. This official historical marker was erected in 1971 in the present community of Augusta, located on FM 2022. Photo by Marshall L. Moore Jr.

Caledonia Edens, were killed as were two of his grandsons, Robert and Seldon Madden, both sons of James and Lucinda Madden. A fifth child, Nancy Madden's three-year-old daughter Mary, was also killed.[14] A sixth child, Mary Sadler's infant daughter Sophia, is believed to have been killed and her body left in the house, although many sources do not list her. Noted Texas historian Louis W. Kemp, in a biographical sketch of William Sadler obtained from the Texas State Library, noted that "Mrs. Sadler and her infant child were killed by Indians October 18, 183[8]."

Prior to fleeing from their scene of butchery, the Indians set fire to the Edens home. They ripped into the bedding and emptied the feathers into the room to fuel the blaze, then started the fire by spreading the remaining coals from the fireplace in the center of the room. In the confusion of flying feathers, rapidly spreading fire, and Indians busily scalping, severely wounded Lucinda Madden regained consciousness long enough to escape from the room shortly before the Indians departed. As she later related to her grandson, she crawled through the legs of an Indian guard at the door who was wrapped up in the excitement of the moment.[15]

There is little left of the old Edens cemetery at the site of the massacre, but the Edens family still maintains the remnants, located about 150 yards south of where the old home burned. The land, about 2.5 miles southwest of Augusta, is now owned by the Champion Paper Company. This 1994 photo shows Edens family historian Art Hall beside the original marker erected by the State at the massacre site. Photo courtesy of Arthur H. Hall.

According to this same account, Lucinda found the strength to pull herself far out of the view of the Indians to save her own life.

    Crawling to the corner of a fence, she lay there, bleeding, while the Indians set fire to the buildings and destroyed the entire group of houses with the exception of one little out building. As she lay in this fence corner, my grandfather leaped the fence right by her, hotly pursued by the Indians, but she was not seen by either. My grandfather escaped into the woods. After the fire had died down and the Indians [had] gone, my grandmother pulled herself into this little building which had been left, and lay there alone all night. I have heard from her own lips the remarkable statement that she "never slept better in all her life," a fact probably due to the severe loss of blood.[16]

She would not be the only survivor from among the women and children, however. Lucinda Madden's four-year-old son Balis Erls

Madden observed his mother's slithering past the Indian guard and followed suit. Young Balis slipped through, apparently unnoticed, and ran off behind the slaves' quarters to hide all night in what he described as a "hog bed." The young boy remained safe here because the Indians did not molest the negro slaves.[17]

The Indians stole the guns from the women's room and took all but one of the horses tied up near the Edens home. Some of their own inferior guns were discarded in favor of those of the settlers before the attackers retired in the direction of Fort Houston.[18] One account claims some of the children may have been carried off by the Indians, while another states that some had their brains smashed out against the side of the home before being tossed into the fire.[19]

Captain Sadler's first child was among those whose fate in the confusion of the massacre remains unclear. According to the story he later passed on to his family, however, he had lost his wife, child and mother-in-law in the attack. This source states that "the bodies of Mary Murchison Sadler and her child were never found. They were presumably burned in the fire which destroyed the house."[20] Supporting the child's loss is the testimony of Lula Sadler Davis, a niece of W. T. Sadler who later lived near her uncle for many years, who told Robert H. Sadler that Mary *and her baby* were killed by Indians.[21]

There is yet another baby that has possibly been missed in the reporting of the Edens home depredation. Nacogdoches County records show that Martin Murchison's wife delivered a son named Lycurgus in 1837, prior to Houston County's creation that year.[22] What became of this child is unknown; he is not directly mentioned in any accounts.

Undoubtedly the bravest among the survivors of what became known as the "Edens-Madden Massacre" was the old servant woman named Patsy, called "Betsy" in some accounts. She had been with the Edens family since 1813, when she had joined them in Illinois as a sixteen-year-old indentured servant.[23] When the slayings began, Patsy had been quick to gather up infant Melissa Edens, daughter of John Edens, and flee from the home. Her escape was no doubt aided by the fact that the Indians rarely killed negro servants in Texas. Patsy carried young Melissa the one and a half mile distance to the home of William Davis, leaving her in the care of that family.

Wasting no time for help, this "angel of mercy" struck out through the cold woods again on the brutal night of October 18, determined to help as many people as possible.[24] She found Nancy

Madden lying unconscious and badly wounded on a bed in the men's room and pulled her from the flaming log home seconds before the roof fell in, carried her to the servants' cabin which had been left untouched by the Indians, and placed the woman in her own bed. Searching for more survivors, the elderly servant next discovered Lucinda Madden crawling near the burning buildings, suffering from three nasty tomahawk wounds.[25]

As the remnants of the John Edens home turned to glowing coals in the cold October night air, Patsy kept the two injured Madden women in her cabin and cared for them as best she could until help could arrive.

Other settlers in the area had fled for their lives during the Indian assault. One family, John Aspley Jr., his wife Melinda and their six children, fled with several others some fifteen miles through the night to reach safety at Fort Houston.[26]

* * * *

Aftermath At San Pedro Creek

Sunrise on October 19, 1838, near San Pedro Creek in Houston County, revealed the Edens home still smoldering. The smell of charred flesh still lingered. Neighbors and some of the older men returned after sunrise to search for survivors. They found the servant Patsy in the only remaining structure, the slaves' cabin, where she was carrying for Nancy and Lucinda Madden. Young Balis Madden had also emerged from his hiding place by this time.

Later that day, Captain Sadler returned from Fort Houston, fresh from his fight at Kickapoo three days earlier. With him were a number of the men from his company and from that of Captain Box, including William Y. Lacy, Balis Edens, Darius Edens, Daniel Parker and Robert Madden. Both Sadler and Madden had lost their wives and young daughters. As one resident who knew him personally later wrote of the ranger captain, "Instead of meeting with the cheerful reception of his young wife, as fondly anticipated, he was doomed to behold only her charred remains, as they still lay in the smoldering ruins of the house."[27]

The initial grief soon turned to rage as the details of the bloody assault were unveiled. It soon became obvious that the attack was not made for plunder because the Indians had made no effort to steal any personal effects of the settlers other than arms and horses. One item of interest that they left behind was a young boy's cap that old Patsy found in the yard. This same cap had been discovered missing after a band of Indians had camped near the Edens home quite some time before the October 18 massacre.[28]

After it had been determined that no one else was alive in the vicinity and that little remains would ever be found of some of the victims, those gathered held a small burial ceremony that was likely presided over by Elder Daniel Parker. Sadler helped bury his wife and the other bodies in a small cemetery on the Edens property about 150 yards south of the charred remains of the John Edens home. Small markers were made for each person, although several crosses were only representative of unidentifiable ashes. Today, few of these markers still exist and some have fallen victim to vandalism.

The State of Texas erected a Centennial Marker at the massacre site in 1936. It is located in the woods a few miles off FM 2022 near Augusta on the south side of San Pedro Creek, about thirteen miles northeast of Crockett, Texas.

> In a log cabin built here in 1832, by James Madden, seven white women and their children were killed by Indians in 1838 while their husbands were held captives in the adjoining cabin. Known as the Madden Massacre. Erected by the State in 1936.[29]

This marker is not accessible to the general public, but a more accurate marker with more information was erected in 1972 in the community of Augusta. Both of the Madden women recovered from their wounds. Nancy Madden outlived her husband Robert and later married Stephen Bennett, who was a future brother-in-law to Captain Sadler. Lucinda Madden recovered, despite terrible tomahawk wounds and the loss of one ear. After the death of her husband James, she continued to live alone until the age of seventy-seven in 1883, remaining on the old Edens homestead where her life had nearly been taken.

John Edens also continued to live on the San Pedro Creek homestead until his death in 1857. His sons Balis, Darius and John Silas continued to live nearby, as did his other daughters, Laurie and Olive. The Edens family does not know who raised little Melissa, the infant rescued from the slaughter, but it may have been her saviour, Patsy.

Chapter Ten

THE REPUBLIC'S NEW FIRST REGIMENT OF INFANTRY

October 1838 - January 1839

The brutal murders on San Pedro Creek did not go unnoticed in Texas. Known at the time as the Massacre of San Pedro Creek, this event served to rally the citizens of Houston County to drive the Indians from the area. One of the area residents, David H. Campbell, wrote to President-Elect M. B. Lamar. Campbell's graphic letter was dated October 22, 1838, and was certainly one of the first accounts of this tragedy. Published in the *Papers of Mirabeau Buonaparte Lamar*, Volume III, pages 263-65, Campbell wrote that:

> It is with pain and regret that I inform you, that on Thursday night last, the 18th Inst. one of the most shocking and barbarous massacres took place in this immediate vicinity, that has happened on this continent since that of Wyoming during the Revolutionary War in the United States – the particulars of which were detailed to me by Major Elisha Clapp on yesterday.
>
> On Tuesday the 16th Inst. Genl. Rusk with a detachment of the Militia had a meeting with the combined Mexican and Indian enemy and had with him the most of the men from the immediate frontier on which they were. The relatives and several of the neighbors, with their wives and children, congregated at the house of John Edens, when on the night of the 18th, whilst preparing for repose, the house was broken into (it being a double one) where the women and children were, and the four men who were there were in the other end of the house, and barred the doors against the women and children as well as savages – whilst the blood hounds went on with their cruelties, too great for language to depict.

Six Matrons were either killed and mangled directly or wounded so they will die. The little children were thrown into the flames, which they kindled, alive, or their brains dashed out against the walls of the house. Edens has lost his wife and eldest daughter killed dead; another married daughter so wounded she will die, and an infant child of his own besides a number of grandchildren. Your old friend and acquaintance William T. Sadler has lost his wife and his wife's stepmother, Mrs. Murchison, who were mangled and burned in the house. Also a Mrs. Robert Madden was so wounded she cannot possibly live . . . .

Universal detestation and execration has fallen on Edens and his son-in-law, Jim Madden, for their basely, cowardly conduct in the affair – such has been the Massacre of San Pedro Creek.

This letter was received by Lamar on October 22. Campbell also urged the President-Elect of Texas to raise a regiment of one-thousand mounted men for a one-year period to drive the hostile Indians from the republic. Campbell joined Captain John Wortham's Houston County Rangers two weeks later on November 9.

Following Kickapoo, General Rusk determined to expel all hostile Indians from northeastern Texas and contemplated a three-pronged attack against them. He wanted to use John Dyer's Fourth Brigade moving from the Red River area toward the Brazos, Moseley Baker's Second Brigade moving up the Trinity, and his own forces under Kelsey Douglass moving northwest from Nacogdoches.[1]

President Houston, however, refused to release any money from the Treasury to organize and equip these troops, thus stalling Rusk's planned October thrust. General Rusk was encouraged to pursue his campaign against the Indians without the president's funding or approval. He promised his men only that they could expect to be paid for their service sometime in the future. Reports from an Indian trader near the Three Forks on the Trinity placed some seven-hundred warriors in one village, including Caddos, Cherokees, Wacos, Tawakonis, Hainais, Kichais, and some Seminoles.[2]

Rusk's volunteer Texas Militia moved from Nacogdoches back to Fort Houston by late October, and there the general set up a temporary headquarters. Undaunted by the lack of presidential support, the local citizens helped to provide for the army. Captain Sadler, likely motivated by the loss of his family, offered what livestock and food crops he had for Rusk's troops.

As of the end of October, Captain Sadler's company was located at Murchison's Camp, the headquarters of Colonel Willis Landrum. In the quartermaster's file of October 30, 1838, appraiser Leander E. Tipps recorded that W. T. Sadler was owed $497 for having supplied 142 bushels of corn from his farm at the rate of $3.50 per bushel "for the use of the troops now in the field." Of this total, it appears that he was paid for forty-five bushels up front, totaling $157.50. Although he was not paid the balance at this time, he was issued a promisary note that Texas would one day honor.

A second note was dated November 1, 1838, signed by Tipps and Colonel Landrum commanding Third Brigade, showing that Sadler supplied fourteen "beeves" (cattle) and three hogs. For the livestock, Tipps signed a promissory note which stated that "the above written was received by the troops" and that Sadler was due $242.[3]

RECEIPTS FOR DONATIONS TO THE TEXAS ARMY
BY CAPTAIN W. T. SADLER
OCTOBER 30 - NOVEMBER 1, 1838

142 bushels of corn at $3.50		$497.00
45 bushels of corn at $3.50	(paid)	157.50
		$339.50
14 Beeves (cattle)		220.00
3 Hogs		22.00
	(sub total)	$581.50

Public debt records show that he had been paid for just over a quarter of the value of his supplies for Colonel Landrum's command. Due to the economic woes of his young republic, however, Sadler would not be paid by Texas on the remaining $581.50 for these donations until 1848!

Sadler was not alone in supplying these troops. John Edens, who had also lost family members in the massacre, supplied the militia with two-hundred dollars worth of corn fodder and beef in late 1838. This receipt was witnessed by his son Darius Edens before Stephen E. Kennedy, a Houston County Justice of the Peace for the San Pedro area. Edens had previously supplied provisions for ranger companies operating from Fort Houston in September and December 1836. He had also supplied beef to Captain Sadler's rangers under Major Mabbitt's command on October 1, 1838, just prior to their Kickapoo battles. Edens was paid by the Republic of Texas for some of these debts in October 1839 but did not receive full payment until a joint resolution of Congress for his relief was signed by President Lamar on January 21, 1840.[4] Others supplying army forces with food during October and December at Murchison's Camp in Houston County were Armstead Bennett, Martin Murchison, Daniel Parker and Joel Daniel Leathers.[5]

During early November, General Rusk's volunteer forces dwindled as companies were mustered out and volunteers returned to their families. Command of Captain Sadler's rangers passed to John Wortham on November 8; Sadler was apparently more interested in going on the offensive against the Indians than in protecting the immediate settlements. Wortham's revamped Houston County ranger unit included some new volunteers and three men from William's Brookfield's rangers, who had been disbanded soon after the Kickapoo battle. Like Wortham, a number of his men came from Sadler's former company, including Solomon Adams, William H. Adams and Thomas Hays. General Rusk was disappoint to find that only forty-five of the men with him were willing to proceed to the Trinity to attack the Indians. Since Houston had not given the Texas Militia officers official commissions, however, men could not be threatened with court martials for failure to obey orders.[6]

While Rusk struggled with his meager army near Fort Houston, the newly seated Third Congress of the Republic of Texas had convened on November 6. A joint resolution was passed to appropriate $20,000 to buy arms, ammunition, clothing and provisions for the troops under Rusk's command. Another $20,000 was appropriated to fit out 250 men from the Second Brigade. To avoid delay, Rusk was authorized to use $10,000 from the customs collector at San Augustine at once.[7] Congress soon passed other resolutions, one requesting President Houston to issue commissions to all duly elected and appointed militia officers, and another promising to legalize the position of militia officers elected by their men (such as Sadler) in the absence of regularly commissioned officers. Congress pledged to pay all citizens who volunteered for frontier service.[8]

With the passage of these militia laws, the Congress of Texas thereby removed Sam Houston as an obstacle to the combat of the Indian threat in East Texas by Rusk's men. Rusk soon found, however, that the majority of his Third Brigade men were not willing to follow him to the Three Forks, likely because this brigade had already furnished the men who had followed Rusk on his previous expeditions of 1838.[9]

Rusk returned to Nacogdoches in November and had the balance of his Third Brigade members discharged. En route to Nacogdoches was a 150-volunteer detachment under Major George Washington Bonnell which included some sixty well-equipped men of the Milam Guards of Houston. These men followed Rusk into the cold, wet lands around the area between the Falls of the Brazos and the Colorado River. After several frustrating weeks, Rusk and Bonnell's men returned home in December.[10]

From Nacogdoches, Rusk then moved toward the Red River settlements, meeting Captain Edward H. Tarrant of the Fourth Brigade, under General Dyer. With Tarrant's men, Rusk pursued a raiding band of sixty Caddos into Louisiana, an act which was considered by some to be an invasion upon U.S. territory. The men commanded by Rusk during this expedition eventually swelled to more than 450 from General Dyer's Fourth Brigade. These forces swept through the present areas of Fort Worth and Dallas, driving the Caddos toward Louisiana. Only a few Kickapoos were actually encountered, but Rusk's troops burned a few villages found in the Cross Timbers and on the Brazos. After a fruitless six-week expedition, provisions ran low and all the volunteers of the Fourth Brigade were discharged at Clarksville on January 9, 1839.[11]

Rusk finally returned to Nacogdoches following this crusade and was criticized by some for his intrusion upon U.S. soil in pursuit of the Indians. The Indian War was far from over, but it had become bitterly apparent that it would not be solidly addressed until the new President of Texas took office.

* * * *

SADLER'S TEXAS LAND GRANTS

Even as he mourned the loss of his wife, William Sadler's personal land holdings continued to grow in late 1838. Having originally purchased his one-third league of 1,476 acres in 1835, he had then been granted Headright Certificate No. 26 for a league and labor (4,606.5 acres) in Houston County after he had married. Ironically, one upper corner of the Sadler Headright was bordered by the land of John Norris, who had been one of the instigators of the Cordova Rebellion which had been one of the factors in the death of Sadler's wife.

With more than six-thousand acres considered his rightful property, the Republic of Texas would provide him an additional 960 acres, bringing his total property holdings to slightly more than

Donation land grant Certificate No. 713 was issued to W. T. Sadler on December 22, 1838. This document granted him 640 acres for being a veteran of the Battle of San Jacinto.

seven-thousand acres. This additional land came in the form of two donation grants.

Sadler was issued both grants on December 22, 1838, after supplying the required documentation of his service to the Secretary of War. At this time, Albert Sidney Johnston filled this position and signed papers for William Sadler which acknowledged his 1836 army service and the fact that he was indeed a veteran of the Battle of San Jacinto.

By virtue of an act of the Third Congress signed by President Sam Houston on December 21, 1837, all men who were actually engaged in the Battle of San Jacinto, and those men who had been detached by Houston to guard the baggage near Harrisburg prior to the battle, were granted 640 acres of public land for their service.[12] One year after Houston's act to honor these veterans, Sadler was issued Donation Certificate No. 713 by the Secretary of War for 640 acres. He would eventually use this certificate to obtain a tract of land that bordered the southwestern corner of his league and labor

THE REPUBLIC'S NEW FIRST REGIMENT OF INFANTRY

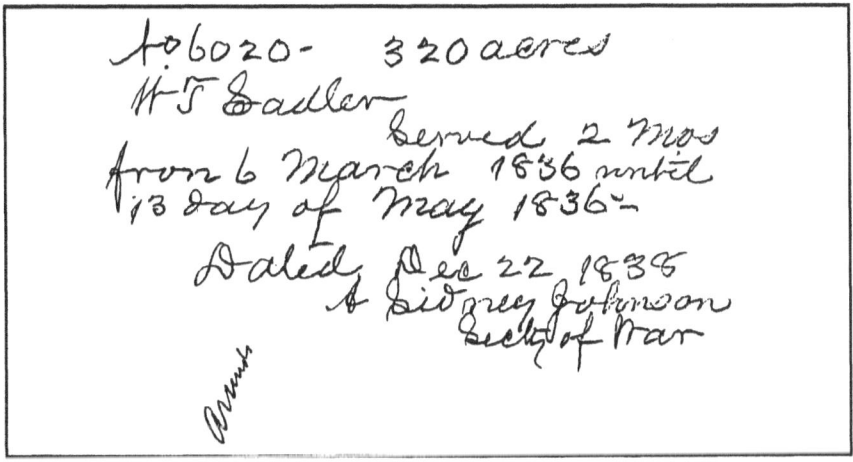

This document from the War Department of Texas shows that William T. Sadler was entitled to pay for his service in the volunteer army of Texas in 1836. The document below shows that Sadler was entitled to 320 acres of land for completing two months of service (dates are inaccurate) with Captain Arnold's company in 1836. Both documents are signed by newly appointed Secretary of War Albert Sidney Johnston. From W. T. Sadler Pension Papers, courtesy of Howard C. Sadler.

in Houston County. By the time Sadler obtained clear patent to this donation land grant on April 14, 1848, the largest portion of this property would lie north of the border of present Anderson and Houston counties.

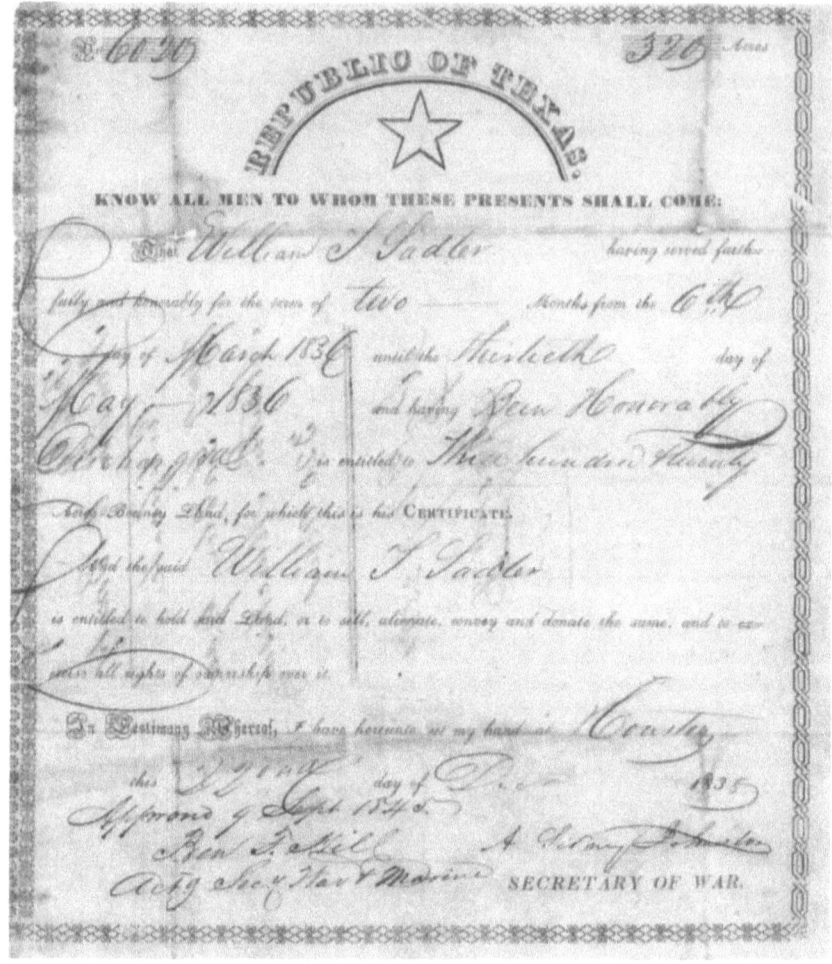

Bounty Certificate No. 6020 was also issued to Sadler on December 22, providing payment in the form of 320 acres of land for his service in the Texas Army in 1836.

This first 640-acre donation was intended to honor the San Jacinto veterans and was therefore not open for sale or trade during the donee's lifetime. Sadler's certificate specifies that this land "cannot be sold, alienated or mortgaged, and is exempt from execution during the life-time of the person to whom it is granted."

Also granted on December 22, 1838, Bounty Certificate No. 6020 was issued to Sadler for 320 acres of land by the Secretary of War for his having served in the army from March 6 to May 30, 1836 (dates inaccurate). This land quantity had been determined by the March 1836 convention at Washington on the Brazos, which had established bounties of 320 acres of land for at least three months' service in the army, 640 acres to those serving at least six months, and 1,280 acres for those who had served longer terms.[13]

His second land grant had different specifications. As a bounty grant, this certificate merely entitled him to the 320 acres as owner but did not restrict his use of the land. In fact, Sadler's Certificate 6020 states that he was "entitled to hold said land, or to sell, alienate, convey and donate the same, and to exercise all rights of ownership over it." The 320-acre tract assigned in Houston County was just east and slightly south of his league and labor headright. Between and touching both of these two properties was a one-quarter league owned by Sam Houston. Sadler's land tract would eventually straddle the county lines of Anderson and Houston counties, with sixty-six acres in Houston and 254 in Anderson. He would, however, later exercise his right to assign the use of this land to his ex-father-in-law, Martin Murchison. As he would later pass this land along to his daughter, their arrangements with this tract were not permanent. In any event, Martin Murchison was listed as the assignee of W. T. Sadler for this 320-acre tract, which he had surveyed by Houston County Surveyor William Dickerson on March 6, 1844.

Aside from his land grants, Sadler was also concerned with keeping track of the money owed him by the Republic of Texas. George W. Browning, who had served in his ranger company during the first skirmish with Cordova's rebels, became Sadler's acting attorney. As such, Browning used his power of attorney to file for pay owed Sadler for service in the Texas Army. As a private in Captain Arnold's company beginning March 6, 1836, he had received his final payment on May 30, 1836, but was still due $22.40 for his continued military service. This backpay certificate, filed by Browning on December 22, 1838, had Sadler's military service authorized by the signature of Secretary of War Albert Sidney Johnston. This payment was authorized on December 31, 1838, by the acting comptroller and was returned to the law offices of Browning.

* * * *

President Lamar Revamps The Texas Military

While General Rusk flailed about after the Indians, Sam Houston's term as President of the Republic of Texas ended on December 9, 1838. He was succeeded by Mirabeau B. Lamar, who held a vastly different policy than his predecessor concerning treatment of Indians. Lamar and Vice President David Burnet were inaugurated on December 10. In his first message to Congress, Lamar stated, "As long as we continue to exhibit our mercy without showing our strength, so long will the Indians continue to bloody the tomahawk and move onward in the work of rapacity and slaughter."[14] Lamar quickly made it known that he intended to remove the Western Cherokees from Texas, and on December 13 he appointed General Albert Sidney Johnston, a strong advocate of the regular army, as Secretary of War to help deal with these tensions.

Once Lamar entered office, the Third Congress immediately adopted a new move to combat the Indian threat. It authorized a new regular army and many short-term ranger units, appropriated necessary funds and also strengthened the militia organization. The new regular army on December 21 was designated the "Frontier Regiment" and was to consist of fifteen companies, a total of 840 men who would be stationed along a military road that would be laid out from the Red River on the United States border to the Nueces River near the Mexico border. Along this route would be a string of forts for the protection of nearby settlements. Congress appropriated $300,000 in Republic promissory notes to help Lamar organize the army.[15]

Each of these fifteen army companies would have a captain, a first lieutenant and a second lieutenant. The army would consist of one regiment divided into two battalions, the First Battalion being all detachments west of the Brazos River and the Second Battalion including all detachments east of the Brazos. The army's regiment would be headed by a colonel, one lieutenant colonel and a major, followed by the company captains.[16] William T. Sadler would be among the earliest officers to be commissioned into this new army.

While the regular army was being organized, Congress passed a bill the following week on December 29 which authorized President Lamar to use $75,000 to press eight mounted volunteer companies into service for six months' ranging duty. Each company would consist of a captain, a first and a second lieutenant, three sergeants and fifty privates, each for six month terms. Each would be paid monthly in the same fashion as Mounted Riflemen in the Ranging Service, which had been established by an act passed December 10, 1836.[17]

Houston County was one of the primary counties that was in need of special protection. The Congress on January 1, 1839, appropriated $5,000 for the purpose "of raising and supporting a Company of 56 Rangers for three months, to be commanded by

Captain John Wortham, whose duty it shall be to range on the frontier of Houston, or any frontier Counties, and to protect the settlements." It was also enacted that it would be the duty of Wortham, whose company was already in service, to report at least every two weeks to Brigadier General Kelsey Douglass on the actions and movements of his company.[18]

In addition, fifty-six-man local ranger companies were authorized for the frontier counties of Bastrop, Gonzales, Goliad, Milam, Refugio, Robertson and San Patricio. Terms of these companies were from three to six months, enlistments were volunteer, and each man was bound to supply his own horse, arms and other equipment.[19]

The cost of maintaining the militia and a regular army had become a sizable burden on Texas. Paper currency issued by President Houston had been backed by the value of public land and the credit of the republic, but this was soon considered shaky.[20] Lamar approved a new congressional plan to issue a large quantity of non-interest bearing notes which would be discounted almost sixty-three cents on the dollar when first issued. These notes would pay for the expanded military expenditures of Texas. For 1839, the Third Congress appropriated a budget of $1,520,455. Of the military appropriation, the amount of $1,140,000 earmarked for support of the army exceeded the Texas government's total expenditures of fiscal year 1838, which had amounted to $831,401.[21]

The new Frontier Regiment of Lamar and his Third Congress became known as the "First Regiment of Infantry"; the designations "Frontier Regiment" or "Texas Army" were rarely used. The First Regiment was placed under command of Colonel Edward "Ned" Burleson, a popular leader who had commanded the First Militia Brigade during 1838 and the the First Regiment of Texas Volunteers at San Jacinto. Headquarters for the First Regiment became Bastrop, near the home of Burleson. A former San Jacinto captain and later a Secretary of War, William S. Fisher was appointed his lieutenant colonel and Peyton S. Wyatt as major. Command of the cavalry for the new army passed to Colonel Lysander Wells, who had previously served as commander of mounted forces on the southwestern frontier.[22]

With Ned Burleson's heading the army, the other senior Texas military officer during 1839 was Hugh McLeod, a New York-born Georgian who had been graduated last in the 1835 class at West Point and who had previously served in the U.S. Army. Having been named Adjutant General of the Texas Army in May 1838, McLeod had served with his friend Tom Rusk during the campaigns

Colonel Edward Burleson, original commander of the Texas First Regiment of Infantry. This original daguerreotype portrait was made in San Marcos, Texas, in 1850. Burleson had previously served as Colonel of the First Regiment of Texas Volunteers at San Jacinto, and he later served as Vice President of the Republic of Texas from 1841 through 1844.

Courtesy of the Archives & Information Services Division, Texas State Library.

against the Indians and Mexicans in 1838. With the new laws of the Texas Army passed by the congress, it was necessary for President Lamar to reappoint McLeod as adjutant general. In this billet, McLeod held the rank colonel, was responsible for keeping army records, and handled administrative matters.

The other chief staff officers of the First Regiment had served in the army during the revolution with Mexico. Those appointed were Quartermaster General William Gordon Cooke, Paymaster General Jacob Snively, Inspector General Peter Hansbrough Bell, Commissary General of Subsistence William L. Cazneau and Surgeon General William R. Smith.

Recruiting began earnestly in early January of 1839 and major recruiting posts were permanently staffed in Houston and Galveston. Later in 1839, officers were stationed in New Orleans to forward new recruits from the United States to Galveston for enlistment.[23] Several of these recruiting captains later took command of their own companies as enlistment grew in late 1839 and early 1840.

Other recruiting stations were opened in smaller Texas towns. From muster roll records, it appears that Nacogdoches and Crockett may have briefly served as stations for their respective counties of Nacogdoches and Houston. East of the Brazos River, new recruits fell under the Second Battalion of the First Regiment of Infantry superintended by Lieutenant Colonel Fisher and Major Wyatt, while Colonel Burleson commanded the First Battalion.[24]

As an early volunteer of the revamped army of the Republic of Texas, W. T. Sadler also became one of its first captains. Having lost his family in the recent Edens-Madden Massacre in October and having thereafter used most of his food crops and livestock to provision the militia, he was dedicated to the expulsion of the hostile Indians of East Texas. By virtue of his previous army experience, his ranger command, his having fought at San Jacinto and having led a company against the Indians, Sadler was commissioned as captain of Company A of Fisher's Second Battalion of the First Infantry.

Captain Sadler and the other army officers previously commissioned into the First Regiment during late December 1838 and early January 1839 were officially commissioned by President Lamar during the latter part of January. The Third Congress confirmed these appointments, and on January 30, 1839, Secretary of War Sidney Johnston issued a memorandum from the War Department, which was reprinted a week later in the February 6 issue of the *Telegraph and Texas Register* in Houston.

> The following appointments have been conferred on the gentlemen herein named, and are announced by command of the president. [See list on following pages.]
> The officers of the general staff and other corps whose appointments are hereby promulgated and confirmed, will take rank, each grade respectively, in the order in which they now stand on the list, without regards to commissions given to them previous to the 23rd inst., all of which are declared null and void.
> The officers named in the foregoing order will immediately signify their acceptance to the adjutant general of the same. Col. E. Burleson, Lt. Col. Wm S. Fisher and Maj. P. S. Wyatt are designated to conduct the recruiting of the 1st regiment of infantry, to be raised in conformity with the act for the protection of the frontier, approved 21st December, 1838.

The newly commissioned captains were directed to report for duty without delay in order "that the ranks of the regiment may be filled with all possible despatch." Sadler no doubt became involved in the recruiting process within Houston County during January. Fortunately, there were enough men willing to join in on the Indian

Original Officer Appointments Of The Frontier Regiment The Army Of The Republic Of Texas
(As of January 30, 1839)

NAME:	OFFICE:	APPOINTED:
Edward Burleson	Colonel, First Regiment, Infantry	January 23, 1839
Lysander Wells	Colonel, First Regiment, Cavalry	January 30, 1839
Hugh B. McLeod	Adjutant General	January 30, 1839
Isaac Watts Burton	Quartermaster General	January 30, 1839
William Gordon Cooke	Commissary Gen. of Subsistence	January 30, 1839
Peter Hansbrough Bell	Inspector General	January 30, 1839
William S. Fisher	Lt. Colonel, First Reg., Infantry	January 23, 1839
Peter Bartelle Dexter	Lt. Colonel, First Reg., Cavalry	January 30, 1839
Peyton S. Wyatt	Major, First Regiment, Infantry	January 23, 1839
William Jefferson Jones *	Major, First Regiment, Cavalry	January 30, 1839
Pinckney C. Caldwell	Quartermaster	January 30, 1839
Benjamin H. Johnson	Assistant Adjutant General	January 30, 1839
Benjamin B. Sturgess	Paymaster	January 30, 1839
John Forbes	Major, Commissary of Subsistence	January 30, 1839
Hillequist Landers	Major, Commissary of Subsistence	January 30, 1839
William Henry Dangerfield*	Commissary of Purchases	January 23, 1839
Ezra Read	Surgeon	January 30, 1839
Thomas P. Anderson	Surgeon	January 30, 1839
Shields Booker	Surgeon	January 30, 1839
William Davis Redd	Captain, First Regiment Infantry	January 23, 1839
Adam Clendenin	Captain, First Regiment Infantry	January 23, 1839
Samuel W. Jordan	Captain, First Regiment Infantry	January 23, 1839
George Thomas Howard	Captain, First Regiment Infantry	January 23, 1839
H. W. Davis	Captain, First Regiment Infantry	January 23, 1839
John J. Holliday	Captain, First Regiment Infantry	January 23, 1839
Benjamin Y. Gillen	Captain, First Regiment Infantry	January 30, 1839
Martin Kingsley Snell	Captain, First Regiment Infantry	January 30, 1839
Robert Oliver	Captain, First Regiment Infantry	January 30, 1839
Mark Blake Skerrett	Captain, First Regiment Infantry	January 30, 1839
George F. Laurence	Captain, First Regiment Infantry	January 30, 1839
George Washington Morgan	Captain, First Regiment Infantry	January 30, 1839
William H. Moore	Captain, First Regiment Infantry	January 30, 1839
William Turner Sadler	Captain, First Regiment Infantry	January 30, 1839
James Belvarde Pope January	Captain, First Regiment Infantry	January 30, 1839
James C. P. Kennymore	1st Lt., First Regiment Infantry	January 23, 1839
Palmer Job Pillans	1st Lt., First Regiment Infantry	January 23, 1839
William Green Kerley	1st Lt., First Regiment Infantry	January 23, 1839
James Goodall	1st Lt., First Regiment Infantry	January 23, 1839
O. P. Kelton	1st Lt., First Regiment Infantry	January 30, 1839
Samuel Price Carson	1st Lt., First Regiment Infantry	January 30, 1839
Duncan Campbell Ogden	1st Lt., First Regiment Infantry	January 30, 1839
Edward A. Thompson	1st Lt., First Regiment Infantry	January 30, 1839
William N. Dunnington	1st Lt., First Regiment Infantry	January 30, 1839

NAME:	OFFICE:	APPOINTED:
Joseph M. Wiehl	1st Lt., First Regiment Infantry	January 30, 1839
Robert Simpson Neighbors	1st Lt., First Regiment Infantry	January 30, 1839
Martin Morann	1st Lt., First Regiment Infantry	January 30, 1839
Davis Verplank Ackermann	1st Lt., First Regiment Infantry	January 30, 1839
Alenson T. Miles	1st Lt., First Regiment Infantry	January 30, 1839
William H. Crutchir	1st Lt., First Regiment Infantry	January 30, 1839
George N. Palmer	2nd Lt., First Regiment Infantry	January 23, 1839
William D. Houghton	2nd Lt., First Regiment Infantry	January 23, 1839
John Schuyler Sutton	2nd Lt., First Regiment Infantry	January 23, 1839
William Redfield	2nd Lt., First Regiment Infantry	January 23, 1839
John Brown	2nd Lt., First Regiment Infantry	January 23, 1839
Henry L. Grush	2nd Lt., First Regiment Infantry	January 30, 1839
Daniel Lacry	2nd Lt., First Regiment Infantry	January 30, 1839
Collier C. Hornsby	2nd Lt., First Regiment Infantry	January 30, 1839
Timothy O'Neil	2nd Lt., First Regiment Infantry	January 30, 1839
W. Hufton	2nd Lt., First Regiment Infantry	January 30, 1839
Daniel Lewis	2nd Lt., First Regiment Infantry	January 30, 1839

* Not included on Secretary of War Johnston's memo, but known to have been commissioned as indicated.

FRONTIER REGIMENT OFFICERS APPOINTED IN 1839 AFTER JANUARY 30:

Jacob Snively	Paymaster General	March 23, 1839
William Lewis Cazneau	Commissary General of Subsistence	October 25, 1839
George Washington Hockley	Commissary General of Ordnance	March 23, 1839
William R. Smith	Surgeon General	July 20, 1839
Edmund Tucker	Surgeon	April 6, 1839
Richard Cochran	Assistant Surgeon	April 6, 1839
James M. Alexander	2nd Lt., First Regiment Infantry	February 20, 1839
Matthew McGovern	2nd Lt., First Regiment Infantry	Nov. 15, 1839
Abram H. Scott	2nd Lt., First Regiment Infantry	March 23, 1839

campaign. During late December, Brigadier General Kelsey Douglass had rallied troops in his Third Brigade Militia District to join General Tom Rusk's present Indian campaign. He reported to Secretary of War Johnston by the end of the month that he had readied some eight-hundred volunteers to join Rusk. Word soon came that Rusk had called off the Caddo expedition, however, and the Third Brigade volunteers were not needed.[25]

The First Regiment thus had some of these volunteers to pull from, as well as numerous men in the Red River area who had been discharged at Clarksville on January 9 after Rusk's Indian expedition was ended. Although no complete roster of Captain Sadler's Company A remains today, there is evidence that some of the First Regiment's earliest recruits were from Clarksville. (It appears that many of Sadler's early Texas military records were destroyed in a deliberately set fire that consumed many valuable records in 1855 in the Adjutant General's office.)

Other army officers actively involved in the early recruiting were Captain Martin K. Snell in Matagorda, Captain Benjamin Y. Gillen and First Lieutenant Joseph M. Wiehl at New Orleans, Captain James January at Velasco, Colonel Hugh McLeod and Captain George F. Laurence at Galveston, plus captains William D. Redd, Adam Clendenin, and Mark Skerrett and Second Lieutenant Henry L. Grush at other Texas stations. Captain George W. Morgan was stationed at the Galveston post for some time and returned home to Pennsylvania in 1839.[26]

The enlisted soldiers of Lamar's new army were generally paid sixteen dollars per month. The earliest of these recruits were taken during late 1838 from the stations at Houston, Galveston and Matagorda. During the early months of 1839, enlistment picked up in Clarksville and Velasco. Later in the year, probably spurned by the subsequent Indian wars, enlistments from the United States increased dramatically.

Of the fifteen new frontier regiment captains, Sadler was by far the oldest at age forty-one. Most were in their twenties. They were better provided for than they had been with the ranger service. According to a receipt issued Sadler on May 28 by Quartermaster Benjamin B. Sturgess, his pay was forty dollars per month, which was supplemented by eight dollars per month for clothing, $2.50 for forage for his horse, plus thirty dollars per month for food rations.

The enlisted men among the new recruits were issued two pairs of wool trousers, three pairs of cotton trousers, a woolen and cotton jacket, two cotton and two flannel shirts, three pairs of boots, three pairs of stockings, two sets of underwear, three different outer coats including a dresscoat, a blanket, and a leather stock.[27] Those not in possession of a horse were issued one by the army.

As an infantry captain, Sadler was issued a double-breasted coat of dark blue cloth with two rows of ten buttons. According to a Republic of Texas document entitled *Uniforms of the Army of the Republic of Texas* concerning the new 1839 look, the captain's formal uniform was "framed with half inch silver lace, two loops of quarter inch lace, four and a half inches long on each side of the collar, with one small uniform button at the end of each loop." The trousers worn were also dark blue with two stripes of white cassimere three-fourths of an inch wide up each outward seam. Captain Sadler's uniform was complemented by Wellington boots, a white vest, white gloves, a black patent leather waist-belt, and a crimson and a silver sword-knot with bullion tassels. His cap was made of beaver pelt with a bell crown and plated scales and displayed a silver star surrounded by rays in the front, with the regiment's number beneath and the company letter "A" within the star.

The First Regiment of Infantry, according to one historian, became "the 'elite' unit of the new republic. The men were uniformed and armed with the best equipment. The First would serve on the Cherokee Campaign, man the western garrisons, build the new military road, participate in the Council House Fight, and after being disbanded, provide the nucleus of the military escort for the Santa Fe Expedition."[28]

Captain Sadler's company, one of the first to form, was not nearly so well equipped because no new arms were purchased for the Texas Army until 1839 due to the heavy debt incurred by the Texas Revolution. During the period of time that President Houston had advocated peace with the Indians, there had been an ample supply of Yeager and Saber rifles remaining from the 1836 revolution.[29]

As the new First Regiment was being formed in December, 1838, Colonel Lysander Wells had sent Colonel William Henry Dangerfield, the Commissary of Purchases, to the United States to purchase arms and equipment. This mission was deemed successful; receipts show Dangerfield purchased U.S. Army-specified weapons, uniforms, cartridge pouches, saddles, six-pound artillery cannons and even wagons for the new Army of the Republic of Texas. Many from

Early Texas firearm. This flintlock rifle is an 1834 U. S. Springfield. It was later converted to a cap and ball setup prior to its use in the Civil War.
Photo courtesy of Howard C. Sadler.

the First Infantry were known to be armed with the new Colt repeating pistol during 1839.

As for firearms, most of the men under Sadler's command supplied their personal pistols, rifles or muskets. A few months later, on May 29, 1839, the Secretary of War instructed the Colonel of Ordnance, George Washington Hockley, to contract with Tryon Son & Company for five-hundred muskets for the army. The George W. Tryon family of Philadelphia had become a well-established manufacturer of arms by 1839 and would remain in business until 1964. An additional one-thousand muskets would be ordered on June 7th, although the first contract with Tryon would not be signed until November 1.

The weapon of choice to be manufactured by Tryon for the Texas Army was the 1816 Model, Type III flintlock musket, which was a .69 caliber smoothbore, of 57 and 11/16 inches in length, with a 42-inch barrel. It was an important step for the arming of the Texas military, but these muskets would not be available until the early months of 1840 after the crisis with the Cherokees had passed.

Aside from its initial shortages in arsenal, this new army was the strongest showing of regulars in the Republic of Texas in two years. The creation of the new First Regiment of Infantry was an important step in defending the frontier settlements, and for William T. Sadler it provided an opportunity to settle a score.

Chapter Eleven

SADLER'S APPEAL
TO PRESIDENT LAMAR

January - February 1839

By mid-January of 1839, Houston County's major settlements were protected by a number of armed forces. Captain John Wortham's new ranging company covered the areas near Crockett while Captain James Box remained in command of Fort Houston, where his company had been operating since the Kickapoo fights three months earlier. Both volunteer companies fell under the command of Major Baley C. Walters of the Third Militia Brigade. The company of Captain James W. Cleveland, under direction of Lieutenant Colonel Jacob Snively, was stationed farther north on the Neches River at the Neches Saline on the fringe of Cherokee territory.

While recruiting for the new First Regiment of Infantry proceeded in January, Captain Sadler and his first recruits took up station at Fort Brown in the little community of Brownsville. Located near the banks of San Pedro Creek about five miles east of present Grapeland, Fort Brown was named for Reuben Brown, son-in-law of Elder Daniel Parker. Brown and the Parkers had built this group of post oak cabins in 1834 when the Pilgrim Predestinarian Regular Baptist Church traveled through the area.[1] This post was located just a few miles from the site of the Edens-Madden Massacre in which Sadler had so recently lost his wife. The army troops in the area were supplied with provisions by local residents. Armstead Bennett and Thomas Lagow were later compensated by Texas for providing corn. One of their receipts was signed "Brown's Fort, Feb. 28, 1839."[2]

As his company began taking shape, so began the requirements of a more regimented lifestyle. The daily routine for a First Infantry company consisted of assemblies, drill and duty patterned after the

First Regiment Receipt. Shortly after the murder of his wife by Indians, Captain Sadler was commissioned into the new Army of the Republic of Texas. In January 1839, he assumed command of Company A of the First Regiment of Infantry. This pay receipt from May 28, 1839 shows his allowances for pay, clothing, forage and subsistence for the period of January 30 - April 30, 1839. Texas Archives, courtesy of Howard Sadler.

U.S. Army's doctrine. Reveille was sounded at daybreak, breakfast was called at 7:00 a.m., and assembly was called at 8:00 a.m. for drills, inspections or assignments of duty. Camp was generally secured at sunset and all men were required to be in their quarters when tattoo was sounded at 9:00 p.m. Any off-duty periods were occupied by the men in hunting, gambling, writing letters or drinking from secret stashes of whiskey.[3]

Although the army's quartermaster, subsistence and purchasing departments were charged with providing sufficient food for the company, the daily meals generally centered around the local availability of corn, beef, beans, pork, bread and coffee. In camp, the enlisted men slept six to a tent with each such group issued a mess kit for cooking. The company was also issued six axes and four spades. Officers were issued axes and hatchets.

While stationed in Brownsville, Captain Sadler assumed duties as the official postmaster of this little community. A report of Texas Postmaster General Robert Barr to President Lamar on February 27, 1839, lists Sadler as Postmaster of the Brownsville Post Office in Houston County.

The postal system of the republic had been in place just over two years, its structure adopted from that of the United States Post Office Department. In a report made to President Lamar, Barr detailed the duties of Sadler and his fellow postmasters.

> Post Masters are required to send with each package of letters forwarded to other offices a way-bill containing a correct amount of the same, and to enter the amount, date, and name of the office, to which it is sent in his account of mails sent. Each Post-Master is also required to keep an account of mails received, in which he enters every way-bill received at his office, showing the date, amount and office from which it was received. The necessary blanks are furnished them for these purposes. In making their returns, they are required to forward with every quarters return a correct copy of mails sent and received at their office, also the way-bills received during the time for which the return is made. By comparing the way-bills with these accounts, I am enabled to detect any errors or frauds that may be attempted to be practiced on the department.

Barr also informed Lamar that occasional complaints arising against such postmasters for neglect in their duties "are unjust." He cited

Postmasters of East Texas [4]
In Service as of February 27, 1839

Name of Office	County	Postmaster
Beaumont	Jefferson	Joseph E. Pulsiver
Brownsville	Houston	William T. Sadler
Clarksville	Red River	John W. Fowler
Crockett	Houston	John H. Kerchoffer
Dekalb	Red River	Hiram Allen
Franklin	Red River	Samuel Moore Fulton
Fort Houston	Houston	William S. McDonald
Gaines Ferry	Sabine	James Gaines
Geneva	Liberty	Francis W. Johnson
Hamilton	Sabine	James A. Chafin
Johnsons	Red River	Livley Johnson
Jonetts	Red River	J. G. Jonett
Jonesboro	Red River	William Scurlock
Jasper	Jasper	John Bevil
Liberty	Liberty	Henry Wise Farley
Lagrange	Red River	Samuel W. Simms
Mustang Prairie	Houston	Collin Aldrich
Mount Sterling	Nacogdoches	John Durst
Milam	Sabine	William H. Harris
Menards Mills	Liberty	Michael B. Menard
Mount Holland	Jefferson	R. E. Boothe
Myrtle Springs	Red River	R. Peters
Nacogdoches	Nacogdoches	John S. Roberts
Neches	Nacogdoches	James Bradshaw
Patillos	Jefferson	George A. Patillo
Pine Island	Jefferson	David Cole
Pollygatcho	San Augustine	Burrell J. Thompson
Richardsons	Jasper	Benjamin Richardson
Richland	Jefferson	Thomas H. Brennan
Salem	Jasper	Seth Swift
Shelbyville	Shelby	Joseph Puve
San Augustine	San Augustine	Ebenezer Kellogg
Spring Hill	Shelby	William Woods
Whites	Sabine	James T. White
Wrights	Jasper	James Quinn
Zavalla	Jasper	Thomas B. Huling

[4]

the young age of the postal system, the unimproved roads over which mail was carried, swollen streams without proper bridges, bad weather, and the heavy volume of such post offices as that of Galveston as factors that at times slowed the mail process between the Republic's thirty-one counties.

The duty of carrying the mail between the established post offices was contracted out to carriers who were paid an annual fee. Barr's report for 1839 shows that George W. Browning was the contractor of the mail route between Cincinnati on the Trinity River and Fort Houston, for which he was paid a fee of one-thousand dollars. There were twenty-six total contracted mail routes in Texas during early 1839, maintained for the collective fee of $35,137.[5]

* * * *

NEW DEPREDATION BRINGS CALL TO ACTION

In the months following the expulsion of Cordova's rebels from Houston County, this frontier area had enjoyed relative peace with the local Indian tribes. The calm came to an abrupt end on January 23 with a new assault in the vicinity of Fort Houston, where Captain Wortham's volunteer ranger company had recently moved to join the company of Captain Box.

Acting upon reports of Indians on the move, Wortham's rangers had departed Fort Houston on January 22 for Hall's trading place on the Trinity River, located about twelve miles away. Shortly after their departure, an express arrived from Lieutenant Colonel Snively at the Neches Saline, who stated that he expected to be attacked by Indians this day.

This express managed to catch Captain Wortham before his company crossed the Trinity. By 3:00 a.m. on January 23, his company was back at Fort Houston and by 9:00 a.m. they had departed to meet Captain Snively at the Neches Saline.[6] That afternoon, the Fort Houston citizens discovered the tracks of horses in two different directions; one set of these tracks proved to be those of Indians. While the Fort Houston company was in the field on January 23, another depredation was made nearby against the Campbell family, whose home was less than a mile from the fort.

Charles C. Campbell and his family had settled near Fort Houston in 1837 on Town Creek, three miles east of present Palestine. He built a home and worked his fields with his wife, five children and two negro slaves. Charles Campbell had passed away the previous week, and at about 10:00 p.m. on a bright moonlight night his home was attacked by approximately fifteen Indians. The neighing of the horses alerted the family that intruders were approaching. Mrs. Campbell and several of the others attempted to hold the wooden door closed while the Indians began chopping into it with tomahawks.[7]

Malathiel Campbell, twenty, tried to defend his family with an old rifle but found that it had a defective flint lock. His mother managed to pull up two of the puncheon boards from the floor and ordered her seventeen-year-old daughter Pamelia to crawl under the house with her four-year-old brother George. As these two children made their escape, one of the Indians forced open the door far enough to nearly sever Mrs. Campbell's arm with a tomahawk. The Indians then burst into the room and tomahawked to death Mrs. Campbell and two of her children, fourteen-year-old Hulda and eleven-year-old Fountain.[8]

Malathiel escaped into the yard with a knife in his hand but was shot down by those outside. The negro servants were allowed to escape unharmed. That evening, the negro man ran to Fort Houston where he "alarmed the citizens by giving a relation as near as he could relate of the massacre."[9] Pamelia Campbell and her young brother George crawled out from under the house and slipped away unnoticed but, as she was entering a nearby thicket, one of the Indians shot an arrow which glanced across her forehead without penetrating her skull. Bleeding heavily from the arrow wound which would leave a scar for the rest of her life, Pamelia and her brother also managed to reach Fort Houston to report the slaughter of their family.

The Indians ransacked the Campbell house, ripping open six feather beds and scattering the feathers, and stealing a keg of gunpowder, a trunk containing four-hundred dollars in silver, some clothing, bedding and some paper money. An armed pursuit party was hastily organized at Fort Houston, set out after the Indians, and found the Campbell's trunk, paper money and the empty keg discarded about a mile from the home. The men followed the trail of the Indians eight miles to the Trinity River, where the small band had to give up the chase because the lands on the west side of the river were filled with hostile Indians.[10]

From Fort Houston, postmaster William S. McDonald wrote a letter to the care of Captain Sadler at Fort Brown, addressing it to the citizens of Houston County. It was written during the late hours of January 23 after the survivors of the Campbell Massacre had arrived at the fort. McDonald acknowledged that the volunteer companies were still in the field and might see action but added the following plea: "We think our situation is quite critical, and would like to get as much assistance as can be afforded us." Before he mailed this letter the following morning, McDonald apparently visited the Campbell home to find the bodies of the victims. "I saw them myself," he wrote Sadler, "and such a scene I never saw before."

This latest act of violence against his Fort Houston neighbors, coupled with the recent murder of his own wife, child and relatives, was apparently more than Captain Sadler could stand. He wanted vengeance. He had seen the mutilated survivors of previous Indian attacks and had himself been involved in two battles with Cordova's rebels the previous fall. It became clear to him that anything attempted to stop these killings would have to involve a commitment from hundreds of citizens who were supported in their actions by the Republic of Texas.

With President Houston out of office, the frontier settlements hoped that new and more forceful methods would be employed to achieve safety. To this end, Sadler wrote to his old friend and fellow Georgian, President Mirabeau Lamar, concerning the rising Indian threat in East Texas. The letter was postmarked in Crockett.

Houston County Texas Febr. 22nd 1839

His Excellency M. B. Lamar

Sir, many have been the vicissitudes th[r]ough which I have pas'd since I saw you, not having saw you since soon after the Battle of San Jacinto. I returned to this neighborhood and commenced farming and married in March following and was doing well until the 18th of October last, at which time my wife was murdered by the Indians. Being at the time in the army myself in the command of a small company of volunteers by the order of Major E. Clapp, having left my companion in the care of her father.

I still remain in this country as yet, but if something efficient is not done to check the Indians, this county will have to break entire[ly]. A large portion of the inhabitants are already gone. There has been some futile attempts made to protect this county, but all the good they have done had been to impoverish the country, for so as they have destroyed the corn [and] beef in the neighborhood. They curse the people and leave them to shift for themselves and we are too weak now and daily becoming weaker so that I fear we shall have to break entire[ly]. And if this county should go, the county of Nacogdoches will follow and where it will stop God only knows.

It may be demanded, "What can be done?" for it is said the men cannot go from the Settlement for want of provisions and that the Troops cannot stay in the Settlement only so long as the corn and beef [of] the same lasts. When they are compelled to leave them without the means [of] substance and without protection.

What then is to be done in this case? All say something must be done and I say so too, but it is with great diffidence that I attempt to hint your Excellency what I think should be done. We cannot check the Indians unless we follow them to their place of rendezvous or where they have their familys and visit them with the same kind of warfare that they give us. We should spare neither age, sect nor condition, for they do not. I know it will be said this is barbarous and too much like the savage. And it certainly is harsh, but it is the only means in my view that will put them down and as such should be resorted to.

The plan of calling on the country for volunteers to go against the Indians will not do unless they are kept under better discipline and more subordination than they have been heretofore, for they only go so far as they think proper and swear they will go no farther and so go home and do nothing toward cowing the enemy; but I must stop, having said so much more than I expected when I sat down.

With every good wist for your health and prosperity and success in the important station to which you have been called, I have the honor to be

               Your Excellencys Obedient
               and humble servant

                        William T. Sadler[11]

Sadler's angry letter, received by Lamar in Houston three days later on February 25, reflected the state of emotions in East Texas in early 1839. Many families had been destroyed by savage attacks in the past two years and many others lived in constant fear. While his plea to "visit them with the same kind of warfare that they give us" was admittedly "harsh," Captain Sadler's patience with the hostile Indian tribes had long since expired.

With President Mirabeau Lamar in office, the resolution to the Indian problems he and others sought would not be long in coming.

Chapter Twelve

FRONTIER FREEDOM: THE CHEROKEE WAR

February 25 - July 16, 1839

After mailing his pugnacious letter to President Lamar, Captain Sadler stopped in Crockett long enough on February 25 to take care of some financial business. Having previously provided corn and livestock to the Third Militia Brigade in the field, he had been issued only a promissory note from the militia's quartermaster. Sadler now appeared before Houston County Justice of the Peace Elijah Gossett to authenticate his receipts.

In a document endorsed with "Republic of Texas, Houston County," Sadler swore "that the attached receipts from previous furnishing the army are just, true and original and the only ones were furnished for settlement and that he is not in any manner indebted to the government except as Endorser on the back of the above receipts."

The month of February 1839 saw Indian conflict in areas of Texas other than Houston County. Near Waterloo, the growing community that would soon be renamed Austin and surveyed for the capital city, Comanche Indians were attacking settlers more frequently. On February 15, Colonel John H. Moore of La Grange had led sixty-three volunteer rangers from La Grange and Bastrop under captains Noah Smithwick and William M. Eastland, plus sixteen Lipan Apaches under Chief Castro, against a hostile Comanche camp on the banks of the San Saba River. In the ensuing battle, Moore reported that his forces killed or wounded at least eighty Comanches with only seven rangers wounded, although one mortally.[1]

As was their custom, the Comanches sought revenge. On February 24 they attacked the home of widow Elizabeth Coleman, whose late husband Robert had been on Sam Houston's staff at San Jacinto, killing her and one of her sons while kidnapping her youngest son and some slaves from a neighboring home. Captain Jacob Burleson, brother of Colonel Edward Burleson, was killed this same day while leading a small band of men against the Indians in the vicinity of Brushy Creek northeast of Waterloo. Soon after his brother's demise, Colonel Burleson arrived on the afternoon of February 24 with another thirty-one men, including Captain Jesse Billingsley. Together, they led a two-pronged attack on the Comanches that ended in a sniping contest from protected positions. Three of the Texas Rangers were killed during the day before the Indians gathered up their own battle casualties and scattered under cover of the darkness.[2] The Battle of Brushy Creek was another example of the frontier depredations that were beginning to take their toll on volunteer groups.

The rise in violence on the frontier in early 1839 reached the point that it had to be dealt with using more disciplined military forces. Urged both by Captain Sadler's letter on February 25 and the pleas of others, President Lamar in Houston began by attempting to strengthen military presence on the prairies. On February 28, Lamar issued an appeal for volunteers to aid "the suffering conditions" of the "brave and energetic" Texans who were becoming overwhelmed by the increasing numbers of hostile Indians.[3] Due to the small size of the Texas Army, he put out a requisition in March 1839 on the counties of Harrisburg, Brazoria, Matagorda, Colorado, Liberty and Galveston to furnish six companies of volunteers to serve for a six month period on the Texas frontiers. An active recruiting campaign was undertaken using the incentives of paid salaries and land grants for those who served.[4]

The major responsibility for recruiting and commanding the frontier ranging companies of Texas was given to Colonel Henry Karnes, who had led the spy units at San Jacinto. Devereaux Woodlief, his former San Jacinto cavalry friend, was commissioned as the lieutenant colonel, and Lamar's friend William Jefferson Jones was named major. Secretary of War Johnston announced their appointment and informed the public that volunteer companies would be accepted for immediate service. County ranging companies were quickly organized, and by April 1839 there were at least twenty mounted volunteer companies and government-authorized ranger units in existence on the Texas frontiers.[5]

The Texas Revolution had provided ample incentive for volunteers to join the regular army, but Colonel Burleson soon found that sufficient forces did not exist for the current Indian crisis. The peak enlistment in the First Regiment of Infantry between 1839 and 1840 was 560 men, including company officers, with a shortage of five full companies. However, by March of 1839 only four total infantry companies were in existence although there were fifteen commissioned captains.

In Lieutenant Colonel Fisher's Second Battalion, there was Captain Sadler's Company A at Fort Brown in Houston County and Captain Adam Clendenin's Company B at Houston in present Harris County. Clendenin was a veteran of the 1836 army whose current company was recruited largely from stations in Houston, Galveston and Velasco. Colonel Burleson's First Battalion consisted of the other two companies. Company C was originally commanded by Captain John Kennymore until May, at which time Captain Samuel W. Jordan took acting command of a newly organized Company C recruited mainly from Houston. Company D was under Captain George Thomas Howard, whose enlistments were from Galveston, Houston, Brazoria, Gonzales and Velasco.[6]

During the early months of 1839, the frontier settlements of East Texas were protected primarily by volunteer militia units, with the one notable exception of Captain Sadler's infantry company. In response to a request from Secretary of State Sam Houston in March, Houston County was divided into separate militia districts to better protect its citizens. Captain Sadler's regulars were assigned to the area surrounding Fort Brown at Brownsville. Captain John Crist's district included Crockett and Mustang Prairie while the San Pedro-Neches district fell under Captain Benjamin W. Davis. Captain James Box's company remained on duty at Fort Houston, and these companies fell under the regional command of Major John Wortham, who had been promoted after his militia company's three-month period of service had expired in February.

Also in response to Secretary Houston's request, Houston County had elected justices of the peace for the various militia districts. In a letter to Sam Houston addressed April 7, 1839, from Mustang Prairie, Houston County Chief Justice Collin Aldrich noted the new justices of the peace for these districts.

> Dear Sir:
> Yours of the 5th of March came to hand, and in answer I will state to you that so far as I can understand the law, that justices of the peace should be elected for two years from the time of their election, but that there shall be elected on the

first Monday in February, 1837, and every two years after, one sheriff and also one coroner at the same time and in the same manner as sheriffs, but I cannot find any law saying the justices of the peace shall be elected at that time. The acting justices of the peace for the County of Houston are as follows:

For Fort Houston, C. T. Minza [McKenzie] and G. W. Browning in and for Capt. John Crist's militia district for Crockett and Mustang Prairie.

Elijah Gossett and William Dillard in and for Capt. B. W. Davis' militia district, for San Pedro and Neches; S. E. Kennedy and Ruben R. Russell, in and for Capt. William T. Sadler's militia district. The county has been laid off in militia districts under the new organization, and elections of company officers will take place immediately and in answer to yours of the 9th of March, I will answer that three copies of abstracts of original titles upon record only have been received, one by the politeness of Mr. G. W. Henchett, and two by mail. Your letter states that ten copies were sent. The journals referred to in yours of the 7th February, came to hand and have been distributed.

I am, Gentlemen, very respectfully,

Your "Obedient Servant,

"Collin Aldrich,

Chief Justice, Houston County."[7]

With the new President of Texas in power, efforts began in the spring of 1839 to remove the Indian threat for the settlers. While Chief Bowles, leader of the Cherokees, tried to convince the Texans that he was working on peace with his Indian leaders, he secretly met again with Mexican rebels.

The efforts of Vicente Cordova and his rebels had been beaten down in East Texas in 1838 by the Battle of Kickapoo, but their efforts to stir the local Indians continued. Cordova wrote to Mexican agent Manuel Flores in Matamoros, and these two instigators planned to meet in Texas to discuss their plans and future movements. Cordova was discovered en route, however, and was attacked by Colonel Burleson's forces near Seguin on March 28, 1839. With captains Micah Andrews and Jesse Billingsley each leading a division, Burleson's men killed about a third of the sixty-five rebels near the Guadalupe River. Although wounded, Cordova and his surviving members made it back into Mexico to regroup.[8]

Mexican agent Flores returned to Texas, departing in April of 1839 from Matamoros with about thirty Indians and Mexicans, but this time he was attacked by Texas Rangers under Lieutenant James O. Rice on May 18. A battle ensued on the San Gabriel River twenty-five miles from present-day Austin, and the rangers killed Flores and two of his followers. From his body the rangers recovered a packet of letters which revealed the Indian/Mexican intentions to attack the Texans.

The discovery of these letters was significant. These documents, sent to Texas Secretary of War Albert Sidney Johnston and General Burleson, commander of the First Regiment of Infantry, showed that Flores had letters for Big Mush and Chief Bowles of the Cherokees and that he had also been in contact with the chiefs of the Caddoes, Kickapoos, Shawnees and other tribes. The letters also proved that Flores and Cordova had been commissioned by Mexican authorities to "harass the Texans persistently, burn their habitations, lay waste their fields, steal their horses, and pursue and punish all Indians friendly to the Texans and all Mexicans who traded with them."[9]

These captured letters caused President Lamar to consider the Cherokees to be conspirators working with Mexico to forge another assault on his young republic. In May, Lamar sent an armed force under Major Baley Walters, a veteran of the Kickapoo battle, to occupy the Neches Saline located inside the Cherokees' claim. The village of Chief Bowles was located just east of the Neches River, near the saline which is in present Smith County.

Bowles' village had moved several times since the Cherokees had first entered Texas. Their total number of three to four-hundred in 1828 had made their home on the Sabine River in northeastern Texas. In 1836 for the Sam Houston treaty, Bowles had been in the village that was about fifteen miles southwest of present Henderson. As many as six other Cherokee villages existed north of Nacogdoches during the late 1830s, including that of Chief Big Mush ("Gatunwali" in the Cherokee tongue) south of present Rusk.[10]

By 1838, the large tribe of Cherokees under Chief Bowles had moved their village to its location near the Neches Saline in the area known as Cherokee Nation by an 1836 treaty with Sam Houston. In the course of operating his salt business at the saline, Bowles entered into partnership with Dr. Elisha DeBard, who had been wounded at nearby Kickapoo the previous year and now lived near the saline. The Cherokees thus considered this great saline their

Chief Bowles, the eighty-three-year-old leader of the Texas Cherokees, was the lead negotiator between the Indians and the Texas couriers during 1839. Neither side could reach a compromise, ending in the heated Battle of the Neches in July in which Chief Bowles would be slain. Captain Sadler is among those soldiers who later claimed to have fired one of the shots that killed Bowles.
Courtesy of the Archives and Information Division of the Texas State Archives.

tribe's business source, and Chief Bowles threatened Major Walters' troops with forceful resistance if they tried to occupy the saline.

Chief Bowles also wrote a letter to General Rusk in Nacogdoches, complaining that his people were alarmed by the presence of Walters' troops.[11] Major Walters and his company had set up a working camp that became known as Fort Saline, in present Henderson County, from which Captain Snively's company had previously operated. Pressure from the Indians, however, compelled Walters to move his men back to the west side of the Neches to the old Kickapoo village, site of the previous year's battle. There they established Fort Kickapoo, which would soon became a major assembling point for Texan troops.[12]

The capture of the Mexican rebels' papers in late May had thus started a turn of events that would lead to a showdown with the Cherokees in Texas.

* * * *

THE ASSEMBLY OF TEXAN TROOPS

This latest threat toward the security of the Texas frontiers helped President Lamar to support the various military forces in place throughout the outlying settlements. Efforts were made to maintain the frontier militia units as well as the revamped regular army. A letter dated May 22, 1839, to Major Hillequist Landers, Commander of Subsistence, from Quartermaster General William G. Cooke demonstrates the provisioning for the two Houston County volunteer companies under Major John Wortham. This letter informed Major Landers that he would be issued contracts for the purchase of food supplies for these troops and that these contracts would be paid by the Texas government.[13]

Cooke's subsistence orders provided for a one month's supply of corn and beef "for four hundred men to be placed under the immediate charge of Major John Wortham, and only subject to the order of Colonel Burleson." Cooke also ordered that corn and beef be provided to Captain Box's thirty-one-man outfit at Fort Houston and to the Honorable Isaac Parker in Crockett. Parker at this time was the Houston County elected representative in the House for the Third Congress. It appears that the same provisions were used by Captain Sadler's Company A at Fort Brown. His payroll records show his company being paid their dues for service, subsistence, forage and clothing on May 29.

Maintenance of the various military forces in East Texas was becoming increasingly important during the end of May as events began moving quickly with the Cherokee situation. After Major Walters was threatened by Chief Bowles, President Lamar sent the Cherokees an ultimatum which denied them their right to live in Texas as a nation within a nation. This letter was delivered to Bowles' village by Texas Indian agent Martin Lacy, twenty-one-year-old Private John Henninger Reagan, Dr. William G. W. Jowers who was a surgeon attached to Walters' range company, and a half-breed interpreter named Cordray, who all went to meet with the Indians.

While the Texan troops were working on Fort Kickapoo, this small party made their way to another village of Bowles that was located farther south of the saline during 1838 and 1839. This second village was located about four miles northwest of the present town of Alto, about five miles north of the old San Antonio Road, or King's Highway, and about three miles north of Lacy's Fort. This particular Cherokee camp was located 150 feet from a spring now called Bowles Creek and about five-hundred yards northwest of the small community of Red Lawn, several miles northwest of present Alto along Highway 69.[14]

The meetings were conducted using interpreters. According to John Reagan, neither Chief Bowles nor the Texan agent, Martin Lacy, "could read or write, except that Mr. Lacy could sign his name mechanically; and neither could speak the language of the other."[15]

Modern view of the Neches River in extreme northeastern Anderson County, near the site of old Fort Kickapoo, where Texas forces assembled in July 1839 during what was known as the Cherokee War. Author's Collection.

In addition to the ultimatum, Bowles was advised that he had no authority to order Major Walters to leave the Neches Saline. As for the Indian depredations in East Texas, Reagan said that Bowles "made a denial of the charges contained in that communication, and said the wild Indians had done the killing and stealing, and not his people."[16] The result of the meeting was Bowles' agreement to confer with his chiefs for ten days to debate the effects of the letter.[17]

As the tensions began building in the Cherokee Nation, efforts were made to reinforce Major Walters and his small company of men. By late May, President Lamar had already ordered Colonel Edward Burleson and his regular army at "Camp Burleson" to march to East Texas to join the other forces being gathered. Captain Martin Snell had resigned from the First Infantry on May 17, having served in the army since the Texas Revolution. On May 27, two volunteer companies under the direction of Lieutenant Colonel Devereaux Woodlief, who had been wounded at San Jacinto, and Major William Jones departed Bastrop to join with Burleson. (Ironically, the Battle of Bird's Creek occurred on the western frontier on this same date on the Little River. Captain John Bird and six other rangers were killed or wounded in a major fight with Comanche braves.)

Burleson's 1st Battalion of the First Regiment of Infantry included Captain Samuel Jordan's Company C and Captain George Howard's

Company D. These regular forces were augmented by Woodlief's two volunteer companies under captains Mark B. Lewis and James P. Ownby. In addition, Burleson's close friend Chief Placido would lead twenty-four of his Tonkawa braves as a small scouting company. Preparation of some of his more rebellious troops had taken longer than expected, but Burleson departed his Mount Pleasant plantation on June 27 and began the move northeastward toward Cherokee lands. Including the Tonkawa company, his forces numbered more than 260 men. This total number increased slightly when they were joined en route by Lieutenant Colonel William Fisher of the Second Battalion from the Brazos area.[18]

About ten days after receiving Lamar's ultimatum, Chief Bowles finally reported that he and Chief Big Mush were unable to reach a peaceful agreement. From Lacy's Fort, agent Martin Lacy, Dr. Jowers, John Reagan and their interpreter Cordray again visited the Cherokee leader near present Alto. Bowles told them that the younger men of his tribe were ready for war, although he and Big Mush wished to avoid it.

According to Reagan, Bowles told them that the young braves "believed they could whip the whites; that he knew the whites could ultimately whip them, but it would cost them ten years of bloody frontier war." The Cherokee leader said that he had no choice but to stand by his people's wishes, for "if he fought, the whites would kill him; and if he refused to fight, his own people would kill him."[19]

Although negotiations would soon be resumed, both the Texans and the Indians were now quietly preparing for conflict. After this meeting in June, Chief Bowles hurriedly conferred with his chiefs and began to gather forces, including Shawnees and Delawares, in Cherokee Nation east of the Neches River in present Smith County. It appears that after this last conference on Bowles Creek, the elder Cherokee leader ceased to use his village near Lacy's Fort and began to operate from his village near the Neches Saline.[20]

Mirabeau Lamar wasted no time in making known his intentions, and the publishers of the *Telegraph* in Houston agreed with his thinking. In an editorial printed on June 19, the newspaper stated that the Cherokees were "unwelcome intruders among us." The *Telegraph* also stated that the Cherokees' connections with Mexican rebels "have already cost us much blood and suffering", and that the time had come to put "an end to these things."

In Houston County, Lamar ordered troops to be assembled to prepare for battle with the Cherokees. According to John Reagan, these troops were first assembled and organized into companies and regiments at Fort Kickapoo in present northeast Anderson County.[21] Among those moving up to Kickapoo was Captain Sadler's Company A of the First Regiment. At Fort Houston, Captain Box's company was relieved by Captain Adam Clendenin's Company B until his men later joined the rest of Burleson's regulars. Box's company is known to have joined the forces at Fort Kickapoo, while Clendenin's became commander of the Fort Houston post from June 28-July 12, 1839.[22]

Aside from Houston County militia companies under Majors Walters and Wortham, a large force of the Second Regiment, Third Brigade of the Texas Militia arrived from Nacogdoches. This force was headed by Colonel Tom Rusk, the veteran Indian campaign leader and San Jacinto hero. As of June 27, President Lamar had appointed Rusk and four others -- Vice President David Burnet, Secretary of War Albert Sidney Johnston, Isaac Watts Burton and James S. Mayfield -- as members of a presidential commission which was specifically charged with removing the Cherokee Indians and all other emigrant tribes residing in Texas.

Heading the roughly three-hundred men from Nacogdoches, Rusk's Third Brigade staff included Lieutenant Colonel James Smith, Major Elisha Clapp, Adjutant Major William N. Dunnington, Sergeant Major Ira Munson, Surgeon Lemuel B. Brown, Quartermaster Edward B. Noble and James Carter, captain of a special spy company that was formed en route. Most of his companies were formed between June 21 and June 28, at which time Rusk marched his regiment to the old Kickapoo village. The company leaders under Rusk's command were captains Carter, Alexander Jordan, Robert W. Smith, Peter Tipps and Jackson Todd. Most of these men had been involved in Rusk's previous 1838 Indian campaigns, and Bob Smith, a former first lieutenant in Sadler's San Jacinto company, had commanded a company in the Kickapoo battle.

At the same time, Colonel Willis Landrum hurriedly assembled his Third Regiment of the Third Brigade of the Texas Militia. His forces consisted of four companies of volunteers from the counties of Harrison, Sabine, San Augustine and Shelby. While Colonel Burleson's main body of the regular Texas Army marched in from the west, Landrum's volunteer companies marched in from the east during early July toward Fort Kickapoo.

General Rusk's troops joined the negotiations near the Indian village and the general immediately immersed himself in the

The Cherokee War of 1839
July 15-16, 1839
Composition of Texan Forces

Command Staff

Kelsey Harris Douglass	Brig. General
Albert Sidney Johnston	Sec. of War
Hugh McLeod	Adj. General
David Spangler Kaufman	Major
Jacob Snively	Brig. Major
David G. Burnet	Vice President
Isaac Watts Burton	Commissioner
James S. Mayfield	Commissioner
Samuel Davis	Aide de Camp
Leonard H. Mabbitt	Aide de Camp
James H. Millroy	Aide de Camp
Palmer Job Pillans	Aide de Camp
Benjamin B. Sturgess	Aide de Camp
John Wortham (Major)	Quartermaster
Martin Lacy	Indian Agent

Douglass' Volunteer Regiment

Baley C. Walters	Major
Solomon Adams	Captain
James Edward Box	Captain
Greenberry H. Harrison	Captain
Henry Madison Smith	Captain
Benjamin A. Vansickle	Captain
John Thayer	Commissary
William G. W. Jowers	Surgeon

Texas Army
First Regiment of Infantry

Edward Burleson	Colonel
William Jefferson Jones	Major
William D. Houghton	1st Lieutenant
Benjamin B. Sturgess	Quartermaster
Shields Booker	Surgeon
Richard Cochran	Ast. Surgeon

Second Battalion
William Jefferson Jones Major
Company C
Samuel W. Jordan Captain
Company D
George Thomas Howard Captain

Volunteer Battalion
Devereaux J. Woodlief Lt. Col
Volunteer Companies
Mark B. Lewis Captain
James P. Ownby Captain
Tonkawa Braves
Chief Placido Captain

First Battalion
William S. Fisher Lt. Colonel
Company A
William Turner Sadler Captain
Company B
Adam Clendenin Captain

Rusk's Nacogdoches Regiment
(2nd Reg., 3rd Brigade Texas Militia)

Thomas Jefferson Rusk	Colonel
James Smith	Lt. Colonel
Elisha Clapp	Major
William N. Dunnington	Adjutant Major
Ira Munson	Sgt. Major
Lemuel B. Brown	Surgeon
L. Martin	Ast. Surgeon
Edward B. Noble	Quartermaster
Alex McIver	Commissary
James Carter	Captain of Spies

Rusk's Volunteer Regiment

Alexander Jordan	Captain
Lewis Sanchez	Captain
Robert W. Smith	Captain
Peter Tipps	Captain
Jackson Todd	Captain

Col. Landrum's Mounted Regiment
(3rd Reg., 3rd Brigade Texas Militia)

Willis H. Landrum	Colonel
Moses L. Roberts	Lt. Colonel
James M. Thompson	Major
George English	Adjutant Major
Thomas Haugh	Serg. Major
Robert O. Lusk	Quartermaster
John M. Hansford	Surgeon
J. R. Robertson	Ast. Surgeon

Harrison/Shelby Counties Company
John Inman Captain
Sabine County Company
James McKim Captain
Shelby County Company
Mitchell Garrison Captain
San Augustine County Company
William Kimbro Captain

Note: See Appendix C for Roster of the Participants in the Cherokee War of East Texas.

negotiations with the Cherokees. By early July Brigadier General Kelsey Douglass, overall commander of the Texas Militia's Third Brigade, had also arrived in camp with his own staff and additional volunteers. Major John Wortham joined Douglass' staff on July 1 as his quartermaster, leaving Major Walters in charge of the volunteer companies previously under his charge. In camp, Captain Sadler's pension papers show that he took advantage of Wortham's new post by giving him power of attorney to settle some of the claims he had outstanding for providing food to the Texas Militia the previous year.

In further talks, Rusk and the other commissioners, Burnet, Johnston, Burton and Mayfield, formally notified Chief Bowles on July 9 of the presidential committee's decision to remove his people.[23] As the ensuing days passed, it allowed time for the Texans to gather their troops against the rising number of Cherokee warriors. In truth, most of the men felt that any further negotiations with the Indians would do little more than buy time for their own reinforcements.

* * * *

"Between Two Fires": Final Negotiations Fail

Rusk finally invited Chiefs Bowles and Big Mush to meet the Texas commissioners on July 10 for talks at a spot near the Saline Creek, just off the Neches River, that became known as "Council Creek." Colonel Hugh McLeod and others delivered this message, approaching the Cherokee village under a white flag because Bowles considered any large group to be hostile. After a brief discussion, the elder Cherokee chief agreed to come to Camp Johnston to which, in anticipation of this meeting, the growing number of Texas forces had moved their camp from Fort Kickapoo on the west side of the Neches. The new camp established was located on Council Creek, just east of the Neches about six miles from the camp of Chief Bowles, and was named after the current Secretary of War.

On July 10, Bowles arrived with twenty-one Indians, including Chief Key of the Cherokees and Chief Spy Buck, representing Chief Linney, of the Shawnees, to meet with the Texan delegates. The Cherokee representatives would not speak until Big Mush had been summoned to join. Chief Harris of the Delawares joined on July 11. Rusk said that the Cherokees' friendship with both the wild Indians and the Mexicans forced the Texans into a no-choice situation. He told Bowles that "you are between two fires" and that "if you remain you will be destroyed."[24]

Chief Bowles had no comment until Big Mush could appear. Bowles gave a speech on July 12, saying that his people would leave just as soon as they could gather enough supplies for the move. Spy Buck, representing the Shawnee's Chief Linney, said that his people would need two months to prepare to move. General Rusk broke up the meeting after all agreed to gather again in two days.

On July 14, the final meeting at Council Creek was held between Rusk, Johnston, Burnet, Burton and Mayfield for Texas and Bowles and twenty Indians. Bowles and Chief Key at first refused to sit on blankets on the ground in traditional Cherokee fashion, although Bowles finally did give in. Rusk noted with apprehension that the Indian leaders had painted their faces black for this meeting and they carried war clubs in their hands.[25]

The Texas commissioners laid out their plan for the Cherokees and their associated bands, the Delawares and Shawnees, to leave in peace with Texas paying them "just compensation" for their improvements, crops and properties. Texas would help the less fortunate Indians, but in return the Cherokees must leave the locks from their guns with Texas troops until they had crossed into the United States. At this point, Bowles strenuously objected to the armed guard and the loss of gunlocks, refusing to sign the Texas agreement. He said that he would call a council to present the articles to the other chiefs, promising their answer to Mayfield in the following morning.[26]

A significant event on July 14, and one that may have served to further discourage the Indians from negotiating, was the arrival of the rest of the Texan troops. Burleson's four companies of regulars and volunteers had marched steadily, stopping briefly at Fort Milam on the Brazos in early July before pushing across the Neches River for Rusk's camp. His men had arrived in Houston County and stopped at Fort Houston on July 13 before pushing on. Captain Clendenin, who had commanded Fort Houston for the previous two weeks, and his Company B of the First Regiment joined Burleson at this time for the march to Camp Johnston. The large force under Burleson arrived at Camp Johnston in Cherokee country on the afternoon of July 14, shortly behind Colonel Willis Landrum's four-company militia regiment.[27]

Burleson and Landrum found Rusk, Douglass and other East Texas forces already in camp in negotiations. With the arrival of Landrum's men, the number in camp had reached approximately eleven-hundred, more troops than had engaged the Mexican army at San Jacinto! Disagreements immediately arose as to who would command the vast force which had been gathered to fight the Cherokees. There were many different sentiments, but the volunteers generally wanted Rusk to lead while the regulars demanded Burleson.

Refusing to oppose each other, Rusk and Burleson agreed to let General Kelsey Douglass, commander of the militia of that part of the Republic, take overall command.[28] Douglass' own staff included Brigadier Major Jacob Snively and James Mayfield, Samuel Davis, Palmer J. Pillans, James H. Millroy, Benjamin Sturgess and Leonard Mabbitt as his volunteer aides.

A large number of the men comprising the fighting forces of the Texans were from Fort Houston and surrounding communities in Houston County. Ben Vansickle's mounted company included many Houston County men that Captain Sadler knew well such as Samuel Box, Darius Edens, Balis Edens and John Parker. Captain James Box's company also included men with whom Sadler had previously fought in the Indian engagements of 1838, including Daniel M. Crist, Stephen Crist, Eli Faulkenberry, William Frost, Daniel McKenzie, Lacy McKenzie, Jacob Morrow, Payten Parker, William Perry, and Humphries Ussery. Two of the men criticized for not doing more for their families in the Edens-Madden Massacre were also present: James Madden, a member of Captain William Kimbro's San Augustine company, and Martin Murchison, a member of Captain Jackson Todd's Nacogdoches company.

On July 15, Colonel Mayfield and several officers tried again to force Bowles to sign the peace agreement, but he refused without the signatures of Chief Harris and Chief Big Mush. At noon on July 15, Burnet, Rusk, Burton, Mayfield and Johnston came back to the Texas camp and announced that they had failed to reach a settlement in the peace talks with Chief Bowles. Apparently, the Indian warriors were prepared to put their fates in the hands of the Great Spirit and fight to their deaths to stay in Texas.

While the negotiations proceeded on July 15, General Douglass dispatched Captain William Kimbro's seventy-man company of San Augustine volunteers to the village of the Shawnees to enforce neutrality by demanding the surrender of their gunlocks.[29] When they arrived the following afternoon, the gunlocks were promptly delivered. Private "Rip" Ford of Kimbro's company, however, believed that Chief Spy Buck had just returned from battle and that the Shawnees had removed the locks from only their "ordinary pieces, and kept the best concealed."[30]

Following the final negotiations on July 15, Chief Bowles sent his son John, accompanied by a prominent half-breed Cherokee named

Fox Fields, to Camp Johnston under a truce flag. True to his word, the old chief was honoring the agreement that both sides keep each other notified on moves. These messengers informed Albert Sidney Johnston that the Cherokees would break camp this day and move to the west of the Neches River. Johnston thanked John Bowles and informed him that the Texas Army would break camp and follow the Cherokees. When approached by Texas forces, the Indians were to display a white flag and surrender their gun locks or be attacked. Bowles and Fields were then accompanied half a mile beyond the Texas picket lines.[31]

July 15: The Evening Engagement

From camp, General Kelsey Douglass wrote a report to Secretary of War Johnston of the ensuing action, stating, "Under your orders the whole force was put in motion towards the encampment of Bowles on the Neches – Col. Landrum crossed on the west side of the Neches and up the river."[32]

The Texas troops had orders to proceed to the Cherokee village but, however, not to fire upon the Indians until the warriors had been summoned for a chance to accept the terms of the government. Upon discovery that Bowles' warriors had deserted their village, the Texan troops moved out shortly after 1:00 p.m. from Camp Johnston and advanced quickly over the sixteen mile distance toward the Delaware village, where it was believed that the Cherokees had retreated only hours before.

Colonel Landrum's Third Regiment was dispatched to the west side of the Neches with "orders to reunite with the main body as soon as he could ascertain that the Indians had not crossed over."[33] This left General Douglass with nearly nine-hundred men, including his staff, his and Rusk's volunteer regiments and the regulars under Ned Burleson. Finding the trail of the enemy's horses and cattle easy to track, these troops pushed forward toward the Delaware village.

It was about 5:00 p.m. when the Texas spies under Captain James Carter discovered the position of the Indians and were fired upon by the enemy's advance guard. The remainder of Captain Jack Todd's company, from which Carter's spies were largely pulled, of Rusk's regiment was ordered to move forward rapidly to support the spy company.[34]

In the vicinity of the Delaware village near a small creek, the Indians were spotted on the point of a hill at the head of a prairie. According to battle participants James D. Long and Jeff Wallace, the

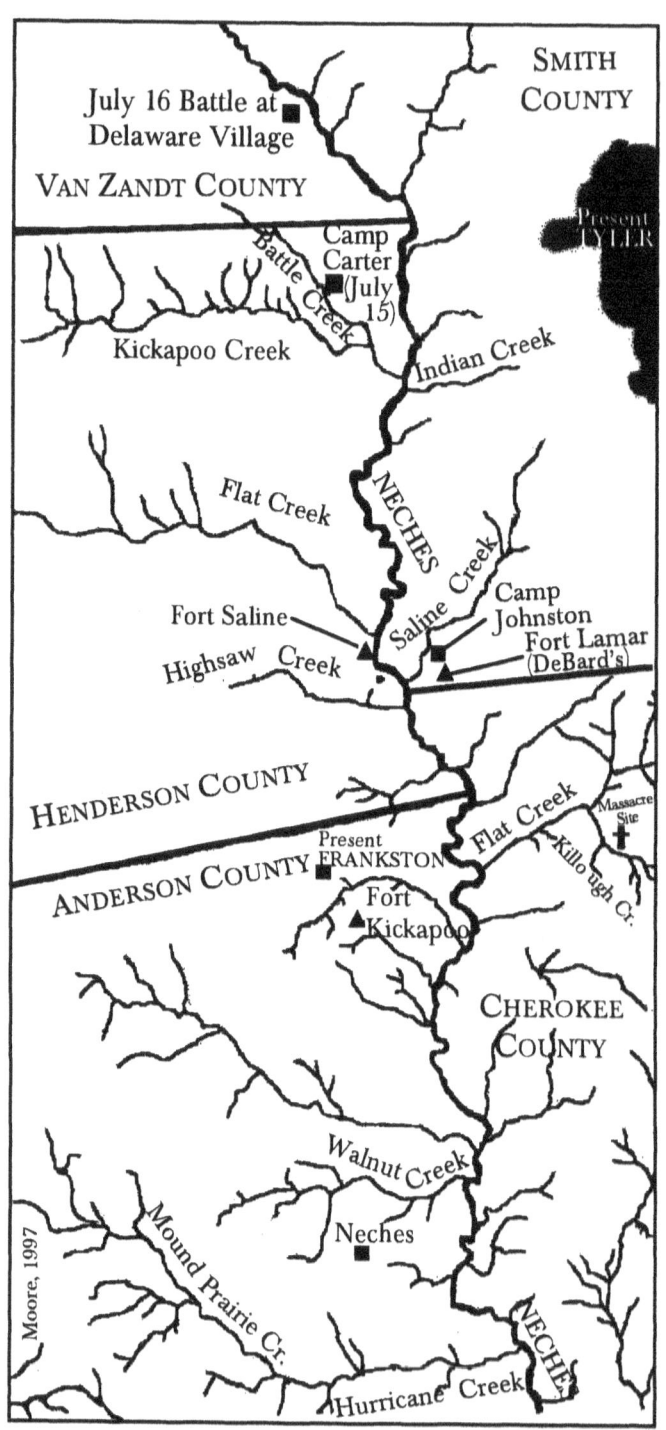

Cherokee War of East Texas July 1839

This map shows the location of the key areas related to the Cherokee War of 1839. All areas east of the Neches River on this map were considered to be Cherokee Indian lands at that time.

After peace negotiations with Chief Bowles began to deteriorate, Texan troops were gathered at Fort Kickapoo in present Anderson County and later at Camp Johnston in present Smith County. These forces included companies of the Texas Militia and the regular army, or First Regiment of Infantry.

The main battle of the Cherokee War became known as the Battle of the Neches. The first day's fight on July 15 occurred near the present town of Chandler, Texas, along Battle Creek. This site afterwards became the Texans' "Camp Carter".

The main battle occurred on July 16 near a Delaware Indian village in present Van Zandt County. Chief Bowles and one-hundred of his Indians were killed and the Cherokees were thereafter driven from Texas.

Indians had broken their camp on July 15 and retreated west across the Neches at a spot about one-hundred yards south of where Indian Creek empties into the river. The principal fight this day occurred along Battle Creek about 3.5 miles northwest of present Chandler, in Henderson County.[35]

Chief Bowles had sent the women and children ahead of the battle area while leaving the braves behind to fight.[36] Rusk motioned toward the enemy to come into action while the Texan forces advanced. The Indians were well entrenched behind a high creek bank. Behind them lay thick woods which would provide them a safe retreat or a good secondary line of defense. On the other hand, Douglass' troops had before them an open prairie with only a thicket of gum bushes, to their right, which paralleled the creek from which to advance. The Indian warriors clearly had an advantage in terms of positioning.[37]

The firing which commenced upon Carter's company was taken as a signal to action by the anxious volunteer Texans. An account of the action on July 15 printed in the *Telegraph* on August 7 relates:

> Great impatience was manifested by our troops and orders loosely given were not clearly understood and but imperfectly obeyed. The hideous yells of the savages, instead of startling our soldiers, excited their spirit for the combat, and they rushed to it pell-mell, determined to drive the enemy from the cover of the timber and brushwood.

General Rusk ordered his companies to advance across the field. Carter's spy company and a twenty-five-man detachment of Captain Todd's company charged the Indians in front. The second portion of Burleson's army regiment, Lieutenant Colonel Woodlief leading Captain Samuel Jordan's regulars and Captain Mark Lewis' Harrisburg volunteers, also charged toward the enemy in the ravine. The Indians taking shelter in the ravine were instantly charged and flanked on the left by Colonel Burleson and the first portion of his regiment, which included the companies of George Howard, James Ownby and Chief Placido.

The Indians commenced firing on the troops of Douglass, Rusk and Burleson as they advanced across the prairie. "As we advanced, the lines were immediately formed and the action became general," wrote Douglass. Aside from captains Todd and Carter's companies, the rest of Tom Rusk's troops and Captain Sadler's Company A took a position on a point of a hill to the right and

July 15th Cherokee Engagement
Texan Casualties

Name	Rank	Company	Remarks:
Joseph S. Anderson	Pvt.	Capt. Lewis	Wounded.
Solomon Allbright	Pvt.	Capt. Vansickle	Wounded.
James Ball	Pvt.	Company D	Shot in the eye.
John Crane	Pvt.	Capt. Harrison	Killed.
Henry P. Crowson	Pvt.	Capt. Harrison	Mortally wounded.
John Day	Pvt.	Company D	Fatally hit in the head.
John A. Harper	Pvt.	Capt. Madison Smith	Wounded.
James McAnulty	Pvt.	Capt. Tipps	Wounded.
Henry M. Rogers	Dr.	Capt. Tipps	Killed.
George T. Slaughter	Pvt.	Capt. Box	Slightly wounded.
John B. Thacker	Pvt.	Capt. Bob Smith	Wounded.
James R. Wilehart	Pvt.	Capt. Tipps	Wounded.

drove a party of Indians which attempted to flank General Douglass' main body of troops on the field from that quarter. By thus splitting their troops, the Texans were able to drive the Indian forces from their ravine and thicket. This action occurred about half an hour before sundown and was quite lively for many.

Private John Reagan, from Bob Smith's seventy-five-man Nacogdoches company, and Major David S. Kaufman charged on their horses toward an Indian who fired upon them and then sought refuge in the creek. The two were quickly ambushed by the fire of other Indians in the creekbed and forced to ride through a gauntlet of enemy fire before escaping to the open prairie. Both men managed somehow to emerge uninjured, rejoining a portion of their regiment that included Chief Placido's Tonkawa company and several of Captain Smith's company: Smith, First Sergeant Andrew Caddell, his sons John and Jeremiah Caddell, Ambrose H. Crain, Martin Lacy and David Rusk of Captain Carter's company.

As the Texans advanced, the enemy's firing was intense. Dr. Henry M. Rogers from Captain Tipps' forty-six-man company was shot three times and fell dead. John Crane from Captain Greenberry Horras Harrison's mounted gunmen was shot through the body as his horse reared up, and he also fell mortally wounded to the battlefield. (Captain Harrison had moved to Houston County in late 1835 and later served in the Texas Congress.) From General Douglass' command, Private Solomon Allbright of Captain Ben Vansickle's fifty-one-man company was wounded. Also wounded in the action was George T. Slaughter of Captain Box's command.

Both sides suffered casualties during the firing that continued in the failing sunlight. Many of the Texans dismounted their horses and proceeded on foot while driving the Cherokees from their defensive positions. The Indians soon fled the battlefield under cover of darkness, carrying off their fallen warriors as usual as witnessed by many of the Texan troops.

Despite many Indians' being removed from the field, eighteen Cherokees were left. From Douglass' command, three men were killed, one man was wounded mortally and ten men were wounded in some fashion. Dr. Albert Woldert, author of a detailed 1920s article on the Cherokee War, had large iron pins placed in the ground where Dr. Rogers and John Crane were buried about two-hundred yards due west of a bend in Battle Creek.[38]

General Douglass' action report was later considered to be biased toward his own command, neglecting the contributions of Burleson's regular army. Burleson wrote a letter to the *Telegraph and Texas Register* which was published on October 23, 1839, in which he gave credit largely to his four companies for driving the Indians from the ravine. They were joined, he wrote, by the spy company of Captain Carter, a portion of Captain Jack Todd's company, and "some few scattering volunteers from other companies."[39] Adjutant General McLeod explained that Rusk and Douglass' regiments had been given credit for some of the attack that Burleson's men had made, but that Rusk's men had also fought valiantly. The casualty list shows that there were actually twice as many volunteer casualties as those from Burleson's regiment.

As night fell on the July 15 battle, the fighting stopped while Texan forces hurriedly gathered Indian lead, powder and provisions abandoned by Bowles' forces. The report of Douglass of the following morning shows:

> Col. Landrum was not able [to join this fight], having so much farther to march to participate in the engagement, but has been ordered to join this morning. All behaved so gallantly it would be invidious to particularize; the action commenced about half an hour before sundown which prevented pursuit. Most of their baggage was captured: five kegs of powder, 250 lbs. lead, many horses, cattle, corn and other property.

Doctors took care of the Texan casualties into the night while Douglass and his fellow leaders regrouped their men for the fight they expected to continue the following morning. The Texas army made camp that night near the battleground and named it Camp Carter in honor of James Carter, whose spy company had first engaged the Indians.

A large number of the men were sent out to guard the exposed frontier settlements in the path of the Cherokee retreat.[40] Captain Sadler and those who had fought in the previous Indian battles of 1838 knew well of the possibilities of a surprise Indian attack during the cover of darkness. A vigilant guard was thus maintained at the Texan camp throughout the night. There were likely few who slept peacefully; all expected full-fledged combat with the Cherokees at any moment.

July 16: Finale at the Delaware Village

The Indians and their allies were on the move before dawn the next morning, retreating up the Neches River. The Indians stopped at the Delaware village above the Neches River northwest of the present town of Chandler, located in the extreme northeastern corner of Henderson County just west of Tyler. The early morning hours in the Texas camp were spent burying the dead and detaching a guard with the wounded to Fort Lamar.

Fort Lamar was actually the home of Dr. Elisha DeBard, who had recently been in the salt-making business near the Neches with Chief Bowles and his Cherokees. Captain Adam Clendenin's Company B of the First Regiment of Infantry had been detached on July 15 to construct a more durable fort. Colonel Burleson obviously expected the Cherokee War to carry on for some time and likely knew that a less-disciplined volunteer company would not allow itself to miss the fight to work on a military structure.

Clendenin's company began building several cabins around DeBard's house and salt-producing warehouse, with the perimeter eventually surrounded by a stockade fence. Following the first battle, the army's surgeons set up a field hospital at the new Fort Lamar named for the new President.[41]

The two regiments under Burleson and Rusk broke camp at 10:00 a.m. on July 16 and renewed their march against the enemy. With those detached to frontier settlements or to DeBard's, the Texan forces had dwindled considerably. In his official report, General Douglass wrote,

> The effective force of the two regiments this morning amounted to about 500, an escort having been sent with the

The Neches battlefield *as it now appears in present Van Zandt County, near Tyler, Texas. This view looks down from the old Delaware village to the upper portion of a hill where the first fighting occurred on July 16, 1839. Beyond the thicket to left is a ravine the Indians occupied as a defensive position until driven into the Neches bottomland beyond.* Author's collection.

wounded to Debards (now Fort Lamar), and many other upon detached service. Col. Landrum not having reached Headquarters the evening previous, orders now dispatched to him to continue his march up the east side of the Neches, which it was understood he had crossed, and joined the main body on its march in the direction of Harris."[42]

The Delaware village of Chief Harris, located on a hill above the Neches River in the extreme southeastern corner of present Van Zandt County just west of present Tyler, occupied an eminence in a scattered group of post oaks. A heavily-timbered bottom land of the Neches stretched out below this village. According to Major William Jones of the Texas Army, it had become "apparent that the reinforcements looked for by Bowles had not reached him and that he was falling back to meet them."[43]

Douglass' forces moved toward the Delaware village with Burleson's regiment on the right and Rusk's to the left. At about 11:00 a.m., after moving about five miles from Camp Carter, they were met by William Nobbitt, a spy from Captain Carter's company who had been dispatched with the intelligence that Carter's men had discovered the enemy's spies a short distance ahead. In the event the enemy made a stand, Colonel Burleson with one battalion was ordered to move forward and sustain the spy company. If the enemy was engaged, Rusk was to rush forward with one battalion of his regiment to support both Burleson and Carter's men, while the balance of the Texan forces marched forward.[44]

Ned Burleson quickly moved forward with the regular companies of captains George Howard and Samuel Jordan plus his steadfast Tonkawa braves under Chief Placido. Over the hill and beyond the vacant Delaware village, Captain Carter's spies had actually discovered the main body of Chief Bowles' forces which had taken up a defensive position in a ravine on the lower side of the hill that descended down toward the river bottom. As Burleson's battalion rode to the brow of the hill and prepared to dismount, the cracking of rifle fire could be heard as Carter's men were taken under fire by the warriors.

As the Texans scrambled to dismount their horses, the Indians at the forefront managed to shoot seven horses and fatally wound one of Burleson's men, Private Martin Tutts of Captain Jordan's Company C. Carter and Burleson's forces soon repulsed the Indian attack and drove them back into the ravine with the main enemy forces for better shelter.

Just behind at the Delaware village, General Rusk quickly formed up his regiment to the front of the troops and led the companies of captains Tipps and Todd to the aid of the men under Carter and Burleson. "The position the enemy occupied was a very favorable one for defense," according to the report of Douglass, "they occupying a ravine and thicket, and our troops having to advance upon them through open woods and down a considerable hill."

As the Texas troops moved forward, they burned the Delaware village. Amidst the terrific noonday July heat, the smoke swirled in black clouds. The Indians below the village were occupying a dry creek bed that ran from the north to the south downhill before turning to the east and heading for the Neches bottom. Just above this bend was a prairie, about half a mile long, located to the east of the part of the creek that ran south. Near the lower end of the prairie and running north, parallel to the creek, was a thicket of hackberry bushes and rattan vines of about three-hundred yards in length.[45]

The Texan forces quickly formed near the Delaware village. The decision was made to leave behind every sixth man of the remaining troops to hold and guard the horses while the rest of the soldiers advanced on foot.[46] Rusk and his lead battalion quickly occupied the point of the hill on both sides of the road leading toward the ravine where the enemy's heavy fire was concentrated. Moving in quickly on the ground next was Lieutenant Colonel James Smith with the First Battalion of Rusk's regiment, consisting of Captain Bob Smith's Nacogdoches company on the right and Captain Madison Smith's company on the left side. General Douglass' lively report continues.

> Col. Burleson in the meantime having obliqued to the left and engaged the extreme right of the Indians; Lt. Col. Woodlief, with the two volunteer companies under Captains Lewis and Ownby had been ordered to deploy and form upon the extreme right, which order was promptly obeyed. The men were brought up in good order, and formed directly on the right. Rusk occupying the center, in which a brisk fire was kept up for about an hour and a half and returned with spirit and animation by our men, who continued to advance upon the enemy.

David Rusk of Carter's company was slightly wounded early in this action. Captain Jordan of Burleson's command was also wounded yet bravely continued to command his men while lying on the ground. From Captain Bob Smith's company, young John Reagan passed over the top of the ridge and spotted the enemy warriors entrenched in the ravine below him. His friend David Kaufman was struck in the face and knocked down by a rifle ball. Despite heavy bleeding Kaufman was not mortally wounded, and Reagan soon continued with the battle.

The rest of Colonel Rusk's regiment, including Captain Sadler's regulars, advanced down from the burning Delaware village and took positions to fire upon the Indian forces barricaded in the ravine below. General Douglass was later convinced that the enemy his men were facing numbered "not less than" seven to eight-hundred warriors. These braves were known to have included those of Chief Bowles and Big Mush plus a number of Delawares, Shawnees and Kickapoos.

The weather was extremely hot and the men ignored their thirst to continue advancing upon the Indian positions. The Texans charged the Cherokees several times but had to withdraw back up the slope or into the nearby woods each time under heavy counter-

Neches Battle Casualties of July 16, 1839

These casualty lists based on: the July 16 Medical Report of Surgeon Shields Booker of the First Infantry for Colonel Edward Burleson's troops, the July 16 Medical Report of Surgeon Lemuel B. Brown of the Texas Militia and company roster research by author.

JULY 16 CASUALTIES FROM TEXAS ARMY UNDER BURLESON:

Rank	Name	Company	Wound
Cpl.	Ferdinand Booker	Infantry Company D	Shot in the arm.
Pvt.	William Joseph Campbell	Infantry Company D	Wounded.
Pvt.	J. J. Caskey	Captain Lewis	Shot in the shoulder.
Cpl.	William Clements	Infantry Company C	Shot in the shoulder.
Capt.	Samuel W. Jordan	Infantry Company C	Shot in the hip.
Pvt.	Thomas McLaughlin	Captain Lewis	Shot in the arm.
Sgt.	Millard M. Parkerson	Infantry Company D	Shot in leg and thigh.
Pvt.	Edward S. Ratcliffe	Captain Lewis	Shot in the arm.
Pvt.	J. M. Smith	Captain Lewis	Shot in the side.
Pvt.	Martin Tutts	Infantry Company C	Fatally shot in chest.
Pvt.	George Willman	Ownby's Volunteers	Intermittent fever.
Pvt.	Joseph B. Young	Infantry Company C	Slightly grazed.

JULY 16 CASUALTIES FROM THE TEXAS MILITIA:

Rank	Name	Company	Remarks
Pvt.	Henry W. Augustine	Capt. Bob Smith	Seriously wounded.
Pvt.	William Bell	Capt. Todd	Wounded.
Pvt.	John N. Brimberry	Capt. Todd	Wounded.
Pvt.	John Ewing	Capt. Harrison	Mortally wounded.
Pvt.	James Gilliland	Capt. Todd	Wounded.
Maj.	David S. Kaufman	Capt. Bob Smith	Wounded.
Pvt.	F. G. Limans	Capt. Todd	Slightly wounded.
Pvt.	George F. Martin	Capt. Todd	Mortally wounded.
Gnl.	Hugh McLeod	Staff	Slightly wounded.
Pvt.	David Rusk	James Carter's spies	Wounded.
Capt.	Henry Madison Smith	Capt. Madison Smith	Wounded.
Pvt.	M. Tansell	Capt. Madison Smith	Wounded.
Pvt.	John S. Thompson	Capt. Madison Smith	Mortally wounded.

fire. Bowles and his men stood firmly. The only course of action became a combined charge by the Texan forces, which was ordered by General Douglass. In this charge, the Indian forces were finally overrun and forced to retreat toward the river bottom back toward their main body. Their entire force was "terrorized and fell back in great disorder upon the cornfields, then in full bearing, and the dense timber of the river bottom. It was here that Bowles evinced the most desperate intrepidity and made several unavailing attempts to rally his trusted warriors."[47] Private Reagan later recorded, "Len

Williams and Ben A. Vansickle, who were with us, and who understood and could speak the Cherokee language, told us that at that time they could hear Bowles, who was urging his warriors to charge, and telling them that the whites were whipped if they would charge."[48]

During this advance, Captain Madison Smith was badly wounded and turned command of his sixty-seven-man company over to First Lieutenant Albert G. Corbin. The enemy was driven for half a mile and took refuge in a swamp in the Neches bottom.[49] They were again charged with Woodlief leading the right, Rusk the center and Burleson the left. This time the enemy offered no resistance but broke and ran in every direction away from their assailants.

According to Private Reagan, "Chief Bowles displayed great courage in these battles," remaining on the field on horseback during the second engagement. Bowles wore a military hat, silk vest, and a handsome sword and sash which had been given to him by Sam Houston. "He was a magnificent picture of barbaric manhood and was very conspicuous during the whole battle, being the last to leave the field when the Indians retreated."[50]

After the Texan charge had scattered his forces toward the open plain and cornfields, Chief Bowles tried valiantly to rally his forces. He remained on horseback on the battlefield, conspicuously exposed to Texas fire. His horse, with a blazed face and four white feet, was eventually shot seven times, and he was shot in the hip before his forces began retiring.[51]

Bowles, suffering from his wound, finally dismounted his dying horse and was reportedly walking away when he was shot again. According to Major Jones, he was hit in the back near the spine by one of Captain Henry M. Smith's privates, Henry Conner, with "a musket ball and three buckshot. He breathed a short while only after his fall."[52]

Second Sergeant Charles N. Bell of Captain Tipps' Nacogdoches company later wrote that he and Captain Bob Smith found Bowles "sitting in the edge of a little prairie on the Neches River." The chief had a bowie knife, a sword and a holster of pistols but, according to Bell "asked for no quarter. Under the circumstances the captain was compelled to shoot him."[53] Bell then witnessed Smith put his pistol to Bowles' head and shoot him dead before taking his sword.

By John Reagan's account, he and his men came upon Chief Bowles as he was shot in the back while walking away. As the eighty-three-year-old chief sat up with his face toward the approaching Texas soldiers, Reagan started toward him to secure his surrender. He wrote:

As I approached him from one direction, my captain, Robert Smith, approached him from another, with his pistol drawn. As we got to him, I said, "Captain, don't shoot him," but as I spoke he fired, shooting the chief in the head, which caused instant death. It ought to be said for Captain Smith that he had known of the many murders and thefts by the Indians, and possibly did, in the heat of battle, what, under other circumstances, he would not have done, for he was esteemed as a most worthy man and citizen.[54]

The account by Reagan of Captain Smith's delivering the fatal head shot to Chief Bowles is generally accepted by most historians. Beyond this, it has not been definitively established as to who shot the Cherokee leader from his horse. As related to his children, Captain Sadler was among those who fired a musket shot which struck the old chief. In an historical sketch of him, an East Texas newspaper stated, "There is evidence that Sadler fought with great bravery, [and] he may have fired the shot that killed Chief Bowles."[55]

Early Texas historian John Henry Brown, who knew many of the men who fought in the Neches battles, wrote, "I well remember in those days, however, that the names of half a dozen men were paraded as the champions, who, under as many different circumstances, had killed Bowles."[56] That Bob Smith finished off Bowles and removed his sword is not disputed. Sadler, who had lost family to the Indians, would have been less interested in collecting war souvenirs than in exacting revenge. Due to his reserved nature, he would not have been likely to boast of such a feat.

After the fall of their leader, the Indians retreated in squads into the thickets around the Neches River. Although Bowles had claimed his Indians were short of arms and ammunition, they held off two charges by the Texans before being overrun.[57] In addition to the death of Chief Bowles, Chief Big Mush and about one-hundred other Indians were killed on the Neches battlefield.

General Douglass halted his men and ordered them to collect the wounded and form on high ground. The Texan forces lost four men mortally wounded: John Ewing, George F. Martin, John S. Thompson and Martin Tutts. In addition, at least twenty other men were listed as wounded on battle reports for July 16. Among the Texans wounded on the battlefield were Vice President Burnet, General Johnston and Adjutant General McLeod, although none was seriously wounded. Henry Augustine, who had been a major of General Rusk's field staff during a previous 1838 Indian campaign,

The Battle of the Neches was fought on July 16, 1839, in Van Zandt County, Texas. Today a Centennial Marker erected in 1936 (inset) remains as a tribute to Chief Bowles and "the last engagement between Cherokees and whites in Texas." Beyond the little field where Bowles fell can be seen the treeline of the Neches River.

Photos by Marshall L. Moore Jr., courtesy of Kenneth Cade, who is working with The American Indian Heritage Center of Texas, Inc. to preserve the Neches battlefield.

suffered an arrow through the leg which necessitated an amputation at the knee. The Republic of Texas rewarded him with a special wooden leg.[58]

In his report, Douglass credited Dr. Shields Booker (who had also treated the wounded at San Jacinto) of the First Infantry, plus Doctors Lemuel Brown and William Jowers and the other surgeons for tending to the wounded men of their respective regiments throughout the hottest of the action. Concerning the officers involved in the Neches battle, Douglass wrote:

> Rusk and Burleson behaved with that gallantry and coolness that has so often distinguished them on the field of battle in Texas. Lt. Colonels Woodlief and James Smith behaved handsomely and lead their commands gallantly into action, obeying circumspectly all orders, and maintaining their respective positions. The Brigadier General cannot invoke too earnestly the thanks of the country to those officers and men who participated in this action, for the bravery and determination they displayed.

Douglass also thanked the men of his staff: Adjutant General McLeod, Major Snively, and volunteer aides Davis, Mabbitt, Sturgess, Millroy and Pillans. The men who had participated in the battle claimed that it had been "amongst the hardest contested battles of the country."

After the death of Chiefs Bowls and Big Mush, the surviving Cherokees fled to the old camp of Bowles. At dusk the survivors returned to recover the bodies of the wounded and the slain. Throughout the night, the sounds of mourning among the defeated Indians could be heard. By dawn's first light on July 17, however, the sounds had ceased and the Indian camp was deserted. The Indians had started their journey toward present Oklahoma in the United States territory.[59]

Advocates for the Cherokee, such as Sam Houston, were appalled and openly critical of Rusk and others for the Cherokee War campaign. However, this battle largely ended the Indian depredations in East Texas that had terrorized the early settlers, and it gave the Republic of Texas all of the former Indian land. The Battle of the Neches has been described as second only to San Jacinto as the most important conflict fought on Texas soil.[60]

Chapter Thirteen

TRANSITION YEARS OF A YOUNG NATION

July 17, 1839 - November 1844

On July 17, 1839, the Texas Army of General Douglass marched across the Neches River "at the encampment the Indians had occupied and abandoned the day previous, and encamped on its banks preparatory to sending the wounded back under an escort."[1] The regiment of Colonel Landrum's command, which had marched up the east side of the Neches and missed the battle, was making its way back to the main body of Texan forces.

Arriving about a week after the battle with Captain Jacob E. Hamilton's company, which had been created on July 22, was San Jacinto veteran Walter Lane who noted that some Texans were collecting grisly battlefield souvenirs. He encountered a "festive cuss" who proudly displayed a strip of skin he had cut from Bowles' back to use as a razor strip and good luck charm. Lane doubted the value of such a charm; he felt that the skin's original owner "had remarkably bad luck."[2]

First of Colonel Landrum's companies to return to the Neches battleground had been that of Captain Kimbro from Chief Linney's Shawnee village. Lieutenant Joseph Burleson stated that he "saw Judge Alfred Polk dismount to scalp a dead Indian." After Burleson "told him not to do it as it seemed barbarious and uncivilized, he refused to do it and took my advice."[3] Another member of Kimbro's company, Private John "Rip" Ford, gazed silently with several others of his company at the unburied body of Chief Bowles. "It was not difficult to accord to him the deed of bravery and to believe he sacrificed himself to save many of his people," Ford later wrote. "Under other circumstances history would have classed him among heroes and martyrs."[4]

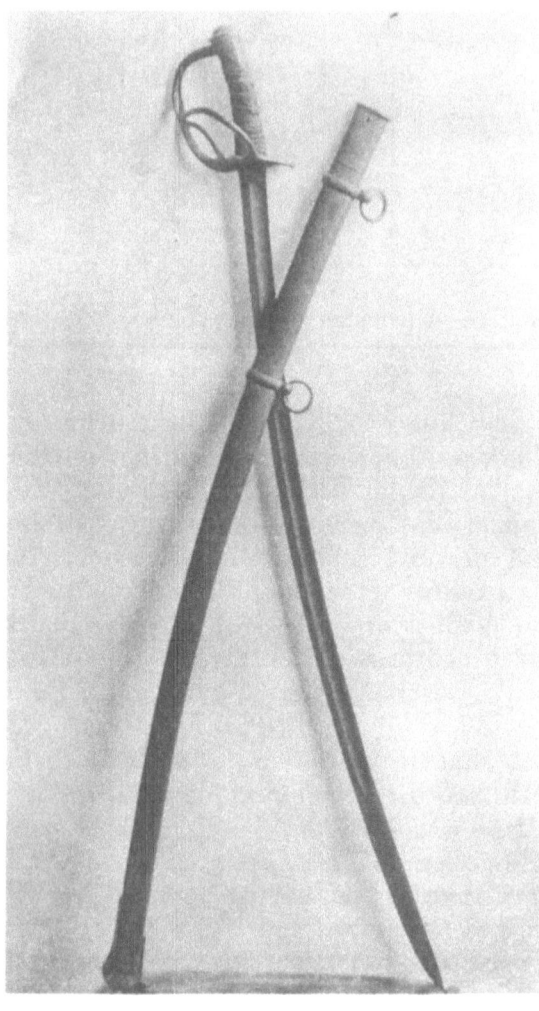

This single-edged steel military sword of Chief Bowles is just over three feet in length, with a brass hilt and shield. After the chief's death on the Neches battlefield, the sword was presented to Captain Bob Smith and was on display for years in the Clinton Lodge in Henderson, Texas. It was turned over to the Cherokee Nation around 1892 and has been placed in their archives in Tahlequah, Oklahoma. Courtesy of the Texas State Archives.

Many Texans, particularly those such as Sadler who had experienced Indian depredations in the past years, did not share young Ford's awe of the fallen Cherokee leader. Pieces of his body were cut away for charms or souvenirs, and a September 1, 1841 article in the *Telegraph and Texas Register* reported that "Some rude chaps scalped the poor chief after his death." The body of Chief Bowles was left on the Neches battlefield, and one early settler recalled that his skull and skeleton were visible in this spot for many years thereafter. It was believed that his body was left on the battlefield by a tribal custom which said that braves who had been scalped were not given funeral honors.[5]

* * * *

EXPULSION OF THE CHEROKEES

On the morning of July 18, the wounded were moved to Fort Lamar by Captain Jack Todd in command of a detail of eighty men. The Texas Army moved forward two miles this day to good water and sent out scouts to look for signs of the defeated Cherokees. At a small branch, Douglass' men camped for two days until Landrum's companies rejoined on the evening of July 20, and Captain Todd returned the next morning. At this point, the entire command was ordered to take up the line of march in pursuit of the Indians.

According to the action report of General Douglass,

> The trail of the Indians bore westward to the headwaters of the Sabine, which was followed and brought us about 4 o'clock in the evening to some Indian huts and cornfields. Several villages and several hundred acres of corn were discovered. We encamped at one of them -- destroyed their houses and cut down their corn. On the 22nd, we again took the trail, which brought us in a few miles to several more villages, and yet more extensive corn fields and improvements; here we encamped, burnt the houses and cut down the corn.

On the morning of July 23, the army again marched in pursuit of its retiring enemy, destroying villages and corn fields it passed. Secretary of War Albert Sidney Johnston reported that the Indians had carried off their wounded men slung across horses. During their retreat, many of these men died and their dead bodies were found for miles dumped like discarded baggage along the trail.[6]

In the afternoon, the advance spies brought back word they had spotted ahead an Indian encampment with signs of life. The Texas troops were thrown into battle order and marched hurriedly to the scene only to find that this encampment had been hastily abandoned. The Indians had left behind a yoke of oxen, some tools and other plunder. A force of scouts sent back toward the Neches battlefield now reported Indian signs near Chief Harris' old village, where they had captured a horse and killed an Indian.

At this point, Chief Placido's Tonkawa scouts reported to General Douglass that the Cherokee trails had scattered ahead. Having laid waste to the Indian villages along his path, Douglass now found it advisable to turn back toward the old Delaware village to prevent an Indian counterattack against frontier settlements. The Texas Army turned back toward the Neches battlefield on July 24 and was rejoined by Captain Kimbro's company, which had been trying to rejoin the army since first being sent to the Shawnee village more than a week previous.

Also arriving this day were two companies of San Augustine volunteers under captains Andrew Jackson Berry and Jacob Hamilton, who reported to Douglass for service to their country. Their service would not be required, however, because the general was already ordering his troops to be disbanded. The army camped that night on a beautiful lake which they called Lake Burleson, located above Harris' old village and near present Tyler.

On the morning of July 25, Douglass dispatched scouts in every direction to ascertain if there were any recent trails of an enemy. All agreed that the remaining Indians were divided and well scattered and that further pursuit would be fruitless. Secretary of War Johnston therefore had General Douglass issue a command to the leaders of the volunteer regiments that they should march their companies home and then muster the troops out of service. About four-hundred troops, including Sadler's Company A, were left on routine duty under Colonel Burleson to protect against a return of the Cherokees.[7]

Defeated, the Cherokees and their allies split into small groups and wandered for weeks without provisions. Some ended up remaining in Texas in small numbers, others joined with Mexican forces on the frontier over the next year, but the majority crossed into the southeastern portion of Indian Territory and settled in present day Oklahoma.[8]

During the Cherokee War, Sam Houston had been out of the country visiting President Andrew Jackson. In a meeting after his return to Nacogdoches, he condemned the Texans who had fought this war and said that Chief Bowles was a better man than his killers. Houston's own life was threatened by angry men before peace could be restored to the meeting.[9]

Ned Burleson's troops departed for the Austin area on August 12, believing that East Texas was secure enough to leave to the local militia companies. Adam Clendenin's Company B left Fort Lamar on August 12 and rejoined Colonel Burleson's First Regiment at Fort Houston on August 14, where two deserters were court-martialed. These men were sentenced to death, but their sentences were later commuted to less severe punishments.

Following the battles on the Neches, many of the hastily assembled militia companies were quickly disbanded. In the months following the conflict in 1839, ranger companies under Joseph L. Bennett were known to have used Fort Houston as a base, and

Captain James Box's long-standing company remained in command of this post until being finally disbanded on October 18, 1839.[10]

In August 1839, the bulk of the regular army followed Colonel Burleson back to the western frontier, stopping briefly at Fort Milam, located on the Brazos River in present Fall County southeast of Waco, then part of Robertson County and near the little community of Marlin near the Falls of the Brazos River. Lieutenant Colonel Fisher ordered this frontier post renamed Camp Burleson and it was garrisoned without interruption by Captain George Howard's Company D into late 1840. During October, the remaining infantry established Camp Walnut Creek a few miles east of present Austin near some settlements on the Colorado River. The army operated from this camp, commanded by Burleson or by Lieutenant Colonel Fisher in his absence, for a short period of time in late 1839.[11]

As of August 29, the army's fifteen infantry commanders were captains Redd, Clendenin, Jordan, Howard, Holliday, Gillen, Skerrett, Laurence, Morgan, Moore, Sadler, January, Mathew Caldwell, John Kennymore and Palmer Pillans (the last three being the most newly appointed). The First Regiment also had two cavalry captains on payroll by this time, Samuel A. Plummer and James H. Millroy.

Captain Jordan resigned from his post September 2 and was replaced as captain of Company C by John Kennymore on October 23, 1839. Captain Kennymore and his men had orders from Burleson to establish Camp Caldwell in response to renewed attacks on immigrants to the Austin area. The site of this camp is in present Williamson County on the south bank of Brushy Creek, about 2.5 miles east of present Round Rock. During October Burleson remained in the new headquarters camp on Walnut Creek, which served as a base camp until about November 16, 1839.[12]

While the bulk of the existing army took up stations around Austin, under construction as the new capital following the Cherokee War, new companies were being formed in Galveston. Probably boosted by the recent Indian conflicts, the recruiting process was in full swing in the United States. Recruits sailed from New Orleans and were enlisted in Galveston during the fall of 1839.

It is unknown how long Company A remained under command of Captain Sadler, but a completely revamped Company A was put together in Galveston through December 14. It was eventually placed under command of Captain William Redd and would not arrive in the Austin area for service until after year's end.

From Galveston, Captain Skerrett estimated to Secretary of War Johnston in November that within a few weeks "there will be in service ten companies" of the Frontier Regiment.[13] In the end, enough recruits were received to fill out five new companies. Captain John Holliday took command of the new Company E in Galveston on September 17. The other new companies were Company F under Captain James January, G under Captain William Sadler, H under Captain George Laurence, and I under Captain Benjamin Gillen.

Audited Republic Claims of Joseph Schleiter shows that he was "a private in Captain Sadler's Company G, 1st Regiment of Infantry" and had been enlisted by Captain Mark Skerrett at Galveston on November 11, 1839.[14] Muster roll records reveal that Michael H. Chevallie was first lieutenant of Sadler's new Company G.[15] Chevallie was later to become a major in the Texas Rangers and to serve with Sadler in the House of the Ninth Congress.

These new companies moved in November and early December from Galveston to Houston, where they obtained provisions and uniforms. Company F under Captain January was the first new company to arrive at Camp Caldwell on December 5, 1839. Sadler's Company G, recruited between October 18 and November 11, 1839, arrived about a week behind January's company.[16] A letter from Secretary of War Johnston on December 12 stated that Sadler's company was "expected hourly" in Austin.[17]

Protecting Austin's Frontier Settlements

As the new companies were arriving from Galveston, Indian hostilities in the Austin area forced Texas leaders to take up a new offensive. On December 11, Secretary of War Johnston ordered Burleson to undertake a campaign against the Comanches and other hostile Indians. At this time, Burleson had four infantry companies available at Camp Caldwell: Adam Clendenin's Company B, John Kennymore's Company C, John Holliday's Company E and James January's Company F. Captain Sadler's Company G apparently took up station at Camp Caldwell, arriving just after the army's departure. Other First Regiment forces active as of this date were Captain George Howard's Company D stationed at Fort Burleson at the Falls of the Brazos; Company A, completing recruitment at Galveston; and Captain Laurence's H and Captain Gillen's I en route from Galveston.[18] An additional small wagon guard under Captain William Moore operated from Fort Burleson during this time.[19] Total army strength in mid-December was about 440, including staff and field officers.[20]

Colonel Burleson's Northwestern Campaign departed on December 16 and included a small band of mounted volunteer scouts under Captain Mathew Caldwell, plus the assistance of some Tonkawa and Lipan scouts. Among Caldwell's volunteers was ranger John L. Lynch, who had previously served as a captain of a Spy Detachment employed by the First Regiment earlier in 1839.[21] An Indian camp was discovered by scouts on December 23, and the braves proved to be Cherokees under Chief John Bowles, son of the old war chief who had been slain in East Texas. Chief Bowles was attempting to reach Mexico with his people by passing beyond the outermost white settlements.[22]

Near the mouth of the San Saba River, Burleson's troops surrounded the camp on Christmas morning. In the ensuing running fight, one Tonkawa brave was wounded and John Lynch was fatally shot in the chest. At least six Indians were killed and left dead on the field, including two chiefs, Egg and John Bowles, while the remainder made the best of the dense, rough terrain to escape the battlefield. The Texans captured the Cherokees' camp equipage, horses, cattle, one elderly man, five women and nineteen children.[23] Among the written documents captured was an account book belonging to the Killough family of East Texas, which belied Sam Houston's claim that Cherokees had never killed white men in Texas.[24]

Burleson's forces chased Indian trails for two weeks until exhausted horses and dwindling supplies forced him to close his campaign. Companies arrived back from this campaign to Camp Caldwell on January 12, 1840. Thereafter, the various companies of the First Regiment were placed into frontier duties.

From remaining muster roll records, it is possible to trace the movements of each of these companies. Captain Redd's Company A was posted briefly at Camp McLeod then moved to San Antonio to man nearby Mission San Jose. Captain Kennymore's C and Captain Gillen's Company I were also moved to Mission San Jose, where all three fell under the supervision of Lieutenant Colonel Fisher.[25] Company B under Captain Clendenin was stationed at San Gabriel, and Company D under Captain Howard and later John Holliday manned Fort Burleson. Company E under Captain Holliday remained at Camp Caldwell until marching for Camp Cazneau on February 22, by then commanded by Captain Mark Lewis.[26] Captain Skerrett's Company H was at Camp Lamar near Austin at year end 1839 and was sent to Cherokee Nation in East Texas during early 1840, where it established Fort Skerrett.[27]

The other two First Regiment companies, F under Captain January and G under Captain Sadler, marched from Camp Caldwell on their new assignment on January 13, 1840. They were designated to man the remote outpost called Little River Fort, which was located just above where the Leon River intersects the Lampasas River. Their men were at this fort by January 20 and remained on duty there until February 10 when, due to winter conditions and "on account of the total failure of subsistence stores," January and Sadler's companies evacuated the Little River Fort completely.[28]

Attributable to the poor conditions, both companies suffered a severe crisis in the form of desertions. During the three weeks at the fort, at least nine men of Company F deserted from their post. Even after evacuating the fort, Captain January lost at least thirty-three more men to desertion between February 12-17, 1840. Captain Sadler's Company G also suffered a high desertion rate. The companies returned to Little River Fort on February 20 and an effort was made to round up as many of the deserters as possible on February 21.

On the night of February 21, Private James W. Brown was the acting corporal of the guard for Captain Sadler's company in camp. He and a number of other soldiers deserted from the camp near Austin. Brown and four others from Company G, captured several days later by a citizen near Nashville-on-the-Brazos, faced court martials before a five-man First Regiment panel. The court martial panel consisted of Colonel William Cazneau, Jacob Snively, Captain Howard, Captain Mark Lewis, and lieutenants A. C. Holmes and Dunnington. The hearings were held on February 29 at eleven o'clock in the camp of Company E at Camp Cazneau.

Colonel Cazneau, president of the court martial panel, found that these desertions of Captain Sadler's men were attributable to a

> temporary want of supplies, and the extreme difficulties attending the transportation when procured, added to the inclemency of the winter, at times when the troops were suffering.

The panel sentenced Brown and the others of Company G to death but later reduced their sentences to serving out their terms with Company E. Most of the other deserters from Sadler and January's companies were also captured. Those who were returned received pay cuts for desertion and some were kept on confinement.[29]

Lieutenant Colonel Fisher apparently stepped in from Mission San Jose to defray the chaos. Company E departed Camp Caldwell on February 22 and by March 5 was stationed at Camp Cazneau on Onion Creek. Fisher placed Captain Mark Lewis in charge of

Company E while he sorted out the remnants of companies F and G. From Little River Fort, Fisher ordered at least twenty-four of Sadler's soldiers transferred into Lewis' Company E on February 26. He also ordered Sadler's First Lieutenant, Michael Chevallie, into Company C on the same date.[30]

Two days later, the remainder of Company F was ordered by Adjutant General McLeod to march to Fort Burleson while the revamped Company E moved on to Camp Cazneau near Austin.[31] In the midst of this confusion, most of the regulars on the western front were being ordered into San Antonio for an impending meeting with Comanche leaders on the frontier hostilities. Three First Regiment companies under captains Howard, Redd and Holliday were stationed in San Antonio and were involved in the famous Council House Fight on March 19, 1840, when the Comanches refused to release their white hostages. At least thirty-five Indians, including most of their leaders, were killed. The Texans lost seven men, including Lieutenant William Dunnington of Company E.[32] As a result of the Council House Fight, the Comanches continued to be a hostile force on the western plains of Texas for several years.

While in the hill country area of Texas, Sadler was able to take care of some land business. Somewhere in the shuffle of events of the previous three years, he had lost the original land Certificate 492 granted to him on March 30, 1838, in Nacogdoches County for the one-third league from Severio Arocha. He was able to secure Duplicate Certificate No. 246/345 from Commissioner Thomas William Ward of the General Land Office in Austin. This document, which would later enable him to have the land surveyed for sale, had been approved February 14, 1840, and was issued to Sadler on March 23.

His further roll with the First Regiment of Infantry in 1840 is unknown. The 1840 census of the Republic of Texas shows William T. Sadler to be a single man without slaves and resident of Houston County who had immigrated to Texas in 1835.[33] Sadler's land holdings at this time showed him to have clear patent on 6,131 acres, not including the 320-acre and 640-acre grants he had received for his 1836 military service, which were not yet patented.

THE EARLY 1840S IN HOUSTON COUNTY

While Sadler's frontier service continued in the army, Houston County had experienced only occasional encounters with straggling bands of Indians. Nathaniel W. Smith, a former U. S. general who had come to Texas in 1838 from Tennessee with his family, had led a party of eighteen on a scouting expedition in December 1839. Their party entered into a gunfight about forty miles north of Fort Houston with a band of Indians believed to be Cherokees. Only one man was wounded by a rifle ball in the thigh before the Indians were driven away.[34]

The only sizable force of frontier defense known to have used Fort Houston in 1840 was that of Major James H. Durst's ranger corps. This consisted of a company under Captain Adolphus Sterne and another smaller one under Lieutenant Daniel Woodlaw which used Fort Houston from July through October.[35] This area had become a popular settlement, as recorded by Fort Houston's Dr. James Hunter in a letter to his father in North Carolina dated January 12, 1840. He described the weather as warm, the climate very pleasant with a natural breeze at most times, the soil extremely productive and good land in abundance. Hunter described the ease of plowing the fertile soil and in fencing in the prairie land. "The water here is excellent," he wrote. "The finest bold running springs as you ever saw are all over the country."[36]

Hunter's letter also detailed that the Fort Houston settlers provided the only protection against Indians or Mexican rebels at this point. "There are about 100 men capable of using arms so that we apprehend no danger from any force they can bring against us," he wrote.[37] During the winter months of 1840-1841, the residents were plagued by a serious fever epidemic which claimed the lives of a number of the community's prominent citizens. Among those dying were General Nat Smith, his wife Martha, their son-in-law Dr. James Hunter, Virginia and William Glenn, who were children of Captain Nathan Glenn, and some of Captain Glenn's slaves.[38]

The early days of 1841 also saw the passing of the First Regiment of Infantry, in which Captain Sadler had been among the earliest officers. Albert Sidney Johnston had resigned in March of 1840 and Ned Burleson had been succeeded as its commander on August 18 by Colonel William G. Cooke. During the Fifth Congress (November 2, 1840 - February 5, 1841), Sam Houston's return to power ensured that the army never prospered. By year end 1840, total enlistments had dropped to 465 men from its peak of 560 during that year. When the Fifth Congress adjourned, it had not passed an act to provide for continued support of the army, thereby destroying the old "Frontier Regiment." Thus ended the last serious effort of the Republic of Texas to maintain a regular army.[39]

Skirmishes with raiding Indians persisted into 1841. Ranger companies, later popularly known as "Texas Rangers," under captains

John Coffee Hays and John T. Price were sent on expeditions to the Nueces River to monitor Mexican resistance. Near Laredo, Hays' men fought several battles with Mexican rebels and Indian warriors over the next few months. Between June 1841 and September 1842, both Mexico and Texas sent expeditions into each other's lands. One of the more ill-fated, the Texan Santa Fe Expedition, failed in its goal to take over Santa Fe and thereby open trade between that city and Texas. A Mexican force retaliated in March 1842, taking over San Antonio and forcing a showdown on September 17 of that year.[40]

In the resulting conflict known as the Battle of Salado Creek, Texas Rangers under Captain Hays and volunteers under Captain Mathew Caldwell defeated Mexican forces under General Adrian Woll and recaptured San Antonio. Among the sixty-odd Mexicans killed was Vicente Cordova, leader of the Cordova Rebellion in East Texas in 1838. During late 1842, President Houston sanctioned the so-called Mier Expedition into the little adobe town located south of the Rio Grande. Following an attack on the border town of Mier, the surviving Texans were forced to surrender and were marched in February 1843 beyond Saltillo and into Mexico. President Santa Anna ordered many of these men executed, although a number of the pitiful survivors were liberated in time.[41]

The last documented raid into the Houston County area was made in 1843. A small band of Indians stole some horses and were pursued by William Frost and three others. Frost shot and killed one Indian before he himself was fatally wounded. The other three managed to kill four more Indians and recover the horses.[42] The once important post called Fort Houston eventually became little more than an historic monument to the early years of battles. Cherokee War veteran John Reagan, who had become the deputy surveyor in 1840 of northern Houston County, later purchased the land surrounding old Fort Houston.

Sadler's land at this time was still located in Houston County. The northernmost settlers of this county had attempted to establish Burnet County in 1841 in honor of David G. Burnet. When the new "county" sent its representatives to congress in Austin, however, they were threatened with imprisonment if they did not return home and disband the effort.[43] It would be five more years before the Fort Houston area residents would be able to establish their own county.

After retiring from the army life, W. T. Sadler returned to his property and resumed farming in the early 1840s. He began building what would become known as Sadler Plantation on the land that had been largely neglected for more than two years. From stories related to his children and grandchildren, he was known to have been visited on occasion by old acquaintances, including President Sam Houston who owned a one-quarter league of land bordering that of Sadler's Headright. Using the good creek water and his corn crop for supplies, he was also known to have made whiskey. Great-great-grandson Howard Sadler recalled seeing an old brass-colored coil that he was told was W. T. Sadler's whiskey coil, kept in an old smokehouse on his grandpa's property in Anderson County. According to family stories, Sadler would take some of his better whiskey out from his little storage house, and then he and Houston would sit out on the porch to drink big and talk big.[44]

In early 1844, Captain Sadler at the age of forty-seven finally decided to settle down again and married twenty-six-year-old Permelia Bennett. Permelia was the daughter of Armstead and Faith Bennett, who had brought their family to Texas in 1835 with some of the Parker family, who had established the early Pilgrim Primitive Baptist Church. The Bennett family had settled a few miles south of present Elkhart on the southern Anderson County border, near Fort Brown.[45]

Following the Parker's Fort Massacre, the Pilgrim Church resumed meeting in the home of Elder Daniel Parker on February 25, 1837, with the Bennetts and children Stephen and Permelia listed as members. Armstead was an early Clerk of the church, and meetings during 1841-1842 were held in his home in Houston County. Stephen Bennett served on a committee which eventually selected a site for a new building to be constructed on the land of Dickerson Parker.[46]

William and Permelia Sadler settled on Sadler's Plantation, located near the settlement known as Ioni, located on Ioni Creek,

These Indian artifacts, testament to the area's earliest settlers, were found on Sadler land in present Anderson County. Photo courtesy of Howard C. Sadler.

twenty miles southeast of Palestine and ten miles east of Elkhart in southeastern Anderson County. Arrowheads and other Indian artifacts from the early Ionis and other Indians have been found about this site. This little community had disappeared from county highway maps by the 1930s. In its prime, however, Ioni had a post office from 1848 to 1900, a population of about sixty in 1884, and was served by three churches, a steam gristmill, a cotton gin, a general store, and a district school.

HOME FRONT POLITICS

Shortly after his second marriage, Captain Sadler entered the political arena of the Republic of Texas in 1844. He would be elected as the representative for Houston County in the House of the Ninth Congress of the republic, and he would remain in office into the early years of statehood of Texas.

Houston County had been first been served in the House of Representatives by Isaac Parker during the Third and Fourth Congresses. Greenberry Horras Harrison, captain of a company of Houston County volunteers during the Cherokee War, was elected to the House for the Fifth Congress but chose to stay in Austin following his term to publish the *Austin Weekly Texian*, later the *Austin Daily Texian*.[47] The county reelected Isaac Parker to replace Harrison for the Sixth and Seventh Congresses. Following this, Parker had served in the Senate for the Eighth Congress and returned to represent Nacogdoches, Rusk and Houston counties for the Ninth Congress. He continued to serve the Texas Senate for an additional four terms, and a county was later named for him.[48]

In Parker's place in the House, a lawyer and politician named Selden L. B. Jasper, who had arrived in Texas after the revolution with Mexico, was elected to represent Houston County in the Eighth Congress.[49] Following Jasper's term in 1844, Captain William Turner Sadler successfully campaigned against him in Houston County. Based on his long tenure in the county, his being a veteran of San Jacinto and his popularity as a leader during the Indian wars, Sadler won the election to represent his county in the House of the Ninth Congress of the Republic of Texas. Jasper, who would be credited with founding Trinity Lodge (later Lathrop Lodge) in Crockett, would run against Sadler again in the future.

The Eighth Congress passed an act on February 1, 1844, creating a District Court for the Northern Division of Houston County at the town of Fort Houston. The act created the boundary to run as follows: beginning at Houston Mound, north of Murchison's Prairie;

moving west to Ioni Village on Elkhart Creek; then to the Trinity River; and from Houston Mound to the Neches River; then up the Neches to the north boundary of Houston County; then west with the county line to the Trinity River; then down the Trinity to the above-named line that ran directly from the Neches to the Trinity.[50]

This act also provided for Fort Houston Division to hold Probate Court on the third Monday of every month for one week or until business was finished. The District Court for Houston County's Northern Division would commence on the second Monday after the fourth Monday in May and November and continue in session until business was finished. These two divisions would remain in place until the establishment of Anderson County in 1846.

The Eighth Congress closed out its session soon thereafter. Campaigns for the next session commenced in the fall of 1844, and W. T. Sadler was elected to office by the voters on September 2. The county's election returns were mailed from Crockett, Texas on September 19 to the Honorable Anson Jones, Secretary of State in Washington, Texas.

> Republic of Texas
> County of Houston
>
> To Hon. Anson Jones
> Secretary of State
>
> The undersigned, Chief Justice of the County aforesaid, certifies that, at an election held in said county on the second day of September, 1844, in accordance with the provisions of existing laws, and in obedience to the Proclamation of His Excellency the President being dated this sixth day of July, 1844, ordering said election, William T. Sadler was elected to the office of Representative for the said county. In testimony whereof I have affixed my office's seal, signed under my hand this twelfth day of September A.D. 1844.
>
> Cyrus H. Randolph
> Chief Justice of Houston County

Chapter Fourteen

THE END OF A REPUBLIC:
THE NINTH CONGRESS

December 2, 1844 - June 1845

In the House, forty elected congressmen would represent the republic's thirty-five current counties. The more heavily populated counties of Bexar, Brazoria, San Augustine and Shelby were represented by more than one delegate. The Republic of Texas, as established by its Constitution, was governed by a two-house Congress. The House was to be made up each session with no more than forty members until the population exceeded 100,000. State population at this time was about 125,000, so the House had latitude in its number of representatives and could be composed of as few as forty or as many as one-hundred representatives, provided that each county was entitled to at least one representative. House members served one-year terms and were required to be at least twenty-five years of age, a citizen of the republic, and a citizen of his district for at least six months. The House chose its own speaker and had sole power of impeachment in the Congress.[1]

THE TEXAS CAPITAL IN WASHINGTON

From its beginnings at Washington-on-the-Brazos in 1836, the Republic of Texas had been headed by David Burnet as president until October 22 of that year, after which time Sam Houston and Mirabeau Lamar had presided over the Republic. Houston would remain in office until December 9, 1844. The first permanent government of Texas had begun its operations in October 1836 in Columbia-on-the Brazos in a small wooden building.

The new city of Houston was then selected as the temporary capital, and President Houston ordered the government there.

Houston served as the Texas capital city from April 19, 1837, until the meeting of the Congress in 1840. Austin became the capital city in 1840 but Sam Houston, fearing an attack by Mexico, ordered the government to return to Houston on March 13, 1842. After the capture of San Antonio, Houston called for a special session of Congress in the town named after him. Encountering heavy resistance from the legislators, he was soon forced to order Congress to meet at Washington-on-the-Brazos as the makeshift capital in September. When Houston tried to have the republic's archives moved to Washington, however, the citizens of Austin refused to release them, resulting in what was called the Archives War.[2]

Senate members were chosen from the districts of Texas, one senator from each district. They served three-year terms, and one-third of the Senate was reelected each year. Each senator had to be thirty or older, a citizen of the republic, and a resident of his district for at least one year. The Senate had the sole responsibility to try impeachments. The House of Representatives elected and judged the qualifications of its own members. A quorum in the House, as with the Senate, was two-thirds of the membership. Members

Washington-on-the-Brazos *was the site of the capital of the Republic of Texas in 1844 when Sadler served in the Ninth Congress. Washington became the capital in September 1842 when the government was moved from Houston. A replica of the unfinished wood frame building called Independence Hall (below), site of the signing of the 1836 Declaration of Independence, was later reconstructed and now stands in the Washington-on-the Brazos State Historical Park, located about 8 miles west of Navasota, Texas.* Author's collection.

received pay as fixed by law, but this salary could not be changed during a session in progress.³

When Sadler entered the Ninth Congress, the Texas government was still meeting at Washington-on-the-Brazos, located on a high bluff overlooking the Brazos River at a point approximately seventy miles northwest of Houston and one-hundred miles southeast of Austin. For Sadler, it was a one-hundred-mile journey from his home in Houston County to the capitol. The meeting quarters were crude at best, and aside from two hotels, Washington-on-the-Brazos offered few luxuries for the congressmen.

The town of Washington had been established in 1834 on the west banks of the Brazos near an early ferry operated by Andrew Robinson. When the Convention of 1836 drafted the Texas Declaration of Independence, the town had boasted two hotels, about fifty houses, and a resident population of more than one hundred. Washington had been evacuated during the Runaway Scrape but had since been incorporated in 1837.⁴

Interestingly enough, the only building in town large enough to hold the Ninth Congress was Hatfield's Grocery, actually a saloon with a large upstairs gambling hall. When not in use by Congress, this room alternately served as a gambling den, a social hall, and even for church. Because it was considered unbecoming for Texas congressmen to enter and exit through a saloon, the stairway to the upstairs gambling hall was moved to the outside of the building and the interior stairway was covered over.⁵

In accordance with the law, the Ninth Congress opened in Washington on Monday, December 2, 1844, for its annual session. The Honorable Dr. Anson Jones, Secretary of State, took the chair and proceeded to organize the House. The former Chief Clerk, James H. Raymond, officiated as Chief Clerk Pro Tem for the proceedings. A roll of the Texas counties was called in alphabetical order, with each member coming forward to present his credentials and take the constitutional oath of office. As only Sadler and eighteen other representatives were present on December 2, a motion was then made to adjourn the House until the following day at 3:00 p.m.⁶

Thirteen more representatives were sworn in on December 3, enough members for a quorum of the House to be declared present. In a close vote, the members then proceeded to elect John M. Lewis of Montgomery County as the Speaker of the House of the Ninth Congress. President Sam Houston gave his final message before the assembled House the following day. He called for a new frontier

NINTH CONGRESS of the REPUBLIC OF TEXAS
WASHINGTON-ON-THE-BRAZOS
DECEMBER 2, 1844 TO FEBRUARY 3, 1845 - REGULAR SESSION
JUNE 16, 1845 TO JUNE 28, 1845 - CALLED SESSION

SENATE of the NINTH CONGRESS

Senator	District / Counties Represented:
John Caldwell	Bastrop, Fayette, Gonzales, Travis
John Alexander Greer	San Augustine
Jesse Grimes	Washington, Montgomery, Brazos
David Spangler Kaufman	Sabine, Shelby, Harrison
Henry L. Kinney	San Patricio, Goliad, Refugio
William Lawrence	Harris, Galveston, Liberty
Samuel H. Luckie *	Bexar
James K. McCrearey	Austin, Colorado, Fort Bend
Henry J. Munson	Robertson, Milam
Isaac Parker	Nacogdoches, Rusk, Houston
George A. Pattillo	Jasper, Jefferson
Timothy Pillsbury	Brazoria
Richard Roman	Matagorda, Jackson, Victoria
John William Smith *	Bexar
George W. Wright	Red River, Fannin, Bowie, Lamar

* Smith died on Jan. 13, 1845 and was succeeded by Luckie on Feb. 1, 1845.

OFFICERS OF THE SENATE OF THE NINTH CONGRESS

Edward Burleson	Vice President until December 9, 1844
Kenneth Lewis Anderson	Vice President, inaugurated Dec. 9, 1844
John Alexander Greer	President Pro Tempore
Henry J. Jewett	Secretary
Alfred W. Luckett	Assistant Secretary
Henry Walton Raglin	Engrossing and Enrolling Clerk
Samuel W. Pipkin	Sergeant-at-Arms
James Neely	Doorkeeper
Orcenith Fisher	Chaplain

patrol force, blamed the whites for the Council House Fight and Comanche hostilities of 1840, and asked for increased trade with the Indians. Houston concluded with the hope

> that your deliberations may be characterized by that wisdom and harmony so essential to the attainment of those great ends for which you are here assembled; with my fervent desire that your labors may, under the guidance of Heaven, give additional force and energy to all those principles of

NINTH CONGRESS of the REPUBLIC OF TEXAS
WASHINGTON-ON-THE BRAZOS
DECEMBER 2, 1844 TO FEBRUARY 3, 1845 - REGULAR SESSION
JUNE 16, 1845 TO JUNE 28, 1845 - CALLED SESSION

HOUSE OF REPRESENTATIVES of the NINTH CONGRESS

Representative	County		
James Armstrong	Jefferson	Hugh McLeod	Bexar
William H. Bourland	Lamar	Evans Mabry	Bastrop
William Leslie Cazneau	Travis	William Means	Sabine
Wilds K. Cooke	Robertson	William Menefee	Colorado
William Gordon Cooke	Bexar	Elliott M. Millican	Brazos
Abel Seymour Cunningham	Victoria	John H. Moffitt	Nacogdoches
John Dunn	Refugio	Duncan Campbell Ogden	Bexar
George Bernard Erath	Milam	Gustavus A. Parker	Fort Bend
John Salmon Ford	San Augustine	Stephen W. Perkins	Brazoria
David Gage	Rusk	Tod Robinson	Brazoria
Benjamin Watson Hardin	Liberty	William Turner Sadler	Houston
James W. Henderson	Harris	William Thomas Scott	Harrison
Stephen B. Johns	Bowie	William R. Scurry	Red River
Isaac W. Johnson	Goliad	Thomas F. Smith	Fannin
Middleton Tate Johnson	Shelby	George Washington Smyth	Jasper
Augustus H. Jones	Gonzales	George Sutherland	Jackson
Simeon L. Jones	San Patricio	James Truitt	Shelby
John M. Lewis	Montgomery	Benjamin Rush Wallace	San Augustine
Samuel K. Lewis	Austin	Augustus Williams	Fayette
Dugald MacFarlane	Matagorda	Robert McAlpin Williamson	Washington

OFFICERS OF THE HOUSE OF THE NINTH CONGRESS

John M. Lewis	Speaker of the House
James Hervey Raymond	Chief Clerk
John Milton Swisher	Assistant Chief Clerk
Benjamin F. Hill	Engrossing Clerk
Michael H. Chevallie	Enrolling Clerk
James M. Alexander	Sergeant-at-Arms
Francis Hughes	Doorkeeper
John Haynie	Chaplain

private and public virtue so indispensable to the stability, prosperity, and success of the Government and people of the Republic.[7]

Following role call on Thursday, December 5, the House adopted the journals of the preceding day before moving on to the establishment of standing committees for their present session.

They were the committees of Judiciary, Public Printing, State of the Republic, Claims and Accounts, Foreign Relations, Enrolled Bills, Public Lands, and Contingent Expenses. The Committee on Public Printing was announced as Stephen Perkins, Dugald MacFarlane, Augustus Jones, William Sadler and James Armstrong. Sadler was also later added to the Committee on Finance, which was chaired by George W. Smyth and which also included John S. Ford, John Dunn and Simeon L. Jones.

On December 9, Anson Jones was sworn in as the fourth and final President of the Republic of Texas, with Kenneth Lewis Anderson as the Vice President. Anderson and James Pinckney Henderson, later the State of Texas' first governor, both came from Lincolnton, North Carolina, the county seat of the county in which W. T. Sadler had been born. Henderson, Thomas Rusk and Anderson were all lawyers with a prominent Texas law firm. President Jones' inaugural ball was held that night above Hatfield's, with many prominent guests in attendance.[8]

The business of passing legislation for the Republic of Texas proceeded over the following weeks, and other necessary committees were formed to debate the various acts. The final motion for the first session of December 16 was the second reading on a bill for the relief of the Sheriff of Houston County. Sadler moved for this bill to be engrossed, or copied to law. Further debate occurred before the Houston County bill was finally carried and the House adjourned for the day.[9]

Among the more unpopular resolutions of the Ninth Congress was one passed by vote on December 20, 1844, that would move the republic's capital back to Austin, as a central location for the next legislature in hopes of ending the Archives War. Nine of the members, Sadler, "Rip" Ford, William R. Scurry, Gustavus A. Parker, James Truitt, Elliott M. Millican, Stephen B. Johns, John M. Lewis and Benjamin Hardin, entered a signed, formal protest against this move. Their motion to keep the capital in Washington was backed by a number of justifications.

> The situation of the city of Austin, on the extreme Northwestern frontier, liable at any moment to hostile incursions from the Indian and Mexican foe, renders that point at all times an insecure repository for the Archives of the nation; and its remoteness from the main body of the people, subjects the citizen, having business with the government, to great danger and inconvenience in going to and from that place.[10]

Sadler and his fellow protesters called upon previous congressional acts which had forbade the movement of the seat of government without the consent of the people they represented. They argued that Washington had been named as the first real capital and should remain the place of business and public affairs transactions concerning the people of Texas. The exception for moving the seat of business had been as deemed necessary in case of emergency by the threat of war, which was not found to be present at this time. This appeal was summed up with their key points.

> The undersigned, then, protest against the passage of this "Joint Resolution;" 1st, because they believe that, under the Constitution, Washington is, Provisionally, the seat of Government, until such time as the same shall be located by the people; 2nd, because they believe there is no emergency now existing, requiring a removal of the President and Heads of Departments, from this, the Provisional Seat of Government; 3rd, because if such emergency does exist, the city of Austin is not, for the reasons shown, a proper point to which to remove them.[11]

Disagreements as to the location of the nation's capital had been a sore issue in the past and would continue to be, but the Ninth Congress would ultimately be the last to use the little river town of Washington for the seat of government in Texas.

Among the bills Sadler would introduce for passage during his first term of office were one creating a new road, another authorizing Houston County's surveyor to transcribe the archives of his office into a bound book, and a bill for the relief of payment due to Mr. William Legare. He was also involved in legislation pertaining to the practice concerning plaintiffs and defendants in district courts.

The Committee on Finance to which Sadler was assigned had been charged with inquiring into the total repeal of all tariff and tonnage duties and into the portion of President Houston's farewell message that related to the finances of the country. On January 6, 1845, the Finance committee presented their signed report before the Speaker of the House. They found that the current taxation methods did not raise nearly enough money to cover the republic's current debt and that those currently levied would have to be increased nearly six-fold to provide such funding.

This report found that "it will be almost impossible to make but [even] a small reduction in the current expenses of the government for the present year" of 1845. There was also found to be a direct proportion between the amounts of exports from Texas for the year ending July 31, 1844, ($615,119) and imports for the same period ($686,503).[12] Based on the abundance of the nation's leading export, cotton, the present year's exports were not expected to exceed the previous year's net. The Committee on Finance thus found that only a very small, if any, reduction could be made on the current impost duties.

Fellow committee member John Ford made a speech on January 25 concerning the protection of the whole frontier of the Republic of Texas. "It is beyond the powers of calculation to compute the losses of life and property which have thus occurred," he stated. "It remains our duty to protect those who are left, to throw a shield between them and their ruthless destroyers, and prevent a recurrence of those bloody tragedies." The Ninth Congress thus passed legislation to provide funds for continued protection of the westernmost frontier counties, an area of Texas land which was still in dispute with the United States.[13]

Sadler's finance group on January 30 also recommended to postpone indefinitely a bill to provide for the duty free importation of printed books. "The poverty and embarrassment of the government is such that we do not feel justified in recommending any farther reductions of imposts, though called for by the crying necessities of an oppressed population," they wrote. They also commented on the "mass of carelessly written books" that did not encourage sound education, saying "three-quarters of the light literature which now encumbers our library shelves and bookstores" could be discarded and "the cause of public learning and public morals would suffer no material damage."[14]

The regular session of the Ninth Congress ended on February 3, 1845, after which time W.T. Sadler returned to his home in Houston County. He found his wife to be progressing nicely in her pregnancy with the couple's first child. Following the close of the Ninth Congress, the long-debated annexation of Texas was in full swing. In the United States, President James Polk had been elected in November 1844 on his annexation platform. Before he could take office, the U.S. Congress argued bitterly over the contested annexation of Texas and barely passed the resolution with a majority of two votes by the Congress on February 28, 1845. Outgoing U. S. President John Tyler signed this resolution on March 1, only three days before his term in office expired.[15]

By this annexation resolution, Texas would become a new state of the United States which could retain her public lands but must pay her own debts. Texas was in grave financial trouble at this time, with the currency of the Republic worth only about fifteen cents on the dollar and fluctuating.[16] As the annexation progressed in the U.S. Capitol, Anson Jones called on the Ninth Congress of the Republic of Texas to hold a special two-week session commencing on June 16, 1845.

With his wife only a week away from her due date, William Sadler traveled the one-hundred miles back to the capitol in Washington. This two-week session met again in the upstairs gambling hall of Hatfield's Grocery on June 16, with Anson Jones asking Congress to reject annexation. Both the House and Senate voted unanimously for immediate annexation, in accordance with the sentiment of the public of Texas whom they represented.[17] This decided, Congress proceeded to elect delegates to frame a republican form of government to submit to the people of Texas for ratification. The publishing of a constitution was required by the United States Congress. After proper evidence of its adoption, this Constitution was to be sent to the United States for submission to Congress on or before January 1, 1846.[18]

Among the items passed during this session was the payment of members of Congress for their service. Payment for travel was decided upon as three dollars for every twenty-five miles traveled to and from Congress, and a per dium rate of three dollars was paid to the representatives for their thirteen days of service. Sadler's receipt from the House's Chief Clerk shows:

House of Representatives
Washington June 28, 1845

This certificate entitles William T. Sadler to pay as member of the House from 16th last to date inclusive and to mileage from the County of Houston to this place and back - in all two hundred miles.

James H. Raymond

$24 Mileage
$39 Per dium
$63

Due to his family affairs back home, Sadler apparently decided that he could not be part of the Constitutional Convention. He nominated a friend and former militia company mate during the Cordova Rebellion, Pledias O. Lumpkin, who had helped survey Austin as the capital site, to take his place as the other Houston County representative with Isaac Parker. The special session ended on Saturday, June 28, 1845, and Sadler immediately struck out for home.

Chapter Fifteen

THE FIRST LEGISLATURE SHAPES THE NEW STATE

1846 - 1847

Upon his return to Houston County in early July from the special session of the Ninth Congress that ended June 28, 1845, Sadler found that his wife had already delivered their first child on June 25. Nathaniel Fletcher Sadler was born on this day in Houston County to Permelia Bennett Sadler and to a statesman whose pride in being a new father obviously outweighed the opportunity of placing his signature on one of the most historic documents in the history of Texas.

During the special two-week session ending June 28, Anson Jones had effectively ended the long-standing Archives War by promising the citizens of Austin that the historic Constitutional Convention would be held in their city. From the Senate, Isaac Parker traveled to Austin to represent Houston County, and P. O. Lumpkin arrived as Sadler's replacement in the House. In fact, only seven of the original members of the Ninth Congress' House of Representative returned for this convention.

Thomas Jefferson Rusk was the unanimous choice for President of the Convention that assembled on July 4, 1845. The delegates resolved to wear crape on their left arm for one month in honor of President Andrew Jackson, who had passed away on June 8. A similar resolution was reached four days later when word was received that Vice President of Texas Kenneth Anderson had also passed away.[1] After the June special session of the Ninth Congress, where Anderson had presided over the Senate, he had returned home to the town of Fanthorpe but suddenly became ill and died on July 3, 1845. The town was later named Anderson in his honor.

Proceeding with business, the Convention on August 19 completed and passed a Bill of Rights, and on its final day, August 28, the delegates signed the Constitution of the State of Texas. The 1845 Constitution remained in effect for fifteen years with only one amendment, although it was rewritten several times in the 1860s before the 1876 Constitution was passed which remains in effect today.[2]

The Texas Constitution was submitted to the voters on October 10, 1845, and the people overwhelmingly approved it by a vote of 7,527 to 536. On the issue of annexation, the vote was 7,664 to 430. The first general election held for state office fell on Monday, December 10, 1845. Lawyer James Pinckney Henderson, prevailed upon to fill the void left by Anderson's death, received more than 80 percent of the votes cast and was elected as the first governor of the new state.[3]

Henderson had been born on March 31, 1808, in Lincolnton, North Carolina, where he had established himself as a prominent lawyer. During the Texas Revolution, he had helped organize a company of United States volunteers from North Carolina, but these men arrived shortly after the Battle of San Jacinto. Under Sam Houston's presidency, he had been appointed attorney general and secretary of state. Henderson had also served in the recent Texas Constitutional Convention.[4] Albert C. Horton, a former cotton farmer and senator from Alabama who had later served in the Congress of the Republic of Texas from 1836-1838, was eventually declared the first lieutenant governor.

Shortly after the first elections for the new state, the United States Congress voted to annex on December 29, 1845. President Polk in Washington then added his signature to the bill which extended the laws of the United States of America over Texas, which became the 28th state.

Under the Third Article of the new Constitution, concerning the Legislative Department, members of the new Legislature of the State of Texas were elected by voters who were at least twenty-one years of age and Texas residents for at least six months prior to the acceptance of the Constitution. A representative had to be at least twenty-one years of age, to have been an inhabitant of the state for at least two years preceding his election and the last year thereof a citizen of the county or town from which he was elected. Excepting treason, felony or breach of the peace, senators and representatives were privileged from arrest during the session of the legislature and during their travel to and from Congress. Senators were elected for four year terms, while members of the House were elected for two year terms commencing on the date of their election.

Texas House of Representatives
The First Legislature

Regular Session:
February 16 - May 13, 1846

Governor: James Pinckney Henderson
Speaker: William E. Crump

MEMBER	COUNTY	MEMBER	COUNTY
Adams, George W.	Robertson	McCullough, Benjamin	Gonzales
Barry, Lewis D.	Red River	McFarland, Samuel	Fannin
Bourland, William H.	Lamar	McNeill, Archibald	Montgomery
Branch, Edward T. [2]	Liberty	Miller, Steward Alexander	Houston
Brown, John [1]	Nacogdoches	Millican, Elliott M.	Brazos
Burroughs, James M.	Sabine	Muckleroy, Daniel	Nacogdoches
Cazneau, William L.	Travis	Mullins, Charles	Fayette
Charlton, Napoleon B.	Liberty	Noble, Jamerson S.	Sabine
Clark, Edward	Harrison	Ogden, Duncan C.	Bexar
Cooke, Wilds K.	Robertson	Pattillo, George A.	Jefferson
Cronican, James	Galveston	Pease, Elisha M.	Brazoria
Dickson, David C.	Montgomery	Perkins, Stephen W.	Brazoria
Dupree, Lewis G.	Washington	Perry, William B.	Colorado
Durham, Berry H.	Bowie	Railey, Charles	Austin
Echols, William F.	Shelby	Rayner, William S.	Fort Bend
Eddy, Z. Williams	Jasper	Redgate, Samuel J.	Colorado
Edwards, Hayden Harrison	Nacogdoches	Rose, John W.	Victoria
Edwards, William C.	San Augustine	Russell, Andrew J.	Bowie
Erath, George Bernhard	Milam	Ryburn, Hiram W.	Fannin
Gillet, James S.	Red River	Sadler, William Turner	Houston
Gilliam, James	Lamar	Savage, Israel S.	Galveston
Gooch, Ben F.	Red River	Smith, James	Rusk
Gray, Peter W.	Harris	Smith, John N. O.	Harris
Holland, Spearman	Harrison	Stevenson, Alexander	San Patricio
Howard, Volney E.	Bexar	Stewart, Charles B.	Montgomery
Hudson, James P.	Fayette	Sublett, Henry W.	San Augustine
Irion, Van R.	Washington	Swift, Arthur	Gonzales
Jones, Henry	Matagorda	Tankersly, Benjamin F.	Harris
Keenan, Charles G.	Montgomery	Truitt, James	Shelby
Mabry, Evans	Bastrop	White, Francis M.	Jackson
McClarty, Charles F.	Rusk	Williams, Augustus	Goliad
McCown, James B.	Harrison	Willie, James	Washington

[1] *Second Speaker of the House*
[2] *Third Speaker of the House*

Each House was required to keep and publish a journal of its proceedings, which included the yeas and nays of the members of each House on voting. The doors of each House were required to be kept open, and neither House could adjourn for more than three days without consent. Bills could be originated in either House and be amended, altered or rejected by the other. The House of Representatives was charged with originating all bills concerning revenue, but the Senate had the power to amend or reject them.

The new Constitution also specified that the First Legislature's House would consist of sixty-six elected representatives: one for each of thirteen counties; two for each of seventeen counties, including Houston County; three representatives each for the counties of Red River, Harrison, Nacogdoches, Harris and Washington; and four representatives for Montgomery County. The Senate would be staffed with twenty-one senators, representing nineteen congressional districts.

In the elections held on December 10, Houston County voted in favor of William Sadler and Steward Alexander Miller to fill the two seats in the House of Representatives for the First and Second Legislatures. Miller, born in Campbell County, Virginia, on July 4, 1805, and orphaned at an early age, had come to Texas in 1839, studied law under James Carr and had reached the rank of colonel while enlisted in Colonel Jacob Snively's expedition of 1843.[5]

After the admission of Texas into the Union, Houston County was placed into a district which included Houston, Nacogdoches and Rusk counties. For this district, there were two senators elected: Isaac Parker of Houston County and Joseph L. Hogg of Rusk County. The new members of the Texas Legislature would be paid from the Treasury of the State a compensation of three dollars for each day they were in attendance and three dollars for every twenty-five miles traveled to and from the place of convening of the legislature.

Much of their time in Congress would be spent shaping the laws into those that would govern the new state into its future. They would also be faced with the important decision of electing the first members of the U.S. Congress to represent Texas. The Constitution also provided that the legislature would be held in the city of Austin, where it was to remain until an election on the permanent seat of government could be held on the first Monday in March 1850.

The Republic of Texas had purchased more than seven-thousand acres of land on the Colorado River and began surveying it in May 1839 for the layout of a new capital town. As streets

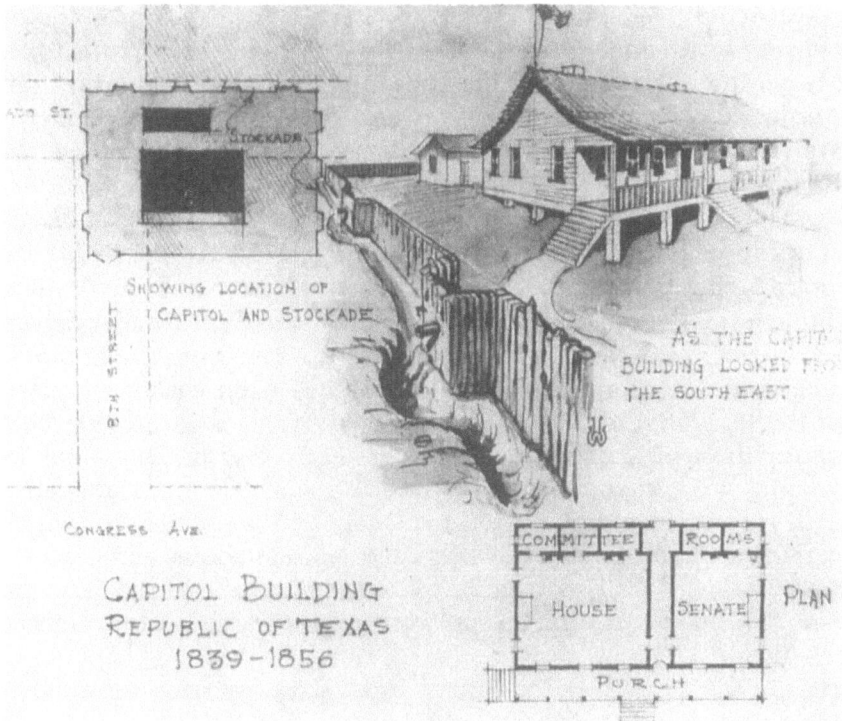

The Capitol of the Republic of Texas in Austin, as seen in an early sketch. The House and Senate met in the same building, which was surrounded by a stockade fence. After being moved in 1842, Austin was reinstated as the capital city prior to the convening of the First Legislature of the State of Texas in 1845. Courtesy of the Archives Division - Texas State Library.

began taking shape, a temporary capitol building had been constructed in 1840. Austin's north-south streets were named for rivers, except for the center street of Congress Avenue. East-west streets were named for native Texas trees with three exceptions: Water Avenue beside the river, College Avenue and North Avenue, the latter on the northern extreme of town. These east-west streets were later given numbers instead of tree names.[6]

When Sadler arrived in Austin with Steward Miller in early 1846, he found his new capitol building to be a far cry from the crude facilities he and his fellow congressmen had endured at Washington-on-the-Brazos the previous year. The capitol building was located on a small rise of ground on Colorado Street between Hickory (present 8th) Street and Ash (9th) Street, just west of Congress Avenue. The structure itself was a one-story building constructed from pine planks from Bastrop with a roof made of cypress and cedar shakes, three foot shingles split from logs. Measuring about one-hundred feet long by sixty feet wide, the Austin capitol occupied three lots and served as the joint government building for both the Texas Senate and House of Representatives.[7]

The wooden building, with a covered porch running along its entire front length, faced east toward Congress Avenue, with the larger House Chamber on the south side. A large hallway running through the building from east to west separated the smaller Senate Chamber, and on the back side of the building were small committee rooms which opened off the two main chambers. Each of the legislative chambers had its own fireplace to provide heat during the winter months. During the early days of the capitol, its grounds were surrounded by a protective stockade made of twelve-inch logs, held together by hewn slabs and wooden pins, which extended three feet into the earth and ten feet above. Embrasures were provided for heavy artillery at two points of each side and the entire stockade was surrounded by a ditch five feet wide and three feet deep.[8]

On the grounds of the capitol about sixty feet west was another building measuring seventy feet by twenty feet which had a kitchen and dining room at one end. In the center were a number of beds and cots, and on the north end a "refreshment" room. Between the two buildings were two water wells, and when the Congress was not in session the Capitol Building was used as a school.

Near the capitol on Congress Avenue were a number of other buildings in the early town of Austin: a log house for the quartermaster general; offices for each of the major government agencies; the office of the vice president; dry goods stores and other businesses; and the president's mansion, the town's first two-story building. Two early residences for visitors and congressmen in Austin were also located nearby: the Bullock family operated a two-story building of rental rooms on Pecan (6th) Street and Congress, and a two-story log boarding house operated by Mrs. Angelina Eberly was a block away.

* * * *

One of the first things Sadler accomplished upon arrival in Austin was to take care of some land business with the General Land Office of Texas. Having already transferred his 320-acre bounty land grant to Martin Murchison, he needed the proper title to this land. Presenting his bounty certificate and the surveyor's notes of the property to President Anson Jones and Commissioner Thomas William Ward, he was issued Patent No. 212 of the Republic of Texas. Jones issued the patent letter on February 10, 1846, which reads in part:

> To all to whom these presents shall come know ye I Anson Jones, President of the Republic aforesaid, by virtue of the power vested in me by law and in accordance with the Statutes of said Republic in such case made and provided do by these presents grant William T. Sadler, his heirs or assigns forever Three Hundred and Twenty acres of land.

Jones, another San Jacinto veteran, affixed the seal of the Republic of Texas and that of the General Land Office. Sadler's land patent was among the last issued by the Republic of Texas prior to its becoming a state and was certainly among the last signed by President Jones.

The First Legislature of the State of Texas met on Monday, February 16, 1846, and the House was organized by the Honorable Ebenezer Allen, Secretary of State. An alphabetical role of the counties was called, at which time Sadler and his fellow representatives presented their credentials and took their oaths. General Ned Burleson was elected President Pro Tempore of the Senate and William E. Crump of Austin County was chosen Speaker of the House. James H. Raymond was appointed as Chief Clerk of the House. The Congress then appointed joint committees to wait on the governor-elect. [9] Governor-elect Henderson reported his choice for inauguration day as Thursday, February 19.

Three days after the First Legislature opened, President Anson Jones' tenure as President of the Republic of Texas ended and J. Pinckney Henderson was sworn in as the State of Texas' first governor on February 19, 1846. On this date, the seats were removed from the House and Senate chambers and placed on the long gallery on the east side of the capitol, where the members of the legislature took their seats. Hundreds of citizens gathered to witness the flag-decorated capitol, which now was flying both the Lone Star Flag and the Stars and Stripes of the United States. Governor-elect Henderson and outgoing President Jones were both present, escorted by a joint committee from both houses and military officers of the United States who were in Austin for the occasion.[10]

"The Republic of Texas is no more!" *In his valedictory address of February 19, 1846, President Anson Jones spoke these historic words as Texas became the 28th state of the United States. Congressman Sadler and his fellow members of the First Legislature were among those assembled on the porch of the capitol in Austin for this occasion as Jones lowers the Lone Star Flag. James Pinckney Henderson also became the first governor of Texas this day.*
Illustration courtesy of the Archives and Information Services Division - Texas State Library.

Judge Robert E. B. Baylor, co-founder of Baylor University, delivered the invocation, followed by Anson Jones' delivery of a well-received valedictory address. With the changing of the Texas government, Jones stated to applause that "the sovereignty of the nation is surrendered and incorporated with that of another." The Lone Star of Texas had proudly flown for ten years since independence from Mexico had first been declared in 1836, but he declared that the flag would now blend "its rays with its sister States" in a great consummation of two republics. "The final act in the great drama is now performed," said Jones in a famous statement. "The Republic of Texas is no more!"

With this utterance, the Lone Star was lowered to the boom of nearby artillery and the Stars and Stripes were briskly run to the top of the standard to take its place. For W. T. Sadler and his fellow freedom fighters, it was the moment of a lifetime, the realization of past dreams come true. All the revolutions, frontier depredations and Indians wars of the past decade were replaced by a new association with a powerful nation.

House Speaker William Crump delivered the oath of office to thirty-seven-year-old James Pinckney Henderson, and the first governor of the new state of Texas proceeded to deliver his inaugural address.

> Gentlemen of the Senate and the House of Representatives: This day and within this hour has been consummated the great work of annexation. This consummation, it seems to me, should be a full compensation to our citizens for all their toils and sufferings endured for ten long years.... We have this day fully entered the Union of the North American States. Let us give our friends, who so boldly and nobly advocated our cause, no reason to regret their efforts in our behalf. Henceforth, the prosperity of our sister states will be our prosperity -- their happiness -- their quarrels, our quarrels, and in their wars we will freely participate....

With the completion of the ceremonies in Austin, the Republic of Texas ceased to exist. In its place now stood a proud young state, whose congressmen of the First Legislature of 1846 were faced with shaping the laws and standards upon which its citizens would build their futures.

Governor Henderson quickly appointed his cabinet, and the House and Senate set about establishing their committees to begin passing legislation. On February 20, many of the regular House committees were formed. W. T. Sadler was elected to the Committee on Claims and Accounts with Evans Mabry, James Truitt, George Adams, Napoleon Charlton and Arthur Swift. Sadler would later be elected to several other committees.

Among the first orders of business was the election of Texas' very first representatives to the United States Congress in Washington. On Saturday, February 21, 1846, a joint session of the House and Senate in Austin overwhelmingly elected Thomas Rusk and Sam Houston as these senators. Timothy Pillsbury and David S. Kaufman were elected to serve Texas in the U.S. House of Representatives. In order that one-third of the Senate retire each year, one of the two Texas senators would have to serve a short term. Houston drew the short term, which would end in 1847, while Rusk would remain in the U.S. Congress until 1851. With its latest additions, the United States Senate now boasted fifty-six members.[11]

In his first message before the legislature, Governor Henderson put forth his three foremost goals: economy in government, improvement of the court system and the establishment of a public school system. Concerning the court system, he advised Congress to immediately revise criminal and civil laws to provide for public peace and safety.[12]

On public schools, Henderson stated that the prosperity, happiness and permanence of the Texas government greatly depended "upon the intelligence and moral and religious characters of its citizens." He warned the Congress that many of its sister states had suffered slow progress in maturing plans for and collecting sufficient funds for proper school systems. He therefore charged the First Legislature:

> By the constitution it is made the duty of the Legislature to make suitable provision for the support of public schools, and to set apart not less than one-tenth of the annual revenue of the State as a perpetual fund for that purpose, and as soon as practicable to furnish other means for the support of the free schools throughout the State by taxation.

* * * *

CREATING A NEW COUNTY

Congressman Sadler's greatest accomplishment during the First Legislature was his work with his Houston County Senate counterpart Isaac Parker to create a new county in their home area. Years earlier in 1841, an abortive attempt to create Burnet County with Fort Houston as the county seat had been presented to the Fifth Congress. Although this county had not been allowed, it was clear to Sadler and Parker that Houston County now needed restructuring. On Monday, February 23, Sadler introduced a bill that was entitled "An Act Providing the Mode of Establishing County Seats, For New Counties." This bill was then read before the House for its first time and for its second time on February 25. The standing Rule of the House was that all bills must be read on "three several days" before passage.

In a joint session of the House and Senate, the First Legislature on the morning of February 24 elected James H. Raymond as the first State Treasurer and James B. Shaw as the first Comptroller of Public Accounts for Texas. Sadler's efforts to create a new county continued as he presented a memorial from the citizens of Houston County on Monday, March 2, who were "praying for the creation of a new county." After the reading of this memorial, it was referred to the Committee on County Boundaries.[13] This committee had its hands full during this session of Congress with the large number of new counties being petitioned for including Anderson, Angelina, Burleson, Calhoun, Cass, Cherokee, Collin, Comol, Dallas, DeWitt, Grayson, Guadalupe, Henderson, Hopkins, Lavaca, Leon, Limestone, Navarro, Newton, Nueces, Panola, Polk, Smith, Tyler, Upshur and Wharton.

On March 3, the House held an election for Speaker Pro Tem. James Burroughs, Williams Eddy and Sadler were appointed as Tellers for this election of the Second Speaker of the House. In a ballot vote, the House elected John Brown of Nacogdoches County to this position. The following day, Sadler's act to provide for the mode of establishing new county seats was read a third time and then laid upon the table for passage.

Through the efforts of Parker and Sadler, "An Act Organizing the County of Anderson" was introduced before the First Legislature. For the name of the county to be carved from Houston County, Congressman Sadler had suggested "Anderson County" in honor of Kenneth Lewis Anderson, the last Vice President of the Republic of Texas. Anderson, like Sadler originally from Lincolnton, North Carolina, had become familiar to Sadler during the Ninth Congress. As related, Anderson had been heavily favored to become the first governor of the new state but had passed away shortly after the Ninth Congress had closed its session.

In the House, Sadler's bill was taken up and read for a second time on Saturday, March 7. The only objection to the Anderson County bill concerned the right of the county automatically to be granted separate representation in Congress. The House's journals record the rectification to this point.

> Mr. [Francis] White offered the following as an amendment to the bill.
> "Except, as to right of separate Representation, until entitled by numbers."
> Mr. Sadler offered the following, as an amendment to the amendment, just proposed:
> "Except the right of electing a separate County Surveyor and the right of having a separate Land District."
> Which amendment was adopted.
> Question: Shall the amendment, to the bill now under consideration of the House, as amended, be adopted?
> The House decided in the affirmative.[14]

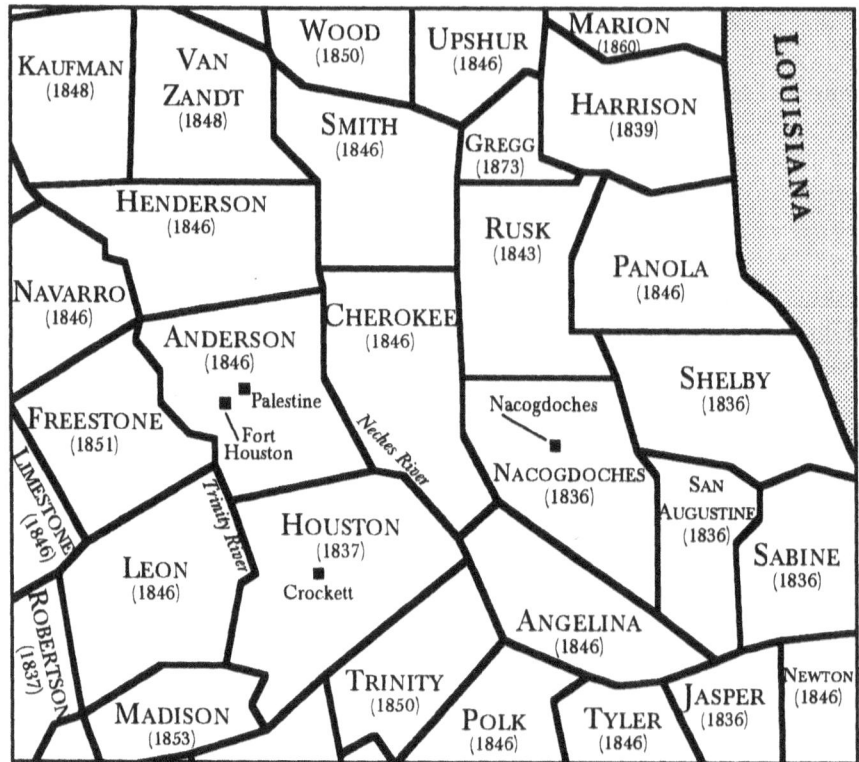

Anderson County, Texas, was created during the First Legislature of 1846 by an act introduced in the House of Representatives by William Sadler and in the Senate by Isaac Parker. By its established boundaries, Anderson County comprised a total area of 1,088 square miles. Many other counties in this area were also created in 1846 during the First Legislature.

It would be another three weeks before the Anderson County bill completed its journey through the House and Senate. Other larger counties of Texas were similarly proposed to be broken up into smaller counties during the First Legislature. Among these was an act to divide Montgomery County, which already had four representatives. This bill was passed to a select committee on March 13 which consisted of Sadler, Truitt, White, Swift and Jones.

The act "To Create the County of Anderson" introduced by Sadler and Isaac Parker was finally passed by the First Legislature on March 24, 1846. Establishing the line between Houston and Anderson counties, Congressman Sadler had the survey specify that the boundary line would start at the summit of Houston Mound, a hill that the militia and citizens gathered around in an emergency, and proceed east to the Neches River and west to the Trinity River.

The act creating the new county reads:

Section 1. Be it enacted by the Legislature of the State of Texas, That all portion of territory comprised in the following limits, constitute a new county to be called the County of Anderson, to wit: Beginning at a place in the county of Houston, known as Houston Mound, about one mile north of Murchison's Prairie; thence, westwardly by a direct line running through the old Ioni village, on the North Elkhart Creek, to the Trinity River; thence, beginning again at Houston's Mound, continuing said direct line eastwardly to the Neches River; thence, up said river with the meanders thereof, to the northeast corner of John Ferguson's league of land; thence, by a direct line parallel to the first above named line, to the Trinity River; thence, down said river with the meanders thereof, to the intersection of said first named line with the Trinity River.

Section 2. Be it further enacted, That the inhabitants of said county shall be entitled to all the privileges and immunities in common with other counties of this State, except the right of electing a separate county surveyor, the right of having a separate land district, and the right of separate representation, until entitled by numbers.

Section 3. Be it further enacted, That Samuel G. Wells, Esq., be, and he is hereby authorized and required as soon as practicable after the passage of this act, to order an election for the Commissioners, giving at least ten days notice thereof, in writing, to be posted up at two or more of the most public places in each magistrate's jurisdiction, the election to be held and managed according to law, and the three individuals voted for, having the highest number of votes, shall be authorized to fill said commission.

Section 4. Be it further enacted, That the said commissioners when so elected, shall have power to select a place for the location of the county seat for said county, having due regard to the general interest of the people of said county, and to receive donations for county purposes, to purchase if necessary for the use of said county, a tract of land not exceeding one hundred acres, on which to place the public buildings for said county; to have laid off, and dispose of any portion of said lot of land, the proceeds to be applied to the building of a court house and jail; and after paying the incidental expenses, said buildings and the county fund thus raised, to be under the direction of the county court, to whom the fund thus raised shall be turned over by the commissioners.

Section 5. Be it further enacted, That the county officers of said county, shall be elected in accordance with the law on this subject made and provided.

Section 6. Be it further enacted, That the said county of Anderson, shall be held responsible for the payment of its equitable proportion of the now existing debt of the county of Houston, from which said county is stricken.

Section 7. Be it further enacted, That in no event shall the county seat of said county be located more than three miles from the center of said county, and that this act take effect from and after its passage.

Approved, March 24th, 1846.[15]

Another important piece of legislation to which Sadler was assigned was that of ceding the vacant territory of the State of Texas to the United States. This special committee was chaired by Volney Howard and also included William Cazneau, Evans Mabry,

This granite marker, located 4.7 miles northeast of Palestine, Texas, on U.S. 79, commemorates the creation of Anderson County in 1846. Photo by Marshall L. Moore Jr.

Jamerson Noble and Sadler. This committee finalized their report on March 1, which was presented before the House on March 28.

> ... It is now more than ten years since Texas achieved and established her independence by a successful revolution. ... Texas came triumphantly out of the struggle, with less loss of blood and treasure than have ever attended a revolution of as much magnitude recorded in the annals of history, but yet it has entailed upon her a considerable debt, which is strongly recommended to our sense of justice and honor for the earliest practicable payment.... Her resources and ability for raising revenue from direct taxation, cannot for many years to come exceed the urgent and indispensable wants of her domestic administration.... However strong, therefore, may be the desire of the country to provide for its creditors, it has no ability of doing so, except through the means of the public lands.[16]

The committee found the present vacant domain of Texas to amount to 180,000,000 acres of land, which would require almost $500,000 just to survey and sectionalize. This process would also force further bloody collisions between surveying parties and roving tribes of Indians, which would necessitate further expensive military intervention. The committee also found that "If Texas is compelled to issue Land Scrip to her public creditors, it will be thrown in a mass upon the market, and sold at such a low rate, that the public lands of Texas will not cost more than a few cents per acre."

In a compromise with the United States in 1850, Texas did give up 67,000,000 acres of land in exchange for a payment which eventually amounted to $12,750,000. The new boundaries of Texas thereafter included the Rio Grande River and the 42nd parallel after surrendering claims to territory that included parts of the present states of New Mexico, Oklahoma, Kansas, Colorado and Wyoming.[17]

Sadler and his companions also found that the state's public debt, composed largely of Treasury Notes issued to provide for the expenses of the years of revolutions and military actions, was approximately $10,000,000. Of this total, the holders of these notes would be reimbursed at a rate just under half their value. A Board of Commissioners was recommended "in order to arrive at any practical result" which would have the right of appeal to the Supreme Court of Texas on questions of law. Claimants seeking amounts less than one-thousand dollars would be allowed to file their claims before their county's Judge of Probate, who would in turn present the necessary papers before the Board for adjudication.[18]

Chairman Howard and his committee thus presented before Congress a resolution that the legislature

> be requested and authorized forthwith to open a negotiation with the Government of the United States, in such forms they may think fit, for the cession of the public lands of Texas to the United States, for an adequate consideration, to enable Texas to pay her public debt; any negotiation to be subject to the ratification of the Legislature of the State of Texas, according to the ordinary forms of legislation.[19]

Other acts taken up during this session included an act to raise state revenue by direct taxation, an act to appropriate funds for the contingent expenses of both Houses of the Legislature, an act to make provisions for Public Education, an act to revise and arrange the state's criminal and civil laws, an act incorporating the city of Austin, and an act to provide for the establishment of peace and the regulation of friendly intercourse with the Indians of Texas.

W. T. Sadler was named Chairman of a Select Committee to which was referred a bill to establish the county of Cass in extreme northeastern Texas. After investigating this matter, Sadler reported before the House that his committee had "instructed me to report the bill back to the House, and to recommend the adoption of the amendments, proposed by the committee on County Boundaries."[20]

Sadler was unafraid to oppose bills that he found to favor one party or another, as evidenced by some of his protests. With Henry Sublett and Williams Eddy, he entered a formal protest on April 13 against an act organizing county courts which was believed to be in conflict with the Texas Constitution. This trio protested the fact that these courts were to be offered the power to levy different rates of taxation upon properties within their county boundaries. They felt it to be the duty of the legislature to decide upon a plan for raising revenues for county purposes and that it was wrong for county courts to possess the power of levying taxes upon properties of citizens of the county when those same citizens did not even have a voice in electing the officers of the Court. Sublett, Sadler and Eddy concluded their protest with "Taxation is authorized when there is no representation -- a principle, the most repugnant of all others to the genius of American Institutions."[21]

A resolution arrived from the Senate that same day announcing that a special committee had been appointed to destroy the seals of the late Republic of Texas. From the House, Representatives Sadler, Charles Stewart and John Smith were appointed to assist in this duty.

While the First Legislature continued its session, another crisis had erupted in Texas. Mexico had warned that annexation of Texas would be considered an act of war, and in response the country had moved troops to the Rio Grande in 1846 to enforce its threat. The United States had then responded by sending out army troops under General Zachary Taylor, and fighting commenced on April 25, 1846. When Taylor called for Texas troops to assist in the fighting, four regiments of infantry and cavalry and two regiments of Texas Rangers were quickly equipped to fight. Colonel George Tyler Wood, who later became Texas' second governor, and Jack Hays took command of the rangers. About eight-thousand Texans served in the Mexican War.

The legislature did not adjourn but continued working on bills concerning the public debt, the library system, the duties and offices of elected officials, the organization of justice courts, provisions for the publication of laws, the regulation of elections, and the ceding of all Texas forts and arsenals to the jurisdiction of the United States, among others.

The Committee on Claims and Accounts to which Sadler had long been assigned faced the arduous task of considering a large number of joint resolutions and relief claims for various citizens. "After mature deliberation" the committee found that it was expedient for the legislature not to take any action yet on these claims. They found that "during the short period allotted to their labors, sufficient time or means to obtain an accurate, or even a general knowledge of all the claims" had not been possible. It was therefore recommended that a proper tribunal should be instituted "with sufficient power to investigate and pass over all claims or demands against the Republic of Texas." This report of May 8 was signed by representatives Rayner, Russell, Eddy, Adams, Truitt, Charlton, Dickson, Muckleroy, Swift, Redgate and Sadler.[22]

By request of this committee all claims and papers would be returned to the House for future consideration by a proper tribunal. This report was then adopted by a vote of the House. All those still submitting claims against the late Republic of Texas for past payments due, including Sadler himself for his supply donations to the military in 1838, would be forced to wait even longer.

Another act affecting Sadler's new home counties passed on May 8, 1846, entitled "An Act To Apportion the Liabilities of the County of Houston Between Said County and the County of Anderson."

According to this legislation, any "existing debt and liabilities of whatever description" of former Houston County citizens who now lived in the new Anderson County would be the financial responsibility of those citizens now in Anderson County. These debts would be due on the second Monday in July 1846.[23] Other debts payable to persons or corporations located outside of either county would be equally payable by both Houston and Anderson counties.

In addition, all taxes owed to the county after the second Monday in July would go to the appropriate county to which the citizen belonged. It was also enacted that the chief justices of both counties would meet in Crockett before the second Monday in January 1847 for a joint court session between Anderson and Houston counties for the purpose of

> ascertaining the debts and credits of said county of Houston, existing on the said second Monday in July, and for the purpose of making an equitable partition of said debts, credits and liabilities, according to the provisions of this act, and for the purpose of transferring to Anderson County her just proportion of said debts, credits and liabilities.[24]

Finally, this act provided that a majority of the members of the county courts for Anderson and Houston should form a quorum to transact the debt business. They should meet daily until the duty was completed, and their respective counties would pay each member a fee of two dollars per day for their services.

During these last days of session of Congress, the ongoing Mexican War required special attention. On May 9, the First Legislature passed a resolution that Governor James Henderson would be given a commission as major general in charge of the Texas Volunteers. Among his staff was Mirabeau Lamar, General Ned Burleson, Henry L. Kinney and Edward Clark, who later became a governor of Texas. Lamar was stationed in Laredo with a volunteer force with Hamilton P. Bee as his second-in-command. Henderson fell ill at the time Texan troops departed for Mexico, but he later left in an unescorted carriage to catch up with the main Texas forces on September 18.[25]

As the regular session of Congress drew near its close, House Speaker John Brown presented a valedictory address to his sixty-five fellow members, congratulating them on enduring "the storms of Legislation" with such good conduct that was trusted would "ever characterize the deliberate assemblies of this State."

Gentlemen, the great number of bills that have passed this Legislature, and the short time in which they have passed them, displays a talent for business, that would do honor to the oldest State of this confederacy, and will amply remunerate your constituents for the confidence reposed in you . . . .

Gentlemen, in a few more days, you will separate, to scatter yourselves over this vast country, again to commingle with those who honored you with seats in this Hall. On Monday next, will end your political labors, and perhaps, 'ere two more years roll round, many of us will pass into eternity. Let not these considerations blunt your ardor for the prosperity and happiness of our State. Remember that it was industry and perseverance that gave Texas existence as a State, and bade every breeze bear on its bosom the glad tidings, that another Star had arisen in the West which forms a new asylum for the oppressed, that are bowed down by the insolence of tyranny and oppression.[26]

Brown also thanked the House members for having overcome the worst bit of controversy that had troubled their session: the appointment in February of Albert C. Horton as lieutenant governor. The declared results of the voting had been for this position to have been filled by Nicholas Henry Darnell, who had later offered a formal resignation from this post prior to his acceptance. This resignation had stemmed from a protest that a number of counties' election results had not yet been received when Darnell was so designated on February 17. Sadler and fourteen of his constituents had not protested Horton as the replacement, but they had protested the method used by the legislature to fill his position.

In a signed protest presented to the House journals following Brown's speech, these men respectfully submitted their case which included the summation, "Towards the individual holding the station, we have not, nor have we ever had, any unkind feelings. We had full confidence in his ability and honesty, and protest alone against the *manner* in which he has been placed in office."[27]

The First Legislature of Texas ended its session on the night of Monday, May 13, 1846, and its members retired to their respective home counties after an exhausting three months of passing the early laws that would help to shape their new state.

Captain William Turner Sadler *(1797-1884), a Texas pioneer, early Texas Ranger captain, San Jacinto veteran, postmaster, company leader during the 1838 Indian campaigns, and officer of the First Regiment of Infantry during the Cherokee War of 1839. Sadler went on to represent Houston County in the Ninth Congress (the final session of the Republic of Texas) and in the first two legislatures of the State of Texas. Reproduction of an early charcoal portrait.* Courtesy of Howard C. Sadler.

Chapter Sixteen

EARLY ANDERSON COUNTY AND THE SECOND LEGISLATURE

June 1846 - March 1848

Following the session of Congress, Sadler did not participate in the Mexican War but instead returned home during the late days of May 1846 to help organize his newly created county. His first task was to help create a town to serve as the county seat. Since the passage of the act in March, the two leading towns in the newly established area, Fort Houston and Mound Prairie, had begun feuding over which would become the county seat. Former militia Major Elisha Clapp was among Mound Prairie's leading citizens at this time. Both towns were quick to offer land and various inducements for the coveted designation.[1]

According to legislation that Sadler had introduced, however, any newly organized county's county seat could not be more than three miles from the geographic center of the county. Since Fort Houston and Mound Prairie were both more than three miles from the center, a new town would have to be formed to serve as the county seat. During Sadler's absence in Austin, Samuel Wells had held the required election for county commissioners in April.

James Box, John Parker and Micham Main were the three men receiving the highest number of votes and therefore became the commissioners who would select a site for the county seat. With his civil engineering education, Sadler also assisted in establishing the boundaries of Houston County as it is today. He gave the readings of latitude and longitude for the northeast corner and northwest corner of this neighboring county.[2]

About two miles north and east of Fort Houston was an old log trading post, at about the site of the present Palestine jail, established in the 1830s west of Gum Springs and operated by James R. Fulton and Johnston Shelton. From this store the men, later joined by

Soon after Sadler and Parker helped pass the legislation to create Anderson County, the county seat of Palestine was established in 1846. Measuring 20 x 32 feet, the first county courthouse (left) was then erected in early 1847 in the center of the town square.
Illustration courtesy of the Anderson County Historical Commission.

settler William Bigelow, had traded with early settlers in furs, hides and general supplies they brought in regularly from Shreveport. Near this log store led a road from Fort Houston that ran to the Thomas Goss Headright on the Neches River.[3]

At this central Anderson County location, on a one-hundred-acre tract of land on the southwest corner of the Samuel G. Wells Headright League, the new county seat would be laid out. The deed for this town was from Fulton and Bigelow and the price paid was five-hundred dollars for the one-hundred acres, quite a premium at the time.

The first session of the Anderson County court was held shortly thereafter, on July 30, 1846, and among the first jurors was Dr. Henry H. Link, a physician newly arrived in Texas from Tennessee. Among the items approved were the building of a courtroom and a jail under supervision of James E. Box and deputy surveyor Darius H. Edens with an underground dungeon, and the building of proper roads to connect the county seat town to Fort Houston, Parker's Bluff, Cannon's Ferry and Kingsboro in nearby Henderson County. In August a county tax was levied and Thomas Hanks was appointed County Treasurer.[4]

Other first officials appointed for the new County of Anderson were D. H. Edens as chief justice (equivalent of county judge), William Wright, James W. Gardner, Valentine S. Anglin and Allen Killough as commissioners, John Crawford Grigsby as clerk, Peyton Parker as sheriff, William M. Gibson as the assistant tax collector, and Alexander E. McClure as district clerk.

The first public building constructed in Anderson County was the new County Jail (left). Standing on the south end of the courthouse square, the jail measured 20 x 20 feet square and featured a dungeon for prisoners on the ground level with small grills for light and ventilation. Illustration courtesy of the Anderson County Historical Commission.

The first store of Anderson County was operated by Fulton and Shelton, while Alexander Joost had later become Fort Houston's first merchant. In the new town, a large new store was built on the north and west sides of the courthouse plaza. Among the operators of this store was John Murchison, Sadler's first brother-in-law.

The county seat was surveyed as a townsite by Johnston Shelton on October 15, 1846. James Box and D. H. Edens are credited with drawing the first maps of the town and for naming the streets. A committee consisting of Congressman Sadler, P. O. Lumpkin and John Parker met to lay out and name the new county seat. At the request of Parker, the town was named Palestine in honor of the small town in Crawford County, Illinois, where Sadler's wife had lived as a little girl before coming down with the Parkers and the Pilgrim Church. Many of these immigrants, of course, had been killed in 1836 during the Parker's Fort Massacre. Sadler's new wife, Permelia Bennett, and her family were among the earliest members of the Parkers' church.

The Anderson County court arranged election precincts in October. District court for the 6th Judicial District of Texas was held on November 9, 1846, with Judge William B. Ochiltree presiding. Civil cases involving title to land and slaves were the first cases heard.

During the early months of 1847, Palestine grew rapidly and the first public buildings were soon completed. William and Permelia Sadler's second child, Martha Tucker Sadler, was born into the new county on April 12, 1847. Judge Edens maintained his surveying business between court duties, and he was hired by Sadler to survey the 640-acre land grant received for his San Jacinto service. According to Houston County Land Donation File 108, Edens completed this survey on September 3, 1847, and filed these papers on September 8. Edens also surveyed Sadler's claim to the one-third league of land near Fort Houston on November 25, 1847, as evidenced by File 177 filed November 27.

Having been elected to two-years terms, William Sadler and Stewart Miller departed Palestine for Austin during the winter 1847 for the Second Legislature of Texas. Both men returned representing Houston County, as Anderson was not yet qualified for its own representative. Due to the Mexican War, some nineteen months had passed since the previous Congress had ended its session.

The members of the Second Legislature convened at the capitol in Austin on Monday, December 13, 1847. Congress was organized by the Honorable David Burnet, Secretary of State, who was assisted by former Chief Clerk of the House Ben F. Hill. Each representative came forward to take his seat alphabetically by county after presenting his credentials and taking the state's constitutional oath of office. James W. Henderson of Harris County was elected as the new Speaker of the House.[5]

Sadler's old friend Mirabeau Lamar, who had been elected as representative for San Patricio and Nueces Counties, was defeated by Henderson in the voting for the Speaker position. Following his term as president, Lamar had returned to his farm near Richmond in Fort Bend County, but his personal tragedies had continued when he found that his sixteen-year-old daughter Rebecca Ann had died in Georgia. He had then been elected to Congress soon after his return to Texas.

Speaker Henderson took the chair on December 13 and addressed the assembled House, directing its members to conduct their deliberations toward the advancement, happiness and honor of the people, to whom they all owed a strict accountability.

During the next two days, the House proceeded to appoint members to its various standing committees. Sadler was assigned to the Finance Committee, along with Hamilton Stuart, Charles Keenan, James Taylor, O. M. Wheeler, William Bourland, Archibald McNeill, James Shaw and William Fields. Sadler was also appointed to the Committee on Public Buildings with Shaw, Wheeler, Adolphous Sterne, William Stout, Mark Potter, William Webb, Clinton Winkler and Thomas Shannon. He was also appointed to the newly created Committee on the Penitentiary with Potter, M. A. Dooley, John Anderson, W. H. Crutchir, William Edwards, E. M. Wilder, Benjamin Epperson and Samuel Mosely.

On Wednesday December 15, acting upon a report of the committee on Printing, the House decided that there would be ten copies of the *Texas Democrat* printed for each member for use of the House. That afternoon, seats were prepared in the larger House chamber to make room for the Senators. The lieutenant governor was given a seat on the right by Speaker James W. Henderson and then a biennial message of Governor J. Pinckney Henderson was read.

Henderson opened by greeting the legislature with a congratulation for "the prosperous and happy condition of our country." He informed them that future matters would be up to his successor as governor, but that he would limit his message to matters acted upon since the adjournment of the First Legislature. His message recapped the previous year's battle with Mexican troops on the Rio Grande, the attachment of Texas to the Union, and his belief that "Northern people are the aggressors, and it is our duty to join with the other States of the South, in resisting their efforts with manly firmness."[6]

Following the reading of Henderson's farewell message as Governor of the State of Texas, the joint assembly of the House and Senate took up the business of electing a senator to the Congress of the United States of America. Elisha Lott of Nacogdoches nominated General Sam Houston, while others nominated a half dozen other candidates , including General Edward Burleson and Henderson, the outgoing governor. Sadler and fifty-four others voted in favor of returning Houston to his expired post, and he was declared duly elected Texas Senator to the U. S. Congress for the next six years, rejoining Tom Rusk.[7]

John H. Reagan, who had been a negotiator with Chief Bowles during the Cherokee War, had subsequently started practicing law before being elected to the Second Legislature as the representative of Nacogdoches County. Reagan later wrote of this Texas Congress:

> More was done at this session than at any other since the organization of the State government. All the organic laws were re-enacted and perfected, having been hurriedly passed by the First Legislature. The organization of the supreme, district, county and justice courts was provided for. The

duties of sheriffs, assessors and collectors of taxes, of constables and coroners were defined. A very elaborate probate law was passed, a law providing for the assessment and collection of taxes, and a law for apportioning senators and representatives, and for defining the senatorial and representative districts; besides much other general and special legislation.[8]

Another law passed by the Second Legislature introduced by Reagan gave each county of the state its own land records and land office.

As with most typical days in the Texas House, countless bills, pertaining to everything from granting land to immigrants to ascertaining the outstanding liabilities of Texas, were read on successive days before they could be passed. Due to the time consumed by this process, William Bourland introduced a resolution on January 4 that a five-man committee be appointed by the House Chairman. The chair appointed congressmen Bourland, Elisha Pease, William Sadler, Benjamin Tankersley and James Willie to make up this committee. Sadler was a natural choice, as he had often referred various legislation to its proper committees to avoid lengthy debates on the floor. Their job would be to present at a later date any "amendments to the standing rules of the House as they may deem expedient for the dispatch of business."[9]

In addition to his work on various committees, Congressman Sadler helped introduce a number of new bills during his tenure. One such act that he put before the House on December 31, 1847, was a joint resolution authorizing the Comptroller of Public Accounts to provide a residence in the city of Austin for the use of the Executive of the State.

His office in the Second Legislature did not go unchallenged, however. With the recent creation of Anderson County, his home now fell outside of the new county boundaries of his actual represented county of Houston. Following the 10:00 a.m. roll call on Monday, January 3, 1848, the House took up the issue of Sadler's office. During the early days of this legislature, disgruntled former Houston County politician Seldon Jasper had sent a letter to the House informing them that he felt William Sadler had been improperly returned to Congress from Houston County for his third term. This letter had been previously read and referred to the House Privilege and Elections Committee for consideration.

After studying the issue, it was found that there was no injustice in Sadler's return to the House. The committee's report was read by

TEXAS HOUSE OF REPRESENTATIVES
THE SECOND LEGISLATURE

Regular Session:
December 13, 1847 - March 20, 1848
Governor: George T. Wood
Speaker: James W. Henderson

MEMBER	COUNTY	MEMBER	COUNTY
Allen, James L.	Gonzales	Millican, Elliott M.	Brazos
Anderson, John D.	Gonzales	Mosely, Samuel F.	Bowie
Armstrong, James	Jefferson	Neal, Benjamin F.	Refugio
Bogart, Sam	Fannin	Pease, Elisha M.	Brazoria
Bourland, William H.	Lamar	Perry, William B.	Colorado
Bryan, Guy M.	Brazoria	Potter, Mark M.	Galveston
Burroughs, James M.	Sabine	Railey, Charles	Austin
Caruthers, Thomas	Montgomery	Rains, Emory	Shelby
Crump, William E.	Austin	Rayner, William S.	Fort Bend
Crutchir, William H.	Fayette	Reagan, John H.	Nacogdoches
Cunningham, Abel Symour	Victoria	Renfro, J.	Sabine
Davis, James M.	Robertson	Robertson, Jerome B.	Washington
Davis, John H. (Jack)	Liberty	Rogers, Magnus T.	Harris
DeCordova, Jacob R. [2]	Harris	Runnels, Hardin R.	Bowie
Dennis, Thomas M.	Matagorda	Sadler, William Turner	Houston
Dooley, M. A.	Bexar	Shannon, Thomas J.	Fannin
Eddy, Z. Williams	Jasper	Shaw, James	Milam
Edwards, William C.	San Augustine	Sterne, Adolphous	Nacogdoches
Epperson, Benjamin H.	Red River	Stewart, William H.	Gonzales
Fields, William	Liberty	Stoddard, Jesse W.	Goliad
Gilliam, James	Red River	Stout, William B.	Red River
Goode, Richard N.	Harrison	Stuart, Hamilton	Galveston
Hardiman, Thomas J.	Bastrop	Tankersly, Benjamin F.	Harris
Haynie, Samuel G.	Travis	Taylor, James F.	Harrison
Irion, Van R.	Washington	Truitt, James	Shelby
Keenan, Charles G.	Montgomery	Walling, Jesse	Rusk
Lamar, Mirabeau B. [1]	San Patricio	Webb, William G.	Fayette
Lewis, Henry M.	Bexar	Wheeler, O. M.	San Augustine
Lott, Elisha E.	Nacogdoches	White, Benjamin J.	Jackson
Lyons, James H.	Rusk	Wilder, E. M.	Harrison
McCown, James B.	Montgomery	Willie, James	Washington
McNeill, Archibald	Montgomery	Winkler, Clinton M.	Robertson
Miller, John F.	Colorado	Wren, Johnson	Lamar
Miller, Steward A.	Houston		

[1] Resigned in January, 1848.   [2] Joined Congress on February 19, 1848.

Chairman Abel Cunningham of Victoria County before the House on January 3.

> The committee on Privileges and Elections, to whom were referred certain communications from S. L. B. Jasper, Esq., in relation to the election of the Hon. Wm. T. Sadler, to the Legislature, have had the same under consideration, and a majority of said committee have instructed me to report that there is no evidence before the committee to show that the said Sadler was improperly returned as a member elect from the county of Houston, and to recommend that said communications be laid upon the table.[10]

Cunningham's report was adopted by the State Legislature and the issue concerning Congressman Sadler's election was dropped.

Representative Mirabeau Lamar submitted his resignation to Speaker James Henderson on January 28, which was read before the assembled House. After being excused from Congress, he returned to his home in Laredo and was later replaced by Jacob Raphael DeCordova, who had been born in Jamaica in 1808 before making his way to Texas. DeCordova later joined the House on Saturday, February 19, and was added to the committees of Public Lands and Finance.

Among the important elections conducted by the Second Legislature was the appointment of the state's district attorneys, which was accomplished on Saturday, February 5. With both the House and Senate assembled in the Representative Hall, Speaker James Henderson directed the proceedings to fill the state's ten judicial districts.

For filling the Ninth Judicial District, Sadler nominated Andrew Jackson Fowler, a graduate of LaGrange College in Alabama who

First Judicial District	*Sixth Judicial District*
Hiram Waller	David W. Fields
Second Judicial District	*Seventh Judicial District*
John A. Green	Samuel D. Hay
Third Judicial District	*Eighth Judicial District*
Thomas Johnson	William C. Young
Fourth Judicial District	*Ninth Judicial District*
C. W. Peterson	Andrew Jackson Fowler
Fifth Judicial District	*Tenth Judicial District*
Richard S. Walker	William S. Glass

had come to Texas in 1837 and who had seen action during the numerous Indian battles. He had represented Lamar County in the House of Representatives of the Sixth Congress (1841-42) and had recently served as chief justice of Henderson County.[11] Fowler won with twenty-eight votes to twenty-five for another nominee, John C. McCoy. Sadler voted in favor of nine of these ten district attorneys, who were declared by Speaker Henderson to all be "duly and constitutionally elected" to two-year terms.

In other elections, the Congress selected the new Commissioner of the General Land Office on February 28. Sadler voted in favor of long-standing incumbent Thomas William Ward, but George W. Smyth won this appointment. For the election of a Comptroller of Public Accounts and a State Treasurer, Sadler moved that a committee be appointed to invite the Senate to meet with the House for said election. Speaker Henderson then appointed Sadler as Chairman of the Special Committee, which also included James McCown and Samuel Haynie.

While another bill to incorporate the Houston Mechanics' Institute was being read, the special committee conferred. Sadler thereafter announced to Henderson that his committee had gone before the Senate and invited them to a joint meeting in the Representative Hall for said election at noon that day.[12] Following a fifteen-minute recess, the House and Senate assembled for the required election. Sadler and fifty-one others voted overwhelmingly in favor of James B. Shaw to head the office of Comptroller of Public Accounts.

Beyond such standard legislation as county boundaries, taxation, and public debt, the Second Legislature also tackled a number of resolutions pertaining to the advancement of transportation in Texas. These included public roads, the clearing of a raft on the Colorado River, a bill incorporating the Galveston Steam, Ferry, Freight and Tow-Boat Company, and the incorporation of two of the earliest railroad companies, the Galveston and Red River Railroad Company and the Colorado and Brazos Railroad Company. Additionally, the Committee on the Penitentiary to which Sadler was assigned presented a plan for the erection of a state penitentiary, along with regulations to effect the organization and conduct of the system.

Congress met on Saturday, March 18, pursuant to adjournment and then held its final roll call of the session on Monday, March 20. Throughout the session, there had been work done to help take care of the unfair apportionment of senators and representatives. About two-thirds of the population of Texas lived east of the Trinity River, yet about two-thirds of the members of the Texas Congress came from the west side of the river.[13] The House did manage to pass a bill on its final day which apportioned the representation equally.

Another matter facing the Second Legislature was the fact that it did not have a public printer to make public the laws and acts passed. All proceedings were thus maintained only in manuscript form. The original copy of the important Congress equalization bill was stolen before its could be approved by the House. John Reagan, William Bourland and James Willie were directed to make a duplicate of the stolen bill, which they completed and had passed successfully by both houses of Congress on the day of adjournment, although it would later take a court decision by the State Supreme Court to make it official.[14]

On his last day of service in the Congress of the State of Texas, Sadler benefited from one of the acts they passed. He was finally authorized payment for some of the supplies he had furnished the Texas Army ten years prior, thanks to the provisions of a resolution of the legislature entitled "An Act to Provide for ascertaining the Debt of the late Republic of Texas." The state auditor and the comptroller of public accounts had been instructed by the Second Legislature to ascertain jointly the various items of debt of the republic. All debts were rated, or scaled down.

In Sadler's case, his claim for having provided food for the troops following the Battle of Kickapoo was ordered reduced to seventy cents on each dollar owed. In the final accounting, he was paid $481.50, or about 84.5 percent of what he was owed. His document reads:

Public Debt
of the
Republic of Texas

This is to certify that William T. Sadler has, under the provisions of an act of the LEGISLATURE OF THE STATE OF TEXAS, entitled "An Act to Provide for ascertaining the Debt of the late Republic of Texas," approved 20th March, 1848, filed with the Auditor and Comptroller an accounting for supplies furnished Col. Landrum's command in October and November 1838, amounting to four hundred and eighty one 50/100 dollars, which is sufficiently authenticated to authorize the auditing of the same under the laws of the late Republic of Texas. The said claim, according to the data before us, is reduced to four hundred and seven 00/100 dollars, in par funds, as having been at that sale so available to the Government.

In testimony whereof we have hereunto set our hands and affixed our Seals of Office, this Twelfth day of October, A. D. 1848.

After the adjournment on March 20, many of the members of the House and Senate went down to the main street in Austin for a farewell drink together to celebrate the close of another session.[15] For Sadler, it was the end of his service in the Texas Congress. His home life in East Texas was calling him.

Shortly after his departure for Anderson County, he received clear patent to the 640 acres of land for fighting at San Jacinto that he had been granted in Houston and Anderson counties. Governor George Wood and Commissioner of the General Land Office George Smyth signed Patent No. 85 on April 14, 1848, in Austin, which stated, "This grant is made in consideration of the said William T. Sadler having fought at the Battle of San Jacinto 1836, and the land hereby granted is not subject to sale, alienation, mortgage or execution during the lifetime of the said William T. Sadler."

The new county seat town of Palestine had grown rapidly in his absence. Town lots had been auctioned off in December 1847, and residents of many other area communities bought property in town as an investment. After the first residences and businesses were established Mrs. Susan Scott Mallard, wife of Judge John B. Mallard, took the first town census in 1848. She found only fourteen households living within the central town itself, those of Judge Mallard, George W. Tuggle, Reuben A. Reeves, Alexander Joost, Alexander E. McClure, John C. Grigsby, Elisha J. DeBard, William Jowers, Seldon Jasper, John G. Ratcliffe, Mrs. Ann White, Peter Galloway, Andrew Jackson Fowler and John Ratcliffe. The census total was sixty-two whites and twenty-one negro slaves.[16]

This census also recorded an additional eighty-six whites and ten negroes in unnamed households, bringing the town's total population to 179. Other families known to have settled in or near Palestine by 1848 include James Box, Daniel M. Crist, Darius H. Edens, Charles Gilliam, Dr. Berria Graham, George W. Hanks,

James Steele Hanks, Thomas Hanks, David C. Hunter, William Jones, Levi Jordan, Carter T. McKenzie, Peyton Parker, James M. Perry, John E. Pinson, Ira Prewitt, Joseph Rainey, William R. Rogers and Tom Scott.

Early in 1848, John Crawford Grigsby was killed while on a trading expedition on the Trinity River. His position as the first county clerk was temporarily filled by Dr. Jowers. The first district clerk became Alexander McClure, Joseph Rainey became the coroner and the first notary public was William Jones. With Anderson County's first election in 1848, John Mallard was chosen county judge, Samuel Cravens became the new county clerk, and William R. Rogers was elected sheriff.

Congressman Sadler did not run for office again this year, having already served three consecutive terms. In the 1848 elections in Houston County, he was succeeded in the House of Representatives by his friend Dr. William Jowers. During the 1849 session of the Third Legislature, Anderson and Houston counties fell into a one-representative district with Jowers' representing both. By the Fourth Legislature, however, Anderson County elected its own representative, with Jowers' filling the role once again. He would continue in Texas Congress service for a number of years.

Chapter Seventeen

CALIFORNIA GOLD, TEXAS RAILROADS AND THE CIVIL WAR

1849-1865

The city of Palestine and county of Anderson continued to grow as settlers moved in from all over the country. Captain Sadler's young son, Nathaniel Fletcher (who went by "Fletch"), often told his grandchildren about his early years of growing up on Sadler Plantation. Young Fletch was amused by the frequent travelers along the road which ran in front of his home. There were freight wagons usually driven by negro slaves, and there were also horse-drawn carriages, buckboards, ox wagons and horseback riders. Long before the oxen came into sight, Fletch could hear the cracking of the whips which the drivers used to guide the animals.[1]

Shortly after his return home, Sadler's brother-in-law Miles Bennett was married to Laura Jordan on May 29, 1848. He had just missed another Bennett family wedding prior to his return; his young niece Icephenia, daughter of brother-in-law Stephen Bennett, had married his former Senate counterpart, Isaac Parker on February 11, 1848, in Anderson County. An even more joyous event to commemorate his return home was the arrival of a new member of his family. Daughter Mary Ann Sadler was born to him and wife Permelia on December 16, 1848, on Sadler Plantation, the couple's third child.

The new state of Texas grew rapidly in the years following its annexation into the United States. A census taken in 1848 gave the state population as 158,356, of whom 42,455 were slaves.[2] In Anderson County, the little town of Elkhart was established west of Sadler's league and labor. This town's first church was made of logs in December 1848 and Ben Parker, son of Elder Daniel Parker, served as pastor until his death in 1896. Several other churches of more permanent structure were built over the years.

Soon after the county was firmly established with its own courthouse and judicial system, the leaders of Anderson County set up a formal postal system. The first two postal offices in Anderson County were established on March 8, 1847. Charles Shelton was named postmaster in Palestine and Valentine S. Anglin was named postmaster at Anglins. A third post office was added in March 1848 at Beaver with Hansford Hanks its postmaster. When the county's fourth post office was established at Ioni, William T. Sadler was named postmaster for this community. He had previously served as a postmaster at Fort Brown in Houston County during 1838-1839.

Three more post offices were established in Anderson County in 1850 with Joseph Kennedy the postmaster at Elkhart, William Stewart at Sand Springs and James Steele Hanks at the short-lived community of Plentitude.[3] Nine more post offices would later be established in Anderson County prior to the Civil War.

Sadler served as community postmaster for the village of Ioni from November 30, 1848, to April 2, 1858. This public service was interrupted only by his trip to California in search of a personal fortune during the historic Gold Rush of 1849.

THE CALIFORNIA GOLD RUSH

More than 100,000 gold-seekers swarmed into the lands of the new state of California and made their way up the western slopes of the Sierra. These prospectors, arriving between 1848 and 1852 and collectively dubbed the "forty-niners", sought personal wealth in the beautiful and rare metal called gold. Although only a small percentage of those arriving actually found enough gold to make any money, the craze caused a boost in the national economy and created a large number of businesses in California. The peak of the rush in terms of mining population and mineral output was in 1852, when $81 million worth of gold was mined from California soil.[4]

James Wilton Marshall, owner of a sawmill on the south fork of the American River east of San Francisco, is credited with discovering the first significant pieces of gold on January 24, 1848. Marshall shared the find with the mill's operator, Captain John Augustus Sutter, and news of the discovery at Sutter's Mill soon spread. A San Francisco newspaper, the *Californian*, reported "GOLD MINE FOUND" on March 15, and by mid-summer about four-thousand gold-seekers had flocked to the fields. This number more than doubled by year's end as prospectors panned the American River and began collecting bits of gold in bottles, tins, buckskin bags and even shoes.

News of the discovery of gold in California began reaching U. S. newspapers in late 1848, but it was not until an official report reached Washington that the news really hit home. In his opening message to the second session of the 30th Congress on December 5, 1848, President James Knox Polk reported on the acquisition of California and the valuable discovery of gold mines. "The accounts of the abundance of gold in that territory," he stated, "are of such an extraordinary character as would scarcely command belief were they not corroborated by authentic reports."

President Polk's message helped to spread the fever that became known as the Gold Rush. During the early months of 1849, men began selling their businesses and quitting jobs to strike out by land or by sea for California. The ports along the coast of Texas were soon packed with forty-niners seeking passage by sea from such points as Galveston, Indianola, Port Lavaca, Corpus Christi and Brownsville. The ships, however, became plagued with disease from the dirty travelers and many died en route.

News of the great Gold Rush reached W. T. Sadler in Anderson County and spurned him to join the trek to California in 1849. Like so many others, he began making preparations by raising money for supplies and provisions. To do so, he sold off some of his excess land; to James M. Douthit he sold one-hundred acres and to John and Jasper Starr, he sold 106 acres at the rate of one dollar per acre.

By the survey document Sadler presented to the Starrs, the land sold to them began at "a stake in the East boundary line of Severo Arocho Third of a League and at the SE corner of a Survey of one hundred acres made for James M. Douthit." This land's eastern boundary was the line of the one-third league and included waterfront access to Frost Creek for cattle. In these handwritten records Sadler wrote that "I do hereby bind myself, my heirs, executors and administrators to warrant and forever defend all and singular" the written promises made to these purchasers. Sadler signed and affixed his personal seal to each document.

The sale of the 106 acres to the Starrs was signed on March 22, 1849, and was witnessed by James M. Perry and Congressman William J. W. Jowers. As Sadler had apparently departed for California and Jowers was serving in the Texas Congress at the time, James Perry appeared with the Starrs before Anderson County

Clerk John P. Walton in Palestine on July 7, 1849, as a witness to the signing of the Sadler document.

It is unclear when Sadler actually struck out west. The 1850 Census of Texas lists him in Anderson County as of October 1850, but this may have been because he was the head of the household and was traveling somewhere along the way where no census takers could possibly find him. The following shows the census listing for Family No. 352 in Anderson County, whose total population was given as 2,884, including some six-hundred slaves.

NAME	AGE	OCCUPATION	PLACE BORN
Sadler, William T.	53	Farmer	North Carolina
Permelia	32	-	Indiana
Nathaniel F.	5	-	Houston County, TX
Martha Tucker	3	-	Anderson County, TX
Mary Ann	2	-	Anderson County, TX
Bennett, Benjamin	24	-	Illinois

His family was doing well at the time and his financial status was stable, as the 1850 Census show his financial holdings to have been valued at $5,000. Although his wife was pregnant with their fourth child, Sadler left his family in the care of Permelia and his youngest brother-in-law, Benjamin Bennett. According to one family story he left with two old mules, one of which he rode and the other he led. Upon his return, he is said to have brought back both mules.[5]

The trip to California was rugged, but Sadler is said to have chosen to travel alone. Most gold-seekers chose to form companies of a hundred or more and elected captains to lead their expeditions across the continent. To a man accustomed to making long journeys into the unknown, such a company would have only served to slow Sadler down. He probably departed about June 1849, as his second son, William Peterson Sadler, was born to Permelia on January 9, 1850, in Anderson County.

Many others from Houston and Anderson County would make similar expeditions. Palestine's Darius Edens arrived at the gold camps in 1849, was said to be only "somewhat successful" in his gold search, and eventually returned to his family's land in the community of Augusta, Texas, site of the horrible massacre of 1838, where he opened his own mercantile business.[6]

Sadler's former brother-in-law John Murchison had departed earlier and elected to join a company. At the Colorado River at LaGrange, Murchison and other immigrants for California formed a

Captain Sadler returned from the California Gold Rush in 1851 with only a buckskin pouch of nuggets and golddust. From one of the larger nuggets, he created a ring by having it attached to a band. This ring (left) is crudely etched with the numerals "49" and is in the possession of Sadler's great-great-granddaughter, Jane Taylor Linkswiler.
Photo by Lee Lusby, courtesy of Jane Linkswiler and JoAnn Day Freeman.

company on May 28, 1949, and Murchison was elected captain. An article in the March 31, 1849, *Texas Democrat* stated that "Companies of five persons may report to Capt. John Murchison at LaGrange, where they will register for the expedition."⁷

His company was one of the first to attempt the Guadalupe Mountains beyond El Paso. In a letter dated June 23, 1849, Murchison described some of the fatal first attempts made by early companies. Some men had become lost in the mountains, while others were reduced to eating their horses, mules and even snakes.⁸ It was not uncommon to go days without water in some of the more desolate stretches of travel. Murchison's company was one of the few that was considered well organized for the long haul, having properly provisioned itself and having carefully selected its followers. ⁹

The trail to the gold mines led most land travelers through El Paso and across the New Mexico territory formerly claimed by Texas. After a trying journey, most "forty-niners" made their way through the settlement of Santa Cruz before arriving in the large town of Tucson. Beyond, many tribes of friendly Indians were encountered through the Gila Desert before entering California and arriving in the thriving city of Los Angeles to reprovision. From there, the forty-niners made their way for the Stockton mines in Southern California. The company of John Murchison made it to the gold fields, although he was killed by an accidental discharge of his own gun on July 24, 1849, and buried along the trail near San Bernadino.¹⁰

Following the wide Sacramento River up north from San Francisco Bay, the forty-niners worked the waters and tributary creeks of such rivers as the Feather, Yuba and American, which ran westward from the northern Sierras. After the arduous journey through the mountains and deserts to California, gold-seekers such as Sadler found the toil of separating gold dust from rock and sand to be backbreaking work. For the independent prospector, the tools of the trade were generally a shovel and a wash pan to sift through the silt for glittering nuggets.

Those who were lucky enough to collect worthwhile hauls from the rivers found that they could sell their gold in San Francisco for sixteen dollars per ounce. Many worked for years for naught and returned home penniless. As for Sadler, he did not strike it rich nor even recover all the money he certainly must have spent on travel and provisions. He did, however, return home in 1851 with a small buckskin poke of gold dust and a crude ring which he had carved out of a pure gold nugget. This ring was passed down from Geneva Sadler Taylor, daughter of Sadler's oldest son Nathaniel Fletcher, to her granddaughter, Jane Colclough Taylor Linkswiler.

LIFE IN 1850S ANDERSON COUNTY

Sadler returned from California in 1851 with the same two mules he had left with almost two years prior. His new son, William Peterson, was already a year old and soon came to be called "Billy." He and wife would later celebrate the birth of their fifth child, daughter Elizabeth Ann "Betty" Sadler on August 19, 1852, in Anderson County.

Farming and his duties as the Ioni community postmaster were resumed by Sadler. His oldest daughter Martha later gave the following statement to Mary Kate Hunter of her early life on Sadler Plantation.

> I was raised at the old Ioni Village, born in 1847. My mother was W. T. Sadler's second wife and her name was Permelia Bennett, daughter of Armstead Bennett, who lived about a mile south of what is now Elkhart. My grandfather, Armstead Bennett, settled near the Brown's Fort when he first came to Texas with the Parkers in 1833 from Illinois. He was one of the Pilgrim Church. My mother was a member of the Pilgrim, born in Illinois [Indiana].
>
> I remember when it was five miles to our nearest neighbor, one being Uncle Joe Crawford, north of us and Martin Murchison who lived down at Murchison Prairie, five miles south; this was in Houston County. I was born in 1847, and these were the only neighbors we had when I was a child.

The Edens home was set fire and burned [in 1838]. It was eight or ten miles south of us in Houston County, not far from what is now Augusta. When I was small I went five miles to school in Providence, a church and a school house northeast from the Ioni Village – just a primary school, and a missionary Baptist Church. Mr. and Mrs. George Gresham moved in near us later and she taught a primary school. I've been to Fort Houston School House and Church, to the northeast.[11]

In January 1852, Sadler signed and sealed a deed to Daniel Parker Jr. for the sum of $1,000 for the sale of the final 590 acres of his original land purchase of 1835. The deed showed that this was a portion of his one-third league purchased from Severo Arocha, and that the land included a mill built by Levi Jordan and Owens. This document was signed and sealed in the presence of Judge Reuben A. Reeves. Although Daniel Parker had bought out the remainder of this land in 1852, it was not until 1858 that the last deed document pertaining to this land was filed by Sadler in Palestine.

Aside from being a retired soldier and congressman, a local farmer, and a postmaster, William Turner Sadler was listed as a charter member of the Ioni Lodge Number 93, AF&AM, which was chartered January 23, 1852, by local Masons, of which Sadler was a member. The original officers of the Ioni Lodge were James L. Richards, warden, Robert B. Lewis, senior warden, and John Blair, junior warden. Prior to building a proper lodge, the Masons often gathered to meet in the home of Dr. Elisha DeBard on Church Street in Palestine. DeBard's daughter, Mrs. Flora Josephine "Sammie" DeBard Phillips, later recalled that Judge Jowers and Charles Adolphus Sterne, son of Texas Congressman Adolphus Sterne, were among the early Masons who also met upstairs in her home.[12]

The Masons were credited with establishing the first Masonic Institute in 1855, described as "large, commodious and well equipped." One house was apparently made for the males and another for the females.[13] The first formal school building, the Palestine Female Institute, was later erected in 1858. On June 6, 1860, the Ioni Lodge accepted a resolution to change its name to Augusta Lodge. The lodge was later rebuilt further south and still stands in the community of Augusta near Crockett, Texas.

In 1852 Sadler received news from his family's home in Putnam County, Georgia, that his father, Nathaniel Milton Sadler, had passed away on his plantation at the age of eighty-two. Sadler travelled from Texas back to Georgia for the first time in seventeen years to help take care of his father's effects. When he returned to Anderson County, his younger brother Nathaniel Sadler II came along, both men bringing their share of their father's slaves, cattle, horses, mules, wagons, furniture and other belongings distributed to the children after their father's funeral. At least ten known servants were known to have traveled back with Sadler: Allen, his wife Charity and three small children; Louis; Jordan; and Stuart, with his wife Harriet, and first son Alex.

Nathaniel Sadler II/Jr. bought two 640-acre parcels of land from Daniel Parker Jr. in Anderson County west of Elkhart. The total cost was $6,400 for 1,280 acres. Parker had obtained his land originally from William Greenwood and Peyton Parker; this land was situated on Box's Creek. This deed of November 4, 1853 was between Daniel Parker and "Nathaniel M. Sadler of the County of Putnam and State of Georgia." William T. Sadler and Stephen Bennett signed this document as witnesses, but it was not filed in the Palestine county clerk's office until January 6, 1858, when W. T. Sadler brought in the document for authentication. Nathaniel Sadler returned to Georgia to sell his property to raise money, after which he brought his entire family and their possessions to live in Anderson County.

EARLY RAILROADS IN TEXAS

In an effort to improve transportation, communication and population, the state of Texas had struggled for years with building railways to connect some of its major cities. During the republic years, a number of railroad charters had been issued to companies hoping to connect Galveston, Harrisburg and the Brazos Valley, but none had been able to complete their objectives. The first railroads in the United States had been built in the 1820s in Massachusetts and Pennsylvania to transport granite and coal for short distances. Early tracks had rails made of pine timbers, set on stone ties that were laid on beds of stones.

The oldest railroad in the country still in existence is the Baltimore and Ohio, which was chartered on February 28, 1827, in Maryland. The first mile of this track had been completed in January 1829. In 1830-1831, the Mohawk and Hudson, from Albany to Schenectady, had completed a 16.1-mile line, and in Richmond, Virginia, another early line had run a distance of twelve miles to the Chesterfield mines. The first railroad to use the T-line had been a five-mile line built from New Orleans to Lake Ponchartrain in the early 1830s.[14] W. T. Sadler had taken his first train ride aboard this train with Mirabeau Lamar in June 1835 while traveling to Texas.

General Sidney Sherman is credited with attracting capital to the first successful railroad project in Texas, the Buffalo Bayou, Brazos and Colorado Railway Company which was chartered on February 11, 1850. Construction began in 1851 and the first locomotive, named for Sherman, arrived in 1852. The first twenty-mile section of this line was opened between present Houston and Stafford on September 7, 1853. This railway was the first to operate in Texas, was the second railroad west of the Mississippi River, and is the oldest component of the present Southern Pacific.[15]

Other early charters in the 1850s included the Galveston and Red River Railway Company, which later became the Houston and Texas Central Railway Company. Due to insufficient capital in Texas to finance the early railroads, most of the early charters were created by local groups. William Sadler was among one such early group which received a charter to form a company to bring a railroad to Palestine in Anderson County.

An act to encourage Texas railroad construction was passed on January 30, 1854, and soon thereafter Sadler and his partners began working on the Palestine Tap Railway Company. Following is a summary of the act incorporating their company.

> Sec. 1. Be it enacted by the Legislature of the State of Texas, that R. M. Bonner, William J. Miller, W. G. W. Jowers, John G. Googh, F. S. Jackson, W. T. Sadler, P. L. Quarles, Josiah King Sr., P. G. Oldham, W. C. Kinney and Nathan Glenn be, and they are hereby created and established a body corporate and politic under the name and title of "The Palestine Tap Railway Company," and the said corporation are invested with the right and power to contract and to be contracted with, to sue and be sued, plead and be impleaded, to take, buy and sell real and personal property.
>
> Sec. 2. That the said corporation are hereby invested with the right and power of locating, constructing and maintaining a railroad, extending from the town of Palestine in Anderson County, to a point intersecting with the railroad of Houston, Trinity and Tyler Railroad Company, the point of intersection to be fixed upon by the Board of Directors of the Company hereby created.
>
> Sec. 3. That the capital stock of the corporation shall not exceed the sum of $400,000, divided into shares of $100 each.

Sec. 14. That the said Company shall be entitled to all grants, rights, privileges and immunities of an act entitled "act to encourage the construction of railroads in Texas by donation of land," approved January 30th, 1854.

Sec. 15. That this act take effect and be in force from and after its passage, and continue for 99 years.

Approved February 9, 1860.

It appears that Sadler was active in the organization and management of this early railway charter in East Texas. Like so many early ventures, however, the Palestine Tap Railway Company was later purchased by a larger rail company, and it would the 1870s before Texas railroads made their way into Palestine.

* * * *

On October 25, 1855, Sadler's brother-in-law Stephen Bennett married Nancy Madden, who was a crippled survivor of the 1838 Edens-Madden Massacre in which Sadler's first wife had been slain. Sadler's daughter Martha later related:

> I saw two women who escaped from the Eden House. One was tomahawked in the side, Mrs. Lucinda Madden, and the other, Mrs. Bob Madden, was tomahawked behind the ear. They both lived .... The way Mrs. Bob Madden escaped was: an Indian was standing with both hands on the door facing, directing the massacre, and she crawled between his legs and escaped. She married my Uncle Stephen Bennett later.

Land records and pension documents of William Sadler show some of his legal dealings during the late 1850s. On January 21, 1857, he appointed Palestine lawyer John E. Cravens as his agent and attorney. Acting on Sadler's behalf, Cravens was given power of attorney to claim money owed his client on certain audited papers dating back to October 8, 1848. Cravens and Sadler took a legal document before W. E. Vaughan, clerk of the Anderson County Clerk, to have the power of attorney legally acknowledged.[16] Receipts from Sadler's pension papers show that Cravens succeeded in securing payment in full for this claim by February 3, 1857.

On January 6, 1858, Sadler and a farm worker of his, Stephen Bryant, appeared before Anderson County Clerk A. G. Cantley at noon to authenticate his brother Nathaniel's 1,280-acre land purchase in 1853 from Daniel Parker Jr. Months later, he worked on finalizing the deed documents to pass ownership of his original one-third league of land to its rightful purchasers. County surveyor James E. Teague had surveyed this land on September 10, 1853, and this survey had been followed by another on October 26, 1857, by Anderson County Surveyor George W. Tuggle.

Portions of his original 1835 purchase from Severo Arocha had previously been sold to several others. To George Parks and J. P. Parker, Sadler sold approximately 750 acres for $1,200 dollars. Joseph Parker was already living on the northwest corner of this land. This deed, signed July 17, 1858, shows the breakdown of sales that finalized the passing of this land from Sadler's hands. To Parks and Parker was conveyed

> the following described tract or parcel of land lying and being situated in the County of Anderson and State above mentioned on Parker's Creek about 7 miles South of Palestine, a tributary of the Trinity River. The remainder of One Third of a League of land after deducting: 320 acres to Stephen Crist on the South Boundary line; 100 acres to James M. Douthit on the North Boundary line; and near 200 acres to John and Jasper Starr on the East Boundary line. The remainder being 750 acres, more or less. It being the Headright claim of Severo Rocha and by him sold and transferred to the said Wm. T. Sadler by which means the patent came out in the name of the said Wm. T. Sadler.

The balance of the 1,476-acre tract of property not mentioned was a one-hundred-acre sale to R. M. Wragg. Sadler filed the last of these deeds on August 3, 1858, with the Anderson County court clerk. These documents were witnessed and sealed with the notation, "Before me, A. G. Cantley, Clerk of the County Court in and for the County of Anderson this day personally came W. T. Sadler the grantor of the foregoing deed, who is to me well known, and acknowledged that he signed, sealed and delivered the same for all the uses and purposes therein set forth." Thus, his one-third league of land over a ten-year period had sold for a collective sum of approximately $1,900, or about $1.29 per acre.

William and Permelia Sadler's large family grew even larger on September 8, 1858, with the arrival of daughter Laura J. Sadler. Their seventh child and fifth daughter, Celestia "Lessie" Sadler, was born in September 1860. The couple's first six children are listed on the 1860 Census of Texas. Anderson County's population had more than tripled in the past decade, swelling to 10,398 by the new census, including 3,668 slaves. Cotton production had grown from 784 bales in the 1850 census to 7,517 bales in the new census. The state's total population of 604,215 was nearly triple the 1850 census.[17]

Stephen Bryant was shown to be a farm laborer living on the Sadler Plantation at the time the census was taken. It is said that this young man and his mother had come to live on Sadler land in the 1850s, but the mother had passed away while there and was buried in the little Sadler cemetery on the property.[18] Sadler was listed as a farmer of sixty-two years, whose financial worth had increased dramatically in the past ten years. From a value of $5,000 in 1850, the new census assessed his real estate at $20,000 in 1860, a 400 percent increase. Aside from land, Sadler held $14,393 in personal property, much of which included the value of his father's slaves.

1860 CENSUS OF ANDERSON COUNTY

NAME		AGE	OCCUPATION	PLACE BORN
Sadler, William T.		62	Farmer	North Carolina
	Permelia	42	-	Indiana
	Nathaniel F.	15	-	Houston County, TX
	Martha Tucker	13	-	Anderson County, TX
	Annie	11	-	Anderson County, TX
	William P.	9	-	Anderson County, TX
	Elizabeth	7	-	Anderson County, TX
	Laura	1	-	Anderson County, TX
Bryant, Stephen		28	Farm laborer	Alabama

W. T. Sadler's brother Nathaniel came down with typhoid fever in late May 1860. Since acquiring his land on Box's Creek in 1853, Nathaniel Sadler had brought his wife and children to Texas from Putnam County, Georgia, but died after a month's illness in June 1860. William T. Sadler went before the Anderson County court soon after his brother's death and asked to be named administrator of his brother's estate. He was appointed administrator after posting a bond of $45,000. County records show that during 1860, Nathaniel Sadler's land was appraised and the administrator, William T. Sadler, was ordered to buy provisions, clothing and seed for the use of the farm and its negroes, supporting the family of the deceased for the present year and to sell cotton to the best advantage and to thereafter report his success. Nathaniel's widow remarried in

1861 and they thereafter moved the children out of the county to a new home, leaving William to handle the land holdings of his brother. With the upcoming Civil War, it would be many years before Sadler was able to handle the estate properly.

* * * *

FINAL CALL TO DUTY: THE CIVIL WAR

The issue of freedom or "emancipation" for the slaves of the United States became increasingly turbulent in 1860. Those considered to be "slave states" became a virtual powderkeg with the election that fall of the first Republican president, Abraham Lincoln, who received no votes at all in Texas.[19] In December 1860, South Carolina voted unanimously to secede from the Union of the United States, and within five weeks Mississippi, Florida, Alabama, Georgia and Louisiana followed suit.

Leaders from these states met in Montgomery, Alabama, in February 1861 to adopt a constitution and set up a provisional government they called the Confederate States of America, which would be joined by Arkansas, North Carolina, Tennessee and Virginia. The original states elected Jefferson Davis as President of the Confederacy.

Sam Houston was Governor of Texas when the Secession Convention he much opposed convened in Austin on March 2, 1861, to canvass the popular vote on the secession ordinance that had been brought forth. The state's voters, 46,129 to 14,697, voted in favor of uniting Texas with the Confederate States of America. Sam Houston paid a visit to Palestine's citizens, speaking from the steps of the Osceola Hotel against secession, but Anderson County was eager to fight for states rights.[20] Of fifteen-hundred votes cast, only seven voted against secession.[21]

To modify the state government to conform with the Confederacy, an oath of allegiance was required for all state officials. Houston and his secretary of state refused to take this oath and the Convention voted to depose him from office on March 16. "By reason of the refusal of the late Governor, Sam Houston, to take the official oath," his office was vacated and then filled by Lieutenant Governor Edward Clark, with whom Sadler had served in the First Legislature.[22]

The county's only local newspaper, the *Trinity Advocate*, had advised the men to begin preparing for war. When the Civil War did break out at South Carolina's Fort Sumter on April 12, companies began forming up in Anderson County. Captain James W.

Gardner's cavalry Company I of the 7th Texas Cavalry (Henry Sibley's Brigade) was the first to march to war in May 1861.

Also moving toward war in 1861 were other companies organized of Anderson and Cherokee County volunteers, including those of captains John Aycock (Company A, 2nd Texas Cavalry), Marsh Glenn (whose company saw service along the Texas coast), Alex T. Rainey (later promoted to colonel, originally captain of Company H, 1st Texas Infantry, Hood's Brigade), and Dr. John R. Woodward (commander of Company G of Hood's Brigade). The largest number of Anderson County troops were assigned to Hood's Brigade, in which the county's residents suffered their greatest losses. The most prominent resident from Palestine to serve the Confederacy was Judge John Reagan, who became Postmaster General of the Confederacy for the duration of the war.[23]

During 1862, Anderson County fielded a number of other Confederate companies to the war between the states. Captain Bedford F. Parks (later promoted to major), with *Trinity Advocate* publisher Alexander W. Ewing as his first lieutenant, was dispatched to Louisiana and Arkansas in charge of the revamped Company H of Hood's Brigade (originally under Captain Rainey). Also being sent to Louisiana were companies under captains J. M. Hanks and John Bussey. Captain William H. Tucker took command of Company G of the 28th Texas Cavalry in April for service in Virginia and the East. Finally, two volunteer cavalry companies were created in Anderson County in 1862 with Judge William Jowers and Reuben A. Reeves elected as their captains. Each company was designated for service in Missouri.[24] The volunteer company of Captain Bill Frazier also served in the Tyler area during the war. All told, Anderson County furnished as many as one-thousand men for service during the Civil War.

In Anderson County, the citizens not fighting did their part by sewing uniforms, knitting socks and blankets and producing ammunition and gun parts at a Mound Prairie factory. A makeshift hospital for wounded Confederate soldiers was established at the Hunter House, and a group of skillful women nurses was supervised by Mrs. Louisiana Catherine Small McClure, wife of Alexander McClure and known as "Aunt Bee."[25]

After Governor Sam Houston was deposed from office in 1861, sixty-four-year-old W. T. Sadler took his fourteen-year-old son Nathaniel Fletcher Sadler on horseback some sixty miles to see him. Houston, almost seventy, lived in Huntsville and had settled into the Steamboat House as of December 1862. He was quite ill at the time

Nathaniel Fletcher Sadler, the oldest son of W. T. Sadler, fought with his father in the Civil War for the Confederacy. "Fletch" served briefly in Major Gould's Battalion from Grapeland, Texas, before enlisting in Company E of Colonel Alexander Terrell's Texas Cavalry at the age of eighteen. He was never wounded during the many engagements of Terrell's regiment in the Red River Campaign in Louisiana. This photo was taken in 1916 when he was seventy-one years old. Courtesy of Howard C. Sadler.

Sadler and son came to see him. According to Nathaniel Sadler, Houston was bedridden and in poor shape. He defiantly predicted that he would return to fight again in 1863 once he had shaken his ailments, but the elder Sadler felt that Houston had seen his last fight. He even told him, "I'm willing to bet the last words on your lips will be 'Texas.'"[26]

In fact, the last words spoken by Sam Houston when he passed away in Huntsville on July 26, 1863 at the age of seventy were almost as predicted. As his wife knelt beside his bed that evening, Houston said, "Texas. Texas. Martha," before slipping away.[27]

During the Civil War, the Texas Congress continued to function. Sadler's old militia buddy, W. G. W. Jowers, followed his early military duty by serving as senator for the collective counties of Anderson, Houston and Trinity between 1864 and 1865. Jowers continued to hold this seat through the Eleventh Legislature of 1866-1867.[28]

Houston County in the Civil War lists Nathaniel Fletcher Sadler as serving in Captain James McLean's Company C from Grapeland, Texas. "Fletch" Sadler was 4th Corporal of Company C, which was part of Major Robert S. Gould's Battalion in Colonel Horace Randal's Brigade. He enlisted on March 12, 1862, at age sixteen in Anderson County, is shown on a muster roll dated May 28, 1862 and he left this company on May 23, 1862 during its reorganization.

The Steamboat House in Huntsville, Texas, where William T. Sadler and his son Fletcher went to visit Sam Houston during his final days. This renovated building is now part of the Sam Houston Memorial Park. Author's collection.

TERRELL'S 34TH TEXAS CAVALRY REGIMENT

Although he is not formally listed on the only surviving muster rolls, William T. Sadler was said to have sworn his allegiance to the Confederacy and to have fought in Company E of the 34th Regiment of Colonel Alexander's Terrell's Texas Cavalry. Perhaps because of his advanced age, sixty-six in August of 1863, Sadler may not have been an official enlistment. By the acts of the Confederate Congress, able-bodied men between the ages of eighteen and forty-five were conscripted to join the formation of regiments. Those not within this age range, however, were authorized to volunteer for local defenses and special services.

There are no service records of Sadler's son Fletch to indicate where he served after transferring from Gould's Battalion in 1862. His pension records, however, show that he enlisted soon after turning eighteen in Company E of the 37th Regiment as a private on August 6, 1863, in Palestine when the company was formed. N. F. Sadler is listed on the muster rolls of Terrell's Company E for January and February 1864, the only rolls of Company E on file. No later muster record of him is available.

Alexander Watkins Terrell was born in November 1828 in Virginia and was a licensed lawyer before the age of twenty-one. A former City Attorney of St. Joseph, Missouri, Terrell moved to Austin in 1852 and entered law practice. In 1857 he was elected District Judge and remained on the bench in the Austin District until 1863.[29] Terrell resigned his bench to organize a regiment of cavalry for the Confederate service. His regiment fought valiantly in Louisiana, and a few weeks before the end of the Civil War in Texas, Terrell was commissioned by General Edmund Kirby Smith as a brigadier general in recognition of his accomplishments as a leader.[30]

Terrell's Texas Cavalry was originally organized to be a battalion, but the large number of enlistments saw this unit mustered into Confederate service as a regiment. Terrell had previously served in the First Texas Cavalry, or Arizona Brigade. This regiment is listed incorrectly as the 37th Texas Cavalry Regiment in some sources, but the men of Terrell's regiment always referred to themselves as the 34th and so signed their paroles at war's end.[31]

Company E of Terrell's Texas Cavalry was organized in Palestine on April 11, 1863. Judge Reuben A. Reeves was elected captain. This company fell under Terrell's 34th Regiment (or commonly known as the 37th) and was later designated an infantry unit. The other senior officers of this regiment were Lieutenant Colonel John C. Robertson and Major Miram S. Morgan. Sadler's son, Fletch, was shown as present on the only muster rolls taken for this unit during January - February, 1864. His father was not listed as present during these muster rolls, although William Sadler is known to his family to have served with his son. One East Texas newspaper serving Anderson, Smith and Cherokee counties in 1981 relates, "During the Civil War, he again rode off to war, this time with his young son, N. F. Sadler, as one of his recruits."[32]

Terrell's regiment was originally organized to serve west of the Colorado River and the unit was first assigned on June 25, 1863, as part of the Second Brigade, First Division (District of Texas, New Mexico and Arizona) in what was known as the Trans-Mississippi Department, under General Kirby Smith. In July, this regiment was detached as part of the Northern Sub-District, and as of September 30 it was assigned as a cavalry detachment of the Eastern Sub-District assigned to defend Galveston, Texas.

During the late summer of 1863 while under temporary command of Lieutenant Colonel Robertson, the regiment was ordered to be dismounted, an order that was so unpopular that two officers and more than sixty enlisted men mutinied and left the unit during September. These men were quickly tracked down and many of them ended up in a prison camp at Tyler, Texas. Fletcher Sadler later related that his horse Reuben, being the tallest in the company, was designated as the hanging horse for deserters who were captured, although there is no evidence to suggest that his mount was ever pressed into service.[33]

During the roundup of deserters, most of Terrell's regiment was moved to a camp near Columbus, Texas, before being ordered in November to march toward Matagorda. In December 1863, the unit was stationed at Camp Wharton and by January was operating from Camp Dixie and Camp Albert Sidney Johnston near the mouth of the Caney River. Private J. K. M. Dumas died while at Camp Dixie on January 28, 1864, according to Company E war rolls. In mid-March, 1864, the regiment was remounted to assist in the operations against General Nathaniel P. Banks' Red River Campaign and it would remain a mounted regiment for the remainder of its service. Banks' federal troops had been issued orders to invade the interior of Louisiana to effect the capture of Shreveport. Terrell's Texas Cavalry saw the balance of its action in the Civil War in Louisiana during the period of March 25 - June 1, 1864.

Union cavalry troops occupied Natchitoches on March 31, which led to a skirmish at Crump's Hill on April 2 near Many, Louisiana. General Banks' Union troops gathered near Natchitoches, while farther northwest up the Red River the Confederate troops under General Kirby Smith prepared for battle. Smith's forces made a stand against the superior Federal force on the afternoon of April 7 at Wilson's farm, three miles north of Pleasant Hill. On the morning of April 8, three Confederate regiments, including Terrell's, formed a wide battle line for a stand at Mansfield. Also participating along Pleasant Hill Road were John Walker's and Horace Randal's Texas Infantry Brigades.

Amidst the thunder of muskets and cannons, a deadly clash was fought throughout April 8 near Mansfield, during which Terrell's regiment dismounted and charged headlong into the Union flank. Through the dense forest, the Confederates advanced while driving back the Union troops with bullets and bayonets. By dark, the dead and dying from both sides lay scattered over several miles of battlefield as Terrell's men made camp for the night at a small creek.[34]

Terrell's regiment and all of the Texas cavalry pursued the fleeing Federal Army for twelve miles. On April 9 near the village of Pleasant Hill, the Union Army took up a defensive position and they were engaged beginning at 4:30 p.m. by several Texas regiments. In a fast charge through the piney woods, the Confederates advanced so fast that they soon found themselves virtually surrounded by their blue-uniformed enemies. The deadly fire continued until darkness,

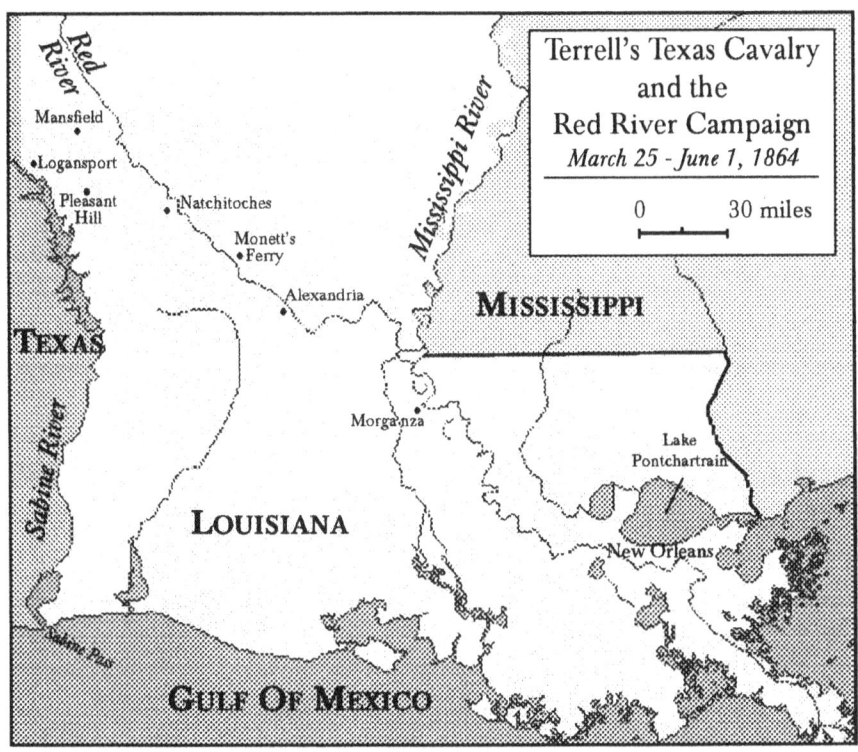

at which time Terrell's regiment was ordered pulled back to Mansfield. About 15,300 Confederate troops and about 12,600 members of the Union Army were engaged at various strengths over the two day battle at Mansfield and Pleasant Hill. Union losses were 150 killed, 844 wounded and 375 missing. Confederate losses were about 1,000 killed or wounded and 500 missing.[35]

From Terrell's command, Major Morgan had been seriously wounded in the arm. Sadler's Company E's suffered several casualties during these actions on April 8 and 9. Private Elisha Maine was killed. Private R. H. Gilmore was wounded in the hand and another private was wounded on April 8 or 9. During the same action, Company E's Lieutenant Nathan C. Gunnels suffered a broken arm.

Fighting erupted again on April 12-13 at Pleasant Hill Landing and Blair's Landing. Several skirmishes and an engagement were fought at Monett's Ferry at Cane River Crossing in Louisiana between April 22-24. After a week's break, skirmishes broke out on Hudnot's Plantation and continued for the period of May 1-9 on several other plantations around Alexandria. Another skirmish was fought on May 12, but a retreat from Alexandria to Morganza,

Louisiana, was effected between May 13-20, during which time a number of battles were fought. Private R. C. McKenzie was wounded in the left side on May 13 and Private Samuel T. Owens was wounded in the shoulder. Operations against the expeditions from Morganza to the Atchafalaya River proceeded between May 30 and June 5. One skirmish fought at the river on June 1, 1864, was the last action recorded for Terrell's regiment in the Civil War.

Throughout these engagements, neither W. T. Sadler nor his son was ever wounded, although Fletcher Sadler was hospitalized at one point for an unnamed sickness. Although Sadler never filed for pension claims during his remaining years after the Civil War, his son did present his own claim in 1915 at the age of seventy. These papers were witnessed by two fellow Company E soldiers, Private William Zachariah Day and Corporal Thomas W. Moore, who stated that Fletcher was "a good soldier, and never deserted and never voluntarily abandoned his post of duty."

Although Terrell's regiment later received little acclaim for having fought in the Civil War, they had indeed played an important role in the Red River Campaign. One historian credits these men with turning the tide at the battles of Mansfield and Pleasant Hill, thus saving the Western Department and Texas itself from a sad fate.[36]

During the summer of 1864, Sadler's Company E returned to Texas. En route, Private John T. Rice was captured near Morganza, Louisiana, on August 8 and was sent to New York for the balance of the war.[37] Upon return, Captain Reeves resigned from the company in September, 1864, to take his newly elected position as associate judge of the Supreme Court of Texas. As no muster rolls exist for Company E after early 1864, it is unknown who became captain of the unit from this point on.

Terrell's Texas Cavalry completed its Civil War service around Houston and Hempstead, and Company E was disbanded in May at Hempstead when news of the surrender of eastern Confederate armies was received. Fletcher Sadler's pension papers reflect that he surrendered in April 1865. Longtime Palestine resident Alexander Joost was shown as a sergeant of Company E on a prisoner of war roll of May 26, 1865.

General Kirby Smith, commander of the Trans-Mississippi Department, signed an order for his forces to surrender on May 26, 1865, in New Orleans. The balance of the men under his command surrendered after receiving the word in June 1865 at Galveston.

Chapter Eighteen
FINAL YEARS OF A TEXAS VETERAN
1866-1884

W. T. Sadler returned home to Palestine to find new hostilities in the makings. President Abraham Lincoln's Emancipation Proclamation was declared to be in effect in Texas by General Gordon Granger on June 19, 1865, from Galveston. Not all slaves received the word immediately, but the news eventually spread by word of mouth.[1] Although the Civil War brought about freedom for the slaves, it also created new problems for them. In Anderson County, District Judge Reuben Reeves, former captain of Company E, refused to let the county's blacks participate as jurors in the judicial process.

Sadler, known throughout his life as a man who looked out for the well being of his fellow citizens, was the only known Anderson County resident to offer a new start to some of the free blacks. Upon his return to Sadler Plantation, he granted freedom to all of the slaves, who had worked for his family most of their lives. To each male head of household, he donated more than one-hundred acres of prime farmland.

At least ten of these freed blacks had traveled with him from Georgia some fourteen years prior. Some of these families continued for years to work paying jobs for Sadler and his children's families in Anderson County. One former slave, known as "Aunt Charlotte" Sadler to many of Sadler's descendants, lived in Anderson County until her death in early January 1936. Many of these former slaves took on the last name "Sadler" as their own, and descendants of these Sadlers still reside in the county.

Captain Sadler's great-grandson Jerry Sadler later wrote of the good river bottom farmland his ancestor gave to his former slaves.

This may seem odd considering W. T. Sadler favored secession and fought in the Civil War, but the Civil War was not fought entirely over the issue of slavery, and he was a man who believed in the law. When the South lost, he abided by the defeat, unlike many of his neighbors. The negroes weren't just slaves to him, but people who were part of his extended family, suddenly broken free from home. With little education or training for independence and responsibility, they faced more than enough difficulty surviving without the

SADLER'S ASSISTANCE TO EMANCIPATED BLACKS

The 1870 Census for Anderson County, Texas shows William Sadler's family and four former slave families to which he had given a new start in life. The male head of household's personal estate value indicates the acreage he was given by Sadler. Each newly freed family took the last name of Sadler (all names mistakenly spelled "Saddler"). Ten of the former slaves were born in Georgia before coming to Texas with Sadler in 1853.

Name	Age	Sex	Color	Profession/ Trade	Value of Real Estate	Value of Personal Estate	Place of Birth
Sadler, William T.	73	M	W	Farmer	1197	4000	NC
Fletcher	25	M	W	Farmer			TX
William P.	18	M	W				TX
Elizabeth	16	F	W				TX
Laura	9	F	W				TX
Celestia	7	F	W				TX
Joseph	13	M	B	Farm laborer			TX
Sadler, Jordan	31	M	B	Farmer		125	GA
Jane	24	F	M	Keeping House			TX
Alice	1	F	M	At Home			TX
Sadler, Louis	24	M	B	Farmer		150	GA
Rebecca	25	F	B	Keeping House			TX
Mary	9	F	B	At Home			TX
Lucy	6	F	B	At Home			TX
Mary	18	F	B	Domestic Servant			TX
Jackson	8 mos.	M	B	At Home			TX
Sadler, Allen	70	M	B	Farmer		175	GA
Charity	60	F	B	Keeping House			GA
Jane	25	F	B	Domestic Servant			GA
Emiline	19	F	B	Domestic Servant			GA
John	17	M	B	Farm Laborer			GA
Nettie	4	F	B	At Home			TX
James	1	M	B	At Home			TX
Sadler, Alex	18	M	B	Farm Laborer			GA
Sadler, Stuart	48	M	B	Farmer		125	GA
Harriet	44	F	B	Keeping House			GA
Stuart	14	M	B	Farm Laborer			TX
Joe	13	M	B	At Home			TX
Anderson	9	M	B	At Home			TX
Adelia	5	F	B	At Home			TX

* W = White, B = Black, M = Mulatto, I = Indian.

added burden of trying to make a living farming rocky, lifeless soil. For generations, the white Sadlers continued to be friendly toward the black Sadlers and the other black families of the area.[2]

A large number of the new black citizens soon rose up in rebellion against their former white masters. Opportunistic "carpetbaggers" and "scalawags" who swarmed into Texas after the war were credited with organizing many of the former slaves into a force known as the "Loyal League." Fearing the bold new black organization, a white group known as the "Defensive League" was formed to oppose the Loyal League. Wearing white outfits with red dunce caps, the Defensive League, an early form of the Ku Klux Klan, even adorned their horses with paper masks and forced cayenne pepper in the horses' nostrils to force them to snort in an evil fashion.[3]

Martial law was declared in Palestine and the Reconstruction Governor of Texas, Edmund J. Davis, sent an armed force to operate from Palestine's school house to keep the peace. The Defensive League, however, took matters into its own hands and rode in force on one occasion to Mound Prairie to break up a meeting of the black Loyal Leaguers. In a bloody clash, the freed blacks were broken up. Relations remained tense in East Texas for some time but, as Anderson County's early history relates, "In time the new relations between ex-slave and former master adjusted themselves, and the two races found that they could live and work harmoniously in the same section without either harming or imposing on the other."[4]

DEADLY TWISTER ON SADLER PLANTATION

Following the Civil War, Sadler resumed his quiet life of farming and raising his children on his Anderson County plantation. At this time, he had eight children from his wife Permelia of twenty-two years: Nathaniel Fletcher, William Peterson, Martha, Mary Ann, Betty, Laura, Celestia and an infant son, Joseph.

A surviving issue of the *Trinity Advocate* of August 8, 1866, indicates that the nearby county seat of Palestine was well along its way to recovering from the Civil War. At this time, there were twelve dry goods stores, six grocery stores selling everything from hard candy to barrels of bourbon, three saloons, three drug stores, one hotel, one cabinet shop, one watch maker's shop, three blacksmith's shops, a shoe shop, a barber shop, a saddler's shop, a tailor's shop, two printing shops, and a number of doctor and lawyer offices. A few modern brick buildings had appeared, including the court house and the clerk's office.[5]

This paper also showed a call for a meeting in nearby Tyler for a railroad convention to begin the Great Northern Railroad through East Texas. Sadler had been involved in an earlier railroad venture in the 1850s, but the Civil War had halted railroad construction for a time. It was not until 1872 that the International-Great Northern Railroad (I&GN) came into Anderson County, establishing the town of Neches. The I&GN railway which built through Anderson County was composed of numerous predecessor railroad companies, including the Houston Tap and Brazoria Railway Company.[6] Many of the early railroad companies were bought out by larger groups. It is likely that Sadler and his partners sold their Palestine Tap prior to the Civil War for a fair sum, because the 1860 Census of Texas shows him to have a healthy bank account. Early residents of Anderson County were treated to a big picnic and firework show upon the arrival of the first train in town. "All Palestine and the country round came streaming into town at sound of the first railroad whistle."[7] The coming of the railroads brought Palestine new life, and the county seat that Sadler had helped establish continued to flourish in the late 1800s.

Although Palestine was becoming more and more modernized, it was still a frontier town. The area's settlers were still subject to the mercy of mother nature. The streets were dusty in the dry times but turned to virtually impassible red mud with each heavy rain. Snow and ice made appearances during the winters, summers were very hot and humid, and tornadoes occasionally came with the more violent thunderstorms in East Texas.[8]

Soon after the end of the Civil War, one such violent storm swept across the Sadler Plantation with deadly results during the night of December 6, 1866. The storm spurned a powerful tornado that appeared without warning and ripped into the Sadler home. The voracious winds tore away the entire upper story of the early two-story log home. W. T. Sadler and most of his children escaped the destruction with only bruises but, to his grief, his wife Permelia and infant son Joseph disappeared with the upper floor.

It was not until the light of the following morning that the Texas veteran found the bodies of young Joseph and his mother, Permelia Bennett Sadler. Both tornado victims were buried in the family's little cemetery a short distance from their home. It was an especially cruel loss to Sadler, whose first wife and child had been violently taken from him in the 1838 Edens-Madden Massacre.

Providing For The Children

Following this tragedy, Sadler's family continued to farm in Anderson County. His oldest son, Nathaniel Fletcher, established his own plantation after the Civil War a few miles from his father's home. As a minor he had never owned his own slaves, but some of his father's ex-slaves came to live and work on Fletch's farm. One bright spot for W. T. Sadler was the marriage of his eighteen-year-old daughter, Mary Ann, to Civil War veteran William Zachariah Day, who served as a sheriff and county commissioner of Anderson County, on February 2, 1867, in their home county. Another of his daughters, Martha Tucker Sadler, married William Thomas Kennedy on July 26, 1869. William's mother, Abigail Parker Kennedy, was the daughter of Elder Daniel Parker.

Life was difficult in the Reconstruction Era following the great war between the states. The county was run by opportunists, generally called carpetbaggers or scalawags, who rigged elections and attempted to penalize those Southerners who had participated in the war. The 1870 Texas Census showed the population of Anderson County to have declined slightly over the past decade to 9,229, of which 52 percent were white and 48 percent were black.[9] Texas population for 1870 was figured as 818,579.[10]

During this time, Sadler helped provide for his childrens' futures by dividing up tracts of his vast land holdings for their own residences. On December 27, 1869, Sadler gave his daughter Mary Ann Day and her husband a 320-acre tract of land, his bounty land grant from San Jacinto, on Caney Creek, that began at the upper left corner of his original survey and was bordered by the south end of the William R. Wilson League. This land deed was given "for and in consideration for the love and affection" Sadler had for his child. He signed and sealed this document in the presence of Ben Parker and Daniel Parker Jr. and filed it with Anderson County Clerk W. H. King on November 23, 1870. Interestingly, Sadler was paid one dollar for this sale of land.

While at the Anderson County court in Palestine on November 23, Sadler also filed paperwork for his pension due from the Republic of Texas for his prior military service. The State Legislature passed an act in 1870 providing for the surviving veterans of the Texas Revolution. He filed his claim with Justice of the Peace William T. Smith, who acknowledged that before him

> personally appeared W. T. Sadler, aged 73 years, who being duly sworn declares that he is the identical W. T. Sadler who

was a private soldier in the Company commanded by Captain Leander Smith in the 2nd Regiment, commanded by Sidney Sherman, Colonel. That he enlisted in the Army of Texas on the 8th day of April AD 1836 before the Battle of San Jacinto at or near the Dewee Crossing on the Colorado River for three months and was honorably discharged at Victoria, Texas by General T. J. Rusk on or about the 1st day of July AD 1836 and that he has not before made application for pension under the act of the Legislature of the State of Texas approved 1870 and that he makes the application and declaration for the purpose of obtaining his pension under the said act as one of the surviving veterans in the war that separated Texas from Mexico.

This document was signed by Sadler and Smith and was witnessed by Dr. Henry H. Link and Miles Bennett. Both men swore that they were personally acquainted with Sadler, had witnessed him sign this document, "that they know him to be the person that he represents himself to be and that they are disinterested in the claim and that they reside in said county of Anderson."

Over the next few years, Sadler's children continued to start their own families. Daughter Elizabeth Ann "Betty" Sadler married Gilbert Russell Day Jr. on December 27, 1872, in Anderson County. The elder Sadler continued to help his children by providing them with their own land.

On October 20, 1873, Sadler gave his first son, Nathaniel Fletcher, a tract of land from the original Sadler Headright of 963 acres. This land began at the southeast corner of Sadler's Survey, then ran north with the eastern boundary line of this survey to the west corner of the Sam Houston Survey, then west across Sadler Creek to the corner in the western boundary line of the survey, then south to the southwest corner of the survey; then east to the place of beginning. This deed was witnessed by W. H. Campbell and W. P. Sadler and signed by notary public on Oct. 28, 1873, and filed on December 23, by District Clerk G. R. Howard.

On the same day (October 20, 1873), Sadler gave his second son, William Peterson, a tract of land from his original headright. The boundaries of this transfer ran from Sadler Creek to Gilbert Day's northeast corner line, then up the creek to where Nathaniel F.'s line crossed the creek, then east to the northwest corner of the Sam Houston Survey, then northeast to the southeast corner of the Sadler Survey, then followed this survey to a branch that led to the place of beginning. This document was witnessed by W. H. Campbell and Nathaniel F. Sadler on October 28, and also filed on December 23, 1873.

Also on October 20, Sadler gave his daughter Betty and her husband Gilbert Day, brother of the Zach Day who had married her sister Mary Ann, a portion of the W. T. Sadler Headright equalling six-hundred acres. This property began at the northwest corner of the N. F. Sadler Survey, then south to Sadler's Creek, and eventually back down the southwest direction with the meander of Sadler Creek to the place of beginning. This paper was handwritten by Sadler, witnessed by W. H. Campbell and N. F. Sadler and filed in the same manner as the previous two documents.

Two weeks after the preceding three transfers, Sadler on November 3, 1873, gave his daughter Laura another portion of his headright. Laura's land began at the west bank of Sadler's Creek going to the north boundary of the Sadler Headright, then west along the Sadler Headright boundaries to the William Wilson Survey. It also bordered the Gilbert Day Survey before finally turning back to its point of beginning. This deed was witnessed by W. H. Campbell and Gilbert Day, was notarized on February 6, 1874, and was filed in the district clerk's office of Jim Conaway at 9:00 a.m. on May 5, 1874.

Finally, Sadler deeded land to his other two daughters, Martha Tucker Sadler Kennedy and to Celestia "Lessie" Sadler. Although Lessie would later marry Alonzo "Lon" Foster in 1886, she remained with her aging father and lived with him through his final years. The land he gave to her included his own homestead, which began on the west banks of Sadler's Creek at the southeast corner of the Laura Sadler Survey, ran along the original headright's boundaries to the northeast corner of the William Peterson Sadler Survey, and eventually followed Sadler's Creek back to its point of origin. This deed was witnessed before the Anderson County clerk's office by W. H. Campbell and Gilbert Day.

PENSION PAPERS AND A NEW LAND GRANT

In his latter years, W. T. Sadler took steps to establish the pension he was due from Texas for his years of early service. On June 17, 1874, he appeared before his attorneys in Anderson County to fill out paperwork giving them power of attorney in carrying out his pension claims. The document they signed specified that the attorneys would sell a fractional bond for one-hundred dollars as their payment after the pension was issued. During the same time,

Pension Claim No. 290 was issued to William T. Sadler on June 20, 1874, by the State of Texas for his service in the Texas Army during the Battle of San Jacinto in 1836. Pension Papers of Sadler from Audited Claims microfilm series, reel 237, frame 105.

Sadler and Thomas T. Gammager served as witnesses to an affidavit of service for Daniel Parker Jr. on June 20, when Parker filed his own pension papers for service in the Texas Army in 1836. Gammager has been Master Sergeant and Quartermaster Sergeant on the Field and Staff of Terrell's Texas Cavalry Regiment.

Sadler's Pension Claim No. 290, filed earlier on December 2, 1870, had been approved on June 28, 1871, for the amount of $250. This payment was issued on June 20, 1874, and was received by DeCordova, Withers and Co. attorneys, as witnessed by friends Ben Parker and Isaac Parker. The certificate he received showed that Sadler, seventy-seven years old on July 1, was eligible for $250 of pension per year for the rest of his life. This last part, however, was scratched out and listed as payable through only July 1, 1874, the current date. By laws of the State of Texas passed August 13, 1870, and April 21, 1874, these payments were to be made to the veterans each year on or after December 31.

A new law was passed in the Reconstruction years that required the real property of a deceased head of family to be auctioned on the public square. W. T. Sadler had been left as administrator of his deceased brother Nathaniel Milton's estate following his death in June 1860. The District Court of Anderson County on September

> **LOST.**
>
> THE HEADRIGHT DUPLICATE CERTIFICATE No. 247—346, issued to the undersigned on the 23rd day of March, 1846, for one League and Labor of land, and unless intelligence of it is received at the proper department within three months I will apply to the proper officer for a triplicate of said lost certificate. W. T. SADDLER.
> July 8, 1376. ·2m

Sadler ran this classified ad for three successive months in the Palestine Advocate *during the summer of 1876 in order to obtain a triplicate copy of his Headright Certificate. Note the typo on the date and the misspelling of his name.*

18, 1872, had passed a decree directing Sadler to auction off certain tracts of land from his brother's estate. Sadler was notified of this decree on December 17, 1872, and was given a credit of six months in which to comply with the orders. He was directed to advertise this property in the local newspaper for a length of time before conducting the public auction.

The date for the auction of N. M. Sadler's land was set as the first Tuesday of March 1873, on which date Captain Sadler stood on the steps of the courthouse in Palestine and conducted the auction. When possible, citizens with money helped others to bid on their own property, but courthouse auctions became very commonplace and much land was acquired at cheap prices by the hated carpetbaggers. Sadler had broken up his brother's land into at least eighteen separate forty-acre tracts which were purchased by local residents for an average rate of $165 per forty-acre tract, yielding a total income of just over $3,000. Mr. L. Helm purchased two tracts for $350 dollars, Henry E. Diggs purchased two forty-acre tracts for $310 and W. A. Hagood purchased fourteen of the forty-acre tracts. These sales were finalized by Sadler before D. A. Calhoun, Justice of the Peace and Notary Public of Anderson County on May 15, 1874, and before Anderson County District Court Clerk Jim Conaway on May 15 and September 15, 1874.

Sadler went before the Anderson County court on November 15, 1876, to authenticate a triplicate certificate to his league and labor of land. His duplicate certificate had been lost and, according to law, he had to advertise for three months in the local newspaper to make sure that no one else had a claim against this land. James W. Ewing, one of the proprietors of the *Palestine Advocate*, appeared in court with Sadler this day to show proof that he had indeed advertised this notice in his paper for the required time period. The General Land Office then issued Triplicate Certificate No. 34/57 to him on November 18.

Transportation helped Palestine continue to flourish in the 1870s. Under the leadership of Judge Reagan, Palestine and Anderson County voted in 1875 on a bond issue of $150,000 to be given as a bonus to the International-Great Northern Railroad to locate their machine and repair shops and general offices to Palestine. This bond act brought three-hundred jobs to Palestine and resulted in the city's population's doubling in size to more than four-thousand people. The county was traversed north to south by the railroad, which branched at Palestine, one set of tracks running south to Houston and Galveston and the other to Laredo.[11] The I&GN Railroad is currently called the Missouri Pacific and still serves Palestine, which is still a hub of the Texas State Railroad.

One of Sadler's close neighbors, and soon-to-be relatives by marriage, at this time was the family of Robert Owen Roach. The Roachs had migrated from Tennessee to the Arkansas Territory, where they had operated a trading post for the Indians. The family left behind this business to travel by boat to New Orleans, and then on to Texas around 1849 via the little port town of Indianola. After selling their boat and loading their personal possessions into wagons, the Roachs had then traveled by land to Seguin, Texas, where they lived for about a year.

Dissatisfied, the family moved on to the Sadler settlement near Palestine, where Mr. Roach somehow acquired land from Captain Sadler. The Roach family had five children, three boys and two girls. "Billy" Sadler, youngest son of W. T. and Permelia Sadler, was married on May 31, 1876, in the little community of Ioni to Josephine Roach, who had been born in Anderson County on October 23, 1852. Billy's older brother Fletch had already married Josephine's sister, Martha Roach Gibson, on December 6, 1871.

In a small settlement of this type in the early days of Texas, in which the nearest neighbor might be several miles away, it was only natural for members of neighboring families to marry each other. A study of pre-1900 Anderson and Houston County families shows many marriages where two or more siblings of one family married siblings from another family. When a spouse was killed, it was also not uncommon for the in-law to become the survivor's next spouse.

A Final Wish Observed

For the remainder of his life, Captain Sadler returned to farming. He "deprecated all attempts to honor him for his services under the Republic of Texas, protesting that he had only done what was his duty," according to one published historical sketch.[12]

For his service during the Texas Revolution of 1836, Sadler was awarded Veteran Donation No. 612 on August 17, 1881, for 1,280 acres in Mason County.

The state he had served for so many years was rapidly recovering and the scars from the many battles were slowly healing. The 1880 census listed the total population of Texas as 1,591,749, almost double that of the previous decade.[13] Total population had been less than five thousand when Sadler first came to scout out land in 1822!

In the last years of his life, Sadler was honored by the State of Texas as one of the surviving veterans of the Texas Revolution. As such, the State Congress had passed legislation entitled "An act granting a land certificate of 1,280 acres to each of the surviving soldiers of the Texas Revolution." This act also provided for surviving signers of the Declaration of Texas Independence, and the widows of such soldiers and signers. The Congress had passed a similar act on July 28, 1876, which provided 640 acres to each of the indigent veterans who had been involved in the Battle of San

Jacinto. The new act approved March 15, 1881, therefore provided the 1,280 acres to a greater number of honorees.

These applications were submitted by veterans who had served in the Texas Army between the commencement of the Texas Revolution in 1835 and the period prior to January 1, 1837. W. T. Sadler went before his old friend William Jowers, now County Judge of Anderson County, on July 20, 1881, to procure his land certificate. He filed the necessary papers stating that he had served in Captain Hayden Arnold's company in the Battle of San Jacinto and that he had previously received a bounty warrant for 320 acres for his army service. Jowers affixed his seal of the County Court that Sadler was indeed "a bona fide Texas veteran," and this document was witnessed by Ben Parker and Miles Bennett.

Sadler's document was filed by Stephen H. Darden in Austin on July 26, one day before his eighty-fourth birthday, and was forwarded by the Commissioner of the General Land Office. Sadler had previously gone before the Anderson County Court on July 6 to file a power of attorney document giving Darden authority to act as "my Agent and Attorney to prosecute before any Court or Commission and the Commissioner of the General Land Office, my right to any Land Certificate or an annual pension to which I may be or may become entitled for military services rendered by me." After Darden filed the necessary application in Austin, the Texas Board of Veterans then issued Sadler's land certificate on August 11, 1881.

Sadler was granted his 1,280 acres in Mason County, situated on the waters of Honey Creek, a tributary of the Llano River. This property was situated about 3.5 miles southwest of the town of Mason, about thirty-five miles northwest of Fredericksburg, Texas. Due to his age and the location of this land grant, Sadler obviously had no interest in maintaining this land.

His agent, Stephen Darden, was instructed to sell his Veteran Donation Land Certificate No. 612 to the top bidder. Sadler's certificate was sold by Darden to Ben F. Gooch and W. P. Lockhart of Mason County on November 7, 1881, for the sum of $230. After taking care of the necessary surveys, Gooch and Lockhart filed on October 31, 1882, a document titled "File 2101, Bexar Donation W. T. Sadler by Atty."

At the age of eighty-six as he was dying, Captain Sadler requested to be buried quietly and without any demonstration. According to his great-grandson Jerry Sadler, he left a letter instructing that "the world not be notified of my death, because there are too many people claiming credit for things they didn't do."[14] This

The State of Texas in 1936 erected this Centennial Marker on the old Sadler Plantation to honor the service of Captain William Turner Sadler. The little cemetery is maintained by the Sadler family and is surrounded by a fence that was erected courtesy of Howard C. Sadler. Note that his place of birth is incorrectly listed as Tennessee.
Author's collection.

request perhaps stemmed from the fact that this humble, dedicated Texas servant had received little recognition for his achievements during his lifetime. Many significant events with which this member of the Texas Veteran's Association had been involved during the early years of Texas went largely unrecorded in state history.

The fact that he commanded one of the earliest Texas Ranger companies formed during the Texas Revolution is not recorded in any published ranger history. The battle at Kickapoo Village in which his militia company and others ended the Cordova Rebellion has received little attention in histories of the Indian wars. The fact that he commanded a company of the First Regiment of Infantry during the Cherokee War has been virtually erased through time and the loss of many early Republic records. His involvement with Santa Anna following his capture at San Jacinto and his claim of firing one of the shots which fatally wounded Chief Bowles at the Neches battle have survived as merely footnotes of Houston County history. In the House of Representatives, he had helped create Anderson County and was actively involved in the committee whose legislation would help Texas eliminate its enormous debts through the sale of public lands to the United States.

Sadler's children considered his request of privacy to be a strange one but were loyal enough to honor it. He died in his home near Elkhart, in Anderson County, on February 18, 1884, and was buried beside his second wife, Permelia Bennett Sadler, in the Sadler cemetery. A granite Centennial Marker to honor San Jacinto veterans was erected by the State of Texas in 1936.

The Sadler cemetery is located where his plantation, sometimes called the "Sadler League", and home once stood. It now stands in an old cornfield on a sunny hill off Highway 2022 near Percilla. This spot is south of the present community of Slocum and is just across the northern boundary line of Houston County. The exact spot is 4.3 miles north of the intersections of Highway 228 and Farm Road 2022.

His younger son, William Peterson Sadler, who died of pneumonia at an early age, and his wife, Josephine Roach Sadler, are both buried alongside W. T. and Permelia Sadler. Graves of some of the plantation's early slaves are on the east side of the cemetery enclosure, and there are also a number of graves with crude rock headstones which bear no inscriptions. One of these is said to be the marker for W. T. Sadler's youngest son Joseph, who was lost with his mother in the 1866 tornado on the family plantation.

Although Sadler's wishes of a quiet burial were carried out, the news did finally make it to the rest of the state. The Thursday, March 6, 1884 edition of the *Galveston Daily News* carried a special front-page tribute which it had picked up from Palestine the previous day.

CAPTAIN SADLER DEAD.

An Old Veteran and Worthy Citizen Gone To Rest.

[SPECIAL TO THE NEWS.]

PALESTINE, March 5. – Captain W. T. Sadler, one of the veterans of San Jacinto, died last week at his home, about four miles below Elkhart, in this county. He was 86 years of age, and had been a member of the Texas Congress and of the legislature of the State after annexation.

He was of singularly modest and retiring disposition, and had never taken any part in the proceedings of the Veterans association, being desirous of avoiding, as he stated to his children, all glorification for the past.

Indeed, he was so sensitive on this point that he left special instructions with his son to have his funeral conducted quietly and not to have the news of his death circulated until after he was laid in his grave, and his wishes were respected by the family, so that it was only to-day the news reached Palestine, to the sincere regret of all his old friends here.

The *Austin Statesman* picked up on the news via telegram and carried a notice in its March 7 issue. Judge Jowers of the Elkhart area stated that Sadler had served in both the Texas Congress and the Texas Legislature just after annexation. The *Statesman*'s obituary related that Sadler "during the fading years of his life declined having anything to do with public demonstrations in connection with his fellow soldiers, claiming such demonstrations were uncalled for and useless. He was 86 years of age, and connected with nearly all the prominent families in this section of the state."

APPENDIX A: RANGER/FRONTIER COMPANIES IN SERVICE REPUBLIC OF TEXAS, 1835-1839 (INCLUDING TEXAS MILITIA)

For those companies whose exact tenure of service is unknown, an approximation is given using months or periods when the company *was* known to be in service. All commanders listed held the rank of captain unless otherwise noted. The key source for this list is author's research of muster rolls, audited claims, and pension papers from the Republic of Texas era from the Texas State Library Archives.

1835-1837

UNIT COMMANDER	TYPE OF COMPANY/AREA & DATES OF SERVICE
Micah Andrews	Company C of Major Smith's battalion; December 14, 1836 - August 1837.
William W. Arrington	Appointed captain on November 28, 1835. No evidence that company was mustered into service.
George W. Barnett	Ranger company; July 20 - August 28, 1835.
Thomas H. Barron	Briefly commanded ranger company during February and March 1836. Captain of Company B of Colonel Coleman's battalion; August 15 - December 14, 1836. Company A of Major Smith's ranger battalion from December 14, 1836 - November 1837.
William Bicknell	Red River Volunteers; July 14 - October 14, 1836.
Jesse Billingsley	Ranger company of Colonel Burleson's battalion; July 1 - October 1, 1836.
Calvin Boales	Ranger company; September 11 - November 14, 1836. Company formerly under Captain Sterling Robertson.
John M. Bowyer	Harrisburg County Mounted Gunmen; June 18 - December 18, 1837.
Isaac Watts Burton	Ranger Company; December 19, 1835 - June 24, 1836. Burton promoted to major on June 24.
Joseph Bell Chance	Washington County Guards; March 20 - June 1, 1836.
Elisha Clapp	Volunteer Rangers; September 10 - December 12, 1836. Houston Couny Mounted Gunmen; authorized June 12, 1837, for six months' service.
John Clarke	San Augustine Mounted Gunmen; authorized June 12, 1837.
Philip Haddox Coe	Ranger company; July 9 - August 31, 1835.
Robert Morris Coleman	Ranger company; June 12 - August 29, 1835. Ordered to raise three ranging companies on August 13, 1836, for protecting area between the upper Brazos and Guadalupe rivers. Commanded Company C briefly; served as colonel commanding battalion until January 1837.
Michael Costley	Nacogdoches County Ranger Company; September 11 - December 11, 1836.
John Robert Craddock	Red River County Mounted Gunmen; authorized June 12, 1837.
Charles Curtis, Lt.	Led ranger company and was in temporary command of Fort Coleman as of January 1837.
George Washington Davis	Superintendent of twenty-man ranger company authorized in November 1835 to patrol between Colorado and Guadalupe rivers during Texas Revolution.

Appendix A: Ranger/Frontier Companies 1835-1839

Nicholas Mosby Dawson	Company B, 1st Regiment Volunteers; January 29 - November 12, 1836.
John H. Dyer	Red River County Mounted Gunmen; June 12 - December 12, 1837.
William Mosby Eastland	Company B of Colonel Coleman/Major Smith's battalion; December 14, 1836 - March 2, 1838.
George English	Shelby County Mounted Gunmen; May 31 -November 31, 1837.
Louis B. Franks	Ranger company; February 1 - March 1836.
Daniel Boone Friar	Superintendent and captain of ranger company based in Viesca in Robertson's Colony. Served from November 1, 1835 - February 1, 1836.
Jasper Good	Jasper County Mounted Gunmen; authorized June 12, 1837 for six months' service.
Garrison Greenwood	Appointed superintendent on October 17, 1835, of ten-man ranger company based at Fort Houston.
Squire Haggard	Promoted to captain of George Jewel's ranger company when Jewel was promoted to major. Served at Fort Houston from late 1836 through March 19, 1837.
Franklin Hardin	Liberty County Company; July 7 - October 7, 1836.
James A. Head	Ranger company; January 27 - March 27, 1836.
William Warner Hill	Ranger company of Colonel Burleson's battalion; July 3 - October 3, 1836. Fought Indian battle in August 1836.
Eli Hillhouse	Ranger company of twenty-five men under superintendent Silas M. Parker. Served October 23 - December 24, 1836.
John C. Hunt	Bastrop County volunteers; July 1 - October 1, 1836.
George Washington Jewel	Volunteer ranger company mustered into Texas service on September 19, 1836. Jewel promoted by his men and served as major through March 19, 1837.
Henry Wax Karnes	Commanded cavalry company March 20 - September 26, 1836. Served as colonel of cavalry from January 2, 1837 - March 14, 1838.
George C. Kimbell	Thirty-two-man Gonzales Mounted Ranger Company. Formed February 23, 1836; most lost their lives at Alamo.
Byrd Lockhart	Mounted Spy Company; July 4 - August 16, 1836.
John L. Lynch	Company A of Major Smith's ranger battalion; November 28, 1837 - March 3, 1838. Formerly served as first lieutenant under Captain William Eastland.
Joseph Mather, Lt.	Acting commander of Company E of Major William Smith's ranger battalion; September 17 - October 1, 1837.
John Gilmore McGehee	Ranger company of Colonel Burleson's battalion; July 1 - November 20, 1836.
Jose Antonio Menchaca	Mounted Bexar Company; October 1836 - March 1837.
Daniel Monroe	Company B of Major William Smith's ranger battalion; January 1 - December 14, 1837.
William H. Moore, Lt.	Acting commander of Company B of Major William Smith's ranger battalion; December 1837 - April 30, 1838.
James W. Parker	Ten-man ranger company under superintendent Silas M. Parker. Served January 1 - May 19, 1836.
Silas M. Parker	Superintendent of two ranger companies patrolling frontier

Appendix A: Ranger/Frontier Companies 1835-1839

	between Brazos and Trinity rivers during Texas Revolution.
James Perry	Galveston County Mounted Gunmen; June 12 - December 12, 1837.
John G. W. Pierson	Post Washington Mounted Company; June 30 - September 30, 1836. Also Washington County Mounted Gunmen; June 12 - December 12, 1837.
Dickinson Putnam	Second Company of Rangers under Major Burton; in service June 24 - November 1, 1836.
Henry Reed	San Augustine Volunteer Company organized June 4, 1836, for three-month period.
Thomas Robbins	Mounted cavalry/ranger company; April 25 - August 13, 1836. Robbins had previously served as a lieutenant under captains Isaac Burton and William H. Smith.
Sterling Clack Robertson	Ranger company; January 17 - February 1836 and July 25 - September 11, 1836 in Colonel Burleson's battalion.
Alexander Robless, Lt.	Company A of Coleman's Battalion of Rangers; October 5 - December 31, 1836. Robless assumed command from Captain Walden.
William Turner Sadler	Houston Company #10 of Mounted Rangers. Based at Fort Houston and ranged between Neches and Trinity rivers from January 1 - March 16, 1836.
Eli Seale	Ranger company; December 25, 1835 - January 25, 1836. Seale assumed command after Captain Hillhouse died.
William R. Scurlock	San Augustine Volunteer Company; July 4 - October 4, 1836.
Erastus "Deaf" Smith	Spy company in service during Texas Revolution. Formed cavalry company in December 1836 that served near San Antonio through June 10, 1837.
James Smith	Nacogdoches Mounted Volunteers; April 11 - July 11, 1836.
Lee C. Smith	Ranger Company E of Major Smith's battalion; March 17 - September 17, 1837.
Samuel Smith, Lt.	Third Company of Rangers under Major Burton; August 6 - October 25, 1836.
William H. Smith	Cavalry/Ranger company originally attached to army; March 10 - July 18, 1836. Served as major of Battalion of Rangers from December 14, 1836 - December 14, 1837.
Jacob Snively	Ranger company; known to have operated in Nacogdoches County post-San Jacinto into 1837.
William C. Swearingen	Ranger company stationed at post on Sabine River; May 6 - August 20, 1837.
Benjamin R. Thomas, 2nd Lt.	Commanding Company C of Coleman's Battalion of Rangers from September - December 31, 1836.
Stephen Townsend	Ranger company; February 1 - March 16, 1836.
John James Tumlinson	Ranger company; January 17 - August 16, 1836. Command of company fell briefly to Second Lieutenant George M. Petty during the Runaway Scrape.
A. B. Van Benthuysen, Lt.	Commanded eighteen-man detachment from Captain Bowyer's company; engaged Indians in October - November 1837.
Alfred P. Walden	Company A of Coleman's Battalion of Rangers; August 15 - October 5, 1836. Sent to Louisiana for supplies and arms.

Eleazor Louis R. Wheelock Ranger company; May 8 - September 15, 1836.
Robert McAlpin Williamson Ranger company; July 1 - September 15, 1835.
William C. Wilson Ranger company under Lieutenant Colonel Griffin Bayne; March 1 - June 1, 1836.
Nicholas Wren, Lt. Ranger Company C under command of Lieutenant Wren at Fort Houston from at least August 8 - September, 1837.
John York Ranger company of Colonel Burleson's battalion; July 1 - November 20, 1836.

1838-1839

Solomon Adams Houston County Rangers; February 8 - August 9, 1839.
Micah Andrews La Grange Rangers; March 10 - June 10, 1839.
John Applegate Mounted Volunteers, 3rd Brigade, Texas Militia, Fall 1838.
Hayden S. Arnold Nacogdoches Town Infantry Company, Texas Militia; October 5 - November 16, 1838.
Hugh W. Augustine * Mounted Volunteers, 3rd Brigade, Texas Militia; August 8 - August 22, 1838.
Joseph L. Bennett Mounted Gunmen, Texas Milita; July 28 - September 3, 1839.
Andrew Jackson Berry San Augustine County Mounted Volunteers, 1st Regiment, 3rd Brigade, Texas Militia; July 19 - August 10, 1839
Jesse Billingsley Bastrop Volunteer Rangers; fought in Battle of Brushy Creek in February 1839 and also fought Vicente Cordova's men in March 1839.
John Bird Mounted rangers from Austin and Fort Bend counties; April 24 - May 26, 1839; Bird killed in battle on May 26 and succeeded by Nathaniel Brookshire.
George Birdwell Mounted Riflemen, 1st Regiment, 4th Brigade, Texas Militia; November 17, 1838 - January 7, 1839.
William Bicknell * RedRiver mounted volunteers in service for fourteen days during July 1838.
George H. Black Mounted rangers; October 22, 1839 - January 29, 1840.
Champaign Blythe Mounted Gunmen, 4th Brigade, Texas Militia; August 30 - September 21, 1838.
Thomas J. Bowen, 1st Lt. Bexar Area "Jordan's Company"; April 11 - June 11, 1838.
James Edward Box Mounted Volunteers, 2nd Regiment, 3rd Brigade, Texas Militia; October 14, 1838 - March 25, 1839. Also Houston County Rangers; March 26 - October 18, 1839.
Samuel Charles Box * Mounted militia company; August 7 - September 24, 1838.
James Bradshaw Mounted Riflemen, 3rd Brigade, Texas Militia; October 10 - December 1, 1838.
Thomas H. Brennan, 1st Lt. Mounted Gunmen, 1st Regiment, Texas Militia; September 2 - December 4, 1839.
George C. Briscoe Fannin County Rangers under General Bonnell; November 16, 1838 - January 9, 1839.
William Charles Brookfield Mounted rangers; October 12 - 24, 1838.
Thomas G. Brooks San Augustine Volunteers, 3rd Brigade, Texas Militia; October 29 - November 29, 1838.
Nathaniel Brookshire Mounted volunteers from Austin and Fort Bend counties;

Appendix A: Ranger/Frontier Companies 1835-1839

	May 26 - July 24, 1839; Suceeded Captain Bird when he was killed in battle on May 26, 1839.
Squire Brown	Mounted Gunmen, 1st Regiment, 4th Brigade, Texas Militia; August 30 - December 28, 1838. Company formerly under Captain Blythe.
Benjamin Franklin Bryant	Forty-eight-man volunteer company organized near the falls of the Brazos; fought Indians on January 16, 1839.
Jacob Burleson	Volunteer company of twenty-five men from Well's Fort area near present Austin; Burleson killed in Battle of Brushy Creek on February 24, 1839.
Andrew Caddell *	Mounted Volunteers, 2nd Regiment, 3rd Brigade, Texas Militia; August 16 - August 29, 1838; and 1st Regiment, 3rd Brigade, November 1 - 15, 1838.
Mathew Caldwell	Gonzales Rangers; March 16 - June 16, 1839.
Nathaniel H. Carroll	Mounted Gunmen, 1st Regiment, Texas Militia; September 15 - December 1, 1839.
James Carter	Spy Company, Texas Militia; July, 1839.
Capt. Castro	Lipan Indians volunteering against Comanches; January 25 - February 25, 1839.
Claiborn Chisholm	Mounted Rangers, 1st Regiment, 4th Militia Brigade; June 9 - September 9, 1838.
James W. Cleveland	Mounted rangers; January 6 - February 5, 1839.
Stephen Collins	Mounted Volunteers, Texas Milita; October 12 - November 26, 1838.
John R. Craddock	Mounted Riflemen, Company B, 1st Regiment, 4th Brigade, Texas Militia; September 6, 1838 - January 7, 1839.
J. A. Creery, Lt.	Houston Volunteers, Harrisburg County, Texas Militia; June 10 - August 8, 1839. Lieutenant Creery replaced Captain John Garrett on June 10.
John Crist	Houston County Volunteers, Texas Militia; early 1839.
Joseph Daniels	Milam Guards of Houston, Company A, 2nd Brigade, Texas Militia; November 15, 1838 - February 15, 1839.
Benjamin W. Davis	Houston County Volunteers, Texas Militia; early 1839.
Samuel Davis	Mounted Gunmen, Company D, 1st Regiment, Texas Militia; September 10 - November 27, 1839.
John B. Denton	Volunteer Mounted Riflemen, 1st Regiment, Texas Militia, July 15 - August 15, 1839.
Nimrod Doyle	Volunteer Rangers, Robertson County; March 8 - June 10, 1839.
James H. Durst	Mounted Rangers, 3rd Brigade, Texas Militia; December 1, 1838 - January 25, 1839.
John Durst *	Mounted Gunmen of Mt. Sterling Settlement, Nacogdoches County, Texas Militia; October 10 - 20, 1838, and November 17 - December 11, 1838.
Joseph Durst *	Mounted Rangers, 3rd Brigade, Texas Militia; August 15 - September 27, 1839.
Dickson Dyer	Mounted Riflemen, 1st Regiment, 4th Brigade, Texas Militia; December 5, 1838 - January 7, 1839. Dyer took command after Captain Gillian resigned.

William Mosby Eastland	La Grange Volunteers; January 25 - February 25, 1839; fought battle at San Gabriel River on February 15, 1839.
Balis Edens	Commanding small volunteer company at Brown's Fort as of February 1839.
William Edmondson	Mounted Riflemen, 1st Regiment, 4th Brigade, Texas Militia; September 6, 1838 - January 7, 1839.
John Emberson	Volunteer Ranger Company, Red River and Fannin counties, 2nd Regiment, 4th Brigade, Texas Militia; March 16 - September 16, 1839.
George English *	Mounted Volunteers, 3rd Regiment, 3rd Brigade, Texas Militia; August 6 - 26, 1838 and October 10, 1838 - January 13, 1839.
George Bernard Erath	Milam County Rangers; March 8 - June 8, 1839.
William G. Evans, Lt.	Commanded thirty-four-man volunteer unit recruited in Houston March 20, 1839; on duty at Fort Milam or Marlin's Fort from April 3 - September 12, 1839.
John Ferguson	Mounted Volunteers, 3rd Regiment, 3rd Brigade, Texas Militia; December 8, 1838 - March 8, 1839.
James Fisher	Mounted Gonzales Company (under Major Baley C. Walters) stationed on the Angelina River, Nacogdoches County, 2nd Regiment, 3rd Brigade, Texas Militia; September 14 - October 3, 1838.
John B. Gaines	Mounted Gunmen, 3rd Regiment, 3rd Brigade, Texas Militia; November 1, 1838 - February 1, 1839.
John Garrett	Houston Volunteers, Harrisburg County, Texas Militia; April 8 - June 10, 1839. Garrett resigned on June 10 and was replaced by Lieutenant J. A. Creery.
Mitchel Garrison	Shelby County Volunteers, 3rd Regiment, 3rd Brigade, Texas Militia; June 28 - August 10, 1839.
John Porter Gill	Mounted Gunmen of Brazoria County, Company B, 1st Regiment, Texas Militia; September 14 - December 1, 1839.
James Gillian	Mounted Riflemen, 1st Regiment, 4th Brigade, Texas Militia; September 6 - December 5, 1838. Gillian resigned December 5 and was replaced by Captain Dickson Dyer.
Robert Kemp Goodloe *	Mounted Gunmen, San Augustine Volunteers, 3rd Brigade, Texas Militia; August 12 - September 1, 1838.
Jose Maria Gonzales	Mounted Volunteers, Texas Militia; September 8 - November 21, 1839.
John J. Grumbles	Elected captain of fourteen-man ranging company formed February 22, 1839, near Bastrop during Comanche hostilities.
Richard Haley	Shelby County Mounted Company, 3rd Regiment, 3rd Brigade, Texas Militia; October 14, 1838 - January 10, 1839; July 9 - August 10, 1839.
William V. R. Hallund	Mounted Gunmen, 1st Regiment, Texas Militia; October 4 - November 22, 1839. Hallund became captain after William Young was elected major.
Jacob E. Hamilton	San Augustine County Mounted Rangers, 3rd Brigade, Texas Militia; July 22 - August 10, 1839.
Robert S. Hamilton	Mounted Riflemen, 1st Regiment, 4th Brigade, Texas

Appendix A: Ranger/Frontier Companies 1835-1839 293

	Militia; September 6, 1838 - January 7, 1839.
Wesley W. Hanks *	Volunteer Riflemen, 1st Regiment, 3rd Brigade, Texas Militia; August 6 - 22, 1838.
Greenberry Horace Harrison	Mounted Riflemen recruited by Colonel Karnes; June 28 - August 10, 1839.
John Hart	Fannin County Mounted Gunmen, 2nd Regiment, 4th Brigade, Texas Militia; November 19, 1838 - January 7, 1839.
James Hoggart	Mounted Volunteers, 1st Regiment, 3rd Brigade, Texas Militia; November 1 - 18, 1838.
George W. Hooper *	Mounted Volunteers, Texas Militia, August 9- 27, 1838.
James E. Hopkins	Mounted Riflemen, 1st Regiment, 4th Brigade, Texas Militia; September 6, 1838 - January 7, 1839.
Alexander Horton *	Mounted Volunteers, San Augustine County, 1st Regiment, Texas Militia; August 8 - 22, 1838.
James G. Hyde, 1st Lt.	Mounted Gunmen, 3rd Brigade, Texas Militia; July 9 - August 10, 1839.
John Inman	Mounted Volunteers, 3rd Brigade, 3rd Regiment, Texas Militia; July 9 - August 10, 1839.
Alexander Jordan	Mounted Rangers, Nacogdoches County, 3rd Brigade, Texas Militia; June 21 - August 5, 1839.
Nathaniel T. Journey	Fannin County Mounted Rangers, 2nd Regiment, 4th Brigade; September 14, 1838 - March 13, 1839.
Henry Wax Karnes	Colonel of cavalry during 1838 and 1839.
William M. Keeling *	Volunteer Infantry Company, 3rd Regiment, Texas Militia; August 9 - 23, 1838.
William Kimbro	Mounted Volunteers, 1st Reg., 3rd Brigade, Texas Militia; Oct. 24 - November 25, 1838 and July 15 - August 10, 1839.
David Laird *	Volunteer Infantry Company, 1st Regiment, 3rd Brigade, Texas Militia; August 6 - 22, 1838.
Mark B. Lewis	Volunteer mounted rangers; March 2 - September 9, 1839.
George W. Long	Mounted Gunmen, Company F, 1st Regiment, Texas Militia; September 9 - November 30, 1839.
James D. Long	Mounted Volunteers, Nacogdoches County, 2nd Regiment, 3rd Brigade, Texas Militia; August 5 - 25, 1839.
Isaac Lyday	Third Red River County Ranging Company, 4th Militia Brigade; November 29, 1838 - February 28, 1839.
John L. Lynch	Captain of rangers, January 6 - February 20, 1838. Ranger spy company; June 26 - August 25, 1839. Lynch killed December 25, 1839 in Cherokee fight with Chief John Bowles.
James D. Matthews	Robertson County Mounted Rangers; March 8 - June 8, 1839.
James McKim	Sabine County Mounted Company, 3rd Brigade, Texas Militia; July 9 - August 10, 1839.
Ephraim W. McLean	Galveston Mounted Volunteers, Texas Militia; November 19 - December 8, 1839. McLane elected to command after Captain William Wilson resigned on November 19.
Isam Medford	Mounted Gunmen, 2nd Regiment, 3rd Brigade, Texas Militia; October 16, 1838 - January 3, 1839.
Nelson Merrill	Bastrop County Rangers; June 10 - September 10, 1839.

John W. Middleton	Sabine County Ranging Company; July 1 - August 14, 1839.
Joseph R. Mix	Mounted Riflemen, 1st Regiment, 4th Brigade, Texas Militia; September 6 - November 28, 1838. Mix promoted to colonel November 28, succeeded by William R. Scurlock.
John Henry Moore	Named colonel in charge of two Bastrop and La Grange companies under Smithwick and Eastland; led Indian fight on San Gabriel River on January 26, 1839.
William H. Moore, Lt.	Senior ranger officer commanding at Fort Houston on the Colorado River as of April 1838.
David Muckleroy *	Nacogdoches Mounted Company, 3rd Regiment, 2nd Brigade, Texas Militia; August 9 - 22, 1838.
Merrill Nelson	Bastrop Rangers; June 10 - September 10, 1839.
James R. O'Neal	Fannin County Frontier Volunteer Company of Spies; June 8 - September 8, 1838.
Clark L. Owen	Mounted ranger company of about thirty men; served for six months beginning about May 1839.
James P. Ownby	Volunteer mounted ranger company; March 2 - September 9, 1839.
Panther	Shawnee Indians, Mounted Company, 3rd Brigade; November 25, 1838 - January 25, 1839.
Placido	Twenty-four-man Tonkawa Indian scouting company; served under Colonel Edward Burleson during 1839's Cherokee War and Northwestern Campaign.
George Pollitt	Guard company for General Thomas Rusk's Indian Campaign, Texas Milita; October 12, 1838 - January 2, 1839.
Henry Reed	Mounted Gunmen, 1st Regiment, Texas Militia; October 3 - November 22, 1839.
James Reily *	Mounted Nacogdoches Guards, 2nd Regiment, 3rd Brigade, Texas Militia; September 9 - 24, 1838.
David Renfro *	Sabine County Mounted Volunteers, 3rd Regiment, 3rd Brigade, Texas Militia; August 12 - 26, 1838; October 17 - November 9, 1838.
James O. Rice, Lt.	Participated in Cordova fight in March, 1839; commanded a seventeen-man detachment of Captain Andrew's men into battle on May 18, 1839.
Mark R. Roberts	Fannin County Rangers, 2nd Regiment, 4th Brigade, Texas Militia; January 14 - April 13, 1839 and September 16, 1839 - March 16, 1840.
James Rogers	Commanded twenty-seven-man company from Fort Wilbarger and fought in Battle of Brushy Creek on February 24, 1839.
David Rusk *	Mounted Riflemen, Texas Militia; August 8 - 22, 1838.
Eli Russell	Mounted Company under Major Baley Walters, Texas Militia; September 2 - November 15, 1838.
William Turner Sadler	Houston County Mounted Volunteers, 3rd Brigade, Texas Militia; September - November 8, 1838.
Lewis Sanchez *	Mounted Gunmen, 3rd Brigade, Texas Militia; August 5 - 27, 1838; September 7, 1838 - January 27, 1839; and June 15 - July 22, 1839.

Appendix A: Ranger/Frontier Companies 1835-1839

William R. Scurlock	Mounted Riflemen, 1st Regiment, 4th Brigade, Texas Militia; November 28, 1838 - January 7, 1839. Scurlock promoted to captain on November 28, after Captain Joseph R. Mix was promoted to colonel.
R. H. Shearer, Lt.	Volunteer Infantry Platoon; August 30 - November 30, 1838.
Isham Sims	Guard company for Mexican prisoners in Nacogdoches, Texas Militia; August 22 - October 21, 1838.
James W. Sims	Mounted Riflemen, Red River County, 1st Regiment, 4th Brigade, Texas Militia; August 2 - November 2, 1839.
Robert Sloan	Fannin County Mounted Rangers, 2nd Regiment, 4th Brigade, Texas Militia; September 14, 1838 - January 14, 1839.
James Smith	Mounted Volunteers/Spies, 2nd Regiment, 3rd Brigade, Texas Militia; October 7 - Dec. 1, 1838.
Henry Madison Smith	Volunteer Rangers, Nacogdoches County; March 1 - September 2, 1839.
Robert W. Smith *	Mounted Nacogdoches Volunteers, 3rd Brigade, Texas Militia; August 8 - 21, 1838; October 10 - 21, 1838; November 8 - 20, 1838; and June 28 - August 5, 1839.
Noah Smithwick	Bastrop Ranger Company; January 25 - February 25, 1839; involved in fight on San Gabriel River on February 15, 1839.
Jacob Snively	Mounted Rangers, Houston County; September 14, 1838 - March, 1839.
Joseph Sowell	Fannin County Militia Company, 2nd Regiment, 4th Brigade; August 1 - 31, 1839.
Hiram B. Stephens *	Mounted Rangers, Nacogdoches County, 2nd Regiment, 3rd Brigade, Texas Militia; August 4 - September 15, 1838.
Jesse Stiff	Fannin County Mounted Rangers, 2nd Regiment, 4th Brigade, Texas Militia; December 2 - 30, 1838.
Henry B. Stout	Red River County Rangers, 1st Regiment, 4th Brigade; November 20, 1838 - May 26, 1839.
Edward H. Tarrant	Mounted Riflemen, 4th Brigade, Texas Militia; September 6, 1838 - January 7, 1839.
James F. Timmins *	Mounted Gunmen, 3rd Brigade, Texas Militia; August 14 - 25, 1838; October 12, 1838 - February 6, 1839.
Peter Tipps	Mounted Nacogdoches Volunteers, 2nd Regiment, Texas Militia; July 13 - August 5, 1839.
Jackson Todd	Mounted Nacogdoches Volunters, 2nd Regiment, 3rd Brigade, Texas Militia; November 19 - December 1, 1838.
John James Tumlinson	Mounted Gunmen/Spy Company, 1st Regiment, Texas Militia; October 13 - November 22, 1839.
Benjamin A. Vansickle	Mounted Volunteers, 3rd Brigade, Texas Militia; July 1 - August 5, 1839.
Charles Mote Walters *	Mounted Volunteers, Nacogdoches, 2nd Regiment, 3rd Brigade, Texas Militia; August 10 - 30, 1838; September 4 - October 12, 1838.
Daniel Weeks	Mounted Nacogdoches Volunteers, 2nd Regiment, 3rd Brigade, Texas Militia; August 22 - September 14, 1838.

Madison Guess Whitaker	Mounted Volunteers, Nacogdoches County, Texas Militia; October 30 - November 11, 1838.
Joseph Williams	Mounted Volunteers, 2nd Regiment, 3rd Brigade, Texas Militia; October 9 - 19, 1838.
Samuel Williams	Mounted Gunmen, 1st Regiment, Texas Militia; September 11 - December 2, 1839.
Jason Wilson	Mounted Gunmen, 1st Regiment, 4th Brigade, Texas Militia; May 27 - August 27, 1838.
William F. Wilson	Galveston Mounted Volunteers, Texas Militia; September 8 - November 19, 1839. Wilson resigned on November 19 and was succeeded by Ephraim McLean.
John Wortham	Houston County Rangers, 3rd Regiment, Texas Militia; November 9, 1838 - February 8, 1839. Promoted to major.
William P. Wyche	Sabine County Mounted Volunteers, 3rd Brigade, Texas Militia; November 4, 1838 - February 4, 1839.
William Foster Young	Mounted Gunmen, 1st Regiment, Texas Militia; September 14 - October 4, 1839. Young elected major on October 4.

* Indicates a company that was formed for Colonel Thomas J. Rusk's August Indian Campaign from Nacogdoches or Rusk's Winter 1838 Indian Campaign. Most of these units were disbanded immediately after the campaign.

APPENDIX B: COMPLETE MUSTER ROLL OF CAPTAIN ARNOLD'S COMPANY OF NACOGDOCHES VOLUNTEERS: MARCH - MAY 1836

Officers:	Date Enrolled:
Captain	
Hayden S. Arnold	March 6
1st Lieutenant	
Robert W. Smith	March 6
2nd Lieutenant	
Isiah Edwards	March 6
1st Sergeant	
Thomas D. Brooks	April 12
2nd Sergeant	
Samuel Leeper	March 6
1st Corporal	
William P. Kincannon	March 6
2nd Corporal	
Samuel Phillips	March 6

Privates:	Date Enrolled:
Howard W. Bailey	April 12
John T. Ballard	March 6
Seaborn Berry	March 6
James Edward Box	March 6
John Andrew Box	March 6
Nelson A. Box	March 6
Samuel Charles Box	May 8
Stillwell Box [1]	March 6
Thomas Griffin Box	March 6
Henry Mitchell Brewer	April 12
John W. Carpenter	March 6
John Francis Cheairs Jr.	May 6
Henry Larkin Chapman	April 12
Simon Contras	March 6
Thomas Donahoo	March 6
Daniel Doubt	
William T. H. Fitzamier	May 19
G. W. Gibbons	April 30
John V. D. Gossett [2]	March 6
John Crawford Grigsby	
Alfred M. Hallmark [1]	March 6
William Calvert Hallmark	
Elias Edley Hamilton	March 6
John W. Harvey	March 6
Samuel G. Holderness	May 19
Peter W. Holmes	March 15
Keeton McLemore Jones [1]	
William S. Kennard	March 6
James Madden [3]	
Philip C. Martin	
James McAnulty	May 19
John McCoy	March 6
John W. McHorse	March 6
Alexander McKenzie	May 8
Stephen McLinn	
George R. Mercer	March 6
James Mitchell	March 6
Jose Molino [4]	March 6
John Moss	March 6
Robert W. Nabors	May 6
William Nabors	March 6
Daniel Parker Jr.	
Dickerson Parker	
Samuel H. Perry	April 26
Leroy Pruett	March 7
Martin Pruett	March 7
William S. Rinard	May 6
David Rusk	April 6
William Turner Sadler	
William Bennett Scates	March 20
Stephen Franklin Sparks	April 12
Robert G. Stadler	May 12
John B. Trenary	March 6
Henry William Vardeman [1]	March 6
Jesse Walling	March 6
John C. Walling [1]	March 6
Madison Guess Whittaker	March 6
William F. Williams	March 6
Benjamin F. Wood	May 21
Elisha Pierce Wright	March 6
Archibald Yancy	May 7
John Yancy	March 6
John Swanson Yarbrough Sr. [5]	March 6
John Swanson Yarbrough Jr. [6]	March 6
Joseph Randolph Yarbrough [1]	March 6

1 Had enlisted before Battle of San Jacinto, but was left with sick and baggage at Harrisburg.
2 On furlough for 30 days as of April 17, 1836.
3 Discharged from company April 22 after battle.
4 Due to mistakes in spelling and in transcribing muster rolls, Jose Molino is variously listed as Hosea Malina Alexin or Hosea Maloney, Mexican.
5 Spelled Yarborough on San Jacinto rolls
6 Son of Yarbrough Sr. Not listed on any official rosters, as his name was likely considered a duplicate. Family records indicate that he was killed at San Jacinto.
NOTE: John Marvey is listed on some rosters for this unit, but this name does not appear in the *Muster Rolls of the Texas Revolution*. Probably was John Harvey listed twice by error.

APPENDIX C: THE CHEROKEE WAR OF EAST TEXAS
ROSTER OF KNOWN PARTICIPANTS AS OF JULY 15, 1839

Kelsey Harris Douglass	Brig. General	Leonard H. Mabbitt	Aide de Camp
Hugh B. McLeod	Adjutant Gen.	James H. Millroy	Aide de Camp
David Spangler Kaufman	Major	Palmer J. Pillans	Aide de Camp
Jacob Snively	Brig. Major	Benjamin B. Sturgess	Aide de Camp
David G. Burnet	Vice President	John Wortham (Major)	Quartermaster
Isaac Watts Burton	Commissioner	Albert Sidney Johnston	Sec. of War
James S. Mayfield	Commissioner	Martin Lacy	Indian Agent
Samuel Davis	Aide de Camp	William G. W. Jowers	Surgeon

DOUGLASS' VOLUNTEER REGIMENT – TEXAS MILITIA
Baley C. Walters   Major

CAPTAIN S. ADAMS' HOUSTON COUNTY RANGERS

John Wortham ...... Major	Charles Ellis	Marshall B. McIver
Solomon Adams ..... Capt.	Charles Erwin	John McLaughlin
Ira P. Ellis .... 1st Lt.	John Erwin	Albert A. Nelson
Henry Masters .... 2nd Lt.	Elijah Gossett	Avery Nolan
William J. B. Ford . 1st Sgt.	Lee C. Gossett	Henry Ovender
William D. F. Adams 2nd Sgt.	James M. Hall	Greenberry Pate
John Walker ..... 3rd Sgt.	John B. Hall	John Powers
PRIVATES:	William V. Hall	William Riley
John Adams	Daniel Hand	James R. Russell
Sephus Adams	Samuel Harrison	George L. Short
Edward Allbright	William D. Harrison	Ira Shute
Jacob Allbright	John Hartgrave	George M. Stewart
Alfred Benge	William Harvey	Abraham Stroud
John P. Barnett	Thomas Hayes	Philip Walker
James W. Brent	James B. Horten	William White
Joel Clapp	Alfred M. Liles	William W. Wilkinson
John E. Clapp	Jose de Marteres Maria	George Wolverton
Miles I. Eason	Simon Matthews	
Benjamin B. Ellis	Edry McCoy	

CAPTAIN J. E. BOX'S MOUNTED RANGERS

James Edward Box ... Capt.	Harrison Farmer	Lacy McKenzie
Daniel M. Crist .... 1st Lt.	Eli Faulkenberry	Jacob Morrow
Elijah B. Reneau. ... 2nd Lt.	William Frost	John Morton
Gibson Gastin ..... 1st Sgt.	Devereaux Gatewood	Payton Parker
PRIVATES:	Spencer Hobbs	William Perry
Thomas Berry	Levi Hopkins	Mark Roberts
Jeremiah Blackwell	Solomon Hopkins	George T. Slaughter
Benjamin Cannon	Samuel Huffer	John Smith
Stephen Crist	William Killian	William Smith
Richard C. Dixon	Levi Martin	Humphries Ussery
Arnold Evans	Daniel McKenzie	

CAPTAIN G. H. HARRISON'S MOUNTED GUNMEN

Greenberry H. Harrison Capt.	Nicholas Henry Darnell *	William L. Longstreet
PRIVATES:	John E. Dusenberry	William M. Love
William F. Allison	Richard Duty	Oliver Lund
Abram Anglin *	John Ewing	John Robbins
Roland William Box	John W. Harrison	James Ross
Asa Brigham	Sam Harrison	Wesley Selman *
Anderson Buffington *	Benjamin Highsmith *	Jeff Wallace *
John Crane	George E. Hunter	Samuel G. Wells
Stephen Crist	Joseph Jordan	George W. Wilson
Henry P. Crowson	Peterson Lloyd	

* Known participant not in service with the First Regiment. No complete roster available for Capt. Harrison's company. Partial roster from Republic of Texas audited and unpaid claims.

APPENDIX C: Cherokee War Participants (Continued)

CAPTAIN H. M. SMITH'S VOLUNTEER RANGERS

Henry Madison Smith Capt.
Albert G. Corbin . . . . 1st Lt.
Jackson War . . . . . . 2nd Lt.
William W. Wade. . 1st Sgt.
John F. Grigsby . . . 2nd Sgt.
John C. Snow . . . . . 3rd Sgt.
Jeremiah Ball . . . . . 4th Sgt.
Elijah H. Moore . . . 1st Cpl.
William Mayfield . 2nd Cpl.
J. W. Robertson . . . 3rd Cpl.
J. B. McDonald . . . 4th Cpl.
PRIVATES:
John Anderson
Durham Avant
William Avant
Samuel Baker
T. C. Barnes
William M. Berryhill
M. L. Boyd
George Box
Alfred Bright
Charles Brimmingham
Andrew J. Click

Henry C. Conner
William T. Davis
Morgan Egleson
Peter Elliott
Daniel Eskens
Elisha A. Evans
John A. Evans
G. W. Floyd
Henry Geough
Thomas Gower
John A. Harper
Benjamin C. Harrill
Samuel Huffer
John Hunter
John Jacobs
George Kimbro
Thomas Larkins
Mapers Lennix
Jesse H. Looney
William Loyd
Joseph Martin
L. H. Matthis
W. H. Matthis

David F. O'Kelly
George W. Payne
Z. F. Petty
Richard Pollard
John Pollitt
William A. Ravy
John Ridens
T. F. Rodden
John Rome
Samuel D. Sansom
William Saper
John Shepherd
John Smith
Conrad Snider
Thomas Spears
John Stokely
M. Tansell
John S. Thompson
James Triplett
Elisha Tubbs
Henry M. Vardeman
S. W. Vardeman
G. Xavier

CAPTAIN B. A. VANSICKLE'S MOUNTED VOLUNTEERS

Benjamin A. Vansickle Capt.
Hiram C. Vansickle . 1st Lt.
Green B. Hardwick 2nd Lt.
John D. Miller . . . . 1st Sgt.
PRIVATES:
Solomon Allbright
William Allison
Lewis Borkerdah
Samuel C. Box
James W. Brown
William Butler
William Calwell
Wily Calwell
Bird Carr
Charles Chevallier
William Connor
David Cook
William Crawson
Balis Edens
Darius H. Edens

John N. Elliott
Abraham Frizly
John Garceo
Samuel Gililland
John Griffin
John Gregg
John Crawford Grigsby
Daniel Harrison
Stephen Hatter
James Hill
Abel Hodges
George Isaacs
Leon Jones
James Kuykendahl
John Lennix
Robert Lennix
John Little
Micham Main
Jacob Masters
James McLean

Daniel Meredith
Samuel Miller
Joseph R. Moore
John Parker
James Patten
Samuel Patten
E. J. Pinkett
Edgar Pollitt
Clinton A. Rice
Ransom Rucker
Ruben R. Russell
Edwin Sims
Luther Smith
Charles Taylor
Peter Towns
Robert Walters
Alexander White
Leonard Houston Williams
Robert Williams
Thomas Williams

2ND BRIGADE, THIRD REGIMENT OF VOLUNTEERS – TEXAS MILITIA
STAFF:

Thomas Jefferson Rusk	Colonel	Edward B. Noble	Quartermaster
James Smith	Lt. Colonel	Alex McIves	Commissary
Elisha Clapp	Major	Dr. Lemuel B. Brown	Surgeon
William N. Dunnington	Adjutant Major	Dr. L. Martin	Surgeon
Ira Munson	Sergeant Major	James Carter	Captain, Spies

(Note: Captain Carter's spy company was formed after General Rusk's regiment left Nacogdoches, with the majority of his men pulled from the ranks of Captain Todd's company.)

CAPTAIN A. JORDAN'S MOUNTED RANGERS

Alexander Jordan .... Capt.
F. C. Haynie .... 1st Lt.
Russell Kelley .... 2nd Lt.
David Gage .... Sgt.
PRIVATES:
Edward Abshire
Elijah Alred
Henry Awalt
Thomas Berryhill
William Bruce
Joseph Buffington
Hesituah Charty
R. Chisum
A. Dill
Augustin Duncan
Alston Ferguson

Elijah Ferguson
John Ferguson
John Grace
Jackson Grayson
Henry Hilton
James Hutton
Thomas Jones
Andrew Jordan
Armstead Jordan
Samuel Jordan
Isaac Lemans
John Lollar
Thomas Maxwell
Matthew Mays
James McWilliams
Farris Montgomery

William Reagan
S. J. Sims
William T. Smith
H. J. Stackman
Hardy F. Stackman
Henry Stackman
G. W. Starr
Samuel R. Stephenson
Corbin Tansell
William W. Umsted
David Vanwinkle
William Vardeman
William Washburne
Francis Williams
William Williams
James Woodworth

CAPTAIN SANCHEZ'S MOUNTED GUNMEN

Captain:
Lewis Sanchez
1st Lieutenant:
Juan Monsola
Orderly Sergeant:
Santiago Rabia
Privates:
Francisco Accosta
Watkene Adomades
Lusino Anandas
Howard Bailey
Thomas Berryhill
Candelario

Henry Chapman
Santiago Comarche
Santiago Carro
Manuel Garcia
Manuel Gouteras
Francisco Lacerine
Cornelias Lopes
Feliciano Lopez
Sylvester Luna
Dolores Martinez
Juan Matto
Jose Maria Mendes
Jacinto Miganio

Jose Maria Monsola
Poular Monsola
Jose Maria Montes
Anastacio Mora
Maximo Salasar
David Sanchez
Ignacio Sanchez
Pedro Sanchez
Secusmoonda Sepulvado
James Solar
Berry Smith
William Smith
Incarnacion Wharres

CAPTAIN R. W. SMITH'S MOUNTED VOLUNTEERS

Robert W. Smith ..... Capt.
Stephen F. Sparks .. 1st Lt.
Daniel Weeks .... 2nd Lt.
Andrew Caddell ... 1st Sgt.
Henry C. Cook ... 2nd Sgt.
W. L. Song ...... 3rd Sgt.
S. A. Askew ...... 4th Sgt.
Robert W. Watkins 1st Cpl.
Eli G. Sparks .... 2nd Cpl.
Henry Rogers .... 3rd Cpl.
Benjamin F. Sills Bugleman
PRIVATES:
G. G. Alfred
Elijah Anderson
W. Barton
John Baskus
Isaac Bean
Robert Bean
Samuel M. Bean
S. L. Burns
William W. Burrows
Jeremiah D. Caddell
John Caddell
George W. Click
Ambrose Hulen Crain

Colby W. Crawford
Asa Dorsett
Calvin Eaton
Jesse F. Ellington
Malcolm Given
Archabald C. Graham
John F. Graham
Vincent Hamilton
Thomas Hawkins
Daniel Lacey
Joshua Leach
James D. Long
William Manor
George Martin
Alexander McIver
William McKaughn
Francis C. McKnight
James McKnight
Samuel A. McNutt
Penson Miles
Elijah Mosley
Kindred Henry Muse
William Nelson
J. G. Parker
Moses L. Patten

George Pottitt
John Henninger Reagan
Dimer W. Reaves
John Roark
Russell Roark
R. M. Roark
John Rowan
Martin Rugmupff
Henry Sably
James S. Shanks
Alfred Sims
M. Sims
Thomas Sims
William Sims
David Skelton
James H. Sparks
H. Stovall
J. B. Thacker
Leander Erwin Tipps
Benjamin Franklin Whitaker
Madison Guess Whitaker
Samuel W. Wilds
Owen C. Williams
Maston Windsor
James S. Windsor

APPENDIX C: Cherokee War Participants (Continued) 301

CAPTAIN P. TIPPS' MOUNTED VOLUNTEERS

Peter Tipps .... Capt.	William Davis	Thomas Perry
George K. Black ... 1st Lt.	Berry L. Dunkley	Charles L. Price
James W. Cleveland 2nd Lt.	William Hart	George Riddle
N. Adolphus Sterne 1st Sgt.	John B. Holman	Samuel Rodgers
Charles N. Bell ... 2nd Sgt.	Henry Jacobs	Dr. Henry M. Rogers
Charles S. Taylor . 3rd Sgt.	James Jacobs	John Steward
PRIVATES:	R. L. Lance	William W. Taylor
Henry P. Barron	J. C. Lane	Alfred G. Walling
Bennett Blake	Robert M. Long	Zeke Walling
J. M. Bradshaw	John B. Martin	James R. Wilehart
John Caddell	James McAnulty	Jason Williams
John Caruthers	Thomas T. McIver	William F. Williams
Charles Chevaillier	John B. Murray	Zach F. Worley
John Chisolm	Richard Parmalee	John Wright
William Chisolm	Robert S. Patterson	Archabald Yancy
William H. Crutchir	R. H. Penney	

CAPTAIN J. TODD'S MOUNTED VOLUNTEERS

Jackson Todd .... Capt.	S. B. Eubanks	Walter Murray
Isham Chisum ..... 1st Lt.	S. D. Fulton	J. L. Patilla
John C. Walling .. 2nd Lt.	James Gilliland	Barnard Pantallion
Isham R. Chisum .. 1st Sgt.	Isaac Hamby	L. L. Rogers
Presly M. Walling . 2nd Sgt.	Joshua B. Hanks	Lewis Rose
James R. Goodin .. 3rd Sgt.	Blackstone Hardiman	John Rowan
Bradford Shorter .. 4th Sgt.	Rinaldo Hotchkis	Milton Rowan
PRIVATES:	William F. Humberson	David Rusk
William Bell	Galland Jones	L. L. Shroder
John F. Brown	John Kryson	James Simpson
Robert P. Brown	Jacob Lewis	John M. Sullivan
Isaac M. Brimberry	F. G. Limons	John S. Thorn
William M. Bruce	George Long	Leo M. Thorn
John C. Childers	George W. Martin	W. M. Tigner
Claiborne Chisum	Neil Martin	Asa Walling
Elijah Chisum	A. McAlpin	Benjamin White
Madison Chisum	Thomas McClure	Elbert L. Williams
Matthew Colewell	R. B. Merritt	Jamail Wilson
Samuel L. Davis	George H. Millikin	William N. Wingfield
John Dorsett	Lorenzo M. Mills	George H. Wright
James H. Durst	John C. Morrison	Louis L. Wright
Gibson J. Dyer	David Muckleroy	John S. Yarbrough
R. Eubanks	Martin Murchison	

3RD BRIGADE, THIRD REGIMENT OF VOLUNTEERS – TEXAS MILITIA
STAFF:

Willis H. Landrum	Colonel	Thomas Haugh	Sergeant Major
Moses L. Roberts	Lt. Col.	Robert O. Lusk	Quartermaster
James M. Thompson	Major	Dr. John M. Hansford	Surgeon
George English	Adjutant Major	Dr. J. R. Robertson	Surgeon

(Note: Colonel Landrum's Mounted Regiment arrived at Camp Johnston on July 14, 1839, and was subsequently detached to march up the west side of the Neches River. His regiment therefore missed directly fighting in the Battle of the Neches on July 15-16, 1839.)

APPENDIX C: Cherokee War Participants (Continued)

CAPTAIN J. INMAN'S HARRISON/SHELBY COUNTY COMPANY

John Inman .... Capt.
R. B. English ...... 1st Lt.
Edward A. Merchant 2nd Lt.
R. S. Biggers ...... 1st Sgt.
PRIVATES:
James Alford
William Arnold
George A. Ashabrane
Daniel Brown
James Brown
Joseph Butler
H. B. Cannon
John Choat
Levi Cole
James T. Denton
George H. Duncan
F. M. Fellows
Alfred A. George
Joseph G. Goodbread
G. L. Graham
James M. Graham

Sherman Grosviner
William H. Hart
Samuel C. Heinight
Samuel C. Henderson
Elijah Hill
James Hinton
John Howard
Hiram Inman *
John H. Inman *
Thomas Jester
Thomas P. Kennedy
Charles Lawden
Aman Lewellen
Aaron Lowry
John Lowry
Andrew Martin
John Mason
Thomas P. Meers
Frederic H. Miller
M. B. Phillips
R. E. Price

Augustus Ryan
Evan Sanford
Snider Sanford
William T. Scott
Benjamin F. Smith
Jackson Smith
Bently Stewart
Leander Truett
William Turbin
James B. Tutt
L. D. Vance
Masan M. Vann
John Vanriper
James M. Vaughn
Zachariah C. Walker
L. C. Wharton
W. T. White
William Winn
John Wood
Soloman Wood

* *Transferred in from Captain Garrison's company.*

CAPTAIN J. MCKIM'S SABINE COUNTY COMPANY

James McKim .... Capt.
George W. Slaughter 1st Lt.
William H. Ridgeway 2nd Lt.
J. H. Ridgeway .... 1st Sgt.
A. B. Capps ...... 2nd Sgt.
William Payne .... 3rd Sgt.
PRIVATES:
P. W. Barber
T. M. Brown
J. Buchannon
William B. Burks
Phillip Burrow
J. B. Cameron
D. Carpenter
John D. Cathey
Frank F. Chaney
J. R. Chatham
William R. Coner
James A. Currie
Richard Currie
David Damewood

H. B. Damewood
J. W. Damewood
William Donaho
John Easley
C. Fitzpatrick
B. Foster
J. F. Gomer
M. Goff
William J. Gomley
O. P. Hains
E. R. Harris
William Harris
William D. Harris
W. Hester
James Horton
S. Horton
Jackson Hudson
David Huffman
Isaac Ivey
Curtis M. Jackson
H. A. Kendal

J. Knight
R. S. Love
John Marshall
Job Mason
F. McLamore
John H. McRey
G. W. Milton
A. Montgomery
P. C. Ragsdale
George Reaves
Samuel M. Slaughter
John Sterling
H. A. Taylor
William P. Thompson
H. V. Towner
William H. Vories
A. J. Wait
B. F. Weathers
F. M. Weathers
James W. Williams

CAPTAIN W. KIMBRO'S SAN AUGUSTINE COUNTY COMPANY

William Kimbro ..... Capt.
William D. Ratcliff .. 1st Lt.
Joseph M. Burleson 2nd Lt.
L. A. Temple ..... 1st Sgt.
PRIVATES:
John Blair
Alan V. Braden

Hiram Brown
Samuel T. Burns
J. Cartwright
William H. Castleberry
Armstead Chumney
R. Davidson
S. L. Davidson

H. Davies
G. Davis
William C. Duffield
W. D. Ewing
William Fisher
John Salmon Ford
G. L. Foreman

APPENDIX C: Cherokee War Participants (Continued) 303

CAPTAIN W. KIMBRO'S COMPANY (Cont.)

John B. Foreman
A. G. Frazier
B. Fuller
D. W. Gilbert
John A. Gilbreath
D. G. Griggs
Calvin Hamilton
J. R. Hanks
Wiley Hanks
Amos Harris
J. M. Harris
Travis Harris
D. Hays
B. D. Hendrick
Thomas Hendrick
James Higgins
John Hunt

Samuel M. Hyde
Curtis Jesup
Samuel Jordan
W. B. Kelly
Isaac Kendrick
G. W. Lakey
William Lakey
Toles Landus
Walter P. Lane
E. W. Lucas
James Madden
James Marshall
J. A. Martin
M. McCabe
Milton Moore
Henry Morgan
Thomas Payne

P. O. Pitman
R. Platt
Amos Roark
Solomon Rule
C. R. Sassamon
L. D. Simmons
William R. Scurrie
B. Smith
William Thompson
J. B. Wafford
M. D. Wafford
A. L. Wilson
John A. Winn
Charles Worthington
Levi York

CAPTAIN M. GARRISON'S SHELBY COUNTY COMPANY

Mitchell Garrison .... Capt.
Thomas Haley ..... 1st Lt.
Charles L. Haley .. 2nd Lt.
William Cook ..... 1st Sgt.
PRIVATES:
Thomas G. Anderson
Joseph Ashton
John Boulden
Andstatia Carr
Arthur A. Clingman
William J. Crain
John Crain
Joseph Dial
W. G. Dial
George English *
Joshua D. English
T. M. Ewell
Allen Haley

John R. Haley
John Haley Jr.
S. N. Hall
John M. Hansford *
John Harden
Daniel Hasel
Zachus Hasel
Thomas Haugh *
A. W. O. Hicks
James M. Hooper
William M. Hooper
Thomas Jackson
William Jacobs
Thomas James
R. A. Jordan
Joseph King
J. A. McFarland **
James S. W. Merchant

C. L. Main
R. E. Mayfield
G. L. Moore
Robert Palmer
Dickerson Parker
John Parker
William Porter
J. E. Pugh
S. R. Richardson
Everett Ritter
Andres Roches
S. S. Runnels
William G. Runnels
John Shoemaker
Peter Stockman
William C. Vaun
J. W. Whitaker
Isaac Wisehart

* Promoted into Colonel Landrum's Command Staff.   ** Later transferred into Captain Todd's Company.

FIRST REGIMENT OF INFANTRY – TEXAS ARMY

GENERAL STAFF:
Edward Burleson   Colonel
William S. Fisher   Lt. Col.
William Jefferson Jones   Major
William D. Houghton   1st Lt.
Benjamin B. Sturgess   Quartermaster
Dr. Shields Booker   Surgeon
Dr. Richard Cochran   Ast. Surgeon

COMPANY A: CAPTAIN W. T. SADLER

William T. Sadler ..... Capt.
Duncan C. Ogden . 1st Lt.[1]
Collier C. Hornsby 2nd Lt.[1]
Peter Flanley .... 1st Sgt.[2]
Lewis Reaves ... 2nd Sgt.[2]
John Carroll .... 1st Corp.[2]
John J. Johnson .. 2nd Corp.[2]
PRIVATES:
William Benson[3]
Thomas Casey[3]
John Cavitt[3]
Joseph Cecil[3]
Thomas D. Clark[3]
John Dennison[2,3]
William Dial[2,3]
Joseph Dubignon[2]
John Hamrick[2]
Henry Judd[2]

CAPTAIN SADLER'S COMPANY A (Cont.)

Ross B. Jelkyl [2]
James Martin [2]
Alex McDonald [2]
Stephen A. McLeary [3]
Andrew Moore [3]
John P. Moseley [2]
James H. Pollard [2]
Francis Rosendale [2]
Thomas Simpson [3]
Ephraim Stanberry [2,3]

Charles Stroud [3]
William Waterson [2]
James Wyatt [3]

(THIS ROSTER BASED ON AUTHOR'S COMPILATION.)
[1] Known First Regiment participant of Cherokee War.
[2] Previously attached to Company C under Captain Kennymore until April 30, 1839.

Not listed on any other existing company's muster roll at this time.
[3] Records show this man to have been enlisted in the First Regiment during this period and to have been part of Company A when temporarily commanded by Captain Clendenin in late 1839.

COMPANY B: CAPTAIN A. CLENDENIN

Adam Clendenin .... Capt.
Edward A. Thompson 1st Lt.
James M. Alexander 2nd Lt.
Mathew McGovern 1st Sgt.
James Alston .... 2nd Sgt.
William Walker ... 3rd Sgt.
Richard Nixon ... 4th Sgt.
John J. Johnson ... 1st Cpl.
Casper Lewiston.. 2nd Cpl.
Robert Morris.... 3rd Cpl.
William Berry .... 4th Cpl.
PRIVATES:

Mathew Anderson
John Cassidy
Michael Daily
Henry S. Day
Cornelius Diggons
Joseph Dubignon
Oliver Farnsworth
William Gray
Henry Hays
Thomas Harrison
John Horan
Horace H. Houghton

John Humrich
M. Henry Judd
William Kelly
James H. Pollard
William Redfield
John Riley
John Shaw
Daniel Smith
Humphrey Sullivan
George Wilburton
(NO COMPLETE ROSTER AVAILABLE.)

CAPTAIN PLACIDO'S TONKAWA BRAVES

Twenty-four of Chief Placido's Tonkawa Indian braves formed a scouting company, riding and fighting with Colonel Burleson's regular army during the Cherokee War. No roster available.

COMPANY C: CAPTAIN S. W. JORDAN

Samuel W. Jordan ... Capt.
Wm. N. Dunnington 1st Lt.
John Brown ..... 2nd Lt.
Washington Stephens . Sgt.
Henry Carhart ...... Sgt.
William Hill .... Sgt.
Louis Neil .... Sgt.
Washington Beatty .. Cpl.
William Clements ... Cpl.
PRIVATES:
Charles S. Anderson
Alexander Bell
James Bird
Abraham Bradley
Alfred M. Cooper

Peter F. Craft
Michael Dunn
Louis Dunning
Michael Fanning
John Hare
John Harper
John Harris
Jacob Hoodle
Zephelin Islin
Augustus Kemper
James Kimberly
John Lewis
John Martin
John McDonald
David Miller

George W. Miller
Joseph W. Mott
William Oliver
John Robinson
Adolphus Rousette
William Scott
Harrison Simpson
Christopher Trouts
Martin Tutts
William Tyndall
James Tweed
James White
Mark Wilks
Joseph B. Young
Samuel Young

COMPANY D: CAPTAIN G. T. HOWARD

George T. Howard ...Capt.
Samuel B. Carson .. 1st Lt.
John S. Sutton ... 2nd Lt.
William S. Johnson 1st Sgt.
Eli Phillips ..... 2nd Sgt.
Millard M. Parkerson 3rd Sgt.

Townsend Gardner 4th Sgt.
Phillip Lyons .... 1st Cpl.
Ferdinand Booker 2nd Cpl.
PRIVATES:
James Ball
William Barker

James Burk
Daniel Burns
William Joseph Campbell
James Castillo
Stephen Cook
Martin Coyle

APPENDIX C: Cherokee War Participants (Continued) 305

CAPTAIN HOWARD'S COMPANY D (Cont.)

W. C. N. Creed
John Day
John Downes
Horatio N. Eldridge
James Eldridge
John Garrett
Nehemiah Hauckenbury
Joshua Hudson
George Jenkins
Jesse Jones
Lewis Joseph

R. Knight
George Leonard
Robert P. Little
J. W. McCormack
William McKain
Lewis C. Morrison
Charles Mossenton
Richard D. Newman
John O'Neal
James Parker
John R. Richardson

Francis Riley
John Taite Smith
John Snider
William Stewart
William Taylor
William Thompson
William Wallace
James Warmsley
John A. Wimble

VOLUNTEER REGIMENT ALSO UNDER COLONEL BURLESON'S COMMAND
Lt. Col. Devereaux Jerome Woodlief   Commanding Officer

CAPTAIN M. B. LEWIS' VOLUNTEERS

Mark B. Lewis ...... Capt.
A. L. McCoy ...... 1st Lt.
J. S. Jones .... 2nd Lt.
J. Woodward ..... 1st Sgt.
J. Artoff .... 2nd Sgt.
H. F. Hazenthine. . 3rd Sgt.
James Horie ..... 4th Sgt.
William Cockburn 1st Cpl.
John N. Webster 2nd Cpl.
PRIVATES:
A. Adams
J. L. Adams
W. M. Adams
J. S. Anderson
J. H. Baker
William Baker
William M. Bifset
Frank Bissaro
M. Blood
Ambrose H. Boles
W. S. Brandenbush
John Brian
J. Brian
H. Cambray
A. Campbell
Pedro Cantrero
Simon Casbacon
J. J. Caskey
R. W. Cecil
William Chambers
C. H. Chevallier
J. S. Claiborne
William Coltron

Alton A. Crane
John Davis
Robert Deludy
James Doherty
Thomas Drumgold
Maria Durano
Jacob Ellis
Lawrence Erbil
Perry Fielson
John Flazer
Olmar Frederick
Harvey Garms
Emil Girard
Frank Girard
George Graddel
D. Harper
James Hawthorne
Jose Maria Hermes
Thomas Hernandez
H. C. Holmes
Ratcliffe Hudson
D. G. Humblin
William Jergot
Charles Johnson
John Kerackner
George Kesnan
William Kresinka
Casper Leger
James Lowe
J. B. Marshall
Frederick Marter
J. P. Mayfield
R. S. Mayfield

William McKenzie
J. B. McKernen
Thomas McLaughlin
Francis Milheisler
William Oltman
James S. Phinneas
Ramon Piedas
C. J. F. Prales
Edward S. Ratcliffe
C. Reid
W. H. Reid
C. C. Rhodes
James Rhohm
M. C. Rountree
John Schneider
Andrew Scott
George Scott
Abraham Smith
J. M. Smith
R. Steel
Floyd Stillman
B. O. Stout
John Study
John Stumpskie
Wabria Taierte
Jeremiah Tarbon
Louis Thurman
Carlos Velasquez
A. Wade
W. D. Walk
J. B. Williams
J. H. Williams

CAPTAIN J. P. OWNBY'S VOLUNTEERS

James P. Ownby .... Capt.
W. P. Woodhouse .. 1st Lt.
Daniel Murphy ... 2nd Lt.
Hanibal A. Low ... 1st Sgt.
Harvey Homan .. 2nd Sgt.
Kirkman Green ... 3rd Sgt.
R. H. Waddell .... 4th Sgt.
John Saunders .. 1st Cpl.
John Hilbert .... 2nd Cpl.
James Lindsay ... 3rd Cpl.
John Robinson ... 4th Cpl.

PRIVATES:
Joseph Artoff
George Atkinson
J. G. Barrett
James Boyle
Isaac Brane
J. F. Butler
E. S. Cocran
George Cooke
Richard Copeland
W. B. Craddock
Samuel Crogran
Samuel Crooks
Horatio Cunningham
John Daniels
Edward Daley
Henry Dibble
W. P. Dikeman
Richard Dillon
James Edgy
James M. Everett
Fidel Faholser
William Findley
Robert Follett
Alexander Frazer
W. Rhea Gillmer (surgeon)
Moses Hand
B. C. F. Harrell
James Hays
Samuel Haynes
William Horsler
Francis Hughes (surgeon)
William Johnson
Francis Jones
W. H. Kennedy
A. D. Kilker
James King
Francis Labrick
John Lafayette
J. C. Lockhart
E. B. Lockridge
John Lysaught
W. Mail
Hugh Mathewson
M. McCartney
J. C. McDermott
Daniel McKay
N. McRaney
James Moore
David Morrison
C. A. Ogsbury
J. H. Padget
William Rayhouse
Alexander Reiley
Henry Rinehart
Thomas Russell
R. G. Saunders
John Talbot
E. B. Thomas
T. J. Vitch
William D. Walker
F. Warnicke
J. D. Watkins
Thomas J. Watkins
T. K. Whaler
George Willman
E. Woodruff

CAPTAIN J. B. DENTON'S COMPANY OF MOUNTED VOLUNTEERS

John B. Denton ...... Capt.
Edward Hunter .... 1st Lt.
John D. Bloodworth 2nd Lt.
Thomas R. Wilson . 1st Sgt.
Gilbert Reagan ... 2nd Sgt.
Edward West ..... 3rd Sgt.
PRIVATES:
Samuel Borten
John Brewer
William Brinten
J. M. Buchannon
James Burn
William Crowder
Barshot Feguns
A. N. Graham
J. N. Gray
Robert Haley
William C. Hamilton
J. C. Hart
H. B. Hutchinson
Andrew Jackson Fowler
John N. King
W. C. Lunney
John H. Matthis
James M. Patten
A. J. Price
H. S. Procter
William B. Stout
J. J. Venning
Leory Venning
B. Washbourn

SOURCES FOR CHEROKEE WAR ROSTERS:

Each roster was compiled from muster roll and pay roll records furnished courtesy of the Archives and Information Services Division of the Texas State Library. Author has attempted to record names as accurately as possible, but these documents were generally handwritten with poor penmanship and frequently misspelled names. No guarantee is made as to complete accuracy of this compilation, but it is hoped that this effort will assist others who are interested in further researching the Cherokee campaign.

For the First Regiment General Staff and the companies of *Captains William T. Sadler, Adam Clendenin, Samuel W. Jordan* and *George T. Howard*, the key source was the Daughters of the Republic of Texas' *Defenders of the Republic of Texas, Volume I* (edited by Karen R. Thompson). No muster roll for Sadler's army company is known to exist. Roll presented here constructed by author (see notes previously listed).

APPENDIX D:
TEXAS LAND RECORDS OF WILLIAM TURNER SADLER
Source: General Land Office of Texas

Class:	First Class Headright
Certificate #:	246/345 (Duplicate of # 492)
Certificate Date:	March 23, 1840
Issued By:	Commissioner of the General Land Office
Assigned To:	Wm T. Sadler in July 1835 by Severo Arocha
Acres Granted:	1/3 League
Survey Date:	October 26, 1857 for 1,460 acres
Located in:	Anderson County
Patented:	To William T. Sadler on March 27, 1858
Patent Number:	929

Class:	First Class Headright
Certificate #:	34/57 (Triplicate of Original # 26) Triplicate Copy issued by Commissioner of General Land Office
Certificate Date:	December 22, 1838
Acres Granted:	One League and One Labor
Original Survey:	February 8-9, 1838 of 3,552.66 acres
Secondary Survey:	January 12, 1897 of 977.86 acres
Located in:	Present Anderson County
Patented:	To William T. Sadler on January 16, 1878
Patent Number:	356

Class:	Donation Land Grant
Certificate #:	713
Granted for:	Having Fought at the Battle of San Jacinto
Certificate Date:	December 22, 1838
Issued By:	Secretary of War Albert S. Johnston
Acres Granted:	640

Survey Date:	September 3, 1847
Located in:	Anderson and Houston counties
Patented:	To William T. Sadler on April 14, 1848
Patent Number:	85

Class:	Bounty Land Grant
Certificate #:	6020
Granted for:	Service in Army of Republic of Texas for period of March 6 - May 30, 1836
Certificate Date:	December 22, 1838
Issued By:	Secretary of War Albert S. Johnston
Acres Granted:	320
Survey Date:	March 6, 1844
Located in:	Anderson and Houston counties
Patented:	To William T. Sadler on February 10, 1846
Patent Number:	212

Class:	Donation Land Grant
Certificate #:	612
Granted for:	Surviving Soldiers of the Texas Revolution
Certificate Date:	August 17, 1881
Issued By:	Commissioner of the General Land Office
Acres Granted:	1,280
Survey Date:	January 10, 1882
Located in:	Mason County
Transferred:	By William T. Sadler's attorney (Stephen H. Darden) to Ben F. Gooch and W. P. Lockhart on November 7, 1881
Patent Number:	85

APPENDIX E: *The Sadler Family In Lincoln County, North Carolina*

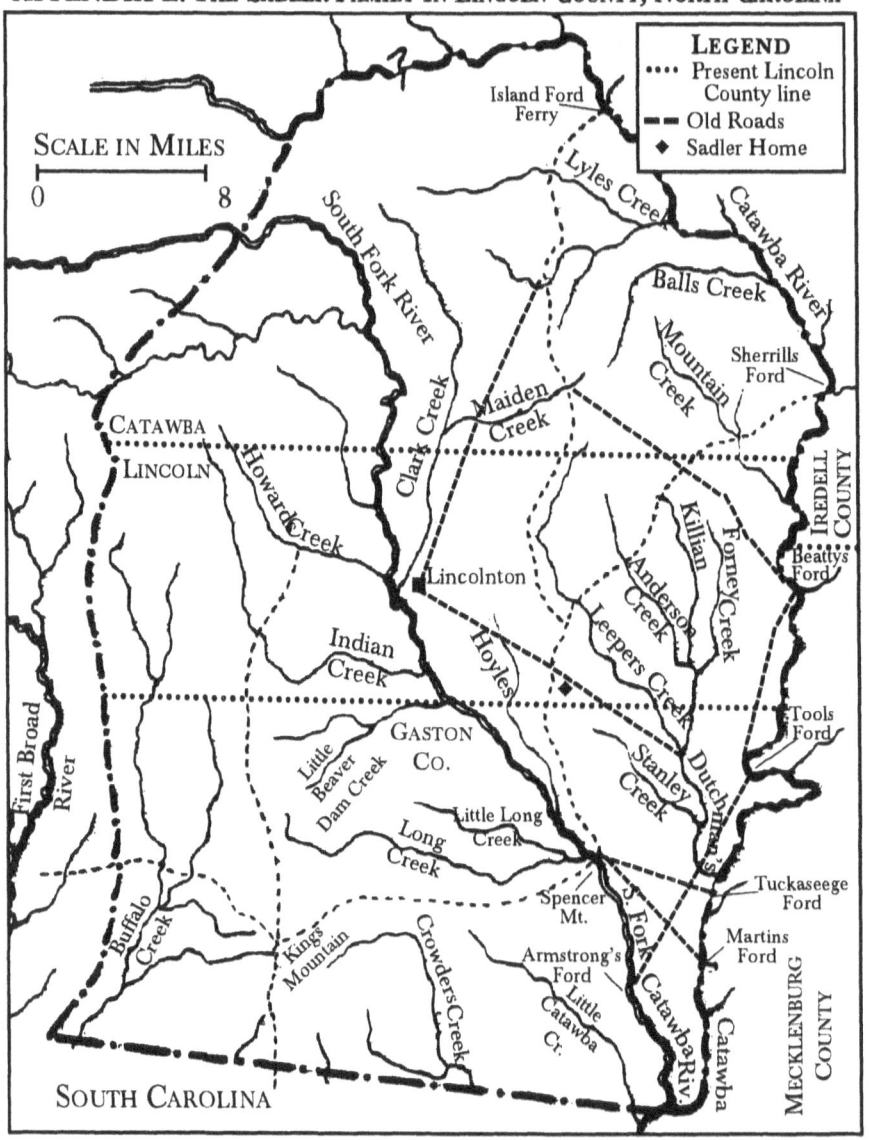

William T. Sadler was born in Lincoln County, North Carolina on July 27, 1797, and lived in this area until his family moved to Georgia in 1818. His father, Nathaniel Milton Sadler, owned property west of the Catawba River near the present southern border of the county. Originally extending to the border of South Carolina, Lincoln County was reduced significantly in 1846 by the creation of present Gaston County.

A study of the Court of Pleas and Quarter Sessions for early Lincoln County provides some interesting insight into the area where the Sadlers lived upon

APPENDIX E: Sadler Family In North Carolina (Continued) 309

moving from Virginia. By all appearances, Nathaniel Sadler and his family lived in a hilly area just north of the present Lincoln and Gaston county lines. His property lay at the origination point of one of the early roads, which typically ran toward a crossing point (or ford) in the local creeks and rivers.

Some of the major Catawba River crossings on the eastern side of Lincoln County were Beattys Ford, Island Ford, Sherrills Ford, Tools Ford, and Tuckaseege Ford. One of the major roads that led southwesterly to Armstrong's Ford, on the South Fork of the Catawba in present Gaston County, North Carolina, originated at the top of a stoney hill on Sadler's property. This hill was then called Mt. Pleasant or sometimes Stoney Knob. Neither of these names is currently used and the area is now known as Little Mountain. Another fork of the road from Sadler's hill led to Hunt's Ford on Dutchman's Creek. Yet another fork led from Martins Ford Ferry to Sadler's, and from there into Lincolnton.

Nathaniel's uncle, Henry Sadler, lived farther south in Lincoln County, near Armstrong's Ford. Here Henry was known since the 1790s to have owned and operated a grist and sawmill known as Sadler's Mill alongside the waters of the South Fork. Henry's oldest son, Jeremiah Sadler, was a Constable of Lincoln County as of 1812.

The early county roads were patrolled, maintained and protected by the local citizens as ordered by the court. Records for April 1796 show that Nathaniel Sadler, Benjamin Pucket, James Abernathy, Samuel Carman and Sterling Abernathy were ordered to serve as Patrollers in Captain John Walker's District for one year.

In October 1805, Nathaniel was given a deed of sale by the court for eighty-five acres purchased from Nathan Abernathy on August 20, 1803, as proved by his brother William Rose. He took up residence in a nearby old stone house previously owned by James Nelson. In April 1805, Nathaniel, his brother William Rose Sadler, Robert Johnston, Alexander Baldridge, George Abernathy, and Drury Kimbol were ordered to serve as Patrolers in Captain Beal's Company for one year's period. New overseers were appointed each year to maintain the roads.

Court of pleas records for April 1807 record the results of Case # 60: Nathaniel Sadler vs. Reverend Humphrey Hunter as "Jury sworn & charged find there were no payments nor setoffs & that the Defendant owes & detains $84 equal in value to L42 currency to the Plaintiff's damage L3.1.7 & 6d costs." In July 1808, the court also recorded a deed of sale from William R. Sadler to Nathaniel Sadler for 126 acres, dated November 13, 1806.

The lure of cheap land prices no doubt compelled most of the Sadlers to move on to Georgia, Missouri and elsewhere over the next twenty years. There are, however, some Sadler descendants still living in this same area of Lincoln and Gaston counties. There is also still a 1.3-mile stretch of Sadler Road that originates from the Mount Zion Church Road in southern Lincoln County and terminates into Alexis Road in northern Gaston County.

Of interest to Sadler family genealogists are the old tombstones in the nearby Stanley, North Carolina, cemetery bordering the Christ's Lutheran Church and Revival Tabernacle Church on Highway 27. The ten Sadler family members buried here are in two distinctly separated family plots. The first is that of J. A. Sadler and the other is that of Henry Sadler. By my best estimation, these two families were both descendants of John Sadler, son of the Henry Sadler who was Nathaniel Milton Sadler's uncle.

That the Sadlers still living in the area of Sadler Road descend from John Sadler is based on interviews with these living Sadlers, research of Lincoln and Gaston County census information, court records, cemetery marker inscriptions, and information in Joan Smola's *Sadler/Saddler Family* book. John Sadler was born in 1776 or 1777 in Brunswick County, Virginia, the second son of Henry and Mary Scarboro Sadler. Henry purchased the mill and land on Killian's Creek in Lincoln County in 1791 and would live in this area until he and his wife both passed away in October 1824.

Census records for 1800-1820 show a large number of Sadlers living in Lincoln County. There were the families of Nathaniel Milton Sadler Sr., his brother William Rose Sadler Sr., another brother, Thomas Sadler III, and a fourth brother, Anderson Sadler. Nathaniel's uncle Henry and his children composed the other bunch of Sadlers in the county during this time. Several of Henry's boys (Zachariah, Jeremiah, James and John) had started raising their own families in separate households before their father's death.

From Nathaniel Milton's branch, all the families moved elsewhere by 1830 except for his brother Thomas Sadler III. Thomas maried Lucy Hansell/Williams and they had two daughters and a son named Merrit, whose wife's name was Mamie. After the death of Henry and Mary Sadler in 1824, all of their children were known to have married and moved on to Missouri and other states.

The exception is John Sadler, whose life's course has remained largely unknown. According to page 438 of the *Sadler/Saddler Family* book, John was born about 1777 and died before October 1824. This would have made him about forty-three at the time of the 1820 census, which shows a John Sadler, in Lincoln County between the age of 26-45, listed on the same page as father Henry and brother Jeremiah's families.

In the 1830 census, John is not shown. There is, however, a Widow Sadler with six young children. In 1840, the Widow Sadler is named as Susan Sadler and five of her children are still living with her. Two of these children were girls (Mary, eighteen, and Elizabeth, sixteen); the other three are boys between the ages of fifteen and thirty. They were named James Alexander, Henry (after John's father) and George.

Daughter Mary Sadler was married to William Nance, and in 1880 they were still living in Lincoln County with three of their older children and Mary's sister, Elizabeth Sadler. Elizabeth lists Virginia as her parents' place of birth. The youngest of John and Susan Sadler's boys died at the early age of twenty-three and is buried in Stanley, NC. George Sadler was born about January 19, 1824, and died October 12, 1847.

The middle son of John and Susan was Henry Sadler, who was born on December 16, 1819 and died on November 15, 1869. His wife, Susan A. Sadler, was born on October 25, 1828, and died on May 8, 1905 at seventy-six years of age. The 1850 Gaston County cenus shows Henry and Susan to have two daughters: Mary E. at two years of age and Susan Sadler at two months of age. Also living with thirty-year-old Henry at this time was his sixty-one-year-old mother and twenty-two-year-old sister Elizabeth. Henry's agricultural schedule showed him to have seventy acres of improved land, three hundred

APPENDIX E: *Sadler Family In North Carolina (Continued)*

This old wood frame house still stands on Sadler Road in Lincoln County, North Carolina, on the property of Kenneth and Lucille Sadler. It was built by their parents, Bill and Julie Sadler, in the late 1800s. These Sadlers appear to descend from the Henry Sadler who was an uncle to William T. Sadler's father. Author's collection.

acres unimproved land, two horses, fourteen cows, seven sheep, twenty swine, and a sizable quantity of corn, wheat, cotton, oats, potatoes, beef, bee's wax, butter, hay and wool. After 1850, Henry and Susan had three more boys, two of whom died very young. John F. Sadler was born December 28, 1854 and died at the age of one on November 13, 1855. Miles A. Sadler was born September 11, 1856, and died on August 8, 1857. The only boy to survive childhood was James H. Sadler, who was born November 4, 1858 and died on March 15, 1910. All three of these boys are buried alongside Henry and Susan in the Stanley cemetery.

The oldest son of John and Susan Sadler left behind the descendants who still reside in this area of North Carolina. James Alexander "Alex" Sadler was born in Lincoln County on November 8, 1817, and died on August 26, 1899. He and his wife, Sarah H. Sadler (born April 2, 1819 and died on December 14, 1902), are also buried in the Stanley cemetery. According to census records and Lelia Sadler Long, James and Sarah Sadler had ten known children: John Michael (born on October 24, 1847 and died in November 1894); Henry (born 1848); Mary Ann (born 1849); Laney (born 1850, married Mr. Queen and lived in Lowell, NC); Belzia (born 1852 and died on Sadler land); Sarah L. (born October 10, 1853, and died unmarried on February 18, 1889, buried beside her parents); William A. Sadler (born on April 4, 1856 and died on April 14, 1933); Fannie (born 1857); George (born 1858); and Rachel (born 1860 and married John Barnett).

Of Alex Sadler's boys, little is known of Henry Sadler's descendants. He and his wife, Catherine R. Sadler (born 1852), settled in Lincoln County on their own farm slightly farther south in northern Gaston County, NC. By 1880, they had at least three daughters: Corna (born 1873); Eunice (born 1874); and Leckie B. Sadler (born August 10, 1879 and died April 26, 1922). Henry, Catherina and younger daughter Leckie are all buried in adjoining plots in the Stanley cemetery. There is a twenty-year-old Annie Sadler shown on Gaston County's 1900 census who is probably another daughter of Henry and Catherine.

The youngest boy of James and Sarah Sadler apparently lived long enough to inherit the family's six-hundred-acre farm. William A. "Bill" and wife Julie Helderman Sadler (born on May 25, 1871 and died on September 7, 1938) are buried in the Mount Zion cemetery close to their property. Bill and Julie are survived by two of their children who still live together on Sadler Road: Kenneth and Lucille Sadler (who had a twin brother named John). According to Kenneth (eighty-two in 1997) and his sister, the property their home resides upon was that of their grandparents. The old wooden Sadler home that still stands on the property was constructed by their grandparents upon enormous rock cornerstones which were dragged up from the nearby creekbed by mules.

The oldest son of James and Sarah Sadler died fairly young at forty-seven, but left behind another descendant who still lives in this area. John Michael Sadler married Mary E. McClure, who was born on April 14, 1870, and died on May 31, 1943. Both are buried at the Mount Zion Church cemetery. Mary remarried a Ballard after John's death. John Michael and Mary Sadler had two children: Katherine Elizabeth "Katie" Sadler, who married a Marlow; and Edgar Alexander Sadler, who was born on March 5, 1891, and died on May 11, 1987.

His wife, Virgie Lelia Hager Sadler, was born on June 3, 1888, and died on April 18, 1944. This couple had four children: Edith Anna Sadler White (who passed away during the summer of 1997); Charles E. Sadler; Lelia Sadler (born in 1920); and David Vance Sadler (who passed away in 1978). Lelia Sadler married Cull Long and they acquired property from one of her relatives just south of the Gaston/Lincoln County line. Mrs. Long is active in the Mount Zion Church near Sadler Road and was very helpful in compiling this background on the North Carolina Sadlers of Lincoln and Gaston counties.

APPENDIX F:
DESCENDANTS OF WILLIAM TURNER SADLER

Sources: Serving as a basis point was the book *Sadler/Saddler Family: A Record of the Family and the Descendants of Thomas Sadler Sr. (1720-1796) and Rebeccah Featherston (1722-1796/99) of Brunswick County, Virginia*, 145-94, compiled by Joan Coker Smola, 1994. Patrick D. Sadler and JoAnn Day Freeman were instrumental in correcting, clarifying and updating names and dates for this appendix. Others who helped to update the information for their family were Howard C. Sadler, Kathy Moore and Marlene Moore Phillips.

William Turner Sadler: born July 27, 1797, in Lincoln County, North Carolina, son of Nathaniel Milton Sadler Sr. and Phebe Tucker Moreland. Died on February 18, 1884, and was buried in the Sadler Cemetery on the original William Turner Sadler Survey in Anderson County, Texas, near the community of Slocum. First married in March 1837 to Mary Murchison (daughter of Martin Murchison), who was murdered by Indians in the Edens-Madden Massacre on October 18, 1838. Married in 1844 to second wife **Permelia Bennett**, a daughter of Armstead and Faith Bennett. Permelia was born in Indiana on March 13, 1818, and died in a tornado on Sadler Plantation along with one of her children on February 6, 1866.

[1] Children of William T. and Permelia Sadler
[2] Grandchildren of William and Permelia Sadler
[3] Great-grandchildren of William and Permelia Sadler
[4] Great-great-grandchildren of William and Permelia Sadler
[5] Great-great-great-grandchildren of William and Permelia Sadler
[6] Great-great-great-great grandchildren of William and Permelia Sadler

DESCENDANTS OF NATHANIEL FLETCHER SADLER AND MARTHA ROACH GIBSON:

[1] **NATHANIEL FLETCHER SADLER** (first son of William T. and Permelia B. Sadler), born June 25, 1845 in Houston County, TX. Died April 9, 1917 in Anderson County, TX. Married MARTHA ROACH GIBSON (born March 29, 1850; died March 6, 1911) on December 6, 1871. Children: 9.

[2] **ROBERT ROACH "TAB" SADLER**, born January, 1872 in Anderson County, TX. Died January 27, 1940. Married MARGUERITTE J. "MAGGIE" DAUGHTERY GOODNER on January 1, 1906 in McLennan County, TX (Waco). Maggie (born 1871 in Philadelphia, PA; died October 11, 1919) was daughter of Patrick Joseph Daughtery and Margaret O'Donnell Kinney. Children: 3.

[3] **ROBERT FLETCHER SADLER SR.**, born January 19, 1907 in Palestine, TX. Died September 25, 1940 in New York, NY. Married LOUISE MARIE WATERMULDER on December 29, 1932 in Yonkers, NY. Louise (born October 29, 1909 in Bronx, NY; died September 24, 1983 in Providence, RI) was daughter of Ludwig and Marie Watermulder. Children: 2.

[4] **LOUISE MARGUERITTE SADLER**, born August 5, 1934 in Utica, NY. Married CHARLES KESSLING, divorced in June, 1970. Married CHARLES FAIR on May 3, 1980. Children: None.

[4] **ROBERT FLETCHER SADLER JR.**, born July 27, 1940 in Bronxville, NY.

[3] **CHARLES ROACH SADLER**, born December 31, 1914 in Anderson County,

314   *APPENDIX F: Descendants of William T. Sadler (Continued)*

TX. Died July 29, 1983. Married VELMA GOODWIN. Children: 2.
   ⁴ CHARLES ROBERT SADLER.
   ⁴ TIMOTHY GOODWIN SADLER.
  ³ PATRICK DAUGHERTY SADLER, born October 10, 1916 in Palestine, TX. Married WELDON LOUISE WATSON on March 22, 1941. Louise born December 22, 1920. Children: 5.
   ⁴ WILLIAM PATRICK SADLER, born May 13, 1942 in Dallas, TX.
   ⁴ ROBERT ROACH SADLER, born May 26, 1943, in Greenville, TX. Married BARBARA "BONNIE" JORDAN on March 13, 1969, in Houston, TX. Bonnie (born September 3, 1942) was daughter of Jay and Edna Jordan. Children: 2.
    ⁵ BABY BOY SADLER, stillborn March 11, 1970.
    ⁵ ROBERT PAYNE SADLER, born July 29, 1971, in Houston, TX.
   ⁴ GERALD ALVIN "JERRY" SADLER, born July 28, 1944, in Dallas, TX. Married ANN MORGAN PHILLIPS on July 19, 1980.
   ⁴ JAMES WELDON SADLER, born October 2, 1946, in Dallas, TX. Married LINDA MELANSON on September 1, 1972. Linda born in May, 1954.
   ⁴ KERMIT MICHAEL SADLER, born February 18, 1951, in Dallas, TX.
 ² WILLIAM THEOPHILUS SADLER SR., born December 5, 1873 at Ioni, TX. Died October 4, 1901. Married LULA BELLE CHILDRESS on May 28, 1898. Lula died on unknown date in Merkle, TX. Children: 2.
  ³ CHILDRESS SADLER, born February 28, 1899, in Palestine, TX. Died September 14, 1925, in Palestine, TX.
  ³ WILLIAM THEOPHILUS SADLER JR., born in Palestine, TX. Died in Merkle, TX. No specifics available. Children: 1.
   ⁴ DAUGHTER SADLER. No specifics available.
 ² OWENA SADLER, born July 1, 1875, at Ioni, TX. Died in Pecos, TX, on unknown date. Married JOHN DURANT JOHNSTON in 1891. Children: 4.
  ³ R. BRUCE JOHNSTON. Specifics unknown. Married ANNIE ZUBER. Child: 1.
   ⁴ DORIS RUTH JOHNSTON. Specifics and dates unknown. Was married to TED GROTEN.
  ³ TED JOHNSTON, born March, 1901. Died May 10, 1992. Married LAURA ADAMS. Laura was born in 1903 and died in 1986. Children: 4.
   ⁴ J. KENNETH JOHNSTON. Specifics unknown. Children: 3.
   ⁴ LAURA LOU JOHNSTON. Specifics unknown. Married CHARLES L. BOMAR.
   ⁴ DOROTHY JOHNSTON. Specifics unknown. Married Mr. STEPKEN.
   ⁴ TED SADLER JOHNSTON. Specifics unknown.
  ³ VERNA JOHNSTON. Specifics unknown. Married JOHN BOX. Children: 3.
   ⁴ BILLY BOX. Specifics unknown.
   ⁴ FRANCES BOX. Specifics unknown.
   ⁴ GRACE ANN BOX. Specifics unknown.
  ³ GRACE JOHNSTON. Specifics unknown.
 ² CLAUDIUS C. "CLAUDE" SADLER, born May 13, 1877, in community of Ioni, TX. Died March 2, 1939, in Anderson County in community of Hickory Grove, TX. Married MAYBELLE VIRGINIA ANTHONY on May 28, 1896, in Grapeland, TX. Maybelle born May 13, 1878, in Percilla, TX, and died on July 7, 1966, in Hickory Grove. Children: 5.
  ³ ROBERT HOWARD SADLER, born January 27, 1899, in Palestine, TX. Died in Percilla, TX, on unknown date. Married MARY BRANCH ROBINSON on June 26, 1920. Children: 2.
   ⁴ GLADYS SADLER. Specifics unavailable. Married Mr. COHENHOUR.

APPENDIX F: Descendants of William T. Sadler (Continued) 315

⁵ **PAMELA COHENHOUR.** Specifics unavailable.
⁴ **HOWARD CLAUDE SADLER**, born July 19, 1924, in Anderson County, TX. Died September 3, 1997, in Port Arthur, TX. Married MICHELE DELVECK on July 6, 1946, in Passau, Germany. Michele born January 27, 1927, in Lille, France. Children: 2.
⁵ **ROBERT JERRY SADLER**, born July 25, 1947, in Port Arthur, TX. Married JANE ALICE CRAIG on July 10, 1971, in Port Arthur, TX. Jane was born on October 19, 1948. Children: 3.
⁶ **KIMBERLY MICHELE SADLER**, born December 3, 1974.
⁶ **KELLY DIANE SADLER**, born September 27, 1977.
⁶ **CHRISTOPHER RYAN SADLER**, born November 8, 1983.
⁵ **PATRICIA BEVERLY SADLER**, born October 24, 1964, in Port Arthur, TX. Married FRED ANTHONY NEPVEUX on October 29, 1991, in Port Arthur, TX. Fred was born on September 11, 1957. Children: 1.
⁶ **WALTER HOWARD NEPVEUX** was born on March 23, 1993, in Port Arthur, TX.
³ **LORETTA VIOLA SADLER**, born July 7, 1902, in Grapeland, TX. Died April 11, 1971, in Dallas, TX. Married HOMER PARK WATKINS on May 30, 1928. Homer was born in Anderson County, TX community of Denson Springs on January 31, 1897. Loretta later remarried twice. Children of first marriage: 1.
⁴ **MARTHA LUCILLE WATKINS**, born September 29, 1926 in community of Hickory Grove, TX. Married FELIX U. WATSON on December 21, 1950, in Dallas, TX. Felix was born on February 27, 1922 in Oray, OK. Children: 2.
⁵ **WILLIAM HOMER "BILL" WATSON**, born on August 1, 1957.
⁵ **JO ANN WATSON**, born on September 17, 1959, in Dallas, TX. Married JOE D. CAMPBELL on July 11, 1978. Children: 1.
⁶ **JULIE ANN CAMPBELL**, born March 17, 1978.
³ **ROY CLAUDE SADLER**, born December 9, 1903, in Kountz, TX. Died July 28, 1951, at Hickory Grove community in Anderson County, TX. Never married.
³ **NATHANIEL FLETCHER "NAT" SADLER**, born February 6, 1905, in Kountz, TX. Died April 13, 1979, in Houston, TX. Married RUBY ELSIE WOOLEY on March 21, 1935, in Houston, TX. Ruby born June 9, 1909, in Oberlin, LA, and died in Houston, TX, on unknown date. Children: 1.
⁴ **CLAUDIA ANN SADLER**, born November 16, 1946, in Port Arthur, TX. Married NOLAN JAMES CHALINE on November 20, 1964, in Dallas, TX. Nolan born on July 7, 1944, in Houston, TX. Children: 2.
⁵ **KATHRYN DENISE CHALINE**, born on November 10, 1966. Later married. Children: 2.
⁵ **NATALIE NOLAN CHALINE**, born on November 6, 1978, in Houston, TX.
³ **GERALD ANTHONY "JERRY" SADLER**, born September 8, 1907, in Kirbyville, TX. Died on February 25, 1982, in community of Hickory Grove in Anderson County, TX. Married LAURA EMMA JONES on September 4, 1942. Laura born on August 24, 1920, in Rising Star, TX. Children: 2.
⁴ **JERRY WILLIAM "BILL"SADLER**, born August 1, 1946, in Houston, TX. Married twice. No children.
⁴ **SAMUEL THOMAS "SAM" SADLER**, born March 15, 1950, in Beaumont, TX. Died December 5, 1987, in automobile accident in Lufkin, TX. Married wife CHRISTIE on unknown date. Children: 2.
⁵ **GENA MARIE SADLER**, born on unknown date.

⁵ **WILLIAM TRAVIS SADLER**, born on unknown date.

² **GENEVA SADLER**, born January 23, 1879, in community of Ioni, TX. Died February 16, 1965, in Hollywood, FL. Married THOMAS RUSSELL "TOM" TAYLOR SR. on September 10, 1911, in San Antonio, TX. Tom born in Summerfield, OH, and died on August 9, 1953, in Miami, FL. Children: 1.

³ **THOMAS RUSSELL "TOMMY" TAYLOR JR.**, born October 5, 1912, in Ashville, NC. Married HOPE COLCLOUGH WALDEN on July 1, 1938. Hope born on February 13, 1918. Children: 2.

⁴ **JANE COLCLOUGH TAYLOR**, born May 23, 1941. Married JOHN GARY "LINK" LINKSWILER SR. on September 22, 1961, in Tucson, AZ. Link born on February 10, 1941, in Lake Charles, LA. Children: 2.

⁵ **JOHN GARY LINKSWILER JR.**, born on September 26, 1975.

⁵ **THOMAS COLCLOUGH LINKSWILER**, born on October 28, 1981.

⁴ **THOMAS RUSSELL "TOM" TAYLOR III**, born May 10, 1943, in Oakland, CA. Married MARJORIE LYNN MCCOY on November 27, 1965, in Bakersfield, CA. Marjorie born May 20, 1943, in Bakersfield, CA. Children: 2 sons.

⁵ **NICHOLAS RUSSELL TAYLOR**, born February 1, 1983, in Burlington, IA.

⁵ **MATTHEW LYNN TAYLOR**, born in November, 1985, in Burlington, IA.

² **HILDA SADLER**, born November, 1881, in Anderson County community of Ioni, TX. Died April 20, 1969, in Alpine, TX. Married LOUIS ARTHUR TITTLE on October 9, 1906. Louis born on February 17, 1885, in Mt. Vernon, TX, and died on unknown date in Dallas, TX. Children: 1.

³ **WANDA GRETCHEN TITTLE**, born February 4, 1912, in Mt. Vernon, TX. Died on January 23, 1992, in Ft. Stockton, TX. Married MAX CHAMPIE in December, 1934. Max died on October 22, 1954. Gretchen married BUD FRAZER BAKER on December 20, 1955. Bud was born on September 1, 1911. No children.

² **OLGA SADLER**, born December, 1884, in Anderson County community of Ioni, TX. Died on unknown date in Franklin, TX. Married FRANK WOODS. Children: 2.

³ **JACQUALYN WOODS**. Birth date unknown. Never married.

³ **MARTHA FRANCES WOODS**. Birth date unknown. Married MARIO RODRIGUEZ. No children.

² **NATHANIEL LAMAR "MORRY" SADLER**, born 1886 or 1887 in Anderson County community of Ioni, TX. Died after 1940 in Travis County, TX. Never married.

² **KIRBY SADLER**, born March 6, 1889, in Anderson County community of Ioni, TX. Died on January 13, 1980.

* * * *

DESCENDANTS OF MARTHA TUCKER SADLER AND WILLIAM THOMAS KENNEDY:

¹ **MARTHA TUCKER SADLER** (first daughter and second child of William T. and Permelia B. Sadler), born April 12, 1847 in Anderson County, TX. Died November 3, 1931. Married WILLIAM THOMAS KENNEDY on July 26, 1869. William born February 18, 1842, and died June 30, 1905. Children: 7.

² **HENRIETTA ELIZABETH KENNEDY**, born May 14, 1866. Died in 1948. Married MILES PARKER. Miles born in 1852 and died in 1901. Hettie later married RICHARD F. HENDRIX. Richard born on March 8, 1870 and died March 16, 1920.

APPENDIX F: *Descendants of William T. Sadler (Continued)* 317

²**WILLIAM JOSEPH KENNEDY**, born June 11, 1870. Died on November 26, 1924. Married ICIPHENIA PARKER (born December 5, 1869, and died on November 10, 1900. William later married IDA MAY WALLING. Ida born May 12, 1882, and died January 22, 1929.

²**STEPHEN BANNISTER KENNEDY**, born July 21, 1872. Married ELLEN DAVIS.

²**DOCIA PERMELIA KENNEDY**, born August 18, 1874. Died on March 13, 1956. Married BENJAMIN J. PARKER. Ben born January 1, 1868, and died January 1, 1956. Children: 7.

    ³**LILA PARKER.**
    ³**ESTELLA PARKER.**
    ³**CHARM PARKER.**
    ³**JOE BAILEY PARKER.**
    ³**LORENE PARKER.**
    ³**JACK PARKER.**
    ³**DALE PARKER.**

²**ROBERT LEE KENNEDY**, born February 3, 1877. Died on May 20, 1956. Married LILLIAN WALLING. Lillian born 1886 and died 1966.

²**PHOEBE TUCKER KENNEDY**, born June 6, 1881. Died on December 29, 1968. Married a Mr. SMITH.

²**ICIPHENIA IRENE KENNEDY**, born February 16, 1884. Died on June 29, 1970. Married WILLIAM ROBERT BENNETT on March 28, 1901. William born on September 29, 1879 and died 1941-1943. One known child.

    ³**ADELLE BENNETT.** Date of birth unknown. Married ARCHIE LEE TRIGG on unknown date.

        ⁴**DANIEL ROBERT "DANNY" TRIGG.**
        ⁴**(DAUGHTER) TRIGG.**

* * * *

DESCENDANTS OF MARY ANN SADLER AND WILLIAM ZACHARIAH DAY:

¹**MARY ANN SADLER** (second daughter and third child of William T. and Permelia B. Sadler), born December 16, 1848 in Anderson County, TX. Died December 8, 1914. Married WILLIAM ZACHARIAH "ZACH" DAY on February 7, 1867. Zach was born on November 28, 1848, and died November 19, 1920. Children: 4.

²**JAMES F. "JIM" DAY**, was born in 1868. Married BEATRICE "BEE" HANKS on February 2, 1896. Children: 3.

    ³**GETTYS NORMAN DAY**, born in 1896. Married TOM MILLER.
    ³**ELIZABETH MAE "LIZZIE" DAY**, born in 1899. Married FITZHUGH PRICE. Fitzhugh was born in 1897 and died in 1973.
    ³**WILLIAM ZACH DAY**, born on November 11, 1902. Married LUDIE DAVIS.

²**WILLIAM RUSSELL DAY**, born February 23, 1870. Died on January 20, 1940. Married JOSIE CHAMBERS on December 1, 1887. Josie was born on December 23, 1870, in Anderson County, TX, and died on October 11, 1938, in Anderson County. Children: 4.

    ³**GLADYS OLA DAY**, born on November 11, 1888. Died on September 3, 1971. Married CLAUDE THOMAS MCIVER. Claude born on May 2, 1888, and died on September 29, 1959. Children: 5.

        ⁴**WELDON MCIVER**, born in 1910. Married VIOLA NEEDHAM.

APPENDIX F: Descendants of William T. Sadler (Continued)

⁴ **EVA MAE MCIVER**, born August 16, 1912, in Anderson County, TX. Married OZZIE CECIL WOLF on October 27, 1932. Ozzie was born on February 15, 1912, in Anderson County, TX, and died on August 30, 1976, in Anderson County, TX. Children: 1.

⁵ **GORDON WAYNE WOLF**, born July 19, 1943. Married BEATRICE KAY WATKINS on May 12, 1962. Beatrice was born on May 13, 1943.

⁴ **ORA DAY MCIVER**, born September 13, 1915. Married NORMAN POLK.

⁴ **H. W. MCIVER**, born on September 20, 1918. Died on January 17, 1983. Married ROSA RICHTER. Later married to MARY ALICE DOBBS.

⁴ **ALTON RUSSELL MCIVER**, born on October 13, 1921. Killed in a tornado in community of Slocum in Anderson County on April 24, 1929.

³ **ZOLA DAY**, was born in September, 1891. Died on June 20, 1979. Married JAMES ELMER MCIVER. James was born in February, 1886, and died in 1952. Children: 2.

⁴ **GERALD MCIVER**. Specifics unknown. Married FREDDIE MAE HARRISON.

⁴ **CLETE MAE MCIVER**. Specifics unknown. Married ERNIE BREWSTER.

³ **R. L. DAY SR.**, was born in March, 1894. Married YUNA REBECCA SORRAY/SORY. Children: 3.

⁴ **R. L. DAY JR.** Specifics unknown.
⁴ **ELOISE DAY**. Specifics unknown.
⁴ **PATSY DAY**. Specifics unknown.

³ **CLARA DAY**, was born on November 11, 1898. Died on December 12, 1979. Married HENRY MCIVER. Children: 3.

⁴ **WADE MCIVER**. Specifics unknown. Married FLORENCE FRANKLIN.
⁴ **KENNETH MCIVER**. Specifics unknown. Married LOYCE JOHNSTON.
⁴ **OUIDA FAY MCIVER**. Specifics unknown. Married K. W. JACOBE.

² **LULA SADLER DAY**, was born in 1872. Married SAMUEL "SAM" QUARLES on December 20, 1888. Sam born in 1866 and died in 1906. Lula later married a Mr. KNOX. Children with Quarles: 6.

³ **ETHEL QUARLES**. Specifics unknown. Married SAMUEL "SAM" SHERIDAN.
³ **ZELMA QUARLES**. Specifics unknown. Married HENRY FRANKS.
³ **IVA QUARLES**. Specifics unknown. Married W. G. DICKEY.
³ **LISA QUARLES**. Specifics unknown. Married WILLIAM "WILL" ELLIS.
³ **SAMANTHA "SAMMIE" QUARLES**. Specifics unknown. Married S. G. LAWRENCE.
³ **CLARICE QUARLES**. Specifics unknown. Married KENMORE HUNTER.

² **CORA THOMAS DAY**, was born on September 24, 1876. Died on April 8, 1961. Married HARRY DANIEL DEATON on August 9, 1892. Harry was born on February 3, 1872, and died on May 26, 1897. Children: 2.

³ **MARY LORAINE DEATON**, born on July 18, 1894. Died on April 24, 1977. Specifics unknown. Married THOMAS "TOM" TURNER and later married JOHN R. WEISER. Children with Tom Turner: 2.

⁴ **HARRY DEATON TURNER**. Specifics unknown. Married HESTER _____. Children: 1.

⁵ **THOMAS PATRICK TURNER**. Specifics unknown.

⁴ **JANICE TURNER**. Specifics unknown, but died at age 18.

³ **HARRYETTA DEATON**, was born on June 10, 1897. Died on September 7, 1983. Married ALBERT GEORGE RUSSELL on December 7, 1918. Albert born on May 9, 1897, and died on March 25, 1969. One child.

⁴ **MADALINE CONSTANCE RUSSELL**, was born on January 22, 1921. Married G. W. DICKEY (born in 1919). Children: 2.
⁵ **MICHAEL GEORGE DICKEY**, specifics unknown. Married GLORIA ANN SAUCIER. Children: 3.
⁶ **MICHAEL WAYNE DICKEY**, born in 1961.
⁶ **KENNETH LEE DICKEY**, born in 1962.
⁶ **ELIZABETH ANN DICKEY**, born in 1969.
⁵ **G. W. DICKEY JR.**, specifics unknown. Married SHARON ANN RICKERTON (born in 1914). Children: 3.
⁶ **BRENT JASON DICKEY**, born in 1966.
⁶ **CRAIG MANNING DICKEY**, born in 1969.
⁶ **JULIE ANN DICKEY**, born in 1971.

CORA THOMAS DAY, was married a second time to WILLIAM FRANK DENSON. William was born on January 5, 1877, and died on December 12, 1960. Cora and her second husband had one child.

³ **LOTA PEARL DENSON**, born on June 29, 1902. Died on December 22, 1976. Married FRED JAKE SCHNORR on August 16, 1916. Children: 2.
⁴ **DORIS ANITA SCHNORR**, born on November 21, 1917. Married JESSE LEONARD COLE and later CHARLES WHEATON.
⁴ **FRANKYE EVELYN SCHNORR**, born on November 10, 1919. Married ALBERT OLEN JOHNSON. Albert was born on March 30, 1917. Children: 1.
⁵ **DORIS LYNN JOHNSON**. Specifics unknown. Married KENNETH HOYT. Children: 2.
⁶ **DEBRA LYNN HOYT**. Specifics unknown.
⁶ **KENNETH HOYT**. Specifics unknown.

LOTA PEARL DENSON was married a second time to ELDRED EARL BRALEY. Eldred born on December 4, 1893, and died on March 6, 1973. Lota and Eldred had one child together.

⁴ **ROSE MARY BRALEY**, born on August 30, 1927. Married JIM WARREN "JIMMIE" MIMS on August 20, 1949. Jimmie born on March 30, 1917.

* * * *

DESCENDANTS OF WILLIAM PETERSON SADLER AND JOSEPHINE ROACH:

¹ **WILLIAM PETERSON SADLER** (second son and fourth child of William T. and Permelia B. Sadler), born January 9, 1850 in Anderson County, TX. Died March 7, 1885. Married JOSEPHINE ROACH on May 31, 1876, in Anderson County, TX. Josephine was born on October 23, 1852, in Anderson County, TX, and died on October 30, 1932. Josephine was a daughter of Robert Owen Roach and Martha Anderson. Josephine was also a sister of Martha Roach, who married Nathaniel Fletcher Sadler. Children: 5.

² **BIRDIE SADLER**, was born on March 11, 1877, in Anderson County, TX. Died on April 21, 1879. No children.

² **DIAMOND SADLER**, was born on February 5, 1879, in Anderson County, TX. Died on June 24, 1966. Married WILLIAM HENRY KOLB. William was born on February 10, 1866, and died on July 7, 1955. Children: 6.

³ **LUCILLE KOLB**, was born on May 7, 1902. Died on February 24, 1990.

APPENDIX F: Descendants of William T. Sadler (Continued)

Married JOHN G. GEE on May 22, 1927. John was born on March 13, 1899, and died on January 8, 1979. Children: 4.

 ⁴ EVERETT WAYNE GEE, born January 14, 1931. Died on April 27, 1933.

 ⁴ DOLORES GEE, was born on November 11, 1934. Married ROBERT U. MCCURLEY JR., on December 21, 1952. Robert was born on May 11, 1929. Children: 2.

  ⁵ LORI ANN MCCURLEY, was born on September 27, 1956. Married GARY ALLEN BURNS on August 2, 1991. Children: 3.

   ⁶ J. ROBERT MCCURLEY BURNS, was born on July 2, 1992.

   ⁶ JOHN ROCCO MCCURLEY BURNS, was born on August 22, 1994.

   ⁶ EMILY CAROLINE BURNS, was born on June 16, 1997.

  ⁵ LAURA SUSAN MCCURLEY, born December 3, 1959. Married MALCOLM FORREST ANDERSON, on June 1, 1985. Forrest was born on July 3, 1957. Children: 2.

   ⁶ FORREST NICOLE ANDERSON, was born on July 25, 1987.

   ⁶ ALGERA LEE ANDERSON, was born on December 25, 1991.

 ⁴ MELVIN DOYLE GEE, was born on March 19, 1936. Died on February 14, 1994, in Waco, TX.

 ⁴ YMELDA GEE, was born on August 3, 1938. Married GEORGE HARRELL LEWIS on January 19, 1958. George was born on October 18, 1932. Children: 3.

  ⁵ HARRELL WAYNE LEWIS, was born on October 18, 1958.

  ⁵ DAVID BRIAN LEWIS, was born on July 27, 1960.

  ⁵ LAJEANA LYNN LEWIS, was born on December 1, 1971.

 ³ WILLIAM BOYCE KOLB, was born on April 1, 1906 and died in 1996. Married MABEL MORRISON on August 5, 1931. Mabel was born on September 20, 1907. Children: 2.

 ⁴ CARMEN KOLB, was born on January 18, 1938. Married LAWRENCE MARVIN WALKER on August 30, 1957. Laurence was born on March 18, 1935. Children: 4.

  ⁵ VICTOR LAURENCE WALKER, was born on February 6, 1959.

  ⁵ VAN MARVIN WALKER, was born on January 24, 1961.

  ⁵ DEVONNA DAWN WALKER, was born on September 4, 1962.

  ⁵ WILLIAM KEVIN WALKER, was born on November 29, 1964.

 ⁴ WILLIAM BOYCE "BILL" KOLB JR., was born on June 16, 1940. Married GAYLE INEZ ELLIOTT on September 9, 1960. Gayle was born on November 21, 1941. Children: 2.

  ⁵ KYLE BOYCE KOLB, was born on January 6, 1963.

  ⁵ WADE KOLB, was born on July 18, 1967.

 ³ ELSIE KOLB, born August 5, 1908. Married GRIFFIN RICHARDSON on August 17, 1943. Griffin born on June 30, 1904, and died on unknown date. No children.

 ³ EVALINE KOLB, was born on March 2, 1911. Died on May 11, 1994, in Tyler, TX. Married MARSHALL LEE MOORE SR. on September 20, 1927. Marshall was born at community of Liberty Hill in Houston County, TX, on February 8, 1903, and died on May 22, 1985, in Houston County, TX. Marshall was the son of William Lee Moore and Nancy Annie Ferguson of Houston County. Children: 2.

 ⁴ MARLENE MOORE, was born on June 20, 1936, in Lubbock, TX. Married JOHN RAY KUBITZ on June 26, 1954. John was born on May 17, 1933, and died in a plane crash on May 3, 1968. Marlene later married Kenneth Phillips on June 26, 1988. Children with John Ray Kubitz: 3.

APPENDIX F: Descendants of William T. Sadler (Continued)   321

⁵ **KAREN ANNETTE KUBITZ**, was born on June 17, 1957. Married RANDALL BURKE SCOTT on July 12, 1980. Randy was born on March 19, 1957. Children: 3.
    ⁶ **MICHAEL BURKE SCOTT** was born on February 4, 1989.
    ⁶ **PRESTON BURKE SCOTT** was born on March 22, 1991.
    ⁶ **KATRINA ANNETTE SCOTT** was born on November 13, 1993.

⁵ **ERIC SCOTT KUBITZ**, was born on August 22, 1959. First married to Lou Ann _____ and later divorced. Next married LESLIE HARRIS in June, 1984; later divorced. Children: 2.
    ⁶ **JACQUELINE MICHELLE KUBITZ** was born on February 17, 1985.
    ⁶ **JENNIFER PAIGE KUBITZ** was born on February 1, 1988.

⁵ **CAROL ALLISON KUBITZ**, was born on October 6, 1965, and was adopted by Marlene and John. Allison married STEVE GOUDY, later divorced. Children by Steve Goudy: 2. Allison married Kevin Nye in April, 1996. Children by Kevin Nye: 1.
    ⁶ **STEFANIE CAROL GOUDY** was born on July 24, 1988.
    ⁶ **ELIZABETH JANE GOUDY** was born on November 12, 1990.
    ⁶ **BRIAN TODD NYE** was born on June 13, 1994.

⁴ **MARSHALL LEE "CHUCK" MOORE JR.**, was born on December 17, 1940, in Dallas, TX. Married FLORENCE KATHLEEN "KATHY" MCGUIRE on May 16, 1964. Kathy was born on July 9, 1944, in Hearne, TX. She is the daughter of Beverly Hartzog McGuire Jr. and Florence Caroline Birkner. Children: 2.
    ⁵ **STEPHEN LEE MOORE**, was born on July 24, 1967, in Houston, Texas. Married CYNTHIA LYNN HUNT on March 20, 1993, in Houston, Texas. Cindy was born on April 23, 1966, in Durant, OK. She is the daughter of David H. Hunt and Patsy Louise Norman. Children: 2.
    ⁶ **KRISTEN TAYLOR MOORE**, was born at Columbia West Houston Medical Center on August 14, 1996, in Houston, TX.
    ⁶ **EMILY KATELYN MOORE**, was born at Northeast Medical Center on November 4, 1997, in Concord, NC.
    ⁵ **SUSAN JANETTE MOORE**, born on June 7, 1971, in Lufkin, TX.

³ **VIRGIL YANCEY KOLB**, was born on June 5, 1913, in Grapeland, TX. Died on July 21, 1989, in El Paso, TX. Married MARTHA FLORINE ROBERTS on September 25, 1943. Martha born on April 30, 1920, in El Paso, TX. Children: 3.
    ⁴ **SHELDON ANDREW KOLB** was born on June 16, 1947, in El Paso, TX. Married MARCENE LOUISE GOLL in Enid, OK. Children: 1.
    ⁵ **RYAN ANDREW KOLB** was born on May 6, 1986, in Enid, OK.
    ⁴ **RONALD VIRGIL KOLB** was born on November 30, 1950, in El Paso, TX. Married MARTHA LOUISE BLAIR on September 18, 1971. Martha born in Guatamala. Children: 6.
    ⁵ **RONALD ANDREW KOLB**, born June 21, 1973, in El Paso, TX.
    ⁵ **BRIAN PETER KOLB**, born on April 22, 1975, in El Paso, TX.
    ⁵ **AARON MATTHEW KOLB**, born May 30, 1978, in El Paso, TX.
    ⁵ **BENJAMIN EDWARD KOLB**, born April 7, 1981, in El Paso, TX.
    ⁵ **JEREMIAH ALLEN KOLB**, born October 30, 1984, in El Paso, TX.
    ⁵ **PHILIP MARSHALL KOLB**, born December 18, 1990, in El Paso, TX.
    ⁴ **DAVID STERLING KOLB** was born on April 23, 1954, in El Paso, TX. Married JUDITH EILEEN CARVER. Judith born on November 20, 1953, in Harlingen, TX. Children: 2.
    ⁵ **ISIAH JONATHAN KOLB**, born June 4, 1987, in Pasadena, CA.

⁵ ANGELA CHERISE KOLB, born May 2, 1989, in Pasadena, CA.

³ WINSTON C. KOLB, was born on April 1, 1919. Married ORETHA OLDFIELD on July 12, 1947. Oretha born on December 4, 1915. Children: 1.

⁴ JANIE KOLB was born on April 4, 1942, and was adopted by Winston and Oretha Kolb. Married JERRY L. BAUGHMAN on April 4, 1959. Jerry was born on November 12, 1939. Children: 2.

⁵ DE LEE BAUGHMAN was born on August 9, 1960.

⁵ DELLA MARIE BAUGHMAN was born on January 6, 1962.

² IVA SADLER was born on November 24, 1880, in the community of Ioni in Anderson County, TX. Died on August 17, 1969, in Palestine, TX. Was never married.

² EDNA SADLER was born on January 19, 1883, in Anderson County, TX. Died on August 19, 1921, in Grapeland, TX. Was never married.

² WILLIAM CLEVELAND SADLER was born on December 26, 1884, in the community of Ioni in Anderson County, TX. Died on April 12, 1940, in Palestine, TX. Married ANNIE MAUD MCCARTY on August 17, 1919. Annie was born on June 18, 1893, in Houston County, TX, and died on September 25, 1955, in Eustace, TX. Children: 5.

³ AGNES WILLANETTE SADLER was born on December 5, 1920, in Grapeland, TX. Died on April 20, 1992, in Lufkin, TX. Married NEWTON HEROD and later to JOHN P. HICKS. Child with Netwon Herod: 1.

⁴ STEPHEN EARL HEROD was born on November 2, 1945, and was adopted by Agnes and Netwon Herod. Married twice.

³ IVA JOSEPHINE SADLER was born on October 6, 1922, in Anderson County, TX. Married JAMES A. EDWARDS on February 21, 1943, but was later divorced. Married HOWARD E. METCALF on July 2, 1973. Children: 6.

⁴ SONDRA JO EDWARDS was born on February 7, 1944. Married CRAIG SCHLOTTERBACK on December 18, 1966. Children: 2.

⁵ LEAH DANIEL SCHLOTTERBACK was born on March 25, 1970. Married JASON BRENT VARNADORE on August 17, 1991. Children: 1.

⁶ AARON LEE VARNADORE was born on October 17, 1992. Died on January 19, 1993.

⁵ JULIE CHRISTINE SCHLOTTERBACK was born on January 12, 1976.

⁴ BEVERLY KAY EDWARDS was born on July 18, 1947. Married BRUCE DAVEY on June 3, 1967, but was later divorced. Later married CHARLES "CHUCK" NEELY, but was later divorced. Children with Bruce Davey: 1.

⁵ HEATHER RENE DAVEY was born on May 31, 1969.

⁴ JAMES MICHAEL EDWARDS was born on June 5, 1955.

⁴ VICKI LYNN EDWARDS was born on January 23, 1959. Married KENNETH SCHMATIAN on October 4, 1975, but was later divorced. Children: 3.

⁵ ROBERT MITCHELL SCHMATIAN was born on August 24, 1976.

⁵ JAMES EDWARD EDWARDS, born October 12, 1980, to Vicki Lynn Edwards.

⁵ JAMES TRAVIS ADAMS III was born on October 9, 1989, to Vicki Lynn Edwards and her second husband, JAMES TRAVIS ADAMS JR.

³ (INFANT) SADLER was stillborn on December 9, 1924, to William Cleveland Sadler and Annie Maud McCarty.

³ BETTY JEAN SADLER was born on February 11, 1928, in Grapeland, TX. Married DONALD EDWARD REED. Children: 4.

⁴ VINCENT DONALD REED was born on March 23, 1947. Married

APPENDIX F: *Descendants of William T. Sadler (Continued)*   323

Rhonda Kieffer on March 12, 1977. Children: 1.
        [5] **Garrett Donald Reed** was born on August 2, 1979.
    [4] **Linda Marian Reed** was born on December 16, 1948.
    [4] **Donna Jean Reed** was born on August 16, 1950. Married Russell Fisher on March 6, 1971. Children: 2.
        [5] **Crystal Leanne Fisher** was born on September 28, 1974.
        [5] **Tracy Jean Fisher** was born on April 4, 1976.
    [4] **Patricia Karen Reed** was born on August 22, 1956. Married Charles Montgomery Lennox. Children: 2.
        [5] **Joseph Reed Lennox** was born on January 18, 1980.
        [5] **John Charles Lennox** was born on August 27, 1986.
  [3] **Laverne Sadler** was born on March 19, 1930, in Grapeland, TX. Married Carl James Marsh on June 9, 1951, in Grapeland, TX. Carl was born on November 24, 1927. Children: 3.
    [4] **Lenora Kay Marsh** was born on October 15, 1953, in Tyler, TX. Married Ronald Van Harbuck on January 29, 1972, but was later divorced. Married William Wood "Bill" Davis on November 12, 1983.
    [4] **William Edward Marsh** was born on December 30, 1955, in Como, TX. Married Cathey Marie Busby on December 18, 1982. Children: 3.
        [5] **Amanda Rae Marsh** was born on August 14, 1983, and was adopted by William Marsh.
        [5] **Robert Carl "Bobby" Marsh**, born on April 22, 1986, in Tyler, TX.
        [5] **Catelyn Elaine Marsh** was born on August 29, 1990.
    [4] **Monica Lynn Marsh** was born on April 14, 1957.

* * * *

DESCENDANTS OF ELIZABETH ANN SADLER AND GILBERT RUSSELL DAY:

[1] **Elizabeth Ann "Betty" Sadler** (third daughter and fifth child of William T. and Permelia B. Sadler), born August 19, 1852 in Anderson County, TX. Died October 14, 1896, in Slocum, TX. Married Gilbert Russell "Gib" Day Jr. on June 22, 1872, in Slocum, TX. Gib born on September 14, 1852, in Slocum, TX, and died on April 16, 1917, in Slocum, TX. Children: 6.
  [2] **John Frank Day Sr.**, born February 27, 1874, in Slocum, TX. Died on September 12, 1858, in Roswell, NM. Married Flora Adell Gray in April, 1902, in Slocum, TX. Flora was born on October 3, 1880. Children: 4.
    [3] **Gilbert Gray Day**, born May 15, 1903, in Slocum, TX. Died on December 23, 1970, in Lubbock, TX. Married Audna Paulene Shoemaker on December 31, 1924, in Fort Worth, TX. Audna was born on January 23, 1906, in Pawnee, OK, and died in an auto-train collision on December 1, 1929, in Santa Fe Springs, CA. Gilbert later married Ann Louise Kannady on August 2, 1932. Ann was born in 1905. Children by Audna Paulene Shoemaker: 1.
      [4] **Jo Ann Day**, born October 11, 1927, in Abilene, TX. Married Orland Estmer Freeman Jr. on September 22, 1946, in Florence, AZ. Orland was born on March 22, 1924, the son of Orland Estmer Freeman Sr. and Occa Jefferson Cunningham. Children: 4.
        [5] **Constance Elaine "Connie" Freeman**, born November 5, 1946, in Phoenix, AZ. Married Richard Watchhorn Iannella on September 6, 1969,

APPENDIX F: Descendants of William T. Sadler (Continued)

in Phoenix, AZ. Richard was born on May 18, 1948, in Phoenix, AZ. Children: 2.

⁶ RICHARD CHAYNE IANNELLA, was born on November 28, 1970, in Scottsdale, AZ. Married JENNIFER PATRICIA MOORE on September 30, 1995, in Phoenix, AZ. Children: 1.

⁷ HAYLEY ANNE IANNELLA, born May 1, 1996, in Albuquerque, NM.

⁶ TRACY ANN IANNELLA, born January 23, 1975, in Scottsdale, AZ.

⁵ SHERI CANDUS FREEMAN, born on May 21, 1951, in Montebello, CA.

⁵ JOHN DOUGLAS FREEMAN, born on April 5, 1955, in Stockton, CA. Married LISA JOYCE RIECK SINASON on May 15, 1987, in Carrollton, TX. Lisa was born on December 19, 1958. Children: 4.

⁶ JEFFREY DEAN SINASON FREEMAN, born on August 15, 1982, in Dallas, TX.

⁶ HUNTER FREDRICK FREEMAN, born on December 23, 1987, in Carrollton, TX.

⁶ TAYLOR DAY FREEMAN, born on April 25, 1991, in Phoenix, AZ.

⁶ PIPER JOY FREEMAN, was born on May 11, 1996, in Gross Pointe Farm, MI.

⁵ SCOTT DAY FREEMAN, born on November 12, 1965, in Phoenix, AZ.

³ ALTA PEARL DAY, born January 21, 1907, in Eden, TX, and died on February 10, 1997, in Great Falls, MT. Married DIAZ DAY on November 20, 1927, in Eden, TX. Diaz was born December 3, 1903, in Black Fork, AR, and died on October 7, 1980, in Lubbock, TX. Children: 3.

⁴ JOHN CHARLES DAY (M.D.), born March 14, 1930, in Eden, TX. Married CLARA ALBERTA MCCORD on October 4, 1959, in Seminole, OK. Clara was born on October 19, 1935. Children: 3.

⁵ CYNDY LYNN DAY, born March 14, 1961, in Tulsa, OK. Married JOHN PHILIP WILSON on April 10, 1988, in Boise, ID. John was born on November 5, 1953, in Gardena, CA. Children: 2.

⁶ KAITLYNN MARIE WILSON, born May 17, 1993, in San Diego, CA.

⁶ JOHN CONNOR WILSON, born March 11, 1997, in San Diego, CA.

⁵ JOHN DIAZ DAY, born December 8, 1962, in Tulsa, OK.

⁵ SARAH LOU DAY, born October 31, 1973, in Boise, ID.

⁴ PATRICIA ANN DAY, born October 10, 1932, in Eden, TX. Married KEITH LEROY CASNER on August 14, 1953, in Heavener, OK. Keith was born on November 11, 1930, in Wichita, KA. Children: 4.

⁵ KAY DIANE CASNER, born September 4, 1958, in Oklahoma City, OK. Married STEPHEN CLEVE OVERLEY on October 27, 1984, in San Antonio, TX. Stephen born on September 17, 1952, in San Antonio, TX. Children: 1.

⁶ SAMUEL CLAY OVERLEY, born December 27, 1985, in San Antonio, TX.

⁵ RICHARD KEITH CASNER, born June 25, 1960, in Sebastian County, AR. Married PENNY JEAN PEEK on February 14, 1981, in Comfort, TX. Penny born on May 8, 1962, in Rosenberg, TX. Children: 2.

⁶ JENNIFER BRETTE CASNER, born April 14, 1983, in Lubbock, TX.

⁶ KAMEE JEAN CASNER, born January 11, 1985, in Lubbock, TX.

⁵ STEVEN JAMES CASNER (M.D.), born April 18, 1964, in Lubbock, TX. Married CARMEN VIDAL. Carmen was born in 1966.

⁵ AMY ELIZABETH CASNER, born December 30, 1966, in Lubbock, TX.

APPENDIX F: *Descendants of William T. Sadler (Continued)* 325

⁴ **JAMES LAWRENCE DAY**, born October 5, 1946, in Ft. Smith, AK. Married JEAN MARIE LUNDBERG on November 29, 1968, in Dallas, TX. Children: 3.

⁵ **JAMES CHRISTOPHER DAY**, born August 22, 1972, in Topeka, KS.

⁵ **CATHERINE TERESA DAY**, born December 17, 1975, in Great Falls, MT.

⁵ **KELLY MARIE DAY**, born August 27, 1978, in Great Falls, MT.

³ **JOHN FRANK DAY JR.**, born March 3, 1909, in Eden, TX. Married CORNELIA LUCILLE HACKLEY on November 22, 1934, in Bonham, TX. Cornelia was born in 1915 in Bonham, TX, and died in 1948, in Bonham, TX. Children with Cornelia Hackley: 1.

⁴ **JOHN FRANK DAY III**, born August 2, 1936, in Bonham, TX. Married STEPHANIE RUTH "STEVIE" MALONE on October 3, 1959, in Kalamazoo, MI. Stephanie was born on April 26, 1936, in Kalamazoo, MI. Children: 2.

⁵ **CYNTHIA LYNN DAY**, born in 1963. Married PETER SIDNEY SABIN, JR. on August 25, 1990, in Menlo Park, CA. Children: 1.

⁶ **CHRISTINA ELIZABETH SABIN**, born December 21, 1995, in Washington.

⁵ **ELIZABETH ANN DAY**, born July 6, 1965, in Mountain View, CA.

JOHN FRANK DAY JR., later married JOSEPHINE POLITO "JO" CARSTEN. Jo born on November 27, 1918. Children: 3.

⁴ **ELLEN JANE CARSTEN DAY**, born May 13, 1944, and adopted by John and Jo Day. Married RICHARD KUCERA and later OLIE NIELSEN.

⁴ **ROBERT FRANCIS DAY**, born September 21, 1951. Married CINDIE SUE COATES; later divorced.

⁴ **JAMES RUSSELL DAY**, born July 12, 1957, in New Haven, CN. Married LESLIE HOGE on July 18, 1981, in North Palm Beach, FL. Children: 3.

⁵ **JAMES RUSSELL DAY JR.**, born April 29, 1982, in North Palm Beach, FL.

⁵ **KEVIN BRADLEY DAY**, born August 26, 1986, in West Palm Beach, FL.

⁵ **LINDSAY DAY**, born September 23, 1990, in West Palm Beach, FL.

³ **CARL RUSSELL DAY**, born May 2, 1912, in Eden, TX. Died on September 4, 1989, in Arabella, NM. Married HAZEL DAWN GREEN on June 27, 1939, in Eden, TX. Hazel was born on November 20, 1916. Children: 3.

⁴ **CARL EDWARD DAY**, born December 15, 1940, in Roswell, NM. Married LOMA DEAN HAYS on February 28, 1964, in Abilene, TX. Loma was born on March 30, 1942, in Dora, NM. Children: 3.

⁵ **MITZI LYNN DAY**, born November 3, 1965, in Roswell, NM. Married TIMOTHY REESE on October 8, 1988, in Ft. Worth, TX. Children: 1.

⁶ **JEREMY WALKER REESE**, born May 27, 1996, in Fort Worth, TX.

⁵ **STEPHANIE EILEEN DAY**, born October 6, 1967, in Roswell, NM. Married JIM WILSON on May 25, 1991, in Roswell, NM.

⁵ **CRISTY DAWN DAY**, born August 18, 1970, in Roswell, NM.

⁴ **GILBERT RUSSELL DAY**, born September 25, 1943, in Roswell, NM. Died October 6, 1982, in airplane crash in Hebbronville, TX. Married SARA ELIZABETH POWELL on January 21, 196_ in Quanah, TX. Sara was born on February 27, 1944, in Quanah, TX. Children: 2.

⁵ **ELIZABETH ANN DAY**, born July 4, 1970, in Abilene, TX.

⁵ **JOHN RUSSELL DAY**, born November 28, 1972, in Abilene, TX.

⁴ **BILLY REX DAY**, born February 20, 1953, in Roswell, NM. Married MARTHA GAIL REYNOLDS on August 3, 1974, in Houston, TX. Martha was born on November 12, 1952, in Houston, TX. Children: 2.

⁵ **AMANDA JEAYN DAY**, born on December 6, 1976.

APPENDIX F: *Descendants of William T. Sadler (Continued)*

⁵ **JENNIFER DAWN DAY**, born on July 24, 1978.

² **IDA ELIZABETH DAY**, born January 7, 1876, in Slocum, TX. Died on October 12, 1965, in Crockett, TX. Married GEORGE BURTON WALLACE on May 15, 1901, in Slocum, TX. George born on February 6, 1875, in Anderson County, TX, and died on June 15, 1959, in Grapeland, TX. Children: 4.

³ **EMA WALLACE**, born February 19, 1902, in Slocum, TX. Died on February 25, 1981, in Brownfield, TX. Married DALLAS L. PATTON in 1925. Dallas born in 1901 and died in 1959. No children.

³ **GILBERT BURTON WALLACE**, born July 19, 1904, in Anderson County, TX. Died on July 7, 1982, in Crockett, TX. Married EFFIE HODGES on November 3, 1923, in Anderson County, TX. Effie born July 25, 1905 and died April 13, 1973. Children: 4.

⁴ **GILBERT BRUCE WALLACE**, born in 1926. Married ANNA MELBA HALTON on October 13, 1943. Melba born on May 4, 1926. Children: 3.

⁵ **GEORGE A. WALLACE**, born in 1947. Married RICKIE PARKER in 1972. Rickie was born in 1955.

⁵ **DAVID L. WALLACE**, born in 1949. Married SHARON L. KUNITZ in 1979. Sharon was born in 1955.

⁵ **PATRICK B. WALLACE**, born in 1952. Married CHRISTINE WIGGINS in 1973. Christine born in 1953.

⁴ **MILDRED N. WALLACE**, born in 1931. Married LEON DOYLE in 1943. Children: 5.

⁵ **NELDA L. DOYLE**, born in 1950.
⁵ **SUE D. DOYLE**, born in 1954.
⁵ **GREGORY L. DOYLE**, born in 1955.
⁵ **LETHA A. DOYLE**, born in 1960.
⁵ **DAVID R. DOYLE**, born in 1961.

⁴ **RICHARD L. WALLACE**, born in 1941. Died May 12, 1988. Never married.

⁴ **ANN E. WALLACE**, born in 1946. Married CHARLES WILLIAMS and later married WILLIAM E. DAVIS. No children.

³ **JOHN DAY WALLACE**, born March 1, 1907, in Grapeland, TX. Died in 1991. Married OLETA NICHOLS. Children: 2.

⁴ **DARRELL WALLACE**, born in 1936. Married MARY WILLIAMS in 1957. Mary born in 1939.

⁴ **CURTIS R. WALLACE**, born in 1945. Married SUE CHANDLER. Sue born in 1946.

³ **LOUISE WALLACE**, born September 3, 1911, in Grapeland, TX. Married WILLIAM W. CASKEY in 1959.

² **MARY PERMELIA DAY**, born March 19, 1878, in Slocum, TX. Died on April 24, 1929, in Anderson County, TX. Married EDMOND PINK MCDANIEL in Anderson County, TX. Edmond was born on September 27, 1874, in Columbia, AR. Children: 6.

³ **LILLIE MAE MCDANIEL**, born April 1, 1902. Died November 16, 1973. Married GORDON GUINN "BUD" EVERETTE SR. first and later ARTHUR VAUGHN. Child by Bud Everette: 1.

⁴ **GORDON GUINN EVERETTE JR.**, born May 3, 1924. Married JEAN WHITE and later ANN BURG. Children by Ann Burg: 4.

⁵ **JOHN ALBERT EVERETTE**. Married KATHY ____. Children: 1.

⁶ **SHARON EVERETTE**.

⁵ **MICHAEL EVERETTE**. Married PENNY STEWART. Children: 1.

APPENDIX F: Descendants of William T. Sadler (Continued)

      ⁶ MANDY EVERETTE.
    ⁵ MARLA EVERETTE. Married DON RUSHING.
    ⁵ WILLIAM EVERETTE. Married CAROLINE _____. Children: 1.
      ⁶ B. J. EVERETTE.
  ³ TROY RAYMOND MCDANIEL, born October 9, 1903. Died on January 4, 1961. Married JULIA KIMBLE in 1927. Children: 2.
    ⁴ RICHARD LYNN MCDANIEL, born February 19, 1937. Married BARBARA PARNELL. Barbara born on April 30, 1938. Children: 3.
      ⁵ DOUGLAS LYNN MCDANIEL, born December 23, 1960. Married ELLEN _____. Children: 1.
        ⁶ ASHLEY MCDANIEL.
      ⁵ SCOTT TROY MCDANIEL, born September 18, 1963.
      ⁵ PATRICIA MCDANIEL, born August 23, 1969.
    ⁴ GAIL MCDANIEL, born December 17, 1942. Married EDMUND NIELS ANDERSON. Children: 2.
      ⁵ JULIE ANDERSON, born March 26, 1970.
      ⁵ NIELS ANDERSON, born April 5, 1975.
  ³ EUNA MCDANIEL, born February 25, 1907. Married W. D. RIGBY. W. D. was born on January 8, 1905. No children.
  ³ LOIS HELEN MCDANIEL, born October 22, 1910. Married ERNEST "BONES" JONES. Ernest born on June 6, 1900. Children: 2.
    ⁴ LOERNA JONES, born August 11, 1930. Married ROBERT TAYLOR. Robert born on March 21, 1925. Children: 2.
      ⁵ CRAIG TAYLOR, born May 16, 1952. Married BRENDA CLARK. Brenda was born on June 17, 1955.
      ⁵ PAMELA LYN TAYLOR, born in 1958.
    ⁴ GORDON WAYNE JONES. Date of birth unknown. Married BRENDA _____.
  ³ HAROLD EDMUND MCDANIEL, born September 2, 1915. Married HELEN JUNE WILLINGHAM. Helen was born on July 1, 1918, and died on May 13, 1981. Harold later remarried. Children by Helen June Willingham: 1.
    ⁴ NANETTE MCDANIEL, born December 20, 1944. Married HOMER ARMSTRONG.
  ³ GILBERT WAYNE MCDANIEL, born August 18, 1919. Died in 1993. Married MARY MOZELLE PERRY. Mary was born on December 10, 1918, and died on June 10, 1989. Children: 2.
    ⁴ JEROLD WAYNE MCDANIEL, born June 11, 1951. Married SUSAN ELIZABETH MORROW. Susan was born on March 10, 1952.
    ⁴ MARY ANN MCDANIEL, born February 16, 1954. Married BRADFORD WAYNE HENDLEY. Brad was born on June 3, 1953.
² JEWELL DAY, born in Anderson County, TX, between 1879 and 1885. Married JOHN ALLEN. Children: 5.
    ³ OTIS ALLEN.
    ³ OLEN ALLEN.
    ³ HATTIE FAYE ALLEN. Died at age 9.
    ³ VIVIAN ALLEN.
    ³ BENNETT ALLEN.
² LEILA DAY, born on September 1, 1886, in Slocum, TX. Died in 1949. Married THOMAS VICKERY. Thomas was born on November 9, 1878, and died in 1959. Children: 6.

APPENDIX F: Descendants of William T. Sadler (Continued)

   ³ **BOYD VICKERY.** Died young.
   ³ **MILDRED VICKERY.**
   ³ **MARGIE VICKERY,** born June 30, 1919. Married ATMAR PELHAM. Atmar was born on October 6, 1912. Children: 1.
      ⁴ **LARRY PELHAM.**
   ³ **OTHELL VICKERY.** Married BEATRICE _____. Children: 6.
      ⁴ **TRAVIS VICKERY.**
      ⁴ **LOUISE VICKERY.**
      ⁴ **PEGGY VICKERY.**
      ⁴ **RITA VICKERY.**
      ⁴ **BOBBY VICKERY.**
      ⁴ **MIKE VICKERY.**
   ³ **O. B. "OBEE" VICKERY.** Killed on August 19, 1944 in World War II.
   ³ **OZELL VICKERY,** born May 16, 1925. Married LOUISE SEYMOUR. Louise born on March 4, 1925. Children: 2.
      ⁴ **RONNIE VICKERY.**
      ⁴ **TERESA ANN VICKERY.**
 ² **GILBERT ROY DAY,** born on June 6, 1895, in Slocum, TX. Died on December 16, 1982, in Lubbock, TX. Married CORA VICTORIA BETSILL on May 31, 1918. Cora was born on February 11, 1900, in Anderson County, TX, and died on July 22, 1955, in Dallas, TX. Gilbert was later married to LULA CURTIS in 1965. Lula died in 1981. Children with Cora Victoria Betsill: 5.
   ³ **EVELYN ELIZABETH DAY,** born March 12, 1919. Married RANDY LYNN LEWIS SR. Randy was born on January 1, 1913, and died on November 29, 1981. Evelyn later married EARL CASWELL. Earl was born on February 7, 1922. Children by Randy Lewis: 1.
      ⁴ **RANDY LYNN LEWIS JR.,** born on July 2, 1947. Married DEBORRAH MARKETT on August 25, 1973.
   ³ **HAZEL ELENDER DAY,** born October 25, 1920, in Slocum, TX. Married WELDON GORDON on February 1, 1941. Weldon was born on November 3, 1920, in Bowie, TX. Children: 1.
      ⁴ **LINDA JOYCE GORDON,** born February 1, 1943, in Brownfield, TX. Married BOBBY JOE HARKINS on June 21, 1962. Bobby was born on August 25, 1943, in Abernathy, TX. Children: 2.
         ⁵ **PAMELA LYNN HARKINS,** born June 25, 1964.
         ⁵ **KAYLA JO HARKINS,** born February 11, 1968.
      ⁴ **JUDY GORDON,** born August 15, 1946. Married CHARLES GRANTHAM on June 17, 1965..
   ³ **GLEN RUSSELL DAY SR.,** born August 16, 1922. Married JOY SHEPHERD on September 27, 1924. Joy was born on October 8, 1928. Children: 3.
      ⁴ **DEBRA DAY,** born August 2, 1952. Married BOBBY FLIPPO on June 13, 1970. Children: 2.
         ⁵ **RENEE' FLIPPO,** born March 9, 1973.
         ⁵ **KAYLA FLIPPO,** born March 3, 1977.
      ⁴ **CARLA DAY,** born December 30, 1955. Married DAVID CANNON on February 8, 1975. Children: 3.
         ⁵ **CODY KENT CANNON,** born February 15, 1978.
         ⁵ **CRAIG LEE CANON,** born June 5, 1981.
         ⁵ **CRYSTAL LACHELLE CANNON,** born December 9, 1982.
      ⁴ **GLEN RUSSELL DAY JR.,** born April 19, 1958. Married KIM BEAVERS

APPENDIX F: Descendants of William T. Sadler (Continued) 329

on June 1, 1979.

³ **OLETA JOYCE DAY**, born June 22, 1928, in Gilliland, TX. Married BILL RICHARDSON on October 1, 1946. Bill was born on July 29, 1926 and died on unknown date. Children: 4.
    ⁴ **RONNIE GIL RICHARDSON**, born December 14, 1948. Married FAY SHIPLEY on November 19, 1967. Children: 4.
        ⁵ **KARRI LYNN RICHARDSON**, born January 30, 1969.
        ⁵ **LACY LANE RICHARDSON**, born January 30, 1971.
        ⁵ **ERIC MACY RICHARDSON**, born October 22, 1973.
        ⁵ **TISH RENEE' RICHARDSON**, born February 7, 1979.
    ⁴ **RICKY LYNN RICHARDSON**, born January 30, 1951. Married BECKY MILLER on November 24, 1976. Children: 2.
        ⁵ **ROBERT LYNN RICHARDSON**, born August 2, 1977.
        ⁵ **KEITH LYNN RICHARDSON**, born September 27, 1979.
    ⁴ **GILBERT LAYNE RICHARDSON**, born November 15, 1952. Married PAM BRITTON on October 22, 1976. Children: 2.
        ⁵ **WILLIAM LAYNE RICHARDSON**, born November 19, 1976.
        ⁵ **BRANDY KAY RICHARDSON**, born December 9, 1977.
    ⁴ **MARK RICHARDSON**, born May 5, 1959.
³ **VICTOR ROY DAY**, born February 14, 1936. Married SUSAN "SUZY" DEAN on February 14, 1973. Susan was born on March 1, 1944.

* * * *

DESCENDANTS OF LAURA J. SADLER AND GILBERT RUSSELL DAY:

¹ **LAURA J. SADLER** (fourth daughter and sixth child of William T. and Permelia B. Sadler), born September 8, 1858 in Anderson County, TX. Died November 1, 1925. Married Gilbert Russell "Gib" Day Jr. on November 23, 1897 as his second wife after her sister died. No children were born to Laura and Gib Day.

* * * *

DESCENDANTS OF CELESTIA SADLER AND ALONZO FOSTER:

¹ **CELESTIA "LESSIE" SADLER** (fifth daughter and seventh child of William T. and Permelia B. Sadler), born September, 1860 in Anderson County, TX. Date of death unknown. Married ALONZO "LON" FOSTER on November 4, 1886. Children: 6.
    ² **LENA FOSTER**. Never married.
    ² **CLYDE FOSTER**. Married IDA STUBBLEFIELD. No specifics available.
    ² **EDWINA FOSTER**. Married CHARLIE LIVELY. No specifics available.
    ² **BONNIE FOSTER**. Married _____ KNOWLES. No specifics available.
    ² **CLIFTON FOSTER**. No specifics available.
    ² **WINNIE FOSTER**. No specifics available.

* * * *

APPENDIX F: Descendants of William T. Sadler (Continued)

OTHER CHILDREN OF WILLIAM TURNER SADLER:

¹ **SOPHIA SADLER.** Died during infancy. Believed by author to have been born in 1838 and killed by the Indians during the Edens-Madden Massacre on October 18, 1838. Mother would have been Mary Murchison Sadler.

¹ **JOSEPH SADLER** (third son and eighth child of William T. and Permelia B. Sadler). Died during early childhood on February 6, 1866. Believed by Sadler family to be the child that died with Permelia Bennett Sadler during a tornado which ripped the second floor off their home.

CHAPTER NOTES

CHAPTER 1
TEXAS BOUND: LAMAR AND THE "UNASSUMING GENTLEMAN"

1. Drago, Harry Sinclair. *The Steamboaters: From the Early Side-Wheelers to the Big Packets* (New York: Dodds, Mead & Company, 1967), 6-7.
2. Ibid, 125.
3. *Steamboats on the Mississippi*. Written for American Heritage Junior Library (Mahwah, N.J.: Troll Associates), 57.
4. Mirabeau Buonaparte Lamar kept at least two known journals of his travel to Texas in 1835. One, a sixty-eight-page holograph diary he titled "Journal of My Travels," is in private possession by his great-granddaughter, Kate Calder Pauls of Galveston, at this date. Pages of the document were obtained from microfilm from the Rosenberg Library in Galveston, Texas, courtesy of Anna B. Peelber of the Galveston & Texas History Center. Lamar's "Journal of My Travels" was edited by Philip Graham and printed in the July 1936 issue of *Southwest Review*, Volume XXI, No. 4. Notes from this abbreviated journal will be referenced as Lamar's "Journal of My Travels."
    The second, untitled journal that Lamar kept en route to Texas is a 194-page handwritten journal purchased by Rice University from a dealer in New York City in 1952 which is on file on campus in the Woodson Research Center of Fondren Library. Mr. Steven Johns of the Woodson Research Center was very cooperative in researching the Lamar papers and in providing a copy of the original manuscript. This extended journal, full of the history of each of the towns encountered along the route to Texas, is hereafter referred to as Lamar [Journal].
    The fact that Lamar spelled his companion's name as "Saddler" in his journal is typical of this time. Many documents on Texas list Sadler as Saddler.
5. Ramsay, Jack C. Jr. *Thunder Beyond the Brazos: Mirabeau B. Lamar* (Austin, Tex: Eakin Press, 1985), 9-10.
6. Lamar [Journal].
7. Smola, Joan Coker. *Sadler/Saddler: A Record of the Family and Descendants of Thomas Sadler Sr. (1720-1796) and Rebeccah Featherston (1722-1796/99) of Brunswick County Virginia* (Tulsa, Okla.: Privately Published, 1994), 33.
8. Sherrill, William L. *The Annals of Lincoln County, North Carolina* (Charlotte, N.C.: The Observer Printing House Inc., 1937), 29-31.

9. Smola, 139-40. Additional updated information supplied by Patrick D. Sadler.
10. Sadler descendant Ted Johnston wrote a three-page account of his great-grandfather that was based on the testimony of his mother, Owena Sadler Johnston, and his grandfather, Nathaniel Fletcher Sadler (the oldest son of Captain Sadler). According to this account, W. T. Sadler was employed at one time by the U. S. Army to help build a string of forts along the southern border of the United States. Florida was still owned by Spain, with Georgia being the United States border to this Spanish territory. This account claims that W. T. came to know the Spanish Governor of Florida, who put him to work surveying and mapping areas which Spain intended to claim. This source also claims that Sadler's surveying and mapping work eventually took him into the Texas territory which he became interested in. Johnston's account says that this surveying work helped enable Sadler to earn the right to his first piece of land in Texas, courtesy of Spain. This is included as an interesting footnote; unfortunately, none of Sadler's original headright documents survived to bear out this claim. William Turner's middle name was the maiden name of his maternal grandmother, Martha Turner Sadler.
11. Smola, 1312. Original research done by Joan Coker Smola at Florida State Archives in Tallahassee in 1981.
12. Ibid, 146-47 from Patrick D. Sadler's narrative on William Turner Sadler. Patrick also provided his unedited draft of this narrative for the author's review.
13. Ibid, 147.
14. White, Gifford. *1830 Citizens of Texas: A Census of 6,500 Pre-Revolutionary Texians* (Austin, Tex: Eakin Press, 1983), 1.
15. Barker, Eugene C. *The Life of Stephen F. Austin: Founder of Texas, 1793-1836* (Austin, Tex: University of Texas Press, 1985), 83-88.
16. Ibid, 131.
17. Ibid, 131-32.
18. Ibid, 132.
19. Ibid, 132-33.
20. White, *1830 Citizens of Texas*, 2.
21. Barker, 121.
22. *History of Houston County: 1687-1979*. Compiled and edited by the History Book Committee of Houston County Historical Commission of Crockett, Texas (Tulsa, Okla: Heritage Publishing Company, 1979), 6-7.
23. Ibid, 10.
24. Lamar [Journal], 153-55.
25. Graham, Philip. "Mirabeau B. Lamar's First Trip to Texas." *Southwest Review*, XXI No. 4 (July 1936): 374.
26. Ramsay, 10-11.
27. Ibid, 11-15.
28. Ibid, 17-22.
29. Lamar [Journal], 9.
30. Ibid, 9-10. See also Lamar's "Journal of My Travels" and Graham, 374-75.
31. Lamar's "Journal of My Travels."
32. Lamar [Journal], 377.
33. Ibid, 377-78.
34. Ibid, 381-82.
35. Although Lamar writes in both of his journals that this steamboat's name was the *Romeo*, this boat was likely the *Rover*. *The Louisiana Historical Quarterly*'s 1942 article "The Red River of the South" by N. Philip Norman lists all known steam-

boats to have used the Red River from the first trip by Henry Shreve in 1814 to well into the early 1900s. There is no listing of a *Romeo*, but the Natchitoches-Alexandria packet boat *Rover*, built in 1830, was in service at this time on the Red River. Nancy Boothe Parker points out that neither of Lamar's journals were kept as true day-by-day diaries during the course of these travels. Rather, they appear to have been thoughtfully compiled after the fact with thoughts of publishing them. Over time, memory may have changed the *Rover* to "*Romeo*" in Lamar's mind.
36. Lamar [Journal], 13.
37. *Steamboats on the Mississippi*, 121-24.
38. Lamar [Journal], 31.
39. Ibid, 32-33.
40. Drago, 78-81.
41. Lamar [Journal], 34.
42. Graham, 383.
43. Ibid.
44. Ibid.
45. Lamar's "Journal of My Travels."
46. Parker, Nancy Boothe. "Mirabeau B. Lamar's Texas Journal." *Southwestern Historical Quarterly* LXXXIV No. 2 (October 1980). Article continued in Vol. LXXXIV No. 3 (January 1981): 205.

CHAPTER 2
PIONEERS OF THE FORT HOUSTON SETTLEMENT

1. Webb, Walter Prescott. *Handbook of Texas*, Vol. II, 256.
2. Ibid.
3. Ibid.
4. Letter of Rusk courtesy of The Center For American History at The University of Texas in Austin, Texas.
5. Ericson, Carolyn Reeves. *Nacogdoches Headrights: A Record of the Disposition of Land* (New Orleans: 1977), 15.
6. "Records of an Early Texas Baptist Church." Original records published in *The Quarterly of the Texas State Historical Association.* Part I, covering 1833-1847, is printed in the Vol. XI, No. 2 edition (85-156) from October 1907, and Part II, covering 1847-1869, is printed in the Vol. XII, No. 1 edition (1-60) from July 1908.
7. Parker family history from Pauline Buck Hohes' *A Centennial History of Anderson County, Texas* (San Antonio, Tex: Naylor, 1936), 21-22.
8. Notes on Parker-Bennett family research, courtesy of Laverne Sadler Marsh.
9. Wylie, Edna McDonald. "The Fort Houston Settlement." A Thesis from August 1958, p. 7. Available in the Clayton Branch of the Houston Public Library. Other key source for this period is privately published work of Hulen M. Greenwood entitled *Garrison Greenwood: Ancestors and Descendants* (Houston, Tex: 1986), 57-61.
10. Wylie, 7-8.
11. Ibid, 8.
12. *Supplement to Pioneer Families of Anderson County Prior to 1900* (Palestine, Tex: Anderson County Genealogical Society, January 1991), 73-74.
13. Wylie, 8-9.
14. Ibid.

15. Mary Kate Hunter Notebooks in Palestine Library. "Statement of Mr. R. R. Sadler - Taken Down by Kate Hunter, June 20, 1923."
16. Mary Kate Hunter Notebooks, Vol. IX. Statement of Mr. T. J. Starr from November 16, 1941.
17. *The New Handbook of Texas* (Austin: The Texas State Historical Association, 1996, Six Volumes) Vol. 3, 866.
18. Fowler, Andrew J. "Historical Sketches of Anderson County," in Mary Kate Hunter Papers of Carnegie Library in Palestine, Tablet 8-L, pp. 2-3A.
19. Statement of Mr. T. J. Starr from November 16, 1941 in Mary Kate Hunter Notebooks, Vol. IX. See also Greenwood, 60.
20. Wylie, 10.
21. Ibid, 11.
22. Ibid, 12-13.
23. Greenwood, 60. See also Wylie, 17.
24. Webb, Walter Prescott (Editor-in-Chief). *The Handbook of Texas: A Dictionary of Essential Information* (Austin, Tex: The Texas State Historical Association, 1952) Vol. 2, 757.
25. Boyd, Bob. *The Texas Revolution: A Day-by-Day Account* (San Angelo, Tex: San Angelo Standard, Inc., 1986), 4-5.
26. Ibid, 7.
27. Ibid, 8-9.
28. Ibid, 30.
29. Ibid, 41.
30. Ibid, 42-48.
31. Wylie, 51-52.
32. Webb, Walter Prescott. *The Texas Rangers: A Century of Frontier Defense* (Austin, Tex: The University of Texas Press, 1935), 22-23.
33. Ibid, 20-21.

CHAPTER 3
SADLER'S RANGERS AND THE NACOGDOCHES VOLUNTEERS

1. Smithwick, Noah. *The Evolution of a State/Recollections of Old Texas Days* (1900. Reprint. Austin, Tex: The University of Texas Press, 1983), 82. Smithwick states that his ranger captain, John James Tumlinson, was commissioned to raise his own company.
2. Webb, *The Texas Rangers*, 23.
3. Gammell, Karl Hans Peter Marius Nielsen. *The Laws of Texas, Vol. I.* (Austin, Tex: The Gammel Book Company, 1898), 526-27.
4. Webb, *The Texas Rangers*, 23-24.
5. Pension Papers of Daniel L. Crist, courtesy of the Texas State Library and Archives Commission. All Audited Claims and Pension Papers of the Republic of Texas are contained in microfilm series OCLC#37449683. For statements of Crist on Sadler's company, see reel 211, frames 19-23.
6. Parker affirmed the service of Samuel G. Wells in Sadler's ranger company and stated that he was present at the formation of the unit on January 1, 1836. See Wells Pension Papers, reel 244, frames 650-54.
7. The Pension Papers of Samuel Wells and Daniel Crist indicate that the privates enlisted for a three-month period ending April 1, 1836. Due to the Alamo crisis, however, their service would be cut short.

8. Based on author's research of Audited Claims of the Republic of Texas and a study of the Nacogdoches Volunteers who later served at San Jacinto. For more details on this basis, see footnote 45 in this chapter.
9. Hohes, Pauline Buck. *A Centennial History of Anderson County, Texas* (San Antonio, Tex: Naylor, 1936), 22-23.
10. *The History of Houston County*. For John Crawford Grigsby family, see pp. 376-77. Dr. Frank Edens also furnished information on his ancestor, John Grigsby Sr. John Grigsby Sr. and John Crawford Grigsby are frequently confused, including in a biographical sketch in *The History of Houston County*, 376-77. Crawford Grigsby fought at San Jacinto, but the league of land located in present Dallas in the name of John Grigsby was actually that of his father for being an early Texas settler. For info on the Hallmarks, see pp. 385-87.
11. James Madden info based on his Audited Claims.
12. Wells and Crist both named Sadler's unit as "Company No. 10" in their pension papers. Sadler signed a document on March 19, 1836 as "Paymaster for the Houston Company." For further information on this document, see page 49 in this chapter.
13. Gammell, Vol. I, 526-27 and 924-25.
14. Smithwick 82. See also Wilkins, Frederick. *The Legend Begins: The Texas Rangers, 1823-1845* (Austin, Tex: State House Press, 1996), 16.
15. "Statement of Mr. R. R. Sadler - Taken Down by Kate Hunter, June 20, 1923." Mary Kate Hunter Notebooks, Palestine, Texas. Robert Roach "Tab" Sadler, first grandchild of W. T. Sadler, was born in 1872, making him old enough to have heard his grandpa's stories first-hand. Tab Sadler stated that at the time his grandfather heard of the Alamo's plight, he and a party of men "were working on the house." For more info on this quote, see footnote 23 in this chapter.
16. Pension Papers of Silas H. Bates, whose service in Captain Hillhouse's company was certified by Abram Anglin and Andrew McMillan. See Republic of Texas Audited Claims microfilm series, reel 202, frame 316. Other Audited Claims of Silas Parker and James W. Parker show that Hillhouse served as captain of this first unit through December 31, 1835. He was succeeded by Captain Eli Seale, and James Parker served as captain of a ten-man unit under Silas Parker's superintendence.
17. Boyd, 87-88.
18. Ibid, 88.
19. Wilkins, 18, from Williamson dispatch which can be found in John Henry Brown's *History of Texas*, Vol I, 537.
20. Smithwick, 87.
21. "Statement of Mr. R. R. Sadler - Taken Down by Kate Hunter, June 20, 1923." Robert Roach Sadler's reference to "Fannin's men" at the Alamo should really be "Travis' men." Fannin and his men fought and were captured on March 19, a time when it is known that Sadler's men were already en route to join the army.
22. See Samuel Wells Pension Papers on reel 244, frames 650-54 and those of Daniel Crist, reel 211, frames 19-23. The Alamo, of course, had not fallen by March 1. It is also important to note that these pension papers were filed in July 1873, when the chronology of events was not fresh at hand.
23. Grigsby and his wife Louisa were received into the Pilgrim Church on Saturday, February 6, and he was elected Clerk Protem on March 5, 1836. See "Records of an Early Texas Baptist Church," in *The Quarterly of the Texas State Historical Association*. Part I, Vol. XI, No. 2 edition (October 1907): 100. For info on Sadler's men crossing Robbins' Ferry on March 19, 1836, see page 42. Biographical sketch of Captain Townsend in Sam Houston Dixon and Louis Wiltz

Kemp's *The Heroes of San Jacinto* (Houston, Tex: The Anson Jones Press, 1932). Townsend's first name is mistakenly given as Spencer in this source.
24. Wells info from his audited claims and muster roll of McFarland's company, which is published in *Muster Rolls of the Texas Revolution*, 251-52.
25. Crist Pension Papers, reel 211, frame 8.
26. Boyd, 91-92 and Walter Lord's *A Time To Stand*, 125-28. At least three of these men (Martin, Almeron Dickinson and Jacob C. Darst) had been in the October 2 Gonzales fight.
27. Huston, Cleburne. *Towering Texan: A Biography of Thomas J. Rusk* (Waco, Tex: Texian Press, 1971), 30-32.
28. Ibid, 33-34.
29. Boyd, 92-94.
30. Ibid, 95.
31. The Republic of Texas pension papers of Alfred M. and William Calvert Hallmark show that the brothers both joined the Texas Army at different times. In Alfred's papers (reel 218, frame 608) he states that he joined Captain Hayden Arnold's company on March 6, 1836, and marched with them until joining the Texas Army of Sam Houston at the Colorado River. William's papers (reel 218, frames 640-42) show that he did not join Arnold's company until about April 1, 1836, at which time the army was stationed at Groce's Retreat near the Brazos River.
32. Family sketches of these Nacogdoches Volunteers obtained from *The History of Houston County*. For Yarbrough, see page 633.
33. For Box family information see *The History of Houston County*, 262-67. Also referenced: Edna Box Riley's "Stephen Box Family" sketch.
34. Dixon, Sam Houston and Louis Wiltz Kemp. *The Heroes of San Jacinto* (Houston, Tex: The Anson Jones Press, 1932). Additional biographical sketch of Captain Hayden Arnold by Kemp was furnished by Brian Butcher, Research Director for the San Jacinto Museum of History.
35. Information on the Nacogdoches Volunteers drawn largely from biographical sketches in *The Heroes of San Jacinto*, 339-54.
36. Purcell, Robert Allen. *The History of the Texas Militia* (Austin, Tex: University of Texas, 1981), 75-78.
37. Ibid, 77.
38. Boyd, 98-99.
39. Lord, Walter. *A Time To Stand: The Epic of the Alamo as a Great National Experience* (New York: Harper & Row Publishers, 1961), 175 and 206-207. He also presents the controversial account that one of these victims executed may have been the fabled Davy Crockett. Aside from the three Americans who survived, at least ten Hispanic women and children inside the fortress were spared.
40. Boyd, 99.
41. Huston, 35-37.
42. Lord, 178-81.
43. Bate, W. N. *General Sidney Sherman: Texas Soldier, Statesman and Builder* (Waco, Tex: Texian Press, 1974), 34-35. The two blacks were Travis' ex-slave Joe and Ben, Colonel Almonte's black orderly, who was sent along as an escort.
44. Boyd, 104-105.
45. Daniel Parker Jr.'s pension papers (mircrofilm reel 232, frames 300-302) state that he enrolled in Captain Arnold's Company of Sherman's regiment at the Colorado River. One of the witnesses to his pension in 1874 was William T. Sadler, who in his own pension papers, lists that he joined the Texas Army at the

Dewees Crossing of the Colorado River. Crawford Grigsby joined the army about April 1, according to Dixon and Kemp, 344. William Hallmark also joined about April 1, according to his pension papers. Philip Martin also joined the army at the Colorado River, serving briefly with Captain William Smith's spy company before joining Arnold's company just prior to the Battle of San Jacinto. See Martin's pension papers, reel 227, frame 299. James Madden also joined the Nacogdoches Volunteers after their formation, although date is unknown. His audited claims show that he was discharged from Arnold's company on April 26, 1836. One of Arnold's muster rolls states that Madden was "discharged 22 April after battle." See *Muster Rolls of the Texas Revolution*, 66 and James Madden Audited Claims, reel 63, frame 647.
46. Tolbert, Frank X. *The Day of San Jacinto* (New York: McGraw-Hill Book Co., 1959), 49-51.
47. Boyd, 107-109.
48. Ibid, 109.
49. Ibid, 111.
50. Dixon and Kemp, 345.

CHAPTER 4
A TIME TO FIGHT: THE FORK IN THE ROAD

1. Tolbert, 87-88.
2. Bate, 40.
3. Ibid, 41.
4. Tolbert, 51-52.
5. Ibid, 52.
6. Huston, 37.
7. Tolbert, 80-82.
8. Bate, 45.
9. "Recollections of S. F. Sparks." *Quarterly of the Texas State Historical Association* XII No. 1 (July 1908): 61.
10. Tolbert, 82-83.
11. Huston, 38 and Tolbert, 90.
12. Dixon, 345.
13. Tolbert, 91.
14. Huston, 38-40.
15. "Recollections of S. F. Sparks," 67.
16. Pohl, James W. *The Battle of San Jacinto* (Texas State Historical Association, 1989), 25-26.
17. "Recollections of S. F. Sparks," 69.
18. Tolbert, 94-96.
19. Bate, 57.
20. Dixon, 345.
21. Tolbert, 97.
22. Ibid, 99.

CHAPTER 5
RENDEZVOUS WITH SANTA ANNA: THE BATTLE OF SAN JACINTO

1. "Recollections of S. F. Sparks," 70.
2. Bate, 57.

3. "The Battle of San Jacinto. By One Who Fought In It." Anonymous early account of the battle written by a cavalry member. Published in Little's *Living Age*, September 7, 1844, 259-65.
4. Pohl, 29.
5. Tolbert, 113.
6. Ibid, 113-15.
7. Ibid, 116-17.
8. Ibid, 117.
9. Bate, 62-63.
10. "The Battle of San Jacinto. By One Who Fought In It," 10.
11. Dixon, 345.
12. Tolbert, 124-39.
13. Tolbert on page 144 describes Emily as being a slave girl of James Morgan. According to more recent research, Emily D. West was actually a free mulatto (or mixed black and Caucasian). Apparently Sam Houston himself helped spread the story of Santa Anna's involvement with this woman at the moment of the attack on the San Jacinto battlefield. See Bob Tutt's "New Twists Discovered in Saga of 'Yellow Rose of Texas.' Researcher discovers that Sam Houston played a role in one of Texas' greatest stories." Originally printed in *Houston Chronicle*, reprinted in *Port Arthur News* on Thursday, March 13, 1997, 4B.
14. "Recollections of S. F. Sparks," 70-71.
15. Original letter of Heard from May 18, 1859 was quoted in the 1860 *Texas Almanac* and is also quoted in Bate's *General Sidney Sherman*, 70.
16. Tolbert, 141.
17. Dixon, 341.
18. *History of Houston County*, 633.
19. Tolbert, 145-46.
20. "Recollections of S. F. Sparks," 71.
21. Ibid, 71.
22. Hohes, Pauline Buck. *A Centennial History of Anderson County, Texas* (San Antonio, Tex: Naylor, 1936), 23.
23. Huston on page 48 discusses the Rusk brothers assisting Houston. David Rusk, of course, was from Sadler's company, indicating that the Nacogdoches Volunteers were at or near this scene. The story of Sadler also assisting General Houston is plausible and had been told to the author's great-grandmother, Diamond Sadler Kolb. Her recollections were later typed up as "Roach-Sadler History," courtesy of Laverne Sadler Marsh.
24. Ibid, 49. Dr. N. D. Labadie quote from "The Battle of San Jacinto" which was published in the 1859 issue of the *Texas Almanac*.
25. Letter of Sidney Sherman letter published in the *Galveston Weekly News*, September 15, 1857.
26. Tolbert, 165-75.
27. "Recollections of S. F. Sparks," 72.
28. This story was related to author by his grandmother, Evaline Kolb Moore, and her cousin, former Texas Land Commissioner Jerry Sadler.
29. "The Battle of San Jacinto. By One Who Fought In It," 264.
30. Tolbert, 179.
31. *History of Houston County* describes this event on pages 10 and 558. This account is related by Nathaniel F. "Nat" Sadler from Nathaniel F. "Fletch" Sadler, the latter being the first son of W. T. Sadler.

32. Huston, 52.
33. Tolbert, 184-86.

CHAPTER 6
POST-SAN JACINTO: A NEW THREAT IN EAST TEXAS

1. Tolbert, 192-93.
2. "Recollections of S. F. Sparks," 73.
3. Bate, 112.
4. Jenkins, John H. *Papers of the Texas Revolution*, Vol. 7, 152-53.
5. Pierce, Gerald Swetnam. *The Army of the Republic of Texas, 1836-1845*. A dissertation from the University of Mississippi, copyright 1964, on file in the Texas Room of the Houston Public Library, 47-49.
6. Ibid, 50-51.
7. Pierce, *Texas Under Arms*, 168.
8. Bate, 125-27.
9. Pierce, *Texas Under Arms*, 168.
10. Pierce, *The Army of the Republic of Texas*, 64.
11. Ibid, 59-61.
12. Ibid, 63.
13. Letter of Leander Smith to Brigadier Gen. Thomas J. Rusk in Jenkins, Vol. 7, 433.
14. De Shields, James T. *Border Wars of Texas* (Austin, Tex: State House Press, 1993), 135. Originally printed in 1912 by the Herald Company of Tioga, Texas.
15. Woldert, Albert, M.D. "The Last of the Cherokees in Texas, and the Life and Death of Chief Bowles." *Chronicles of Oklahoma*, Issued by the Oklahoma Historical Society in Oklahoma City, Okla. Vol. I, No. 3, (June 1923): 193.
16. Ibid, 182-83.
17. De Shields, 173-74.
18. "The Records of an Early Texas Baptist Church." *The Quarterly of the Texas State Historical Association*. Volume I (1833-1847) of the church's history is published in the Vol. XI, No. 2 issue of October 1907. Quote from 100.
19. Brown, John Henry. *Indian Wars and Pioneers of Texas*, 40-43.
20. *New Handbook of Texas*, Vol. 2, 348.
21. Pierce, *Texas Under Arms*, 72-73.
22. *History of Cherokee County*.
23. Everett, Dianna Everett. *The Texas Cherokees: A People Between Two Fires, 1819-1840* (Norman: University of Oklahoma Press, 1990), 80.
24. *History of Houston County*, 505 and 11 (Letter of Daniel McLean to his son James McLean, who was attending school in Natchitoches, Louisiana). Due to the quality of such early grammar, the author has included minor editing.
25. DeShields, 223-25.
26. Brown, 55-56.
27. Ibid, 56.
28. Wylie, 36.
29. Webb, et. al. *The Handbook of Texas*, Vol II, 250.
30. DeShields, 207-208.
31. *History of Houston County*, 11, 504-505, and 564-65.
32. "A Brief Study of Thomas J. Rusk Based on His Letters to His Brother, David, 1835-1856," *Southwestern Historical Quarterly* XXXIV (April, 1931): 278-79.
33. Ibid.
34. Pierce, *The Army of the Republic of Texas*, 127-28.

35. DeShields, 211.
36. Woldert article, including special notes included by the author in a copy held by the Texas State Archives. Woldert's quotes from Congressman Burton are taken from "First Biennial Report of the Texas Library, and Historical Association from March 29th, 1909, to August 31st, 1910," which contained excerpts from the *Secret Journals of the Senate of the Republic of Texas* (2nd Congress).

CHAPTER 7
CORDOVA'S REBELLION AND GENERAL RUSK'S TEXAS MILITIA

1. Everett, 83-84.
2. Ibid, 85-89.
3. Purcell, Robert Allen. *The History of the Texas Militia* (Austin, Tex: University of Texas, 1981), 81-82.
4. Ibid, 73-74.
5. Ibid, 311.
6. Everett, 90.
7. Ibid, 90-91.
8. Brown, 62-63.
9. Ibid, 56.
10. Everett, 91.
11. Pierce, *The Army of the Republic of Texas*, 135-36.
12. Everett, 94.
13. *Lone Star State*, 238-39.
14. "A Brief Study of Thomas J. Rusk Based on His Letters to His Brother, David, 1835-1856," *Southwestern Historical Quarterly* XXXIV (April, 1931): 279.
15. Ibid, 280.
16. Everett, 94-96.
17. Pierce, *The Army of the Republic of Texas*, 137-38.
18. DeShields, 272.
19. Letter from Citizens of Fort Houston to President Sam Houston, from Original Rusk Papers, Stephen F. Austin State University Library in Nacogdoches, Texas.
20. Pierce, *Texas Under Arms*, 74-75.
21. Original muster roll of Captain Squire Brown's Mounted Gunmen, August 30, 1838 - December 28, 1838.
22. John Wortham came to Houston County, Texas in 1837 with his first wife and first three children. His biography in *History of Houston County*, 627-28, also relates that the Walkers were closely tied to him. The Walkers are found on Captain Wortham's ranger muster roll when his unit was created on November 7, 1838. Wortham was promoted to major in early 1839 and Solomon Adams took command of the Houston County Rangers (see muster roll of Adams' unit in appendix for Cherokee War). John Nite brought his wife and first three children from Alabama in 1837 and settled west of Crockett near Porter Springs in Houston County. Nite was first lieutenant of Wortham's rangers. See *History of Houston County*, 512.
23. *History of Houston County*, 504.
24. Pierce, *Texas Under Arms*, 75.
25. Original Rusk Papers.
26. *Cherokee County History*. First Edition, 1986.
27. Everett, 96.

28. Brown, 56.
29. Pierce, *Texas Under Arms*, 86.
30. Pierce, *The Army of the Republic of Texas*, 139-40.
31. Everett, 96.
32. Pierce, *The Army of the Republic of Texas*, 140.
33. Mabbitt's forces based on rosters of Captain Brown; Captain James Bradshaw's Mounted Riflemen, October 10 - December 1, 1838; Captain Jacob Snively's Mounted Rangers, September 4 - December 13, 1838; and Captain James E. Box's Mounted Riflemen, October 14, 1838 - January 14, 1839. Sadler's company roster is constructed by author's research, including Republic of Texas audited claims on microfilm. Many of his men became part of Captain Box's company when it was formed on October 14. The others are men who are known to have participated in Cordova's Rebellion from around the Fort Houston and Fort Brown areas.

CHAPTER 8
MABBITT'S SKIRMISH AND THE BATTLE OF KICKAPOO

1. Avera, Carl. *Centennial Notebook: A Collage of Reminenece of Palestine's First Century* (Palestine, Tex: Royall National Bank, 1976), 2.
2. Brown, 56.
3. *Telegraph and Texas Register*, letter of Major General Thomas J. Rusk, November 3, 1838.
4. Lacy account from *Memorial and Biographical History of Navarro, Henderson, Anderson, Limestone, Freestone and Leon Counties, Texas*, 240. Lacy's account is also contained in the Mary Kate Hunter Notebooks in the Palestine Library.
5. Ibid.
6. Wylie, 103.
7. Letter of Major General Thomas J. Rusk printed in the *Telegraph and Texas Register*, November 3, 1838. For roll of participants in the Battle of Kickapoo, author relied upon sources previously noted in Chapter 7. These additional muster rolls were also used: Major General Thomas J. Rusk's General Staff, Campaigns of 1838 and 1839 (August 4, 1838 - February 1, 1839); Captain William C. Brookfield's Mounted Rangers, October 12 - 24, 1838; Captain John Durst's Mounted Volunteers of Mt. Sterling Settlement (Nacogdoches County), October 10 - 20, 1838; Captain Robert W. Smith's Mounted Nacogdoches Volunteers, August 8 - 21, 1838; and Captain Joseph Williams' Mounted Volunteers (2nd Regiment, 3rd Brigade, Texas Militia), October 9 - 19, 1838.
8. "A Brief Study of Thomas J. Rusk," *Southwestern Historical Quarterly* XXXIV (April 1931), 279-80.
9. Gulick, *The Papers of Mirabeau Buonaparte Lamar*, Vol II, 263-67.
10. Brown, 56.
11. Rusk letter from *Telegraph and Texas Register*, November 3, 1838.
12. Brown, 56, and letter of Col. Hugh McLeod to M. B. Lamar from Gulick, *The Papers of Mirabeau Buonaparte Lamar*, Vol II, 266.
13. McLeod letter from Gulick, Vol. II, 266.
14. Brown, 56.
15. McLeod letter from Gulick, Vol. II, 266.
16. Ibid.
17. Judge Andrew J. Fowler article on "The Edens Massacre" from Historical

Sketch of Anderson County in Palestine Library.
18. McLeod letter from Gulick, Vol. II, 266.
19. Ibid.
20. Rusk letter from *Telegraph and Texas Register*, November 3, 1838.
21. Ibid.
22. McLeod letter from Gulick, Vol. II, 266.
23. *Republic of Texas Pension Application Abstracts.* Published by the Austin Genealogical Society (Austin, Tex: Morgan Printing and Publishing, 1987), 89. In Daniel L. Crist's pension papers, Dr. Perry stated that he was the surgeon of Major Mabbitt's battalion and that he operated on Crist to remove the rifle balls from his hip and hand. See Audited Claims reel 211, frames 9-16.
24. Woldert, 201-205.
25. Everett, 96.
26. McLeod letter from Gulick, Vol. II, 266.
27. *The New Handbook of Texas, Vol. 4* (Austin, Tex: The Texas State Historical Association), 891.
28. Wylie, 84.
29. Audited Republic Claims of Texas from the Texas State Library and Archives Commission series OCLC#37449683. Claim of John Walker may be found on reel 108, Frames 499-500. For Robert Madden's claim, see reel 63, frame 652.
30. Audited Republic Claims of Texas, series OCLC#37449683. See claims of John Murchison, located on reel 126, frames 304-306.

CHAPTER 9
THE EDENS-MADDEN MASSACRE

1. Judge Andrew J. Fowler's "The Edens' Massacre" account, from the Mary Kate Hunter Notebooks in Palestine, Texas, states that the armed and mounted Indians were "supposed to be Anadarkos." De Shields on 107 of *Border Wars of Texas* claims that these Indians were the Caddos.
2. McLean, Malcolm D. (ed.). *Papers Concerning Robertson's Colony in Texas* (Arlington: The University of Texas at Arlington, 1991), Vol. XVII, 260-61.
3. *The Edens Adventure: A Brief History of the Edens Family in America* (Published by the Edens Family Association, 1992), 40.
4. Fowler's "The Edens' Massacre" account. Fowler's writing is based on a personal interview with Mrs. Ruth Ann Grigsby Edens of Palestine, who was 16 years old at the time and in the Davis house that night. She later married Balis Edens, who escaped the massacre with his life.
5. *History of Houston County*, 12.
6. DeShields, 107.
7. Ibid.
8. Fowler's "The Edens Massacre."
9. DeShields, 107.
10. *History of Houston County*, 12.
11. Fowler's "The Edens Massacre."
12. Ibid.
13. *History of Houston County*, 12.
14. *The Edens Adventure*, 39-40.
15. Account of Lucinda Madden's grandson, James William Madden, which has

been published in the *History of Houston County* on page 13 and in *The Edens Adventure* on pages 34-37.
16. Ibid.
17. Ibid.
18. DeShields, 107-108.
19. David H. Campbell letter to President-Elect Mirabeau B. Lamar in Gulick's *The Papers of Mirabeau Buonaparte Lamar*, Vol. II, 263-65.
20. "Notes Relative to the Edens Massacre," written by Robert H. Sadler on January 1, 1971. Courtesy of Howard C. Sadler collection. The sources of Robert Sadler's writeup, are, in his words: "I was told many times of the Edens Massacre in my early childhood by my father and grandfather, Nathaniel F. Sadler, who was the son of W. T. Sadler, whose wife, child and mother-in-law were killed in the raid." A *Palestine Herald-Press* article on Captain Sadler from 1969 also states that Mary Sadler and her "infant child" were killed in the massacre. Former Texas Land Commissioner Jerry Sadler, a great-grandson of Captain Sadler, was told by his grandfather that W. T.'s wife and child had been killed in the massacre. This fact Jerry related to the author in a 1980 interview and also included in the introduction of his memoirs, published in 1984.
21. Sadler family notes prepared by Robert H. Sadler, a great-grandson of Captain Sadler. Robert Sadler heard Lula Sadler Davis' account at her home in Grapeland, Texas.
22. Ericson, Carolyn Reeves. *Nacogdoches - Gateway to Texas, Vol. I: A Biographical Directory, 1773 - 1849* (Nacogdoches, Tex: Ericson Books, 1991).
23. *The Edens Adventure*, 40.
24. Brown, *Indian Wars and Pioneers of Texas*, 57.
25. Ibid.
26. *History of Houston County*, 240.
27. Fowler's "The Edens Massacre."
28. Ibid.
29. *Houston County Cemeteries*, 895.

CHAPTER 10
THE REPUBLIC'S NEW FIRST REGIMENT OF INFANTRY
1. Pierce, *Army*, 142.
2. Ibid.
3. William T. Sadler Pension Papers, courtesy of Howard C. Sadler.
4. *The Edens Adventure*, 41-44.
5. Captain Jacob Snively received 38 bushels of corn on October 30, 1838, from Armstead Bennett and 3 bushels of corn from Daniel Parker. This is evidenced by Audited Claims of the Republic of Texas on microfilm reel 7. Joel Daniel Leathers of the Mustang Prairie community in Houston County also furnished 700 bushels of corn to the Texas Army, as evidenced by a receipt from December 29, 1838, which was endorsed by Quartermaster Martin Lacy. See *History of Houston County*, 445. Martin Murchison submitted a claim for furnishing fodder, hay and five cattle to the army on October 22, 1838. Murchison had previously supplied Captain Jewel's Fort Houston rangers in 1836. See Audited Claims microfilm series, reel 126, frames 307-14.
6. On Rusk's lack of volunteers, see Pierce, 143. Captain Wortham's Houston

County Rangers Muster Roll of November 9, 1838 - February 8, 1839 courtesy of the Texas State Library and Archives Commission. John P. Barnett, John E. Clapp and Ira P. Ellis transferred into Wortham's company from that of Captain Brookfield's previous command.
7. Pierce, *Army*, 143.
8. Gammell, Vol. II, 3-5.
9. Pierce, 144.
10. Ibid.
11. Ibid, 145-46.
12. Dixon and Kemp, *The Heroes of San Jacinto*, 32.
13. Ibid, 31.
14. Gulick, *The Papers of Mirabeau Buonaparte Lamar*, Vol. 2, 352.
15. See Pierce, *Army*, 153-54; also Gammel, Vol. II, 15-17.
16. Gammell, "An Act to provide for the protection of the Northern and Western Frontier," Vol. II, 15-17.
17. Ibid, Vol. II, 29-30.
18. Ibid, Vol. II, "An Act For the Protection of a Portion of the Frontier," 31.
19. Ibid, Vol. II, 44, 78, and 93.
20. Pierce, 154.
21. Ibid, 154-55.
22. Pierce, *Army*, 155-57.
23. Thompson, Karen R. (Editor). *Defenders of the Republic of Texas* (Austin, Tex.: Laurel House Press by the Daughters of the Republic of Texas, 1989), 15.
24. Ibid, 16.
25. Pierce, 146.
26. Webb, *The Handbook of Texas*, Vol. 2, 233.
27. Thompson, 15.
28. Ibid, 15.
29. Koury, Michael J. *Arms For Texas: A Study of the Weapons of the Republic of Texas* (Fort Collins, Colo.: The Old Army Press, 1973), 8, 14 and 39-40.

CHAPTER 11
SADLER'S APPEAL TO PRESIDENT LAMAR

1. *History of Houston County*, 280.
2. Bennett and Lagow supplied the army with 11 bushels of corn at $2.50 each for a receipt of $27.50. For this and other provisions to the military forces in East Texas, Bennett and Lagow were finally reimbursed by a joint resolution approved January 17, 1842. This document was signed by Speaker of the House of Representatives Kenneth Anderson, President of the Senate Edward Burleson and by Sam Houston.
3. Thompson, *Defenders of the Republic of Texas*, 15-16.
4. Letter of Post Master Barr to President Lamar in Day, James M. *Post Office Papers of the Republic of Texas, 1836-1839* (Austin, Tex: Texas State Library, 1966), 215-18.
5. Ibid, 213-15.
6. William S. McDonald letter to Captain Sadler of January 23, 1839 from Wortham Papers, now located in the University of Texas' Center for American History.

7. Wylie, 49.
8. Brown, 57-58.
9. McDonald to Sadler letter of January 23, 1839.
10. Brown, 58.
11. Copy of original letter obtained from Texas State Archives. Sadler's appeal to Lamar is also printed in Gulick's *The Papers of Mirabeau Buonaparte Lamar*, Vol. II, 464-65. Author has made minor punctuation and spelling corrections for ease of readership.

CHAPTER 12
FRONTIER FREEDOM: THE CHEROKEE WAR

1. Crosby, David F. "Texas Rangers in The Battle of Brushy Creek." *Wild West* Vol. 10, No. 2 (August 1997): 62-63.
2. Ibid, 89-90.
3. Jenkins, John H. and Kenneth Kesselus. *Edward Burleson: Texas Frontier Leader* (Austin, Tex: Jenkins Publishing Co., 1990), 186.
4. Nance, Joseph M. *After San Jacinto: The Texas-Mexican Frontier, 1836-1841* (Austin, Tex: University of Texas Press, 1963), 90-91.
5. *Telegraph and Texas Register*, January 9, 1839. For more details on the frontier companies of this period, see Appendix A.
6. For the surviving rosters of the First Regiment of Infantry for 1839-1841, see Thompson's *Defenders of the Republic of Texas*.
7. Aldrich, Armistead Albert. *History of Houston County, Together with Biograhical Sketches of Many Pioneers* (San Antonio, Tex: The Naylor Co., 1943), 16. P. O. Lumpkin had been named the new Chief Justice on January 23, 1839, by the Third Congress, but he resigned this position on March 12 to serve as a government agent to select and survey the site of the republic's permanent capital. Aside from Aldrich, John Kerchoffer also briefly filled this position in 1839 before John Collins assumed the duties of Houston County Chief Justice for the next year and a half.
8. Brice, Donaly E. *The Great Comanche Raid: Boldest Indian Attack of the Texas Republic* (Austin, Tex: Eakin Press, 1987), 10-13.
9. Richardson, T. C. *East Texas*, Vol. 1, 116.
10. Everett, *The Texas Cherokees*, 51.
11. Everett, 102-103 and Clarke, Mary Whatley. *Thomas J. Rusk: Soldier, Statesman, Jurist* (Austin, Tex: Jenkins Publishing Company, 1971), 124.
12. Pierce, *Texas Under Arms*, 125.
13. Quartermaster's Orders of May 22, 1839. Letter courtesy of Archives Division of the General Land Office of Texas.
14. Woldert, 197-98.
15. Reagan, John H. *The Memoirs of John H. Reagan*. Edited by John F. Jenkins (Austin, Tex: The Pemberton Press, 1968), 32.
16. Reagan, John H. "Expulsion of the Cherokees from East Texas." *Quarterly of the Texas State Historical Association* Vol. I (1897): 40. Hereafter sited as Reagan "Expulsion."
17. Everett, 103-104.
18. Jenkins, *Burleson*, 197-99.
19. Reagan, "Expulsion" 41.
20. Woldert, 209-12.

21. Procter, Ben H. *The Life of John H. Reagan* (Austin, Tex: The University of Texas Press, 1962), 22-23.
22. Pierce, *Texas Under Arms*, 76.
23. Everett, 104.
24. Ibid, 104-105.
25. Clarke, *Thomas J. Rusk*, 130.
26. Everett, 106.
27. Jenkins, *Burleson*, 200.
28. Reagan, *Memoirs*, 32.
29. DeShields, 300.
30. Ford, 29.
31. Reagan, *Memoirs*, 33.
32. "Report of K. H. Douglass of the Campaign Against the Cherokees," August, 1839. Provided by Donaly E. Brice, Supervisor of Reference Services with the Texas State Library and Archives Commission. Hereafter referred to as Douglass Cherokee Campaign Report. See also Winfrey, Dorman, and James M. Day. *The Texas Indian Papers, 1825-1843*. 4 volumes (Austin, Tex: Austin Printing Co., 1911), 76-77.
33. Cherokee War from *Telegraph and Texas Register* of August 7, 1839.
34. The August 7, 1839 *Telegraph and Texas Register* states that this company was that of a "Captain Ford," but it is likely that this was intended to be Captain Todd.
35. Woldert in "The Last of the Cherokees in Texas" from the *Chronicles of Oklahoma* gives the location of the battles of the Cherokee War. Some of Woldert's research after publishing this article was made available to the author by Donaly E. Brice of the Texas State Archives.
36. Winfrey and Day, 77.
37. Procter, 24-25.
38. Woldert, 217-18.
39. Jenkins, *Burleson*, 202.
40. Procter, 25.
41. Pierce, *Texas Under Arms*, 89-90 and 205-206.
42. Douglass Cherokee Campaign Report.
43. Brown, *Indian Wars and Pioneers of Texas*, 68.
44. Douglass Cherokee Campaign Report.
45. Reagan, *Memoirs*, 33.
46. Procter, 26.
47. Jones quote from Brown, 68.
48. Reagan, "Expulsion" 45.
49. DeShields, 302.
50. Reagan, *Memoirs*, 34.
51. Clarke, *Thomas J. Rusk*, 133.
52. Jones quote from Brown, 68.
53. Letter dated Nacogdoches, July 27, 1885, published by Brown, 68.
54. Reagan, "Expulsion" 45-46.
55. Jones, Ernest. "Captain W. T. Sadler Helped Create County." *Palestine Herald-Press*, Wednesday, February 5, 1969, 10. Sadler's involvement in the death of Chief Bowles was also related to the author by his grandmother, Evaline Kolb Moore, her cousin and former Texas legislator Jerry Sadler and relative Howard C. Sadler.

56. Brown, 68.
57. Everett, 108.
58. Ericson, 45-46.
59. Clarke, *Thomas J. Rusk*, 134.
60. Clarke, Mary Whatley. *Chief Bowles and the Texas Cherokees*. Civilization of the American Indian Series, No. 113 (Norman: University of Oklahoma Press, 1971), 111.

CHAPTER 13
Transition Years Of A Young Nation

1. Douglass Cherokee Campaign Report.
2. Lane, Walter Paye. *The Adventures and Recollections of General Walter P. Lane* (Austin, Tex: Pemberton Press, 1970), 41.
3. *Republic of Texas Pension Application Abstracts*. Published by the Austin Genealogical Society (Austin, Tex: Morgan Printing and Publishing, 1987), 49.
4. Ford, 30.
5. Clarke, *Chief Bowles and the Texas Cherokees*, 110.
6. Clarke, *Thomas J. Rusk*, 135-36.
7. Jenkins, *Edward Burleson*, 206-209.
8. Everett, 108-109.
9. Clarke, *Thomas J. Rusk*, 135.
10. Pierce, *Texas Under Arms*, 76.
11. Ibid, 104-105, 175. Camp Walnut Creek was located within a few miles of Austin, a little more than 2 miles northeast of the Montopolis bridge over the Colorado River.
12. For the August 29, 1839 First Infantry officer roster, see Gulick, No. 1425, Vol. 3, 84-86. Kennymore with an 18-man detachment had been ordered by Burleson on October 18 to establish what became Camp Caldwell. See Jenkins, 215. Company C passed to Kennymore on October 23, 1839, according to muster roll records published in Thompson's *Defenders of the Republic of Texas*. This camp was believed to be named for Mathew Caldwell, a noted frontiersman and volunteer captain for a time in the First Infantry Regiment. This Camp Caldwell was adjacent to Kenney's Fort, a private fort built by Dr. Thomas Kenney and Joseph Barnhart in the spring of 1839, while construction of Austin's capitol was underway some 25 miles south. It was described as consisting of a single blockhouse and three or four log cabins, surrounded by an eight foot stockade. For Camp Caldwell and Kenney's Fort see Pierce's *Texas Under Arms*, 25-26, 81-82.
13. Secretary of War Albert Sidney Johnston to President Lamar, from the War Department, City of Austin, December 12, 1839. From the Army Papers (Correspondence, 1837-1839), Texas State Archives, Texas State Library, Austin.
14. Audited Claims of the Republic of Texas. See microfilm reel 92, frame 311, for claim of Joseph Schleiter. Audited Claims for Mark Skerrett show that he had been in charge of the new army's artillery corps from December 7, 1838 - January 23, 1839, at which time he was promoted to captain. Pay records for the period of September - December 30, 1839, show Skerrett to be in command of Post Galveston.
15. Thompson, *Defenders of the Republic of Texas*, 99. Chevalllie was transferred to Company E from Company G on February 26, 1840.
16. Ibid. See muster rolls for Company F. January's Company F was recruited through October 30, left Galveston on November 5, 1839, then left Houston for

Austin on November 12. Company F arrived at Camp Caldwell on December 5, 1839. Muster rolls records of those men who transferred from Company G indicate their enlistment between October 18 and November 11 at Galveston.

17. Johnston to Lamar, December 12, 1839. Johnston's letter does not mention any company commanders by name. He lists four companies under Burleson stationed on the Colorado River above Austin, one company marching toward Austin that was expected hourly, one company stationed at the Falls of the Brazos, and one and a half more companies en route from Galveston.

18. Author's research of muster roll records and known activities of each company. Companies H and I were recruited through December 4th (see Thompson, *Defenders*, 223-27, 243-47) and thereafter en route from Galveston on December 12.

19. Captain George Howard lists Captain Moore as being in charge of a wagon guard from Fort Burleson during late October and early November. See "Document A: Engagement with Indians on the 24th, Oct., 1839, - Captain George T. Howard's Command," written on October 29, 1839. Published in *Appendix to the Journals of the House of Representatives: Fifth Congress* (Printed at the Gazette Office, courtesy of the Texas State Archives), 125-26.

20. Pierce, *The Army of the Republic of Texas*, 179.

21. Jenkins, 216. John Lynch had been captain of a special six-man Spy Detachment which had been paid $25 a month per man to serve as scouts for Burleson's troops from 6/25 - 8/25/39.

22. Jenkins, 216 and Pierce, *Army*, 179.

23. Details of this battle taken from Edward Burleson's report, written on December 26, 1839, from Camp Lynch. See *Appendix to the Journals of the House of Representatives: Fifth Congress*, 126-28.

24. Jenkins, 218.

25. For Redd's Company A, see Thompson's *Defenders of the Republic of Texas*, 27 - 37. His company left Camp McLeod on February 2, arrived in San Antonio on February 9 and marched from San Antonio to Mission San Jose on the 10th. Company A would remain at Mission San Jose through April of 1840. Muster roll records place Company C (Thompson, 99 - 103) under Kennymore and Company I under Captain Benjamin Gillen (Thompson, 248-53) at Mission San Jose on February 29, 1840, where they remained through April. A muster roll of the First Regiment's Field and Staff shows William Fisher commanding companies A, C and I and the Southwestern Frontier from January through February 29, 1840 (Thompson, 257).

26. Company B is shown to be stationed at San Gabriel through February 29. Records place them in San Gabriel by at least February 12. Adam Clendenin left on furlough on February 7 and Lt. Collier Hornsby took over as acting commander. See Thompson, 76-80. Company D remained stationed at Fort Burleson continuously until May 28. On January 28, 1840, Captain John Holliday assumed command from George Howard. See Thompson, 131-142. Company E was under Holliday through January of 1840 and command was assumed by Mark B. Lewis on February 26, 1840, following serious desertions from two other companies. E was at Camp Caldwell on Feb. 12, 1840, where several men deserted. Lewis' men departed Camp Caldwell on February 22 and arrived at Camp Cazneau on Onion Creek on March 5, 1840. See Thompson, 162-169.

27. A muster roll signed by Captain Laurence places Company H at Camp Lamar near Austin on December 31, 1839. Under Captain Skerrett, H established Fort Skerrett in Cherokee Nation during early 1840. They remained there until July 11,

CHAPTER NOTES 349

when they began their march back to the Austin area. See Thompson, 223-38.
28. No muster roll has survived for Captain Sadler's Company G. Its actions are based on the likely turn of events which encouraged so many men to desert. Muster rolls from other First Regiment companies show many men from G being transferred in around February 26, 1840, when Lt. Col. Fisher apparently stepped in to sort out the crisis. For the movements of Company F and its own high desertion rate, see Thompson 188-93.
29. Thompson, 188-93. One man joined Company I under Lt. Col. Fisher's command after having been returned from desertion on February 25. At least two other men joined Company B after having deserted from Company G in February. See Thompson, 81-82. For an account of the court martial of the five captured men from Sadler's Company G, see *Malcolm D. McLean's Papers Concerning Robertson's Colony in Texas* (Arlington: The University of Texas at Arlington Press, 1991), Vol. XVI, 523-27. The five captured men were Sergeant Oliver P. Gale, Corporal Jacob McMindus, and privates James W. Brown, Josiah R. Edgar and Charles Ladoucer. They were tried at Camp Cazneau by Colonel William Cazneau, Colonel Jacob Snively, Captain George Howard, Captain Mark Lewis and Lieutenant A. C. Holmes. Lieutenant William Dunnington acted as special Judge Advocate. The five men were all found guilty and were sentenced to be shot to death. The men were ultimately pardoned, released from arrest and ordered to return to duty in Company E on February 26. Dunnington cited in these men's favor the "temporary want of supplies, and the extreme difficulties attending the transportation when procured, added to the inclemency of the winter, at times when the troops were suffering."
30. Thompson's *Defenders of the Republic of Texas* is again the key source for information on the desertions of Companies F and G. The twenty-four men of Company G who were transferred into Captain Lewis' Company E on February 26 were: 3rd Sergeant Edward Smith, 4th Corporal Henry Sandcular, and privates T. W. Brown, John Brown, Michael Campbell, Daniel Carlin, John Dalton, Lewis Duval, Peter Davison, Josiah R. Edgar, Thomas Denning, Albert Germar, Thomas Haskins, Wilson C. Hamilton, Charles Ladoucer, Conrad Lundell, Jacob McMindus (demoted), Thomas O'Brien, John Quinn, Michael Riley, James Simms, Hiram Summers, Joseph Schleiter, and Henry Ward. See 163-69. First Lieutenant Michael Chevallie is shown to have been transferred by Fisher to Company C on 26 Feb 1840. See 109. Two more men, privates James W. Brown and Oliver P. Gale, were charged with deserting Company G and were reassigned to Company B on March 11, 1840. See 81-82.
31. Thompson, 169, 193. Camp Cazneau, in honor of Commissary General William L. Cazneau, was on Onion Creek near Austin in Travis County, probably near the present Bergstrom Air Force Base. For description, see Pierce's *Texas Under Arms*, 27.
32. Brice, 21-26.
33. White, *1840 Census of Texas*, 154.
34. Original letter to Col. Archibald R. S. Hunter of Murphy, North Carolina was presented to the University of Texas by Mary Kate Hunter, granddaughter of Dr. Hunter. This letter is also included in Wylie's "Fort Houston Settlement" as Appendix B.
35. Pierce, *Texas Under Arms*, 76.
36. Hunter letter previously cited.
37. Ibid.

38. Wylie, 77.
39. Thompson, *Defenders of the Republic of Texas*, 16.
40. Webb, Walter Prescott. *The Texas Rangers: A Century of Frontier Defense* (Austin, Tex: University of Texas Press, 1991), 67-73.
41. Ibid, 73-77.
42. Brown, 58.
43. Neyland, James. *Palestine (Texas): A History* (Palestine, Tex: Empress Books), 1.
44. Related by Howard Sadler from his grandfather Claude Sadler, who was a grandson of W. T. Sadler.
45. *Supplement to Pioneer Families of Anderson County Prior to 1900* (Palestine, Tex: Anderson County Genealogical Society, January, 1991), 15-17. Armstead and Faith Bennett had brought the following children with them to Texas: thirty-year-old son Stephen Bennett, his wife and four-year-old daughter Icephenia; daughter Sarah Bennett, who later married Thomas Lagow; D. W. Bennett, a son who had died on November 30, 1836, while in the service of the Texas Army; son Miles Bennett, who had also served in the post-San Jacinto Texas Army; daughter Permelia; daughter Judith, who married Daniel Parker Jr.; youngest son Benjamin; and daughter Elizabeth, who married William Grigsby. Elizabeth married Bannister Edens in 1857 after Grigsby had passed away.
46. "The Records of an Early Texas Baptist Church." *The Quarterly of the Texas State Historical Association*, Volume I (1833-1847), published in the Vol. XI, No. 2 issue (October 1907): 155. The congregation was not without its vices, as evidenced by one entry in the Primitive Church's records. In a meeting on September 5, 1846, "Brother Armstead Bennett informed the church that he had been overtaken in a fault by drinking too much arden spirits whereupon the church hearing the acknowledgement of Brother Bennett unanimously forgave him."
47. *The New Handbook of Texas*, Vol. 3, 484.
48. Ibid, Vol. 2, 336.
49. Ibid, Vol. 3, 914.
50. Gammel, *Laws of the Republic of Texas*, Vol. II, 967-68.

CHAPTER 14
THE END OF A REPUBLIC: THE NINTH CONGRESS

1. *New Handbook of Texas*, Vol. 2, 267.
2. *The Texas Capitol: Symbol of Accomplishment* (Austin, Tex: The Texas Legislative Council in Cooperation with The Texas Highway Department, 1967), 22.
3. *New Handbook of Texas*, Vol. 2, 267.
4. Webb, *The Handbook of Texas*, Vol. 2, 865.
5. DeBruhl, Marshall. *Sword of San Jacinto: A Life of Sam Houston* (New York: Random House, 1993), 298-99.
6. *Journals of the House of Representatives of the Ninth Congress of the Republic of Texas* (Washington, Tex: Miller & Cushney, Public Printers, 1845), 3-4.
7. Ibid, 4-16.
8. Gambrell, Herbert. *Anson Jones: The Last President of Texas* (1947; reprint, Austin, Tex: University of Texas Press, 1988), 372.
9. *Journals of the House of Representatives of the Ninth Congress of the Republic of Texas.*, 56.
10. Ibid, 93-97.
11. Ibid, 97.
12. Ibid, 172.

13. Ford, 32-33.
14. *Journals of the House of Representatives of the Ninth Congress of the Republic of Texas,* 354-56.
15. *Journals of the Convention, Assembled at the City of Austin on the Fourth of July, 1845, For the Purpose of Framing a Constitution for the State of Texas* (Austin, Tex: Miner & Cruger, Printers to the Convention, 1845), I-III.
16. Ibid, III.
17. DeBruhl, 316.
18. *Journals of the Convention, Assembled at the City of Austin on the Fourth of July, 1845, For the Purpose of Framing a Constitution for the State of Texas,* IV.

CHAPTER 15
THE FIRST LEGISLATURE SHAPES THE NEW STATE

1. *Journals of the Convention, Assembled at the City of Austin on the Fourth of July, 1845, For the Purpose of Framing a Constitution for the State of Texas,* vi.
2. Ibid, vi - xi.
3. Winchester, Robert Glenn. *James Pickney Henderson: Texas' First Governor* (San Antonio, Tex: The Naylor Company, 1971), 70.
4. Sherrill, William L. *The Annals of Lincoln County, North Carolina* (Charlotte, N.C.: The Observer Printing House Inc., 1937), 163-64.
5. *History of Houston County,* 475.
6. Clark, Sara. *The Capitols of Texas: A Visual History* (Austin, Tex: Encino Press, 1975), 23.
7. Ibid.
8. Connor, Seymour V., et. al. *Capitols of Texas* (Waco, Tex: Texian Press, 1970), 85-87.
9. Winchester, 70 and *Journals of the House of Representatives of the First Legislature of the State of Texas* (Clarksville, Tex: Standard Office, 1848).
10. Winchester, 71-73.
11. Huston, 126-27.
12. Winchester, 78-79.
13. *Journals of the House of Representatives of the First Legislature of the State of Texas,* 66.
14. Ibid, 100.
15. Gammell, *Laws of the State of Texas,* Vol. II, 1326-27.
16. *Journals of the House of Representatives of the First Legislature of the State of Texas,* 302-309.
17. Miller, *The Public Lands of Texas, 1519-1970,* 60.
18. *Journals of the House of Representatives of the First Legislature of the State of Texas,* 308.
19. Ibid, 309.
20. Ibid, 330.
21. Ibid, 488-89.
22. Ibid, 683-84.
23. Gammell, *Laws of the State of Texas,* Vol. II, 182.
24. Ibid, 183.
25. Winchester, 80-81.
26. *Journals of the House of Representatives of the First Legislature of the State of Texas,* 719-21.
27. Ibid, 722-26.

CHAPTER 16
EARLY ANDERSON COUNTY AND THE SECOND LEGISLATURE
1. Neyland, *Palestine (Texas): A History*, 1.
2. *History of Houston County*, 558.
3. "Splendid Program Marks Unveiling of Markers by the Woman's Foundation," *Palestine Daily Herald*, November 29, 1926.
4. *The New Handbook of Texas*, Vol. 1, 172.
5. *Journals of the House of Representatives of the State of Texas, Second Legislature* (Houston, Tex: Published at the *Telegraph* Office, 1848), 3-5.
6. Ibid, 19-28.
7. Ibid, 29.
8. Reagan, *Memoirs*, 53-54.
9. *Journals of the House of Representatives of the State of Texas, Second Legislature*, 203.
10. Ibid, 190-91.
11. *The New Handbook of Texas*, Vol. 2, 1143.
12. *Journals of the House of Representatives of the State of Texas, Second Legislature*, 553-54.
13. Reagan, *Memoirs*, 54.
14. Ibid, 54-55.
15. Ibid, 55.
16. Neyland, 5-9.

CHAPTER 17
CALIFORNIA GOLD, TEXAS RAILROADS AND THE CIVIL WAR
1. Family writeup by Ted Johnston, a great grandson of W. T. Sadler.
2. *The New Handbook of Texas*, Vol. 2, 12.
3. "Century-Old Records Reveal Names of First Postmasters in County" from Mary Kate Hunter Notebooks, Vol. II.
4. Johnson, William Weber. *The Old West Series: The Forty-Niners* (Alexandria, Va.: Editors of Time-Life Books, 1974), 19, 23-38.
5. Related by Howard Sadler, whose father Robert heard the story from William Sadler's son Nathaniel Fletcher.
6. *The Edens Adventure*, 347.
7. Martin, Mabelle Eppard (Editor). "From Texas to California in 1849: Diary of C. C. Cox." *Southwestern Historical Quarterly*: 3rd Installment in Vol. VIII (January 1926): 213.
8. Ibid, 3rd Installment, 213-14.
9. Ibid, 2nd Installment from October 1925, Vol. VII, 132.
10. Webb, *The Handbook of Texas*, Vol. 2, 250.
11. Martha Tucker Sadler statement of July 17, 1927, in Volume IX of Ms. Hunter's unpublished notebooks in Palestine's Carnegie Library. Her statements are also published in the *Sadler/Saddler Family* history, 163-64.
12. Hohes, 44-45.
13. Ibid, 136.
14. Patrick D. Sadler research provided to author.
15. *The New Handbook of Texas*, Vol. 5, 411.
16. W. T. Sadler Pension Papers, courtesy of Howard C. Sadler.
17. *The New Handbook of Texas*, Vol. 2, 12.
18. Source: Parker-Sadler-Bennett research provided by Laverne Sadler Marsh.

19. Page, Dave. *Ships Versus Shore: Civil War Engagements Along Southern Shores and Rivers* (Nashville, Tenn.: Rutledge Hill Press, 1994), 345.
20. Weyland, 15.
21. Hohes, 50.
22. *Documents of Texas History*, 196.
23. Hohes, 50-51. Captain Gardner, captain of the county's first Civil War company, died on June 28, 1862. Additional information on Anderson County's participation in the Civil War courtesy of Marshall L. Moore Jr.'s research of Mary Kate Hunter's Notebooks in Palestine's Carnegie Library.
24. Ibid, 51.
25. Neyland, 16-17.
26. Sadler, Jerry with James Neyland. *Politics, Fat-Cats & Honey-Money Boys: The Mem-Wars of Jerry Sadler* (Santa Monica, Cal: Roundtable Publishing, Inc., 1984), 2-4. This story was related to Jerry Sadler by his grandfather, N. F. Sadler. The author also heard this story from Jerry in 1980. In his autobiography, he goes on to relate the conversation of Sam Houston and William Sadler, as roughly recalled by 14-year-old Nathaniel Fletcher Sadler. Sadler implied that Houston had been drunk at San Jacinto and not even commanding his troops at the time he was wounded. Various stories, in fact, emerged over the years from different San Jacinto veterans that Sam Houston (a known drinker) may have been under the influence. Other stories indicate that he tried to halt the Texan charge and may have left the battlefield. More than a few stories have been told over the years as to how he was actually wounded and as to whether he was shot by friend or foe. Jerry Sadler indicates that his great-grandfather had immense respect for the Texas leader and thus chose never to speak out against his courage in battle. Similarly, few who fought Santa Anna's army at San Jacinto chose to believe him to be anything less than the hero of Texas independence.
27. De Bruhl, Marshall. *Sword of San Jacinto: A Life of Sam Houston* (New York: Random House, 1993), 402.
28. Aldrich, *History of Houston County*, 21-22.
29. Brown, *Indian Wars and Pioneers of Texas*, 581.
30. Ibid.
31. Spencer, John. *Terrell's Texas Cavalry: Wild Horsemen of the Plains in the Civil War* (Austin, Tex: Eakin Press, 1982), v-vi.
32. Briggs, Osjetea. "Jerry Sadler – Statesman." *The Dogwood Express*, Vol. 3, No. 48 (Wednesday, December 2, 1981): 10.
33. Related to author in 1980 by Jerry Sadler, a grandson of N. F. Sadler.
34. Spencer, 14-22.
35. Livermore, Thomas L. *Numbers & Losses in the Civil War in America, 1861-1865* (Carlisle, Pennsylvania: John Kallmann Publishers, 1996), 109-10.
36. Spencer, vi-vii, quoting C. H. Jackson in *Texans Who Wore Gray*.
37. Ibid, 132, 103, 130.

CHAPTER 18
FINAL YEARS OF A TEXAS VETERAN
1. Weyland, 19.
2. Sadler with Neyland, *Politics, Fat-Cats & Honey-Money Boys: The Mem-Wars of Jerry Sadler*, 8. Many of these blacks who took on the name of Sadler continued to

live in Anderson County. From his youth in the county, Patrick Sadler remembers Harriet Sadler, the elderly wife of Stuart Sadler, both of whom had been born in Georgia and had traveled to Texas in the early 1850s. Pat and Howard Sadler both remembered Sherman, George and Abraham Lincoln "Linc" Sadler, who were sons of "Aunt Charlotte" Sadler. "Aunt Charlotte" is probably the nineteen-year-old Emiline Sadler shown on Anderson County's 1870 census. Since she passed away in January 1936 at age 84, she is the only Georgia-born former slave of the right age in the county. Charlotte must have been her middle name or nickname. She worked for some time on the farm of Captain Sadler's son Fletcher. A grandson of "Aunt Charlotte" named Harvey Sadler still lives in Anderson County at the present time. For more info on Aunt Charlotte Sadler, see *The Tracings*, Volume XII, No. 2 (June 1993): 21. Published by the Anderson County Genealogical Society.
3. Hohes, 52-53.
4. Ibid, 52.
5. Ibid, 221.
6. Ibid, 440-41.
7. Ibid, 443.
8. Neyland, 10.
9. *The New Handbook of Texas*, Vol. 1, 172.
10. Ibid, Vol. 2, 12.
11. Ibid, Vol. 1, 172.
12. *Biographical Directory of the Texan Conventions and Congresses, 1832 - 1845* (Austin, Tex: Book Exchange, 1941), 166-67.
13. *The New Handbook of Texas*, Vol. 2, 12.
14. Sadler with Neyland, 1.

BIBLIOGRAPHY

Personal Contacts:
This book is possible thanks largely to the support and assistance of others. Chief on the list of those who went of their way to help gather materials was my father, Marshall L. Moore Jr., who spent time in Tyler, Palestine, Austin and other cities while researching various portions of this text. He spent a good deal of time digging up information from Anderson County and also provided a number of photos from such historical sites as Fort Houston and the old Parker's Fort.

Other members of my family have been of great assistance in compiling this history. Patrick D. Sadler has shared the wealth of his genealogical research, his insights and his Sadler documents. He also served as an advisor throughout the process of researching this text, encouraging me to look further into various areas. The late Howard C. Sadler of Port Arthur allowed me to study and copy many of his family archives, including W. T. Sadler's Pension Papers and Audited Military Claims, N. F. Sadler's Pension Papers, newspaper clippings and compilations by his father, and several illustrations contained within this text. Howard also served as an avid supporter of this project and gave me encouragement to complete the work.

Joan Coker Smola furnished a copy of her exhaustive family compilation on the *Sadler/Saddler* family history. Laverne Sadler Marsh of Tyler also provided copies of a number of the Sadler family documents she has collected. From the Edens family, Dr. Frank N. Edens, Arthur Hall and Mrs. Jack W. Schoultz of Grapeland provided input concerning Sadler's ties to the horrible Edens-Madden Massacre of Houston County. In my youth, I also listened to a number of stories concerning Captain Sadler from my grandmother, Evaline Kolb Moore. Her cousin, former Texas Land Commissioner Jerry Sadler, related much of his insight on his great-grandfather for a school paper I was working on in 1980.

Donaly E. Brice, Supervisor of Reference Services at the Texas State Library and Archives Commission in Austin, went out of his way to help answer questions, to look up historical data and to provide documents which he felt would be helpful in my efforts. Mr. Brice and his staff, including Preservation Officer John Anderson, were also very generous in the time they spent reproducing requested muster rolls, journals of Congress and illustrations.

Research Director Brian Butcher of the San Jacinto Museum of History supplied assistance on the Battle of San Jacinto and biographical research of Louis Kemp concerning Sadler. Mr. Butcher was also instrumental in securing approval from the museum for reproduction of a number of illustrations.

For Sadler's travels to Texas with Mirabeau Buonaparte Lamar in 1835, I relied upon two little known journals that Lamar kept. One, a sixty-eight-page holograph diary he titled "Journal of My Travels," currently is in the possession of his great-granddaughter, Kate Calder Pauls of Galveston. Pages of the document were obtained from microfilm from the Rosenberg Library in Galveston, Texas, courtesy of Anna B. Peebler of the Galveston & Texas History Center. Lamar's "Journal of My Travels" was edited by Philip Graham and printed in the July 1936 issue of *Southwest Review*. The second, untitled journal that Lamar kept is a 194-page handwritten journal, acquired by Rice University in 1952 from a dealer in New York City, which is on file on the campus in the Woodson Research Center of Fondren Library. Mr. Steven Johns of the Woodson Research Center was very cooperative in researching the Lamar papers, in providing a copy of the original manuscript and in offering other articles for research.

Mr. Kenneth R. Cade took the time to escort my wife, father and me around the Neches battlegrounds, located on private property, near present Tyler, Texas. Mr. Cade is working with The American Indian Heritage Center of Texas, Inc., to preserve this historic site as a state monument in the future.

For Anderson County information, I must thank Mrs. Elizabeth Neel of the Anderson County Genealogical Society and Brenda Ladd of the Palestine Public Library's Specials.

Doug Weiskopf and his associates of the Houston Public Library's Texas Room were helpful in locating political and historical references to Captain Sadler. The Clayton Genealogy Division of the Houston Public Library also proved to be an invaluable source for family histories, county histories, early Texas census data, and numerous Republic of Texas documents.

For Appendix F: Sadler Family Tree, I relied heavily upon the research of Patrick Sadler and the lengthy *Sadler/Saddler Family* book. Special thanks go to JoAnn Day Freeman for editing this section and encouraging me to contact Patrick for clarifications on many of the dates. Howard Sadler, Kathy Moore and Marlene Phillips also helped to update their family's particular sections. JoAnn Freeman and Jane Linkswiler went out of their way to have a close-up photo taken of Sadler's Gold Rush ring.

Printed Government Documents:
Appendix to the Journals of the House of Representatives: Fifth Congress. Printed at the Gazette Office for the Republic of Texas, 1841.
Journals of the Convention, Assembled at the City of Austin on the Fourth of July, 1845, For the Purpose of Framing a Constitution for the State of Texas. Austin, Tex: Miner & Cruger, Printers to the Convention, 1845.
Journals of the Fourth Congress of the Republic of Texas. Austin, Tex: Von Boeckmann-Jones Co. Printers, 1930.
Journals of the House of Representatives of the First Legislature of the State of Texas. Clarksville, Tex: Printed at the Standard Office, 1848. Pages from this journal were reproduced from the Holdings of the Texas State Archives.
Journals of the House of Representatives of the State of Texas, Second Legislature. Houston, Tex: Published at the *Telegraph* Office, 1848.

Journals of the House of Representatives of the Ninth Congress of the Republic of Texas. Washington, Tex: Miller & Cushney, Public Printers, 1845.
Uniform of the Army of the Republic of Texas. Prescribed and published by order of the President.

Unpublished Materials:
Army Papers, Republic of Texas. Archives and Library Division, Texas State Library in Austin, Texas.
Edens, Dr. Frank N. Unpublished research on Parker and Bennett families.
Hunter, Mary Kate. Unpublished Papers of, located in Carnegie Library in Palestine, Texas. Miss Hunter was a school teacher who collected statements in the early 1900s from many of the county's earliest citizens. Some of her collected works are referenced, including, "Statement of Mr. R. R. Sadler - Taken Down by Kate Hunter, June 20, 1923"; "Some Early History of Palestine" by Bonner Frizzell; and Judge A. J. Fowler's "The Edens' Massacre" and "Historic Sketches of Anderson County."
Lamar, Mirabeau Buonaparte. "Journal of My Travels." This sixty-eight-page holograph diary of his 1835 journey to Texas is in the private possession by his great-granddaughter, Kate Calder Pauls of Galveston, at this date. Pages of the document were obtained from microfilm from the Rosenberg Library in Galveston, Texas, courtesy of Anna B. Peelber of the Galveston & Texas History Center. A second, untitled 194-page hand-written journal that Lamar kept is in the possession of Rice University in Houston, Texas, in the Woodson Research Center of Fondren Library.
Muster Rolls of the Texas Army and the Texas Militia, courtesy of the Texas State Archives. See individual chapter footnotes and appendices for those referenced.
Riley, Edna Box. "Stephen Box Family" sketch of 1971 in the collections of the Clayton Genealogy Branch of the Houston Public Library.
Rusk, Thomas Jefferson, letter to President D. G. Burnet of April 22, 1836, from the Headquarters of the Army of Texas at San Jacinto. Courtesy of The Center for American History, The University of Texas at Austin.
Sadler, Robert H. "Notes Relative to the Edens Massacre." Written on January 1, 1971. "Facts related to Robert H. Sadler by Lula Sadler Davis of Grapeland, Texas, widow of John A. Davis." Courtesy of Howard C. Sadler collection.
Sadler, William Turner. Texas Pension Papers and Audited Military Claims. Provided courtesy of Howard C. Sadler. Also referenced: William Turner Sadler land documents provided by the General Land Office of Texas.
Wimberly, Dan B. "Daniel Parker: Pioneer Preacher and Political Leader." History dissertation submitted to the Graduate Faculty of Texas Tech University in May 1995. Courtesy of Dr. Frank N. Edens.
Wylie, Edna McDonald. "The Fort Houston Settlement." A Thesis from August 1958 in the collections of the Houston Public Library's Clayton Genealogy Branch.

Articles/Newspapers:
"The Battle of San Jacinto. By One Who Fought In It." Anonymous early account of the battle written by a member of the cavalry. Published in Little's *Living Age*, (September 7, 1844): 259-65.
"A Brief Study of Thomas J. Rusk Based on His Letters to His Brother, David, 1835-1856." *Southwestern Historical Quarterly*, XXXIV (April 1931).

Briggs, Osjetea. "Jerry Sadler – Statesman." *The Dogwood Express*, Vol. 3, No. 48, (December 2, 1981): 10.
Brown, Jennifer. "Their Spirits Still Live On Battleground: Indian Group Buys East Texas Site of Famed Battle of Neches." *Tyler Morning Telegraph*, (December 14, 1997).
Crosby, David F. "Texas Rangers in The Battle of Brushy Creek." *Wild West*, Vol. 10, No. 2, (August 1997): 60-64, 89-90.
Fuller, Henry C. "Stirring Events of History Written in Nacogdoches Fort." *Houston Press*, (April 30, 1931).
Graham, Philip. "Mirabeau B. Lamar's First Trip to Texas." *Southwest Review*, Vol. XXI No. 4, (July 1936).
"Jerry Sadler – A Life of Serving the Public." *Palestine Herald Press Midweek Extra*, (November 28, 1979): 2-3.
Jones, Ernest. "Captain W. T. Sadler Helped Create County." *Palestine Herald-Press*, (February 5, 1969): 10.
Martin, Mabelle Eppard (Editor). "From Texas to California in 1849: Diary of C. C. Cox." *Southwestern Historical Quarterly* Vol. VI, (July 1925): 113-38; Vol. VII, (October 1925): 36-50; Vol. VIII, (January 1926): 201-223.
Norman, N. Philip. "The Red River of the South." *The Louisiana Historical Quarterly*, (1942).
Obituary of W. T. Sadler in *Austin American Statesman*, (March 7, 1884).
Parker, Nancy Boothe. "Mirabeau B. Lamar's Texas Journal." *Southwestern Historical Quarterly*, Vol. LXXXIV, No. 2 (October 1980). Article continued in Vol. LXXXIV, No. 3 (January 1981).
Reagan, John Hunter. "Expulsion of the Cherokees from East Texas." *Quarterly of the Texas State Historical Association*, Vol. I (1897), 38-46.
"The Records of an Early Texas Baptist Church." *The Quarterly of the Texas State Historical Association*. Volume I (1833-1847) of the church's history is published in the Vol. XI, No. 2 issue of October 1907 and Volume II (1847-1869) is published in Vol. XII, No. 1 of July 1908.
"Recollections of S. F. Sparks." *Quarterly of the Texas State Historical Association*. Volume XII, No. 1 (July 1908).
"Sadler Descendant of County Pioneer." *Palestine Herald-Press*, (January 10, 1975).
Sherman, Sidney. "Further Defenses Against General Houston's Charges." *The Galveston Weekly News*, (June 23, 1835).
"Slavery Time 'Mammy' Dies Over Week End," *Palestine Daily Herald*, (January 9, 1936). This obituary of "Aunt Charlotte" Sadler and other info on her is also contained in Anderson County Genealogical Society's *The Tracings*, Volume XII, No. 2 (June 1993): 1.
"Splendid Program Marks Unveiling of Markers by the Woman's Foundation," *Palestine Daily Herald*, (November 29, 1926).
Texas Democrat. Published in Austin, Texas, (May 20, 1846), Vol. I, No. 20.
Telegraph and Texas Register. Early Texas newspaper published in Houston. Many articles (see source notes from individual chapters for dates) between 1836 and 1839 copied from microfilm in the Texas Room of the Houston Public Library.
Tutt, Bob. "New Twists Discovered in Saga of 'Yellow Rose of Texas.' Researcher discovers that Sam Houston played a role in one of Texas' greatest stories." Originally printed in *Houston Chronicle*, reprinted in *Port Arthur News* (March 13, 1997): 4B. Courtesy of Howard C. Sadler.
Walter, John F. "Terrell's Texas Cavalry." Courtesy of John F. Walter's Institute for Civil War Research, (March 1978, revised July 1996).

Woldert, Albert, M.D. "The Last of the Cherokees in Texas, and the Life and Death of Chief Bowles." *Chronicles of Oklahoma*, Issued by The Oklahoma Historical Society in Oklahoma City, Okla., Volume I, Number 3, (June 1923): 179-226. Copy provided by the Texas State Archives, which included supplemental notes made by Woldert after the original publication of this article.

Yates, Becky. "Historical Date Line: Edens-Madden Massacre." *The East Texas Roundup*, Crockett, Texas, (December 17, 1970): 6. Courtesy of Howard C. Sadler.

Books:

Aldrich, Armistead Albert. *History of Houston County, Together with Biograhical Sketches of Many Pioneers*. San Antonio, Tex: The Naylor Co., 1943.

Avera, Carl. *Centennial Notebook: A Collage of Reminenece of Palestine's First Century*. Palestine: Royall National Bank, 1976.

———. *From Steamboats to Spacecraft: Between the Neches and the Trinity. A History of Anderson County's First 125 Years*. Palestine, Tex: Express Books, an Imprint of the Word Factory.

Ault, Phil. *Whistles Around the Bend: Travel on America's Waterways*. New York: Dodd, Mead & Company, 1982.

Barker, Eugene C. *The Life of Stephen F. Austin: Founder of Texas, 1793-1836*. Austin: University of Texas Press, 1985.

Barker, Eugene C., and Amelia W. Williams, eds. *The Writings of Sam Houston* (eight volumes). Austin: University of Texas Press, 1938.

Bate, W. N. *General Sidney Sherman: Texas Soldier, Statesman and Builder*. Waco, Tex: Texian Press, 1974.

Battles of Texas. Waco, Tex: Texian Press, 1987.

Biographical Directory of the Texan Conventions and Congresses, 1832 - 1845. Austin, Tex: Book Exchange, 1941.

Biographical Gazetteer of Texas. Austin, Tex: W. M. Morrison Books, 1987.

Blessington, Joseph Palmer. *The Campaigns of Walker's Texas Division*. Austin, Tex: State House Press, 1994. Originally published in New York City in 1875 by Lange, Little & Company.

Boyd, Bob. *The Texas Revolution: A Day-by-Day Account*. San Angelo, Tex: San Angelo Standard, Inc., 1986.

Brice, Donaly E. *The Great Comanche Raid: Boldest Indian Attack of the Texas Republic*. Austin, Tex: Eakin Press, 1987.

Brown, John Henry. *Indian Wars and Pioneers of Texas*. 1880. Reprint. Austin, Tex: State House Press, 1988.

Caughey, John Walton. *The California Gold Rush*. Berkley and Los Angeles, Calif: University of California Press, 1948.

Cherokee County History. First Edition, 1986. Crockett, Tex: Published by the Cherokee County Historical Commission and the Publications Development Co. of Texas.

Clark, Sara. *The Capitols of Texas: A Visual History*. Austin, Tex: Encino Press, 1975.

Clarke, Mary Whatley. *Chief Bowles and the Texas Cherokees*. Civilization of the American Indian Series, No. 113. Norman, Okla.: University of Oklahoma Press, 1971.

Clarke, Mary Whatley. *Thomas J. Rusk: Soldier, Statesman, Jurist*. Austin, Tex: Jenkins Publishing Company, 1971.

Connor, Seymour V., et. al. *Capitols of Texas*. Waco, Tex: Texian Press, 1970.

Day, James M. *Post Office Papers of the Republic of Texas, 1836-1839*. Austin, Tex: Texas State Library, 1966.

De Bruhl, Marshall. *Sword of San Jacinto: A Life of Sam Houston.* New York: Random House, 1993.
De Shields, James T. *Border Wars of Texas.* 1912. Reprint. Austin, Tex: State House Press, 1993.
Dixon, Sam Houston and Louis Wiltz Kemp. *The Heroes of San Jacinto.* Houston, Tex: The Anson Jones Press, 1932.
Drago, Harry Sinclair. *The Steamboaters: From the Early Side-Wheelers to the Big Packets.* New York: Dodd, Mead & Company, 1967.
The Edens Adventure: A Brief History of the Edens Family in America. Published by the Edens Family Association, 1992.
Ericson, Carolyn Reeves. *Nacogdoches Headrights: A Record of the Disposition of Land.* New Orleans: 1977.
———. *Nacogdoches – Gateway to Texas. A Biographical Directory, Vol. I.* Nacogdoches, Tex: Ericson Books, 1977.
Everett, Dianna Everett. *The Texas Cherokees: A People Between Two Fires, 1819-1840.* Norman: University of Oklahoma Press, 1990.
Ford, John Salmon, edited by Stephen B. Oates. *Rip Ford's Texas.* Austin: University of Texas Press, 1994.
Gambrell, Herbert. *Anson Jones: The Last President of Texas.* Austin: University of Texas Press, 1988 reprint. 1947. Reprint.
Gammell, (Karl) Hans Peter Marius Nielsen. *The Laws of Texas.* Austin, Tex: The Gammel Book Company, 1898.
Greenwood, Hulen M. *Garrison Greenwood: Ancestors and Descendants.* Privately published by author in Houston, Tex: 1986.
Gulick, Charles A. Jr., Winnie Allen, Katherine Elliott, and Harriet Smither. *The Papers of Mirabeau Buonaparte Lamar,* 6 Volumes. Austin, Tex: Pemberton Press, 1968.
History of Houston County: 1687-1979. Compiled and edited by the History Book Committee of Houston County Historical Commission of Crockett, Texas. Tulsa, Okla.: Heritage Publishing Company, 1979.
Hohes, Pauline Buck. *A Centennial History of Anderson County, Texas.* San Antonio, Tex: Naylor, 1936.
Houston County (Texas) Cemeteries. Third Edition. Marceline, Mo.: Walsworth Publishing Co, Inc., 1987.
Huston, Cleburne. *Towering Texan: A Biography of Thomas J. Rusk.* Waco, Tex: Texian Press, 1971.
Ingmire, Mrs. Frances Terry. *Anderson County, Texas Land Titles.* Dallas, Tex: Copyright 1979.
James, Marquis. *The Raven: A Biography of Sam Houston.* 1929. Reprint. Atlanta, Ga.: Mockingbird Books, Inc., 1956.
Jenkins, John H. and Kenneth Kesselus. *Edward Burleson: Texas Frontier Leader.* Austin, Tex: Jenkins Publishing Co., 1990.
Jenkins, John H. *Papers of the Texas Revolution 1835-1836.* Ten Volumes. Austin, Tex: Presidial Press, 1973.
Johnson, William Weber. *The Old West Series: The Forty-Niners.* Alexandria, Va.: Editors of Time-Life Books, 1974.
Koury, Michael J. *Arms For Texas: A Study of the Weapons of the Republic of Texas.* Fort Collins, Colo.: The Old Army Press, 1973.
Lane, Walter Paye. *The Adventures and Recollections of General Walter P. Lane.* Austin, Tex: Pemberton Press, 1970.
Livermore, Thomas L. *Numbers & Losses in the Civil War in America, 1861-1865.* Carlisle, Pa.: John Kallmann Publishers, 1996.

Lord, Walter. *A Time To Stand: The Epic of the Alamo as a Great National Experience*. New York: Harper & Row Publishers, 1961.
Mainer, Thomas Nelms. *Houston County in the Civil War*. Houston County Historical Commission: Publications Development Company of Texas, 1981.
McAllister, Anne Williams and Kathy Gunter Sullivan. *Court of Pleas and Quarter Sessions: Lincoln County, North Carolina. 1789 April - 1796 April.* Published by authors, 1987.
———.*Court of Pleas and Quarter Sessions: Lincoln County, North Carolina. April 1805 - October 1808*. Published by authors, 1988.
McLean, Malcolm D. *Papers Concerning Robertson's Colony in Texas*. Published by the University of Texas at Arlington. Arlington, Tex: The UTA Press, Vol. XVI, 1991.
Miller, Thomas Lloyd. *Bounty and Donation Land Grants of Texas: 1835-1888*. Austin: University of Texas Press, 1967.
Muster Rolls of the Texas Revolution. Austin: Daughters of the Republic of Texas, 1986.
Nacogdoches County Families: Texas Sesquisentinneal, Vol. I. Published by The Nacogdoches County Genealogical Society. Dallas, Tex: Curtis Media Corporation, 1985.
Nance, Joseph M. *After San Jacinto: The Texas-Mexican Frontier, 1836-1841*. Austin: University of Texas Press, 1963.
Nevin, David. *The Old West Series: The Texans*. Alexandria, Va: Editors of Time-Life Books, 1975. (Note: This book contains a copy of Sadler's 640-acre land grant from San Jacinto on page 136.)
The New Handbook of Texas. Austin: The Texas State Historical Association, 1996, Six Volumes.
Newcomb, W. W. Jr. *The Indians of Texas: From Prehistoric to Modern Times*. Austin, Tex: University of Texas Press, 1961.
Neyland, James. *Palestine (Texas): A History*. Palestine, Tex: Empress Books.
Page, Dave. *Ships Versus Shore: Civil War Engagements Along Southern Shores And Rivers*. Nashville, Tenn: Rutledge Hill Press, 1994.
Pierce, Gerald Swetnam. *The Army of the Republic of Texas, 1836-1845*. Dissertation from the University of Mississippi, copyright 1964, on file in the Texas Room of the Houston Public Library.
———. *Texas Under Arms. The Camps, Posts, Forts, and Military Towns of the Republic of Texas*. Austin, Tex: Encino Press, 1969.
Pioneer Families of Anderson County Prior to 1900. Palestine, Tex: Anderson County Genealogical Society, 1984.
Pohl, James W. *The Battle of San Jacinto*. Texas State Historical Association, 1989.
Procter, Ben H. *The Life of John H. Reagan*. Austin, Tex: The University of Texas Press, 1962.
Purcell, Robert Allen. *The History of the Texas Militia*. Austin: University of Texas Press, 1981.
Ramsay, Jack C. Jr. *Thunder Beyond the Brazos: Mirabeau B. Lamar.* Austin, Tex: Eakin Press, 1985.
Reagan, John Henninger. *The Memoirs of John H. Reagan*. Edited by John F. Jenkins. Austin, Tex: The Pemberton Press, 1968.
Republic of Texas Pension Application Abstracts. Published by the Austin Genealogical Society. Austin, Tex: Morgan Printing and Publishing, 1987.
Richardson, Rupert N. *Texas, The Lone Star State*. New York: Prentice-Hall, 1943.
Roberts, Madge Thornall (Editor). *The Personal Correspondence of Sam Houston. Volume I: 1839-1845*. Denton: University of North Texas Press, 1996.

Roland, Charles P. *Albert Sidney Johnston: Soldier of Three Republics.* Austin: University of Texas Press, 1964.
Sadler, Jerry with James Neyland. *Politics, Fat-Cats & Honey-Money Boys: The Mem-Wars of Jerry Sadler.* Santa Monica, Calif.: Roundtable Publishing, Inc., 1984.
Sherrill, William L. *The Annals of Lincoln County, North Carolina.* Charlotte, N.C.: The Observer Printing House Inc., 1937.
Sifakis, Stewart. *Compendium of the Confederate Armies: Texas.* New York: Facts On File, Inc., 1995.
Smithwick, Noah. *The Evolution of a State/Recollections of Old Texas Days.* Austin: University of Texas Press, 1983.
Smola, Joan Coker. *Sadler/Saddler: A Record of the Family and Descendants of Thomas Sadler Sr. (1720-1796) and Rebeccah Featherston (1722-1796/99) of Brunswick County Virginia.* Tulsa, Okla.: Privately Published, 1994.
Spellman, Charles E. *The Texas House of Representatives: A Pictorial Roster, 1846-1992.*
Spencer, John. *Terrell's Texas Cavalry: Wild Horsemen of the Plains in the Civil War.* Austin, Tex: Eakin Press, 1982.
Steamboats on the Mississippi. Written for American Heritage Junior Library. Mahwah, N.J.: Troll Associates.
Supplement to Pioneer Families of Anderson County Prior to 1900. Palestine, Tex: Anderson County Genealogical Society, January, 1991.
The Texas Capitol: Symbol of Accomplishment. Austin: The Texas Legislative Council in Cooperation with The Texas Highway Department, 1967.
Thompson, Karen R. (Editor). *Defenders of the Republic of Texas.* Austin, Tex: Daughters of the Republic of Texas via Laurel House Press, 1989.
Tolbert, Frank X. *The Day of San Jacinto.* New York: McGraw-Hill Book Co., 1959.
Uniform of the Army of the Republic of Texas. Prescribed and published by order of the President.
Wallace, Ernest, David M. Vigness and George B. Ward. *Documents of Texas History.* Austin, Tex: State House Press, 1994.
Webb, Walter Prescott (Editor-in-Chief). *The Handbook of Texas: A Dictionary of Essential Information* (Three Volumes). Austin: The Texas State Historical Association, 1952.
———. *The Texas Rangers: A Century of Frontier Defense.* Austin: University of Texas Press, 1991.
White, Gifford. *1830 Citizens of Texas: A Census of 6,500 Pre-Revolutionary Texians.* Austin, Tex: Eakin Press, 1983.
———. *1840 Census of Texas.* Austin, Tex: The Pemberton Press, 1966.
———. *1840 Citizens of Texas Land Grants.* Austin, Tex: 1988.
Wilbarger, John Wesley. *Indian Depredations in Texas.* 1889. Reprint. Austin, Tex: State House Press, 1985.
Wilkins, Frederick. *The Legend Begins: The Texas Rangers, 1823 - 1845.* Austin, Tex: State House Press, 1996.
Williams, Amelia W. and Eugene C. Barker. *Writings of Sam Houston.* Austin: The University of Texas Press, 1939.
Winchester, Robert Glenn. *James Pickney Henderson: Texas' First Governor.* San Antonio, Tex: The Naylor Company, 1971.
Winfrey, Dorman, and James M. Day. *The Texas Indian Papers, 1825-1843.* Four volumes. Austin, Tex: Austin Printing Co., 1911.
Wooster, Ralph A. *Texas and Texans in the Civil War.* Austin, Tex: Eakin Press, 1995.

INDEX

Able, John, 119
Adams, Britton H., 113, 118
Adams, George William, 221, 227, 235
Adams, Sephus, 113, 118
Adams, Capt. Solomon, 108, 113, 118, 144, 177
Adams, William H., 113, 118, 129, 144
Ackermann, Davis Verplank, 155
Agua Dulce, Tex., 48
Aguirre, Capt. Miguel, 61-62
Alabama, 5-6, 15, 46, 92, 131, 220, 246, 262, 263
Alabama Hotel, 19
Alabama Indians, 81, 132
Alabama River, 5, 15, 16, 18-19, 21
Alamo, 2, 37-38, 42, 43, 44-45, 47-48, 49, 50, 54, 57, 58, 59, 60, 67, 70, 95
Albany, N.Y., 258
Aldrich, Collin, 94, 162, 169-70
Aldrich, George, 94, 97, 98
Alexander, J.,
Alexander, James M., 113, 119, 155, 213
Alexandria, 269
Allbright, Jacob, 94
Allbright, John, 117
Allbright, Solomon, 184
Allen, Ebenezer, 225
Allen, Hiram, 162
Allen, James L., 245
Allen, Capt. John M., 64
Allison, James, 112, 117
Allison, William Jr., 112, 117

Almonte, Col. Juan N., 14, 57, 66, 70, 74, 75
Alto, Tex., 99, 111, 173, 175
American Indian Heritage Center of Texas, 193
American Revolution, 7
American River, 252, 253, 255
Anadarko Indians, 100, 132
Anahuac, Tex., 36
Anderson, C. D., 71
Anderson, Columbus, 91, 95
Anderson County, Tex., 1, 2, 3, 11, 14, 27, 29-31, 32, 33, 34, 39, 43, 86, 87, 88, 89, 92, 94, 98, 107, 108, 110-12, 122, 123, 127, 147, 149, 174, 176, 182, 205, 207, 208, 235-36, 239-42, 244, 249-50, 251, 252, 253, 254, 256, 258, 259, 260, 261, 262, 263-64, 265, 267, 271, 272, 273, 274, 275, 276-78, 279, 280, 282, 283, 284;
creation of: 228-32;
named by Sadler: 229
Anderson, Elijah, 118
Anderson, John D., 243, 245
Anderson, Joseph S., 184
Anderson, Kenneth Lewis, 8, 212, 214, 219, 220, 229
Anderson, Tex., 219
Anderson, Dr. Thomas P., 154
Anderson, Washington, 71
Andrews, Capt. Micah, 64, 170
Angelina Co., Tex., 229
Angelina River, 11, 26, 31, 82, 87, 102, 103

Anglin, Abram, 31, 32, 36, 84, 85, 87, 91
Anglin, Elisha, 84, 94
Anglins (post office), 252
Anglin, Valentine S., 31, 240, 252
Anglin, William, 94
Archer, Branch T., 37
Archives War, 210, 214, 219
Arizona, 267
Arkansas, 263, 264, 280
Armstrong, James, 213, 214, 215
Army of Texas (see also First Regiment of Infantry), 2, 37-38, 41, 44, 47, 48, 49, 50, 51-72, 77-80, 87, 89, 93, 99, 108, 143, 149, 150, 151, 157, 160, 168, 181, 186, 187, 195, 197, 248, 276, 278, 282
Arnold, Capt. Hayden S., 45, 46, 47, 49, 50, 51, 53, 64, 65-66, 67, 68-69, 77, 78, 79, 93, 147, 149, 282
Arnold, Hendrick, 53
Arocha, Severio (or Rocha), 27, 30, 32, 33, 99, 203, 253, 257, 261
Arrington, Capt. William W., 39
Artage, L. L., 112, 118
Arthur, John, 31
Ash (9th) Street (Austin, Tex.), 223
Aspley, John Jr., 139
Aspley, Melinda, 139
Atchafalya River, 21, 22, 270
Augusta Lodge, 257
Augusta, Tex., 4, 41, 108, 112, 116, 131, 136, 137, 140, 254, 256, 257
Augustine, Maj. Henry W., 103, 190, 192-193
Augustine, Capt. Hugh W., 103
Austin Colony, 90
Austin Co., Tex., 212, 213, 221, 225, 245
Austin Daily Texian, 207
Austin, Moses, 11
Austin Statesman, 285
Austin, Stephen Fuller, 1, 11-12, 14, 36, 37, 38, 47, 81, 89, 133
Austin, Tex., 3, 41, 167, 171, 198, 199, 200, 201, 203, 205, 207, 210, 211, 214, 218, 219, 222-27, 234, 239, 242, 244, 249, 263, 266, 267, 282
Avant, Durham, 119
Aycock, Capt. John, 264

Bailey, Howard W., 46, 53, 73, 118
Bailey, Jeremiah, 118
Baker, Capt. Moseley, 44, 52, 53, 55, 56, 64, 71, 100, 101, 142

Baldwin Co., Ga., 8, 14
Ball, James, 184
Ballard, John T., 46
Ballensweller, Refugio, 117
Baltimore and Ohio Railroad, 258
Banks, Gen. Nathaniel P., 268
Banks, R. P., 119
Barnett, John P., 117
Barr, Robert, 89, 161-62, 163
Barry, Lewis D., 221
Bascus, John, 113, 117
Bastrop, Baron de, 11
Bastrop Co., Tex., 56, 151, 212, 213, 221, 245
Bastrop, Tex., 95, 151, 167, 174, 224
Bates, Seth, 84
Bates, Silas H., 84, 85, 86
Bates, William, 112, 118
Baton Rouge, La., 21
Battle Creek, 182, 183, 185
Baylor, Judge Robert E. B., 226
Baylor University, 226
Bayne, Lt. Col. Griffin, 43
Bayou Natchitoches, 22
Bayou Sara, La., 21
Bean, Isaac, 118
Bean, Robert, 118
Beaumont, Tex., 162
Beaver, Tex. (community), 252
Bee, Barnard E., 100
Bee, Hamilton P., 236
Bell, Charles N., 191
Bell, Peter Hansbrough, 152, 154
Bell, William, 190
Bennett, Armstead, 27, 29, 108, 113, 118, 144, 159, 206, 256
Bennett, Benjamin, 254
Bennett, Faith, 27, 108, 206
Bennett, Harriet, 27
Bennett, Icephenia, 251
Bennett, Capt. Joseph L., 64, 198
Bennett, Mary, 27
Bennett, Miles, 44, 94, 251, 276, 282
Bennett, Stephen, 27, 44, 94, 113, 118, 140, 206, 251, 258, 260
Benton, Col. Jesse, 43
Berry, Capt. Andrew Jackson, 198
Berry, Thomas, 112, 118, 128
Bevil, John, 162
Bexar Co., Tex., 209, 212, 213, 221, 245
Bexar Department, 14
Bexar Road, 87
Bexar, Tex., 14, 38, 282
Bigelow, William, 240

Big Mush, Chief ("Gatunwali"), 37, 99, 114, 128, 171, 175, 178-80, 189, 192, 194
Big Pine Creek, 94
Billingsley, Capt. Jesse, 64, 71, 168, 170
Biloxi Indians, 81, 110, 127
Bingham, Benjamin Rice, 71
Bird, Capt. John, 174
Bird's Creek, Battle of, 174
Black River, 22
Blair, John, 257
Blair's Landing, La., 269
Blakey, Lemuel Stockton, 71
Blythe, A. J., 113, 119
Blythe, A. W., 113, 119
Blythe, Champain, 113, 119
Bogart, Sam, 245
Bonnel, Maj. George Washington, 145
Bonner, R. M., 259
Bonner's Ferry, 91
Booker, Ferdinand, 190
Booker, Dr. Shields, 64, 154, 177, 190, 193
Boothe, R. E., 162
Borden, John Pettit, 64
Bostick, Sion Record, 72
Bottoms, Zachariah W., 119
Bourland, William H., 213, 221, 242, 244, 245, 248
Bowie Co., Tex., 212, 213, 221, 245
Bowie, James, 26, 37, 42, 45
Bowles, Chief ("Duwali"), 3, 11, 37, 81-82, 89, 96, 100, 103, 104, 114, 128, 170, 171-72, 173-75, 178-81, 182, 183-96, 198, 243, 283
Bowles Creek, 173, 175
Bowles, Chief John, 180-81, 201
Box, George A., 113, 119
Box, Capt. James Edward, 31, 35, 45, 46, 107, 112, 117, 120-21, 125, 129, 139, 159, 163, 169, 173, 176, 177, 180, 184, 199, 239, 240, 241, 249
Box, John Andrew, 45, 46, 94
Box, John M., 45
Box, Nelson A., 45, 46, 94
Box, Roland William, 31, 107
Box, Capt. Samuel Charles, 103, 113, 117, 180
Box's Creek, 258, 262
Box, Sebastian, 113, 119
Box's Fort (see Fort Box)
Box, Stephen F., 45, 94
Box, Stillwell, 45, 46, 57

Box, Thomas Griffin, 45, 46, 94, 113, 117
Boyd, M. D., 113, 119, 128
Bradshaw, Capt. James, 107, 112, 115, 117, 119, 125, 127, 128, 129, 162
Branch, Edward T., 221
Brazoria Co., Tex., 168, 209, 212, 213, 221, 245
Brazoria, Tex., 169
Brazos Co., Tex., 212, 213, 221, 245
Brazos Department, 14
Brazos River, 2, 38, 39, 51, 52, 53, 54, 56, 90, 95, 101, 142, 145, 150, 152, 175, 179, 199, 211, 258
Brennan, Thomas H., 162
Brewer, Henry Mitchell, 46, 53, 119
Brewer, James, 119
Brewer, John, 119
Brewer, William Jr., 119
Brimberry, John N., 190
Briscoe, Capt. Andrew, 64
Bromley, William, 118
Brookfield, Capt. William Charles, 117, 129, 144
Brooks, Samuel, 112, 118
Brooks, Thomas D., 46, 53
Brown's Fort (see Fort Brown)
Brown, James, 119
Brown, James W., 202
Brown, John, 155, 221, 229, 236-37
Brown, John Henry, 192
Brown, John T., 106
Brown, Dr. Lemuel B., 176, 177, 190, 193
Brown, Reuben, 29, 44, 94, 108, 113, 118, 159
Brown, Sally, 27
Brown, Sarah Parker, 108
Brown, Capt. Squire, 107, 112, 115, 116, 118, 119, 120, 128, 129
Brownfield, Newton, 112, 118
Browning, George Washington, 31, 106, 113, 117, 149, 163, 170
Brownsville, Tex. (Cameron Co.), 253
Brownsville, Tex. (Houston Co.), 159, 161, 162, 169
Brunswick Co., Va., 7, 10
Brushy Creek (Battle of), 44, 168, 199
Bryan, Guy M., 245
Bryan, Moses Austin, 75
Bryant, Capt. Benjamin Franklin, 64
Bryant, Stephen, 260, 262
Buffalo Bayou, 57, 59
Buffington, Joseph, 113, 119
Buez, Daniel, 112, 118

Bullock family, 124
Bullock, James W., 25
Bullock, Julius, 112, 116
Burleson Co., Tex., 229
Burleson, Col. Edward "Ned", 1, 3, 37, 48, 53, 60, 64, 65, 66, 72, 100, 101, 152, 153, 154, 168-69, 170, 171, 173, 174-75, 176, 177, 179, 180, 181, 183, 185, 186, 187, 188-90, 191, 194, 198, 199, 200, 201, 204, 212, 225, 236, 243
Burleson, Capt. Jacob, 168
Burleson, Joseph, 195
Burnet Co., Tex., 205, 228
Burnet, David G.,
  as first Texas President: 44, 52-53, 56, 57, 78, 209;
  as Vice President of Texas: 105, 150, 176, 177, 178-80, 192, 205;
  as Secretary of State: 242
Burnham Crossing, 48
Burroughs, James M., 221, 229, 245
Burrow, Wily, 118
Burton, Maj. Isaac Watts, 39, 44, 96, 117, 129, 154, 176, 177, 178-80
Bussey, Capt. John, 264

Caddell, Capt. Andrew, 103, 184
Caddell, Jeremiah D., 184
Caddell, John, 184
Caddo Indians, 34, 81, 90, 95, 102, 105, 116, 120, 124, 126, 127, 131, 142, 145, 155, 171
Cade, Kenneth,
Cadenhead, Levi P., 119
Cahawba (Cahaba), Al., 15-16
Cahawba Press, 16
Caldwell, John, 212
Calder, Capt. Robert James, 64
Caldwell, Capt. Mathew, 199, 201, 205
Caldwell, Pinckney C., 154
Calhoun Co., Tex., 229
Calhoun, D. A., 279
California, 4, 252-56
California Gold Rush, 3, 252-56
Californian, 252
Campbell, Charles C., 163-64
Campbell, Mrs. Charles C., 163-64
Campbell Co., Va., 222
Campbell, David H., 141-42
Campbell, Fountain, 164
Campbell, George, 164
Campbell, Hulda, 164
Campbell, Malathiel, 164
Campbell Massacre, 163-65

Campbell, Pamelia, 164
Campbell, W. H., 276, 277
Campbell, William Joseph, 190
Camp Albert Sidney Johnston, 268
Camp Burleson, 174, 199, 200, 201, 203
Camp Caldwell, 199, 200, 201
Camp Carter, 182, 186, 187
Camp Cazneau, 201, 202, 203
Camp Dixie, 268
Camp Johnston, 178, 179, 181, 182
Camp Lamar, 201
Camp McLeod, 201
Camp Victoria, 79, 80
Camp Walnut Creek, 199
Camp Wharton, 268
Cane River Crossing, 269
Caney Creek, 275
Caney River, 268
Cannon's Ferry, 240
Cantley, A. G., 260, 261
Caro, Ramon, 72
Carpenter, John W., 46, 106, 107, 112, 116, 120
Carper, Dr. William M., 64
"Carpetbaggers", 273, 275
Carr, James, 222
Carson, Samuel Price, 44, 154
Cartenas, Delores, 113, 119
Carter, Capt. James, 176, 177, 181, 183, 184, 185, 186, 188, 189, 190
Carter, M. Theo, 106
Carter, Robert W., 64
Cartwright, James, 112, 118
Caruthers, Thomas, 245
Caskey, J. J., 190
Cass Co., Tex., 229, 234
Castrillon, Gen. Manuel, 68
Castro, Chief, 167
Cazneau, Col. William Leslie, 152, 155, 202, 213, 221, 232
Chafin, James A., 162
Chandler, Tex., 182, 183, 186
Chapman, Henry Larkin, 46, 53
Charlotte, N.C., 8
Charlton, Napoleon B., 221, 227, 235
Cherokee Co., Tex., 82, 229, 264, 267
Cherokee Indians, 2, 3, 11, 37, 81-83, 89-90, 96, 98, 99, 102-104, 105, 110, 111, 114, 124, 127, 128, 131, 132, 142, 150, 158, 159, 170, 171-72, 173-94, 196, 197-98, 201, 204
Cherokee Nation (in East Texas), 81-83, 103, 104, 171, 174, 175, 201;
  in Oklahoma: 196

Cherokee War (Battle of the Neches), 1, 3, 87, 157, 174, 181-94, 198, 199, 205, 207, 238, 243, 283
Chesterfield, Va., 258
Chevallie, Michael H., 200, 203, 213
Chevallier, Charles, 113, 119
Chickasaw Indians, 105
Childers, Josiah Taylor, 113, 119
Choctaw Bayou, 98
Choctaw Indians, 81
Christy, Julious, 27
Christy, Rachel, 27
Christy, Col. William, 77
Church Street (Palestine, Tex.), 257
Cincinnati, Oh., 54
Cincinnati, Tex., 163
Civil War, 1, 8, 157, 252, 263-70, 271, 272, 273, 274, 275
Civil War Units:
    First Texas Cavalry (Arizona Brigade) - 267;
    First Texas Infantry (Hood's Brigade) - 264;
    Gould's Battalion: 265, 266;
    Randle's Brigade - 265;
    Second Brigade, First Division - 267;
    2nd Texas Cavalry - 264;
    7th Texas Cavalry (Sibley's Brigade) - 264; 37th Texas Cavalry Regiment (also known as Terrell's Texas Cavalry or 34th Regiment): 265, 266-270;
    28th Texas Cavalry - 264
Claiborne, Al., 18
Clapp, Maj. Elisha, 71, 88, 94, 109, 110, 111, 141, 165, 176, 177, 239
Clapp, John E., 117
Clark, Edward, 221, 236, 263
Clarksville, Tex., 145, 155, 156, 162
Clements, William, 190
Clendenin, Capt. Adam, 154, 156, 169, 176, 177, 179, 186, 198, 199, 200, 201
Cleveland, James W., 113, 119, 159
Cleveland, Horatio N.,
Click, Andrew Jackson, 112, 117
Clinton Lodge, 196
Cobb, William, 113, 119
Cochran, Dr. Richard, 155, 177
Cole, David, 162
Coleman, Elizabeth, 167-68
Coleman, Robert Morris, 64, 168
Coleto Creek, 50

Collard, Job S., 64
College Avenue (Austin, Tex.), 223
Collin Co., Tex., 229
Collinsworth, James, 64, 105
Colorado, 233
Colorado Co., Tex., 168, 212, 213, 221, 245
Colorado River, 2, 38, 39, 40, 48, 49, 50, 51, 145, 199, 222, 247, 254, 267, 276
Colorado Street (Austin, Tex.), 223
Columbia (on-the-Brazos), Tex., 14, 96, 209
Columbus, Tex., 51, 268
Columbus Enquirer, 18
Comanche Indians, 81, 83, 85, 86, 167, 168, 174, 200, 203, 212
"Come and Take It" Flag, 36, 44
Comol Co., Tex., 229
Conaway, James, 277, 279
Confederacy (Confederate States of America), 3, 62, 86, 263, 265-270
Congress Avenue (Austin, Tex.), 223, 224
Congress of the Republic of Texas,
    First: 82-83, 89, 93;
    Second: 95, 96, 100;
    Third: 94, 144, 146, 150, 151, 153, 173, 207;
    Fourth: 207;
    Fifth: 128, 204, 207, 228;
    Sixth: 207, 247;
    Seventh: 207;
    Eighth: 207-208;
    Ninth: 3, 200, 207-208, 209-18, 219, 229, 238
Conner, Henry, 191
Constitutional Convention of Texas, 44, 52, 148, 211
Convention of 1833, 37
Cook, Davis, 119
Cook, James R., 64
Cook, Thomas, 119
Cooke, Wilds K., 213, 221
Cooke, William Gordon, 64, 152, 154, 173, 204, 213
Cooper's 1st Batallion, 10
Cooper, James, 71
Cooper, Mathias, 71
Corbin, Lt. Albert G., 191
Cordova Rebellion, 102, 103-105, 108-109, 115, 127, 131, 145, 205, 218, 283
Cordova, Vicente, 25, 102, 103-105, 108-109, 110, 111, 114, 115, 120,

122, 123, 125, 127, 132, 163, 165, 170-71, 205
Cordray (interpretor), 173, 175
Corpus Christi, Tex., 253
Cos, Gen. Martín Perfecto de, 36, 37, 63, 66, 68, 77
Costley, Capt. Michael, 44, 87-88, 111
Council Creek, 178, 179
Council House Fight, 157, 203, 212
Coushatta Indians, 81, 100, 102, 103, 124, 126, 127, 132
Craft, James A., 64
Craigheay, William, 106
Crain, Ambrose Hulon, 118, 184
Crane, John, 184, 185
Cravens, John E., 260
Cravens, Samuel, 250
Crawford, Corley T., 112, 118
Crawford Co., Ill., 27, 29, 241
Crawford, Joseph, 256
Creek Indians, 18
Crist, Annie Parker, 27, 31, 108
Crist, Benjamin, 31
Crist, Cicero, 31
Crist Creek, 32
Crist, Daniel LaMora, 31, 35, 39, 43-44, 87, 107, 112, 118, 127, 128
Crist, Daniel Murry, 31, 113, 117, 180, 249
Crist, Elizabeth, 31
Crist, George W., 31
Crist, Jacob, 113, 118
Crist, Capt. John, 29, 30, 31, 32, 36, 106, 108, 113, 118, 169, 170
Crist, Martha "Patsy", 31
Crist, Reason, 31, 94
Crist, Stephen, 27, 31, 94, 106, 108, 113, 118, 180, 261
Crockett, David, 45, 95
Crockett, Tex., 45, 95, 97, 140, 152, 159, 162, 165, 167, 169, 170, 173, 207, 208, 236, 257
Cronican, James, 221
Crowson, Henry P., 184
Crump, William E., 221, 225, 227, 245
Crutchir, William H., 155, 243, 245
Cruz, Juan, 102, 116
Culpepper Co., Va., 28
Cumba, James, 71
Cunningham, Abel Seymour, 213, 245, 246
Curl, William, 119

Dallas Co., Al., 15
Dallas Co., Tex., 229

Dallas, Tex., 89, 145
Dangerfield, William Henry, 154, 157
Darden, Stephen H., 282
Darnell, Nicholas Henry, 237
Davidson, Rebecca, 27
Davidson, Robert, 27
Davidson, Dr. William F., 64
Davis, Capt. Benjamin W., 169, 170
Davis, Gov. Edmund J., 273
Davis, George Washington, 39, 44
Davis, Capt. H. W., 154
Davis, James M., 245
Davis, Jefferson, 263
Davis, John H. "Jack", 113, 119, 245
Davis, Lula Sadler,
Davis, Randolph W., 35
Davis, Samuel, 177, 180, 194
Davis, William P., 132, 138
Dawson, Nicholas Mosby, 64
Day, Elizabeth Ann Sadler "Betty", 256, 262, 272, 273, 276, 277
Day, Gilbert Russell Jr., 276, 277
Day, John, 184
Day, Mary Ann Sadler "Annie", 251, 254, 262, 273, 275, 277
Day, William Zachariah "Zach", 270, 275, 277
DeBard, Dr. Elisha J., 87, 112, 117, 128, 129, 171, 186, 187, 249, 257
DeCordova, Jacob Raphael, 245, 246
DeCordova, Withers & Co., 278
"Defensive League", 273
"Deguello", 60
Dekalb, Tex., 162
Delap, John S., 31, 106
Delaware Indians, 81, 86, 100, 124, 175, 178, 179, 181, 186, 187, 188, 189, 197
Delespine, H. A., 35
Delgado, Col. Pedro Francisco, 61
Deen, John, 119
Denham, M. H., 64
Dennis, Thomas M., 245
Denson, Polly, 27
Denson Springs, Tex., 33
Dewees Crossing, 51, 276
Dewees, William D., 51
DeWitt Co., Tex., 229
Dexter, Lt. Col. Peter Bartelle, 154
Dick (Texas Army drummer), 63
Dickerson, James, 113,119
Dickerson, William, 149
Dickinson, Capt. Almeron, 48
Dickinson, Susanna, 48
Dickson, David C., 221, 235

Diggs, Henry E., 279
Dikes, Levi B., 118
Dillard, William, 170
Dixon, Abigail, 108
Dixon, Levin, 108
Dixon, James G., 113, 119
Dixon, Richard C., 106
Donohue's Farm, 55, 56
Dooley, M. A., 243, 245
Dorset, Theodore, 118
Dorsett, Asa, 118
Doubt, Daniel, 40, 46, 49
Douglass, Gen. Kelsey Harris, 100, 101, 103, 104, 109, 142, 151, 153, 177, 178, 179, 180, 181, 183, 184-94, 195, 197, 198
Douthit, Benjamin W., 35, 91
Douthit, James M., 253, 261
Dumas, J. K. M., 268
Duncan, George Holman, 106
Dunn, John, 213, 214
Dunnington, Maj. William N., 154, 176, 177, 202, 203
Dupree, Lewis G., 221
Durham, Barry H., 221
Durst, Maj. James H., 204
Durst, Capt. John, 118, 129, 162
Durst, Capt. Joseph, 103, 113, 119
Duty, Mrs., 84, 86
Duty, Richard, 115
Duwali (see Chief Bowles)
Dwight, George E., 35, 84, 85
Dwight, Mrs. George E., 84, 85
Dyer, Gen. John, 100, 104, 142, 145

Eason, Mills I., 117
Eastland, Capt. William Mosby, 64, 167
Eaton, Elizabeth, 27
Eaton, Polly, 27
Eaton, Rachel, 27
Eaton, Richard, 27, 29
Eatonton Academy, 16
Eberly, Angelina, 224
Echols, William F., 221
Eddy, Z. Williams, 221, 229, 234, 235, 245
Edens, Balis, 108, 113, 117, 139, 140, 180
Edens, Caledonia, 135-136
Edens, Darius H., 108, 113, 117, 139, 140, 143, 180, 240, 241, 242, 249, 254
Edens, Emily, 135-136
Edens, John, 2, 108, 112, 116, 131-32, 135, 138, 139, 140, 141, 142, 143-44
Edens, Mrs. John, 132, 134, 135
Edens, John Silas, 108, 113, 118, 140
Edens, Laurie, 140
Edens-Madden Massacre, 2, 4, 131-40, 141-42, 153, 159, 180, 257, 260, 274
Edens, Melissa, 135, 138, 140
Edens, Olive, 140
Edgar, Joseph Smith, 71
Edwards, Hayden Harrison, 221
Edwards, Isiah, 45, 46, 64
Edwards, William C., 221, 243, 245
The Egg (Cherokee Chief), 201
El Camino Real (see San Antonio Road)
Elkhart Creek, 208
Elkhart, Tex., 11, 33, 108, 206, 207, 252, 256, 258, 284, 285; establishment of: 251
Ellis, Ira P., 117
Elm Creek Battle, 90
El Paso, Tex., 255
Emancipation Proclamation, 271
English, Capt. George, 103, 197
Epperson, Benjamin H., 243, 245
Erath, Capt. George Bernard, 90, 95, 213, 221
Ewing, Dr. Alexander Wray, 64, 70, 74, 264
Ewing, Williston Edley, 31, 32, 44, 98
Ewing, James W., 279
Ewing, John, 190, 192

Fairfield, Ga., 7
Fall Co., Tex., 199
Falls of the Brazos, 35, 145, 199, 200
Fannin Co., Tex., 212, 213, 221, 245
Fannin, Capt. James Walker Jr., 37, 42, 48, 50, 51, 79
Fanthorpe, Tex., 219
Farley, Henry Wise, 162
Faulkenberry, David, 84, 85, 87, 91, 95
Faulkenberry, Eli, 35, 180
Faulkenberry, Evan, 84, 85, 86, 87, 91, 95
Faulkenberry family, 29
Faulkenberry, Nancy, 27
Fayette Co., Tex., 128, 212, 213, 221, 245
Feather River, 255
Ferguson, John, 231
Fields, David W., 246

Fields, Fox, 181
Fields, William, 242, 245
Filisola, Gen. Vicente, 77, 79, 105
Finch, Matthew, 64
Finch, Richard B., 117
Finley, William, 102
First Infantry Company, Second Regiment of Texas Volunteers (see Nacogdoches Volunteers)
First Regiment of Infantry (Texas Army), 3, 53, 58, 60, 64, 65, 66, 150-61, 169, 171, 174-75, 179, 182, 186, 189, 190, 193, 195-203, 204, 238
Fisher, James, 119
Fisher, Orcenith, 212
Fisher, Samuel Rhodes, 89
Fisher, Lt. Col. William S., 51, 64, 151, 153, 154, 169, 175, 177, 199, 201, 202-203
Fitzhugh, Dr. John P. T., 64
Flores, Juan, 102, 116, 127
Flores, Manuel, 64, 170, 171
Florida, 263
Forbes, Col. John, 64, 81, 96, 154
Ford, John Salmon "Rip", 1, 180, 195, 196, 213, 214, 216
Ford, Levi, 119
Fort Bend, Tex., 52, 56
Fort Bend Co., Tex., 212, 213, 221, 242, 245
Fort Box (Box's Fort), 107
Fort Brown (Brown's Fort), 3, 29, 107-108, 159, 164, 169, 173, 206, 252, 256
Fort Burleson (see Camp Burleson)
Fort Duty, 115
Fort Gibson, 86
Fort Jesup (La.), 23, 91
Fort Houston, 2, 28, 30, 31, 36, 40, 44, 49, 86, 98;
  early work on by Sadler's rangers: 41, 43, 88;
  use of: 88-89, 90, 91, 93, 104, 105-107, 108, 109, 111-14, 115, 116, 120-22, 128-30, 132, 138, 139, 142, 144, 159, 162, 163-65, 169, 170, 173, 176, 179, 180, 198, 205, 207, 208, 228, 240, 242
Fort Houston Settlement, 31-32, 33, 34, 35-36, 38, 39, 41, 84, 88, 100, 107, 204, 239, 241, 257
Fort Kickapoo, 172, 173, 174, 176, 178, 182

Fort Lacy (Lacy's Fort), 99, 103, 111, 173, 175
Fort Lamar, 186, 187, 197, 198
Fort Milam (see also Fort Burleson), 179, 199
Fort Parker (see Parker's Fort)
Fort Saline, 172
Fort Skerrett, 201
Fort Sumter, S.C., 263
Fort Worth, Tex., 145
"Forty-Niners", 252
Foster, James, 119
Foster, Celestia Sadler, 261, 272, 273, 277
Fowle, Thomas Patton, 71
Fowler, Andrew Jackson, 126, 246-47, 249
Fowler, John W., 113, 119, 162
France, 25
Francis, Saint, 14
Franklin County, Ga., 28
Franklin (post office), 162
Frankston, Tex., 122, 127
Frazier, Capt. Bill, 264
Fredericksburg, Tex., 282
Fredonian Rebellion, 36
Freeman, Jo Ann Day, 4
French Quarter, 20
Friar, Daniel Boone, 38
Frontier Regiment (see First Regiment of Infantry)
Frost, Nancy, 30
Frost, Robert, 84, 85, 86
Frost, Samuel M., 84, 85, 86
Frost's Creek, 32, 253
Frost, William M., 29, 30-31, 36, 97, 98, 106, 107, 112, 117, 180, 205
Fuller, Calvin J., 112, 118
Fuller, Ponton, 112, 118
Fulton, James R., 239, 240, 241
Fulton, Robert, 5
Fulton, Samuel Moore, 162

Gage, Calvin, 71
Gage, David, 213
Gaines Ferry, 23, 162
Gaines, James, 23, 162
Gallatin, Albert Edward, 71
Gallion, John C., 113, 117
Galloway, Peter, 249
Galveston Bay, 57, 105
Galveston Co., Tex., 168, 212, 221, 245
Galveston Island, 57, 96
Galveston Steam, Ferry, Freight &

INDEX

Tow-Boat Company, 247
Galveston, Tex., 59, 96, 152, 156, 162, 169, 199, 200, 253, 258, 267, 270, 271, 280
Galveston Weekly (Daily) News, 69, 284-285
Gammager, Thomas T., 278
Gaona, Gen. Antonio, 56, 77
Gardner, Capt. James W., 32, 35, 240, 263-64
Garrison, Capt. Mitchell, 177
Gates, Amos H., 112, 117
Gatunwali (see Chief Big Mush)
General Convention of Texas (1836), 37, 44
General Land Office of Texas, 3, 27, 30, 32, 97, 99, 203, 224-25, 247, 249, 279, 282
Geneva (post office), 162
Georgia, 1, 6-10, 11, 14, 15, 16, 18, 24, 28, 31, 46, 47, 59, 75, 81, 151, 242, 257-58, 263, 271, 272
Gibson, William M., 240
Giddings, Giles Albert, 71
Gila Desert, 255
Gill, John Porter, 64
Gillaspie, Capt. James, 64
Gillen, Capt. Benjamin Y., 154, 156, 199, 200, 201
Gillet, James S., 221
Gilliam, Charles, 249
Gilliam, James, 118, 221, 245
Gilliland, H., 112, 118
Gilliland, James, 112, 190
Gilliland, William P., 118
Gilmore, Charles, 112, 118
Gilmore, R. H., 269
Glass, William S., 246
Glenn, G., 35
Glenn, Capt. Marsh, 264
Glenn, Capt. Nathan, 204, 259
Glenn, Virginia, 204
Glenn, William, 204
Golden Standard (Mexican cannon), 60-61, 68
Goliad Co., Tex., 212, 213, 221, 245
Goliad Massacre (La Bahia), 50, 56, 58, 67, 70
Goliad, Tex., 14, 37, 38, 42, 48, 50, 79, 80, 151
Gonzales Co., Tex., 151, 212, 213, 221, 245
Gonzales, Tex., 14, 36, 42, 43, 44, 48, 67, 169
Gooch, Ben F., 221, 282

Goodall, James, 154
Goode, Richard N., 245
Goodloe, Capt. Robert Kemp, 103
Googh, John G., 259
Goss, Thomas, 240
Gossett, Andrew Edwards, 94
Gossett, Elijah, 94, 167, 170
Gossett, James L., 117
Gossett, Presley, 117
Gossett, William, 117
Gough, Henry, 113, 119
Gould, Maj. Robert S., 265
Graham, Dr. Berria, 249
Granger, Gen. Gordon, 271
Grapeland, Tex., 29, 107, 159, 265
Grayson Co., Tex., 229
Grayson, Peter W., 105, 221
Green, John A., 246
Green, Gen. Thomas Jefferson, 80
Greenwood, Beverly, 112, 117
Greenwood, Elizabeth Jordan, 30
Greenwood, Garrison, 27, 29, 30-31, 36, 38, 39, 90
Greenwood, William, 258
Greer, John Alexander, 212
Gregg Co., Tex., 82
Gregg, John, 27, 94
Gresham, George, 257
Griggs, Asbury, 119
Grigsby, John Jr., 27, 41, 134
Grigsby, John Crawford, 40-41, 43, 46, 49, 113, 118, 129, 240, 249, 250
Grigsby, Louisa Thompson, 27, 41
Grigsby, Ruth Ann, 134
Grimes Co. Tex., 30
Grimes, Jesse, 212
Grison, Thomas, 119
Groce, Jared, 52
Groce's Retreat, 52, 53, 55
Groesbeck, Tex., 29, 83
Grush, Henry L., 155, 156
Guadalupe Co., Tex., 229
Guadalupe Mountains, 255
Guadalupe River, 39, 48, 79, 171
Gulf of Mexico, 10, 21
Gum Springs, 239
Gunnels, Nathan C., 269
Gustine, Dr. Lemuel, 64
Gutierrez-Magee Expedition, 90

Haggard, Capt. Squire, 88
Hagood, W. A., 279
Hainais (Indians), 142
Hale, John C., 64, 71
Hall, Arthur H., 137

Hall, James, 112, 117, 127, 128, 129
Hall's Trading Place, 163
Hall, Warren D. C., 102
Hallmark, Alfred M., 45, 46, 57, 112, 117
Hallmark, George William, 41
Hallmark, Mathew Dewey T., 113, 117
Hallmark, William Calvert, 40, 41, 45, 46, 49, 113, 117
Hamilton, Elias Edley, 46
Hamilton, Capt. Jacob E., 195, 198
Hamilton, Isiah, 112, 118
Hamilton (post office), 162
Handy, Col. Robert Eden, 53, 64
Hanks, Eler D., 112, 118
Hanks, George W., 249
Hanks, Hansford, 252
Hanks, Capt. J. M., 264
Hanks, James Steele, 250, 252
Hanks, Thomas J., 112, 118
Hanks, Thomas, 112, 118, 240, 250
Hanks, Capt. Wesley W., 103
Hansford, John M., 177
Hardemann, Bailey, 44
Hardiman, Thomas J., 245
Hardin, Augustus Blackburn, 112, 118
Hardin, Benjamin Watson, 213, 214
Hardin, Franklin, 64
Hardwick, Green Benjamin, 113, 117
Harkil, Solomon, 118
Harper, John A., 184
Harper, Benjamin J., 64
Harper, Peter, 64, 118
Harris[burg] Co., Tex., 168, 169, 183, 212, 213, 221, 222, 242, 245, 258
Harrisburg, Tex., 46, 53, 54, 56, 57, 78, 146
Harris, Chief, 178, 180, 187, 197, 198
Harris, E. R., 112, 118
Harris, John A., 113, 117
Harris, William H., 162
Harrison, A. L., 64
Harrison Co., Tex., 176, 177, 212, 213, 221, 222, 245
Harrison, Capt. Greenberry Horras, 177, 184, 190, 207
Harvey, John W., 46, 50, 54-55, 57, 62
Hatfield's Grocery, 211, 214, 217
Haugh, Thomas, 177
Hay, Samuel D., 246
Haynie, John, 213
Haynie, Samuel G., 245, 247
Hays, Capt. John Coffee "Jack", 3, 205, 235
Hays, Thomas, 113, 118, 129, 144

Head, James, 113, 117
Heard, Capt. William Jones E., 44, 64, 66-67
Helm, Mrs. L., 279
Hempstead, Tex., 55, 270
Henchett, G. W., 117, 170
Henderson Co., Tex., 172, 183, 186, 229, 240, 247
Henderson, James W., 213, 242, 243, 245, 246, 247
Henderson, Gov. James Pinckney, 1, 8, 89, 214, 220, 221, 225, 226, 227-228, 236, 243
Henderson, Tex., 82, 89, 99, 171, 196
Henderson, William F., 113
Herby, 118
Hickory (8th) Street (Austin, Tex.), 223
Hicks, Isaac, 119
Hill, Benjamin F., 213, 242
Hill, Capt. William Warner, 64
Hillhouse, Capt. Eli, 41
Hobbs, Spencer, 106, 108, 113, 117
Hockley, Col. George Washington, 64, 100, 155, 158
Hogg, Joseph L., 222
Holland, Spearman, 221
Holliday, Capt. John J., 154, 199, 200, 201, 203
Holmes, Lt. A. C., 202
Holmes, Peter W., 46
Honey Creek, 282
Hooper, Capt. George W., 103
Hope, Adolphus, 64
Hopkins Co., Tex., 229
Hornsby, Collier C., 155
Hornsby's Station, 41
Horton, Albert C., 220, 237
Horton, Capt. Alexander, 64, 103
Houghton, William D., 155, 177
Houston County in the Civil War, 265
Houston Co., Tex., 1, 3, 4, 14, 29, 41, 43, 45, 90, 92, 93-95, 97, 98, 100, 107, 108, 109, 114, 130, 131, 132, 133, 136, 138, 139, 141, 142, 143, 144, 145, 147, 149, 150-51, 152, 153, 159, 161, 162, 163, 164, 167, 169-70, 173, 175, 176, 179, 180, 184, 198, 203-208, 211, 212-19, 221, 222, 228-231, 232, 235-36, 238, 239, 242, 244, 245, 246, 249, 250, 252, 254, 256, 262, 265, 280, 283, 284
created from Nacogdoches County - 93-95
Houston, Martha, 265

INDEX 373

Houston Mechanics' Institute, 247
Houston Mound, 107, 207, 208, 230-31
Houston, Sam, 1, 2, 35, 81-82, 168, 169, 171, 191, 194, 201, 264-65, 276;
  as Major General of Texas Army: 37, 48, 49, 50, 51-53, 55, 56, 57-59, 60, 62, 63, 64, 65, 67-70, 71, 72-75, 77, 78;
  as President of Texas: 82-83, 86, 87, 88, 89, 91, 93, 94, 95, 96, 98, 99, 100, 102, 103-104, 105-106, 107, 116, 121, 142, 144, 146, 149, 157, 165, 204, 205, 206, 209, 210-13, 215, 220;
  as U.S. Senator: 227, 243;
  as Governor of Texas: 263
Sam Houston Memorial Park, 266
Houston, Tex. (Anderson Co.), 33, 35-36, 39, 43, 90, 105
Houston, Tex. (Harris Co.), 73, 100, 122, 145, 152, 153, 156, 166, 168, 169, 175, 200, 209, 210, 211, 259, 270, 280
Howard, G. R., 276
Howard, Capt. George Thomas, 154, 169, 174, 177, 183, 188, 199, 200, 201, 202, 203
Howard, Volney E., 221, 232, 234
Hudnot's Plantation, 269
Hudson, James P., 221
Hufton, W., 155
Hughes, Francis, 213
Huling, Thomas B., 162
Hunter, David C., 250
Hunter House, 264
Hunter, Dr. James, 91, 204
Hunter, John, 113, 119
Hunter, Mary Kate (historian), 34, 88, 256
Huntsville, Tex., 264-65
Huston, Gen. Felix, 80, 89, 93
Hyde, James G., 113, 119

Ibarvo, Gil Antonio, 25
Ijams, Basil G., 64
Illinois, 27, 28, 29, 30, 131, 138, 256
Independence Hall, 210
Indian Creek, 183
Indiana, 256, 262
Indianola, Tex., 253, 280
Ingram, Allen, 71
Inman, Capt. John, 177
Ioni Creek, 11, 33-34, 81, 99, 132, 207
Ioni Indians, 11, 33-34, 81, 99, 132, 207
Ioni Lodge (Augusta Lodge), 257
Ioni, Tex., 206-207, 252, 256, 280
Ioni Village, 34, 208, 231, 256, 257
Iowa Indians, 81
Irion, Van R., 221, 245
Isaacs, George, 112, 117, 128

Jackson Co., Tex., 212, 213, 221, 245
Jackson, Pres. Andrew, 37, 198, 219
Jackson, F. S., 259
Jacobs, John, 113, 119
Jamaica, 246
James, W. F., 71
January, Capt. James Belvarde Pope, 154, 156, 199, 200, 201-202
Jasper Co., Tex., 162, 212, 213, 221, 245
Jasper, Seldon L. B., 207, 244, 246, 249
Jasper, Tex., 162
Jefferson Co., Ga., 6, 7
Jefferson Co., Tex., 162, 212, 213, 221, 245
Jesup, Gen. Thomas Sidney, 23
Jewel, Maj. George Washington, 87-88, 91
Jewett, Henry J., 212
Joe (slave at Alamo), 48
Johns, Stephen B., 213, 214
Johnson, Adam, 118
Johnson, Benjamin H., 154
Johnson, Charles, 112, 118
Johnson, Francis W., 162
Johnson, Isaac W., 213
Johnson, Livley, 162
Johnson, Middleton Tate, 213
Johnsons (post office), 162
Johnson, Thomas, 246
Johnston, Gen. Albert Sidney, 1, 93, 146, 147, 149, 150, 153, 155, 168, 171, 176, 177, 178-79, 180, 181, 192, 197, 198-200, 204
Jones, A. T., 112, 118
Jones, Dr. Anson, 1, 64, 208, 211
  as President of Texas: 214, 217, 219, 225, 226
Jones, Augustus H., 213, 214
Jonesboro, Tex., 14, 162
Jones, Henry, 221, 230
Jones, Keeton McLemore, 46, 57
Jones, Simeon L., 213, 214
Jones, Maj. William Jefferson, 154, 168, 174, 177, 187, 191
Jones, William, 250

Jonett, J. G., 162
Jonetts (post office), 162
Joost, Alexander, 35, 176, 249, 270
Jordan, Capt. Alexander, 177, 241
Jordan, Elizabeth Estes, 30
Jordan, James, 27, 30
Jordan, Joseph, 27, 29, 30-31, 33, 35, 36, 94
Jordan, Laura, 251
Jordan, Levi, 30, 250, 257
Jordan, Prudence, 27, 30
Jordan, Capt. Samuel W., 154, 169, 174, 177, 183, 188, 189, 190, 194
Jowers, Dr. William George Washington, 113, 118, 173, 175, 177, 193, 249, 250, 253, 257, 259, 264, 265, 282, 285

Kansas, 233
Karnes, Capt. Henry Wax, 48, 53, 57, 63, 64, 71, 73, 78, 79, 168
Kaufman, Maj. David Spangler, 103, 117, 129, 177, 184, 189, 190, 212, 227
Keeling, Capt. William M., 103
Keenan, Charles G., 221, 242, 245
Kelley, Michael P., 113, 119, 128
Kellogg, Ebenezer, 162
Kellogg, Elizabeth, 84, 85, 86
Kelton, O. P., 154
Kemp, Louis W., 136
Kennedy, Abigail Parker, 108, 275
Kennedy, Joseph, 29, 108, 113, 118, 252
Kennedy, Martha Tucker Sadler, 34, 241, 254, 256-57, 260, 262, 273, 275, 277
Kennedy, Stephen E., 143, 170
Kennedy, William Thomas, 275
Kennymore, Capt. John C. P., 154, 169, 199, 200, 201
Kentucky, 51, 95
"Kentucky Mustangs", 48
Kerchoffer, John H., 94, 162
Kerley, William Green, 154
Key, Chief, 178, 179
Kichai Indians, 34, 81, 95, 105, 106, 124, 126, 142
Kickapoo, Battle of (Kickapoo War), 1, 2, 106, 120, 122-30, 131, 132, 142, 144, 159, 170, 171, 176, 248
Kickapoo Creek (Springs), 94, 115, 122, 124, 125, 127
Kickapoo Indians, 34, 81, 100, 108, 111, 113, 124, 131, 132, 145, 171, 189
Kickapoo Village, 104, 105, 109, 111, 114, 120, 122-27, 129, 172, 176, 283
Killough, Allen, 111, 240
Killough, Isaac Sr., 110
Killough Massacre, 110-11, 114, 127, 201
Killough, Nathaniel, 111, 112, 117, 127, 128
Killough, W. B., 127
Kimbell, Capt. George, 44
Kimbro, Capt. William, 31, 64, 177, 180, 195, 197
Kincannon, Jesse C., 119
Kincannon, William P., 46
King, Capt. Amon, 48
King, Josiah Sr., 259
Kingsboro, Tex., 240
King's Highway (see San Antonio Road)
King, W. H., 275
Kinney, Henry L., 212, 236
Kinney, W. C., 259
Kiowa Indians, 83
Knox, George W., 119
Kolb, Diamond Sadler, 69
Ku Klux Klan, 273

Labadie, Dr. Nicholas D., 64, 69
La Bahía (see Mission La Bahía)
La Bahía Massacre (Goliad Massacre), 48, 50, 58, 70, 79
Lacey, B., 112, 117
Lacry, Daniel, 155
Lacy, Martin, 87, 99, 111, 120, 173, 175, 177, 184
Lacy's Fort (see Fort Lacy)
Lacy, William Young, 104, 117, 120, 139
Lafayette, Marquis de, 18
Lagow, Thomas, 29, 159
LaGrange College, 246
La Grange, Tex., 49, 51, 128, 162, 167, 254
Laird, Capt. David, 103
Lake Burleson, 198
Lake Ponchartrain, 19-20, 258
Lamar Co., Tex., 212, 213, 221, 245, 247
Lamar, Jefferson Jackson, 7
Lamar, John, 6
Lamar, Lucius Quintus Cincinnatus, 6, 18
Lamar, Mirabeau Buonaparte, 1, 2, 6-

INDEX

7, 236, 242, 245, 246;
  in company with Sadler to Texas: 6-7, 15-24, 259;
  at Battle of San Jacinto: 59, 61, 63, 64, 65, 73;
  as Secretary of War: 78;
  as Vice President of Texas: 89, 104, 105, 122, 124, 141-142;
  as President of Republic of Texas: 3, 15, 144, 149-152, 153, 156, 161, 165-166, 167, 168, 170, 171, 172, 173, 174, 175, 176, 186, 209
Lamar, Rebecca Ann, 18, 242
Lamar, Tabitha B. Jordan, 18
Lamar, Thomas Randolph, 7
Lamb, George A., 64, 71
Lamoin, George T., 31
Lampasas River, 202
Landers, Maj. Hillequist, 154, 173
Landrum, Col. Willis H., 103, 143, 176, 177, 179, 181, 185, 187, 195, 197, 248
Lane, Walter Paye, 62, 63, 64, 113, 195
Langham, Joel, 113, 119
Laredo, Tex., 205, 236, 246, 280
La Salle Expedition, 25
Lathrop Lodge, 207
Laucer, William, 119
Laurence, Capt. George F., 154, 156, 199, 200
Lavaca Co., Tex., 229
Lawrence, William, 212
League and labor (land measurements, defined), 12
Leathers, Joel Daniel - 144
Lee, Gen. Robert E., 8
Leeper, Samuel, 46
Legare, William, 215
Legislatures of Texas:
  First: 1, 3, 221-237, 243, 263;
  Second: 3, 222, 239-249;
  Third: 250;
  Fourth: 250;
  Eleventh: 265
Leon, Captain Alonso de, 14
Leon Co., Tex., 229
Leon River, 202
Lewis (slave), 7
Lewis, Archibald, 64
Lewis, Daniel, 155
Lewis, George Washington, 36, 71
Lewis, Henry M., 245
Lewis, John M., 211, 213, 214
Lewis, Capt. Mark B., 175, 177, 183, 184, 189, 190, 201, 202-203
Lewis, Robert B., 257
Lewis, Samuel K., 213
Liberty Co., Tex., 162, 168, 212, 213, 221, 245
Liberty, Tex., 14, 162
Liberty Hill, Tex. (community), 4
Liles, Alfred M., 117
Limans, F. G., 190
Limestone Co., Tex., 29, 83, 229
Lincoln, Pres. Abraham, 263, 271
Lincoln, Benjamin, 7
Lincoln Co., N.C., 1, 7-8
Lincolnton, N.C., 8, 214, 220, 229
Link, Dr. Henry H., 240, 276
Linkswiler, Jane Colclough Taylor, 4, 255, 256
Linney, Chief, 178, 179, 195
Lipan Indians, 81, 167, 201
Little, Jackson, 118
Little River Fort, 202, 203
Little River, Ga., 7
Little River, La., 22
Little River (Tex.), 174
Little Rock (steamboat), 6-7, 15-16, 18-19
Lively, John, 119
Llano River, 282
Lockhart, W. P., 282
Logan, Capt. William M., 64
Logansport, La., 29
Lone Star Flag, 225, 226
Long, James D., 25, 103, 118, 181
Looce, Joseph, 119
Looney, Jesse H., 112, 118
Lopez, Joseph, 117
Lott, Elisha E., 243, 245
Lott, John, 41
Louisiana, 15, 16, 19-24, 25, 45, 46, 91, 145, 263, 264, 265, 267, 268-70
Louisville, Ga., 6
Love, Robert A., 27
"Loyal League", 273
Luckett, Alfred W., 212
Luckie, Samuel H., 212
Lumpkin, Pleiades Orion, 31, 106, 108, 113, 117, 218, 219, 241
Lumpkin, Gov. Wilson, 31
Lund, Oliver, 36, 84
Lusk, Robert O., 177
Lyons, James H., 245
Lynch, John L., 201
Lynch's Ferry, 57, 59, 60

Mabbitt, Major Leonard H., 47, 104, 105, 107, 108, 109, 112, 114, 115-117, 119-22, 125, 129, 143, 177, 180, 194
Mabin, Mathew, 112, 118
Mabry, Evans, 213, 221, 227, 232
MacFarlane, Dugald, 213, 214
Maddan, Zachariah, 117
Madden, Balis Erls, 135, 137-38, 139
Madden, James S., 31, 40, 41, 46, 49, 78, 94, 108, 131, 132, 134, 135, 136, 140, 142, 180
Madden, Lucinda Elizabeth Edens, 132, 134, 135, 136-39, 140, 142, 260
Madden, Mary, 135, 136
Madden (Bennett), Nancy Halhouser, 132, 134, 135, 136, 138-40, 260
Madden, Robert (boy), 135, 136
Madden, Robert, 108, 113, 118, 129, 133, 134, 139, 140, 142
Madden, Seldon, 135, 136
Magnolia Road, 32
Magnolia, Tex., 32
Main, Micham, 31, 239
Maine, Elisha, 269
Mallard, Judge John B., 249, 250
Mallard, Susan Scott, 249
Mansfield, La., 268-269, 270
Mansion House (hotel), 19
Many, La., 268
Marlin, Tex., 199
Marsh, Laverne Sadler, 4
Marshall, James Wilton, 252
Marshall, John, 112, 117
Marteth, Daniel, 112, 118
Martin, Capt. Albert, 44
Martin, George F., 112, 118, 190, 192
Martin, Dr. L., 177
Martin, Philip C., 40, 41, 46, 49
Martin, Capt. Wylie, 52, 55, 56
Martinez, Delores, 118
Maryland, 258
Mason Co., Tex., 282
Masonic Institute, 257
Mason, Tex., 282
Massachusetts, 258
Massacre of San Pedro Creek (see Edens-Madden Massacre)
Matagorda Co., Tex., 168, 212, 213, 221, 245
Matagorda, Tex., 14, 20, 56, 156, 268
Matamoros, Mexico, 79, 89-90, 102, 170, 171
Matthews, Lyman H., 119

Mayfield, Col. James S., 176, 177, 178-79, 180
Mays, Thomas H., 71
McAnulty, James, 118, 184
McCaskey, Capt. Robert D., 64
McClarty, Charles F., 221
McClure, Alexander E., 36, 240, 249, 250, 264
McClure, Louisiana Catherine Small "Aunt Bee", 264
McCown, James B., 221, 245, 247
McCoy, John C., 46, 247
McCrearey, James K., 212
McCullough, Benjamin, 221
McDonald, William S., 31, 32, 35, 106, 162, 164-65
McGovern, Matthew, 155
McFarland, Samuel, 221
McFarland, Capt. Thomas S., 44
McHorse, John W., 46
McIntire, Capt. Thomas H., 64
McIver, Alex, 177
McKaughn, William, 113, 119
McKenzie, Alexander, 106, 107, 112, 117
McKenzie, Carter T., 106, 170, 250
McKenzie, Daniel M., 31, 180
McKenzie, Lacy, 106, 107, 112, 119, 180
McKenzie, Lt., 6, 19
McKenzie, R. C., 270
McKim, Capt. James, 177
McLaughlin, Thomas, 190
McLean, Daniel, 90, 93, 108
McLean, Capt. James, 90, 265
McLean-Sherdian Massacre, 93, 95
McLeod, Col. Hugh, 87, 102, 103, 104, 117, 121, 122, 124, 125-27, 129, 151, 152, 154, 156, 177, 178, 185, 190, 192, 194, 203, 213
McLinn, John, 36
McLinn, Stephen, 46
McNeill, Archibald, 221, 242, 245
McNelly, Bennett, 64
McRoy, Mack, 113, 119, 128
Mead, Marcus P., 97
Means, William, 213
Medford, John A., 119
Medina River, 90
Menard, Michael B., 162
Menards (post office), 162
Menchaca, Antonio, 64
Menefee, William, 213
Meradith, Joseph, 113, 119
Meradith, Stewart, 113, 119

INDEX 377

Mercer, George R., 46
Meredith, Daniel, 119
Meriwether's Company, 10
Mexia, Tex., 83
Mexican Army, 36, 37-38, 42, 43, 47-48, 50, 51, 53, 54, 57, 60-62, 63, 65-72, 77-80, 90, 102
Mexican War of 1846, 235, 236, 239, 242
Mexico, 1, 2, 11, 14, 25, 26, 36, 37, 73, 75, 81, 83, 89, 95, 100, 104, 127, 150, 171, 201, 205, 207, 210, 235, 276
Mexico City, 11, 34, 47
Mier, 205
Mier Expedition, 205
Milam, Col. Ben, 37, 38
Milam Co., Tex., 90, 151, 212, 213, 221, 245
Milam Guards, 145
Milam, Tex., 162
Miles, Lt. Alfred H., 72, 95
Miles, Alenson T., 155
Miles Creek, 4
Millard, Lt. Col. Henry, 60, 64, 65
Milledgeville, Ga., 6
Miller, John D., 112, 118
Miller, John F., 245
Miller, Steward Alexander, 221, 222, 223, 242, 245
Miller, William J., 64, 259
Millican, Elliott M., 213, 214, 221, 245
Millroy, James H., 177, 180, 194, 199
Miracle, Capt. Pedro Julian, 102, 105
Mission Concepcion, 37
Mission La Bahía, 48, 50
Mission Nuestra Señora de Guadalupe de los Nacogdoches, 25
Mission Santísimo Nombre de Maria, 14
Mission San Francisco de los Tejas (Mission Tejas), 14
Mission San Jose, 201, 202
Mississippi, 15, 46, 80, 263
Mississippi River, 5, 20-22, 259
Missouri, 46, 264
Mitchell, James, 46
Mitchell, John, 112, 118
Mitchell, Thomas, 113, 117
Mobile, Al., 5, 6, 7, 19
Mobile Bay, 5
Mobile River, 18, 19
Moffitt, John H., 213
Mohawk and Hudson Railroad, 258
Molino, Jose, 46

Moncolva, Coahuila, 23
Monett's Ferry, 269
Montgomery, Al., 5, 6, 16, 263
Montgomery Co., Tex., 211, 212, 213, 221, 222, 230, 245
Moore, Benjamin, 113, 119
Moore, Elias, 97
Moore, Elisha, 131, 134-135
Moore, Evaline Kolb, 4
Moore, Col. John Henry, 36, 167
Moore Lake, 4
Moore, Marshall L. Jr., 4
Moore, Shadrack H., 36
Moore, Thomas W., 270
Moore, Capt. William H., 154, 199, 200
Moran, Martin, 155
Moreland, Capt. Isaac N., 64
Moreland, William, 7
Morgan, Capt. George Washington, 154, 156, 199
Morgan, Maj. Miram S., 267, 269
Morganza, La., 269, 270
Morris, Oliver, 27
Morrison, John C., 113, 119
Morrow, Jacob C., 106, 107, 112, 117, 180
Mosely, Samuel F., 243, 245
Mosley, J. P., 112, 118
Moss, John, 46
Motley, Dr. Junius William, 64, 67, 69, 71
Mound City, Tex., 107
Mount Pleasant, 175
Mound Prairie, Tex., 239, 264, 273
Mount Holland (post office), 162
Mount Selman, Tex., 110
Mount Sterling, Tex., 162
Muckelroy, Capt. David, 103
Muckleroy, Daniel, 221, 235
Mullins, Charles, 221
Muncriff, John A., 117
Munson, Henry J., 212
Munson, Ira, 176, 177
Murchison, John, 92, 108, 113, 118, 126, 128, 129, 241, 254-55
Murchison, Lycurgus, 135, 138
Murchison, Martin, 94, 131, 134-35, 138, 144, 149, 180, 225, 256
Murchison, Sarah Hall, 132, 134, 135, 142
Murchison's Camp, 143, 144
Murchison's Prairie, 92, 207, 231, 256
Murphree, Capt. David, 64
Muscogee Co., Ga., 18

Mustang Prairie, Tex., 132, 162, 169, 170
Myers, Elias G., 31
Myrtle Springs (post office), 162

Nabors, William, 46
Nacogdoche Indians, 25
Nacogdoches, Battle of, 25, 36
Nacogdoches Co., Tex., 45, 47, 88, 92, 93, 94, 95, 99, 102, 103, 129, 138, 145, 152-62, 165, 203, 207, 212, 213, 221, 222, 229, 243, 245
Nacogdoches Department, 14, 31, 38
Nacogdoches Road, 32, 35, 86
Nacogdoches, Tex., 2, 11, 14, 15, 20, 24, 25-26, 27, 28, 29, 31, 32, 35, 37, 45-47, 49, 50, 53, 55, 56, 71, 80, 86, 87, 89, 91, 99, 102, 103, 104, 105, 108, 109, 115, 120, 121, 128, 132, 142, 152, 162, 171, 172, 176, 180, 184, 191, 198
"Nacogdoches Volunteers" (Second Regiment, Texas Volunteers, First Company Infantry), 2, 40, 45-47, 50, 51, 53, 57, 64, 65-66, 67-68, 73, 77, 78, 79, 107, 120
Nashville, Tenn., 87
Nashville-on-the-Brazos, Tex., 202
Natchez, Miss., 80
Natchez Trace, 34
Natchitoches, La., 20, 21, 22-24, 90, 268
Navarro Co., Tex., 113, 229
Navasota River, 29, 41, 83, 85, 86
Navasota, Tex., 210
Neal, Benjamin F., 245
Neches, Battle of, 11, 14, 27, 31, 32, 33, 37, 38, 39, 82, 87, 92, 94, 98, 107, 108, 115, 122, 127, 159, 171, 174, 174 178, 179, 181, 182, 183-94, 195, 197, 198, 208, 230, 231, 240
Neches River, 3, 11, 14, 27, 31, 32, 33, 37, 38, 39, 82, 87, 92, 94, 98, 107, 108, 115, 122, 127, 159, 171, 174, 175, 178, 179, 181, 182, 183-94, 195, 197, 198, 208, 230, 231, 240
Neches Saline, 99, 110, 122, 132, 159, 163, 171, 174, 175
Neches, Tex., 115, 162, 169, 170, 274
Neely, James, 212
Neighbors, Robert Simpson, 155
Neill, Col. James Clinton, 48, 54, 60-61, 62, 64, 71
Nelson, Allen T., 32
Nelson, Charles H., 97

Nelson, James, 71
New Mexico, 233, 255, 267
New Orleans (steamboat), 5
New Orleans, La., 19-20, 21, 22, 23, 77, 152, 156, 199, 258, 270
Newport, Ky., 51
Newton Co., Tex., 229
New York, N.Y., 151, 270
New Washington, Tex., 56, 57, 60
Nite, John Edward, 108, 113, 118
Nixon, Mrs. Loreno D. Sr., 84, 85
Nixon, Loreno D. Jr., 84, 85, 86
Nixon, Sarah Parker, 84, 85, 86
Nobbitt, William, 188
Noble, Edward B., 176, 177
Noble, Jamerson S., 221, 233
Norris, John, 102, 145
North Avenue (Austin, Tex.), 223
North Carolina, 7, 9, 42, 45, 46, 80, 81, 204, 220, 262, 263
North Elkhart Creek, 231
Northwestern Campaign, 200-201
Nueces Co., Tex., 229, 242
Nueces River, 150, 205

Ochiltree, William Beck, 241
Ogden, Duncan Campbell, 154, 213, 221
Ohio River, 5
O'Kelly, J. D., 113, 119
Oklahoma - 94, 198, 223
Old Fort Parker State Historical Park, 83
Oldham, P. G., 259
Old Stone Fort,
"Old Three Hundred" settlers, 11, 90
Oliver, Capt. Robert, 154
O'Neal, James, 112, 118
O'Neil, Timothy, 155
Onion Creek, 202
Opelika, Al., 6
Osceola Hotel, 263
Otto (steamboat), 20
Ouachita Parish, La., 45
Owens, 257
Owens, Samuel T., 270
Ownby, Capt. James P., 175, 177, 183, 189, 190

Palestine Advocate, 279
Palestine Female Institute, 257
Palestine Herald-Press, 1
Palestine, Ill., 29, 241
Palestine, Tex., 27, 30, 31, 87, 99, 120, 163, 207, 232, 249, 250, 252, 254,

257, 258, 259, 260, 261, 263, 264, 266, 267, 270, 271, 273, 275, 279, 280, 284;
   creation of: 239-42
Palmer, George N., 155
Panola Co., Tex., 229
Park, William A., 71
Parker, Benjamin, 29, 36, 84, 85, 94
Parker, Benjamin F., 29, 113, 118, 251, 275, 278, 282
Parker, Cynthia Ann, 84-86
Parker, Daniel Sr. (Elder), 27, 28-29, 38, 39, 40, 43, 83, 140, 144, 159, 206, 251, 275
Parker, Daniel Jr., 29, 40, 49, 94, 113, 118, 139, 257, 258, 261, 275, 178
Parker, Dickerson, 29, 31, 40, 46, 49, 68, 94, 113, 118, 206
Parker, Francis Marion, 84
Parker, Gustavus A., 213, 214
Parker, Isaac, 27, 29, 86, 94, 173, 207, 212, 218, 219, 222, 228-29, 230, 240, 251, 278
Parker, Isaac Duke, 29
Parker, J. P., 261
Parker, Capt. James W., 27, 29, 83, 84-86, 87
Parker, James W. Jr., 84
Parker, Elder John, 27, 29, 32, 84, 85, 98
Parker, Chief John, 84-86
Parker, John D., 44, 94, 180, 239, 241
Parker, Joe A., 29, 261
Parker, Kalbe, 29
Parker, Lucinda, 27
Parker, Lucy Duty, 84, 85
Parker, Lucy W., 27
Parker, Martha Dickerson "Patsey", 27, 28
Parker, Martha Duty, 84, 85, 86
Parker, Martha Patsy, 84
Parker, Orlena, 84
Parker, Peyton, 180, 240, 250, 258
Parker, Pheby, 27
Parker, Chief Quanah, 86
Parker, Sallie White (Granny), 84-86
Parker's Bluff, 240
Parker's Creek, 97, 261
Parker's Fort, 29, 41, 83-86, 111
Parker's Fort Attack (or Massacre), 83-86, 91, 111, 241
Parker, Silas Mercer, 29, 36, 38, 39, 41, 84, 85
Parker, Silas Mercer Jr., 84
Parkerson, Millard M., 190

Parks, Maj. Bedford F., 264
Parks, George, 261
Paso de Francia, 23
Pate, William H., 113, 118
Patillo, George A., 162, 212, 221
Patillos (post office), 162
Patsy (Edens family servant), 133, 135, 138-140
Patton, William H., 64
Pease, Elisha M., 221, 244, 245
Pecan Point Road, 32, 35
Pecan (6th) Street (Austin, Tex.), 224
Peggy's Lake, 69-70
Pennsylvania, 156, 258
Percilla, Tex., 93, 284
Perkins, J. P., 32
Perkins, Stephen W., 213, 214, 221
Permanent Council of Texas, 38, 39
Perry, James M., 64, 250, 253
Perry, Dr. William B., 36, 113, 118, 127, 180, 221, 245
Persons, Albert G., 106
Persons, Benjamin, 106
Persons, Edmund H., 36
Peters, R., 162
Peterson, C. W., 246
Pettus, John Freeman,
Philadelphia, Pa. - 131
Phillips, Flora Josephine DeBard "Sammie", 257
Philips, Samuel, 46, 98
Phillips, M. L., 112, 118
Piedras, Jose de las, 26
Pilgrim Predestinarian Regular Baptist Church, 27, 29, 31, 43, 83, 84, 107, 108, 159, 206, 241, 256
Pillans, Palmer Job, 154, 177, 180, 194, 199
Pillsbury, Timothy, 212, 227
Pine Island (post office), 162
Pinson, John E., 250
Pipkin, Samuel W., 212
Placido, Chief, 175, 177, 183, 184, 188, 197
Plaquemine, La., 21
Pleasant Hill, La., 268-69, 270
Pleasant Hill Road, 268
Plentitude, Tex. (community), 252
Plummer, James Pratt, 84-86
Plummer, Luther M., 84, 85
Plummer, Rachel Parker, 84-86
Plummer, Samuel A., 199
Polk Co., Tex., 229
Polk, Judge Alfred, 195
Polk, President James Knox, 216, 220,

253
Pollygatcho (post office), 162
Portersville, La., 19
Port Lavaca, Tex., 253
Potter, Mark M., 242, 243, 245
Potter, Robert, 44
Powelton Academy, 16
Prewitt, Ira, 250
Price, Edward, 118
Price, Capt. John T., 205
Providence, Tex. (community), 257
Pruett, Jacob, 112, 117
Pruett, Len, 112, 117
Pruett, Leroy, 46, 47
Pruett, Martin J., 46, 47, 112, 117
Pulsiver, Joseph E., 162
Putnam Co., Ga., 1, 6, 7, 8, 9, 10, 13, 14, 16, 24, 34, 257, 262
Putnam, Michael, 71
Puve, Joseph, 162

Quaker Church, 7
Quapaw Indians, 81
Quarles, P. L., 259
Quesenberry, T. J., 112, 118
Quinn, James, 162

Raglin, Henry Walton, 212
Railey, Charles B., 221, 245
Railroads in Texas, 258-260;
    Buffalo Bayou, Colorado and Brazos Railway Company: 247, 259;
    Galveston and Red River Railroad Company: 247, 259;
    Houston Tap and Brazoria Railway Company: 274;
    Houston and Texas Central Railway Company: 259;
    Houston, Trinity and Tyler Railroad Company: 259;
    International/Great Northern Railroad (I&GN): 274, 280;
    Missouri Pacific Railroad: 280;
    Palestine Tap Railway Company: 259-260;
    Southern Pacific: 274;
    Texas State Railroad: 280
Raines, Isaac, 112, 118
Raines, Joel D., 112, 118
Raines, Jon D., 112, 118
Rainey, Col. Alex T., 264
Rainey, Joseph, 250
Rains, Emory, 245
Randal, Col. Horace, 265, 268

Randolph, Cyrus H., 208
Randolph, Tex., 49
Ratcliffe, Edward S., 190
Ratcliffe, John, 249
Ratcliffe, John G., 249
Raymond, James Hervey, 211, 213, 217, 225, 228
Raymond, Samuel, 64
Rayner, William S., 221, 235, 245
Read, Ezra, 154
Reagan, John Henninger, 1, 87, 173-74, 175-76, 184, 189, 190-92, 204, 243-44, 245, 248, 264, 280
Reconstruction Era, 273, 275, 278
Rector, Elbridge Gerry, 71
Redd, Capt. William Davis, 154, 156, 199, 201, 203
Redfield, William, 155
Redgate, Samuel J., 221, 235
Red Lawn, Tex., 173
Red River, 14, 20, 21, 22, 23, 32, 105, 142, 145, 150, 155, 221, 268
Red River Campaign, 265, 268-70
Red River Co., Tex., 162, 212, 213, 221, 222, 245
Reeves, Judge Reuben A., 249, 257, 264, 270, 271
Refugio Co., Tex., 151, 212, 213, 245
Refugio, Tex., 48, 50
Reily, Capt. James, 103, 117, 129
Reneau, Elijah B., 113, 117
Renfro, Capt. David, 103
Renfro, J., 245
Rennard, Hugh, 118
Republic of Texas, 1, 2, 3, 4, 8, 14, 25, 52, 82, 89, 95, 96, 97, 99, 102, 105, 128, 129, 144, 149, 152, 153, 156, 158, 165, 167, 194, 207, 209, 214, 217, 222, 225, 229, 235, 238, 248, 249, 275, 280;
    Constitution of: 44;
    Declaration of Independence: 44, 57, 210, 281, 283;
    1840 Census of: 203;
    military of: 47;
    end of: 225-227
Reuben (horse), 267-268
Revolutionary War, 141
Rhodes, Joseph, 64
Rice, Lt. James O., 171
Rice, John T., 270
Richards, James L., 257
Richardson, Benjamin, 162
Richardsons (post office), 162
Richland Creek, 113

Richland (post office), 162
Richmond, Tex., 52, 56, 242
Richmond, Va., 258
Rio Grande River, 23, 89, 205, 233, 235, 243
Ripley, Phineas, 64
Roach, Robert Owen, 280
Roark, John, 118
Roark, Russell, 118
Robbins Ferry, 49
Robbins, Nathaniel, 49
Roberts, Charles, 102
Roberts, John S., 162
Roberts, Matthew, 102
Roberts, Lt. Col. Moses L., 177
Robertson Co., Tex., 151, 199, 212, 213, 221, 245
Robertson, Jerome B., 245
Robertson, Lt. Col. John C., 267
Robertson, J. R., 177
Robertson, Larkin, 106
Robinson, Andrew, 211
Robinson, George Washington, 71
Robinson, P. T., 113, 118, 129
Robinson, Tod, 213
Robinson, William, 112, 117
Robison, Joel Walter, 72
Rocky Point (Rocky Knob), 32
Rogers, Dr. Henry M., 118, 184, 185
Rogers, Magnus T., 245
Rogers, Col. Samuel, 93, 118
Rogers, Wiley, 112, 118
Rogers, William R., 250
Rolling, Asa, 113, 119
Roman, Capt. Richard, 51, 64, 212
Romeo (steamboat), 20-22
Rose, John W., 221
Rose, Louis, 113, 119
Round Rock, Tex., 199
Rovan, John, 113, 119
Rowan, John, 113, 119
Rowe, James, 64
Runaway Scrape, 49, 53, 80, 211
Runnels, Hardin R., 245
Rusk Co., Tex., 82, 207, 212, 213, 221, 222, 245
Rusk, Capt. David, 46, 68-69, 103, 122, 189, 190
Rusk, Gen. Thomas Jefferson, 1, 3, 26, 44, 52, 54, 56, 57-58, 61-62, 63, 64, 65, 67, 68-69, 70, 75, 78, 79-80, 89, 95, 100-103, 104, 105, 107, 108, 109, 111, 114, 115, 117, 120-23, 125-29, 141, 142, 144-45, 151, 155, 171, 172, 176-80, 181, 183, 184-189, 191, 192, 194, 214, 219, 227, 243, 276
Russell, Andrew J., 221, 235
Russell, Reuben R., 170
Rutherford Co., N.C., 7
Ryburn, Hiram W., 221

Sabine Co., Tex., 6, 162, 176, 177, 212, 213, 221, 245
Sabine River, 14, 18, 23, 82, 101, 171, 197
Sacramento River, 255
Sadler, Adelia (freed black), 272
Sadler, Alex (freed black), 258, 272
Sadler, Alice (freed black), 272
Sadler, Allen (freed black), 258, 272
Sadler, Anderson (freed black), 272
Sadler, Charity (freed black), 258, 272
Sadler, Charles Wesley, 8
Sadler Creek (Saddler's Creek), 32, 33, 34, 92, 99, 276, 277
Sadler, Emiline "Aunt Charlotte", 271, 272
Sadler, Gerald Anthony "Jerry", 4, 272-273, 282
Sadler, Harriet (freed black), 258
Sadler, Henry, 8
Sadler Hill, Ga., 9-10
Sadler, Howard C., 4, 206, 283
Sadler, Jackson (freed black), 272
Sadler, James Jr., 9
Sadler, James (freed black), 272
Sadler, Jane (freed black), 272
Sadler, Jeremiah, 8
Sadler, Joe (freed black), 272
Sadler, John, 76
Sadler, John (freed black), 272
Sadler, Jordan (freed black), 258, 272
Sadler, Joseph (farm laborer), 272
Sadler, Joseph (son), 273-274, 284
Sadler, Josephine Roach, 280, 284
Sadler, Laura J., 261, 262, 272, 273, 277
Sadler, Louis (freed black), 258, 272
Sadler, Lucy (freed black), 272
Sadler, Martha Rose, 7
Sadler, Martha Matilda, 8
Sadler, Martha Roach Gibson, 280
Sadler, Mary (freed black), 272
Sadler, Mary Murchison, 92-93, 132, 134, 135, 136, 138
Sadler, Nancy Turner Moreland, 8
Sadler, Nathaniel Fletcher "Fletch", 219, 251, 254, 256, 262, 264-68, 272, 273, 275, 276, 277, 280

Sadler, Nathaniel Milton Sr., 7-10, 14, 257-58
Sadler, Nathaniel Milton II/Jr., 8, 14, 258, 260-61, 262, 278-79
Sadler, Nettie (freed black), 272
Sadler, Patrick D., 4
Sadler, Permelia Bennett, 27, 206-207, 219, 241, 251, 254, 256, 261, 262, 273-74, 280, 284
Sadler, Peterson G., 8, 10
Sadler, Phebe Tucker Moreland, 8
Sadler Plantation, 9, 205, 206, 250, 256, 262, 271, 274, 283, 284
Sadler, Rebecca (freed black), 272
Sadler, Robert H., 138
Sadler, Robert Roach "Tab", 43
Sadler, Sophia, 135, 136
Sadler, Stuart (freed black), 258, 272
Sadler, Theophilus, 8, 10
Sadler, Thomas Sr., 10
Sadler, Thomas Jr., 7
Sadler, William Peterson "Billy", 254, 256, 262, 272, 273, 276, 277, 280, 284
Sadler, William Rose Sr., 8
Sadler, William Turner -
    early life of: 7-11;
    first trip to Texas: 10-11;
    travels to Texas with Lamar: 6-7, 15-24, 259;
    arrives in Nacogdoches: 25-26;
    land dealings/acquisitions of: 13-14, 26-27, 30, 32, 34, 92-93, 97-99, 145-149, 203, 224-225, 242, 249, 253-254, 257, 260-261, 276-280, 281-282;
    with first settlers of Anderson County: 29-32;
    and establishment of Houston: 35-36;
    as captain of early Texas Ranger company during Texas Revolution: 38, 39-41, 43-44, 45, 49, 51, 87;
    member of Nacogdoches Volunteer Company in Texas Revolution: 46, 51, 56, 57, 59, 62, 77, 78, 79;
    at San Jacinto: 62, 65-69;
    and interrogation of Santa Anna: 73-75;
    in Captain Smith's company: 78-80;
    marries Mary Murchison: 92;
    as captain of volunteer ranging company of Texas Militia: 89, 101, 106, 107-108, 110, 111-13, 117, 118, 120-21, 131, 139, 143, 144;
    in skirmish with Cordova's rebels: 115-19;
    in Battle of Kickapoo: 123-30;
    loses family in massacre: 134-40, 142;
    provides for Texas Army: 142-143, 167, 248-49;
    as postmaster in Houston County: 161-63;
    letter to Lamar: 165-66, 168;
    as captain of First Infantry company: 150, 153, 154, 156-61, 164-65, 169, 173, 176, 177, 178, 183, 189, 198, 199, 200-203;
    in Cherokee War: 83-194;
    and death of Chief Bowles: 192;
    marries Permelia Bennett: 206-207;
    and Sam Houston: 206, 264-65;
    in Ninth Congress: 208-18;
    in First Legislature: 221-37;
    naming/creation of Anderson County: 228-32;
    and creation of Palestine: 239-42;
    in Second Legislature: 242-49;
    as early postmaster in Anderson County: 252, 256;
    in California Gold Rush: 253-56;
    as member of Masons: 257;
    returns to Georgia to settle father's estate: 257-58;
    involvement with Texas railroads: 259-60, 274;
    and Civil War: 266-70;
    provides land to freed blacks: 271-73;
    loses second wife/child to a tornado: 274;
    pension papers of: 277-78;
    death of: 283-85;
    descendants of: 313-30
Salado Creek, Battle of, 205
Salem (post office), 162
Saline Creek, 178
Saltillo, 205
San Antonio Road (El Camino Real, or "King's Highway"), 14, 23, 24, 35, 49, 50, 82, 86, 99, 111, 173
San Antonio, Tex., 2, 14, 27, 34, 36, 37-38, 42, 43, 44-45, 47-48, 50,

INDEX

53, 77, 201, 203, 205, 210
San Augustine Co., Tex., 14, 23, 162, 176, 177, 180, 209, 212, 213, 221, 245
San Augustine, Tex., 24, 109, 144, 162
San Bernadino, Cal., 255
Sanchez, Antonio, 118
Sanchez, Capt. Lewis, 103, 118, 176, 177
Sand Springs, Tex. (community), 252
San Felipe de Austin, Tex., 11, 14, 35, 37, 51, 52, 56, 133
San Francisco Bay, 255
San Francisco, Cal., 252
San Francisco de Los Tejas (see Mission Tejas)
San Gabriel, Tex., 171, 201
San Jacinto, Battle of, 1, 2, 4, 15, 40, 43, 44, 47, 52, 55, 60-75, 77, 78, 83, 87, 88, 93, 96, 98, 107, 113, 116, 120, 121, 146, 148, 151, 153, 165, 168, 174, 176, 179, 193, 194, 195, 207, 220, 225, 238, 249, 275, 276, 278, 281, 282, 283, 284
San Jacinto Museum of History - 76
San Jacinto Monument, 73
San Jacinto River, 57, 59
San Marcos, Tex., 152
San Patricio Co., Tex., 48, 151, 212, 213, 221, 242, 245
San Pedro Creek, 29, 107, 112, 130, 131, 132, 134, 139, 140, 141, 143, 159, 169, 170
San Saba River, 167, 201
Santa Anna Perez de Lebron, President Antonio López de (Santa Anna), 4, 25, 26, 36, 38, 41-42, 43, 47-48, 50, 53-57, 60-62, 63, 65, 66, 68, 69, 70-75, 77, 78, 79, 80, 205, 283
Santa Cruz, Az., 255
Santa Fe Expedition, 157, 205
Santa Fe, N.M., 205
Saracen (Sam Houston's horse), 65, 67
Savage, Israel S., 221
Scates, William Bennett, 46
Schenectady, N.Y., 258
Schleiter, Joseph, 200
Scott, Abram H., 155
Scott, Thomas M., 112, 116, 118, 250
Scott, William, 162
Scott, William Thomas, 213
Scurlock, William, 162
Scurry, William R., 213, 214
Second Regiment of Texas Volunteers, 2, 46, 52, 53, 56, 57, 59, 62, 64, 65, 66-67, 68, 79, 276
Seguín, Capt. Juan Nepomuceno, 44, 64, 78
Seguin, Tex., 170, 180
Selma, Al., 15
Seminole and Creek Indian Wars, 10, 37, 39
Seminole Indians, 142
Sesma, Gen. Joaquín Ramírez, 50
Sevier, Elbridge G., 118
Shanks, Charles, 112, 118
Shanks, Joseph, 112, 118
Shannon, Thomas J., 242, 245
Sharp, John, 64
Shaw, James B., 228, 242, 245, 247
Shawnee Indians, 81, 82, 105, 111, 171, 175, 178, 179, 180, 194, 198
Shearer, W. B., 106
Shearwood, Justus, 113, 119
Shelby Co., Tex., 162, 176, 177, 209, 212, 213, 221, 245
Shelbyville (post office), 162
Shelton, Charles, 252
Shelton, Johnston, 239, 241
Sheridan, John, 4, 87, 93, 108
Sheridan, Lucinda, 93
Sherman, Col. Sidney, 1, 2, 48, 51, 52, 53, 56, 60-61, 62, 63, 64, 65, 66-67, 69, 70, 74, 77, 79, 159, 276
Shreve, Capt. Henry Miller, 21
Shreveport, La., 22, 240, 268
Shreve Town Company, 21
Shute, Ira C., 117
Sierra Mountains, 252, 255
Simms, Samuel W., 162
Sims, Charles H., 114
Skerrett, Capt. Mark Blake, 154, 156, 199, 200, 201
Slaughter, George T., 184
Slawson, Augustus W., 113, 119
Slocum, Tex., 93, 284
Slyvester, Sgt. James Austin, 72
Smiley, Daniel, 112, 118
Smith, Gen. Edmund Kirby, 267, 268, 270
Smith, Erastus "Deaf", 48, 53, 57, 63, 71, 74, 77
Smith Co., Tex., 82, 99, 171, 175, 182, 229, 267
Smith, Governor Henry, 37, 44, 89
Smith, Capt. Henry Madison, 177, 184, 189, 190, 191
Smith, J. H., 112, 118
Smith, J. M., 190
Smith, Lt. Col. James, 122, 176, 177,

189, 194, 221
Smith, John, 106, 112, 118
Smith, John N. O., 221, 235
Smith, John William, 44, 212
Smith, Capt. Leander, 54, 78-80, 276
Smith, Martha, 204
Smith, Gen. Nathaniel W., 129, 203-204
Smith, Capt. Robert W., 45, 46, 64, 103, 118, 121, 129, 176, 177, 184, 189, 190, 191-92, 196
Smith, Thomas F., 213
Smith, Capt. William H., 31, 64, 71
Smith, Dr. William R., 152, 155
Smith, William T., 106, 108, 113, 118, 275, 276
Smithwick, Capt. Noah, 43, 167
Smola, Joan Coker, 4
Smyth, George Washington, 213, 214, 247, 249
Snake Creek - 115
Snell, Capt. Martin Kingsley, 64, 154, 156, 174
Snively, Col. Jacob, 31, 107, 113, 115, 119, 125, 128, 129, 152, 155, 159, 163, 172, 177, 180, 194, 202, 222
Snively Expedition, 222
Somervell, Maj. Alexander, 48, 58, 64
South Carolina, 26, 81, 92, 263
Spain, 11, 25
Sparks, Eli G., 118
Sparks, Stephen Franklin, 46, 53, 56, 57, 66, 68, 73, 118
Sparks, Richard, 36
Spring Creek, 79
Springhill, Miss., 19
Spring Hill (post office), 162
Spy Buck, Chief, 178, 179, 180
Stafford, Tex., 259
Starkes, Theodore B., 118
Starr, Jasper, 253, 261
Starr, John, 253, 261
Stars and Stripes Flag, 225, 226
Steamboat House, 264-65
Steele, Alphonzo, 69, 71
Steele, William H., 64
Stephens, Ashley R., 71
Stephens, Capt. Hiram B., 103, 118
Sterne, Charles Adolphus, 257
Sterne, Capt. Adolphus, 242, 245, 257
Stevenson, Alexander, 221
Stevenson, Capt. Robert, 64
Steward, B., 113, 119
Stewart, Charles B., 221, 235
Stewart, William H., 245, 252

Stilwell, William S., 64
Still, Jack, 120
Stills Creek, 115
St. Joseph, Mo., 266
St. Louis, Mo., 34
Stockton, Cal., 255
Stoddard, Jesse W., 245
Stokely, Isaac, 119
Stout, Capt. William B., 242, 245
Strickland, Capt. William, 79
Stuart, Hamilton, 242, 245
Sturgess, Benjamin B., 154, 156, 177, 180, 194
Sublett, Henry W., 221, 234
Summerville, Miss., 19
Surfside, Tex., 78
Sutherland, George, 213
Summers, William M., 64
Sutter, Capt. John Augustus, 252
Sutter's Mill, 252
Sutton, John Schuyler, 155
Swift, Arthur, 221, 227, 230, 235
Swift, Seth, 162
Swisher, Harvey H., 64
Swisher, John Milton, 213

Tail (Cherokee brave), 127
Tallassee, Al., 6
Tankersly, Benjamin F., 221, 244, 245
Tansell, M., 190
Tarrant, Capt. Edward H., 145
Tawakoni Indians, 142
Taylor, Charles S., 103
Taylor, Geneva Sadler, 256
Taylor, James F., 242, 245
Taylor, William W., 118
Taylor, Gen. Zachary, 235
Teague, James E., 261
Teal, Henry, 79
Tehuacana Indians, 34, 81
Tejas Indians, 14
Telegraph and Texas Register, 35, 57, 129, 153, 175, 183, 185, 196
Tennessee, 28, 37, 45, 46, 50, 112, 203, 240
Tensaw River, 18
Terrell, Col. Alexander Watkins, 265, 266-70, 278
Texas,
    under Spanish rule: 11;
    named for Tejas Indians: 14;
    under Mexican rule: 11;
    census info of: 11, 251, 254, 262, 272, 275;

Constitution of the Republic of Texas: 44, 52;
population of: 14;
capitals of: 209-11, 214-15, 222-24;
annexation into United States: 216-217, 225-27;
State Constitution of: 219-20, 222, 234;
use of public lands to pay debts: 232-34;
and Civil War: 263-70
Texas Almanac, 66
Texas Army (see Army of Texas)
Texas Democrat, 243, 255
Texas Militia, 2, 47, 95, 100-102, 103-104, 105, 107, 111-14, 120-29, 141, 142-45, 151, 155, 159, 167, 169, 176, 177, 178, 182, 190; brigade districts defined: 100-101
Texas Navy, 96
Texas Rangers - 2, 3, 38, 39-43, 47, 49, 83, 87-88, 90, 93, 150-51, 168, 171, 174, 200, 204-205, 235, 238, 283
Texas Revolution, 26, 36-38, 41-45, 47-75, 80, 86, 90, 107, 157, 168, 174, 220, 275, 281, 282, 283
Texas State Library, 136
Texas Veterans Association, 3, 53, 282, 283, 284
Thacker, John B., 184
Thayer, John, 177
Tinsley, James W., 64
Thomas, David, 44
Thompson, Burrell J., 162
Thompson, Charles P., 72
Thompson, Edward A., 154
Thompson, John S., 190, 192
Thompson, Maj. James M., 177
Thompson, William, 112, 118
Three Forks of the Trinity, 142, 144
Timmins, Capt. James F., 103
Tipps, Leander Erwin, 143
Tipps, Capt. Peter, 176, 177, 184, 188
Tombigbee River, 18
Todd, Capt. Jackson, 176, 177, 180, 181, 183, 185, 188, 190, 191, 197
Tom, John Files, 71
Tonkawa Indians, 81, 100, 105, 175, 184, 188, 197, 201
Town Creek, 33, 35, 163
Townsend, Capt. Stephen, 43
Trans-Mississippi Department, 267, 270

Trask, Olwyn J., 62, 71
Travis Co., Tex., 212, 213, 221, 245
Travis, Lt. Col. William Barret, 2, 36, 42, 44-45, 47-48, 57
Trenary, John B., 46
Trinity Advocate, 263, 264, 273
Trinity Co., Tex., 265
Trinity Lodge, 207
Trinity River, 2, 31, 32, 35, 38, 39, 48, 88, 89, 91, 94, 95, 98, 101, 102, 104, 108, 132, 142, 144, 163, 164, 208, 230, 231, 248, 250, 261
Triplett, James, 113, 119, 128
Troup, Gov. George MacIntosh, 16, 18
Truitt, James, 213, 214, 221, 227, 230, 235, 245
Tryon Co., N.C., 7
Tryon, George W., 158
Tryon Son & Company, 158
Tucker, Dr. Edmund, 155
Tucker, Capt. William H., 264
Tucson, Az., 255
Tuggle, George W., 249, 261
Tumlinson, Capt. John James, 39, 41, 43, 44
Turner, Capt. Amasa, 51, 64
Turner, Samuel, 113, 119
Tutts, Martin, 188, 190, 192
Twaisime, Heartwell, 118
Twin Sisters (Texas cannon), 54, 59, 60-61, 65, 68, 72, 78
Tyler, President John, 216
Tyler Co., Tex., 229
Tyler, Tex., 186, 187, 198, 264, 267, 274

Umsted, William W., 113, 119
Union Army, 268-270
Upshur Co., Tex., 229
Urrea, Gen. José, 42, 48, 50, 56, 77, 89-90
Ussery, Humphries, 106, 180
Utley, Thomas C., 71

Vanbenthuysen, Lt. A. B., 95
Vandever, Logan - 71
Vansickle, Capt. Benjamin Anderson, 87, 112, 117, 177, 180, 184, 191
Vansickle, Elias, 132
Vansickle, Hiram C., 113, 117
Van Zandt Co., Tex., 82, 182, 187, 193
Vara (*land measurement, defined*), 12
Vardeman, William Henry, 46, 57, 113, 119
Vaughan, W. E., 260

Velasco, Tex., 78, 80, 156, 169
Vermillion, Joseph D., 72
Victoria Co., Tex., 56, 212, 213, 221, 245, 246
Victoria, Tex., 14, 77, 79, 80, 276
Vince Ranch, 72
Vince's Bridge, 63, 72
Virginia, 7, 46, 81, 263, 264, 266
Volunteer Army of the People (Republic of Texas), 47
Votaw, Elijah, 71

Waco Indians, 38, 81, 86, 105, 142
Waco, Tex., 199
Wade, William W., 113, 119
Waggoner, Robert, 112, 118
Walker, Emaline Sophia Sadler, 8
Walker, J., 112, 118
Walker, John, 113, 118, 129
Walker, Lt. Col. John, 268
Walker, Martin A., 71, 108, 113, 118
Walker, Nathaniel Sadler, 8
Walker, Phillip, 108, 113, 118
Walker, Richard S., 246
Walker, William S., 71
Walker, W. G., 112, 118
Wallace, Benjamin Rush, 213
Wallace, Jeff, 181
Wallace, William A. A. "Bigfoot", 3
Waller Co., Tex., 55
Waller, Hiram, 246
Walling, Jesse, 46, 245
Walling, John C., 46, 57, 87
Walnut Creek, 199
Walters, Maj. Baley C., 117, 121, 129, 159, 171, 172, 173, 174, 176, 177, 178
Walters, Capt. Charles Mote, 103
Walters, George T., 119
Walters, Robert, 119
Walters, Tillman, 119
Walters, Wayne, 119
Walton, John P., 254
Ward, Jackson, 113, 119
Ward, Thomas William, 203, 225, 247
Ward, Capt. William, 50
Ware, Dr. James Jefferson, 87, 112, 117, 128
Ware, Capt. William, 64
Washington, Al., 6, 7, 15, 16
Washington Co., Tex., 212, 213, 221, 222, 245
Washington, D.C., 220, 227, 253
Washington-on-the-Brazos State Historical Park, 210
Washington (on-the-Brazos), Tex., 41, 44, 48, 50, 52, 148, 208, 209, 210, 217, 223
Wasnell, William, 119
Water Avenue (Austin, Tex.), 223
Waterloo (Austin), Tex., 167, 168
Waters, George, 71
Watkins, Robert H., 118
Watson, B. W., 118
Webb, David F., 112, 119
Webb, William G., 242, 245
Weeks, Daniel, 118
Weeks, James, 112, 118
Wells, Col. Lysander, 64, 151, 154, 157
Wells, Moses, 113, 119
Wells, Pheby Parker, 108
Wells, Samuel G., 40, 43-44, 94, 108, 113, 118, 231, 239, 240
Welsh, George Washington, 113, 119
West, Emily D., 66, 72
West Point, 151
Wharton Co., Tex., 229
Wharton, Gen. John Austin, 54, 64, 69
Wharton, William Harris, 37
Wheeler, Elijah, 112, 117
Wheeler, O. M., 242, 245
"Whip Handle Dispatch", 79
White, Alexander, 112, 117
White, Ann, 249
White, Benjamin J., 245
White, C. C., 112, 118
White, Francis M., 221, 229, 230
White, James T., 162
White, John, 112, 118
White, Joseph E., 119
Whites (post office), 162
White, Stephen, 32, 94
Whittaker, Madison Guess, 46
Wichita Indians, 95
Wiehl, Joseph M., 155, 156
Wilder, E. M., 243, 245
Wilds, Samuel W., 113, 119
Wilehart, James R., 184
Wilkinson, Leroy, 71
Wilkinson, William W., 117
Williams, Augustus, 213, 221
Williams, Barakias, 110
William Settlement, 53
Williams, John "Young", 112, 117
Williams, Capt. Joseph, 119, 129
Williams, Leonard, 112, 117, 190-91
Williams, Samuel M., 12
Williams, Thomas, 112, 117, 128
Williams, William F., 46
Williamson Co., Tex., 199

Williamson, Maj. Robert McAlpin ("Three-Legged Willie"), 39, 42-43, 44, 213
Willie, James, 221, 244, 245, 248
Willman, George, 190
Wilson, George W., 108
Wilson, James, 36
Wilson, John, 107, 112, 116
Wilson, Robert, 105
Wilson's Farm (La.), 268
Wilson, William R., 36, 98, 275, 277
Windsor, James, 119
Windsor, Martin, 119
Winkler, Clinton M., 242, 245
Winters, William Carvin, 71
Woldert, Dr. Albert, 185
Woll, Gen. Adrian, 205
Wood, Edward B., 64
Wood, George, 110
Wood, Gov. George Tyler, 235, 245, 249
Wood, Capt. William, 64
Woodlaw, Lt. Daniel, 204
Woodlief, Lt. Col. Devereaux Jerome, 62, 71, 168, 174, 175, 177, 183, 189, 191, 194
Woods, William, 162
Woodward, Capt. John R., 264
Wortham, Maj. John, 94, 108, 113, 118, 142, 144, 151, 159, 163, 169, 173, 176, 177, 178
Wragg, R. M., 261
Wren, Johnson, 245
Wright, George W., 212
Wright, John, 113, 119
Wrights (post office), 162
Wright, William, 240
Wyatt, Maj. Peyton S., 151, 153, 154
Wyoming, 141, 233

Yancy, John, 46
Yarbrough, John Swanson Sr., 45, 46, 67-68, 94
Yarbrough, John Swanson Jr., 45, 46, 67-68, 71
Yarbrough, Joseph Randolph, 45, 46, 57, 94
"Yellow Rose of Texas", 66
Yellowstone (steamboat), 52, 53
Young, Joseph B., 190
Young, William C., 246
Young, William Foster, 71
Yuba River, 255

Zavala, Dr. Lorenzo de, 44, 56, 73
Zavala, Lorenzo de Jr., 57, 64, 75
Zavalla, Tex., 162

ABOUT THE AUTHOR

Stephen L. Moore, a sixth generation Texan, graduated from Stephen F. Austin State University in Nacogdoches, where he studied journalism and advertising. He is currently an account manager for a Houston-based firm which serves the retail advertising industry.

His interest in military history and efforts in writing continue to combine as a part-time hobby. He previously combined with William J. Shinneman and Robert W. Gruebel to write *The Buzzard Brigade: Torpedo Squadron Ten at War* (Missoula, Montana: Pictorial Histories Publishing Company).

Steve, his wife Cindy and their two daughters currently make their home in the Dallas area.